To the memory of Robert L. Howard

Contents

Classic and Contemporary Readings in the Philosophy of Education

Steven M. Cahn

Graduate School
The City University of New York

The McGraw-Hill Companies, Inc.
New York   St. Louis   San Francisco   Auckland   Bogotá   Caracas
Lisbon   London   Madrid   Mexico City   Milan   Montreal   New Delhi
San Juan   Singapore   Sydney   Tokyo   Toronto

McGraw-Hill Higher Education

A Division of The **McGraw-Hill** *Companies*

Classic and Contemporary Readings in the Philosophy of Education

Copyright © 1997 by The McGraw-Hill Companies, Inc. All rights reserved. Printed in the United States of America. Except as permitted under the United States Copyright Act of 1976, no part of this publication may be reproduced or distributed in any form or by any means, or stored in a data base or retrieval system, without the prior written permission of the publisher.

Acknowledgments appear on pages 5, 32, 39, 111, 163, 198, 262, 276, 288, 325, 368, 377, 386, 411, 435, 444, 456, 460, 471, 477, 488, 499, 510, 522, 536, and 546, and on this page by reference.

This book is printed on acid-free paper.

11 12 13 14 15 DOC/DOC 0 1 9 8 7 6 5

ISBN 0-07-009619-8

This book was set in Palatino by Ruttle, Shaw & Wetherill, Inc.
The editor was Phillip A. Butcher;
the production supervisor was Leroy Young.
Project supervision was done by Hockett Editorial Service.
The cover was designed by Rafael Hernandez.
R. R. Donnelley & Sons Company was printer and binder.

Library of Congress Cataloging-in-Publication Data

Classic and contemporary readings in the philosophy of education /
    [compiled by] Steven M. Cahn.
        p.   cm.
    Expanded and updated ed. of: The philosophical foundations of education. 1970.
    Includes bibliographical references (p.*).
    ISBN 0-07-009619-8
    1. Education—Philosophy.   I. Cahn, Steven M.   II. Philosophical foundations of
education.
LB41.C18   1997
370'.1—dc20   96-5368

Preface

This volume brings together classic writings on education by leading figures in the history of philosophy, along with notable contributions to the field by a variety of contemporary thinkers. The historical materials are sizable, including the complete texts of Plato's *Meno*, Dewey's *The Child and the Curriculum* and *Experience and Education*, as well as Mill's neglected but remarkably insightful *Inaugural Address at St. Andrews*. The recent materials reflect diverse approaches, such as open education, pragmatism, communitarianism, scholasticism, feminism, analytic philosophy, hermeneutics, critical theory, and multiculturalism.

This book builds on a previous work I edited, *The Philosophical Foundations of Education* (Harper & Row, 1970), which is no longer in print, and I appreciate the encouragement of those who, having used it, urged me to undertake this much expanded and updated version. I still recall with gratitude the kind reception I received from my students at Vassar College, when during the mid-1960s I first taught philosophy of education. The contents of this volume and its predecessor reflect the students' enthusiasm for reading original sources rather than a textbook.

Among those at McGraw-Hill to whom I owe thanks are Cynthia Ward, who undertook the project; Judy Cornwell, who made helpful suggestions; Bill McLane, who offered valuable advice and oversaw the work to completion; his able editorial assistant, Allison McNamara; editorial supervisor, David Damstra; production supervisor, Leroy Young; and design manager, Chuck Carson. Ian Gardiner, my former research assistant at the Graduate School of the City University of New York, provided his proofreading skills.

For suggestions concerning the contents, I am most appreciative to Harvey Siegel of the University of Miami, as well as to additional reviewers chosen by the publisher: Randall Curren of the University of Rochester, Laura Duhan Kaplan of the University of North Carolina at Charlotte, William Whisner of the University of Utah, and several anonymous others.

A final note. This volume is dedicated to an educator who enriched the lives of thousands, myself included, although ours was not a traditional educational setting. While he never wrote down the lessons he sought to impart, they are embodied in the following adaptation of a tribute, written in 1979, by my brother, Victor L. Cahn, now a professor of English at Skidmore College:

Memories from youth tend to be indelible. Happy or sad, they shape and color our lives.

Some time ago someone from my youth died. His name was Robert L. Howard, he was eighty-three, and for fifty years he was an exemplar of a profession that has to an extent faded from American life. He was a camp director. He ran Camp Seneca, which he had founded in 1921 in Pawling, New York.

Seneca was located on picturesque Whaley Lake, amidst acres of gentle hills and abundant trees. I never visited the grounds except in summer, and thus in my mind they are forever green.

The camp was a world unto itself. We moved through the activities of the day to the call of the bugle. Yet we lived in bunks named "Comanche" and "Iroquois" and followed a variety of Native American themes.

The bulk of our days was devoted to sports, but we also spent time in the wood-shop, the crafts shop, and the nature hut. Movies and original stage presentations were a regular part of our lives. Every day we sang songs and yelled cheers.

It all sounds commonplace, I suppose. Yet youngsters kept returning, summer after summer. Then they became counselors. Eventually they sent their children. Why?

The reason, I believe, was Bob's unswerving faith that as young people grew to maturity, they could find fulfillment within a structure and tradition that gave them support. Throughout every summer he used to say, "We're beginning to hit stride." The phrase suggested not only that the camp season was flourishing, that enjoyable and challenging activities were underway, but also that all of us, while learning to share in group efforts, were progressing along our own individual paths.

His unshakeable optimism was inherent in his refrain "The sun always shines on Seneca." We laughed when he said so during rainstorms that kept us huddled inside. But years later I understood. The sun always did shine, because the warmth and light came from within him and was reflected by us. However the rest of my life may proceed, the memories of his affection and encouragement will continue to sustain me.

Steven M. Cahn

Introduction

What should be the goals of education? This question lies at the heart of philosophy of education. A satisfactory answer requires a thorough examination of metaphysical, epistemological, ethical, and political issues. What is human nature? How can a person acquire knowledge? By what moral standards should a person live? How should society be organized? To develop a philosophy of education requires addressing these critical matters.

Furthermore, merely stating goals is insufficient. Unless these are detailed and the methods of carrying them out clarified, the goals themselves remain too vague to be of value. Granted, for example, that students ought to learn to think critically about important bodies of knowledge. But what is critical thinking? Can it be taught? If so, how? What are the important bodies of knowledge? Is virtue a form of knowledge? Can it be taught in the same way as mathematics? A philosophy of education needs to deal with such concerns.

Doing so is an arduous undertaking. Yet it is of vital importance, for on it rest all intelligent decisions about educational policy.

For example, should college students be required to take a course in the history of Western civilization? Resolving this issue depends on answering such questions as: (1) Is it unwise or unfair to require students to take a particular course? (2) What is the proper relationship between students and the educational institutions they attend? (3) Why is the history of Western civilization worth studying? (4) Is that history more important for our students than the history of other civilizations? (5) Is history to be studied to acquire information or to learn a method of inquiry? (6) Does the investigation of historical events necessarily involve an approach that is inapplicable to the scientific study of inanimate objects? A seemingly simple question regarding one course thus leads into complex matters involving ethical and political judgments as well as epistemological and metaphysical commitments.

To make important choices without consideration of one's ends is intellectual irresponsibility. People who are called on to make educational decisions thus are obliged to reflect on the appropriate purposes of their enterprise or, in other words, to study carefully the philosophy of education.

PART I

Classic Theories

1

Plato

The writings of the Greek philosopher Plato (427–347 B.C.) are among the most influential in the history of Western civilization. All work in philosophy of education should be measured against the standard of excellence he established.

He wrote in dialogue form, and in almost every dialogue the major figure is Plato's teacher, Socrates. The extent to which the historical Socrates espoused the views attributed to the character "Socrates" in Plato's dialogues is a matter of long-standing controversy. What is widely agreed is that the historical Socrates was concerned with the search for definitions of such concepts as "justice," "virtue," "piety," and "courage" and that he defended the thesis that "virtue is knowledge." The Theory of Forms, however, as well as the major ideas presented in *The Republic,* appear to be Platonic rather than Socratic in origin.

The *Meno* dialogue is a superb introduction to a number of central issues in the philosophy of education. Among these are: (1) Can virtue be taught? (2) How is it possible for persons who have been taught what is right to act contrary to the principles they have learned? (3) What is the Socratic method of teaching and how effective is it?

In connection with this third issue, special attention should be paid to Socrates' questioning of a boy concerning certain geometric truths. How successful is the method of questioning and to what extent is it applicable to other fields, such as history or science?

Although the *Meno* dialogue concludes with Socrates defending the thesis that virtue cannot be taught, this view is, in fact, not that of Socrates or Plato. Consider the *Protagoras* dialogue, in which Socrates eventually agrees with the opinion of Protagoras, a highly respected teacher in Athens, who argues in a profound speech that virtue can be taught.

The Republic is widely regarded as Plato's greatest work. It presents a fully developed and brilliantly argued, although not necessarily convincing, philosophy of education. Plato's educational views reflect his metaphysical, epistemological, ethical, and political views. His denigration of vocational education, for example, follows from the separation of knowledge and action implicit in his Theory of Forms as well as from his creation of an intellectual and moral elite that rules over and is served by the labor force.

Bertrand Russell, the famed twentieth-century British philosopher, once referred to Plato's *Republic* as a "totalitarian tract." This controversial judgment reflects Plato's policies of strict censorship and his advocacy of oligarchic rule. Defenders of democracy will find *The Republic* a superb whetstone for sharpening the arguments they can bring forth in support of their own opposing political and educational commitments.

Meno*

MENO: Can you tell me, Socrates, whether virtue is acquired by teaching or by practice; or if neither by teaching nor by practice, then whether it comes to man by nature, or in what other way?

SOCRATES: There was a time, Meno, when the Thessalians were famous among the other Hellenes for their riches and their riding; but now, if I am not mistaken, they are famous also for their wisdom, especially at Larisa, which is the native city of your friend Aristippus. And this is Gorgias' doing; for when he came there, he imbued with the love of wisdom the flower of the Aleuadae, among them your admirer Aristippus, and the other chiefs of the Thessalians. And he has taught you the habit of answering questions in the grand and bold style, which is natural to those who know, and may be expected from one who is himself ready and willing to be questioned on any subject by any Hellene, and answers all comers. How different is our lot! my dear Meno. Here at Athens there is a dearth of the commodity, and all wisdom seems to have emigrated from us to you. I am certain that if you were to ask any Athenian whether virtue was natural or acquired, he would laugh in your face, and say: "Stranger, you have far too good an opinion of me, if you think that I can answer your question. For I literally do not know what virtue is, and much less whether it is acquired by teaching or not." And I myself, Meno, living as I do in this region of poverty am as poor as the rest of the world; and I confess with shame that I know literally nothing about virtue; and when I do not know the "quid" of anything how can I know the "quale"? How, if I knew nothing at all of Meno, could I tell if he was handsome, or the opposite; rich and noble, or the reverse of rich and noble? Do you think that I could?

MEN: No, indeed. But are you in earnest, Socrates, in saying that you do not know what virtue is? And am I to carry back this report of you to Thessaly?

SOC: Not only that, my dear boy, but you may say further that I have never come across anyone else who did, in my judgement.

MEN: Then you have never met Gorgias when he was at Athens?

SOC: Yes, I have.

MEN: And did you not think that he knew?

SOC: I have not a good memory, Meno, and therefore I cannot now tell what I thought of him at the time. I dare say that he does know, and that you know what he said: please, therefore, to remind me of what he said; or, if you would rather, tell me your own view; for I suspect that you and he think much alike.

MEN: Very true.

SOC: Then as he is not here, never mind him, and do you tell me. I adjure you, Meno, be generous, and tell me what you say that virtue is; for I shall esteem myself truly fortunate if I find that I have been mistaken, and that you

---

*The translation is by Benjamin Jowett.

and Gorgias do really have this knowledge, when I have been just saying that I have never met anybody who had.

MEN: There will be no difficulty, Socrates, in answering your question. Let us take first the virtue of a man—he should know how to administer the state, and in the administration of it should benefit his friends and harm his enemies; and he must also be careful not to suffer harm himself. A woman's virtue, if you wish to know about that, may also be easily described: her duty is to order her household and keep properly what is indoors, and obey her husband. Every age, every condition of life, young or old, male or female, bond or free, has a different virtue: there are virtues numberless, and consequently there is no difficulty about definitions; for there is a virtue relative to the actions and ages of each of us in all that we do. And I take it the same may be said of vice, Socrates.

SOC: How fortunate I am, Meno! When I ask you for one virtue, you present me with a swarm of them, which are in your keeping. Suppose that I carried on the figure of the swarm, and asked of you, What is the nature of the bee? and you answered that there are many different kinds of bees, and I replied: But are there many different kinds of bees because they differ *quâ* bees; or, not differing *quâ* bees, are they distinguished from one another by something else, some quality such as beauty, or size, or some other such attribute? How would you answer me?

MEN: I should answer that bees do not differ from one another, *quâ* bees.

SOC: And if I went on to say: That is what I desire to know, Meno; tell me what is the quality in which they do not differ, but are all alike;—you would presumably be able to answer?

MEN: I should.

SOC: And so of the virtues, however many and different they may be, they have all a common form which makes them virtues; and on this he who would answer the question, "What is virtue?" would do well to have his eye fixed: Do you understand?

MEN: I am beginning to understand; but I do not as yet take hold of the question as I could wish.

SOC: When you say, Meno, that there is one virtue of a man, another of a woman, and so on, does this apply only to virtue, or would you say the same of health, and size, and strength? Or is the nature of health always the same, whether in man or woman?

MEN: I should say that health is the same, both in man and woman.

SOC: And is not this true of size and strength? If a woman is strong, she will be strong by reason of the same form and of the same strength subsisting in her which there is in the man. I mean to say that strength, as strength, whether of man or woman, is the same. Is there any difference?

MEN: I think not.

SOC: And will not virtue, as virtue, be the same, whether in a child or in an old man, in a woman or in a man?

MEN: I cannot help feeling, Socrates, that this case is different from the others.

Soc: But why? Were you not saying that the virtue of a man was to order a state, and the virtue of a woman was to order a household?

Men: I did say so.

Soc: And can either household or state or anything be well ordered without temperance and without justice?

Men: Certainly not.

Soc: Then they who order a state or a house temperately and justly order them with temperance and justice?

Men: Certainly.

Soc: Then both men and women, if they are to be good men and women, must have the same virtues of temperance and justice?

Men: Clearly.

Soc: And could either a young man or an elder one ever become good, while they were intemperate and unjust?

Men: Certainly not.

Soc: They must be temperate and just?

Men: Yes.

Soc: Then all human beings are good in the same way, and become good by possession of the same virtues?

Men: Such is the inference.

Soc: And they surely would not have been good in the same way, unless their virtue had been the same?

Men: They would not.

Soc: Then now that the sameness of all virtue has been proven, try and remember what Gorgias, and you with him, say that virtue is.

Men: I know not what to say, but that virtue is the power of governing mankind—if you really want to have one definition of them all.

Soc: That is indeed what I want. Now consider this point; can virtue as you define it be the virtue of a child or a slave, Meno? Can the child govern his father, or the slave his master; and would he who governed be any longer a slave?

Men: I think not, Socrates.

Soc: No, indeed; there would be small reason in that. Yet once more, fair friend; according to you, virtue is "the power of governing"; but shall we not add "justly and not unjustly"?

Men: Yes, Socrates; I agree there; for justice is virtue.

Soc: Would you say "virtue," Meno, or "a virtue"?

Men: What do you mean?

Soc: I mean as I might say about anything; that roundness, for example, is "a figure" and not simply "figure," and I should adopt this mode of speaking, because there are other figures.

Men: Quite right; and that is just what I say about virtue—that there are other virtues as well as justice.

Soc: What are they? tell me the names of them, as I would tell you the names of the other figures if you asked me.

MEN: Courage and temperance and wisdom and a noble way of life are virtues, it seems to me; and there are many others.

SOC: Yes, Meno; and again we are in the same case: in searching after one virtue we have found many, though not in the same way as before; but we have been unable to find the common virtue which runs through them all.

MEN: Why, Socrates, even now I am not able to help you in your inquiry and get at one common notion of virtue as in the other cases.

SOC: No wonder; but I will try to get us nearer if I can. You perhaps understand that this reasoning applies universally: suppose that someone asked you the question which I asked before: Meno, what is figure? if you answered "roundness," he would reply to you, in my way of speaking, by asking whether roundness is "figure" or "a figure"; and you would, of course, answer "a figure."

MEN: Certainly.

SOC: And for this reason—that there are other figures?

MEN: Yes.

SOC: And if he proceeded to ask, What other figures are there? you would have told him.

MEN: I should.

SOC: And if he similarly asked what colour is, and you answered whiteness, and the questioner rejoined, Would you say that whiteness is colour or a colour? you would reply, A colour, because there are other colours as well.

MEN: I should.

SOC: And if he had said, Tell me what they are?—you would have told him of other colours which are colours just as much as whiteness.

MEN: Yes.

SOC: And suppose that he were to pursue the matter in my way, he would say: Ever and anon we are landed in particulars, but that is not what I want; tell me then, since you call them by a common name, and say that they are all figures even when opposed to one another, what is that common nature which you designate as figure—which contains round no less than straight, and, you say, belongs to one no more than to the other—that would be your mode of speaking?

MEN: Yes.

SOC: And in speaking thus, do you mean to say that the round is no more round than straight, or the straight no more straight than round?

MEN: Of course not.

SOC: You only assert that the round figure is figure no more than the straight, nor the straight than the round?

MEN: Very true.

SOC: To what then do we give the name of figure? Try and answer. Suppose that when a person asked you this question either about figure or colour, you were to reply, My good sir, I do not understand what you want, or know what you mean; he would look rather astonished and say: Do you not understand that I am looking for that which is identical in all the particulars? And then he might put the question in another form: Meno, he might say, what is there identical in the round, the straight, and everything else that you call a figure? Could you not answer that question, Meno? I wish that you would try; the attempt will be good practice for the answer about virtue.

MEN: I would rather that you should answer, Socrates.

SOC: Shall I indulge you?

MEN: By all means.

SOC: And then you will tell me about virtue?

MEN: I will.

SOC: Then I must do my best, for there is a prize to be won.

MEN: Certainly.

SOC: Well, I will try and explain to you what figure is. What do you say to this answer?—Figure is the only thing which accompanies colour. Will you be satisfied with it, as I am sure that I should be if you would let me have a similar definition of virtue?

MEN: But, Socrates, it is such an artless answer.

SOC: Why artless?

MEN: Because, according to you, figure is that which always accompanies colour. Very well; but if a person were to say that he does not know what colour is, any more than what figure is—what sort of answer would you have given him?

SOC: In my opinion, the truth. And if he were a philosopher of the eristic and contentious sort, I should say to him: You have my answer, and if I am wrong, your business is to take up the argument and refute me. But if we were friends, and were talking as you and I are now, I ought of course to reply in a milder strain and more in the dialectician's vein; that is to say, I should not only speak the truth, but I should make use of premisses which the person interrogated would be willing to admit. And this is the way in which I shall endeavour to approach you. You will acknowledge, will you not, that there is such a thing as an end, or termination, or extremity?—all which words I use in the same sense, although I am aware that Prodicus might disagree on this point: but still you, I imagine, would speak of a thing as ended or terminated—that is all which I am saying—nothing subtle.

MEN: Yes, I should; and I believe that I understand your meaning.

SOC: And you would speak of a surface and also of a solid, as for example in geometry.

MEN: Yes.

SOC: Well then, you are now in a condition to understand my definition of figure. I define figure to be always that in which the solid finds its limit; or, more concisely, the limit of solid.

MEN: And now, Socrates, what is colour?

SOC: You are outrageous, Meno, in thus plaguing a poor old man to give you an answer, when you will not take the trouble of remembering what is Gorgias' definition of virtue.

MEN: When you have told me what I ask, I will tell you, Socrates.

SOC: A man who was blindfolded has only to hear you talking, and he would know that you are a beautiful creature and still have lovers.

MEN: Why do you think so?

SOC: Why, because you always speak in imperatives, like proud beauties who reign with absolute power so long as they are in their prime; and also, I suspect, you have found out that I have a weakness for beauty, and therefore to humour you I must answer.

MEN: Please do.

SOC: Would you like me to answer you after the manner of Gorgias, in which you may find it easier to follow me?

MEN: I should like nothing better.

SOC: Do not he and you and Empedocles say that there are certain effluences from existing things?

MEN: Certainly.

SOC: And passages into which and through which the effluences pass?

MEN: Exactly.

SOC: And some of the effluences fit into the passages, and some of them are too small or too large?

MEN: True.

SOC: And there is such a thing as sight?

MEN: Yes.

SOC: And now, as Pindar says, "read my meaning":—colour is an effluence of figures, commensurate with sight, and palpable to sense.

MEN: That, Socrates, appears to me to be an admirable answer.

SOC: Why, yes, because it happens to be one which you have been in the habit of hearing: and your wit will have discovered, I suspect, that you may explain in the same way the nature of sound and smell, and of many other similar phenomena.

MEN: Quite true.

SOC: The answer, Meno, was in the solemn language of tragedy, and therefore was more acceptable to you than the other answer about figure.

MEN: Yes.

SOC: And yet, O son of Alexidemus, I cannot help thinking that the other was the better; and I believe that you would be of the same opinion, if you would only stay and be initiated, and were not compelled, as you said yesterday, to go away before the mysteries.

MEN: But I will stay, Socrates, if you will give me many such answers.

SOC: Well then, for my own sake as well as for yours, I will do my very best; but I am afraid that I shall not be able to give you very many as good. And now, in your turn, you are to fulfil your promise, and tell me what virtue is in the universal; and do not make a singular into a plural, as the facetious always say of those who break a thing, but leave virtue whole and sound when you tell me its nature. I have given you the pattern.

MEN: Well then, Socrates, virtue, as I take it, is when he, who desires things which are lovely, is able to provide them for himself; so the poet says, and I say too that "virtue is the desire of things that are lovely, with power to attain them."

SOC: And does he who desires the things that are lovely also desire the good?

MEN: Certainly.

SOC: Then are there some who desire the evil and others who desire the good? Do not all men, my dear sir, desire good?

MEN: I think not.

SOC: There are some who desire evil?

MEN: Yes.

SOC: Do you mean that they think the evils which they desire, to be good; or do they know that they are evil and yet desire them?

MEN: Both, I think.

SOC: And do you really imagine, Meno, that a man knows evils to be evils and desires them notwithstanding?

MEN: Certainly I do.

SOC: Desire is of possession?

MEN: Yes, of possession.

SOC: And does he think that evils do good to him who possesses them, or does he know that their presence does harm?

MEN: There are some who think that the evils do them good, and others who know that they do harm.

SOC: And, in your opinion, do those who think that they do them good know that they are evils?

MEN: I would not go so far as that.

SOC: Is it not obvious that those who are ignorant of their nature do not desire them, but desire what they suppose to be goods although they are really evils; and therefore if in their ignorance they suppose the evils to be goods they really desire goods?

MEN: In that case, no doubt.

SOC: Again, those who, as you say, desire evils, and think that evils are hurtful to the possessor of them, presumably know that they will be hurt by them?

MEN: They must know it.

SOC: And must they not suppose that those who are hurt are miserable in proportion to the hurt which is inflicted upon them?

MEN: How can it be otherwise?

SOC: But are not the miserable ill fated?

MEN: Yes, indeed.

SOC: And does anyone desire to be miserable and ill fated?

MEN: I should say not, Socrates.

SOC: But if there is no one who desires to be miserable, there is no one, Meno, who desires evil; for what is misery but the desire and possession of evil?

MEN: That appears to be the truth, Socrates, and I admit that nobody desires evil.

SOC: And yet, were you not saying just now that virtue is the desire and power of attaining good?

MEN: Yes, I did say so.

SOC: But of this definition one part, the desire, is common to all, and one man is no better than another in that respect?

MEN: Clearly.

Soc: It is obvious then that if one man is indeed better than another, he must be better in the power of attaining good?

Men: Exactly.

Soc: Then, according to your definition, virtue would appear to be the power of attaining good?

Men: I entirely approve, Socrates, of the manner in which you now view this matter.

Soc: Then let us see whether what you now say is true from another point of view; for very likely you may be right:—You affirm virtue to be the power of attaining goods?

Men: Yes.

Soc: And the goods which you mean are such as health and wealth?

Men: And the possession of gold and silver, and having office and honour in the state.

Soc: Those are what you would call goods?

Men: Yes, I should include all those.

Soc: Then, according to Meno, who is the hereditary friend of the great king, virtue is the power of getting silver and gold; and would you add that they must be gained piously, justly, or do you deem this to be of no consequence? And is any mode of acquisition, even if unjust, equally to be deemed virtue?

Men: Not virtue, Socrates.

Soc: But vice?

Men: Yes.

Soc: Then justice or temperance or piety, or some other part of virtue, as would appear, must accompany the acquisition, and without them the mere acquisition of goods will not be virtue.

Men: Why, how can there be virtue without these?

Soc: On the other hand, the failure to acquire gold and silver in an unjust way for oneself or another, or in other words the want of them, may be equally virtue?

Men: True.

Soc: Then the acquisition of such goods is no more virtue than the nonacquisition and want of them, but it seems that whatever is accompanied by justice or honesty is virtue, and whatever is devoid of any such quality is vice.

Men: It cannot be otherwise, in my judgement.

Soc: And were we not saying just now that justice, temperance, and the like, were each of them a part of virtue?

Men: Yes.

Soc: And so, Meno, this is the way in which you mock me.

Men: Why do you say that, Socrates?

Soc: Why, because a short while ago I asked you not to break up virtue and offer it to me in little pieces, and I gave you patterns according to which you were to frame your answer; and you have forgotten already, and tell me that virtue is the power of attaining goods with justice; and justice you acknowledge to be a part of virtue.

Men: Yes.

SOC: Then it follows from your own admissions, that virtue consists in doing with one part of virtue whatever a man does do; for justice and the like are said by you to be parts of virtue, each and all of them. Let me explain further. Did not I ask you to tell me the nature of virtue as a whole? And you are very far from telling me this, but declare every action to be virtue which is done with a part of virtue; as though you had told me the nature of virtue as a whole, so that I should recognize it even when you fritter it away into little pieces. And, therefore, my dear Meno, I fear that I must begin again and repeat the same question: What is virtue? for otherwise I can only say that every action done with a part of virtue is virtue; what else is the meaning of saying that every action done with justice is virtue? Ought I not to ask the question over again; for can anyone who does not know the nature of virtue know the nature of a part of virtue?

MEN: No; I do not say that he can.

SOC: Do you remember how, in the example of figure, we rejected any answer given in terms which were as yet unexplained or unadmitted?

MEN: Yes, Socrates; and we were quite right in doing so.

SOC: But then, my friend, do not suppose that while the nature of virtue as a whole is still undetermined, you can explain it to anyone by reference to some part of virtue; or indeed explain anything at all in that fashion. We should only have to ask over again the old question, What is this virtue of yours? Am I not right?

MEN: I believe that you are.

SOC: Then begin again, and answer me, What, according to you and your friend Gorgias, is the definition of virtue?

MEN: O Socrates, I used to be told, before I knew you, that you were always doubting yourself and making others doubt; and now you are casting your spells over me, and I am simply getting bewitched and enchanted and am at my wits' end. And if I may venture to make a jest upon you, you seem to me both in your appearance and in your power over others to be very like the flat torpedo fish, who torpifies whose who come near him and touch him, as you have now torpified me, I think. For my soul and my tongue are really torpid, and I do not know how to answer you; and though I have been delivered of an infinite variety of speeches about virtue before now, and to many persons—and very good speeches they were, as I thought—at this moment I cannot even say what virtue is. And I think that you are very wise in not voyaging and going away from home, for if you did in other places as you do in Athens, you would be cast into prison as a magician.

SOC: You are a rogue, Meno, and had all but caught me.

MEN: What do you mean, Socrates?

SOC: I can tell why you made a simile about me.

MEN: Why?

SOC: In order that I might make another simile about you. For I know that all beautiful youths like to have similes made about them—as well they may, since beautiful images, I take it, are naturally evoked by beauty—but I shall not return the compliment. As to my being a torpedo, if the torpedo is itself torpid as well as the cause of torpidity in others, then indeed I am a torpedo, but not otherwise; for I perplex others, not because I am clear, but because I am utterly perplexed myself. And now I know not what virtue is, and you seem to be in the same case, although you did once perhaps know before you touched me. However, I have no objection to join with you in the inquiry.

MEN: And how will you investigate, Socrates, that of which you know nothing at all? Where can you find a starting-point in the region of the unknown? And even if you happen to come full upon what you want, how will you ever know that this is the thing which you did not know?

SOC: I know, Meno, what you mean; but just see what a tiresome dispute you are introducing. You argue that a man cannot inquire either about that which he knows, or about that which he does not know; for if he knows, he has no need to inquire; and if not, he cannot; for he does not know the very subject about which he is to inquire.

MEN: Well, Socrates, and is not the argument sound?

SOC: I think not.

MEN: Why not?

SOC: I will tell you why: I have heard from certain men and women skilled in things divine that—

MEN: What did they say?

SOC: They spoke of a glorious truth, as I conceive.

MEN: What is it? and who are they?

SOC: Some of them are priests and priestesses, who have striven to learn how to give a reasonable account of the things with which they concern themselves: there are poets also, like Pindar, and the many others who are inspired. And they say—mark, now, and see whether their words are true— they say that the soul of man is immortal, and at one time has an end, which is termed dying, and at another time is born again, but is never destroyed. And the moral is, that a man ought to live always in perfect holiness. "*For in the ninth year Persephone sends the souls of those from whom she has received the penalty of ancient crime back again from beneath into the light of the sun above, and these are they who become noble kings and mighty men and great in wisdom and are for ever called saintly heroes.*" The soul, then, as being immortal and having been born again many times, and having seen all things that exist, whether in this world or in the world below, has knowledge of them all; and it is no wonder that she should be able to call to remembrance all that she ever knew about virtue, and about everything; for as all nature is akin, and the soul has learned all things, there is no difficulty in a man eliciting out of a single recollection all the rest—the process generally called "learning"—if he is strenuous and does not faint; for all inquiry and all learning is but recollection. And therefore we ought not to listen to this eristic argument about the impossibility of inquiry: for it will make us idle, and it is sweet to the sluggard; but the other doctrine will make us active and inquisitive. In that confiding, I will gladly inquire with you into the nature of virtue.

MEN: Yes, Socrates; but what do you mean by saying that we do not learn, and that what we call learning is only a process of recollection? Can you teach me how this is?

SOC: I told you, Meno, just now that you were a rogue, and now you ask whether I can teach you, when I am saying that there is no teaching, but only recollection; and thus you imagine that you will expose me in a contradiction.

MEN: Indeed, Socrates, I protest that I had no such intention. I only asked the question from habit; but if you can prove to me that what you say is true, I wish that you would.

SOC: It will be no easy matter, but I am willing to do my best for you. Suppose that you call one of your numerous attendants, whichever you like, that I may demonstrate on him.

MEN: Certainly. Come hither, boy.

SOC: He is Greek, and speaks Greek, does he not?

MEN: Yes, indeed; he was born in the house.

SOC: Attend now, and observe whether he learns of me or only remembers.

MEN: I will.

SOC: Tell me, boy, do you know that a figure like this is a square?

BOY: I do.

SOC: And you know that a square figure has these four lines equal?

BOY: Certainly.

SOC: And these lines which I have drawn through the middle of the square are also equal?

BOY: Yes.

SOC: A square may be of any size?

BOY: Certainly.

SOC: And if one side of the figure be two feet long, and the other side two feet, how much will the whole be? Let me explain: if in one direction the space was two feet long, and in the other direction one foot, the whole space would be two feet taken once?

BOY: Yes.

SOC: But since this side is also two feet, there are twice two feet?

BOY: There are.

SOC: Then the square is twice two feet?

BOY: Yes.

SOC: And how many are twice two feet? count and tell me.

BOY: Four, Socrates.

SOC: And might there not be another figure twice as large as this, but of the same kind, and having like this all the lines equal?

BOY: Yes,

SOC: And how many feet will that be?

BOY: Eight feet.

SOC: And now try and tell me the length of the line which forms the side of that double square: this is two feet—what will that be?

BOY: Clearly, Socrates, it will be double.

SOC: Do you observe, Meno, that I am not teaching the boy anything, but only asking him questions; and now he fancies that he knows how long a line is necessary in order to produce a figure of eight square feet; does he not?

MEN: Yes.

SOC: And does he really know?

MEN: Certainly not.

SOC: He fancies that because the square is double, the line is double?

MEN: True.

SOC: Now see him being brought step by step to recollect in regular order. *(To the boy.)* Tell me, boy, do you assert that a double space comes from a double line? Remember that I am not speaking of an oblong, but of a figure equal every way, and twice the size of this⎯that is to say of eight feet; and I want to know whether you still say that a double square comes from a double line?

BOY: Yes.

SOC: But does not this line become doubled if we add another such line here?

BOY: Certainly.

SOC: And four such lines, you say, will make a space containing eight feet?

BOY: Yes.

SOC: Let us describe such a figure: Would you not say that this is the figure of eight feet?

BOY: Yes.

SOC: And are there not these four divisions in the figure, each of which is equal to the figure of four feet?

BOY: True.

SOC: And is not that four times four?

BOY: Certainly.

SOC: And four times is not double?

BOY: No, indeed.

SOC: But how much?

BOY: Four times as much.

SOC: Therefore the double line, boy, has given a space, not twice, but four times as much.

BOY: True.

SOC: Four times four are sixteen—are they not?

BOY: Yes.

SOC: What line would give you a space of eight feet—for that gives a fourfold space, of sixteen feet, does it not?

BOY: Yes.

SOC: And the space of four feet is made from this half line?

BOY: Yes.

SOC: Good; and is not a space of eight feet twice the size of this, and half the size of the other?

BOY: Certainly.

Soc: Such a space, then, will be made out of a line greater than this one, and less than that one?

Boy: Yes; I think so.

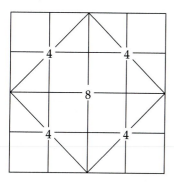

Soc: Very good; I like to hear you say what you think. And now tell me, is not this a line of two feet and that of four?

Boy: Yes.

Soc: Then the line which forms the side of the eight foot space ought to be more than this line of two feet, and less than the other of four feet?

Boy: It ought.

Soc: Try and see if you can tell me how much it will be.

Boy: Three feet.

Soc: Then if we add a half to this line of two, that will be the line of three. Here are two and there is one; and on the other side, here are two also and there is one: and that makes the figure of which you speak?

Boy: Yes.

Soc: But if there are three feet this way and three feet that way, the whole space will be three times three feet?

Boy: That is evident.

Soc: And how much are three times three feet?

Boy: Nine.

Soc: And what was to be the number of feet in the doubled square?

Boy: Eight.

Soc: Then the eight foot space is not made out of a line of three feet?

Boy: No.

Soc: But from what line?—tell me exactly, and if you would rather not reckon, try and show me the line.

Boy: Indeed, Socrates, I do not know.

Soc: Do you see, Meno, what advances he has made in his power of recollection? He did not know at first, and he does not know now, what is the side of a figure of eight feet: but then he thought that he knew, and answered confidently as if he knew, and felt no difficulty; now he feels a difficulty, and neither knows nor fancies that he knows.

Men: True.

Soc: Is he not better off in knowing his ignorance?

MEN: I think that he is.

SOC: If we have made him doubt, and given him the "torpedo's shock," have we done him any harm?

MEN: I think not.

SOC: We have certainly, as would seem, assisted him in some degree to the discovery of the truth; and now he will wish to remedy his ignorance, but then he would have been ready to tell all the world again and again that the double space should have a double side.

MEN: True.

SOC: But do you suppose that he would ever have started to inquire into or to learn what he fancied that he knew, though he was really ignorant of it, until he had fallen into perplexity under the idea that he did not know, and had desired to know?

MEN: I think not, Socrates.

SOC: Then he was the better for the torpedo's touch?

MEN: I think so.

SOC: Mark now the further development. I shall ask him, and not teach him, and he shall share the inquiry with me: and do you watch and see if you find me telling or explaining anything to him, instead of eliciting his opinion. Tell me, boy, is not this a square of four feet which I have drawn?

BOY: Yes.

SOC: And now I add another square equal to the former one?

BOY: Yes.

SOC: And a third, which is equal to either of them?

BOY: Yes.

SOC: Suppose that we fill up the vacant corner?

BOY: Very good.

SOC: Here, then, there are four equal spaces?

BOY: Yes.

SOC: And how many times larger is this space than this other?

BOY: Four times.

SOC: But we wanted one only twice as large, as you will remember.

BOY: True.

SOC: Now, does not this line, reaching from corner to corner, bisect each of these spaces?

BOY: Yes.

SOC: And are there not here four equal lines which contain this space?

BOY: There are.

SOC: Look and see how much this space is.

BOY: I do not understand.

SOC: Has not each interior cut off half of the four spaces?

BOY: Yes.

SOC: And how many such spaces are there in this section?

BOY: Four.

SOC: And how many in this?

BOY: Two.

SOC: And four is how many times two?

BOY: Twice.

SOC: So that this space is of how many feet?

BOY: Of eight feet.

SOC: And from what line do you get this figure?

BOY: From this.

SOC: That is, from the line which extends from corner to corner of the figure of four feet?

BOY: Yes.

SOC: And that is the line which the learned call the diagonal. And if this is the proper name, then you, Meno's slave, are prepared to affirm that the double space is the square of the diagonal?

BOY: Certainly, Socrates.

SOC: What do you say of him, Meno? Were not all these answers given out of his own head?

MEN: Yes, they were all his own.

SOC: And yet, as we were just now saying, he did not know?

MEN: True.

SOC: But still he had in him those notions of his—had he not?

MEN: Yes.

SOC: Then he who does not know may still have true notions of that which he does not know?

MEN: Apparently.

SOC: And at present these notions have just been stirred up in him, as in a dream; but if he were frequently asked the same questions, in different forms, he would know as accurately as anyone at last?

MEN: I dare say.

SOC: Without anyone teaching him he will recover his knowledge for himself, if he is merely asked questions?

MEN: Yes.

SOC: And this spontaneous recovery of knowledge in him is recollection?

MEN: True.

SOC: And this knowledge which he now has must he not either have acquired at some time, or else possessed always?

MEN: Yes.

SOC: But if he always possessed this knowledge he would always have known; or if he has acquired the knowledge he could not have acquired it in this life, unless he has been taught geometry. And he may be made to do the same with all geometry and every other branch of knowledge; has anyone ever taught him all this? You must know about him, if, as you say, he was born and bred in your house.

MEN: And I am certain that no one ever did teach him.

SOC: And yet he has these notions?

MEN: The fact, Socrates, is undeniable.

SOC: But if he did not acquire them in this life, then he must have had and learned them at some other time?

MEN: Clearly he must.

Soc: Which must have been the time when he was not a man?

MEN: Yes.

Soc: And if there are always to be true notions in him, both while he is and while he is not a man, which only need to be awakened into knowledge by putting questions to him, his soul must remain always possessed of this knowledge; for he must always either be or not be a man.

MEN: Obviously.

Soc: And if the truth of all things always exists in the soul, then the soul is immortal. Wherefore be of good cheer, and try to discover by recollection what you do not now know, or rather what you do not remember.

MEN: I feel, somehow, that I like what you are saying.

Soc: And I too like what I am saying. Some things I have said of which I am not altogether confident. But that we shall be better and braver and less helpless if we think that we ought to inquire, than we should have been if we thought that there was no knowing and no duty to seek to know what we do not know;—that is a belief for which I am ready to fight, in word and deed, to the utmost of my power.

MEN: There again, Socrates, your words seem to me excellent.

Soc: Then, as we are agreed that a man should inquire about that which he does not know, shall you and I make an effort to inquire together into the nature of virtue?

MEN: By all means, Socrates. And yet I would much rather return to my original question, Whether in seeking to acquire virtue we should regard it as a thing to be taught, or as a gift of nature, or as coming to men in some other way?

Soc: Had I the command of you as well as of myself, Meno, we should not have inquired whether virtue is given by instruction or not, until we had first ascertained "what it is." But since you never think of self-control—such being your notion of freedom—but think only of controlling me and do control me, I must yield to you, for you are irresistible. And therefore it seems we have now to inquire into the qualities of a thing of which we do not as yet know the nature. At any rate, will you loosen the reins a little, and allow the question "Whether virtue is given by instruction, or in any other way," to be argued upon hypothesis? Let me explain. As the geometrician, when he is asked whether a certain triangle is capable of being inscribed in a certain circle, will reply: "I cannot tell you as yet; but I will offer an hypothesis which may assist us in forming a conclusion: If the figure be such that when you have produced a given side of it, the given area of the triangle falls short by an area corresponding to the part produced, then one consequence follows, and if this is impossible then some other; so let me assume an hypothesis, and I am willing to tell you whether this triangle is capable of being inscribed in the circle."—that is a geometrical hypothesis. And we too, as we know not the nature and qualities of virtue, must ask, whether virtue is or is not capable of being taught, upon some hypothesis, as thus: what kind of spiritual good must virtue be in order that it may be taught or not?

Let the first hypothesis be that virtue is not within the class "knowledge,"—in that case will it be taught or not? or, as we were just now saying, "recollected"? For there is no use in disputing about the name. But is virtue taught or not? or rather, does not everyone see that knowledge alone is taught?

MEN: I agree.

SOC: Then if virtue is a kind of knowledge, virtue will be taught?

MEN: Certainly.

SOC: Then now we have made a quick end of this question: if virtue is of such a nature, it will be taught; and if not, not?

MEN: Certainly.

SOC: The next question is, whether virtue is knowledge or of another species?

MEN: Yes, that appears to be the question which comes next in order.

SOC: Very well then; do we not say that virtue is good?—This is an hypothesis which stands firm?

MEN: Certainly.

SOC: Now, if there be some other good which is separate from knowledge, possibly virtue also is not a kind of knowledge; but if knowledge embraces all good, then we shall be right in supposing that virtue is a kind of knowledge?

MEN: True.

SOC: And virtue is that which makes us good?

MEN: Yes.

SOC: And if we are good, then we are profitable; for all good things are profitable?

MEN: Yes.

SOC: Then virtue is profitable?

MEN: That is the only inference.

SOC: Then now let us take particular examples of things which profit us. Health and strength, and beauty and wealth—these, and the like of these, we call profitable?

MEN: True.

SOC: And yet these same things may also sometimes do us harm: would you not think so?

MEN: Yes.

SOC: And what is the guiding principle which makes them profitable or the reverse? Are they not profitable when they are rightly used, and hurtful when they are not rightly used?

MEN: Certainly.

SOC: Next, let us consider the goods of the soul: they are temperance, justice, courage, quickness of apprehension, memory, a noble way of life, and the like?

MEN: Surely.

SOC: And such of these as are not knowledge, but of another sort, are sometimes profitable and sometimes hurtful; as, for example, courage wanting good sense, which is only a sort of confidence? When a man has no sense he is harmed by such confidence, but when he has sense he is profited?

MEN: True.

Soc: And the same may be said of temperance and quickness of apprehension; whatever things are learned or managed with sense are profitable, but without sense they are hurtful?

Men: Very true.

Soc: And in general, all that the soul attempts or endures when under the guidance of wisdom, ends in happiness; but when she is under the guidance of folly, in the opposite?

Men: That appears to be true.

Soc: If then virtue is a quality of the soul, and is admitted to be profitable, it must be wisdom or good sense, since none of the things of the soul are either profitable or hurtful in themselves, but they are all made profitable or hurtful by the addition of wisdom or of folly; and therefore if virtue is profitable, virtue must be a sort of wisdom?

Men: I quite agree.

Soc: And the other goods, such as wealth and the like, of which we were just now saying that they are sometimes good and sometimes evil, do not they also become profitable or hurtful, accordingly as the soul guides and uses them rightly or wrongly; just as the things of the soul herself become profitable when under the guidance of wisdom and harmful when guided by folly?

Men: True.

Soc: And the wise soul guides them rightly, and the foolish soul wrongly?

Men: Yes.

Soc: And is not this universally true of human nature? All other things hang upon the soul, and the things of the soul herself hang upon wisdom, if they are to be good; and so wisdom is inferred to be that which profits—and virtue, as we affirm, is profitable?

Men: Certainly.

Soc: And thus we arrive at the conclusion that virtue is either wholly or partly wisdom?

Men: I think that what you are saying, Socrates, is very true.

Soc: But if this is true, then the good are not by nature good?

Men: I think not.

Soc: If they were, there would assuredly be discerners of characters among us who would know our future great men; and on their showing we should have adopted them, and should be keeping them in the citadel out of the way of harm, having set a stamp upon them far rather than upon a piece of gold in order that no one might tamper with them; and that when they grew up they might be useful to the state?

Men: Yes, Socrates, that would seem the right way.

Soc: Then if the good are not by nature good, are they made good by instruction?

Men: There appears to be no other alternative, Socrates. On the supposition that virtue is knowledge, there can be no doubt that virtue is taught.

Soc: Yes, indeed; but what if the supposition is erroneous?

Men: I certainly thought just now that we were right.

SOC: Yes, Meno; but a principle which has any soundness should stand firm not only just now, but always.

MEN: Well; and why are you so difficult, so slow to believe that virtue is knowledge?

SOC: I will try and tell you why, Meno. I do not retract the assertion that if virtue is knowledge it may be taught, but I fear that I have some reason in doubting whether it is knowledge. Consider now and say whether virtue, and not only virtue but anything that is taught, must not have teachers and disciples?

MEN: Surely.

SOC: And conversely, may not the art of which neither teachers nor disciples exist be presumed to be incapable of being taught?

MEN: True; but do you think that there are no teachers of virtue?

SOC: I have certainly often inquired whether there were any, and taken great pains to find them, and have never succeeded; and I have had many companions in the search, by preference the persons whom I thought to have the most experience in that line. And here at the moment when he is wanted Anytus has sat down beside us, and we should be well advised to ask him to join us in our search. In the first place, he is the son of a wealthy and wise father, Anthemion, who acquired his wealth, not by gift or without effort, like Ismenias the Theban (who has recently become as rich as Polycrates), but by his own skill and industry, and who is a well-conditioned modest man, not insolent, nor overbearing, nor annoying; moreover, this son of his has received a good education, as the Athenian people certainly appear to think, for they choose him to fill the highest offices. And these are the sort of men with whose help we ought to inquire whether there are any teachers of virtue, and who they are. Please, Anytus, to help me and your friend Meno in answering our question, Who are the teachers? Consider the matter thus: If we wanted Meno to be a good physician, to whom should we send him? Should we not send him to the physicians?

ANYTUS: Certainly.

SOC: Or if we wanted him to be a good cobbler, should we not send him to the cobblers?

ANY: Yes.

SOC: And so forth?

ANY: Yes.

SOC: Let me trouble you with one more question. When we say that we should be right in sending him to the physicians if we wanted him to be a physician, do we mean that we should be right in sending him to those who profess the art, rather than to those who do not, and to those who demand payment for teaching the art, and publicly offer to teach it to anyone who chooses to come and learn? And if these were our reasons, should we not be right in sending him?

ANY: Yes.

SOC: And might not the same be said of flute-playing, and of the other arts? Would a man who wanted to make another a flute-player refuse to send him to those who promise to teach the art and take money for it, and let him go about plaguing other persons to give him instruction, who are not professed teachers and who never had a single disciple in that branch of knowledge which we expect them to teach him—would not such conduct be the height of folly?

ANY: Most certainly, and of ignorance too.

SOC: Very good. And now you are in a position to advise with me about my friend Meno. For some time he has been telling me, Anytus, that he desires to attain that kind of wisdom and virtue by which men order the state or the household, and honour their parents, and know how to receive citizens and strangers and to send them on their way as a good host should. Now, to whom should he go in order that he may learn this virtue? Does not the previous argument imply clearly that we should send him to those who profess to teach virtue and have publicly thrown open their teaching to any Hellene who chooses to come to them and pay the fees they fix?

ANY: Whom do you mean, Socrates?

SOC: You surely know, do you not, Anytus, that these are the people whom mankind call sophists?

ANY: In heaven's name, Socrates, forbear! I only hope that no friend or kinsman of mine, whether from this city or another, will ever be so mad as to allow himself to be corrupted by them; for they are a manifest pest and corrupting influence to those who have to do with them.

SOC: What, Anytus? Among all the people who profess that they know how to do men good, do you mean to say that these are the only ones who not only do them no good, but positively corrupt those who are entrusted to them, and in return for this disservice have the face to demand money? Indeed, I cannot believe you; for I know of a single man, Protagoras, who made more out of his craft than the illustrious Pheidias, who created such noble works, or any ten other sculptors. How could that be? A mender of old shoes, or patcher up of clothes, who returned shoes or clothes in worse condition than he received them, could not have remained thirty days undetected, and would very soon have starved; whereas during more than forty years, Protagoras was corrupting all Hellas, and sending his disciples from him worse than he received them, and he was never found out. For, if I am not mistaken, he was about seventy years old at his death, forty of which were spent in the practice of his profession; and during all that time he had a good reputation, which to this day he retains: and not only Protagoras, but many others are well spoken of—some who lived before him, and others who are still living. Now, when you say that they deceive and corrupt the youth, are we to suppose that they do it consciously or unconsciously? Can those who are deemed by many to be the wisest of men be out of their minds?

ANY: Out of their minds! No, Socrates; the young men who give their money to them are out of their minds, and their relations and guardians who entrust their youth to the care of these men are still more out of their minds, and most of all, the cities who allow them to come in, and do not drive them out, citizen and stranger alike.

Soc: Has any of the sophists wronged you, Anytus? What makes you so angry with them?

Any: No, indeed, neither I nor any of my family has ever had, nor would I suffer them to have, anything to do with them.

Soc: Then you are entirely unacquainted with them?

Any: And I have no wish to be acquainted.

Soc: Then, my dear friend, as you have no acquaintance whatever with the profession, how can you know whether there is any good or bad in it?

Any: Quite well; I am sure that I know what manner of men these are, whether I am acquainted with them or not.

Soc: You must be a diviner, Anytus, for otherwise I really cannot make out, judging from your own words, how you know about them. But I am not inquiring of you who are the teachers who will corrupt Meno (let them be, if you please, the sophists); I only ask you to tell us who there is in this great city who will teach him how to become proficient in the virtue which I was just now describing. He is the friend of your family, and you will oblige him.

Any: Why do you not tell him yourself?

Soc: I have told him whom I supposed to be the teachers of these things; but I learn from you that I am utterly at fault, and I dare say that you are right. And now I wish that you, on your part, would tell me to whom among the Athenians he should go. Whom would you name?

Any: Why single out individuals? Any Athenian gentleman taken at random will do far more good to him than the sophists, if Meno will mind him.

Soc: And did those gentlemen grow of themselves; and without having been taught by anyone, were they nevertheless able to teach others that which they had never learned themselves?

Any: I imagine that they have learned of the previous generation of gentlemen. Have there not been many good men in this city?

Soc: Yes, certainly, Anytus; and many good statesmen also there have been and there are still, in the city of Athens. But the question is whether they were also good teachers of their own virtue;—not whether there are or have been good men in this part of the world, but whether virtue can be taught, is the question which we have been discussing. Now, do we mean to say that the good men of our own and of other times knew how to impart to others that virtue which they had themselves; or is virtue a thing incapable of being communicated by or received from another? That is the question which I and Meno have long been arguing. Look at the matter in your own way: Would you not admit that Themistocles was a good man?

Any: Certainly; no man better.

Soc: And must not he then have been a good teacher, if any man ever was a good teacher of his own virtue?

Any: No doubt,—if he wanted to be so.

Soc: But would he not have wanted? He would, at any rate, have desired to make his own son a good man and a gentleman; he could scarcely have been jealous of him, and have intentionally abstained from imparting to him his own virtue. Did you never hear that he made his son Cleophantus a fine horseman; and had him taught to stand upright on horseback and hurl a javelin, and to do many other marvellous things; and in anything which could be learned from good teachers he was proficient? Have you not heard from our elders of him?

ANY: I have.

SOC: So no one could charge his son with natural incompetence?

ANY: Very likely not.

SOC: But did anyone, old or young, ever say in your hearing that Cleophantus, son of Themistocles, was a wise or good man in the same respects as his father was?

ANY: I have certainly never heard anyone say so.

SOC: And if virtue could have been taught, would his father Themistocles have sought to train him in these minor accomplishments, and allowed him, who was his own son, to be no better than his neighbours in those qualities in which he himself excelled?

ANY: Indeed, indeed, I think not.

SOC: Here was a teacher of virtue whom you admit to be among the best men of the past. Let us take another;—Aristides, the son of Lysimachus: would you not acknowledge that he was a good man?

ANY: To be sure I should.

SOC: And did not he train his son Lysimachus better than any other Athenian in all that could be done for him by the help of masters? But what has been the result? Is he a bit better than any other mortal? He is an acquaintance of yours, and you see what he is like. There is Pericles, again, magnificent in his wisdom; and he, as you are aware, brought up two sons, Paralus and Xanthippus.

ANY: I know.

SOC: And you know, also, that he taught them to be unsurpassed horsemen, and had them trained in music and gymnastics and all sorts of arts—in these respects they were on a level with the best—and had he no wish to make good men of them? Nay, he must have wished it. But virtue, as I suspect, could not be taught. And that you may not suppose the incompetent teachers to have been only the least worthy sort of Athenians and few in number, remember again that Thucydides brought up two sons, Melesias and Stephanus, whom, besides giving them a good education in other things, he trained in wrestling, and they were the best wrestlers in Athens: one of them he committed to the care of Xanthias, and the other of Eudorus, who were celebrated as the finest wrestlers of that day. Do you remember them?

ANY: I have heard of them.

SOC: Now, can there be a doubt that Thucydides, whose children were taught things for which he had to spend money, would have taught them to be good men, which would have cost him nothing, if virtue could have been taught? Will you reply that he was a man of no account, and had not many friends among the Athenians and allies? Nay, but he was of a great family, and a man of influence at Athens and in all Hellas, and, if virtue could have been taught, he would have found some Athenian or foreigner to make good men of his sons, if he could not himself spare the time from cares of state. Once more, I suspect, friend Anytus, that virtue is not a thing which can be taught?

ANY: Socrates, I think that you are too ready to speak evil of men: and, if you will take my advice, I would recommend you to be careful. Perhaps there is no city in which it is not easier to do men harm than to do them good, and this is certainly the case at Athens, as I believe that you know.

SOC: I think, Meno, that Anytus is in a rage. And he may well be in a rage, for he believes, in the first place, that I am defaming these gentlemen; and in the second place, he is of opinion that he is one of them himself. But today he does not know what is the meaning of defamation, and if he ever does, he will forgive me. Meanwhile I will return to you, Meno; for I suppose that there are gentlemen in your region too?

MEN: Certainly there are.

SOC: And will they come forward to teach the young? and do they profess to be teachers? and do they agree that virtue can be taught?

MEN: No indeed, Socrates, they are anything but agreed; you may hear them saying at one time that virtue can be taught, and then again the reverse.

SOC: Can we call those teachers who do not even accept the possibility of their own vocation?

MEN: I think not, Socrates.

SOC: And what do you think of these sophists, who are the only professors? Do they seem to you to be teachers of virtue?

MEN: I often wonder, Socrates, that Gorgias is never heard promising to teach virtue, and when he hears others promising he only laughs at them; but he thinks that men should be taught to speak.

SOC: Then you think that neither are the sophists teachers?

MEN: I cannot tell you, Socrates; like the rest of the world, I am in doubt, and sometimes I think that they are teachers and sometimes not.

SOC: And are you aware that not you only and other politicians have doubts whether virtue can be taught or not, but that Theognis the poet says the very same thing?

MEN: Where does he say so?

SOC: In these elegiac verses:—

> Eat and drink and sit with the mighty, and make yourself agreeable to them; for from the good you will learn what is good, but if you mix with the bad you will lose the intelligence which you already have.

Do you observe that here he seems to imply that virtue can be taught?

MEN: Clearly.

SOC: But in some other verses he shifts about and says:—

> If understanding could be created and put into a man, then they [who were able to perform this feat] would be gaining great rewards.

And again:—

> Never would a bad son have sprung from a good sire, for he would have heard
> the voice of instruction; but not by teaching will you ever make a bad man into a
> good one.

and this, as you may remark, is a flat contradiction of the other.

MEN: Clearly.

SOC: And is there anything else of which the professors, so far from being acknowledged as teachers of others, are admitted to be ignorant themselves,
and incompetent in the very subject which they are professing to teach? or is
there anything else about which even its recognized possessors, in this case
the "gentlemen," are sometimes saying that "this thing can be taught," and
sometimes the opposite? Can you say that they are teachers in any true
sense whose ideas are in such confusion?

MEN: I should say, certainly not.

SOC: But if neither the sophists nor the gentlemen are teachers, clearly there
can be no other teachers?

MEN: No.

SOC: And if there are no teachers, neither are there disciples?

MEN: Agreed.

SOC: And we have admitted that a thing cannot be taught of which there are
neither teachers nor disciples?

MEN: We have.

SOC: And there are no teachers of virtue to be found anywhere?

MEN: There are not.

SOC: And if there are no teachers, neither are there scholars?

MEN: That, I think, is true.

SOC: Then virtue cannot be taught?

MEN: Not if we have argued correctly. But I cannot believe, Socrates, that there
are no good men: And if there are, how did they come into existence?

SOC: I am afraid, Meno, that you and I are not good for much, and that Gorgias has been as poor an educator of you as Prodicus has been of me. Certainly we shall have to look to ourselves, and try to find someone who will
help in some way or other to improve us. This I say, because I observe that,
absurdly enough, in the previous discussion none of us remarked that right
and good action is possible to man under other guidance than that of
knowledge (ἐπιστήμη). Perhaps that is the reason why we have failed to
discover how good men are produced.

MEN: How do you mean, Socrates?

SOC: You will see. Good men are necessarily useful; were we not right in admitting this? It must be so.

MEN: Yes.

SOC: And in supposing that they will be useful if they are true guides to us of
action—there we were also right?

MEN: Yes.

Soc: But when we said that a man cannot be a good guide unless he have knowledge (φρόνησις) in this we seem to have made a wrong admission.

Men: What do you mean by "a good guide"?

Soc: I will explain. If a man knew the way to Larisa, or anywhere else, and went to the place and led others thither, would he not be a right and good guide?

Men: Certainly.

Soc: And a person who had a right opinion about the way, but had never been and did not know, would be a good guide also, would he not?

Men: Certainly.

Soc: And while he has true opinion about that which the other knows, he will be just as good a guide if he only thinks the truth, as he who knows the truth?

Men: Exactly.

Soc: Then true opinion is as good a guide to correct action as knowledge; and that was the point which we omitted in our speculation about the nature of virtue, when we said that knowledge only is the guide of right action; whereas there is also true opinion.

Men: So it seems.

Soc: Then right opinion is not less useful than knowledge?

Men: There is a difference, Socrates; he who has knowledge will always be right, but he who has right opinion will sometimes be right, and sometimes not.

Soc: What do you mean? Can he be wrong who has right opinion, so long as he has right opinion?

Men: I admit the cogency of your argument, and therefore, Socrates, I wonder that knowledge should ever be prized far above right opinion—or why they should ever differ.

Soc: And shall I explain this wonder to you?

Men: Do tell me.

Soc: You would not wonder if you had ever observed the images of Daedalus; but perhaps you have not got them in your country?

Men: What have they to do with the question?

Soc: Because they require to be fastened in order to keep them, and if they are not fastened they will run away like fugitive slaves.

Men: Well, what of that?

Soc: I mean to say that, like runaway slaves, they are not very valuable possessions if they are at liberty, for they will walk off; but when fastened they are of great value, for they are really beautiful works of art. Now this is an illustration of the nature of true opinions: while they abide with us they are beautiful and fruitful of nothing but good, but they run away out of the human soul, and do not care to remain long, and therefore they are not of much value until they are fastened by reasoned understanding of causes; and this fastening of them, friend Meno, is recollection, as you and I have agreed to call it. But when they are bound, in the first place, they attain to be knowledge; and, in the second place, they are abiding. And this is why knowledge is more honourable and excellent than right opinion, because fastened by a chain.

MEN: Indeed, Socrates, something of the kind seems probable.

SOC: I too speak rather in ignorance; I only conjecture. And yet that knowledge differs from right opinion is no matter of conjecture with me. There are not many things which I profess to know, but this is most certainly one of them.

MEN: Yes, Socrates; and you are quite right in saying so.

SOC: And am I not also right in saying that true opinion leading the way perfects any action quite as well as knowledge?

MEN: There again, Socrates, I think that you are correct.

SOC: Then for action right opinion is not a whit inferior to knowledge, nor less useful; nor is the man who has right opinion inferior to him who has knowledge?

MEN: True.

SOC: And surely the good man has been acknowledged by us to be useful?

MEN: Yes.

SOC: Seeing then that men become good and useful to states (if they do), not only because they have knowledge, but because they have right opinion, and that neither knowledge nor right opinion is given to man by nature or acquired by him—do you imagine either of them to be given by nature?

MEN: Not I.

SOC: Then if they are not given by nature, neither are the good by nature good?

MEN: Certainly not.

SOC: And nature being excluded, then came the question whether virtue is acquired by teaching?

MEN: Yes.

SOC: If virtue was practical wisdom, then, as we thought, it could be taught?

MEN: Yes.

SOC: And if it could be taught it was wisdom?

MEN: Certainly.

SOC: And if there were teachers, it could be taught; and if there were no teachers, not?

MEN: True.

SOC: But surely we acknowledged that there were no teachers of virtue?

MEN: Yes.

SOC: Thus we acknowledged that it could not be taught, and was not wisdom?

MEN: Certainly.

SOC: And yet we admitted that it was a good?

MEN: Yes.

SOC: And that which guides aright is useful and good?

MEN: Certainly.

SOC: And for human beings the only right guides are knowledge and true opinion—things which by some happy chance go aright do not do so by human guidance—and when human guidance leads aright, it must be by one of these two, true opinion or knowledge.

MEN: I think so too.

Soc: But if virtue is not taught, neither is virtue knowledge.

Men: Clearly not.

Soc: Then of two good and useful things, one, which is knowledge, has been set aside, and cannot be supposed to be our guide in political life.

Men: I think not.

Soc: And therefore not by any wisdom, and not because they were wise, did Themistocles and those others of whom Anytus spoke govern their states. This was the reason why they were unable to make others like themselves—because their virtue was not grounded on knowledge.

Men: That is probably true, Socrates.

Soc: But if not by knowledge, the only alternative which remains is that statesmen guide their states by right opinion. They stand in the same relation to wisdom as diviners and prophets, who likewise say many things truly when they are inspired, but they know not what they say.

Men: So I suppose.

Soc: And may we not, Meno, truly call those men "divine" who, having no understanding, yet succeed in many a grand deed and word?

Men: Certainly.

Soc: Then we shall also be right in calling divine those whom we were just now speaking of as diviners and prophets, including the whole tribe of poets. Yes, and with these we may class statesmen as no less divine and inspired, being possessed of God and filled with His breath, in which condition they say many grand things, not knowing what they say.

Men: Yes.

Soc: And the women too, Meno, call good men divine—do they not? and the Spartans, when they praise a good man, say "he is a divine man."

Men: And I think, Socrates, that they are right; although very likely our friend Anytus may take offence at the word.

Soc: I do not care; as for Anytus, there will be another opportunity of talking with him. To sum up our inquiry—the result seems to be, if we are at all right in our line of argument, that virtue is neither natural nor imparted by teaching, but an instinct given by God to those to whom it is given. Nor is the instinct accompanied by reason, unless there may be supposed to be among statesmen someone who is capable of educating statesmen. And if there be such a one, he may be said to be among the living what Homer says that Tiresias was among the dead, "he alone has understanding, but the rest are flitting shades"; in point of virtue he will be in like manner a reality among shadows.

Men: That is excellent, Socrates.

Soc: Then, Meno, the conclusion is that virtue comes by the gift of God to those to whom it does come. But we shall never know the certain truth until, before asking how virtue is given, we set ourselves to inquire into the essential nature of virtue. I fear that I must go away, but do you, now that you are persuaded yourself, persuade our friend Anytus. And do not let him be so exasperated; if you can conciliate him, you will have done good service to the Athenian people.

Protagoras*

. . . When we were all seated, Protagoras said: Now that the company are assembled, Socrates, you might repeat what you said to me just now on behalf of this young man.

I replied: I will begin again at the same point, Protagoras, and tell you once more the purport of my visit: this is my friend Hippocrates, who is desirous of your society; he would like to know what will happen to him if he associates with you. I have no more to say.

Protagoras answered: Young man, if you associate with me, on the very first day you will return home a better man than you came, and better on the second day than on the first, and better every day than you were on the day before.

When I heard this, I said: Protagoras, I do not at all wonder at hearing you say this; even at your age, and with all your wisdom, if anyone were to teach you what you did not know before, you would become better no doubt: but please to answer in a different way—I will explain how by an example. Let me suppose that Hippocrates, instead of desiring your society, were suddenly to desire that of the young man Zeuxippus of Heraclea, who has lately arrived on a visit to Athens, and he had come to him as he had come to you, and had heard him say, as he has heard you say, that every day he would grow and become better if he associated with him: and then suppose that he were to ask him, "In what shall I become better, and in what shall I grow?"—Zeuxippus would answer, "In painting." And suppose that he went to Orthagoras the Theban, and heard him say the same thing, and asked him, "In what shall I become better day by day?" he would reply, "In flute-playing." Now I want you to make the same sort of answer to this young man and to me, who am asking questions on his account. When you say that on the first day on which he associates with you he will return home a better man, and on every day will grow in like manner,—in what, Protagoras, will he be better? and about what?

When Protagoras heard me say this, he replied: You ask questions fairly, and I like to answer a question which is fairly put. If Hippocrates comes to me he will not experience the sort of drudgery with which other sophists are in the habit of insulting their pupils; who, when they have just escaped from the arts, are taken against their will and driven back into them by these teachers, and made to learn calculation, and astronomy, and geometry, and music (he gave a look at Hippias as he said this); but if he comes to me, he will learn that which he comes to learn. And this is prudence in affairs private as well as public; he will learn to order his own house in the best manner, and he will be fully qualified to speak and act in the affairs of the state.

Do I understand you, I said; and is your meaning that you teach the art of politics, and that you promise to make men good citizens?

That, Socrates, is exactly the profession which I make.

*The translation is by Benjamin Jowett.

Then, I said, you possess a truly noble art, if there is no mistake about this; for to you, Protagoras, I will speak with entire candour, and admit that I used to think that this art is incapable of being taught, and yet I know not how to disbelieve your assertion. And I ought to tell you why I am of opinion that this art cannot be taught or communicated by man to man. I say that the Athenians are an outstanding people, and indeed they are esteemed to be such by the other Hellenes. Now I observe that when we are met together in the assembly, and the matter in hand relate to building, the builders are summoned as advisers; when the question is one of ship-building, then the ship-wrights; and the like of other arts which they think capable of being taught and learned. And if some person offers to give them advice who is not supposed by them to have any skill in the art, even though he be good-looking and rich and noble, they will not listen to him; but laugh and hoot at him, until either he is clamoured down and retires of himself, or he is dragged away or put out by the constables at the command of the prytanes. This is their way of behaving about that which they deem to be the subject of an art. But when the question is an affair of state, then everybody is free to have a say—carpenter, tinker, cobbler, merchant, sea-captain; rich and poor, high and low—anyone who likes gets up, and no one reproaches him, as in the former case, with not having learned, and having no teacher, and yet giving advice; evidently because they are under the impression that this sort of knowledge cannot be taught. And not only is this true of the state, but of individuals; the best and wisest of our citizens are unable to impart their own excellence to others: as for example, Pericles, the father of these young men, who provided them with admirable instruction in all that could be learned from masters, in his own department of politics neither taught them, nor gave them teachers; but they were allowed to wander at their own free will in a sort of hope that they would light upon virtue of their own accord. Or take another example: there was Cleinias the younger brother of our friend Alcibiades, of whom this very same Pericles was the guardian; and he being in fact under the apprehension that Cleinias would be corrupted by Alcibiades snatched him away from his brother, and placed him in the house of Ariphron to be educated; but before six months had elapsed, Pericles sent him back to Alcibiades, not knowing what to do with him. And I could mention numberless other instances of persons who were good themselves, and never yet made any one else good, whether friend or stranger. Now I, Protagoras, when I contemplate these examples, am of opinion that virtue cannot be taught. But then again, when I listen to your words, I waver; and am disposed to think that there must be something in what you say, because I know that you have great experience, and learning, and invention. And I wish that you would, if possible, show me a little more clearly that virtue can be taught. Will you be so good?

That I will, Socrates, and gladly. But what would you like? Shall I, as an elder, speak to you as younger men in an apologue or myth, or shall I argue out the question?

To this several of the company answered that he should choose for himself.

Well, then, he said, I think that the myth will be more interesting.

Once upon a time there were gods only, and no mortal creatures. But when the appointed time came that these also should be created, the gods fashioned them out of earth and fire and various mixtures of both elements in the interior of the earth; and when they were about to bring them into the light of day, they ordered Prometheus and Epimetheus to equip them, and to distribute to them severally their proper qualities. Epimetheus said to Prometheus: "Let me distribute, and do you inspect." This was agreed, and Epimetheus made the distribution. There were some to whom he gave strength without swiftness, while he equipped the weaker with swiftness; some he armed, and others he left unarmed; and devised for the latter some other means of preservation. Upon those whom he clothed in diminutive bodies, he bestowed winged flight or subterranean habitation: those which he aggrandized with magnitude, he protected by their very size: and similarly with the rest of his distribution, always compensating. These devices he used as precautions that no race should be destroyed. And when he had provided against their destruction by one another, he contrived also a means of protecting them against the seasons of heaven; clothing them with close hair and thick skins sufficient to defend them against the winter cold, yet able to resist the summer heat, and serving also as a natural bed of their own when they wanted to rest; also he furnished them with hoofs and hair and hard and callous skins under their feet. Then he gave them varieties of food,—herb of the soil to some, to others fruits of trees, and to others roots, and to some again he gave other animals as food. And some he made to have few young ones, while those who were their prey were very prolific; and in this manner the race was preserved. Thus did Epimetheus, who, not being very wise, forgot that he had distributed among the brute animals all the qualities which he had to give,—and when he came to man, who was still unprovided, he was terribly perplexed. Now while he was in this perplexity, Prometheus came to inspect the distribution, and he found that the other animals were quite suitably furnished, but that man was naked and shoeless, and had neither bed nor arms of defence. The appointed hour was approaching when man in his turn was to emerge from earth into the light of day; and Prometheus, not knowing how he could devise his salvation, stole the mechanical arts of Hephaestus and Athene, and fire with them (they could neither have been acquired nor used without fire), and gave them to man. Thus man had the wisdom necessary to the support of life, but political wisdom he had not; for that was in the keeping of Zeus, and the power of Prometheus no longer extended to entering into the citadel of heaven, where Zeus dwelt, who moreover had terrible sentinels; but he did enter by stealth into the common workshop of Athene and Hephaestus, in which they used to practise their favourite arts, and carried off Hephaestus' art of working by fire, and also the art of Athene, and gave them to man. And in this way man was supplied with the means of life. But Prometheus is said to have been afterwards prosecuted for theft, owing to the blunder of Epimetheus.

Now man, having a share of the divine attributes, was at first the only one of the animals who had any gods, because he alone was of their kindred; and he would raise altars and images of them. He was not long in inventing articulate speech and names; and he also constructed houses and clothes and shoes and beds, and drew sustenance from the earth. Thus provided, mankind at first lived dispersed, and there were no cities. But the consequence was that they were destroyed by the wild beasts, for they were utterly weak in comparison of them, and their practical attainments were only sufficient to provide them with the means of life, and did not enable them to carry on war against the animals: food they had, but not as yet the art of government, of which the art of war is a part. After a while the desire of self-preservation gathered them into cities; but when they were gathered together, having no art of government, they evilly entreated one another, and were again in process of dispersion and destruction. Zeus feared that the entire race would be exterminated, and so he sent Hermes to them, bearing reverence and justice to be the ordering principles of cities and the bonds of friendship and conciliation. Hermes asked Zeus how he should impart justice and reverence among men:—Should he distribute them as the arts are distributed; that is to say, to a favoured few only, one skilled individual having enough of medicine or of any other art for many unskilled ones? "Shall this be the manner in which I am to distribute justice and reverence among men, or shall I give them to all?" "To all," said Zeus; "I should like them all to have a share; for cities cannot exist, if a few only share in the virtues, as in the arts. And further, make a law by my order, that he who has no part in reverence and justice shall be put to death, for he is a plague of the state."

And this is the reason, Socrates, why the Athenians and mankind in general, when the question relates to carpentering or any other mechanical art, allow but a few to share in their deliberations; and when anyone else interferes, then, as you say, they object, if he be not of the favoured few; which, as I reply, is very natural. But when they meet to deliberate about political virtue, which proceeds only by way of justice and wisdom, they are patient enough of any man who speaks of them, as is also natural, because they think that every man ought to share in this sort of virtue, and that states could not exist if this were otherwise. Such, Socrates, is the reason of this phenomenon.

And that you may not suppose yourself to be deceived in thinking that all men regard every man as having a share of justice or honesty and of every other political virtue, let me give you a further proof. In other cases, as you are aware, if a man says that he is a good flute-player, or skilful in any other art in which he has no skill, people either laugh at him or are angry with him, and his relations think that he is mad and go and admonish him; but when honesty is in question, or some other political virtue, even if they know that he is dishonest, yet, if the man comes forward publicly and tells the truth against himself, then, what in the other case was held by them to be good sense, viz., telling the truth, they now deem to be madness. They say that all men ought to profess honesty whether they are honest or not, and that a man is out of his mind who makes no claim to that virtue. Their notion is, that every man must have it in some degree, or else he ought not to be in the world.

I have been showing that they are right in admitting every man as a counsellor about this sort of virtue, as they are of opinion that every man is a partaker of it. And I will now endeavour to show further that they do not conceive this virtue to be given by nature, or to grow spontaneously, but to be a thing which may be taught; and which comes to those to whom it does come, by taking pains. No one would instruct, no one would rebuke or be angry with those whose calamities they suppose to be due to nature or chance: they do not try to punish or to prevent them from being what they are; they do but pity them. Who is so foolish as to chastise or instruct the ugly, or the diminutive, or the feeble? And for this reason. Because, I take it, everyone knows that good and evil of this kind is the work of nature and of chance; whereas if a man is wanting in those good qualities which are held to be attainable by study and exercise and teaching, and has only the contrary evil qualities, other men are angry with him, and punish and reprove him—of these evil qualities one is impiety, another injustice, and they may be described generally as the very opposite of political virtue. In such cases any man will be angry with another, and reprimand him,—clearly because he thinks that by study and learning the virtue may be acquired. If you think, Socrates, of the effect of punishment upon the wrong-doer, you will see at once that in the opinion of mankind virtue may be acquired; no one punishes the evil-doer under the notion, or for the reason, that he has done wrong,—only the unreasonable fury of a beast acts in that manner. But he who desires to inflict rational punishment does not retaliate for a past wrong, for what has been done cannot be undone; he has regard to the future, and is desirous that the man who is punished, and he who sees him punished, may be deterred from doing wrong again. Now if this is his conception, then he also conceives that virtue may be taught; since it is for the sake of deterrence that he punishes. This is the notion of all who retaliate upon others either privately or publicly. And the Athenians, too, your own citizens, like other men, punish and take vengeance on all whom they regard as evil-doers; and hence we may infer them to be of the number of those who think that virtue may be acquired and taught. Thus far, Socrates, I have shown you clearly enough, if I am not mistaken, that your countrymen are right in admitting the tinker and the cobbler to advise about politics, and also that they deem virtue to be capable of being taught and acquired.

There yet remains one difficulty which has been raised by you about good men. What is the reason why good men teach their sons the knowledge which can be gained from teachers, and make them wise in that, but make them no better than anyone else in the virtues which distinguish themselves? And here, Socrates, I will leave the apologue and resume the argument. Please to consider: Is there or is there not some one quality of which all the citizens must be partakers, if there is to be a city at all? In the answer to this question is contained the only solution of your difficulty; there is no other. For if there be any such quality, and this quality or unity is not the art of the carpenter, or the smith, or the potter, but justice and temperance and holiness and, in a word, manly virtue—if this is the quality of which all men must be partakers, and which is the very condition of their learning or doing anything else, and if he who is wanting in this, whether he be a child only or a grown-up man or woman, must be taught and punished, until by punishment he becomes better, and he who rebels against instruction and punishment must be either exiled or condemned to death as incurable—if what I am saying be true, and yet good men have their sons taught other things and not this, do consider what a strange thing their goodness has become. For we have shown that they think virtue capable of being taught and cultivated both in private and public; and, notwithstanding, they have their sons taught lesser matters, ignorance of which does not involve the punishment of death: but greater things, of which the ignorance may cause death and exile to their own children, if they have no knowledge of virtue or encouragement toward it—aye, and confiscation as well as death, and, in a word, may be the ruin of families—those things, I say, they are supposed not to have them taught,—not to take the utmost care that they should learn. How improbable is this, Socrates!

Education and admonition commence in the first years of childhood, and last to the very end of life. Mother and nurse and father and tutor are vying with one another about the improvement of the child as soon as ever he is able to understand what is being said to him: he cannot say or do anything without their teaching him and setting forth to him that this is just and that is unjust; this is honourable, that is dishonourable; this is holy, that is unholy; do this and abstain from that. And if he obeys, well and good; if not, he is straightened by threats and blows, like a piece of bent or warped wood. At a later stage they send him to teachers, and enjoin them to see to his good behaviour even more than to his reading and music; and the teachers do as they are desired. And when the boy has learned his letters and is beginning to understand what is written, as before he understood only what was spoken, they put on his desk the works of great poets for him to read; in these are contained many admonitions, and many tales and praises and encomia of famous men of old, which he is required to learn by heart, in order that he may imitate or emulate them and desire to become like them. Then, again, the teachers of the lyre take similar care that their young disciple is temperate and gets into no mischief; and when they have taught him the use of the lyre, they introduce him to the poems of other excellent poets, who are the lyric poets; and these they set to music, and make their harmonies and rhythms quite familiar to the children's souls, in order that they may learn to be more gentle, and harmonious, and rhythmical, and so more fitted for speech and action; for the life of man in every part has need of harmony and rhythm. Then they send them to the master of gymnastic, in order that the improvement of their bodies may better minister to the virtuous mind, and that they may not be compelled through bodily weakness to play the coward in war or on any other occasion. This is principally done by those who have the means, and those who have the means are the rich; their children begin to go to school soonest and leave off latest. When they have done with masters, the state again compels them to learn the laws, and live after the pattern which they furnish, and not after their own fancies; and just as the writing-master first traces outlines with a style for the use of the young beginner who is not yet able to write, then gives him the tablet and makes him write along those lines, so the city outlines the laws, which were the invention of good lawgivers living in the olden time, and compels us to exercise and to obey authority in accordance with those; and he who transgresses them is to be corrected, or, in other words, called to account, which is a term used not only in your country, but also in many others, seeing that justice calls men to account. Now when there is all this care about virtue private and public, why, Socrates, do you still wonder and doubt whether virtue can be taught? Cease to wonder, for the opposite would be far more surprising.

But why then do the sons of good fathers often turn out ill? Learn now the cause of this. There is nothing very wonderful in it, if what I said before was true, that the existence of a state implies that no man is unskilled in virtue. If so—and nothing can be truer—then I will further ask you to take as an illustration some other pursuit or branch of knowledge, and reflect upon that. Suppose that there could be no state unless we were all flute-players, as far as each had the capacity, and everybody was freely teaching everybody the art, both in private and public, and reproving the bad player as freely and openly as every man now teaches justice and the laws, not concealing them as he would conceal the other arts, but imparting them—for all of us have a mutual interest in the justice and virtue of one another, and this is the reason why everyone is so ready to propagate and teach justice and the laws;—suppose, I say, that there were the same readiness and liberality among us in teaching one another flute-playing, do you imagine, Socrates, that the sons of good flute-players would be more likely to be good than the sons of bad ones? I think not. Would not their sons grow up to be distinguished or undistinguished according to their own natural capacities as flute-players, and the son of a good player would often turn out to be a bad one, and the son of a bad player to be a good one, but at least they would all play the flute reasonably well in comparison of those who were ignorant and unacquainted with the art of flute-playing? In like manner I would have you consider that he who appears to you to be the worst of those who have been brought up in laws and human society, would appear to be a just man and an artificer of justice if he were to be compared with men who had no education, or courts of justice, or laws, or any constraints forcing them incessantly to the practice of virtue—with savages like those whom the poet Pherecrates exhibited on the stage at last year's Lenaean festival. If you were living among such as the man-haters of his Chorus, you would be only too glad to meet with Eurybates and Phrynondas, and you would sorrowfully long to revisit the rascality of this part of the world. Now you, Socrates, are being fastidious, and why? Because all men are teachers of virtue, each one according to his ability; and you say Where are the teachers? You might as well ask, Who teaches Greek? For of that too there will not be any teachers found. Or you might ask, Who is to teach the sons of our artisans this same art which they have learned of their fathers? He and his fellow workmen have taught them to the best of their ability,—but who will carry them farther in their arts? You would certainly have a difficulty, Socrates, in finding a teacher of them, but there would be no difficulty whatever in finding a teacher of those who are ignorant; this is true of virtue or of anything else. But if there is anyone better able than we are to promote virtue ever so little, we must be content with the result. A teacher of this sort I believe myself to be, excelling all other human beings in the power to raise a man towards nobility and goodness; and I give my pupils their money's-worth, and even more, as they themselves confess. And therefore I have introduced the following mode of payment:—When a man is my pupil, if he likes he pays my fee; if he does not like, he has only to go into a temple and take an oath of the value of the instruction, and he pays no more than that.

Such is my apologue, Socrates, and such is the argument by which I endeavour to show that virtue may be taught, and that this is the opinion of the Athenians. And I have also attempted to show that you are not to wonder at good fathers having bad sons, or at good sons having bad fathers; thus the sons of Polycleitus, who are the companions of our friends here, Paralus and Xanthippus, are nothing in comparison with their father; and this is true of the sons of many other artists. As yet we ought not to bring the same charge against Paralus and Xanthippus themselves, for they are young and there is still hope of them.

Such was the speech of Protagoras, who now held his peace. For a long time I could not take my eyes off him, still spellbound, expecting him to speak further, and eager to hear him. At length, when the truth dawned upon me that he had really finished, not without difficulty I pulled myself together, as it were, and looking at Hippocrates, I said to him: O son of Apollodorus, how deeply grateful I am to you for having urged me to come hither; I would not have missed the speech of Protagoras for a great deal. For I used to imagine that no human care can make men good; but I know better now.

The Republic*
BOOK II

. . . Glaucon, and all the rest with him, requested me by all means to give my assistance, and not to let the conversation drop, but thoroughly to investigate the real nature of justice and injustice, and which is the true doctrine with regard to their respective advantages. So I said what I really felt: The inquiry we are undertaking is no trivial one, but demands a keen sight, according to my notion of it. Therefore, since I am not a clever person, I think we had better adopt a mode of inquiry which may be thus illustrated. Suppose we had been ordered to read small writing at a distance, not having very good eye-sight, and that one of us discovered that the same writing was to be found somewhere else in larger letters, and upon a larger space, we should have looked upon it as a piece of luck, I imagine, that we could read the latter first, and then examine the smaller, and observe whether the two were alike.

*The translation is by John Llewelyn Davies and David James Vaughan.

Undoubtedly we should, said Adeimantus; but what parallel can you see to this, Socrates, in our inquiry after justice?

I will tell you, I replied. We speak of justice as residing in an individual mind, and as residing also in an entire city, do we not?

Certainly we do, he said.

Well, a city is larger than one man.

It is.

Perhaps, then, justice may exist in larger proportions in the greater subject, and thus be easier to discover: so, if you please, let us first investigate its character in cities; afterwards let us apply the same inquiry to the individual, looking for the counterpart of the greater as it exists in the form of the less.

Indeed, he said, I think your plan is a good one.

If then we were to trace in thought the gradual formation of a city, should we also see the growth of its justice or of its injustice?

Perhaps we should.

Then, if this were done, might we not hope to see more easily the object of our search?

Yes, much more easily.

It is your advice, then, that we should attempt to carry out our plan? It is no trifling task, I imagine; therefore consider it well.

We have considered it, said Adeimantus; yes, do so by all means.

Well then, I proceeded, the formation of a city is due, as I imagine, to this fact, that we are not individually independent, but have many wants. Or would you assign any other cause for the founding of cities?

No, I agree with you, he replied.

Thus it is, then, that owing to our many wants, and because each seeks the aid of others to supply his various requirements, we gather many associates and helpers into one dwelling-place, and give to this joint dwelling the name of city. Is it so?

Undoubtedly.

And every one who gives or takes in exchange, whatever it be that he exchanges, does so from a belief that he is consulting his own interest.

Certainly.

Now then, let us construct our imaginary city from the beginning. It will owe its construction, it appears, to our natural wants.

Unquestionably.

Well, but the first and most pressing of all wants is that of sustenance to enable us to exist as living creatures.

Most decidedly.

Our second want would be that of a house, and our third that of clothing and the like.

True.

Then let us know what will render our city adequate to the supply of so many things. Must we not begin with a husbandman for one, and a house-builder, and besides these a weaver? Will these suffice, or shall we add to them a shoemaker, and perhaps one or two more of the class of people who minister to our bodily wants?

By all means.

Then the smallest possible city will consist of four or five men.

So we see.

To proceed then: ought each of these to place his own work at the disposal of the community, so that the single husbandman, for example, shall provide food for four, spending four times the amount of time and labour upon the preparation of food, and sharing it with others; or must he be regardless of them, and produce for his own consumption alone the fourth part of this quantity of food, in a fourth part of the time, spending the other three parts, one in making his house, another in procuring himself clothes, and the third in providing himself with shoes, saving himself the trouble of sharing with others, and doing his own business by himself, and for himself?

To this Adeimantus replied, Well, Socrates, perhaps the former plan is the easier of the two.

Really, I said, it is not improbable; for I recollect, myself, after your answer, that, in the first place, no two persons are born exactly alike, but each differs from each in natural endowments, one being suited for one occupation, and another for another. Do you not think so?

I do.

Well; when is a man likely to succeed best? When he divides his exertions among many trades, or when he devotes himself exclusively to one?

When he devotes himself to one.

Again, it is also clear, I imagine, that if a person lets the right moment for any work go by, it never returns.

It is quite clear.

For the thing to be done does not choose, I imagine, to tarry the leisure of the doer, but the doer must be at the beck of the thing to be done, and not treat it as a secondary affair.

He must.

From these considerations it follows, that all things will be produced in superior quantity and quality, and with greater ease, when each man works at a single occupation, in accordance with his natural gifts, and at the right moment, without meddling with anything else.

Unquestionably.

More than four citizens, then, Adeimantus, are needed to provide the requisites which we named. For the husbandman, it appears, will not make his own plough, if it is to be a good one, nor his mattock, nor any of the other tools employed in agriculture. No more will the builder make the numerous tools which he also requires: and so of the weaver and the shoemaker.

True.

Then we shall have carpenters and smiths, and many other artisans of the kind, who will become members of our little state, and create a population.

Certainly.

Still it will not yet be very large, supposing we add to them neatherds and shepherds, and the rest of that class, in order that the husbandmen may have oxen for ploughing, and the house-builders, as well as the husbandmen, beasts of burden for draught, and the weavers and shoemakers wool and leather.

It will not be a small state, either, if it contains all these.

Moreover, it is scarcely possible to plant the actual city in a place where it will have no need of imports.

No, it is impossible.

Then it will further require a new class of persons to bring from other cities all that it requires.

It will.

Well, but if the agent goes empty-handed, carrying with him none of the commodities in demand among those people from whom our state is to procure what it requires, he will also come empty-handed away: will he not?

I think so.

Then it must produce at home not only enough for itself, but also articles of the right kind and quantity to accommodate those whose services it needs.

It must.

Then our city requires larger numbers both of husbandmen and other craftsmen.

Yes, it does.

And among the rest it will need more of those agents also, who are to export and import the several commodities: and these are merchants, are they not?

Yes.

Then we shall require merchants also.

Certainly.

And if the traffic is carried on by sea, there will be a further demand for a considerable number of other persons, who are skilled in the practice of navigation.

A considerable number, undoubtedly.

But now tell me: in the city itself how are they to exchange their several productions? For it was to promote this exchange, you know, that we formed the community, and so founded our state.

Manifestly, by buying and selling.

Then this will give rise to a market and a currency, for the sake of exchange.

Undoubtedly.

Suppose then that the husbandman, or one of the other craftsmen, should come with some of his produce into the market, at a time when none of those who wish to make an exchange with him are there, is he to leave his occupation and sit idle in the market-place?

By no means: there are persons who, with an eye to this contingency, undertake the service required; and these in well-regulated states are, generally speaking, persons of excessive physical weakness, who are of no use in other kinds of labour. Their business is to remain on the spot in the market, and give money for goods to those who want to sell, and goods for money to those who want to buy.

This demand, then, causes a class of retail dealers to spring up in our city. For do we not give the name of retail dealers to those who station themselves in the market, to minister to buying and selling, applying the term merchants to those who go about from city to city?

Exactly so.

In addition to these, I imagine, there is also another class of operatives, consisting of those whose mental qualifications do not recommend them as associates, but whose bodily strength is equal to hard labour: these, selling the use of their strength and calling the price of it hire, are thence named, I believe, hired labourers. Is it not so?

Precisely.

Then hired labourers also form, as it seems, a complementary portion of a state.

I think so.

Shall we say then, Adeimantus, that our city has at length grown to its full stature?

Perhaps so.

Where then, I wonder, shall we find justice and injustice in it? With which of these elements that we have contemplated, has it simultaneously made its entrance?

I have no notion, Socrates, unless perhaps it be discoverable somewhere in the mutual relations of these same persons.

Well, perhaps you are right. We must investigate the matter, and not flinch from the task.

Let us consider then, in the first place, what kind of life will be led by persons thus provided. I presume they will produce corn and wine, and clothes and shoes, and build themselves houses; and in summer, no doubt, they will generally work without their coats and shoes, while in winter they will be suitably clothed and shod. And they will live, I suppose, on barley and wheat, baking cakes of the meal, and kneading loaves of the flour. And spreading these excellent cakes and loaves upon mats of straw or on clean leaves, and themselves reclining on rude beds of yew or myrtle-boughs, they will make merry, themselves and their children, drinking their wine, wearing garlands, and singing the praises of the gods, enjoying one another's society, and not begetting children beyond their means, through a prudent fear of poverty or war.

Glaucon here interrupted me, remarking, Apparently you describe your men as feasting without anything to relish their bread.

True, I said, I had forgotten:—of course they will have something to relish their food; salt, no doubt, and olives and cheese, together with the country fare of boiled onions and cabbage. We shall also set before them a dessert, I imagine, of figs and peas and beans; and they may roast myrtle-berries and beech-nuts at the fire, taking wine with their fruit in moderation. And thus passing their days in tranquillity and sound health, they will, in all probability, live to an advanced age, and dying, bequeath to their children a life in which their own will be reproduced.

Upon this Glaucon exclaimed, Why Socrates, if you were founding a community of swine, this is just the style in which you would feed them up!

How then, said I, would you have them live, Glaucon?

In a civilized manner, he replied. They ought to recline on couches, I should think, if they are not to have a hard life of it, and dine off tables, and have the usual dishes and dessert of a modern dinner.

Very good; I understand. Apparently we are considering the growth not of a city merely, but of a luxurious city. I dare say it is not a bad plan: for by this extension of our inquiry we shall perhaps discover how it is that justice and injustice take root in cities. Now it appears to me that the city which we have described is the genuine and, so to speak, healthy city. But if you wish us also to contemplate a city that is suffering from inflammation, there is nothing to hinder us. Some people will not be satisfied, it seems, with the fare or the mode of life which we have described, but must have, in addition, couches and tables and every other article of furniture, as well as viands, and fragrant oils, and perfumes, and courtesans, and confectionery; and all these in plentiful variety. Moreover, we must not limit ourselves now to essentials in those articles which we specified at first, I mean houses and clothes and shoes, but we must set painting and embroidery to work, and acquire gold and ivory, and all similar valuables: must we not?

Yes.

Then we shall also have to enlarge our city, for our first or healthy city will not now be of sufficient size, but requires to be increased in bulk, and filled out with a multitude of callings, which do not exist in cities to satisfy any natural want; for example, the whole class of hunters, and all who practice imitative arts, including many who use forms and colours, and many who use music, poets also, with those of whom the poet makes use, rhapsodists, actors, dancers, contractors; lastly, the manufacturers of all sorts of articles, and among others those which form part of a woman's dress. We shall similarly require more personal servants, shall we not? that is to say, tutors, wet-nurses, dry-nurses, tire-women, barbers, and cooks moreover and confectioners? Swineherds again are among the additions we shall require,—a class of persons not to be found, because not wanted, in our former city, but needed among the rest in this. We shall also need great quantities of all kinds of cattle, for those who may wish to eat them; shall we not?

Of course we shall.

Then shall we not experience the need of medical men also, to a much greater extent under this than under the former regime?

Yes, indeed.

The country too, I presume, which was formerly adequate to the support of its then inhabitants will be now too small, and adequate no longer. Shall we say so?

Certainly.

Then must we not cut ourselves a slice of our neighbour's territory, if we are to have land enough both for pasture and tillage, while they will do the same to ours, if they, like us, permit themselves to overstep the limit of necessaries, and plunge into the unbounded acquisition of wealth?

It must inevitably be so, Socrates.

Will our next step be to go to war, Glaucon, or how will it be?

As you say.

At this stage of our inquiry let us avoid asserting either that war does good or that it does harm, confining ourselves to this statement, that we have further traced the origin of war to causes which are the most fruitful sources of whatever evils befall a state, either in its corporate capacity, or in its individual members.

Exactly so.

Once more then, my friend, our state must receive an accession of no trifling extent, I mean that of a whole army, which must go forth and do battle with all invaders in defence of its entire property, and of the persons whom we were just now describing.

How? he asked; are not those persons sufficient of themselves?

They are not, if you and all the rest of us were right in the admissions which we made, when we were modelling our state. We admitted, I think, if you remember, that it was impossible for one man to work well at many professions.

True.

Well then, is not the business of war looked upon as a profession in itself?

Undoubtedly.

And have we not as much reason to concern ourselves about the trade of war as about the trade of shoemaking?

Quite as much.

But we cautioned the shoemaker, you know, against attempting to be an agriculturist or a weaver or a builder besides, with a view to our shoemaking work being well done; and to every other artisan we assigned in like manner one occupation, namely, that for which he was naturally fitted, and in which, if he let other things alone, and wrought at it all his time without neglecting his opportunities, he was likely to prove a successful workman. Now is it not of the greatest moment that the work of war should be well done? Or is it so easy, that anyone can succeed in it and be at the same time a husbandman or a shoemaker or a labourer at any other trade whatever, although there is no one in the world who could become a good draught-player or dice-player by merely taking up the game at unoccupied moments, instead of pursuing it as his especial study from his childhood? And will it be enough for a man merely to handle a shield or any other of the arms and implements of war, to be straightway competent to play his part well that very day in an engagement of heavy troops or in any other military service, although the mere handling of any other instrument will never make anyone a true craftsman or athlete, nor will such instrument be even useful to one who has neither learnt its capabilities nor exercised himself sufficiently in its practical applications.

If it were so, these implements of war would be very valuable.

In proportion, then, to the importance of the work which these guardians have to do, will it require peculiar freedom from other engagements, as well as extraordinary skill and attention.

I quite think so.

Will it not also require natural endowments suited to this particular occupation?

Undoubtedly.

Then, apparently, it will belong to us to choose out, if we can, that especial order of natural endowments which qualifies its possessors for the guardianship of a state.

Certainly; it belongs to us.

Then, I assure you, we have taken upon ourselves no trifling task; nevertheless, there must be no flinching, so long as our strength holds out.

No, there must not.

Do you think then, I asked, that there is any difference, in the qualities required for keeping guard, between a well-bred dog and a gallant young man?

I do not quite understand you.

Why, I suppose, for instance, they ought both of them to be quick to discover an enemy, and swift to overtake him when discovered, and strong also, in case they have to fight when they have come up with him.

Certainly, all these qualities are required.

Moreover, they must be brave if they are to fight well.

Undoubtedly.

But will either a horse, or a dog, or any other animal, be likely to be brave if it is not spirited? or have you failed to observe what an irresistible and unconquerable thing spirit is, so that under its influence every creature will be fearless and unconquerable in the face of any danger?

I have observed it.

We know then what bodily qualities are required in our guardian.

We do.

And also what qualities of the mind, namely, that he must be spirited.

Yes.

How then, Glaucon, if such be their natural disposition, are they to be kept from behaving fiercely to one another, and to the rest of the citizens?

Really it will be difficult to obviate that.

Nevertheless, they certainly ought to be gentle to their friends, and dangerous only to their enemies: else they will not wait for others to destroy them, but will be the first to do it for themselves.

True.

What then shall we do? Where shall we find a character at once gentle and high-spirited? For I suppose a gentle nature is the opposite of a spirited one?

Apparently it is.

Nevertheless a man who is devoid of either gentleness or spirit cannot possibly make a good guardian. And as they seem to be incompatible, the result is, that a good guardian is an impossibility.

It looks like it, he said.

Here then I was perplexed, but having reconsidered our conversation, I said, We deserve, my friend, to be puzzled; for we have deserted the illustration which we set before us.

How so?

It never struck us, that after all there are natures, though we fancied there were none, which combine these opposite qualities.

Pray where is such a combination to be found?

You may see it in several animals, but particularly in the one which we ourselves compared to our guardian. For I suppose you know that it is the natural disposition of well-bred dogs to be perfectly gentle to their friends and acquaintance, but the reverse to strangers.

Certainly I do.

Therefore the thing is possible; and we are not contradicting nature in our endeavour to give such a character to our guardian.

So it would seem.

Then is it your opinion, that in one who is to make a good guardian it is further required that his character should be philosophical as well as high-spirited?

How so? I do not understand you.

You will notice in dogs this other trait, which is really marvellous in the creature.

What is that?

Whenever they see a stranger they are irritated before they have been provoked by any ill-usage; but when they see an acquaintance they welcome him, though they may never have experienced any kindness at his hands. Has this never excited your wonder?

I never paid any attention to it hitherto; but no doubt they do behave so.

Well, but this instinct is a very clever thing in the dog, and a genuine philosophic symptom.

How so, pray?

Why, because the only mark by which he distinguishes between the appearance of a friend and that of an enemy is, that he knows the former and is ignorant of the latter. How, I ask, can the creature be other than fond of learning when it makes knowledge and ignorance the criteria of the familiar and the strange?

Beyond a question, it must be fond of learning.

Well, is not the love of learning identical with a philosophical disposition?

It is.

Shall we not then assert with confidence in the case of a man also, that if he is to shew a gentle disposition towards his relatives and acquaintances, he must have a turn for learning and philosophy?

Be it so.

Then in our judgment the man whose natural gifts promise to make him a perfect guardian of the state will be philosophical, high-spirited, swift-footed, and strong.

Undoubtedly he will.

* * *

This then will be the original character of our guardians. But in what way shall we rear and educate them? And will the investigation of this point help us on towards discovering that which is the object of all our speculations, namely, the manner in which justice and injustice grow up in a state? For I wish us neither to omit anything useful, nor to occupy ourselves with anything redundant, in our inquiry.

Hereupon Glaucon's brother observed, Well, for my part, I fully anticipate that this inquiry will promote our object.

If so, I said, we must certainly not give it up, my dear Adeimantus, even though it should prove somewhat long.

Indeed we must not.

Come then, like idle story-tellers in a story, let us describe the education of our men.

Yes, let us do so.

What then is the education to be? Perhaps we could hardly find a better than that which the experience of the past has already discovered, which consists, I believe, in gymnastic for the body, and music for the mind.

It does.

Shall we not then begin our course of education with music rather than with gymnastic?

Undoubtedly we shall.

Under the term music, do you include narratives, or not?

I do.

And of narratives there are two kinds, the true and the false.

Yes.

And must we instruct our pupils in both, but in the false first?

I do not understand what you mean.

Do you not understand that we begin with children by telling them fables? And these, I suppose, to speak generally, are false, though they contain some truths: and we employ such fables in the treatment of children at an earlier period than gymnastic exercises.

True.

That is what I meant when I said that music ought to be taken up before gymnastic.

You are right.

Then are you aware, that in every work the beginning is the most important part, especially in dealing with anything young and tender? for that is the time when any impression, which one may desire to communicate, is most readily stamped and taken.

Precisely so.

Shall we then permit our children without scruple to hear any fables composed by any authors indifferently, and so to receive into their minds opinions generally the reverse of those which, when they are grown to manhood, we shall think they ought to entertain?

No, we shall not permit it on any account.

Then apparently our first duty will be to exercise a superintendence over the authors of fables, selecting their good productions, and rejecting the bad. And the selected fables we shall advise our nurses and mothers to repeat to their children, that they may thus mould their minds with the fables even more than they shape their bodies with the hand. But we shall have to repudiate the greater part of those which are now in vogue.

Which do you mean? he asked.

In the greater fables, I answered, we shall also discern the less. For the general character and tendency of both the greater and the less must doubtless be identical. Do you not think so?

I do: but I am equally uncertain which you mean by the greater.

I mean the stories which Hesiod, and Homer, and the other poets, tell us. For they, I imagine, have composed fictitious narratives which they told, and yet tell, to men.

Pray what kind of fables do you mean, and what is the fault that you find with them?

A fault, I replied, which deserves the earliest and gravest condemnation, especially if the fiction has no beauty.

What is this fault?

It is whenever an author gives a bad representation of the characters of gods and heroes, like a painter whose picture should bear no resemblance to the objects he wishes to imitate.

Yes, it is quite right to condemn such faults: but pray explain further what we mean, and give some instances.

In the first place, the poet who conceived the boldest fiction on the highest subjects invented an ugly story, when he told how Uranus acted as Hesiod declares he did, and also how Cronus had his revenge upon him. And again, even if the deeds of Cronus, and his son's treatment of him, were authentic facts, it would not have been right, I should have thought, to tell them without the least reserve to young and thoughtless persons: on the contrary, it would be best to suppress them altogether: or, if for some reason they must be told, they should be imparted under the seal of secrecy to as few hearers as possible, and after the sacrifice, not of a pig, but of some rare and costly victim, which might aid to the utmost in restricting their number.

Certainly, these are offensive stories.

They are; and therefore, Adeimantus, they must not be repeated in our city. No: we must not tell a youthful listener that he will be doing nothing extraordinary if he commit the foulest crimes, nor yet if he chastise the crimes of a father in the most unscrupulous manner, but will simply be doing what the first and greatest of the gods have done before him.

I assure you, he said, I quite agree with you as to the impropriety of such stories.

Nor yet, I continued, is it proper to say in any case—what is indeed untrue—that gods wage war against gods, and intrigue and fight among themselves; that is, if the future guardians of our state are to deem it a most disgraceful thing to quarrel lightly with one another: far less ought we to select as subjects for fiction and embroidery, the battles of the giants, and numerous other feuds of all sorts, in which gods and heroes fight against their own kith and kin. But if there is any possibility of persuading them, that to quarrel with one's fellow is a sin of which no member of a state was ever guilty, such ought rather to be the language held to our children from the first, by old men and old women, and all elderly persons: and such is the strain in which our poets must be compelled to write. But stories like the chaining of Hera by her son, and the flinging of Hephaestus out of heaven for trying to take his mother's part when his father was beating her, and all those battles of the gods which are to be found in Homer, must be refused admittance into our state, whether they be allegorical or not. For a child cannot discriminate between what is allegory and what is not; and whatever at that age is adopted as a matter of belief, has a tendency to become fixed and indelible, and therefore, perhaps, we ought to esteem it of the the greatest importance that the fictions which children first hear should be adapted in the most perfect manner to the promotion of virtue.

There is certainly reason in this. But if anyone were to proceed to ask us what these fictions are, and what the fables which convey them, how should we answer him?

To which I replied, My dear Adeimantus, you and I are not poets, on the present occasion, but founders of a state. And founders ought certainly to know the moulds in which their poets are to cast their fictions, and from which they must not be suffered to deviate; but they are not bound to compose tales themselves.

You are right; but to use your own words, what should these moulds be in the case of Theology?

I think they may be described as follows: It is right, I presume, always to represent God as he really is, whether the poet describe him in an epic or a lyrical or a dramatic poem.

Yes, it is right.

Then surely *God* is good in reality, and is to be so represented?

Unquestionably.

Well, but nothing that is good is hurtful, is it?

I think not.

And does that which is not hurtful hurt?

By no means.

And does that which hurts not, do any evil?

I answer as before, no.

And that which does no evil cannot be the cause of any evil either?

How should it be?

Well: is that which is good beneficial?

Yes.

Then it is a cause of well-being?

Yes.

Then that which is good is not the cause of all things, but only of what is as it should be, being guiltless of originating evil.

Exactly so.

If that be so, then God, inasmuch as he is good, cannot be the cause of all things, according to the common doctrine. On the contrary, he is the author of only a small part of human affairs; of the larger part he is not the author: for our evil things far outnumber our good things: and the good things we must ascribe to no other than God, while we must seek elsewhere, and not in him, the causes of the evil things.

That seems to be the exact truth.

Then we must express our disapprobation, if Homer, or any other poet, is guilty of such a foolish blunder about the gods, as to tell us that . . .

Zeus hath been made unto men both of weal and of woe the dispenser.

And if anyone assert that the violation of oaths and treaties, of which Pandarus was the author, was brought about by Athene and Zeus, we shall refuse our approbation: nor can we allow it to be said that the strife and trial of strength between the gods was instigated by Themis and Zeus, nor, again, must we let our young people hear that, in the words of Æschylus,

When to destruction God will plague a house,
He plants among its members guilt and sin.

But if a poet writes about the sufferings of Niobe, as Æschylus does in the play from which I have taken these lines, or the calamities of the house of Pelops, or the disasters at Troy, or any similar occurrences, either we must not allow him to call them the work of a god, or if they are to be so called, he must find out a theory to account for them, such as that for which we are now searching, and must say, that what the god did was righteous and good, and the sufferers were chastened for their profit; but we cannot allow the poet to say, that a god was the author of a punishment which made the objects of it miserable. No: if he should say that because the wicked are miserable, these men needed chastisement, and the infliction of it by the god was a benefit to them, we shall make no objection: but as to asserting that God, who is good, becomes the author of evil to any, we must do battle uncompromisingly for the principle, that fictions conveying such a doctrine as this, whether in verse or in prose, shall neither be recited or heard in the city, by any member of it, young or old, if it is to be a well-regulated city; because such language may not be used without irreverence, and is moreover both injurious to us and self-contradictory.

I vote with you, he said, for this law, which pleases me.

Then one of those theological laws or moulds, in accordance with which we shall require our speakers to speak, and our authors to write, will be to this effect, that God is not the author of all things, but only of such as are good.

You have proved it quite satisfactorily, he replied.

Well, here is a second for you to consider. Do you think that God is a wizard, and likely to appear for special purposes in different forms at different times, sometimes actually assuming such forms, and altering his own person into a variety of shapes, and sometimes deceiving us and making us believe that such a transformation has taken place; or do you think that he is of a simple essence, and that it is the most unlikely thing that he should ever go out of his own proper form?

I cannot answer you all at once. . . .

But surely God and the things of God are in every way most excellent.

Unquestionably.

Then God will be very unlikely to assume many shapes through external influence.

Very unlikely indeed.

But will he change and alter himself?

Clearly he must, if he alters at all.

Does he then, by changing himself, attain to something better and fairer, or to something worse and less beautiful than himself?

Something worse, necessarily, if he alters at all: for we shall not, I presume, affirm that there is any imperfection in the beauty or the goodness of God.

You are perfectly correct; and this being the case, do you think, Adeimantus, that any god or any man would voluntarily make himself worse than he is, in any respect?

It is impossible.

Then it is also impossible for a god to be willing to change himself, and therefore it would seem that every god, inasmuch as he is perfect to the utmost in beauty and goodness, abides ever simply and without variation in his own form.

The inference is inevitable, I think.

Then, my dear friend, let no poet tell us that

> Gods in the likeness of wandering strangers,
> Bodied in manifold forms, go roaming from city to city.

And let no one slander Proteus and Thetis, or introduce in tragedies or any other poems, Hera transformed, collecting in the guise of a priestess,

> Alms for the life-giving children of Inachus, river of Argos.

Not to mention many other similar falsehoods, which we must interdict. And once more, let not our mothers be persuaded by these poets into scaring their children by injudicious stories, telling them how certain gods go about by night in the likeness of strangers from every land; that they may not by one and the same act defame the gods, and foster timidity in their children.

No, let that be forbidden.

But perhaps, I continued, though the gods have no tendency to change in themselves, they induce us, by deception and magic, to believe that they appear in various forms.

Perhaps they do.

Would a god consent to lie, think you, either in word, or by an act, such as that of putting a phantom before our eyes?

I am not sure.

Are you not sure that a genuine lie, if I may be allowed the expression, is hated by all gods and by all men?

I do not know what you mean.

I mean, that to lie with the highest part of himself, and concerning the highest subjects, is what no one voluntarily consents to do; on the contrary, every one fears above all things to harbour a lie in that quarter.

I do not even yet understand you.

Because you think I have some mysterious meaning; whereas what I mean is simply this: that to lie, or be the victim of a lie, and to be without knowledge, in the mind and concerning absolute realities, and in that quarter to harbour and possess the lie, is the last thing any man would consent to; for all men hold in especial abhorrence an untruth in a place like that.

Yes, in most especial abhorrence.

Well, but, as I was saying just now, this is what might most correctly be called a genuine lie, namely, ignorance residing in the mind of the deluded person. For the spoken lie is a kind of imitation and embodiment of the anterior mental affection, and not a pure, unalloyed falsity; or am I wrong?

No, you are perfectly right.

Then a real lie is hated not only by gods, but likewise by men.

So I think. . . .

Then do you grant that a second principle, in accordance with which all speaking and writing about the gods must be moulded, is this: That the gods neither metamorphose themselves like wizards, nor mislead us by falsehoods expressed either in word or act?

I do grant it.

Then while we commend much in Homer, we shall refuse to commend the story of the dream sent by Zeus to Agamemnon, as well as that passage in Æschylus, where Thetis says that Apollo singing at her marriage,

Dwelt on my happy motherhood,
The life from sickness free, and lengthened years.
Then all-inclusively he blest my lot,
Favoured of heaven, in strains that cheer'd my soul.
And I too fondly deem'd those lips divine
Sacred to truth, fraught with prophetic skill;
But he himself who sang, the marriage-guest
Himself, who spake all this, 'twas even he
That slew my son.

When a poet holds such language concerning the gods, we shall be angry with him, and refuse him a chorus, neither shall we allow our teachers to use his writings for the instruction of the young, if we would have our guardians grow up to be as godlike and godfearing as it is possible for man to be.

I entirely acquiesce, said he, in the propriety of these principles, and would adopt them as laws.

BOOK III

Concerning the gods, then, I continued, such, as it would appear, is the language to be held, and such the language to be forbidden, in the hearing of all, from childhood upwards, who are hereafter to honour the gods and their parents, and to set no small value on mutual friendship.

Yes, he said; and I think our views are correct.

To proceed then: if we intend our citizens to be brave, must we not add to this such lessons as are likely to preserve them most effectually from being afraid of death? or do you think a man can ever become brave who is haunted by the fear of death?

No, indeed, I do not.

Well, do you imagine that a believer in Hades and its terrors will be free from all fear of death, and in the day of battle will prefer it to defeat and slavery?

Certainly not.

Then apparently we must assume a control over those who undertake to set forth these fables, as well as the others, requesting them not to revile the other world in that unqualified manner, but rather to speak well of it, because such language is neither true, nor beneficial to men who are intended to be warlike.

We certainly must.

Then we shall expunge the following passage, and with it all that are like it:

> I would e'en be a villein, and drudge on the lands of a master,
> Under a portionless wight, whose garner was scantily furnished,
> Sooner than reign supreme in the realm of the dead that have perished. . . .

These verses, and all that are like them, we shall entreat Homer and the other poets not to be angry if we erase, not because they are unpoetical, or otherwise than agreeable to the ear of most men; but because, in proportion as they are more poetical, so much the less ought they to be recited in the hearing of boys and men, whom we require to be freemen, fearing slavery more than death.

By all means let us do so. . . .

But again, a high value must be set also upon truth. For if we were right in what we said just now, and falsehood is really useless to the gods, and only useful to men in the way of a medicine, it is plain that such an agent must be kept in the hands of physicians, and that unprofessional men must not meddle with it.

Evidently. . . .

To the rulers of the state then, if to any, it belongs of right to use false-hood, to deceive either enemies or their own citizens, for the good of the state: and no one else may meddle with this privilege. Nay, for a private person to tell a lie to such magistrates, we shall maintain to be at least as great a mistake as for a patient to deceive his physician, or a pupil his training-master, con-cerning the state of his own body; or for a sailor to tell an untruth to a pilot concerning the ship and the crew, in describing his own condition or that of any of his fellow-sailors.

Most true.

If then the authorities find anyone else guilty of lying in the city,

> Any of those that be craftsmen,
> Prophet and seer, or healer of hurts, or worker in timber,

they will punish him for introducing a practice as pernicious and subversive in a state as in a ship.

Yes, he said, if performance follow upon profession. . . .

Let us then here close our discussion of the subject matter of narratives: our next task, I imagine, is to investigate the question of their form; and this done, we shall have thoroughly considered both what ought to be said, and the mode of saying it. . . .

I divine, said he, that you are speculating whether we shall admit tragedy and comedy into our city, or not.

It may be so, I replied: and it may be that other claims will be questioned besides those of tragedy and comedy: in fact, I do not yet know myself; but we must go where the argument carries us, as a vessel runs before the wind.

You are quite right.

Here then is a question for you to consider, Adeimantus,—Ought our guardians to be apt imitators, or not? Or does it follow, from our previous ad-missions, that any individual may pursue with success one calling, but not many; or, if he attempts this, by his meddling with many he will fail in all, so far as to gain no distinction in any?

That would undoubtedly be the case.

Does not the same principle apply to imitation, or can the same person imitate many things as well as he can imitate one?

Certainly he cannot.

It is very improbable, then, that one who is engaged in any important calling, will at the same time know how to imitate a variety of things, and be a successful imitator: for even two branches of imitation, which are thought to be closely allied, are more, I believe, than can be successfully pursued together by the same person; as, for instance, the writing of comedy and of tragedy, which you described just now as imitations, did you not?

I did; and you are right in saying that the same persons cannot succeed in both.

Nor yet can a man combine the professions of a reciter of epic poetry and an actor.

True.

Nay, the same actor cannot even play both Tragedy and Comedy; and all these are arts of imitation, are they not?

They are.

And human nature appears to me, Adeimantus, to be split up into yet more minute subdivisions than these, so that a man is unable to imitate many things well, or to do the things themselves of which the imitations are likenesses.

Most true.

If then we are to maintain our first view, that our guardians ought to be released from every other craft, that they may acquire consummate skill in the art of creating their country's freedom, and may follow no other occupation but such as tends to this result, it will not be desirable for them either to practise or to imitate anything else; or if they do imitate, let them imitate from very childhood whatever is proper to their profession,—brave, sober, religious, honourable men, and the like,—but meanness, and every other kind of baseness, let them neither practise nor be skilled to imitate, lest from the imitation they be infected with the reality. For have you not perceived that imitations, whether of bodily gestures, tones of voice, or modes of thought, if they be persevered in from an early age, are apt to grow into habits and a second nature?

Certainly I have.

Then we shall not permit those in whom we profess to take an interest, and whom we desire to become good men, to imitate a woman, being themselves men, whether she be young or old, either reviling a man, or striving and vaunting against the gods, in the belief of her own felicity; or taken up with misfortunes, and griefs, and complaints: much more shall we forbid them to imitate one that is ill, or in love, or in labour.

Exactly so.

Again, they must not be permitted to imitate slaves of either sex engaged in the occupations of slaves.

No, they must not.

Nor yet bad men, it would seem, such as cowards, and generally those whose conduct is the reverse of what we described just now; men in the act of abusing and caricaturing one another, and uttering ribaldry, whether drunk or sober, or committing any of those offences against others, or amongst themselves, of which such men both in word and in deed are wont to be guilty. I think also that we must not accustom them to liken themselves to madmen, in word or in act. For though it is right they should know mad and wicked people of both sexes, they ought not to act like them, nor give imitations of them.

Most true.

Again, may they imitate smiths or any other craftsmen, working at their trade, or rowers pulling at the oars in a galley, or their strokesmen, or anything else of the kind?

Impossible, he replied, since they are not to be permitted even to pay attention to any of these occupations. . . .

And is not this the reason why in a state like ours, and in no other, we shall find the shoemaker a shoemaker, and not a pilot in addition, and the husbandman a husbandman, and not a juryman in addition, and the soldier a soldier, and not a tradesman in addition; and so on throughout?

True.

It is probable then, that if a man should arrive in our city, so clever as to be able to assume any character and imitate any object, and should propose to make a public display of his talents and his productions, we shall pay him reverence as a sacred, admirable, and charming personage, but we shall tell him that in our state there is no one like him, and that our law excludes such characters, and we shall send him away to another city after pouring perfumed oil upon his head, and crowning him with woollen fillets; but for ourselves, we shall employ, for the sake of our real good, that more austere and less fascinating poet and legend-writer, who will imitate for us the style of the virtuous man, and will cast his narratives in those moulds which we prescribed at the outset, when we were engaged with the training of our soldiers.

We shall certainly do so, if it be in our power.

Now then, my dear friend, it would seem that we have completely done with that branch of music which relates to fabulous and other narratives; for we have described both *what* is to be said, and *how* it is to be said.

I think so too. . . .

This being the case, ought we to confine ourselves to superintending our poets, and compelling them to impress on their productions the likeness of a good moral character, on pain of not composing among us; or ought we to extend our superintendence to the professors of every other craft as well, and forbid them to impress those signs of an evil nature, of dissoluteness, of meanness, and of ungracefulness, either on the likenesses of living creatures, or on buildings, or any other work of their hands; altogether interdicting such as cannot do otherwise from working in our city, that our guardians may not be reared amongst images of vice, as upon unwholesome pastures, culling much every day by little and little from many places, and feeding upon it, until they insensibly accumulate a large mass of evil in their inmost souls? Ought we not, on the contrary, to seek out artists of another stamp, who by the power of genius can trace out the nature of the fair and the graceful, that our young men, dwelling as it were in a healthful region, may drink in good from every quarter, whence any emanation from noble works may strike upon their eye or their ear, like a gale wafting health from salubrious lands, and win them imperceptibly from their earliest childhood into resemblance, love, and harmony with the true beauty of reason?

Such a nurture, he replied, would be by far the best.

Is it then, Glaucon, on these accounts that we attach such supreme importance to a musical education, because rhythm and harmony sink most deeply into the recesses of the soul, and take most powerful hold of it, bringing gracefulness in their train, and making a man graceful if he be rightly nurtured, but if not, the reverse? and also because he that has been duly nurtured therein will have the keenest eye for defects, whether in the failures of art, or the misgrowths of nature; and feeling a most just disdain for them, will commend beautiful objects, and gladly receive them into his soul, and feed upon them,

and grow to be noble and good; whereas he will rightly censure and hate all re-
pulsive objects, even in his childhood, before he is able to be reasoned with;
and when reason comes, *he* will welcome her most cordially who can recognize
her by the instinct of relationship, and because he has been thus nurtured?

I have no doubt, he said, that such are the reasons for a musical education. . . .

Gymnastic will hold the next place to music in the education of our
young men.

Certainly.

No doubt a careful training in gymnastic, as well as in music, ought to
begin with their childhood, and go on through all their life. But the following
is the true view of the case, in my opinion: see what you think of it. My belief
is, not that a good body will by its own excellence, make the soul good; but on
the contrary, that a good soul will by *its* excellence render the body as perfect
as it can be: but what is your view?

The same as yours. . . .

Then, Glaucon, am I also right in saying that those who establish a system of education in music and gymnastic, are not actuated by the purpose
which some persons attribute to them, of applying the one to the improvement
of the soul, the other to that of the body?

Why what can be their object, if this is not?

Probably they introduce both mainly for the sake of the soul.

How so?

Do you not observe the characteristics which distinguish the minds of
those who have been familiar with gymnastic all their lives, without any acquaintance with music? and again, of those whose condition is the reverse of
this?

To what do you allude?

To the roughness and hardness which mark the one, and the softness and
gentleness which mark the other.

O yes. Those who have devoted themselves to gymnastic exclusively, become ruder than they ought to be; while those who have devoted themselves
to music are made softer than is good for them.

We know, however, that rudeness is the natural product of the spirited element, which, if rightly nurtured, will be brave; but, if strained to an improper
pitch, will in all probability become harsh and disagreeable.

I think so.

Well, and will not gentleness be a property of the philosophic temperament? and a property which, if too much indulged, will produce in it an excess
of softness; but which, rightly nurtured, will render it gentle and orderly?

True. . . .

To correct then, as it would appear, these two exclusive temperaments,
the spirited and the philosophic, some god, as I for my part shall maintain, has
given to men two arts, music and gymnastic, not for soul and body distinctively, except in a secondary way, but expressly for those two temperaments, in
order that by the increase or relaxation of the tension to the due pitch they may
be brought into mutual accord.

So it would appear.

Then whosoever can best blend gymnastic with music, and bring both to bear on the mind most judiciously, such a man we shall justly call perfect in music, and a master of true harmony, much rather than the artist who tunes the strings of the lyre.

Yes, and with good reason, Socrates.

Then will not some such overseer be always needed in our state, Glaucon, if our commonwealth is designed to endure?

Yes, indeed, such an officer will be quite indispensable.

Such then will be the outlines of our system of education and training. For why should one enter into details respecting the dances which will be in vogue in a state like ours, the hunting and field-exercises, or the sports of the gymnasium and the race-course? It is tolerably clear that these must correspond with the foregoing outlines, and there will be no further difficulty in discovering them.

Perhaps not, he said.

Very good: then what will be the next point for us to settle? is it not this, which of the persons so educated are to be the rulers, and which the subjects?

Unquestionably it is.

There can be no doubt that the rulers must be the elderly men, and the subjects the younger.

True.

And also that the rulers must be the best men among them.

True again.

Are not the best agriculturists those who are most agricultural?

Yes.

In the present case, as we require the best guardians, shall we not find them in those who are most capable of guarding a state?

Yes.

Then for this purpose must they not be intelligent and powerful, and, moreover, careful of the state?

They must.

And a man will be most careful of that which he loves?

Of course.

And assuredly he will love that most whose interests he regards as identical with his own, and in whose prosperity or adversity he believes his own fortunes to be involved.

Just so.

Then we must select from the whole body of guardians those individuals who appear to us, after due observation, to be remarkable above others for the zeal with which, through their whole life, they have done what they have thought advantageous to the state, and inflexibly refused to do what they thought the reverse.

Yes, these are the suitable persons, he said.

Then I think we must watch them at every stage of their life, to see if they are tenacious guardians of this conviction, and never bewitched or forced into a forgetful abandonment of the belief that they ought to do what is best for the state. . . .

Yes.

We must also appoint them labours, and vexations, and contests, in which we must watch for the same symptoms of character.

Rightly so.

And, as a third kind of test, we must try them with witchcraft, and observe their behaviour; and, just as young horses are taken into the presence of noise and tumult, to see whether they are timid, so must we bring our men, while still young, into the midst of objects of terror, and presently transfer them to scenes of pleasure, trying them much more thoroughly than gold is tried in the fire, to find whether they shew themselves under all circumstances inaccessible to witchcraft, and seemly in their bearing, good guardians of themselves and of the music which they have been taught, approving themselves on every occasion true to the laws of rhythm and harmony, and acting in such a way as would render them most useful to themselves and the state. And whoever, from time to time, after being put to the proof, as a child, as a youth, and as a man, comes forth uninjured from the trial, must be appointed a ruler and guardian of the city, and must receive honours in life and in death, and be admitted to the highest privileges, in the way of funeral rites and other tributes to his memory. And all who are the reverse of this character must be rejected. Such appears to me, Glaucon, to be the true method of selecting and appointing our rulers and guardians, described simply in outline, without accuracy in detail.

I am pretty much of your mind.

Is it then really most correct to give to these the name of perfect guardians, as being qualified to take care that their friends at home shall not wish, and their enemies abroad not be able, to do any mischief; and to call the young men, whom up to this time we entitled guardians, auxiliaries, whose office it is to support the resolutions of the rulers?

I quite think so, he said.

This being the case, I continued, can we contrive any ingenious mode of bringing into play one of those seasonable falsehoods of which we lately spoke, so that, propounding a single spirited fiction, we may bring even the rulers themselves, if possible, to believe it, or if not them, the rest of the city?

What kind of fiction?

Nothing new, but a Phoenician story, which has been realized often before now, as the poets tell and mankind believe, but which in our time has not been, nor, so far as I know, is likely to be realized, and for which it would require large powers of persuasion to obtain credit.

You seem very reluctant to tell it.

You will think my reluctance very natural when I have told it.

Speak out boldly and without fear.

Well I will; and yet I hardly know where I shall find the courage or where the words to express myself. I shall try, I say, to persuade first the rulers themselves and the military class, and after them the rest of the city, that when we were training and instructing them, they only fancied, as in dreams, that all this was happening to them and about them, while in reality they were in course of formation and training in the bowels of the earth, where they themselves, their armour, and the rest of their equipments were manufactured, and from whence, as soon as they were thoroughly elaborated, the earth, their real mother, sent them up to its surface; and, consequently, that they ought now to take thought for the land in which they dwell, as their mother and nurse, and repel all attacks upon it, and to feel towards their fellow-citizens as brother children of the soil.

It was not without reason that you were so long ashamed to tell us your fiction.

I dare say; nevertheless, hear the rest of the story. We shall tell our people, in mythical language: You are doubtless all brethren, as many as inhabit the city, but the God who created you mixed gold in the composition of such of you as are qualified to rule, which gives them the highest value; while in the auxiliaries he made silver an ingredient, assigning iron and copper to the cultivators of the soil and the other workmen. Therefore, inasmuch as you are all related to one another, although your children will generally resemble their parents, yet sometimes a golden parent will produce a silver child, and a silver parent a golden child, and so on, each producing any. The rulers therefore have received this in charge first and above all from the gods, to observe nothing more closely, in their character of vigilant guardians, than the children that are born, to see which of these metals enters into the composition of their souls; and if a child be born in their class with an alloy of copper or iron, they are to have no manner of pity upon it, but giving it the value that belongs to its nature, they are to thrust it away into the class of artisans or agriculturists; and if again among these a child be born with any admixture of gold or silver, when they have assayed it, they are to raise it either to the class of guardians, or to that of auxiliaries: because there is an oracle which declares that the city shall then perish when it is guarded by iron or copper. Can you suggest any device by which we can make them believe this fiction?

None at all by which we could persuade the men with whom we begin our new state: but I think their sons, and the next generation, and all subsequent generations, might be taught to believe it.

Well, I said, even this might have a good effect towards making them care more for the city and for one another; for I think I understand what you mean. However, we will leave this fiction to its fate: but for our part, when we have armed these children of the soil, let us lead them forward under the command of their officers, till they arrive at the city: then let them look around them to discover the most eligible position for their camp, from which they may best coerce the inhabitants, if there be any disposition to refuse obedience to the laws, and repel foreigners, if an enemy should come down like a wolf on the fold. And when they have pitched their camp, and offered sacrifices to the proper divinities, let them arrange their sleeping-places. Is all this right?

It is.

And these sleeping-places must be such as will keep out the weather both in winter and summer, must they not?

Certainly: you mean dwelling-houses, if I am not mistaken.

I do; but the dwelling-houses of soldiers, not of moneyed men.

What is the difference which you imply?

I will endeavour to explain it to you, I replied. I presume it would be a most monstrous and scandalous proceeding in shepherds to keep for the protection of their flocks such a breed of dogs, or so to treat them, that owing to unruly tempers, or hunger, or any bad propensity whatever, the dogs themselves should begin to worry the sheep, and behave more like wolves than dogs.

It would be monstrous, undoubtedly.

Then must we not take every precaution that our auxiliary class, being stronger than the other citizens, may not act towards them in a similar fashion, and so resemble savage monsters rather than friendly allies?

We must.

And will they not be furnished with the best of safeguards, if they are really well educated?

Nay, but they are *that* already, he exclaimed.

To which I replied, It is not worthwhile now to insist upon that point, my dear Glaucon: but it is most necessary to maintain what we said this minute, that they must have the right education, whatever it may be, if they are to have what will be most effectual in rendering them gentle to one another, and to those whom they guard.

True.

But besides this education a rational man would say that their dwellings and their circumstances generally should be arranged on such a scale as shall neither prevent them from being perfect guardians, nor provoke them to do mischief to the other citizens.

He will say so with truth.

Consider then, I continued, whether the following plan is the right one for their lives and their dwellings, if they are to be of the character I have described. In the first place, no one should possess any private property, if it can possibly be avoided: secondly, no one should have a dwelling or storehouse into which all who please may not enter; whatever necessaries are required by temperate and courageous men, who are trained to war, they should receive by regular appointment from their fellow-citizens, as wages for their services, and the amount should be such as to leave neither a surplus on the year's consumption nor a deficit; and they should attend common messes and live together as men do in a camp: as for gold and silver, we must tell them that they are in perpetual possession of a divine species of the precious metals placed in their souls by the gods themselves, and therefore have no need of the earthly ore; that in fact it would be profanation to pollute their spiritual riches by mixing them with the possession of mortal gold, because the world's coinage has been the cause of countless impieties, whereas theirs is undefiled: therefore to them, as distinguished from the rest of the people, it is forbidden to handle or touch gold and silver, or enter under the same roof with them, or to wear them on their dresses, or to drink out of the precious metals. If they follow these rules, they will be safe themselves and the saviours of the city: but whenever they come to possess lands, and houses, and money of their own, they will be householders and cultivators instead of guardians, and will become hostile masters of their fellow-citizens rather than their allies; and so they will spend their whole lives, hating and hated, plotting and plotted against, standing in more frequent and intense alarm of their enemies at home than of their enemies abroad; by which time they and the rest of the city will be running on the very brink of ruin. On all these accounts, I asked, shall we say that the foregoing is the right arrangement of the houses and other concerns of our guardians, and shall we legislate accordingly; or not?

Yes, by all means, answered Glaucon.

BOOK IV

Here Adeimantus interposed, inquiring, Then what defence will you make, Socrates, if any one protests that you are not making the men of this class particularly happy?—when it is their own fault, too, if they are not; for the city really belongs to them, and yet they derive no advantage from it, as others do, who own lands and build fine large houses, and furnished them in corresponding style, and perform private sacrifices to the gods, and entertain their friends, and, in fact, as you said just now, possess gold and silver, and everything that is usually considered necessary to happiness; nay, they appear to be posted in the city, as it might be said, precisely like mercenary troops, wholly occupied in garrison duties.

Yes, I said, and for this they are only fed, and do not receive pay in addition to their rations, like the rest, so that it will be out of their power to take any journeys on their own account, should they wish to do so, or to make presents to mistresses, or to lay out money in the gratification of any other desire, after the plan of those who are considered happy. These and many similar counts you leave out of the indictment.

Well, said he, let us suppose these to be included in the charge.

What defence then shall we make, say you?

Yes.

By travelling the same road as before, we shall find, I think, what to say. We shall reply that, though it would not surprise us, if even this class in the given circumstances were very happy, yet that our object in the construction of our state is not to make any one class preeminently happy, but to make the whole state as happy as it can be made. For we thought that in such a state we should be most likely to discover justice, as, on the other hand, in the worst-regulated state we should be most likely to discover injustice, and that after having observed them we might decide the question we have been so long investigating. At present, we believe we are forming the happy state, not by selecting a few of its members and making them happy, but by making the whole so. Presently we shall examine a state of the opposite kind. Now, if someone came up to us while we were painting statues, and blamed us for not

putting the most beautiful colours on the most beautiful parts of the body, because the eyes, being the most beautiful part, were not painted purple, but
black, we should think it a sufficient defence to reply, Pray, sir, do not suppose
that we ought to make the eyes so beautiful as not to look like eyes, nor the
other parts in like manner, but observe whether, by giving to every part what
properly belongs to it, we make the whole beautiful. In the same way do not,
in the present instance, compel us to attach to our guardians such a species of
happiness as shall make them anything but guardians. For we are well aware
that we might, on the same principle, clothe our cultivators in long robes, and
put golden coronets on their heads, and bid them till the land at their pleasure; and that we might stretch our potters at their ease on couches before the
fire, to drink and make merry, placing the wheel by their side, with directions
to ply their trade just so far as they should feel it agreeable; and that we might
dispense this kind of bliss to all the rest, so that the entire city might thus be
happy. But give not such advice to *us:* since, if we comply with your recommendation, the cultivator will be no cultivator, the potter no potter; nor will
any of those professions, which make up a state, maintain its proper character.
For the other occupations it matters less: for in cobblers, incompetency and de-
generacy and pretence without the reality, are not dangerous to a state: but
when guardians of the laws and of the state are such in appearance only, and
not in reality, you see that they radically destroy the whole state, as, on the
other hand, they alone can create public prosperity and happiness. If then,
while *we* aim at making genuine guardians, who shall be as far as possible
from doing mischief to the state, the supposed objector makes a class who
would be cultivators and as it were jovial feasters at a holiday gathering, rather
than citizens of a state, he will be describing something which is not a state. We
should examine then whether our object in constituting our guardians should
be to secure to them the greatest possible amount of happiness, or whether our
duty, as regards happiness, is to see if our state as a whole enjoys it, persuading or compelling these our auxiliaries and guardians to study only how to
make themselves the best possible workmen at their own occupation, and
treating all the rest in like manner, and thus, while the whole city grows and
becomes prosperously organized, permitting each class to partake of as much
happiness as the nature of the case allows to it.

I think, he replied, that what you say is quite right. . . .

Really, my good Adeimantus, these injunctions of ours are not, as one
might suppose, a number of arduous tasks, but they will be inconsiderable, if
the guardians diligently observe the one great point, as the saying is, though it
should rather be called sufficient than great.

What is that?

Education, I said, and rearing. For if by a good education they be made
reasonable men, they will readily see through all these questions, as well as
others which we pass by for the present, such as the relations between the
sexes, marriage, and the procreation of children; in all which things they will
see that the proverb ought, as far as possible, to be followed, which says that
"among friends everything is common property."

Yes, that would be the most correct plan.

And indeed, if a state has once started well, it exhibits a kind of circular progress in its growth. Adherence to a good system of nurture and education creates good natures, and good natures, receiving the assistance of a good education, grow still better than they were, their breeding qualities improving among the rest, as is also seen in the lower animals.

Yes, naturally so. To speak briefly, therefore, the overseers of the state must hold fast to this principle, not allowing it to be impaired without their knowledge, but guarding it above everything;—the principle, I mean, which forbids any innovation, in either gymnastic or music, upon the established order, requiring it, on the contrary, to be most strictly maintained, from a fear lest, when it is said that men care most for the song

Which being newest is sung, and its music encircleth the singers,

it might perhaps be imagined that the poet is speaking not of new songs, but of a new style of music, and novelty should accordingly be commended. Whereas novelty ought not to be commended, nor ought the words to be so understood. For the introduction of a new kind of music must be shunned as imperilling the whole state; since styles of music are never disturbed without affecting the most important political institutions: at least so Damon affirms, and I believe him.

Pray include me too among the believers in this doctrine, said Adeimantus.

Then to all appearance, I continued, it is here in music that our guardians should erect their guard-house.

At any rate, said he, it is here that lawlessness easily creeps in unawares.

Yes, in the guise of amusement, and professing to do no mischief.

No, and it does none, except that gradually gaining a lodgement it quietly insinuates itself into manners and customs; and from these it issues in greater force, and makes its way into mutual compacts: and from compacts it goes on to attack laws and constitutions, displaying the utmost impudence, Socrates, until it ends by overturning everything, both in public and in private.

Good, said I; is this so?

I think it is.

Then, as we said in the beginning, must not our children from the very first be restricted to more lawful amusements, because when amusements are lawless, and children take after them, it is impossible for such children to grow into loyal and virtuous men?

Unquestionably.

Accordingly, when our children, beginning with right diversions, have received loyalty into their minds by the instrumentality of music, the result is the exact reverse of the former; for loyalty accompanies them into everything and promotes their progress, and raises up again any state institution which might happen to have been cast down.

Yes, that is true.

Consequently such persons make the discovery even of those trifling regulations, as they are held to be, which had all been lost by those whom we described before.

What regulations do you mean?

Those, for example, which require the young to maintain a decorous silence in the presence of their elders, stooping to them, and rising up at their entrance, and paying every attention to their parents; together with regulations as to the mode of wearing the hair, the style of dress and shoes, and personal decoration in general, and everything else of the same kind. Is not this your opinion?

It is.

But to legislate on these matters would be foolish, I think: it is never done, I believe; nor could express verbal legislation on such points ever be permanent.

How could it be?

At any rate, it is probable, Adeimantus, that the bent given by education will determine all that follows. For does not like always invite like?

Undoubtedly it does.

And so we should expect our system at last, I fancy, to end in some complete and grand result, whether this result be good or the reverse.

We certainly should.

On these grounds I should not attempt to extend our legislation to points like those.

With good reason. . . .

Then the organization of our state is now complete, son of Ariston: and the next thing for you to do is to examine it, furnishing yourself with the necessary light from any quarter you can, and calling to your aid your brother and Polemarchus and the rest, in order to try if we can see where justice may be found in it, and where injustice, and wherein they differ the one from the other, and which of the two the man who desires to be happy ought to possess, whether all gods and men know it or not.

That will not do! exclaimed Glaucon; it was you that engaged to make the inquiry, on the ground that you would be guilty of a sin if you refused to justice all the aid in your power.

I recollect that it was as you say, I replied: and I must so do, but you also must assist me.

We will. . . .

Now observe whether you hold the same opinion that I do. If a carpenter should undertake to execute the work of a shoemaker, or a shoemaker that of a carpenter, either by interchanging their tools and distinctions, or by the same person undertaking both trades, with all the changes involved in it, do you think it would greatly damage the state?

Not very greatly.

But when one whom nature has made an artisan, or a producer of any other kind, is so elated by wealth, or a large connexion, or bodily strength, or any similar advantages, as to intrude himself into the class of the warriors; or when a warrior intrudes himself into the class of the senators and guardians, of which he is unworthy, and when these interchange their tools and their distinctions, or when one and the same person attempts to discharge all these duties at once, then, I imagine, you will agree with me, that such change and meddling among these will be ruinous to the state.

Most assuredly they will.

Then any intermeddling in the three classes, or change from one to another, would inflict great damage on the state, and may with perfect propriety be described as in the strongest sense a doing of evil.

Quite so.

And will you not admit that evil-doing of the worst kind towards one's own state is injustice?

Unquestionably.

This then is injustice. On the other hand, let us state that, conversely, adherence to their own business on the part of the industrious, the military, and the guardian classes, each of these doing its own work in the state, is justice, and will render the state just.

I fully coincide, he said, in this view.

Let us not state it yet quite positively; but if we find, on applying this conception to the individual man, that there too it is admitted to constitute justice, we will then yield our assent—for what more can we say?—but if not, in that case we will institute a new inquiry. At present, however, let us complete the investigation which we undertook in the belief that, if we first endeavoured to contemplate justice in some larger subject which contains it, we should find it easier to discern its nature in the individual man. Such a subject we recognized in a state, and accordingly we organized the best we could, being sure that justice must reside in a *good* city. The view, therefore, which presented itself to us there, let us now apply to the individual: and if it be admitted, we shall be satisfied; but if we should find something different in the case of the individual, we will again go back to our city, and put our theory to the test. And perhaps by considering the two cases side by side, and rubbing them together, we may cause justice to flash out from the contact, like fire from dry bits of wood, and when it has become visible to us, may settle it firmly in our own minds.

There is method in your proposal, he replied, and so let us do. . . .

Now, can we say that people sometimes are thirsty, and yet do not wish to drink?

Yes, certainly; it often happens to many people.

What then can one say of them, except that their soul contains one principle which commands, and another which forbids them to drink, the latter being distinct from and stronger than the former?

That is my opinion.

Whenever the authority which forbids such indulgences grows up in the soul, is it not engendered there by reasoning; while the powers which lead and draw the mind towards them, owe their presence to passive and morbid states?

It would appear so.

Then we shall have reasonable grounds for assuming that these are two principles distinct one from the other, and for giving to that part of the soul with which it reasons the title of the rational principle, and to that part with which it loves and hungers and thirsts, and experiences the flutter of the other desires, the title of the irrational and concupiscent principle, the ally of sundry indulgences and pleasures.

Yes, he replied: it will not be unreasonable to think so.

Let us consider it settled, then, that these two specific parts exist in the soul. But now, will spirit, or that by which we feel indignant, constitute a third distinct part? If not, with which of the two former has it a natural affinity?

Perhaps with the concupiscent principle.

But I was once told a story, which I can quite believe, to the effect, that Leontius, the son of Aglaion, as he was walking up from the Piraeus, and approaching the northern wall from the outside, observed some dead bodies on the ground, and the executioner standing by them. He immediately felt a desire to look at them, but at the same time loathing the thought he tried to divert himself from it. For some time he struggled with himself, and covered his eyes, till at length, over-mastered by the desire, he opened his eyes wide with his fingers, and running up to the bodies, exclaimed, "There! you wretches! gaze your fill at the beautiful spectacle!"

I have heard the anecdote too.

This story, however, indicates that anger sometimes fights against the desires, which implies that they are two distinct principles.

True, it does indicate that.

And do we not often observe in other cases that when a man is overpowered by the desires against the dictates of his reason, he reviles himself, and resents the violence thus exerted within him, and that, in this struggle of contending parties, the spirit sides with the reason? But that it should make common cause with the desires, when the reason pronounces that they ought not to act against itself, is a thing which I suppose you will not profess to have experienced yourself, nor yet, I imagine, have you ever noticed it in anyone else.

No, I am sure I have not.

Well, and when anyone thinks he is in the wrong, is he not, in proportion to the nobleness of his character, so much the less able to be angry at being made to suffer hunger or cold or any similar pain at the hands of him whom he thinks justified in so treating him; his spirit, as I describe it, refusing to be roused against his punisher?

True.

On the other hand, when anyone thinks he is wronged, does he not instantly boil and chafe, and enlist himself on the side of what he thinks to be justice; and whatever extremities of hunger and cold and the like he may have to suffer, does he not endure till he conquers, never ceasing from his noble efforts, till he has either gained his point, or perished in the attempt, or been recalled and calmed by the voice of reason within, as a dog is called off by a shepherd?

Yes, he replied, the case answers very closely to your description; and in fact, in our city we made the auxiliaries, like sheep-dogs, subject to the rulers, who are as it were the shepherds of the state.

You rightly understand my meaning. But try whether you also apprehend my next observation.

What is it?

That our recent view of the spirited principle is exactly reversed. Then we thought it had something of the concupiscent character, but now we say that, far from this being the case, it much more readily takes arms on the side of the rational principle in the party conflict of the soul.

Decidedly it does.

Is it then distinct from this principle also; or is it only a modification of it, thus making two instead of three distinct principles in the soul, namely, the rational and the concupiscent? Or ought we to say that, as the state was held together by three great classes, the producing class, the auxiliary, and the deliberative, so also in the soul the spirited principle constitutes a third element, the natural ally of the rational principle, if it be not corrupted by evil training?

It must be a third, he replied.

Yes, I continued; if it shall appear to be distinct from the rational principle, as we found it different from the concupiscent.

Nay, that will easily appear. For even in little children anyone may see this, that from their very birth they have plenty of spirit, whereas reason is a principle to which most men only attain after many years, and some, in my opinion, never.

Upon my word you have well said. . . .

Here then, I proceeded, after a hard struggle, we have, though with difficulty, reached the land; and we are pretty well satisfied that there are corresponding divisions, equal in number, in a state, and in the soul of every individual.

True.

Then does it not necessarily follow that, as and whereby the state was wise, so and thereby the individual is wise?

Without doubt it does.

And that as and whereby the individual is brave, so and thereby is the state brave; and that everything conducing to virtue which is possessed by the one, finds its counterpart in the other?

It must be so.

Then we shall also assert, I imagine, Glaucon, that a man is just, in the same way in which we found the state to be just.

This too is a necessary corollary.

But surely we have not allowed ourselves to forget, that what makes the state just, is the fact of each of the three classes therein doing its own work.

No; I think we have not forgotten this.

We must bear in mind, then, that each of us also, if his inward faculties do severally their proper work, will, in virtue of that, be a just man, and a doer of his proper work.

Certainly, it must be borne in mind.

Is it not then essentially the province of the rational principle to command, inasmuch as it is wise, and has to exercise forethought in behalf of the entire soul, and the province of the spirited principle to be its subject and ally?

Yes, certainly.

And will not the combination of music and gymnastic bring them, as we said, into unison; elevating and fostering the one with lofty discourses and scientific teachings, and lowering the tone of the other by soothing address, till its wildness has been tamed by harmony and rhythm?

Yes, precisely so.

And so these two, having been thus trained, and having truly learnt their parts and received a real education, will exercise control over the concupiscent principle, which in every man forms the largest portion of the soul, and is by nature most insatiably covetous. And they will watch it narrowly, that it may not so batten upon what are called the pleasures of the body, as to grow large and strong, and forthwith refuse to do its proper work, and even aspire to absolute dominion over the classes which it has no right according to its kind to govern, thus overturning fundamentally the life of all.

Certainly they will.

And would not these two principles be the best qualified to guard the entire soul and body against enemies from without; the one taking counsel, and the other fighting its battles, in obedience to the governing power, to whose designs it gives effect by its bravery?

True.

In like manner, I think, we call an individual brave, in virtue of the spirited element of his nature, when this part of him holds fast, through pain and pleasure, the instructions of the reason as to what is to be feared, and what is not.

Yes, and rightly.

And we call him wise, in virtue of that small part which reigns within him, and issues these instructions, and which also in its turn contains within itself a true knowledge of what is advantageous for the whole community composed of these three principles, and for each member of it.

Exactly so.

Again, do we not call a man temperate, in virtue of the friendship and harmony of these same principles, that is to say, when the two that are governed agree with that which governs in regarding the rational principle as the rightful sovereign, and set up no opposition to its authority?

Certainly, he replied; temperance is nothing else than this, whether in state or individual.

Lastly, a man will be just, in the way and by the means which we have repeatedly described.

Unquestionably he will. . . .

And so there really was, Glaucon, a rude outline of justice (and hence its utility) in the principle that it is right for a man whom nature intended for a shoemaker to confine himself to shoemaking, and for a man who has a turn for carpentering to do carpenter's work, and so on.

It appears so.

The truth being that justice is indeed, to all appearance, something of the kind, only that, instead of dealing with a man's outward performance of his own work, it has to do with that inward performance of it which truly concerns the man himself, and his own interests: so that the just man will not permit the several principles within him to do any work but their own, nor allow the distinct classes in his soul to interfere with each other, but will really set his house in order; and having gained the mastery over himself, will so regulate his own character as to be on good terms with himself, and to set those three principles in tune together, as if they were verily three chords of a harmony, a higher and a lower and a middle, and whatever may lie between these; and after he has bound all these together, and reduced the many elements of his nature to a real unity, as a temperate and duly harmonized man, he will then at length proceed to do whatever he may have to do, whether it involve the acquisition of property or attention to the wants of his body, whether it be a state affair or a business transaction of his own; in all which he will believe and profess that the just and honourable course is that which preserves and assists in creating the aforesaid habit of mind, and that the genuine knowledge which presides over such conduct is wisdom; while on the other hand, he will hold that an unjust action is one which tends to destroy this habit, and that the mere opinion which presides over unjust conduct, is folly.

What you say is thoroughly true, Socrates.

Very good: if we were to say we have discovered the just man and the just state, and what justice is as found in them, it would not be thought, I imagine, to be an altogether false statement.

No, indeed, it would not.

Shall we say so then?

We will.

Be it so, I continued. In the next place we have to investigate, I imagine, what injustice is.

Evidently we have.

Must it not then, as the reverse of justice, be a state of strife between the three principles, and the disposition to meddle and interfere, and the insurrection of a part of the mind against the whole, this part aspiring to the supreme power within the mind, to which it has no right, its proper place and destination being, on the contrary, to do service to any member of the rightfully dominant class? Such doings as these, I imagine, and the confusion and bewilderment of the aforesaid principles, will, in our opinion, constitute injustice, and licentiousness, and cowardice, and folly, and, in one word, all vice.

Yes, precisely so.

And is it not now quite clear to us what it is to act unjustly, and to be unjust, and, on the other hand, what it is to act justly, knowing as we do the nature of justice and injustice?

How so?

Because these phenomena in the soul are exactly like the phenomena of health and disease in the body.

In what way?

The conditions of health, I presume, produce health, and those of disease engender disease.

Yes.

In the same way, does not the practice of justice beget the habit of justice, and the practice of injustice the habit of injustice?

Inevitably.

Now to produce health is so to constitute the bodily forces as that they shall master and be mastered by one another in accordance with nature; and to produce disease is to make them govern and be governed by one another in a way which violates nature.

True.

Similarly, will it not be true that to beget justice is so to constitute the powers of the soul that they shall master and be mastered by one another in accordance with nature, and that to beget injustice is to make them govern and be governed by one another in a way which violates nature?

Quite so.

Then virtue, it appears, will be a kind of health and beauty, and good habit of the soul; and vice will be a disease, and deformity, and sickness of it.

True.

And may we not add, that all fair practices tend to the acquisition of virtue, and all foul practices to that of vice? Undoubtedly they do.

What now remains for us, apparently, is to inquire whether it is also *profitable* to act justly, and to pursue honourable aims, and to be just, whether a man be known to be such or not,—or to act unjustly, and to be unjust, if one suffer no punishment, and be not made a better man by chastisement.

Nay, Socrates, to me, I confess, the inquiry begins to assume a ludicrous appearance, now that the real nature of justice and injustice has presented itself to us in the light described above. Do people think that when the constitution of the body is ruined, life is not worth having, though you may command all varieties of food and drink, and possess endless wealth and power; and shall we be told that, when the constitution of that very principle whereby we live is going to rack and ruin, life is still worth having, let a man do what he will, if that is excepted which will enable him to get rid of vice and injustice, and to acquire virtue and justice?

Yes, it is ludicrous, I replied. . . .

BOOK V

. . . Polemarchus, who was seated a little further off than Adeimantus, put out his hand to take hold of his brother's dress high up near the shoulder, drew him towards himself, and leaning forwards whispered a few words into his ear, of which we only caught the following:

Shall we let him off then, or what shall we do?

Certainly not, said Adeimantus, beginning to speak aloud. Whereupon I said, Pray what may that be which you are not going to let off?

You, he replied.

And why, pray? I further inquired.

We have an idea that you are lagging, and stealing a whole section, and that a very important one, out of the subject, in order to avoid handling it. . . .

I must recur, then, to a portion of our subject which perhaps I ought to have discussed before in its proper place. But after all, the present order may be the best; the men having quite played out their piece, we proceed with the performance of the women; especially since this is the order of your challenge. . . .

Most assuredly.

Must we not then first come to an agreement as to . . . whether the nature of the human female is such as to enable her to share in all the employments of the male, or whether she is wholly unequal to any, or equal to some and not to others; and if so, to which class military service belongs? Will not this be the way to make the best beginning, and, in all probability, the best ending also?

Yes, quite so.

Would you like, then, that we should argue against ourselves in behalf of an objector, that the adverse position may not be undefended against our attack?

There is no reason why we should not.

Then let us say in his behalf, "Socrates and Glaucon, there is no need for others to advance anything against you: for you yourselves, at the beginning of your scheme for constructing a state, admitted that every individual therein ought, in accordance with nature, to do the one work which belongs to him." "We did admit this, I imagine: how could we do otherwise?" "Can you deny that there is a very marked difference between the nature of woman and that of man?" "Of course there is a difference." "Then is it not fitting to assign to each sex a different work, appropriate to its peculiar nature?" "Undoubtedly." "Then if so, you must be in error now, and be contradicting yourselves when you go on to say, that men and women ought to engage in the same occupations, when their natures are so widely diverse?" Shall you have any answer to make to that objection, my clever friend?

It is not so very easy to find one at a moment's notice: but I shall apply to you, and I do so now, to state what the arguments on our side are, and to expound them for us.

These objections, Glaucon, and many others like them, are what I anticipated all along; and that is why I was afraid and reluctant to meddle with the law that regulates the possession of the women and children, and the rearing of the latter.

To say the truth, it does seem no easy task.

Why no: but the fact is, that whether you fall into a small swimming-bath, or into the middle of the great ocean, you have to swim all the same.

Exactly so.

Then is it not best for us, in the present instance, to strike out and endeavour to emerge in safety from the discussion, in the hope that either a dolphin may take us on his back, or some other unlooked-for deliverance present itself?

It would seem so.

Come then, I continued, let us see if we can find the way out. We admitted, you say, that different natures ought to have different occupations, and that the natures of men and women are different; but now we maintain that these different natures ought to engage in the same occupations. Is this your charge against us?

Precisely.

Truly, Glaucon, the power of the art of controversy is a very extraordinary one.

Why so?

Because it seems to me that many fall into it even against their will, and fancy they are discussing, when they are merely debating, because they cannot distinguish the meanings of a term, in their investigation of any question, but carry on their opposition to what is stated, by attacking the mere words, employing the art of debate, and not that of philosophical discussion.

This is no doubt the case with many: does it apply to us at the present moment?

Most assuredly it does; at any rate there is every appearance of our having fallen unintentionally into a verbal controversy.

How so?

We are pressing hard upon the mere letter of the dogma, that different natures ought not to engage in the same pursuits, in the most courageous style of verbal debate, but we have wholly forgotten to consider in what senses the words 'the same nature' and 'different natures' were employed, and what we had in view in our definition, when we assigned different pursuits to different natures, and the same pursuits to the same natures.

It is true we have not considered that.

That being the case, it is open to us apparently to ask ourselves whether bald men and long-haired men are of the same or of opposite natures, and after admitting the latter to be the case, we may say that if bald men make shoes, long-haired men must not be suffered to make them, or if the long-haired men make them, the others must be forbidden to do so.

Nay, that would be ridiculous.

Would it be ridiculous, except for the reason that we were not then using the words, "the same" and "different," in a universal sense, being engaged only with that particular species of likeness and difference which applied directly to the pursuits in question? For example, we said that two men who were mentally qualified for the medical profession, possessed the same nature. Do you not think so?

I do.

And that a man who would make a good physician had a different nature from one who would make a good carpenter.

Of course he has.

If, then, the male and the female sex appear to differ in reference to any art, or other occupation, we shall say that such occupation must be appropriated to the one or the other: but if we find the difference between the sexes to consist simply in the parts they respectively bear in the propagation of the species, we shall assert that it has not yet been by any means demonstrated that the difference between man and woman touches our purpose; on the contrary, we shall still think it proper for our guardians and their wives to engage in the same pursuits.

And rightly.

Shall we not proceed to call upon our opponents to inform us what is that particular art or occupation connected with the organization of a state, in reference to which the nature of a man and a woman are not the same, but diverse?

We certainly are entitled to do so.

Well, perhaps it might be pleaded by others, as it was a little while ago by you, that it is not easy to give a satisfactory answer at a moment's notice; but that, with time for consideration, it would not be difficult to do so.

True, it might.

Would you like us then to beg the author of such objections to accompany us, to see if we can shew him that no occupation which belongs to the ordering of a state is peculiar to women?

By all means.

Well then, we will address him thus: Pray tell us whether, when you say that one man possesses talents for a particular study, and that another is without them, you mean that the former learns it easily, the latter with difficulty; and that the one with little instruction can find out much for himself in the subject he had studied, whereas the other after much teaching and practice cannot even retain what he has learnt; and that the mind of the one is duly aided, that of the other thwarted, by the bodily powers? Are not these the only marks by which you define the possession and the want of natural talents for any pursuit?

Everyone will say yes.

Well then, do you know of any branch of human industry in which the female sex is not inferior in these respects to the male? or need we go the length of specifying the art of weaving, and the manfacture of pastry and preserves, in which women are thought to excel, and in which their discomfiture is most laughed at?

You are perfectly right, that in almost every employment the one sex is vastly superior to the other. There are many women, no doubt, who are better in many things than many men; but, speaking generally, it is as you say.

I conclude then, my friend, that none of the occupations which comprehend the ordering of a state belong to woman as woman, nor yet to man as man; but natural gifts are to be found here and there, in both sexes alike; and, so far as her nature is concerned, the woman is admissible to all pursuits as well as the man; though in all of them the woman is weaker than the man.

Precisely so.

Shall we then appropriate all duties to men, and none to women?

How can we?

On the contrary, we shall hold, I imagine, that one woman may have talents for medicine, and another be without them; and that one may be musical, and another unmusical.

Undoubtedly.

And shall we not also say, that one woman may have qualifications for gymnastic exercises, and for war, and another be unwarlike, and without a taste for gymnastics?

I think we shall.

Again, may there not be a love of knowledge in one, and a distaste for it in another? and may not one be spirited, and another spiritless?

True again.

If that be so, there are some women who are fit, and others who are unfit, for the office of guardians. For were not those the qualities that we selected, in the case of the men, as marking their fitness for that office?

Yes, they were.

Then as far as the guardianship of a state is concerned, there is no difference between the natures of the man and of the woman, but only various degrees of weakness and strength.

Apparently there is none.

Then we shall have to select duly qualified women also, to share in the life and official labours of the duly qualified men; since we find that they are competent to the work, and of kindred nature with the men.

Just so. . . .

Very well; if the question is how to render a woman fit for the office of guardian, we shall not have one education for men, and another for women, especially as the nature to be wrought upon is the same in both cases.

No, the education will be the same. . . .

But I really think, Socrates, he continued, that if you be permitted to go on in this way, you will never recollect what you put aside some time ago before you entered on all these questions, namely, the task of shewing that this constitution of things is possible, and how it might be realized. . . .

Well, then, I continued, in the first place we ought not to forget that we have been brought to this point by an inquiry into the nature of justice and injustice.

True: but what of that?

Why nothing. But, if we find out what justice is, shall we expect the character of a just man not to differ in any point from that of justice itself, but to be its perfect counterpart? Or shall we be content provided he comes as near it as is possible, and partakes more largely of it than the rest of the world?

The latter: —we shall be content. . . .

Do you think any the worse of the merits of an artist, who has painted a beau ideal of human beauty, and has left nothing lacking in the picture, because he cannot prove that such a man as he has painted might possibly exist?

No, indeed, I do not.

Well, were not we likewise professing to construct in theory the pattern of a perfect state?

Yes, certainly.

Then will our theory suffer at all in your good opinion, if we cannot prove that it is possible for a city to be organized in the manner proposed?

Certainly not.

This then is the true state of the case: but if for your gratification I am to exert myself also to shew in what especial way and on what conditions our ideal might best be realized, I must ask you, with a view to this demonstration, to grant over again your former admissions.

Which do you mean?

In any case, can a theoretical sketch be perfectly realized in practice? or is it a law of nature that performance can never hit the truth so closely as theory? Never mind if some think otherwise; but tell me whether you admit the fact or not.

I do admit it.

Then do not impose upon me the duty of exhibiting all our theory realized with precise accuracy in fact: but if we succeed in finding out how a state may be organized in very close accordance with our description, you must admit that we have discovered the possibility of realizing the plan which you require me to consider. Shall you not be content if you gain thus much? for my own part I shall be.

So shall I.

Then our next step apparently must be, to endeavour to search out and demonstrate what there is now amiss in the working of our states, preventing their being regulated in the manner described, and what is the smallest change that would enable a state to assume this form of constitution, confining ourselves, if possible, to a single change; if not, to two; or else, to such as are fewest in number and least important in their influence.

Let us by all means endeavour so to do.

Well, I proceeded, there is one change by which, as I think we might shew, the required revolution would be secured; but it is certainly neither a small nor an easy change, though it is a possible one.

What is it? . . .

Unless it happen either that philosophers acquire the kingly power in states, or that those who are now called kings and potentates, be imbued with a sufficient measure of genuine philosophy, that is to say, unless political power and philosophy be united in the same person, most of those minds which at present pursue one to the exclusion of the other being peremptorily debarred from either, there will be no deliverance, my dear Glaucon, for cities, nor yet, I believe, for the human race; neither can the commonwealth, which we have now sketched in theory, ever till then grow into a possibility, and see the light of day. But a consciousness how entirely this would contradict the common opinion made me all along so reluctant to give expression to it: for it is difficult to see that there is no other way by which happiness can be attained, by the state or by the individual. . . .

BOOK VI

. . . Here Adeimantus interposed and said . . . a person will tell you, that though at each question he cannot oppose you with words, yet in practice he sees that all the students of philosophy, who have devoted themselves to it for any length of time, instead of taking it up for educational purposes and relinquishing it while still young, in most cases become exceedingly eccentric, not to say quite depraved, while even those who appear the most respectable are notwithstanding so far the worse for the pursuit which you commend, that they become useless to their country.

When he had said this, I replied;—Then do you think this objection untrue?

I am not sure, he answered; but I should be glad to hear what you think of it.

Let me tell you, that I hold it to be a true objection.

How then can it be right to assert that the miseries of our cities will find no relief, until those philosophers who, on our own admission, are useless to them, become their rulers?

You are asking a question, I replied, which I must answer by the help of an illustration.

And you, I suppose, have not been in the habit of employing illustrations.

Ah! you rally me, do you, now that you have got me upon a subject in which demonstration is so difficult? However, listen to the illustration, that you may see still better how stingy I am with the work. So cruel is the position in which those respectable men are placed, in reference to their states, that there is no single thing whose position is analogous to theirs. Consequently I have to collect materials from several quarters for the imaginary case which I am to use in their defence, like painters when they paint goat-stags and similar monsters.

Figure to yourself a fleet, or a single ship, in which the state of affairs on board is as follows. The captain, you are to suppose, is taller and stronger than any of the crew, but rather deaf, and rather short-sighted, and correspondingly deficient in nautical skill; and the sailors are quarrelling together about the pilotage,—each of them thinking he has a right to steer the vessel, although up to that moment he has never studied the art, and cannot name his instructor, or the time when he served his apprenticeship; more than this, they assert that it is a thing which positively cannot be taught, and are even ready to tear in pieces the person who affirms that it can: meanwhile they crowd incessantly round the person of the captain, begging and beseeching him with every importunity to entrust the helm to them; and occasionally, failing to persuade him, while others succeed better, these disappointed candidates kill their successful rivals, or fling them overboard, and, after binding the high-spirited captain hand and foot with mandragora or strong drink, or disabling him by some other contrivance, they remain masters of the ship, and apply its contents to their own purposes, and pass their time at sea in drinking and feasting, as you might expect with such a crew; and besides all this, they compliment with the title of 'able seaman,' 'excellent pilot,' 'skilful navigator,' any sailor that can second them cleverly in either persuading or forcing the captain into installing them in command of the ship, while they condemn as useless every one whose talents are of a different order,—having no notion that the true pilot must devote his attention to the year and its seasons, to the sky, and the stars, and the winds, and all that concerns his art, if he intends to be really fit to command a ship; and thinking it impossible to acquire and practise, along with the pilot's art, the art of maintaining the pilot's authority whether some of the crew like it or not. Such being the state of things on board, do you not think that the pilot who is really master of his craft is sure to be called a useless, star-gazing babbler by the mariners who form the crews of ships so circumstanced?

Yes, that he will, replied Adeimantus.

Well, said I, I suppose you do not require to see my illustration passed in review, to remind you that it is a true picture of our cities in so far as their disposition towards philosophers is concerned; on the contrary, I think you understand my meaning.

Yes, quite.

That being the case, when a person expresses his astonishment that philosophers are not respected in our cities, begin by telling him our illustration, and endeavour to persuade him that it would be far more astonishing if they were respected.

Well, I will.

And go on to tell him that he is right in saying that the most respectable of the proficients in philosophy are of no use to the world; only recommend him to lay the fault of it not on these good people themselves, but upon those who decline their services. For it is not in the nature of things that a pilot should petition the sailors to submit to his authority, or that the wise should wait at the rich man's door. No, the author of that witticism was wrong: for the real truth is, that, just as a sick man, be he rich or poor, must attend at the physician's door, so all who require to be governed must attend at the gate of him who is able to govern,—it being against nature that the ruler, supposing him to be really good for anything, should have to entreat his subjects to submit to his rule. In fact, you will not be wrong, if you compare the statesmen of our time to the sailors whom we were just now describing, and the useless visionary talkers, as they are called by our politicians, to the veritable pilots.

You are perfectly right.

Under these circumstances, and amongst men like these, it is not easy for that noblest of occupations to be in good repute with those to whose pursuits it is directly opposed. But far the most grievous and most obstinate misconstruction, under which Philosophy labours, is due to her professed followers; who are doubtless the persons meant by the accuser of Philosophy, when he declares, as you tell us, that most of those who approach her are utterly depraved, while even her best pupils are useless:—to the truth of which remark I assented, did I not?

Yes, you did.

We have explained the reason why the good are useless, have we not?

Certainly we have. . . .

Well, then, this part of the subject having been laboriously completed, shall we proceed to discuss the questions still remaining, in what way, and by the help of what pursuits and studies, we shall secure the presence of a body of men capable of preserving the constitution unimpaired, and what must be the age at which these studies are severally undertaken?

Let us do so by all means. . . .

Now consider what a small supply of these men you will, in all probability, find. For the various members of that character, which we described as essential to philosophers, will seldom grow incorporate: in most cases that character grows disjointed.

What do you mean?

You are aware that persons endowed with a quick comprehension, a good memory, sagacity, acuteness, and their attendant qualities, do not readily grow up to be at the same time so noble and lofty-minded, as to consent to live a regular, calm, and steady life: on the contrary, such persons are drifted by their acuteness hither and thither, and all steadiness vanishes from their life.

True.

On the other hand, those steady and invariable characters, whose trustiness makes one anxious to employ them, and who in war are slow to take alarm, behave in the same say when pursuing their studies; that is to say, they are torpid and stupid, as if they were benumbed, and are constantly dozing and yawning, whenever they have to toil at anything of the kind.

That is true.

But we declare that, unless a person possesses a pretty fair amount of both qualifications, he must be debarred all access to the strictest education, to honour, and to government.

We are right.

Then do you not anticipate a scanty supply of such characters?

Most assuredly I do.

Hence we must not be content with testing their behaviour in the toils, dangers, and pleasures, which we mentioned before; but we must go on to try them in ways which we then omitted, exercising them in a variety of studies, and observing whether their character will be able to support the highest subjects, or whether it will flinch from the trial, like those who flinch under other circumstances.

No doubt it is proper to examine them in this way. But pray which do you mean by the highest subjects? . . .

Assuredly you have heard the answer many a time; but at this moment either you have forgotten it, or else you intend to find me employment by raising objections. I incline to the latter opinion; for you have often been told that the essential Form of the Good is the highest object of science, and that this essence, by blending with just things and all other created objects, renders them useful and advantageous. And at this moment you can scarcely doubt that I am going to assert this, and to assert, besides, that we are not sufficiently acquainted with this essence. And if so,—if, I say, we know everything else perfectly, without knowing this,—you are aware that it will profit us nothing; just as it would be equally profitless to possess everything without possessing what is good. Or do you imagine it would be a gain to possess all possessible things, with the single exception of things good; or to apprehend every conceivable object, without apprehending what is good,—in other words, to be destitute of every good and beautiful conception?

Not I, believe me.

Moreover, you doubtless know besides, that the chief good is supposed by the multitude to be pleasure,—by the more enlightened, insight?

Of course I know that.

And you are aware, my friend, that the advocates of this latter opinion are unable to explain what they mean by insight, and are compelled at last to explain it as insight into that which is good.

Yes, they are in a ludicrous difficulty.

They certainly are: since they reproach us with ignorance of that which is good, and then speak to us the next moment as if we knew what it was. For they tell us that the chief good is insight into good, assuming that we understand their meaning, as soon as they have uttered the term 'good.'

It is perfectly true.

Again: are not those, whose definition identifies pleasure with good, just as much infected with error as the preceding? For they are forced to admit the existence of evil pleasures, are they not?

Certainly they are.

From which it follows, I should suppose, that they must admit the same thing to be both good and evil.

Does it not?

Certainly it does.

Then is it not evident that this is a subject often and severely disputed?

Doubtless it is.

Once more: is it not evident, that though many persons would be ready to do and seem to do, or to possess and seem to possess, what seems just and beautiful, without really being so; yet, when you come to things good, no one is content to acquire what only seems such; on the contrary, everybody seeks the reality, and semblances are here, if nowhere else, treated with universal contempt?

Yes, that is quite evident.

This good, then, which every soul pursues, as the end of all its actions, divining its existence, but perplexed and unable to apprehend satisfactorily its nature, or to enjoy that steady confidence in relation to it, which it does enjoy in relation to other things, and therefore doomed to forfeit any advantage which it might have derived from those same things;—are we to maintain that, on a subject of such overwhelming importance, the blindness we have described is a desirable feature in the character of those best members of the state in whose hands everything is to be placed?

Most certainly not.

At any rate, if it be not known in what way just things and beautiful things come to be also good, I imagine that such things will not possess a very valuable guardian in the person of him who is ignorant on this point. And I surmise that none will know the just and the beautiful satisfactorily till he knows the good.

You are right in your surmises.

Then will not the arrangement of our constitution be perfect, provided it be overlooked by a guardian who is scientifically acquainted with these sub-jects?

Unquestionably it will. But pray, Socrates, do *you* assert the chief good to be science or pleasure or something different from either? . . .

I will do so, as soon as we have come to a settlement together, and you have been reminded of certain statements made in a previous part of our conversation, and renewed before now again and again.

Pray what statements?

In the course of the discussion we have distinctly maintained the existence of a multiplicity of things that are beautiful, and good, and so on.

True, we have.

And also the existence of an essential beauty, and an essential good, and so on;—reducing all those things which before we regarded as manifold, to a single form and a single entity in each case, and addressing each as an independent being.

Just so.

And we assert that the former address themselves to the eye, and not to the pure reason; whereas the forms address themselves to the reason, and not to the eye.

Certainly. . . .

Suppose you take a line divided into two unequal parts,—one to represent the visible class of objects, the other the intellectual,—and divide each part again into two segments on the same scale. Then, if you make the lengths of the segments represent degrees of distinctness or indistinctness, one of the two segments of the part which stands for the visible world will represent all images:—meaning by images, first of all, shadows; and, in the next place, reflections in water, and in close-grained, smooth, bright substances, and everything of the kind, if you understand me.

Yes, I do understand.

Let the other segment stand for the real objects corresponding to these images,—namely, the animals about us, and the whole world of nature and of art.

Very good.

Would you also consent to say that, with reference to this class, there is, in point of truth and untruthfulness, the same distinction between the copy and the original, that there is between what is matter of opinion and what is matter of knowledge?

Certainly I should.

Then let us proceed to consider how we must divide that part of the whole line which represents the intellectual world.

How must we do it?

Thus: one segment of it will represent what the soul is compelled to investigate by the aid of the segments of the other part, which it employs as images, starting from hypotheses, and travelling not to a first principle, but to a conclusion. The other segment will represent the objects of the soul, as it makes its way from an hypothesis to a first principle which is not hypothetical, unaided by those images which the former division employs, and shaping its journey by the sole help of real essential forms.

I have not understood your description so well as I could wish.

Then we will try again. You will understand me more easily when I have made some previous observations. I think you know that the students of subjects like geometry and calculation, assume by way of materials, in each investigation, all odd and even numbers, figures, three kinds of angles, and other similar data. These things they are supposed to know, and having adopted them as hypotheses, they decline to give any account of them, either to themselves or to others, on the assumption that they are self-evident; and, making these their starting point, they proceed to travel through the remainder of the subject, and arrive at last, with perfect unanimity, at that which they have proposed as the object of investigation.

I am perfectly aware of the fact, he replied.

Then you also know that they summon to their aid visible forms, and discourse about them, though their thoughts are busy not with these forms, but with their originals, and though they discourse not with a view to the particular square and diameter which they draw, but with a view to the absolute square and the absolute diameter, and so on. For while they employ by way of images those figures and diagrams aforesaid, which again have their shadows and images in water, they are really endeavouring to behold those abstractions which a person can only see with the eye of thought.

True.

This, then, was the class of things which I called intellectual; but I said that the soul is constrained to employ hypotheses while engaged in the investigation of them,—not travelling to a first principle, (because it is unable to step out of, and mount above, its hypotheses,) but using, as images, just the copies that are presented by things below,—which copies, as compared with the originals, are vulgarly esteemed distinct and valued accordingly.

I understand you to be speaking of the subject-matter of the various branches of geometry and the kindred arts.

Again, by the second segment of the intellectual world understand me to mean all that the mere reasoning process apprehends by the force of dialectic, when it avails itself of hypotheses not as first principles, but as genuine hypotheses, that is to say, as stepping-stones and impulses, whereby it may force its way up to something that is not hypothetical, and arrive at the first principle of every thing, and seize it in its grasp; which done, it turns round, and takes hold of that which takes hold of this first principle, till at last it comes down to a conclusion, calling in the aid of no sensible object whatever, but simply employing abstract, self-subsisting forms, and terminating in the same.

I do not understand you so well as I could wish, for I believe you to be describing an arduous task; but at any rate I understand that you wish to declare distinctly, that the field of real existence and pure intellect, as contemplated by the science of dialectic, is more certain than the field investigated by what are called the arts, in which hypotheses constitute first principles, which the students are compelled, it is true, to contemplate with the mind and not with the senses; but, at the same time, as they do not come back, in the course of inquiry, to a first principle, but push on from hypothetical premises, you think that they do not exercise pure reason on the questions that engage them, although taken in connexion with a first principle these questions come within the domain of the pure reason. And I believe you apply the term understanding, not pure reason, to the mental habit of such people as geometricians,—regarding understanding as something intermediate between opinion and pure reason.

You have taken in my meaning most satisfactorily; and I beg you will accept these four mental states, as corresponding to the four segments,—namely pure reason corresponding to the highest, understanding to the second, belief to the third, and conjecture to the last; and pray arrange them in gradation, and believe them to partake of distinctness in a degree corresponding to the truth of their respective objects.

I understand you, said he. I quite agree with you, and will arrange them as you desire.

BOOK VII

Now then, I proceeded to say, go on to compare our natural condition, so far as education and ignorance are concerned, to a state of things like the following. Imagine a number of men living in an underground cavernous chamber, with an entrance open to the light, extending along the entire length of the cavern, in which they have been confined, from their childhood, with their legs and necks so shackled, that they are obliged to sit still and look straight forwards, because their chains render it impossible for them to turn their heads round: and imagine a bright fire burning some way off, above and behind them, and an elevated roadway passing between the fire and the prisoners, with a low wall built along it, like the screens which conjurors put up in front of their audience, and above which they exhibit their wonders.

I have it, he replied.

Also figure to yourself a number of persons walking behind this wall, and carrying with them statues of men, and images of other animals, wrought in wood and stone and all kinds of materials, together with various other articles, which overtop the wall; and, as you might expect, let some of the passers-by be talking, and others silent.

You are describing a strange scene, and strange prisoners.

They resemble us, I replied. For let me ask you, in the first place, whether persons so confined could have seen anything of themselves or of each other, beyond the shadows thrown by the fire upon the part of the cavern facing them?

Certainly not, if you suppose them to have been compelled all their lifetime to keep their heads unmoved.

And is not their knowledge of the things carried past them equally limited?

Unquestionably it is.

And if they were able to converse with one another, do you not think that they would be in the habit of giving names to the objects which they saw before them?

Doubtless they would.

Again: if their prison-house returned an echo from the part facing them, whenever one of the passers-by opened his lips, to what, let me ask you, could they refer the voice, if not to the shadow which was passing?

Unquestionably they would refer it to that.

Then surely such persons would hold the shadows of those manufactured articles to be the only realities.

Without a doubt they would.

Now consider what would happen if the course of nature brought them a release from their fetters, and a remedy for their foolishness, in the following manner. Let us suppose that one of them has been released, and compelled suddenly to stand up, and turn his neck round and walk with open eyes towards the light; and let us suppose that he goes through all these actions with pain, and that the dazzling splendour renders him incapable of discerning those objects of which he used formerly to see the shadows. What answer should you expect him to make, if someone were to tell him that in those days he was watching foolish phantoms, but that now he is somewhat nearer to reality, and is turned towards things more real, and sees more correctly; above all, if he were to point out to him the several objects that are passing by, and question him, and compel him to answer what they are? Should you not expect him to be puzzled, and to regard his old visions as truer than the objects now forced upon his notice?

Yes, much truer.

And if he were further compelled to gaze at the light itself, would not his eyes, think you, be distressed, and would he not shrink and turn away to the things which he could see distinctly, and consider them to be really clearer than the things pointed out to him?

Just so.

And if someone were to drag him violently up the rough and steep ascent from the cavern, and refuse to let him go till he had drawn him out into the light of the sun, would he not, think you, be vexed and indignant at such treatment, and on reaching the light, would he not find his eyes so dazzled by the glare as to be incapable of making out so much as one of the objects that are now called true?

Yes, he would find it so at first.

Hence, I suppose, habit will be necessary to enable him to perceive objects in that upper world. At first he will be most successful in distinguishing shadows; then he will discern the reflections of men and other things in water, and afterwards the realities; and after this he will raise his eyes to encounter the light of the moon and stars, finding it less difficult to study the heavenly bodies and the heaven itself by night, than the sun and the sun's light by day.

Doubtless.

Last of all, I imagine, he will be able to observe and contemplate the nature of the sun, not as it *appears* in water or on alien ground, but as it *is* in itself in its own territory.

Of course.

His next step will be to draw the conclusion, that the sun is the author of the seasons and the years, and the guardian of all things in the visible world, and in a manner the cause of all those things which he and his companions used to see.

Obviously, this will be his next step.

What then? When he recalls to mind his first habitation, and the wisdom of the place, and his old fellow-prisoners, do you not think he will congratulate himself on the change, and pity them?

Assuredly he will.

And if it was their practice in those days to receive honour and commendations one from another, and to give prizes to him who had the keenest eye for a passing object, and who remembered best all that used to precede and follow and accompany it, and from these data divined most ably what was going to come next, do you fancy that he will covet these prizes, and envy those who receive honour and exercise authority among them? Do you not rather imagine that he will . . . be ready to go through anything, rather than entertain those opinions, and live in that fashion?

For my own part, he replied, I am quite of that opinion. I believe he would consent to go through anything rather than live in that way.

And now consider what would happen if such a man were to descend again and seat himself on his old seat? Coming so suddenly out of the sun, would he not find his eyes blinded with the gloom of the place?

Certainly, he would.

And if he were forced to deliver his opinion again, touching the shadows aforesaid, and to enter the lists against those who had always been prisoners, while his sight continued dim, and his eyes unsteady,—and if this process of initiation lasted a considerable time,—would he not be made a laughingstock, and would it not be said of him, that he had gone up only to come back again with his eyesight destroyed, and that it was not worthwhile even to attempt the ascent? And if anyone endeavoured to set them free and carry them to the light, would they not go so far as to put him to death, if they could only manage to get him into their power?

Yes, that they would.

Now this imaginary case, my dear Glaucon, you must apply in all its parts to our former statements, by comparing the region which the eye reveals, to the prisonhouse, and the light of the fire therein to the power of the sun: and if, by the upward ascent and the contemplation of the upper world, you understand the mounting of the soul into the intellectual region, you will hit the tendency of my own surmises, since you desire to be told what they are; though, indeed, God only knows whether they are correct. But, be that as it may, the view which I take of the subject is to the following effect. In the world of knowledge, the essential Form of Good is the limit of our inquiries, and can barely be perceived; but, when perceived, we cannot help concluding that it is in every case the source of all that is bright and beautiful,—in the visible world giving birth to light and its master, and in the intellectual world dispensing, immediately and with full authority, truth and reason;—and that whosoever would act wisely, either in private or in public, must set this Form of Good before his eyes.

To the best of my power, said he, I quite agree with you.

That being the case, I continued, pray agree with me on another point, and do not be surprised, that those who have climbed so high are unwilling to take a part in the affairs of men, because their souls are ever loath to desert that upper region. For how could it be otherwise, if the preceding simile is indeed a correct representation of their case?

True, it could scarcely be otherwise.

Well: do you think it a marvellous thing, that a person, who has just quitted the contemplation of divine objects for the study of human infirmities, should betray awkwardness, and appear very ridiculous, when with his sight still dazed, and before he has become sufficiently habituated to the darkness that reigns around, he finds himself compelled to contend in courts of law, or elsewhere, about the shadows of justice, or images which throw the shadows, and to enter the lists in questions involving the arbitrary suppositions entertained by those who have never yet had a glimpse of the essential features of justice?

No, it is anything but marvellous.

Right: for a sensible man will recollect that the eyes may be confused in two distinct ways and from two distinct causes,—that is to say, by sudden transitions either from light to darkness, or from darkness to light. And, believing the same idea to be applicable to the soul, whenever such a person sees a case in which the mind is perplexed and unable to distinguish objects, he will not laugh irrationally, but he will examine whether it has just quitted a brighter life, and has been blinded by the novelty of darkness, or whether it has come from the depths of ignorance into a more brilliant life, and has been dazzled by the unusual splendour; and not till then will he congratulate the one upon its life and condition, and compassionate the other; and if he chooses to laugh at it, such laughter will be less ridiculous than that which is raised at the expense of the soul that has descended from the light of a higher region.

You speak with great judgment.

Hence, if this be true, we cannot avoid adopting the belief, that the real nature of education is at variance with the account given of it by certain of its professors, who pretend, I believe, to infuse into the mind a knowledge of which it was destitute, just as sight might be instilled into blinded eyes.

True; such are their pretensions.

Whereas, our present argument shews us that there is a faculty residing in the soul of each person, and an instrument enabling each of us to learn; and that, just as we might suppose it to be impossible to turn the eye round from darkness to light without turning the whole body, so must this faculty, or this instrument, be wheeled round, in company with the entire soul, from the perishing world, until it be enabled to endure the contemplation of the real world and the brightest part thereof, which, according to us, is the Form of Good. Am I not right?

You are.

Hence, I continued, this very process of revolution must give rise to an art, teaching in what way the change will most easily and most effectually be brought about. Its object will not be to generate in the person the power of seeing. On the contrary, it assumes that he possesses it, though he is turned in a wrong direction, and does not look towards the right quarter; and its aim is to remedy this defect.

So it would appear.

Hence, while, on the one hand, the other so-called virtues of the soul seem to resemble those of the body, inasmuch as they really do not pre-exist in the soul, but are formed in it in the course of time by habit and exercise; the virtue of wisdom, on the other hand, does most certainly appertain, as it would appear, to a more divine substance, which never loses its energy, but by change of position becomes useful and serviceable, or else remains useless and injurious. For you must, ere this, have noticed how keen-sighted are the puny souls of those who have the reputation of being clever but vicious, and how sharply they see through the things to which they are directed, thus proving that their powers of vision are by no means feeble, though they have been compelled to become the servants of wickedness, so that the more sharply they see, the more numerous are the evils which they work.

Yes, indeed it is the case.

But, I proceeded, if from earliest childhood these characters had been shorn and stripped of those leaden, earthborn weights, which grow and cling to the pleasures of eating and gluttonous enjoyments of a similar nature, and keep the eye of the soul turned upon the things below;—if, I repeat, they had been released from these snares, and turned round to look at objects that are true, then these very same souls of these very same men would have had as keen an eye for such pursuits as they actually have for those in which they are now engaged.

Yes, probably it would be so.

Once more: is it not also probable, or rather is it not a necessary corollary to our previous remarks, that neither those who are uneducated and ignorant of truth, nor those who are suffered to linger over their education all their life, can ever be competent overseers of a state,—the former, because they have no single mark in life, which they are to constitute the end and aim of all their conduct both in private and in public; the latter, because they will not act without compulsion, fancying that, while yet alive, they have been translated to the islands of the blest.

That is true.

It is, therefore, our task, I continued, to constrain the noblest characters in our colony to arrive at that science which we formerly pronounced the highest, and to set eyes upon the good, and to mount that ascent we spoke of; and, when they have mounted and looked long enough, we must take care to refuse them that liberty which is at present permitted them.

Pray what is that?

The liberty of staying where they are, and refusing to descend again to those prisoners, or partake of their toils and honours, be they mean or be they exalted.

Then are we to do them a wrong, and make them live a life that is worse than the one within their reach?

You have again forgotten, my friend, that law does not ask itself how some one class in a state is to live extraordinarily well. On the contrary, it tries to bring about this result in the entire state; for which purpose it links the citizens together by persuasion and by constraint, makes them share with one another the benefit which each individual can contribute to the common weal, and does actually create men of this exalted character in the state, not with the intention of letting them go each on his own way, but with the intention of turning them to account in its plans for the consolidation of the state.

True, he replied; I had forgotten.

Therefore reflect, Glaucon, that far from wronging the future philosophers of our state, we shall only be treating them with strict justice, if we put them under the additional obligation of watching over their fellow-citizens, and taking care of them. We shall say: It is with good reason that your compeers elsewhere refuse to share in the labours of their respective states. For they take root in a city spontaneously, in defiance of the prevailing constitution; and it is but fair that a self-sown plant, which is indebted to no one for support, should have no inclination to pay to anybody wages for attendance. But in your case, it is we that have begotten you for the state as well as for yourselves, to be like leaders and kings of a hive,—better and more perfectly trained than the rest, and more capable of playing a part in both modes of life. You must therefore descend by turns, and associate with the rest of the community, and you must habituate yourselves to the contemplation of these obscure objects. For, when habituated, you will see a thousand times better than the residents, and you will recognize what each image is, and what is its original, because you have seen the realities of which beautiful and just and good things are copies. And in this way you and we shall find that the life of the state is a substance, and not a phantom like the life of our present states, which are mostly composed of men who fight among themselves for shadows, and are at feud for the administration of affairs, which they regard as a great boon. Whereas I conceive the truth stands thus: That city in which the destined rulers are least eager to rule, will inevitably be governed in the best and least factious manner, and a contrary result will ensue if the rulers are of a contrary disposition.

You are perfectly right.

And do you imagine that our pupils, when addressed in this way, will disobey our commands, and refuse to toil with us in the state by turns, while they spend most of their time together in that bright region?

Impossible, he replied: for certainly it is a just command and those who are to obey it are just men. No; doubtless each of them will enter upon his administration as an unavoidable duty,—conduct the reverse of that pursued by the present rulers in each state.

True, my friend; the case stands thus. If you can invent for the destined rulers a life better than ruling, you may possibly realize a well-governed city: for only in such a city will the rulers be those who are really rich, not in gold, but in a wise and virtuous life, which is the wealth essential to a happy man. But if beggars, and persons who hunger after private advantages, take the reins of the state, with the idea that they are privileged to snatch advantage from their power, all goes wrong. For the post of magistrate is thus made an object of strife; and civil and intestine conflicts of this nature, ruin not only the contending parties, but also the rest of the state.

That is most true.

And can you mention any life which contemns state-offices, except the life of true philosophy?

No indeed, I cannot.

Well, but the task of government must be undertaken by persons not enamoured of it: otherwise, their rivals will dispute their claim.

Unquestionably it must.

Then what other persons will you compel to enter upon the duties of guardians of the state, if you discard those who understand most profoundly the means of attaining the highest excellence in the administration of a country, and who also possess honours of a different stamp, and a nobler life than that of a statesman?

I shall not discard them, he replied; I shall address myself only to them.

And now would you have us proceed to consider in what way such persons are to arise in the state, and how they are to be carried up to the light, like those heroes who are said to have ascended up to heaven from the nether world?

Certainly I would have you do so.

Apparently this is a question . . . of a soul, which is traversing a road leading from a kind of night-like day up to a true day of real existence; and this road we shall doubtless declare to be true philosophy.

Exactly so.

Then must we not consider what branch of study possesses the power required?

Certainly we must.

Then, Glaucon, can you tell me of a science which tends to draw the soul from the fleeting to the real? Whilst I speak, I bethink myself that we certainly said, did we not, that our pupils must be trained in their youth to war?

Yes, we did say so.

Then the science, which we are in quest of, must possess this feature as well as the former.

What feature?

That it can be turned to use by warlike men.

That is certainly advisable, if it be practicable.

Now in the foregoing discussion we were for training our pupils through the agency of music and gymnastic.

True.

Gymnastic, I believe, is engaged upon the changeable and perishing; for it presides over the growth and waste of the body.

That is evident.

Hence gymnastic cannot be the study for which we are looking.

No, it cannot.

But what do you say to music, considered in the extent in which we previously discussed it?

Nay, he replied, music was only the counterpart of gymnastic, if you remember: for it trained our guardians by the influence of habit, and imparted to them, not science, but a kind of harmoniousness by means of harmony, and a kind of measuredness by means of measure; and in the subjects which it treated, whether fabulous or true, it presented another series of kindred characteristics: but it contained no branch of study tending to any advantage resembling the one of which you are now in quest.

Your memory is very exact, I made answer: for music really did possess nothing of the kind. But, my excellent Glaucon, where are we to find the thing we want? All the useful arts, I believe, we thought degrading.

Unquestionably we did: yet what other study is there still remaining, apart from music and gymnastic and the useful arts?

Come then, if we can find nothing beyond and independent of these, let us take one of those studies which are of universal application.

Pray which?

That general one, for example, of which all arts, trains of thought, and sciences, avail themselves; and which is also one of the first things that everyone must learn.

Tell me the nature of it.

I allude to that common process of distinguishing the numbers, one, two, and three. And I call it briefly, Number and Calculation. For may it not be said of these, that every art and science is compelled to crave a share in them?

Certainly it may.

And is not the science of war one of the number?

Beyond a doubt it is. . . .

Then can we help concluding, that to be able to calculate and count is a piece of knowledge indispensable to a warrior?

Yes, most indispensable, if he is to understand how to handle troops at all, or rather, if he is to be anything of a man.

And does your notion of this science coincide with mine?

Pray what is your notion?

It seems to be by nature one of those studies leading to reflection, of which we are in quest; but no one appears to make the right use of it, as a thing which tends wholly to draw us towards real existence.

Explain your meaning.

I will endeavour to make my own opinion clear to you. And you, on your side, must join me in studying those things, which I distinguish in my own mind as conducive, or not, to the end in view, and express your assent or dissent; in order that we may see more clearly, in the next place, whether I am right in my surmises as to the nature of this science.

Pray go on with your distinctions.

I will. If you observe, some of the objects of our perceptions do not stimulate the reflection into exercise, because they appear thoroughly appreciated by the perception; whereas others urge the reflection strenuously to examine them, because the perception appears to produce an unsound result.

It is plain you are talking of objects seen at a distance, and painting in perspective.

You have not quite hit my meaning.

Then pray what sort of objects do you mean?

I regard as non-stimulants all the objects which do not end by giving us at the same moment two contradictory perceptions. On the other hand, all the objects which do end in that way I consider stimulants,—meaning those cases in which the perception, whether incident from a near or a distant object, communicates two equally vivid, but contradictory impressions. You will understand my meaning more clearly thus:—Here you have three fingers, you say,— the little finger, the middle, and the third.

Very good.

Well, suppose me to be speaking of them as they appear on a close inspection. Now here is the point which I wish you to examine with reference to them.

Pray what is it?

It is evident that they are all equally fingers: and, so far, it makes no difference whether the one we are looking at be in the middle or outside, whether it be white or black, thick or thin, and so on. For, so long as we confine ourselves to these points, the mind seldom feels compelled to ask the reflection, what is a finger? Because in no instance has the sight informed the mind at the same moment, that the finger is the opposite of a finger.

No, certainly not.

Then, naturally, such impressions cannot be stimulating or awakening to the reflection.

True.

But how is it, pray, with the relative sizes of the fingers? Does the sight distinguish them satisfactorily, and does it make no difference to it, whether the position of one of them be in the middle, or at the outside? And in like manner, does the touch estimate thickness and thinness, softness and hardness, satisfactorily? And is there no defect in the similar communications of the other senses? Or, rather do they not all proceed thus? To begin with the perception which takes cognizance of hard things: is it not constrained to take cognizance also of soft things, and does it not intimate to the mind, that it feels the same thing to be both hard and soft?

It does.

In such cases, then, must not the mind be at a loss to know what this perception means by *hard*, since it declares the same thing to be also soft; and what the perception of weight means by light and heavy, when it informs the mind that the heavy is light, and the light heavy?

Why yes he answered; such interpretations will be strange to the mind, and will require examination.

Hence it is natural for the mind in such circumstances to call in the aid of reasoning and reflection, and to endeavour to make out whether each announcement is single or double.

Undoubtedly.

Should it incline to the latter view, is it not evident that each part of every announcement has a unity and character of its own?

It is evident.

If then each is *one*, and both together make *two*, the mind will conclude that the two are separable. For if they were inseparable, it could only conclude that they are *one*, not *two*.

True.

Well; the sense of sight, we say, gave us an impression, in which the sensations of great and small were confounded, instead of being separated. Am I not right?

You are.

But, on the other hand, reflection, reversing the process of the sight, was compelled, in order to make the sensible impression clear, to look at great and small as things distinct, not confounded.

True.

Then is it not some contradiction of this kind that first prompts us to ask, "What then, after all, is greatness, and what smallness?"

No doubt it is.

And thus we are led to distinguish between objects of reflection and objects of sight.

Most rightly so.

This, then, was the meaning which I was just now attempting to convey, when I said that some objects tend to stimulate thought, while others have no bias towards awakening reflection,—placing in the former category everything that strikes upon the senses in conjunction with its immediate opposite; and in the latter, everything of which this cannot be said.

Now I understand you, he replied; and I agree with you.

Well: to which of the two classes do you think that number and unity belong?

I cannot make up my mind.

Indeed! Let our previous remarks help you to a conclusion. If unity, in and by itself, is thoroughly grasped by the sight or any other sense, like the finger we spoke of, it cannot possess the quality of drawing the mind towards real existence. But if some contradiction is always combined with it in all its manifestations, making it appear the opposite of unity quite as much as unity itself, in that case a critic will be immediately required, and the mind will be compelled to puzzle over the difficulty, and stir up the inward faculty of thought to the investigation, and put the question, 'What, after all, is unity in itself?' And thus the study of the unit will be one of the things which turn and lead us to the contemplation of real existence.

You are right, said he: the observation of the unit does certainly possess this property in no common degree: for the same thing presents at the same moment the appearance of one thing, and an infinity of things.

Then, if this is the case with the unit, is it not also the case with all numbers without exception?

Doubtless it is.

Well, but calculation and arithmetic treat of number exclusively.

Certainly they do.

And, apparently, they conduct us to truth.

Yes, in a manner quite extraordinary.

Hence it would appear that the science of numbers must be one of the studies of which we are in quest. For the military man finds a knowledge of it indispensable in drawing up his troops, and the philosopher must study it because he is bound to rise above the changing and cling to the real, on pain of never becoming a skilful reasoner.

True.

But our guardian, as it happens, is both soldier and philosopher.

Undoubtedly he is.

Therefore, Glaucon, it will be proper to enforce the study by legislative enactment, and to persuade those who are destined to take part in the weightiest affairs of state, to study calculation and devote themselves to it, not like amateurs, but perseveringly, until, by the aid of pure reason, they have attained to the contemplation of the nature of numbers,—not cultivating it with a view to buying and selling, as merchants or shopkeepers, but for purposes of war, and to facilitate the conversion of the soul itself from the changeable to the true and the real.

What you say is admirable.

Indeed, I continued, talking of this science which treats of calculation, it has only just occurred to me how elegant it is, and how valuable it may be to us in many ways in carrying out our wishes, provided it be pursued for the sake of knowledge, and not for purposes of trade.

How so? he asked.

Because, as we were saying just now, it mightily draws the soul upwards, and compels it to reason about abstract numbers, steadily declining the discussion when any numbers are proposed which have bodies that can be seen and touched. For I presume you are aware that good mathematicians ridicule and disallow any attempt to part the unit in the course of argument; and if *you* divide it into pieces, like small change, *they* multiply it back again, and take every precaution to prevent the unit from ever losing its unity, and presenting an appearance of multiplicity.

That is quite true.

Now suppose, Glaucon, that someone were to ask them the following question:—My excellent friends, what kind of numbers are you discussing? Where are the numbers in which the unit realizes your description of it, which is, that every unit is equal, each to each, without the smallest difference, and contains within itself no parts? What answer should you expect them to make?

If you ask me, I should expect them to say, that the numbers about which they talk, are only capable of being conceived in thought, and cannot be dealt with in any other way.

Then, my friend, do you see that this science is, in all likelihood, absolutely necessary to us, since it evidently obliges the mind to employ the pure intelligence in the pursuit of pure truth?

It certainly possesses this quality in an eminent degree.

Again; have you ever noticed that those who have a turn for arithmetic are, with scarcely an exception, naturally quick at all sciences; and that men of slow intellect, if they be trained and exercised in this study, even supposing they derive no other benefit from it, at any rate progress so far as to become invariably quicker than they were before?

That is true.

And I am pretty sure, also, that you will not easily find many sciences that give the learner and student so much trouble and toil as arithmetic.

No, certainly you will not.

Then on all these accounts, so far from rejecting this science, we must employ it in the education of the finest characters.

I agree with you, said he.

Then let us consider this as one point settled. In the second place, let us inquire whether we ought to concern ourselves about the science which borders on arithmetic.

What is that? Do you mean geometry?

Even so, I replied.

It is obvious, he continued, that all that part of it which bears upon strategy does concern us. For in encamping, in occupying positions, in closing up and deploying troops, and in executing all the other manoeuvres of an army in the field of battle or on the march, it will make every difference to a military man, whether he is a good geometrician, or not.

Nevertheless, I replied, a trifling knowledge of geometry and calculation will suffice for these purposes. The question is, whether the larger and more advanced part of the study tends at all to facilitate our contemplation of the essential Form of Good. Now, according to us, this is the tendency of everything that compels the soul to transfer itself to that region in which is contained the most blissful part of that real existence, which it is of the highest importance for it to behold.

You are right.

Consequently if geometry compels the soul to contemplate real existence, it does concern us; but if it only forces the changeful and perishing upon our notice, it does not concern us.

Yes, so we affirm.

Well then, on one point at any rate we shall encounter no opposition from those who are even slightly acquainted with geometry, when we assert that this science holds a position which flatly contradicts the language employed by those who handle it.

How so?

They talk, I believe in a very ridiculous and poverty-stricken style. For they speak invariably of squaring, and producing, and adding, and so on, as if they were engaged in some business, and as if all their propositions had a practical end in view: whereas in reality I conceive that the science is pursued wholly for the sake of knowledge.

Assuredly it is.

There is still a point about which we must be agreed, is there not?

What is it?

That the science is pursued for the sake of the knowledge of what eternally exists, and not of what comes for a moment into existence, and then perishes.

We shall soon be agreed about that. Geometry, no doubt, is a knowledge of what eternally exists.

If that be so, my excellent friend, geometry must tend to draw the soul towards truth, and to give the finishing stroke to the philosophic spirit,—thus contributing to raise up what, at present, we so wrongly keep down.

Yes, it will do so most forcibly.

Then you must, in the most forcible manner, direct the citizens of your beautiful city on no account to fail to apply themselves to geometry. For even its secondary advantages are not trifling.

Pray what are they?

Not to mention those which you specified as bearing upon the conduct of war, I would insist particularly upon the fact, of which we are assured,—that, where a ready reception of any kind of learning is an object, it will make all and every difference whether the pupil has applied himself to geometry or not.

Yes, undoubtedly it will.

Shall we, then, impose this, as a secondary study, upon our young men?

Yes, let us do so, he replied.

Again: shall we make astronomy a third study? or do you disapprove?

I quite approve of it, said he. For to have an intimate acquaintance with seasons, and months, and years, is an advantage not only to the agriculturist and the navigator, but also, in an equal degree, to the general.

You amuse me by your evident alarm lest the multitude should think that you insist upon useless studies. Yet indeed it *is* no easy matter, but on the contrary a very difficult one, to believe that in the midst of these studies an organ of our souls is being purged from the blindness, and quickened from the deadness, occasioned by other pursuits,—an organ whose preservation is of more importance than a thousand eyes; because only by it can truth be seen. Consequently, those who think with us will bestow unqualified approbation on the studies you prescribe: while those who have no inkling at all of this doctrine, will think them valueless, because they see no considerable advantage to be gained from them beyond their practical applications. Therefore consider at once with which of the two parties you are conversing: or else, if you are carrying on the discussion chiefly on your own account, without any reference to either party, you surely will not grudge another man any advantage which he may derive from the conversation.

I prefer the latter course: I mean to speak, put my questions, and give my answers, chiefly on my own account.

Then take a step backwards, I continued. We were wrong a moment ago in what we took as the science next in order to geometry.

What did we take?

Why, after considering plane surfaces, we proceeded to take solids in a state of revolution, before considering solids in themselves. Whereas the correct way is, proceed from two dimensions to three; which brings us, I believe, to cubical dimensions, and figures into which thickness enters.

True, Socrates; but these subjects, I think, have not yet been explored.

They have not, I replied; and for two reasons. In the first place, they are difficult problems, and but feebly investigated, because no state holds them in estimation: and, in the second place, those who do investigate them stand in need of a superintendent, without whom they will make no discoveries. Now, to find such a person is a hard task to begin with; and then, supposing one were found, as matters stand now, the pride of those who are inquisitive about the subject would prevent their listening to his suggestions. But if a state, in its corporate capacity, were to pay honour to the study, and constitute itself superintendent thereof, these students would yield obedience, and the real nature of the subject, thus continuously and vigorously investigated, would be brought to light. For even now, slighted and curtailed as it is not only by the many, but also by professed inquirers, who can give no account of the extent of its usefulness, it nevertheless makes progress, in spite of all these obstacles, by its inherent elegance; and I should not be at all surprised if its difficulties were cleared up.

There certainly is a peculiar fascination about it. But pray explain more clearly what you were saying just now.

I think you defined geometry as the investigation of plane surfaces.

I did.

You then proceeded to place astronomy next to geometry; though afterwards you drew back.

Yes, I said, the more I haste to travel over the ground, the worse I speed. The investigation of space of three dimensions succeeds to plane geometry; but because it is studied absurdly, I passed it over, and spoke of astronomy, which implies motion of solid bodies, as the next step after geometry.

You are right.

Then let us assign the fourth place in our studies to astronomy, regarding the existence of the science now omitted as only waiting for the time when a state shall take it up.

It is a reasonable idea, Socrates. And to return to the rebuke which you gave me a little while ago for my vulgar commendation of astronomy, I can now praise the plan on which you pursue it. For I suppose it is clear to everyone, that astronomy at all events compels the soul to look upwards, and draws it from the things of this world to the other.

It is not clear to me, I replied, though perhaps it may be to everyone else: for that is not my opinion.

Then what is your opinion?

It seems to me that astronomy, as now handled by those who embark on philosophy, positively makes the soul look downwards.

How so?

I think you have betrayed no want of intrepidity in the conception you have formed of the true nature of that learning which deals with the things above. For probably, if a person were to throw his head back, and learn something from the contemplation of a carved ceiling, you would suppose him to be contemplating it, not with his eyes, but with his reason. Now, perhaps your notion is right, and mine foolish. For my own part, I cannot conceive that any science makes the soul look upwards, unless it has to do with the real and invisible. It makes no difference whether a person stares stupidly at the sky, or looks with half-shut eyes upon the ground; so long as he is trying to study any sensible object, I deny that he can ever be said to have learned anything, because no objects of sense admit of scientific treatment; and I maintain that his soul is looking downwards, not upwards, though he may be lying on his back, like a swimmer, to study, either in the sea, or on dry land.

I am rightly punished, he rejoined; for I deserved your rebuke. But pray what did you mean by saying that astronomy ought to be studied on a system very different from the present one, if it is to be studied profitably for the purposes that we have in view?

I will tell you. Since this fretted sky is still a part of the visible world, we are bound to regard it, though the most beautiful and perfect of visible things, as far inferior nevertheless to those true revolutions, which real velocity, and real slowness, existing in true number, and in all true forms, accomplish relatively to each other, carrying with them all that they contain: which are verily apprehensible by reason and thought, but not by sight. Or do you think differently?

No, indeed, he replied.

Therefore we must employ that fretted sky as a pattern or plan to forward the study which aims at those higher objects, just as we might employ diagrams, which fell in our way, curiously drawn and elaborated by Daedalus or some other artist or draughtsman. For, I imagine, a person acquainted with geometry, on seeing such diagrams, would think them most beautifully finished, but would hold it ridiculous to study them seriously in the hope of detecting thereby the truths of equality, or duplicity, or any other ratio.

No doubt it would be ridiculous.

And do you not think that the genuine astronomer will view with the same feelings the motions of the stars? That is to say, will he not regard the heaven itself, and the bodies which it contains, as framed by the heavenly architect with the utmost beauty of which such works are susceptible? But as to the proportion which the day bears to the night, both to the month, the month to the year, and the other stars to the sun and moon, and to one another,—will he not, think you, look down upon the man who believes such corporeal and visible objects to be changeless and exempt from all perturbations; and will he not hold it absurd to bestow extraordinary pains on the endeavour to apprehend their true condition?

Yes, I quite think so, now that I hear you suggest it.

Hence, we shall pursue astronomy with the help of problems, just as we pursue geometry: but we shall let the heavenly bodies alone, if it is our design to become really acquainted with astronomy, and by that means to convert the natural intelligence of the soul from a useless into a useful possession.

The plan which you prescribe, said he, is, I am confident, many times more laborious than the present mode of studying astronomy.

Yes, I replied; and I imagine we shall prescribe every thing else on the same scale, if we are to be of any use as legislators. But to proceed: what other science in point can you suggest?

I cannot suggest any, on such short notice.

Well, motion, if I am not mistaken, admits of certainly more than one variety: a perfect enumeration of these varieties may perhaps be supplied by some learned philosopher. Those which are manifest to people like us are two in number.

Pray what are they?

We have already described one; the other is its counterpart.

What is that?

It would seem, I replied, that our ears were intended to detect harmonious movements, just as our eyes were intended to detect the motions of the heavenly bodies; and that these constitute in a manner two sister sciences, as the Pythagoreans assert, and as we, Glaucon, are ready to grant. If not, what other course do we take?

We take the course you mentioned first: we grant the fact.

Then, as the business promises to be a long one, we will consult the Pythagoreans upon this question, and perhaps upon some other questions too,—maintaining, meanwhile, our own principle intact.

What principle do you mean?

Never to let our pupils attempt to study any imperfect branch of these sciences, or anything that ever fails to arrive ultimately at that point which all things ought to reach, as we said just now in treating of astronomy. For you can scarcely be ignorant that harmony also is treated just like astronomy in this,—that its professors, like the astronomers, are content to measure the notes and concords distinguished by the ear, one against another, and therefore toil without result.

Yes, indeed, and they make themselves quite ridiculous. They talk about 'repetitions,' and apply their ears closely, as if they were bent on extracting a note from their neighbours: and then one party asserts that an intermediate sound can still be detected, which is the smallest interval, and ought to be the unit of measure; while the other party contends that now the sounds are identical,—both alike postponing their reason to their ears.

I see you are alluding to those good men who tease and torture the chords, and rack them upon the pegs. But not to make the metaphor too long by enlarging upon the blows given by the plectrum, and the peevishness, reserve and frowardness of the strings, I here abandon this style, and tell you that I do not mean these persons, but those whom we resolved but now to consult on the subject of harmony. For they act just like the astronomers; that is, they investigate the numerical relations subsisting between these audible concords, but they refuse to apply themselves to problems, with the object of examining what numbers are, and what numbers are not, consonant, and what is the reason of the difference.

Why the work you describe would require faculties more than human.

Call it, rather, a work useful in the search after the beautiful and the good, though useless if pursued with other ends.

Yes, that is not unlikely.

In addition to this, I continued, if the study of all these sciences which we have enumerated, should ever bring us to their mutual association and relationship, and teach us the nature of the ties which bind them together, I believe that the diligent treatment of them will forward the objects which we have in view, and that the labour, which otherwise would be fruitless, will be well bestowed.

I have the same presentiment, Socrates. But the work you speak of is a very great one.

Do you allude to the prelude? I replied: or to what? Surely we do not require to be reminded that all this is but the prelude to the actual hymn, which we have to learn? For I presume you do not look upon the proficients in these studies as dialecticians.

No, indeed I do not; bating a very few exceptions that have fallen in my way.

But of course you do not suppose that persons unable to take a part in the discussion of first principles, can be said to *know* a particle of the things which we affirm they ought to know.

No, that again is not my opinion.

Then, Glaucon, have we not here the actual hymn, of which dialectical reasoning is the consummation? This hymn, falling as it does within the domain of the intellect, can only be imitated by the faculty of sight; which, as we said, strives to look steadily, first at material animals, then at the stars themselves, and last of all at the very sun itself. In the same way, whenever a person strives, by the help of dialectic, to start in pursuit of every reality by a simple process of reason, independent of all sensuous information,—never flinching, until by an act of the pure intelligence he has grasped the real nature of good,—he arrives at the very end of the intellectual world, just as the last-mentioned person arrived at the end of the visible world.

Unquestionably.

And this course you name dialectic, do you not?

Certainly I do.

On the other hand, the release of the prisoners from their chains, and their transition from the shadows of the images to the images themselves and to the light, and their ascent from the cavern into the sunshine;—and, when there, the fact of their being able to look, not at the animals and vegetables and the sun's light, but still only at their reflections in water, which are indeed divine and shadows of things real, instead of being shadows of images thrown by a light which may itself be called an image, when compared with the sun; —these points, I say, find their counterpart in all this pursuit of the above-mentioned arts, which possesses this power of elevating the noblest part of the soul, and advancing it towards the contemplation of that which is most excellent in the things that really exist, just as in the other case the clearest organ of the body was furthered to the contemplation of that which is brightest in the corporeal and visible region.

For myself, he replied, I accept this statement. And yet I must confess that I find it hard to accept; though at the same time, looking at it in another way, I find it hard to deny. However, as the discussion of it need not be confined to the present occasion, but may be repeated on many future occasions, let us assume the truth of your present theory, and so proceed to the hymn itself, and discuss it, as we have discussed the prelude. Tell us, therefore, what is the general character of the faculty of dialectic, and into what specific parts it is divided, and lastly what are its methods. For these methods will, in all likelihood, be the roads that lead to the very spot where we are to close our march, and rest from our journey.

My dear Glaucon, I replied, you would not be able to follow me further, though on *my* part there should be no lack of willingness. You would no longer be looking at the similitude of that whereof we speak, but at the truth itself, in the shape in which it appears to me. Whether I am right or not, I dare not go so far as to decide positively: but I suppose I am warranted in affirming that we are not far wrong.

Undoubtedly you are.

And may I not also affirm, that the faculty of dialectic can alone reveal the truth to one who is master of the sciences which we have just enumerated; and that in no other way is such knowledge possible?

Yes, on that point also you are warranted in speaking positively.

At any rate, I continued, no one will contradict us when we assert that there is no other method which attempts systematically to form a conception of the real nature of each individual thing. On the contrary, all the arts, with a few exceptions, are wholly addressed to the opinions and wants of men, or else concern themselves about the production and composition of bodies, or the treatment of things which grow and are compounded. And as for these few exceptions, such as geometry and its accompanying sciences, which, according to us, in some small degree apprehend what is real,—we find that, though they may dream about real existence, they cannot behold it in a waking state, so long as they use hypotheses which they leave unexamined, and of which they can give no account. For when a person assumes a first principle which he does not know, on which unknown first principle depends the web of interme- diate propositions, and the final conclusion,—by what possibility can such mere admissions ever constitute science?

It is indeed impossible.

Hence the dialectic method, and that alone, adopts the following course. It carries back its hypotheses to the very first principle of all, in order to estab- lish them firmly; and finding the eye of the soul absolutely buried in a swamp of barbarous ignorance, it gently draws and raises it upwards, employing as handmaids in this work of revolution the arts which we have discussed. These we have often called sciences, because it is customary to do so, but they require another name, betokening greater clearness than opinion, but less distinctness than science. On some former occasion we fixed upon the term understanding to express this mental process. But it appears to me to be no part of our busi- ness to dispute about a name, when we have proposed to ourselves the consid- eration of such important subjects.

You are quite right, said he: we only want a name which when applied to a mental state shall indicate clearly what phenomena it describes.

Indeed I am content, I proceeded, to call as before the first division sci- ence, the second understanding, the third belief, and the fourth conjecture,— the two latter jointly constituting opinion, and the two former intelligence. Opinion deals with the changing, intelligence with the real; and as the real is to the changing, so is intelligence to opinion; and as intelligence is to opinion, so is science to belief, and understanding to conjecture. But the analogy between the objects of these mental acts, and the twofold division of the provinces of opinion and of intelligence, we had better omit, Glaucon, to prevent burdening ourselves with discussions far outnumbering all the former.

Well, I certainly agree with you upon those other points, so far as I can follow you.

Do you also give the title of Dialectician to the person who takes thought- ful account of the essence of each thing? And will you admit that, so far as a person has no such account to give to himself and to others, so far he fails to exercise pure reason upon the subject?

Yes, I cannot doubt it, he replied.

Then shall you not also hold the same language concerning the good? Unless a person can strictly define by a process of thought the essential Form of the Good, abstracted from everything else; and unless he can fight his way as it were through all objections, studying to disprove them not by the rules of opinion, but by those of real existence; and unless in all these conflicts he trav- els to his conclusion without making one false step in his train of thought,— unless he does all this, shall you not assert that he knows neither the essence of good, nor any other good thing; and that any phantom of it, which he may chance to apprehend, is the fruit of opinion and not of science; and that he dreams and sleeps away his present life, and never wakes on this side of that future world, in which he is doomed to sleep forever?

Yes, he said; I shall most decidedly assert all this.

Then certainly, if you ever had the actual training of those children of yours, whose nature and education you are theoretically superintending, I cannot suppose that you would allow them to be magistrates in the state with authority to decide the weightiest matters, while they are as irrational as the strokes of a pen.

No, indeed I should not.

You will pass a law, no doubt, ordering them to apply themselves especially to that education which will enable them to use the weapons of the dialectician most scientifically?

I shall, with your help.

Then does it not seem to you that dialectic lies, like a coping-stone, upon the top of the sciences, and that it would be wrong to place any other science above it, because the series is now complete?

Yes, I believe you are right, he replied.

Hence, I continued, it only remains for you to fix upon the persons to whom we are to assign these studies, and the principle of their distribution.

That is evidently the case.

Do you remember what kind of persons we selected, when we were choosing the magistrates some time ago?

Of course I do.

Well, I would have you regard the qualities we mentioned, as so far entitling their owners to be selected: that is to say, we are bound to prefer the most steady, the most manful, and, as far as we can, the most comely. But in addition to this, besides requiring in them a noble and resolute moral nature, they must also possess such qualifications as are favourable to this system of education.

Pray which do you determine these to be?

They must bring with them a piercing eye for their studies, my excellent friend, and they must learn with ease. For assuredly severe studies try the mettle of the mind much more than bodily exercises; because the labour comes more home to it in the former case, as it is limited to the mind, instead of being shared by the body.

True.

Then we must include in the objects of our search a good memory, a dauntless demeanour, and a thorough love of work. Else, how can you expect to induce a man to go through with his bodily labours, and to learn and practise so much besides?

No; we can hold out no inducement to a man who does not possess talents of the highest order.

At any rate, I continued, it is certain that the false view of philosophy which at present prevails, and the disrepute into which she has fallen, may be traced, as I said before, to the fact, that people apply themselves to philosophy without any regard to their own demerits: whereas the study of her is the privilege of her genuine sons, to the exclusion of the baseborn.

What do you mean by genuine?

In the first place, he that would study her must not halt in his love of work. He must not be half-laborious, and half-indolent, which is the case when a man loves exercise, and the chase, and all bodily toil, but dislikes study, and feels an aversion for listening and inquiring, and in fact hates all intellectual labour. On the other hand, those people are equally halt whose love of work has taken the opposite form.

What you say is perfectly true.

In the same way, may we not affirm that a soul is crippled with reference to truth, if, while it hates voluntary falsehood, and cannot endure it in itself, and is exceedingly indignant when other people are guilty of an untruth, it nevertheless calmly accepts involuntary falsehood, and instead of being distressed when its lack of knowledge is detected, is fain to wallow in ignorance with the complacency of a brutal hog?

No doubt you are right.

Above all, I proceeded, we must watch the genuine and the baseborn on the side of temperance, fortitude, loftiness of mind, and all the separate virtues. For whenever states or private persons have no eye for qualities like these, they unwittingly employ, as magistrates or as friends, men who are halt and illegitimate in one or other of these respects.

Unquestionably it is so.

Hence we, on our side, must take every precaution in all matters of this description. For, if we can procure persons sound in limb, and sound in mind, and train them up under the influence of these lofty studies and severe discipline, justice herself will find no fault with us, and we shall preserve our state and constitution; whereas, if we select pupils of a different stamp, our success will be turned into failure, and we shall draw down upon philosophy a still heavier storm of ridicule.

That would be indeed a disgrace.

It certainly would. But very likely I made myself ridiculous just this minute.

How so? he asked.

I forgot, replied I, that we were not serious, and spoke too earnestly. For, as I spoke, I looked towards Philosophy, and seeing her assailed with unmerited contumely, I was so indignant, and so angry with those who are responsible for it, that I believe I expressed myself too seriously.

No, indeed you did not: at least, in listening, I did not think so.

Well, in speaking, it struck me that I did. But, to proceed, let us not forget, that it will be impossible in this instance to select persons advanced in years, as we did in the former. For we must not be persuaded by Solon into thinking that a man, as he grows old, can learn many things. On the contrary, an old man can sooner run than learn; and the wide range of severe labours must fall wholly on the young.

Unquestionably so.

Arithmetic, therefore, and geometry, and all the branches of that preliminary education which is to pave the way for dialectic, must be taught our pupils in their childhood;—care being taken to convey instruction in such a shape as not to make it compulsory upon them to learn.

Why so?

Because, I replied, no trace of slavery ought to mix with the studies of the freeborn man. For the constrained performance of bodily labours does, it is true, exert no evil influence upon the body; but in the case of the mind, no study, pursued under compulsion, remains rooted in the memory.

That is true.

Hence, my excellent friend, you must train the children to their studies in a playful manner, and without any air of constraint, with the further object of discerning more readily the natural bent of their respective characters.

Your advice is reasonable.

Do you remember our saying that the children must also be taken on horseback within sight of actual war; and that, on any safe occasion, they must be brought into the field, and made to taste blood, like young hounds?

I do remember it, he replied.

Accordingly we must make a select list, including everyone who has displayed remarkable self-possession in the midst of all these labours, studies, and dangers.

At what age must that be done?

As soon as they are released from the necessary bodily exercises, during which, whether they last two or three years, nothing else can be done. For weariness and sleep are enemies to study. And, besides, the behaviour of each in his exercises is one of the tests of character, and a very important one too.

Doubtless it is.

After this period, I continued, these choice characters, selected from the ranks of the young men of twenty, must receive higher honours than the rest; and the detached sciences in which they were educated as children must be brought within the compass of a single survey, to shew the co-relation which exists between them, and the nature of real existence.

Certainly this is the only kind of instruction which will be found abiding, when it has once effected an entrance.

Yes, and it is also a most powerful criterion of the dialectic character. For according as a man can survey a subject as a whole or not, he is, or is not, a dialectician.

I agree with you.

Hence it will be your duty to have an eye to those who shew the greatest ability in these questions, and the greatest firmness, not only in study, but also in war and the other branches of discipline: and when they are thirty years old and upwards, you must select them out of the ranks of your picked men, and raise them to greater honours, and try them by the test of dialectic ability, in order to see who is able to divest himself of his eyes and his other senses, and advance in company with truth towards real existence. And here it is, my friend, that great caution is required.

For what special reason? he inquired.

Do you not perceive, I said, what an immense evil at present accompanies dialectic?

Pray what is it?

Insubordination, I replied, with which I believe dialecticians to be tainted.

Indeed you are right.

Are you at all surprised at the fact, and do you make no allowance for the persons in question?

Pray explain yourself.

By way of parallel case, figure to yourself a supposititious child, brought up in the midst of great wealth, and extensive connexions of high family, and surrounded by flatterers; and suppose him, on arriving at manhood, to learn that his alleged parents are not his real parents, though he cannot discover the latter. Can you guess what would be his behaviour towards his flatterers and towards his spurious parents, first while he was ignorant of the fact of his substitution, and secondly when he became aware of it? or would you like to listen to my own conjectures?

I should, he replied.

Well, I suspect that, so long as he is ignorant of the truth, he will honour his father and his mother and his other apparent relations, more than his flatterers; and that he will not allow the former to want anything so quickly as the latter; and that he will be more likely to be guilty of insubordination in word or deed and of disobedience in important things towards his flatterers, than towards his supposed parents.

Probably he will.

On the other hand, I suspect that, after he has learned the truth, his esteem and regard for his parents will be diminished, while his respect for his flatterers will be heightened, to whom he will now listen very much more than before, and proceed to live as they would have him live, associating with them undisguisedly, and wholly abandoning all concern for that fictitious father, and those pretended relations, unless his disposition is remarkably good.

Your description is perfectly true to nature. But how does this comparison bear upon those who apply themselves to dialectic?

I will tell you. We have, I believe, from childhood decided opinions about things just and beautiful; and we have been bred up to obey and honour these opinions, just as we have grown up in submission to our parents.

True.

Now these opinions are combated by certain pleasurable pursuits, which flatter our soul and try to draw it over to their side; though they fail to persuade us, if we are at all virtuous; in which case, we honour those ancestral opinions, and continue loyal to them.

True.

Well, but when such a person is met by the question, what is beauty?—and having given the answer, which he used to hear from the legislator, is confuted by the dialectic process; and when frequent and various defeats have forced him to believe that there is as much deformity as beauty in what he calls beauty, and that justice, goodness, and all the things, which he used to honour most, are in the like predicament,—how do you think he will behave thenceforth towards his old opinions, so far as respect and obedience are concerned?

Of course he will not pay them the same respect or the same obedience as before.

And so long as he neither honours nor acknowledges his former belief, as he used to do, while at the same time he fails to discover the true principles, is not that flattering life the only one to which he will be likely to attach himself?

It is.

In other words, he will appear, I suppose, to have abandoned his loyalty, and to have become lawless.

There cannot be a doubt of it.

Well now, is not this a condition of the students of dialectic a natural one, and, as I said just now, does it not deserve to be treated with great forbearance?

Yes, and with pity too, he replied.

Then in order that you may not have to feel this pity for those men of thirty, must you not use every precaution in introducing them to dialectic?

Certainly.

And will it not be one great precaution to forbid their meddling with it while young? For I suppose you have noticed, that whenever boys taste dialectic for the first time, they pervert it into an amusement, and always employ it for purposes of contradiction, and imitate in their own persons the artifices of those who study refutation,—delighting, like puppies, in pulling and tearing to pieces with logic anyone who comes near them.

They do, to an extravagant extent.

Hence, when they have experienced many triumphs and many defeats, they fall, quickly and vehemently, into an utter disbelief of their former sentiments: and thereby both they and the whole cause of philosophy have been prejudiced in the eyes of the world.

That is perfectly true.

The man of more advanced years, on the contrary, will not suffer himself to be led away by such madness; but will imitate those who are resolved to discuss and examine truth, rather than those who play at contradiction for amusement; and, as a consequence of his superior discretion, will increase, instead of diminishing, the general respect for the pursuit.

You are right.

Again; were we not studying precaution throughout, when we said some time back, that the characters, which are to be initiated into dialectic, must be stable and orderly, in opposition to the present system, which allows anybody, however unfit, to enter the field?

Certainly we were.

Would it suffice, then, for the acquisition of dialectic, that a man should continue constantly and strenuously devoted to the study,—resigning every other pursuit for it, just as, in its turn, he resigned everything for gymnastic,—during a period twice as long as that which he bestowed on his bodily exercises?

Do you mean six years, or four?

It does not matter much, I replied; say five. After this you will have to send them down again into the cavern we described, and compel them to take commands in war, and to hold such offices as befit young men, that they may also keep up with their neighbours in practical address. And here again you must put them to the test, to see whether they will continue steadfast notwithstanding every seduction, or whether possibly they may be a little shaken.

And how long a time do you assign for this?

Fifteen years, I replied. Then, as soon as they are fifty years old, those who have passed safely through all temptations, and who have won every distinction in every branch whether of action or of science, must be forthwith introduced to their final task, and must be constrained to lift up the eye of the soul, and fix it upon that which gives light to all things; and having surveyed the essence of good, they must take it as a pattern, to be copied in that work of regulating their country and their fellow-citizens and themselves, which is to occupy each in turn during the rest of life;—and though they are to pass most of their time in philosophical pursuits, yet each, when his turn comes, is to devote himself to the hard duties of public life, and hold office for their country's sake, not as a desirable, but as an unavoidable occupation; and thus having trained up a constant supply of others like themselves to fill their place as guardians of the state, they will depart and take up their abode in the islands of the blessed. And the state will put up monuments to their memory at the public expense, and offer sacrifices to them, as demigods, if the Pythian oracle will authorise it, or at least as highly-favoured and godlike men.

Like a sculptor, Socrates, you have finished off the leading men in a style of faultless beauty.

Say leading women too, Glaucon. For do not suppose that my remarks were intended to apply at all more to men than to women, so long as we can find women whose talents are equal to the situation.

You are right, he said, if they are to share with the men in everything on a footing of equality, according to our account.

Well then, do you agree that our theory of the state and constitution is not a mere aspiration, but, though full of difficulties, capable of realization in one way, and only one, which, as we have said, requires that one, if not more, of the true philosophers shall be invested with full authority in a state, and contemn the honours of the present day, in the belief that they are mean and worthless; and that, deeply impressed with the supreme importance of right and of the honours to be derived from it, and regarding justice as the highest and most binding of all obligations, he shall, as the special servant and admirer of justice, carry out a thorough reform in his own state.

How is that to be done?

All who are above ten years old in the city must be despatched into the country, and their children must be taken and bred up beyond the influence of that common character, which their parents among others possess, in the manners and laws of the true philosophers, the nature of which we have described above; and, tell me, will not this be the quickest and easiest way to enable a state and a constitution, such as we have represented, to establish itself and prosper, and at the same time be a blessing to the nation in which it has taken root?

Yes, quite so, he replied: and I believe, Socrates, you have stated correctly the means that would be employed, if such a constitution were ever realized.

And have we not by this time discussed to satiety this state, and the individual that resembles it? For I presume it is also clear what sort of person we shall expect him to be.

It is clear, he replied; and the present inquiry is, I believe, concluded.

2

Aristotle

The famed Greek philosopher Aristotle (384–324 B.C.) did not formulate a complete philosophy of education, as did his teacher, Plato. He did, however, make vitally important contributions to this field of inquiry.

The *Nicomachean Ethics* (named after Aristotle's son Nicomachus) is one of the most subtle philosophical works ever written. Among its contents are Aristotle's discussion of whether virtue is knowledge, and his arguments in behalf of a life devoted to the exercise of pure reason as the supreme human life.

The crucial distinction he draws between intellectual and moral virtue provides him with an answer to the question raised at the opening of the *Meno* dialogue as to "whether virtue is acquired by teaching or by practice." According to Aristotle, moral virtue, which we might call "goodness of character," is formed by habit; one becomes good by doing good. Intellectual virtue, on the other hand, which we might refer to as "wisdom," is acquired by teaching and requires foresight and sophisticated intelligence.

In opposition to the Socratic doctrine that a person who knows the good will necessarily do the good, Aristotle insists on our acknowledging the phenomenon of moral weakness: the situation in which individuals act contrary to what they believe to be best. He emphasizes that a theory which denies the existence of moral weakness is at variance with observed facts.

Aristotle's conception of the ideal state is presented in *Politics*. Unfortunately, the book concludes abruptly without presenting much of the detailed discussion concerning educational matters we are led to expect. Some of Aristotle's treatises, including *Politics*, are texts of his lectures, perhaps as preserved in his students' notes, thus accounting for the stylistic and organizational difficulties that appear in his writings.

Nicomachean Ethics*
BOOK I

1. Every art and every inquiry, and similarly every action and choice, is thought to aim at some good; and for this reason the good has rightly been declared to be that at which all things aim. . . . Now, as there are many actions, arts, and sciences, their ends also are many; the end of the medical art is health, that of shipbuilding a vessel, that of strategy victory, that of economics wealth. But where such arts fall under a single capacity—as bridle-making and the other arts concerned with the equipment of horses fall under the art of riding, and this and every military action under strategy, in the same way other arts fall under yet others—in all of these the ends of the master arts are to be preferred to all the subordinate ends; for it is for the sake of the former that the latter are pursued. . . .

2. If, then, there is some end of the things we do, which we desire for its own sake (everything else being desired for the sake of this), and if we do not choose everything for the sake of something else (for at that rate the process would go on to infinity, so that our desire would be empty and vain), clearly this must be the good and the chief good. Will not the knowledge of it, then, have a great influence on life? Shall we not, like archers who have a mark to aim at, be more likely to hit upon what we should? If so, we must try, in outline at least, to determine what it is. . . .

Our discussion will be adequate if it has as much clearness as the subject-matter admits of; for precision is not to be sought for alike in all discussions, any more than in all the products of the crafts. Now fine and just actions, which political science investigates, exhibit much variety and fluctuation, so that they may be thought to exist only by convention, and not by nature. And goods also exhibit a similar fluctuation because they bring harm to many people; for before now men have been undone by reason of their wealth, and others by reason of their courage. We must be content, then, in speaking of such subjects and with such premisses to indicate the truth roughly and in outline, and in speaking about things which are only for the most part true and with premisses of the same kind to reach conclusions that are no better. In the same spirit, therefore, should each of our statements be *received*; for it is the mark of an educated man to look for precision in each class of things just so far as the nature of the subject admits: it is evidently equally foolish to accept probable reasoning from a mathematician and to demand from a rhetorician demonstrative proofs.

Now each man judges well the things he knows, and of these he is a good judge. And so the man who has been educated in a subject is a good judge of

*Reprinted from Aristotle's *Nicomachean Ethics* translated by David Ross, revised by J. L. Ackrill and J. D. Urmson (1980) by permission of Oxford University Press. The translation of *Politics* is by Benjamin Jowett.

that subject, and the man who has received an all-round education is a good judge in general. Hence a young man is not a proper hearer of lectures on political science; for he is inexperienced in the actions that occur in life, but its discussions start from these and are about these; and, further, since he tends to follow his passions, his study will be vain and unprofitable, because the end aimed at is not knowledge but action. And it makes no difference whether he is young in years or youthful in character; the defect does not depend on time, but on his living and pursuing each successive object as passion directs. For to such persons, as to the incontinent, knowledge brings no profit; but to those who desire and act in accordance with a rational principle knowledge about such matters will be of great benefit.

These remarks about the student, the way in which our statements should be received, and the purpose of the inquiry, may be taken as our preface. . . .

7. . . . Since there are evidently more than one end, and we choose some of these (e.g. wealth, flutes, and in general instruments) for the sake of something else, clearly not all ends are complete ends; but the chief good is evidently something complete. Therefore, if there is only one complete end, this will be what we are seeking, and if there are more than one, the most complete of these will be what we are seeking. Now we call that which is in itself worthy of pursuit more complete than that which is worthy of pursuit for the sake of something else, and that which is never desirable for the sake of something else more complete than the things that are desirable both in themselves and for the sake of that other thing, and therefore we call complete without qualification that which is always desirable in itself and never for the sake of something else.

Now such a thing happiness, above all else, is held to be; for this we choose always for itself and never for the sake of something else, but honour, pleasure, reason, and every excellence we choose indeed for themselves (for if nothing resulted from them we should still choose each of them), but we choose them also for the sake of happiness, judging that through them we shall be happy. Happiness, on the other hand, no one chooses for the sake of these, nor, in general, for anything other than itself. . . .

Happiness, then, is something complete and self-sufficient, and is the end of action.

Presumably, however, to say that happiness is the chief good seems a platitude, and a clearer account of what it is is still desired. This might perhaps be given, if we could first ascertain the function of man. For just as for a flute-player, a sculptor, or any artist, and, in general, for all things that have a function or activity, the good and the 'well' is thought to reside in the function, so would it seem to be for man, if he has a function. Have the carpenter, then, and the tanner certain functions or activities, and has man none? Is he naturally functionless? Or as eye, hand, foot, and in general each of the parts evidently has a function, may one lay it down that man similarly has a function apart from all these? What then can this be? Life seems to be common even to plants, but we are seeking what is peculiar to man. Let us exclude, therefore, the life of nutrition and growth. Next there would be a life of perception, but *it* also seems to be common even to the horse, the ox, and every animal. There remains, then, an active life of the element that has a rational principle (of this, one part has such a principle in the sense of being obedient to one, the other in the sense of possessing one and exercising thought); and as this too can be taken in two ways, we must state that life in the sense of activity is what we mean; for this seems to be the more proper sense of the term. Now if the function of man is an activity of soul in accordance with, or not without, rational principle, and if we say a so-and-so and a good so-and-so have a function which is the same in kind, e.g. a lyre-player and a good lyre-player, and so without qualification in all cases, eminence in respect of excellence being added to the function (for the function of a lyre-player is to play the lyre, and that of a good lyre-player is to do so well): if this is the case, and we state the function of man to be a certain kind of life, and this to be an activity or actions of the soul implying a rational principle, and the function of a good man to be the good and noble performance of these, and if any action is well performed when it is performed in accordance with the appropriate excellence: if this is the case, human good turns out to be activity of soul in conformity with excellence, and if there are more than one excellence, in conformity with the best and most complete.

But we must add 'in a complete life'. For one swallow does not make a summer, nor does one day; and so too one day, or a short time, does not make a man blessed and happy. . . .

13. Since happiness is an activity of soul in accordance with complete excellence, we must consider the nature of excellence; for perhaps we shall thus see better the nature of happiness. The true student of politics, too, is thought to have studied this above all things; for he wishes to make his fellow citizens good and obedient to the laws. As an example of this we have the lawgivers of the Cretans and the Spartans, and any others of the kind that there may have been. And if this inquiry belongs to political science, clearly the pursuit of it will be in accordance with our original plan. But clearly the excellence we must study is human excellence; for the good we were seeking was human good and the happiness human happiness. By human excellence we mean not that of the body but that of the soul; and happiness also we call an activity of soul. But if this is so, clearly the student of politics must know somehow the facts about soul, as the man who is to heal the eyes must know about the whole body also; and all the more since politics is more prized and better than medicine; but even among doctors the best educated spend much labour on acquiring knowledge of the body. The student of politics, then, must study the soul, and must study it with these objects in view, and do so just to the extent which is sufficient for the questions we are discussing; for further precision is perhaps something more laborious than our purposes require.

Some things are said about it, adequately enough, even in the discussions outside our school, and we must use these; e.g. that one element in the soul is irrational and one has a rational principle. . . .

Of the irrational element one division seems to be widely distributed, and vegetative in its nature, I mean that which causes nutrition and growth. . . .

There seems to be also another irrational element in the soul—one which in a sense, however, shares in a rational principle. For we praise the reason of the continent man and of the incontinent, and the part of their soul that has reason, since it urges them aright and towards the best objects; but there is found in them also another natural element beside reason, which fights against and resists it. For exactly as paralysed limbs when we choose to move them to the right turn on the contrary to the left, so it is with the soul; the impulses of incontinent people move in contrary directions. But while in the body we see that which moves astray, in the soul we do not. No doubt, however, we must none the less suppose that in the soul too there is something beside reason, resisting and opposing it. In what sense it is distinct from the other elements does not concern us. Now even this seems to have a share in reason, as we said; at any rate in the continent man it obeys reason—and presumably in the temperate and brave man it is still more obedient; for in them it speaks, on all matters, with the same voice as reason.

Therefore the irrational element also appears to be two-fold. For the vegetative element in no way shares in reason, but the appetitive and in general the desiring element in a sense shares in it, in so far as it listens to and obeys it; this is the sense in which we speak of paying heed to one's father or one's friends, not that in which we speak of 'the rational' in mathematics. That the irrational element is in some sense persuaded by reason is indicated also by the giving of advice and by all reproof and exhortation. And if this element also must be said to have reason, that which has reason also will be twofold, one subdivision having it in the strict sense and in itself, and the other having a tendency to obey as one does one's father.

Excellence too is distinguished into kinds in accordance with this difference; for we say that some excellences are intellectual and others moral, philosophic wisdom and understanding and practical wisdom being intellectual, liberality and temperance moral. For in speaking about a man's character we do not say that he is wise or has understanding but that he is good-tempered or temperate; yet we praise the wise man also with respect to his state; and of states we call those which merit praise excellences.

BOOK II

1. Excellence, then, being of two kinds, intellectual and moral, intellectual excellence in the main owes both its birth and its growth to teaching (for which reason it requires experience and time), while moral excellence comes about as a result of habit, whence also its name is one that is formed by a slight variation from the word for 'habit'. From this it is also plain that none of the moral excellences arises in us by nature; for nothing that exists by nature can form a habit contrary to its nature. For instance the stone which by nature moves downwards cannot be habituated to move upwards, not even if one tries to train it by throwing it up ten thousand times; nor can fire be habituated to move downwards, nor can anything else that by nature behaves in one way be

trained to behave in another. Neither by nature, then, nor contrary to nature do excellences arise in us; rather we are adapted by nature to receive them, and are made perfect by habit.

Again, of all the things that come to us by nature we first acquire the potentiality and later exhibit the activity (this is plain in the case of the senses; for it was not by often seeing or often hearing that we got these senses, but on the contrary we had them before we used them, and did not come to have them by using them); but excellences we get by first exercising them, as also happens in the case of the arts as well. For the things we have to learn before we can do, we learn by doing, e.g. men become builders by building and lyre-players by playing the lyre; so too we become just by doing just acts, temperate by doing temperate acts, brave by doing brave acts.

This is confirmed by what happens in states; for legislators make the citizens good by forming habits in them, and this is the wish of every legislator; and those who do not effect it miss their mark, and it is in this that a good constitution differs from a bad one.

Again, it is from the same causes and by the same means that every excellence is both produced and destroyed, and similarly every art; for it is from playing the lyre that both good and bad lyre-players are produced. And the corresponding statement is true of builders and of all the rest; men will be good or bad builders as a result of building well or badly. For if this were not so, there would have been no need of a teacher, but all men would have been born good or bad at their craft. This, then, is the case with the excellences also; by doing the acts that we do in our transactions with other men we become just or unjust, and by doing the acts that we do in the presence of danger, and being habituated to feel fear or confidence, we become brave or cowardly. The same is true of appetites and feelings of anger; some men become temperate and good-tempered, others self-indulgent and irascible, by behaving in one way or the other in the appropriate circumstances. Thus, in one word, states arise out of like activities. This is why the activities we exhibit must be of a certain kind; it is because the states correspond to the differences between these. It makes no small difference, then, whether we form habits of one kind or of another from our very youth; it makes a very great difference, or rather *all* the difference.

2. Since, then, the present inquiry does not aim at theoretical knowledge like the others (for we are inquiring not in order to know what excellence is, but in order to become good, since otherwise our inquiry would have been of no use), we must examine the nature of actions, namely how we ought to do them; for these determine also the nature of the states that are produced, as we have said. . . . But this must be agreed upon beforehand, that the whole account of matters of conduct must be given in outline and not precisely, as we said at the very beginning that the accounts we demand must be in accordance with the subject-matter; matters concerned with conduct and questions of what is good for us have no fixity, any more than matters of health. The general account being of this nature, the account of particular cases is yet more lacking in exactness; for they do not fall under any art or set of precepts, but

the agents themselves must in each case consider what is appropriate to the occasion, as happens also in the art of medicine or of navigation.

But though our present account is of this nature we must give what help we can. First, then, let us consider this, that it is the nature of such things to be destroyed by defect and excess, as we see in the case of strength and of health (for to gain light on things imperceptible we must use the evidence of sensible things); both excessive and defective exercise destroys the strength, and similarly drink or food which is above or below a certain amount destroys the health, while that which is proportionate both produces and increases and preserves it. So too is it, then, in the case of temperance and courage and the other excellences. For the man who flies from and fears everything and does not stand his ground against anything becomes a coward, and the man who fears nothing at all but goes to meet every danger becomes rash; and similarly the man who indulges in every pleasure and abstains from none becomes self-indulgent, while the man who shuns every pleasure, as boors do, becomes in a way insensible; temperance and courage, then, are destroyed by excess and defect, and preserved by the mean.

But not only are the sources and causes of their origination and growth the same as those of their destruction, but also the sphere of their activity will be the same; for this is also true of the things which are more evident to sense, e.g. of strength; it is produced by taking much food and undergoing much exertion, and it is the strong man that will be most able to do these things. So too is it with the excellences; by abstaining from pleasures we become temperate, and it is when we have become so that we are most able to abstain from them; and similarly too in the case of courage; for by being habituated to despise things that are terrible and to stand our ground against them we become brave, and it is when we have become so that we shall be most able to stand our ground against them. . . .

4. The question might be asked, what we mean by saying that we must become just by doing just acts, and temperate by doing temperate acts; for if men do just and temperate acts, they are already just and temperate, exactly as, if they do what is grammatical or musical they are proficient in grammar and music.

Or is this not true even of the arts? It is possible to do something grammatical either by chance or under the guidance of another. A man will be proficient in grammar, then, only when he has both done something grammatical and done it grammatically; and this means doing it in accordance with the grammatical knowledge in himself.

Again, the case of the arts and that of the excellences are not similar; for the products of the arts have their goodness in themselves, so that it is enough that they should have a certain character, but if the acts that are in accordance with the excellences have themselves a certain character it does not follow that they are done justly or temperately. The agent also must be in a certain condition when he does them; in the first place he must have knowledge, secondly he must choose the acts, and choose them for their own sakes, and thirdly his action must proceed from a firm and unchangeable character. These are not reckoned in as conditions of the possession of the arts, except the bare knowledge; but as a condition of the possession of the excellences, knowledge has little or no weight, while the other conditions count not for a little but for everything, i.e. the very conditions which result from often doing just and temperate acts.

Actions, then, are called just and temperate when they are such as the just or the temperate man would do; but it is not the man who does these that is just and temperate, but the man who also does them *as* just and temperate men do them. It is well said, then, that it is by doing just acts that the just man is produced, and by doing temperate acts the temperate man; without doing these no one would have even a prospect of becoming good.

But most people do not do these, but take refuge in theory and think they are being philosophers and will become good in this way, behaving somewhat like patients who listen attentively to their doctors, but do none of the things they are ordered to do. As the latter will not be made well in body by such a course of treatment, the former will not be made well in soul by such a course of philosophy. . . .

6. . . . Excellence, then, is a state concerned with choice, lying in a mean relative to us, this being determined by reason and in the way in which the man of practical wisdom would determine it. Now it is a mean between two vices, that which depends on excess and that which depends on defect; and again it is a mean because the vices respectively fall short of or exceed what is right in both passions and actions, while excellence both finds and chooses that which is intermediate. Hence in respect of its substance and the account which states its essence is a mean, with regard to what is best and right it is an extreme.

But not every action nor every passion admits of a mean; for some have names that already imply badness, e.g. spite, shamelessness, envy, and in the case of actions adultery, theft, murder; for all of these and suchlike things imply by their names that they are themselves bad, and not the excesses or deficiencies of them. It is not possible, then, ever to be right with regard to them; one must always be wrong. Nor does goodness or badness with regard to such things depend on committing adultery with the right woman, at the right time, and in the right way, but simply to do any of them is to go wrong. It would be equally absurd, then, to expect that in unjust, cowardly, and self-indulgent action there should be a mean, an excess, and a deficiency; for at that rate there would be a mean of excess and of deficiency, an excess of excess, and a deficiency of deficiency. But as there is no excess and deficiency of temperance and courage because what is intermediate is in a sense an extreme, so too of the actions we have mentioned there is no mean nor any excess and deficiency, but however they are done they are wrong; for in general there is neither a mean of excess and deficiency, nor excess and deficiency of a mean. . . .

9. That moral excellence is a mean, then, and in what sense it is so, and that it is a mean between two vices, the one involving excess, the other deficiency, and that it is such because its character is to aim at what is intermediate in passions and in actions, has been sufficiently stated. Hence also it is no easy task to be good. For in everything it is no easy task to find the middle, e.g. to

find the middle of a circle is not for everyone but for him who knows; so, too, anyone can get angry—that is easy—or give or spend money; but to do this to the right person, to the right extent, at the right time, with the right aim, and in the right way, *that* is not for everyone, nor is it easy; that is why goodness is both rare and laudable and noble.

Hence he who aims at the intermediate must first depart from what is the more contrary to it, as Calypso advises—

Hold the ship out beyond that surf and spray.

For of the extremes one is more erroneous, one less so; therefore, since to hit the mean is hard in the extreme, we must as a second best, as people say, take the least of the evils; and this be done best in the way we describe.

But we must consider the things towards which we ourselves also are easily carried away; for some of us tend to one thing, some to another; and this will be recognizable from the pleasure and the pain we feel. We must drag ourselves away to the contrary extreme; for we shall get into the intermediate state by drawing well away from error, as people do in straightening sticks that are bent.

Now in everything the pleasant or pleasure is most to be guarded against; for we do not judge it impartially. We ought, then, to feel towards pleasure as the elders of the people felt towards Helen, and in all circumstances repeat their saying; for if we dismiss pleasure thus we are less likely to go astray. It is by doing this, then, (to sum the matter up) that we shall best be able to hit the mean.

But this is no doubt difficult, and especially in individual cases; for it is not easy to determine both how and with whom and on what provocation and how long one should be angry; for we too sometimes praise those who fall short and call them good-tempered, but sometimes we praise those who get angry and call them manly. The man, however who deviates little from goodness is not blamed, whether he do so in the direction of the more or of the less, but only the man who deviates more widely; for *he* does not fail to be noticed. But up to what point and to what extent a man must deviate before he becomes blameworthy it is not easy to determine by reasoning, any more than anything else that is perceived by the senses; such things depend on particular facts, and the decision rests with perception. So much, then, makes it plain that the intermediate state is in all things to be praised, but that we must incline sometimes towards the excess, sometimes towards the deficiency; for so shall we most easily hit the mean and what is right. . . .

BOOK VI

1. Since we have previously said that one ought to choose that which is intermediate, not the excess nor the defect, and that the intermediate is determined by the dictates of reason, let us discuss this. In all the states we have mentioned, as in all other matters, there is a mark to which the man who possesses

reason looks, and heightens or relaxes his activity accordingly, and there is a standard which determines the mean states which we say are intermediate between excess and defect, being in accordance with right reason. But such a statement, though true, is by no means illuminating; for in all other pursuits which are objects of knowledge it is indeed true to say that we must not exert ourselves nor relax our efforts too much nor too little, but to an intermediate extent and as right reason dictates; but if a man had only this knowledge he would be none the wiser—e.g. we should not know what sort of medicines to apply to our body if someone were to say 'all those which the medical art prescribes, and which agree with the practice of one who possesses the art'. Hence it is necessary with regard to the states of the soul also not only that this true statement should be made, but also that it should be determined what right reason is and what is the standard that fixes it.

We divided the excellences of the soul and said that some are excellences of character and others of intellect. Now we have discussed the moral excellences; with regard to the others let us express our view as follows, beginning with some remarks about the soul. We said before that there are two parts of the soul—that which possesses reason and that which is irrational; let us now draw a similar distinction within the part which possesses reason. And let it be assumed that there are two parts which possess reason—one by which we contemplate the kind of things whose principles cannot be otherwise, and one by which we contemplate variable things; for where objects differ in kind the part of the soul answering to each of the two is different in kind, since it is in virtue of a certain likeness and kinship with their objects that they have the knowledge they have. Let one of these parts be called the scientific and the other the calculative; for to deliberate and to calculate are the same thing, but no one deliberates about what cannot be otherwise. Therefore the calculative is one part of the faculty which possesses reason. We must, then, learn what is the best state of each of these two parts; for this is the excellence of each.

2. The excellence of a thing is relative to its proper function. Now there are three things in the soul which control action and truth—sensation, thought, desire.

Of these sensation originates no action; this is plain from the fact that beasts have sensation but no share in action.

What affirmation and negation are in thinking, pursuit and avoidance are in desire; so that since moral excellence is a state concerned with choice, and choice is deliberate desire, therefore both the reasoning must be true and the desire right, if the choice is to be good, and the latter must pursue just what the former asserts. Now this kind of intellect and of truth is practical; of the intellect which is contemplative, not practical nor productive, the good and the bad state are truth and falsity (for this is the function of everything intellectual); while of the part which is practical and intellectual the good state is truth in agreement with right desire.

The origin of action . . . is choice, and that of choice is desire and reasoning with a view to an end. This is why choice cannot exist either without thought and intellect or without a moral state; for good action and its opposite cannot exist without a combination of intellect and character. Intellect itself, however, moves nothing, but only the intellect which aims at an end and is practical. . . .

5. Regarding *practical wisdom* we shall get at the truth by considering who are the persons we credit with it. Now it is thought to be a mark of a man of practical wisdom to be able to deliberate well about what is good and expedient for himself, not in some particular respect, e.g. about what sorts of thing conduce to health or to strength, but about what sorts of thing conduce to the good life in general. This is shown by the fact that we credit men with practical wisdom in some particular respect when they have calculated well with a view to some good end which is one of those that are not the object of any art. Thus in general the man who is capable of deliberating has practical wisdom. Now no one deliberates about things that cannot be otherwise nor about things that it is impossible for him to do. Therefore, since knowledge involves demonstration, but there is no demonstration of things whose first principles can be otherwise (for all such things might actually be otherwise), and since it is impossible to deliberate about things that are of necessity, practical wisdom cannot be knowledge nor art; not knowledge because that which can be done is capable of being otherwise, not art because action and making are different kinds of thing. It remains, then, that it is a true and reasoned state of capacity to act with regard to the things that are good or bad for man. For while making has an end other than itself, action cannot; for good action itself is its end. It is for this reason that we think Pericles and men like him have practical wisdom, viz. because they can see what is good for themselves and what is good for men in general; we consider that those can do this who are good at managing households or states. . . .

7. . . . Practical wisdom . . . is concerned with things human and things about which it is possible to deliberate; for we say this is above all the work of the man of practical wisdom, to deliberate well, but no one deliberates about things that cannot be otherwise, nor about things which have not an end, and that a good that can be brought about by action. The man who is without qualification good at deliberating is the man who is capable of aiming in accordance with calculation at the best for man of things attainable by action. Nor is practical wisdom concerned with universals only—it must also recognize the particulars; for it is practical, and practice is concerned with particulars. This is why some who do not know, and especially those who have experience, are more practical than others who know; for if a man knew that light meats are digestible and wholesome, but did not know which sorts of meat are light, he would not produce health, but the man who knows that chicken is wholesome is more likely to produce health. . . .

8. . . . What has been said is confirmed by the fact that while young men become geometricians and mathematicians and wise in matters like these, it is thought that a young man of practical wisdom cannot be found. The cause is that such wisdom is concerned not only with universals but with particulars, which become familiar from experience, but a young man has no experience,

for it is length of time that gives experience; indeed one might ask this question too, why a boy may become a mathematician, but not a wise man or a natural scientist. Is it because the objects of mathematics exist by abstraction, while the first principles of these other subjects come from experience, and because young men have no conviction about the latter but merely use the proper language, while the essence of mathematical objects is plain enough to them? . . .

12. . . . . Again, the function of man is achieved only in accordance with practical wisdom as well as with moral excellence; for excellence makes the aim right, and practical wisdom the things leading to it. . .

As we say that some people who do just acts are not necessarily just, i.e. those who do the acts ordained by the laws either unwillingly or owing to ignorance or for some other reason and not for the sake of the acts themselves (though, to be sure, they do what they should and all the things that the good man ought), so is it, it seems, that in order to be good one must be in a certain state when one does the several acts, i.e. one must do them as a result of choice and for the sake of the acts themselves. Now excellence makes the choice right, but the question of the things which should naturally be done to carry out our choice belongs not to excellence but to another faculty. We must devote our attention to these matters and give a clearer statement about them. There is a faculty which is called cleverness; and this is such as to be able to do the things that tend towards the mark we have set before ourselves, and to hit it. Now if the mark be noble, the cleverness is laudable, but if the mark be bad, the cleverness is mere villainy; hence we call clever both men of practical wisdom and villains. Practical wisdom is not the faculty, but it does not exist without this faculty. And this eye of the soul acquires its formed state not without the aid of excellence as has been said and is plain; for inferences which deal with acts to be done are things which involve a starting-point, viz. 'since the end, i.e. what is best, is of such and such a nature', whatever it may be (let it for the sake of argument be what we please); and this is not evident except to the good man; for wickedness perverts us and causes us to be deceived about the starting-points of action. Therefore it is evident that it is impossible to be practically wise without being good. . . .

BOOK VII

2. Now we may ask what kind of right belief is possessed by the man who behaves incontinently. That he should behave so when he has knowledge, some say is impossible; for it would be strange—so Socrates thought—if when knowledge was in a man something else could master it and drag it about like a slave. For *Socrates* was entirely opposed to the view in question, holding that there is no such thing as incontinence; no one, he said, acts against what he believes best—people act so only by reason of ignorance. Now this view contradicts the plain phenomena, and we must inquire about what happens to such a

man; if he acts by reason of ignorance, what is the manner of his ignorance? For that the man who behaves incontinently does not, before he gets into this state, *think* he ought to act so, is evident. But there are *some* who concede certain of Socrates' contentions but not others; that nothing is stronger than knowledge they admit, but not that no one acts contrary to what has seemed to him the better course, and therefore they say that the incontinent man has not knowledge when he is mastered by his pleasures, but opinion. But *if* it is opinion and not knowledge, if it is not a strong belief that resists but a weak one, as in men who hesitate, we forgive their failure to stand by such convictions against strong appetites; but we do not forgive wickedness, nor any of the other blameworthy states. It is then *practical wisdom* whose resistance is mastered? That is the strongest of all states. But this is absurd; the same man will be at once practically wise and incontinent, but *no one* would say that it is the part of a practically wise man to do willingly the basest acts. Besides, it has been shown before that the man of practical wisdom is one who will *act* (for he is a man concerned with the individual facts) and who has the other excellences. . . .

3. Of some such kind are the difficulties that arise; some of these points must be refuted and the others left in possession of the field; for the solution of the difficulty is the discovery of the truth. . . .

As for the suggestion that it is true opinion and not knowledge against which we act incontinently, that makes no difference to the argument; for some people when in a state of opinion do not hesitate, but think they know exactly. If, then, it is owing to their weak conviction those who have opinion are more likely to act against their belief than those who know, there will be no difference between knowledge and opinion; for some men are no less convinced of what they think than others of what they know; as is shown by the case of Heraclitus. But since we use the word 'know' in two senses (for both the man who has knowledge but is not using it and he who is using it are said to know), it *will* make a difference whether, when a man does what he should not, he has the knowledge but is not exercising it, or *is* exercising it; for the latter seems strange, but not the former.

Further, since there are two kinds of propositions, there is nothing to prevent a man's having both and acting against his knowledge, provided that he is using only the universal and not the particular; for it is particular acts that have to be done. And there are also two kinds of universal; one is predicable of the agent, the other of the object; e.g. 'dry food is good for every man', and 'I am a man', or 'such and such food is dry'; but whether this food is such and such, of this the incontinent man either has not or is not exercising the knowledge. There will, then, be, firstly, an enormous difference between these manners of knowing, so that to know in one way would not seem anything strange, while to know in the other way would be extraordinary.

And further the possession of knowledge in another sense than those just named is something that happens to men; for within the case of having knowledge but not using it we see a difference of state, admitting of the possibility of having knowledge in a sense and yet not having it, as in the instance of a man asleep, mad, or drunk. But now this is just the condition of men under the influence of passions; for outbursts of anger and sexual appetites and some other such passions, it is evident, actually alter our bodily condition, and in some men even produce fits of madness. It is plain, then, that incontinent people must be said to be in a similar condition to these. The fact that men use the language that flows from knowledge proves nothing; for even men under the influence of these passions utter scientific proofs and verses of Empedocles, and those who have just begun to learn can string together words, but do not yet know; for it has to become part of themselves, and that takes time; so that we must suppose that the use of language by men in an incontinent state means no more than its utterance by actors on the stage.

Again, we may also view the cause as follows with reference to the facts of nature. The one opinion is universal, the other is concerned with the particular facts, and here we come to something within the sphere of perception; when a single opinion results from the two, the soul must in one type of case affirm the conclusion, while in the case of opinions concerned with production it must immediately act (e.g. if everything sweet ought to be tasted, and this is sweet, in the sense of being one of the particular sweet things, the man who can act and is not restrained must at the same time actually act accordingly). When, then, the universal opinion is present in us restraining us from tasting, and there is also the opinion that everything sweet is pleasant, and that this is sweet (now this is the opinion that is active), and when appetite happens to be present in us, the one opinion bids us avoid the object, but appetite leads us towards it (or it can move each of our bodily parts); so that it turns out that a man behaves incontinently under the influence (in a sense) of reason and opinion, and of opinion not contrary in itself, but only incidentally—for the appetite is contrary not the opinion—to right reason. It also follows that this is the reason why the lower animals are not incontinent, viz. because they have no universal beliefs but only imagination and memory of particulars.

The explanation of how the ignorance is dissolved and the incontinent man regains his knowledge, is the same as in the case of the man drunk or asleep and is not peculiar to this condition; we must go to the students of natural science for it. Now, the last proposition both being an opinion about a perceptible object, and being what determines our actions, this a man either has not when he is in the state of passion, or has it in the sense in which having knowledge did not mean knowing but only talking, as a drunken man may utter the verses of Empedocles. And because the last term is not universal nor equally an object of knowledge with the universal term, the position that Socrates sought to establish actually seems to result; for it is not what is thought to be knowledge proper that the passion overcomes (nor is it this that is dragged about as a result of the passion), but perceptual knowledge.

This must suffice as our answer to the question of whether men can act incontinently when they know or not, and in what sense they know. . . .

BOOK X

6. Now that we have spoken of the excellences . . . what remains is to discuss in outline the nature of happiness, since this is what we state the end of human nature to be. Our discussion will be the more concise if we first sum up what we have said already. We said, then, that it is not a state; for if it were it might belong to someone who was asleep throughout his life, living the life of a plant, or, again, to someone who was suffering the greatest misfortunes. If these implications are unacceptable, and we must rather class happiness as an activity, as we have said before, and if some activities are necessary and desirable for the sake of something else, while others are so in themselves, evidently happiness must be placed among those desirable in themselves, not among those desirable for the sake of something else; for happiness does not lack anything, but is self-sufficient. Now those activities are desirable in themselves from which nothing is sought beyond the activity. And of this nature excellent actions are thought to be; for to do noble and good deeds is a thing desirable for its own sake.

Pleasant amusements also are thought to be of this nature; we choose them not for the sake of other things; for we are injured rather than benefited by them, since we are led to neglect our bodies and our property. But most of the people who are deemed happy take refuge in such pastimes, which is the reason why those who are ready-witted at them are highly esteemed at the courts of tyrants; they make themselves pleasant companions in the tyrant's favourite pursuits, and that is the sort of man they want. Now these things are thought to be of the nature of happiness because people in despotic positions spend their leisure in them, but perhaps such people prove nothing; for excellence and thought, from which good activities flow, do not depend on despotic position; nor, if these people, who have never tasted pure and generous pleasure, take refuge in the bodily pleasures, should these for that reason be thought more desirable; for boys, too, think the things that are valued among themselves are the best. It is to be expected, then, that, as different things seem valuable to boys and to men, so they should to bad men and to good. Now, as we have often maintained, those things are both valuable and pleasant which are such to the good man; and to each man the activity in accordance with his own state is most desirable, and, therefore, to the good man that which is in accordance with excellence. Happiness, therefore, does not lie in amusement; it would, indeed, be strange if the end were amusement, and one were to take trouble and suffer hardship all one's life in order to amuse oneself. For, in a word, everything that we choose we choose for the sake of something else—except happiness, which is an end. Now to exert oneself and work for the sake of amusement seems silly and utterly childish. But to amuse oneself in order that one may exert oneself, as Anacharsis puts it, seems right; for amusement is a sort of relaxation, and we need relaxation because we cannot work continuously. Relaxation, then, is not an end; for it is taken for the sake of activity.

The happy life is thought to be one of excellence; now an excellent life requires exertion, and does not consist in amusement. And we say that serious things are better than laughable things and those connected with amusement, and that the activity of the better of any two things—whether it be two parts or two men—is the better; but the activity of the better is *ipso facto* superior and more of the nature of happiness. And any chance person—even a slave—can enjoy the bodily pleasures no less than the best man; but no one assigns to a slave a share in happiness—unless he assigns to him also a share in human life. For happiness does not lie in such occupations, but, as we have said before, in excellent activities.

7. If happiness is activity in accordance with excellence, it is reasonable that it should be in accordance with the highest excellence; and this will be that of the best thing in us. Whether it be intellect or something else that is this element which is thought to be our natural ruler and guide and to take thought of things noble and divine, whether it be itself also divine or only the most divine element in us, the activity of this in accordance with its proper excellence will be complete happiness. That this activity is contemplative we have already said.

Now this would seem to be in agreement both with what we said before and with the truth. For this activity is the best (since not only is intellect the best thing in us, but the objects of intellect are the best of knowable objects); and, secondly, it is the most continuous, since we can contemplate truth more continuously than we can *do* anything. And we think happiness has pleasure mingled with it, but the activity of wisdom is admittedly the pleasantest of excellent activities; at all events philosophy is thought to offer pleasures marvellous for their purity and their enduringness, and it is to be expected that those who know will pass their time more pleasantly than those who inquire. And the self-sufficiency that is spoken of must belong most to the contemplative activity. For while a wise man, as well as a just man and the rest, needs the necessaries of life, when they are sufficiently equipped with things of that sort the just man needs people towards whom and with whom he shall act justly, and the temperate man, the brave man, and each of the others is in the same case, but the wise man, even when by himself, can contemplate truth, and the better the wiser he is; he can perhaps do so better if he has fellow-workers, but still he is the most self-sufficient. And this activity alone would seem to be loved for its own sake; for nothing arises from it apart from the contemplating, while from practical activities we gain more or less apart from the action. And happiness is thought to depend on leisure; for we are busy that we may have leisure, and make war that we may live in peace. Now the activity of the practical excellences is exhibited in political or military affairs, but the actions concerned with these seem to be unleisurely. Warlike actions are completely so (for no one chooses to be at war, or provokes war, for the sake of being at war; anyone would seem absolutely murderous if he were to make enemies of his friends in order to bring about battle and slaughter); but the action of the statesman is also unleisurely, and—apart from the political action itself—aims at despotic power and honours, or at all events happiness, for him and his fellow citizens—a happiness different from political action, and evidently sought as being different. So if among excellent actions political and military actions are distinguished by nobility and greatness, and these are unleisurely and aim at an end and are not desirable for their own sake, but the activity of intellect, which is contemplative, seems both to be superior in worth and to aim at no end beyond itself, and to have its pleasure proper to itself (and this augments the activity), and the self-sufficiency, leisureliness, unweariedness (so far as this is possible for man), and all the other attributes ascribed to the blessed man are evidently those connected with this activity, it follows that this will be the complete happiness of man, if it be allowed a complete term of life (for none of the attributes of happiness is *in*complete).

But such a life would be too high for man; for it is not in so far as he is man that he will live so, but in so far as something divine is present in him; and by so much as this is superior to our composite nature is its activity superior to that which is the exercise of the other kind of excellence. If intellect is divine, then, in comparison with man, the life according to it is divine in comparison with human life. But we must not follow those who advise us, being men, to think of human things, and, being mortal, of mortal things, but must, so far as we can, make ourselves immortal, and strain every nerve to live in accordance with the best thing in us; for even if it be small in bulk, much more does it in power and worth surpass everything. This would seem, too, to be each man himself, since it is the authoritative and better part of him. It would be strange, then, if he were to choose not the life of himself but that of something else. And what we said before will apply now; that which is proper to each thing is by nature best and most pleasant for each thing; for man, therefore, the life according to intellect is best and pleasantest, since intellect more than anything else *is* man. This life therefore is also the happiest.

8. But in a secondary degree the life in accordance with the other kind of excellence is happy; for the activities in accordance with this befit our human estate. Just and brave acts, and other excellent acts, we do in relation to each other, observing what is proper to each with regard to contracts and services and all manner of actions and with regard to passions; and all of these seem to be human. Some of them seem even to arise from the body, and excellence of character to be in many ways bound up with the passions. Practical wisdom, too, is linked to excellence of character, and this to practical wisdom, since the principles of practical wisdom are in accordance with the moral excellences and rightness in the moral excellences is in accordance with practical wisdom. Being connected with the passions also, the moral excellences must belong to our composite nature; and the excellences of our composite nature are human; so, therefore, are the life and the happiness which correspond to these. The excellence of the intellect is a thing apart; we must be content to say this much about it, for to describe it precisely is a task greater than our purpose requires. It would seem, however, also to need external equipment but little, or less than moral excellence does. Grant that both need the necessaries, and do so equally, even if the statesman's work is the more concerned with the body and things of that sort; for there will be little difference there; but in what they need for the exercise of their activities there will be much difference. The liberal man will need money for the doing of his liberal deeds, and the just man too will need it for the returning of services (for wishes are hard to discern, and even

people who are not just pretend to wish to act justly); and the brave man will need power if he is to accomplish any of the acts that correspond to his excellence, and the temperate man will need opportunity; for how else is either he or any of the others to be recognized? It is debated, too, whether the choice or the deed is more essential to excellence, which is assumed to involve both; it is surely clear that its completion involves both; but for deeds many things are needed, and more, the greater and nobler the deeds are. But the man who is contemplating the truth needs no such thing, at least with a view to the exercise of his activity; indeed they are, one may say, even hindrances, at all events to his contemplation; but in so far as he is a man and lives with a number of people, he chooses to do excellent acts; he will therefore need such aids to living a human life.

But that complete happiness is a contemplative activity will appear from the following consideration as well. We assume the gods to be above all other beings blessed and happy; but what sort of actions must we assign to them? Acts of justice? Will not the gods seem absurd if they make contracts and return deposits, and so on? Acts of a brave man, then, confronting dangers and running risks because it is noble to do so? Or liberal acts? To whom will they give? It will be strange if they are really to have money or anything of the kind. And what would their temperate acts be? Is not such praise tasteless, since they have no bad appetites? If we were to run through them all, the circumstances of action would be found trivial and unworthy of gods. Still, everyone supposes that they *live* and therefore that they are active; we cannot suppose them to sleep like Endymion. Now if you take away from a living being action, and still more production, what is left but contemplation? Therefore the activity of God, which surpasses all others in blessedness, must be contemplative; and of human activities, therefore, that which is most akin to this must be most of the nature of happiness.

This is indicated, too, by the fact that the other animals have no share in happiness, being completely deprived of such activity. For while the whole life of the gods is blessed, and that of men too in so far as some likeness of such activity belongs to them, none of the other animals is happy, since they in no way share in contemplation. Happiness extends, then, just so far as contemplation does, and those to whom contemplation more fully belongs are more truly happy, not accidentally, but in virtue of the contemplation; for this is in itself precious. Happiness, therefore, must be some form of contemplation.

But, being a man, one will also need external prosperity; for our nature is not self-sufficient for the purpose of contemplation, but our body also must be healthy and must have food and other attention. Still, we must not think that the man who is to be happy will need many things or great things, merely because he cannot be blessed without external goods; for self-sufficiency and action do not depend on excess, and we can do noble acts without ruling earth and sea; for even with moderate advantages one can act excellently (this is manifest enough; for private persons are thought to do worthy acts no less than despots—indeed even more); and it is enough that we should have so much as that; for the life of the man who is active in accordance with excellence will be happy. Solon, too, was perhaps sketching well the happy man when he described him as moderately furnished with externals but as having done (as Solon thought) the noblest acts, and lived temperately; for one can with but moderate possessions do what one ought. Anaxagoras also seems to have supposed the happy man not to be rich nor a despot, when he said that he would not be surprised if the happy man were to seem to most people a strange person; for they judge by externals, since these are all they perceive. The opinions of the wise seem, then, to harmonize with our arguments. But while even such things carry some conviction, the truth in practical matters is discerned from the facts of life; for these are the decisive factor. We must therefore survey what we have already said, bringing it to the test of the facts of life, and if it harmonizes with the facts we must accept it, but if it clashes with them we must suppose it to be mere theory. Now he who exercises his intellect and cultivates it seems to be both in the best state and most dear to the gods. For if the gods have any care for human affairs, as they are thought to have, it would be reasonable both that they should delight in that which was best and most akin to them (i.e. intellect) and that they should reward those who love and honour this most, as caring for the things that are dear to them and acting both rightly and nobly. And that all these attributes belong most of all to the wise man is manifest. He, therefore, is the dearest to the gods. And he who is that will presumably be also the happiest; so that in this way too the wise man will more than any other be happy.

9. If these matters and the excellences, and also friendship and pleasure, have been dealt with sufficiently in outline, are we to suppose that our programme has reached its end? Surely, as is said, where there are things to be done the end is not to survey and recognize the various things, but rather to do them; with regard to excellence, then, it is not enough to know, but we must try to have and use it, or try any other way there may be of becoming good. Now if arguments were in themselves enough to make men good, they would justly, as Theognis says, have won very great rewards, and such rewards should have been provided; but as things are, while they seem to have power to encourage and stimulate the generous-minded among the young, and to make a character which is gently born, and a true lover of what is noble, ready to be possessed by excellence, they are not able to encourage the many to nobility and goodness. For these do not by nature obey the sense of shame, but only fear, and do not abstain from bad acts because of their baseness but through fear of punishment; living by passion they pursue their own pleasures and the means to them, and avoid the opposite pains, and have not even a conception of what is noble and truly pleasant, since they have never tasted it. What argument would remould such people? It is hard, if not impossible, to remove by argument the traits that have long since been incorporated in the character; and perhaps we must be content if, when all the influences by which we are thought to become good are present, we get some tincture of excellence.

Now some think that we are made good by nature, others by habituation, others by teaching. Nature's part evidently does not depend on us, but as a result of some divine causes is present in those who are truly fortunate; while argument and teaching, we may suspect, are not powerful with all men, but the soul of the student must first have been cultivated by means of habits for noble joy and noble hatred, like earth which is to nourish the seed. For he who lives as passion directs will not hear argument that dissuades him, nor understand it if he does; and how can we persuade one in such a state to change his ways? And in general passion seems to yield not to argument but to force. The character, then, must somehow be there already with a kinship to excellence, loving what is noble and hating what is base.

But it is difficult to get from youth up a right training for excellence if one has not been brought up under right laws; for to live temperately and hardily is not pleasant to most people, especially when they are young. For this reason their nurture and occupations should be fixed by law; for they will not be painful when they have become customary. But it is surely not enough that when they are young they should get the right nurture and attention; since they must, even when they are grown up, practise and be habituated to them, we shall need laws for this as well, and generally speaking to cover the whole of life; for most people obey necessity rather than argument, and punishments rather than what is noble.

This is why some think that legislators ought to stimulate men to excellence and urge them forward by the motive of the noble, on the assumption that those who have been well advanced by the formation of habits will attend to such influences; and that punishments and penalties should be imposed on those who disobey and are of inferior nature, while the incurably bad should be completely banished. A good man (they think), since he lives with his mind fixed on what is noble, will submit to argument, while a bad man, whose desire is for pleasure, is corrected by pain like a beast of burden. This is, too, why they say the pains inflicted should be those that are most opposed to the pleasures such men love.

However that may be, if (as we have said) the man who is to be good must be well trained and habituated, and go on to spend his time in worthy occupations and neither willingly nor unwillingly do bad actions, and if this can be brought about if men live in accordance with a sort of intellect and right order, provided this has force,—if this be so, the paternal command indeed has not the required force or compulsive power (nor in general has the command of one man, unless he be a king or something similar), but the law *has* compulsive power, while it is at the same time an account proceeding from a sort of practical wisdom and intellect. And while people hate *men* who oppose their impulses, even if they oppose them rightly, the law in its ordaining of what is good is not burdensome.

In the Spartan state alone, or almost alone, the legislator seems to have paid attention to questions of nurture and occupations; in most states such matters have been neglected, and each man lives as he pleases, Cyclops-fashion, 'to his own wife and children dealing law'. Now it is best that there should be a public and proper care for such matters; but if they are neglected by the community it would seem right for each man to help his children and friends towards excellence, and that they should be able or at least choose, to do this.

It would seem from what has been said that he can do this better if he makes himself capable of legislating. For public care is plainly effected by laws, and good care by good laws; whether written or unwritten would seem to make no difference, nor whether they are laws providing for the education of individuals or of groups—any more than it does in the case of music or gymnastics and other such pursuits. For as in cities laws and character have force, so in households do the injunctions and the habits of the father, and these have even more because of the tie of blood and the benefits he confers; for the children start with a natural affection and disposition to obey. Further, individual education has an advantage over education in common, as individual medical treatment has; for while in general rest and abstinence from food are good for a man in a fever, for a particular man they may not be; and a boxer presumably does not prescribe the same style of fighting to all his pupils. It would seem, then, that the detail is worked out with more precision if the care is particular to individuals; for each person is more likely to get what suits his case.

But individuals can be best cared for by a doctor or gymnastic instructor or anyone else who has the universal knowledge of what is good for everyone or for people of a certain kind (for the sciences both are said to be, and are, concerned with what is common); not but what some particular detail may perhaps be well looked after by an unscientific person, if he has studied accurately in the light of experience what happens in each case, just as some people seem to be their own best doctors, though they could give no help to anyone else. None the less, it will perhaps be agreed that if a man does wish to become master of an art or science he must go to the universal, and come to know it as well as possible; for, as we have said, it is with this that the sciences are concerned.

And surely he who wants to make men, whether many or few, better by his care must try to become capable of legislating, if it is through laws that we can become good. For to get anyone whatever—anyone who is put before us—into the right condition is not for the first chance comer; if anyone can do it, it is the man who knows, just as in medicine and all other matters which give scope for care and practical wisdom.

Must we not, then, next examine whence or how one can learn how to legislate? Is it, as in all other cases, from statesmen? Certainly it was thought to be a part of statesmanship. Or is a difference apparent between statesmanship and the other sciences and faculties? In the others the same people are found offering to teach the faculties and practising them, e.g. doctors or painters; but while the sophists profess to teach politics, it is practised not by any of them but by the politicians, who would seem to do so by dint of a certain faculty and experience rather than of thought; for they are not found either writing or speaking about such matters (though it were a nobler occupation perhaps than composing speeches for the law-courts and the assembly), nor again are they found to have made statesmen of their own sons or any other of their friends. But it was to be expected that they should if they could; for there is nothing better than such a skill that they could have left to their cities, or could choose to have for themselves, or, therefore, for those dearest to them. Still, experience seems to contribute not a little; else they could not have become politicians by familiarity with politics; and so it seems that those who aim at knowing about the art of politics need experience as well.

But those of the sophists who profess the art seem to be very far from teaching it. For, to put the matter generally, they do not even know what kind of thing it is nor what kinds of things it is about; otherwise they would not have classed it as identical with rhetoric or even inferior to it, nor have thought it easy to legislate by collecting the laws that are thought well of; they say it is possible to select the best laws, as though even the selection did not demand intelligence and as though right judgement were not the greatest thing, as in matters of music. For while people experienced in any department judge rightly the works produced in it, and understand by what means or how they are achieved, and what harmonizes with what, the inexperienced must be content if they do not fail to see whether the work has been well or ill made—as in the case of painting. Now laws are as it were the works of the political art; how then can one learn from them to be a legislator, or judge which are best? Even medical men do not seem to be made by a study of text-books. Yet people try, at any rate, to state not only the treatments, but also how particular classes of people can be cured and should be treated—distinguishing the various states; but while this seems useful to experienced people, to the ignorant it is valueless. Surely, then, while collections of laws, and of constitutions also, may be serviceable to those who can study them and judge what is good or bad and what enactments suit what circumstances, those who go through such collections without a practised faculty will not have right judgement (unless it be spontaneous), though they may perhaps become more intelligent in such matters.

Now our predecessors have left the subject of legislation to us unexamined; it is perhaps best, therefore, that we should ourselves study it, and in general study the question of the constitution, in order to complete to the best of our ability the philosophy of human nature. First, then, if anything has been said well in detail by earlier thinkers, let us try to review it; then in the light of the constitutions we have collected let us study what sorts of influence preserve and destroy states, and what sorts preserve or destroy the particular kinds of constitution, and to what causes it is due that some are well and others ill administered. When these have been studied we shall perhaps be more likely to see which constitution is best, and how each must be ordered, and what laws and customs it must use. Let us make a beginning of our discussion.

Politics
BOOK VII

4. . . . In what has preceded I have discussed other forms of government; in what remains the first point to be considered is what should be the conditions of the ideal or perfect state; for the perfect state cannot exist without a due supply of the means of life. And therefore we must presuppose many purely imag-

inary conditions, but nothing impossible. There will be a certain number of citizens, a country in which to place them, and the like. As the weaver or shipbuilder or any other artisan must have the material proper for his work (and in proportion as this is better prepared, so will the result of his art be nobler), so the statesman or legislator must also have the materials suited to him.

First among the materials required by the statesman is population: he will consider what should be the number . . . of the citizens . . . [E]xperience shows that a very populous city can rarely, if ever, be well governed; since all cities which have a reputation for good government have a limit of population. We may argue on grounds of reason, and the same result will follow. For law is order, and good law is good order; but a very great multitude cannot be orderly: to introduce order into the unlimited is the work of a divine power—of such a power as holds together the universe. Beauty is realized in number and magnitude, and the state which combines magnitude with good order must necessarily be the most beautiful. To the size of states there is a limit, as there is to other things, plants, animals, implements; for none of these retain their natural power when they are too large or too small, but they either wholly lose their nature, or are spoiled. For example, a ship which is only a span long will not be a ship at all, nor a ship a quarter of a mile long; yet there may be a ship of a certain size, either too large or too small, which will still be a ship, but bad for sailing. In like manner a state when composed of too few is not, as a state ought to be, self-sufficient; when of too many, though self-sufficient in all mere necessaries, as a nation may be, it is not a state, being almost incapable of constitutional government. For who can be the general of such a vast multitude, or who the herald, unless he have the voice of a Stentor?

A state, then, only begins to exist when it has attained a population sufficient for a good life in the political community; it may indeed, if it somewhat exceeds this number, be a greater state. But, as I was saying, there must be a limit. What the limit should be will be easily ascertained by experience. For both governors and governed have duties to perform; the special functions of a governor are to command and to judge. But if the citizens of a state are to judge and to distribute offices according to merit, then they must know each other's characters; where they do not possess this knowledge, both the election to offices and the decision of lawsuits will go wrong. When the population is very large they are manifestly settled at haphazard, which clearly ought not to be. Besides, in an over-populous state foreigners and resident aliens will readily acquire the rights of citizens, for who will find them out? Clearly then the best limit of the population of a state is the largest number which suffices for the purposes of life, and can be taken in at a single view. Enough concerning the size of a state. . . .

8. . . . Let us then enumerate the functions of a state. . . .

First, there must be food; secondly, arts, for life requires many instruments; thirdly, there must be arms, for the members of a community have need of them, and in their own hands, too, in order to maintain authority both against disobedient subjects and against external assailants; fourthly, there must be a certain amount of revenue, both for internal needs, and for the purposes of war; fifthly, or rather first, there must be a care of religion, which is commonly called worship; sixthly, and most necessary of all, there must be a power of deciding what is for the public interest, and what is just in men's dealings with one another.

These are the services which every state may be said to need. For a state is not a mere aggregate of persons, but, as we say, a union of them sufficing for the purposes of life; and if any of these things is wanting, it is impossible that the community can be absolutely self-sufficient. A state then should be framed with a view to the fulfilment of these functions. There must be farmers to procure food, and artisans, and a warlike and a wealthy class, and priests, and judges to decide what is necessary and expedient.

9. Having determined these points, we have in the next place to consider whether all ought to share in every sort of occupation. Shall every man be at once farmer, artisan, councillor, judge, or shall we suppose the several occupations just mentioned assigned to different persons? or, thirdly, shall some employments be assigned to individuals and others common to all? The same arrangement, however, does not occur in every constitution . . . for in democracies all share in all, in oligarchies the opposite practice prevails. Now, since we are here speaking of the best form of government, i.e. that under which the state will be most happy (and happiness, as has been already said, cannot exist without excellence), it clearly follows that in the state which is best governed and possesses men who are just absolutely, and not merely relatively to the principle of the constitution, the citizens must not lead the life of artisans or tradesmen, for such a life is ignoble and inimical to excellence. Neither must they be farmers, since leisure is necessary both for the development of excellence and the performance of political duties.

Again, there is in a state a class of warriors, and another of councillors, who advise about the expedient and determine matters of law, and these seem in an especial manner parts of a state. Now, should these two classes be distinguished, or are both functions to be assigned to the same persons? Here again there is no difficulty in seeing that both functions will in one way belong to the same, in another, to different persons. To different persons in so far as these employments are suited to different primes of life, for the one requires wisdom and the other strength. But on the other hand, since it is an impossible thing that those who are able to use or to resist force should be willing to remain always in subjection, from this point of view the persons are the same; for those who carry arms can always determine the fate of the constitution. It remains therefore that both functions should be entrusted by the ideal constitution to the same persons, not, however, at the same time, but in the order prescribed by nature, who has given to young men strength and to older men wisdom. Such a distribution of duties will be expedient and also just, and is founded upon a principle of conformity to merit. Besides, the ruling class should be the owners of property, for they are citizens, and the citizens of a state should be in good circumstances; whereas artisans or any other class which is not a producer of excellence have no share in the state. This follows from our first principle, for happiness cannot exist without excellence, and a city is not to be termed happy in regard to a portion of the citizens, but in regard to them all.

And clearly property should be in their hands, since the farmers will of necessity be slaves or barbarian country people.

Of the classes enumerated there remain only the priests, and the manner in which their office is to be regulated is obvious. No farmer or artisan should be appointed to it; for the gods should receive honour from the citizens only. Now since the body of the citizens is divided into two classes, the warriors and the councillors, and it is fitting that the worship of the gods should be duly performed, and also a rest provided in their service for those who from age have given up active life, to the old men of these two classes should be assigned the duties of the priesthood.

We have shown what are the necessary conditions, and what the parts of a state: farmers, artisans, and labourers of all kinds are necessary to the existence of states, but the parts of the state are the warriors and councillors. . . .

14. Since every political society is composed of rulers and subjects, let us consider whether the relations of one to the other should interchange or be permanent. For the education of the citizens will necessarily vary with the answer given to this question. Now, if some men excelled others in the same degree in which gods and heroes are supposed to excel mankind in general (having in the first place a great advantage even in their bodies, and secondly in their minds), so that the superiority of the governors was undisputed and patent to their subjects, it would clearly be better that once for all the one class should rule and the others serve. But since this is unattainable, and kings have no marked superiority over their subjects, such as Scylax affirms to be found among the Indians, it is obviously necessary on many grounds that all the citizens alike should take their turn of governing and being governed. Equality consists in the same treatment of similar persons, and no government can stand which is not founded upon justice. For if the government is unjust everyone in the country unites with the governed in the desire to have a revolution, and it is an impossibility that the members of the government can be so numerous as to be stronger than all their enemies put together. Yet that governors should be better than their subjects is undeniable. How all this is to be effected, and in what way they will respectively share in the government, the legislator has to consider. . . . Nature herself has provided the distinction when she made a difference between old and young within the same species, of whom she fitted the one to govern and the other to be governed. No one takes offence at being governed when he is young, nor does he think himself better than his governors, especially if he will enjoy the same privilege when he reaches the required age.

We conclude that from one point of view governors and governed are identical, and from another different. And therefore their education must be the same and also different. For he who would learn to command well must, as men say, first of all learn to obey. As I observed in the first part of this treatise, there is one rule which is for the sake of the rulers and another rule which is for the sake of the ruled; the former is a despotic, the latter a free government. Some commands differ not in the thing commanded, but in the intention with which they are imposed. That is why many apparently menial offices are an honour to the free youth by whom they are performed; for actions do not differ as honourable or dishonourable in themselves so much as in the end and intention of them. But since we say that the excellence of the citizen and ruler is the same as that of the good man, and that the same person must first be a subject and then a ruler, the legislator has to see that they become good men, and by what means this may be accomplished, and what is the end of the perfect life.

Now the soul of man is divided into two parts, one of which has a rational principle in itself, and the other, not having a rational principle in itself, is able to obey such a principle. And we call a man in any way good because he has the excellences of these two parts. In which of them the end is more likely to be found is no matter of doubt to those who adopt our division; for in the world both of nature and of art the inferior always exists for the sake of the superior, and the superior is that which has a rational principle. This principle, too, in our ordinary way of making the division, is divided into two kinds, for there is a practical and a speculative principle. This part, then, must evidently be similarly divided. And there must be a corresponding division of actions; the actions of the naturally better part are to be preferred by those who have it in their power to attain to two out of the three or to all, for that is always to everyone the most desirable which is the highest attainable by him. The whole of life is further divided into two parts, business and leisure, war and peace, and of actions some aim at what is necessary and useful, and some at what is honourable. And the preference given to one or the other class of actions must necessarily be like the preference given to one or other part of the soul and its actions over the other; there must be war for the sake of peace, business for the sake of leisure, things useful and necessary for the sake of things honourable. All these points the statesman should keep in view when he frames his laws; he should consider the parts of the soul and their functions, and above all the better and the end; he should also remember the diversities of human lives and actions. For men must be able to engage in business and go to war, but leisure and peace are better; they must do what is necessary and indeed what is useful, but what is honourable is better. On such principles children and persons of every age which requires education should be trained. . . .

15. Since the end of individuals and of states is the same, the end of the best man and of the best constitution must also be the same; it is therefore evident that there ought to exist in both of them the excellences of leisure; for peace, as has been often repeated, is the end of war, and leisure of toil. But leisure and cultivation may be promoted not only by those excellences which are practised in leisure, but also by some of those which are useful to business. For many necessaries of life have to be supplied before we can have leisure. Therefore a city must be temperate and brave, and able to endure: for truly, as the proverb says, 'There is no leisure for slaves,' and those who cannot face danger like men are the slaves of any invader. Courage and endurance are required for business and philosophy for leisure, temperance and justice for both, and more especially in times of peace and leisure, for war compels men to be just and temperate, whereas the enjoyment of good fortune and the leisure which comes with peace tend to make them insolent. Those then who

seem to be the best-off and to be in the possession of every good, have special need of justice and temperance—for example, those (if such there be, as the poets say) who dwell in the Islands of the Blest; they above all will need philosophy and temperance and justice, and all the more the more leisure they have, living in the midst of abundance. There is no difficulty in seeing why the state that would be happy and good ought to have these excellences. If it is disgraceful in men not to be able to use the goods of life, it is peculiarly disgraceful not to be able to use them in time of leisure—to show excellent qualities in action and war, and when they have peace and leisure to be no better than slaves. . . .

17. After . . . children have been born, the manner of rearing them may be supposed to have a great effect on their bodily strength. . . . To accustom children to the cold from their earliest years is . . . an excellent practice, which greatly conduces to health, and hardens them for military service. . . . For human nature should be early habituated to endure all which by habit it can be made to endure; but the process must be gradual. . . . Such care should attend them in the first stage of life.

The next period lasts to the age of five; during this no demand should be made upon the child for study or labour, lest its growth be impeded; and there should be sufficient motion to prevent the limbs from being inactive. This can be secured, among other ways, by play, but the play should not be vulgar or tiring or effeminate. The Directors of Education, as they are termed, should be careful what tales or stories the children hear, for all such things are designed to prepare the way for the business of later life, and should be for the most part imitations of the occupations which they will hereafter pursue in earnest. . . . The Directors of Education should have an eye to their bringing up, and in particular should take care that they are left as little as possible with slaves. For until they are seven years old they must live at home; and therefore, even at this early age, it is to be expected that they should acquire a taint of meanness from what they hear and see. Indeed, there is nothing which the legislator should be more careful to drive away than indecency of speech; for the light utterance of shameful words leads soon to shameful actions. The young especially should never be allowed to repeat or hear anything of the sort. A freeman who is found saying or doing what is forbidden, if he be too young as yet to have the privilege of reclining at the public tables, should be disgraced and beaten, and an elder person degraded as his slavish conduct deserves. And since we do not allow improper language, clearly we should also banish pictures or speeches from the stage which are indecent. Let the rulers take care that there be no image or picture representing unseemly actions, except in the temples of those gods at whose festivals the law permits even ribaldry, and whom the law also permits to be worshipped by persons of mature age on behalf of themselves, their children, and their wives. But the legislator should not allow youth to be spectators of iambi or of comedy until they are of an age to sit at the public tables and to drink strong wine; by that time education will have armed them against the evil influences of such representations. . . .

Theodorus, the tragic actor, was quite right in saying that he would not allow any other actor, not even if he were quite second-rate, to enter before himself, because the spectators grew fond of the voices which they first heard. And the same principle applies universally to association with things as well as with persons, for we always like best whatever comes first. And therefore youth should be kept strangers to all that is bad, and especially to things which suggest vice or hate. When the five years have passed away, during the two following years they must look on at the pursuits which they are hereafter to learn. There are two periods of life with reference to which education has to be divided, from seven to the age of puberty, and onwards to the age of twenty-one. The poets who divide ages by sevens are in the main right: but we should observe the divisions actually made by nature; for the deficiencies of nature are what art and education seek to fill up.

Let us then first inquire if any regulations are to be laid down about children, and secondly, whether the care of them should be the concern of the state or of private individuals, which latter is in our own day the common custom, and in the third place, what these regulations should be.

BOOK VIII

1. No one will doubt that the legislator should direct his attention above all to the education of youth; for the neglect of education does harm to the constitution. The citizen should be moulded to suit the form of government under which he lives. For each government has a peculiar character which originally formed and which continues to preserve it. The character of democracy creates democracy, and the character of oligarchy creates oligarchy; and always the better the character, the better the government.

Again, for the exercise of any faculty or art a previous training and habituation are required; clearly therefore for the practice of excellence. And since the whole city has one end, it is manifest that education should be one and the same for all, and that it should be public, and not private—not as at present, when everyone looks after his own children separately, and gives them separate instruction of the sort which he thinks best; the training in things which are of common interest should be the same for all. Neither must we suppose that anyone of the citizens belongs to himself, for they all belong to the state, and are each of them a part of the state, and the care of each part is inseparable from the care of the whole. In this particular as in some others the Lacedaemonians are to be praised, for they take the greatest pains about their children, and make education the business of the state.

2. That education should be regulated by law and should be an affair of state is not to be denied, but what should be the character of this public education, and how young persons should be educated, are questions which remain to be considered. As things are, there is disagreement about the subjects. For men are by no means agreed about the things to be taught, whether we look to

excellence or the best life. Neither is it clear whether education is more concerned with intellectual or with moral excellence. The existing practice is perplexing; no one knows on what principle we should proceed—should the useful in life, or should excellence, or should the higher knowledge, be the aim of
our training?—all three opinions have been entertained. Again, about the
means there is no agreement; for different persons, starting with different ideas
about the nature of excellence, naturally disagree about the practice of it. There
can be no doubt that children should be taught those useful things which are
really necessary, but not all useful things; for occupations are divided into liberal and illiberal; and to young children should be imparted only such kinds of
knowledge as will be useful to them without making mechanics of them. And
any occupation, art, or science, which makes the body or soul or mind of the
freeman less fit for the practice or exercise of excellence, is mechanical; wherefore we call those arts mechanical which tend to deform the body, and likewise
all paid employments, for they absorb and degrade the mind. There are also
some liberal arts quite proper for a freeman to acquire, but only in a certain degree, and if he attends to them too closely, in order to attain perfection in them,
the same harmful effects will follow. The object also which a man sets before
him makes a great difference; if he does or learns anything for his own sake or
for the sake of his friends, or with a view to excellence, the action will not appear illiberal; but if done for the sake of others, the very same action will be
thought menial and servile. The received subjects of instruction, as I have already remarked, are partly of a liberal and partly of an illiberal character.

  3. The customary branches of education are in number four; they are—
reading and writing, gymnastic exercises, and music, to which is sometimes
added drawing. Of these, reading and writing and drawing are regarded as
useful for the purposes of life in a variety of ways, and gymnastic exercises are
thought to infuse courage. Concerning music a doubt may be raised—in our
own day most men cultivate it for the sake of pleasure, but originally it was included in education, because nature herself, as has been often said, requires
that we should be able, not only to work well, but to use leisure well; for, as I
must repeat once again, the first principle of all action is leisure. Both are required, but leisure is better than occupation and is its end; and therefore the
question must be asked, what ought we to do when at leisure? Clearly we
ought not to be playing, for then play would be the end of life. But if this is inconceivable, and play is needed more amid serious occupations than at other
times (for he who is hard at work has need of relaxation, and play gives relaxation, whereas occupation is always accompanied with exertion and effort), we
should introduce amusements only at suitable times, and they should be our
medicines, for the emotion which they create in the soul is a relaxation, and
from the pleasure we obtain rest. But leisure of itself gives pleasure and happiness and enjoyment of life, which are experienced, not by the busy man, but by
those who have leisure. For he who is occupied has in view some end which he
has not attained; but happiness is an end, since all men deem it to be accompanied with pleasure and not with pain. This pleasure, however, is regarded differently by different persons, and varies according to the habit of individuals;

the pleasure of the best man is the best, and springs from the noblest sources. It is clear then that there are branches of learning and education which we must study merely with a view to leisure spent in intellectual activity, and these are to be valued for their own sake; whereas those kinds of knowledge which are useful in business are to be deemed necessary, and exist for the sake of other things. And therefore our fathers admitted music into education, not on the ground either of its necessity or utility, for it is not necessary, nor indeed useful in the same manner as reading and writing, which are useful in money-making, in the management of a household, in the acquisition of knowledge and in political life, nor like drawing, useful for a more correct judgement of the works of artists, nor again like gymnastic, which gives health and strength; for neither of these is to be gained from music. There remains, then, the use of music for intellectual enjoyment in leisure; which is in fact evidently the reason of its introduction, this being one of the ways in which it is thought that a freeman should pass his leisure; as Homer says—

> But he who alone should be called to the pleasant feast,
> and afterwards he speaks of others whom he describes as inviting
> The bard who would delight them all.

And in another place Odysseus says there is no better way of passing life than when men's hearts are merry and

> The banqueters in the hall, sitting in order, hear the voice of the minstrel.

It is evident, then, that there is a sort of education in which parents should train their sons, not as being useful or necessary, but because it is liberal or noble. Whether this is of one kind only, or of more than one, and if so, what they are, and how they are to be imparted, must hereafter be determined. Thus much we are already in a position to say; for the ancients bear witness to us— their opinion may be gathered from the fact that music is one of the received and traditional branches of education. Further, it is clear that children should be instructed in some useful things—for example, in reading and writing—not only for their usefulness, but also because many other sorts of knowledge are acquired through them. With a like view they may be taught drawing, not to prevent their making mistakes in their own purchases, or in order that they may not be imposed upon in the buying or selling of articles, but perhaps rather because it makes them judges of the beauty of the human form. To be always seeking after the useful does not become free and exalted souls. Now it is clear that in education practice must be used before theory, and the body be trained before the mind; and therefore boys should be handed over to the trainer, who creates in them the proper habit of body, and to the wrestling-master, who teaches them their exercises.

4. Of those states which in our own day seem to take the greatest care of children, some aim at producing in them an athletic habit, but they only injure their bodies and stunt their growth. Although the Lacedaemonians have not fallen into this mistake, yet they brutalize their children by laborious exercises

which they think will make them courageous. But in truth, as we have often repeated, education should not be exclusively, or principally, directed to this end. And even if we suppose the Lacedaemonians to be right in their end, they do not attain it. For among barbarians and among animals courage is found associated, not with the greatest ferocity, but with a gentle and lion-like temper. . . . It is notorious that the Lacedaemonians themselves, while they alone were assiduous in their laborious drill, were superior to others, but now they are beaten both in war and gymnastic exercises. For their ancient superiority did not depend on their mode of training their youth, but only on the circumstance that they trained them when their only rivals did not. Hence we may infer that what is noble, not what is brutal, should have the first place; no wolf or other wild animal will face a really noble danger; such dangers are for the brave man. And parents who devote their children to gymnastics while they neglect their necessary education, in reality make them mechanics; for they make them useful to the art of statesmanship in one quality only, and even in this the argument proves them to be inferior to others. We should judge the Lacedaemonians not from what they have been, but from what they are; for now they have rivals who compete with their education; formerly they had none.

It is an admitted principle that gymnastic exercises should be employed in education, and that for children they should be of a lighter kind, avoiding severe diet or painful toil, lest the growth of the body be impaired. The evil of excessive training in early years is strikingly proved by the example of the Olympic victors; for not more than two or three of them have gained a prize both as boys and as men; their early training and severe gymnastic exercises exhausted their constitutions. When boyhood is over, three years should be spent in other studies; the period of life which follows may then be devoted to hard exercise and strict diet. Men ought not to labour at the same time with their minds and with their bodies; for the two kinds of labour are opposed to one another; the labour of the body impedes the mind, and the labour of the mind the body.

5. Concerning music there are some questions which we have already raised; these we may now resume and carry further; and our remarks will serve as a prelude to this or any other discussion of the subject. It is not easy to determine the nature of music, or why anyone should have a knowledge of it. Shall we say, for the sake of amusement and relaxation, like sleep or drinking, which are not good in themselves, but are pleasant, and at the same time 'make care to cease', as Euripides says? And for this end men also appoint music, and make use of all three alike—sleep, drinking, music—to which some add dancing. Or shall we argue that music conduces to excellence, on the ground that it can form our minds and habituate us to true pleasures as our bodies are made by gymnastic to be of a certain character? Or shall we say that it contributes to the enjoyment of leisure and mental cultivation, which is a third alternative? Now obviously youths are not to be instructed with a view to their amusement, for learning is no amusement, but is accompanied with pain. Neither is intellectual enjoyment suitable to boys of that age, for it is the

end, and that which is imperfect cannot attain the end. But perhaps it may be said that boys learn music for the sake of the amusement which they will have when they are grown up. If so, why should they learn themselves, and not, like the Persian and Median kings, enjoy the pleasure and instruction which is derived from hearing others? (for surely persons who have made music the business and profession of their lives will be better performers than those who practise only long enough to learn). If they must learn music, on the same principle they should learn cookery, which is absurd. And even granting that music may form the character, the objection still holds: why should we learn ourselves? Why cannot we attain true pleasure and form a correct judgement from hearing others, as the Lacedaemonians do?—for they, without learning music, nevertheless can correctly judge, as they say, of good and bad melodies. Or again, if music should be used to promote cheerfulness and refined intellectual enjoyment, the objection still remains—why should we learn ourselves instead of enjoying the performances of others? We may illustrate what we are saying by our conception of the gods; for in the poets Zeus does not himself sing or play on the lyre. Indeed we call professional performers artisans; no freeman would play or sing unless he were intoxicated or in jest. But these matters may be left for the present.

The first question is whether music is or is not to be a part of education. Of the three things mentioned in our discussion, which does it produce—education or amusement or intellectual enjoyment?—for it may be reckoned under all three, and seems to share in the nature of all of them. Amusement is for the sake of relaxation, and relaxation is of necessity sweet, for it is the remedy of pain caused by toil; and intellectual enjoyment is universally acknowledged to contain an element not only of the noble but of the pleasant, for happiness is made up of both. All men agree that music is one of the pleasantest things, whether with or without song; as Musaeus says,

Song is to mortals of all things the sweetest.

Hence and with good reason it is introduced into social gatherings and entertainments, because it makes the hearts of men glad: so that on this ground alone we may assume that the young ought to be trained in it. For innocent pleasures are not only in harmony with the end of life, but they also provide relaxation. And whereas men rarely attain the end, but often rest by the way and amuse themselves, not only with a view to a further end, but also for the pleasure's sake, it may be well at times to let them find a refreshment in music. It sometimes happens that men make amusement the end, for the end probably contains some element of pleasure, though not any ordinary pleasure; but they mistake the lower for the higher, and in seeking for the one find the other, since every pleasure has a likeness to the end of action. For the end is not desirable for the sake of any future good, nor do the pleasures which we have described exist for the sake of any future good but of the past, that is to say, they are the alleviation of past toils and pains. And we may infer this to be the reason why men seek happiness from these pleasures. But music is pursued, not only as an alleviation of past toil, but also as providing recreation. And who can say whether, having this use, it may not also have a nobler one? In addition to this common pleasure, felt and shared in by all (for the pleasure given by music is natural, and therefore adapted to all ages and characters), may it not have also some influence over the character and the soul? It must have such an influence if characters are affected by it. And that they are so affected is proved in many ways, and not least by the power which the songs of Olympus exercise; for beyond question they inspire enthusiasm, and enthusiasm is an emotion of the character of the soul. Besides, when men hear imitation, even apart from the rhythms and tunes themselves, their feelings move in sympathy. Since then music is a pleasure, and excellence consists in rejoicing and loving and hating rightly, there is clearly nothing which we are so much concerned to acquire and to cultivate as the power of forming right judgements, and of taking delight in good dispositions and noble actions. Rhythm and melody supply imitations of anger and gentleness, and also of courage and temperance, and of all the qualities contrary to these, and of the other qualities of character, which hardly fall short of the actual affections, as we know from our own experience, for in listening to such strains our souls undergo a change. The habit of feeling pleasure or pain at mere representations is not far removed from the same feeling about realities; for example, if anyone delights in the sight of a statue for its beauty only, it necessarily follows that the sight of the original will be pleasant to him. The objects of no other sense, such as taste or touch, have any resemblance to moral qualities; in visible objects there is only a little, for there are figures which are of a moral character, but only to a slight extent, and all do not participate in the feeling about them. Again, figures and colours are not imitations, but signs, of character, indications which the body gives of states of feeling. The connexion of them with morals is slight, but in so far as there is any, young men should be taught to look, not at the works of Pauson, but at those of Polygnotus, or any other painter or sculptor who expresses character. On the other hand, even in mere melodies there is an imitation of character, for the musical modes differ essentially from one another, and those who hear them are differently affected by each. Some of them make men sad and grave, like the so-called Mixolydian, others enfeeble the mind, like the relaxed modes, another, again, produces a moderate and settled temper, which appears to be the peculiar effect of the Dorian; the Phrygian inspires enthusiasm. The whole subject has been well treated by philosophical writers on this branch of education, and they confirm their arguments by facts. The same principles apply to rhythms; some have a character of rest, others of motion, and of these latter again, some have a more vulgar, others a nobler movement. Enough has been said to show that music has a power of forming the character, and should therefore be introduced into the education of the young. The study is suited to the stage of youth, for young persons will not, if they can help, endure anything which is not sweetened by pleasure, and music has a natural sweetness. There seems to be in us a sort of affinity to musical modes and rhythms, which makes some philosophers say that the soul is a harmony, others, that it possesses harmony.

6. And now we have to determine the question which has been already raised, whether children should be themselves taught to sing and play or not. Clearly there is a considerable difference made in the character by the actual practice of the art. It is difficult, if not impossible, for those who do not perform to be good judges of the performance of others. Besides, children should have something to do, and the rattle of Archytas, which people give to their children in order to amuse them and prevent them from breaking anything in the house, was a capital invention, for a young thing cannot be quiet. The rattle is a toy suited to the infant mind, and education is a rattle or toy for children of a larger growth. We conclude then that they should be taught music in such a way as to become not only critics but performers.

The question what is or is not suitable for different ages may be easily answered; nor is there any difficulty in meeting the objection of those who say that the study of music is mechanical. We reply in the first place, that they who are to be judges must also be performers, and that they should begin to practise early, although when they are older they may be spared the execution; they must have learned to appreciate what is good and to delight in it, thanks to the knowledge which they acquired in their youth. As to the vulgarizing effect which music is supposed to exercise, . . . it is quite possible that certain methods of teaching and learning music do really have a degrading effect. It is evident then that the learning of music ought not to impede the business of riper years, or to degrade the body or render it unfit for civil or military training, whether for bodily exercises at the time or for later studies.

The right measure will be attained if students of music stop short of the arts which are practised in professional contests, and do not seek to acquire those fantastic marvels of execution which are now the fashion in such contests, and from these have passed into education. Let the young practise even such music as we have prescribed, only until they are able to feel delight in noble melodies and rhythms, and not merely in that common part of music in which every slave or child and even some animals find pleasure. . . .

3

John Locke

Not every philosopher who discusses educational policy can be said to have formulated a philosophy of education, for formulating such a philosophy involves considering the aims of education within the context of metaphysical, epistemological, ethical, and political concerns. An author who treats these matters only sketchily has produced not a philosophy of education but suggestions concerning educational policy, or, as the British philosopher John Locke (1632–1704) titled his book, *Some Thoughts Concerning Education*.

Among Locke's major themes are (1) the need to instill self-discipline in the young; (2) the importance of reasoning with children; and (3) the significance of the development of character, not merely intellect. These points seemed heretical to many educators of Locke's time but still exert a powerful influence on modern thought.

Rousseau would later argue against Locke that children are not capable of appreciating reason and should never be treated as if they were. Locke maintained, to the contrary, that children become reasonable by being treated as reasonable persons.

Locke was concerned with education within a social order that enabled a pupil to have a tutor. Locke's insights, however, are equally useful to a teacher facing an entire classroom of students. In either setting the art of teaching, as Locke emphasizes, is to arouse and maintain student interest, while conveying knowledge and skills in such a way as to make clear the significance of what is being taught and the power inherent in this new knowledge. Faults should be corrected gently, with kind words that encourage a desire for further learning.

Some Thoughts Concerning Education

1. A sound mind in a sound body, is a short but full description of a happy state in this world: he that has these two, has little more to wish for; and he that wants either of them, will be but little the better for anything else. Men's happiness or misery is [for the] most part of their own making. He whose mind directs not wisely, will never take the right way; and he whose body is crazy and feeble, will never be able to advance in it. I confess, there are some men's constitutions of body and mind so vigorous, and well framed by nature, that they need not much assistance from others; but, by the strength of their natural genius, they are, from their cradles, carried towards what is excellent; and, by the privilege of their happy constitutions, are able to do wonders. But examples of this kind are but few; and I think I may say, that, of all the men we meet with, nine parts of ten are what they are, good or evil, useful or not, by their education. It is that which makes the great difference in mankind. The little, or almost insensible, impressions on our tender infancies, have very important and lasting consequences: and there it is, as in the fountains of some rivers, where a gentle application of the hand turns the flexible waters into channels, that make them take quite contrary courses; and by this little direction, given them at first, in the source, they receive different tendencies, and arrive at last at very remote and distant places. . . .

32. If what I have said in the beginning of this discourse be true, as I do not doubt but it is, viz. that the difference to be found in the manners and abilities of men is owing more to their education than to anything else; we have reason to conclude, that great care is to be had of the forming children's minds, and giving them that seasoning early, which shall influence their lives always after. For when they do well or ill, the praise or blame will be laid there: and when anything is done awkwardly, the common saying will pass upon them, that it is suitable to their breeding.

33. As the strength of the body lies chiefly in being able to endure hardships, so also does that of the mind. And the great principle and foundation of all virtue and worth is placed in this, that a man is able to deny himself his own desires, cross his own inclinations, and purely follow what reason directs as best, though the appetite lean the other way.

34. The great mistake I have observed in people's breeding their children has been, that this has not been taken care enough of in its due season; that the mind has not been made obedient to discipline, and pliant to reason, when at first it was most tender, most easy to be bowed. Parents being wisely ordained by nature to love their children, are very apt, if reason watch not that natural affection very warily; are apt, I say, to let it run into fondness. They love their little ones, and it is their duty: but they often with them cherish their faults too. They must not be crossed, forsooth; they must be permitted to have their wills in all things; and they being in their infancies not capable of great vices, their parents think they may safely enough indulge their little irregularities, and

make themselves sport with that pretty perverseness, which they think well enough becomes that innocent age. But to a fond parent, that would not have his child corrected for a perverse trick, but excused it, saying it was a small matter; Solon very well replied, "Ay, but custom is a great one." . . .

38. It seems plain to me, that the principle of all virtue and excellency lies in a power of denying ourselves the satisfaction of our own desires, where reason does not authorize them. This power is to be got and improved by custom, made easy and familiar by an early practice. If therefore I might be heard, I would advise, that, contrary to the ordinary way, children should be used to submit their desires, and go without their longings, even from their very cradles. The very first thing they should learn to know, should be, that they were not to have anything, because it pleased them, but because it was thought fit for them. If things suitable to their wants were supplied to them, so that they were never suffered to have what they once cried for, they would learn to be content without it; would never with bawling and peevishness contend for mastery; nor be half so uneasy to themselves and others as they are, because from the first beginning they are not thus handled. If they were never suffered to obtain their desire by the impatience they expressed for it, they would no more cry for other things than they do for the moon.

39. I say not this as if children were not to be indulged in anything, or that I expected they should, in hanging-sleeves, have the reason and conduct of counsellors. I consider them as children, who must be tenderly used, who must play, and have play things. That which I mean is, that whenever they craved what was not fit for them to have, or do, they should not be permitted it, because they were little and desired it: nay, whatever they were importunate for, they should be sure, for that very reason, to be denied. I have seen children at a table, who, whatever was there, never asked for anything, but contentedly took what was given them: and at another place I have seen others cry for every thing they saw, must be served out of every dish, and that first too. What made this vast difference but this, that one was accustomed to have what they called or cried for, the other to go without it? The younger they are, the less, I think, are their unruly and disorderly appetites to be complied with; and the less reason they have of their own, the more are they to be under the absolute power and restraint of those, in whose hands they are. From which I confess, it will follow, that none but discreet people should be about them. If the world commonly does otherwise, I cannot help that. I am saying what I think should be; which, if it were already in fashion, I should not need to trouble the world with a discourse on this subject. But yet I doubt not but, when it is considered, there will be others of opinion with me, that the sooner this way is begun with children, the easier it will be for them, and their governors too: and that this ought to be observed as an inviolable maxim, that whatever once is denied them, they are certainly not to obtain by crying or importunity; unless one has a mind to teach them to be impatient and troublesome, by rewarding them for it, when they are so.

40. Those therefore that intend ever to govern their children, should begin it whilst they are very little; and look that they perfectly comply with the will of

their parents. Would you have your son obedient to you, when past a child? Be sure then to establish the authority of a father, as soon as he is capable of submission, and can understand in whose power he is. If you would have him stand in awe of you, imprint it in his infancy; and, as he approaches more to a man, admit him nearer to your familiarity: so shall you have him your obedient subject (as is fit) whilst he is a child, and your affectionate friend when he is a man. For methinks they mightily misplace the treatment due to their children, who are indulgent and familiar when they are little, but severe to them, and keep them at a distance, when they are grown up. For liberty and indulgence can do no good to children: their want of judgment makes them stand in need of restraint and discipline. And, on the contrary, imperiousness and severity is but an ill way of treating men, who have reason of their own to guide them, unless you have a mind to make your children, when grown up, weary of you; and secretly to say within themselves, "When will you die, father?"

41. I imagine everyone will judge it reasonable, that their children, when little, should look upon their parents as their lords, their absolute governors; and, as such, stand in awe of them: and that, when they come to riper years, they should look on them as their best, as their only sure friends: and, as such, love and reverence them. The way I have mentioned, if I mistake not, is the only one to obtain this. We must look upon our children, when grown up, to be like ourselves; with the same passions, the same desires. We would be thought rational creatures, and have our freedom; we love not to be uneasy under constant rebukes and brow-beatings; nor can we bear severe humours, and great distance, in those we converse with. Whoever has such treatment when he is a man, will look out other company, other friends, other conversation, with whom he can be at ease. If therefore a strict hand be kept over children from the beginning, they will in that age be tractable, and quietly submit to it, as never having known any other: and if, as they grow up to the use of reason, the rigour of government be, as they deserve it, gently relaxed, the father's brow more smoothed to them, and the distance by degrees abated: his former restraints will increase their love, when they find it was only a kindness for them, and a care to make them capable to deserve the favour of their parents, and the esteem of everybody else.

42. Thus much for the settling your authority over children in general. Fear and awe ought to give you the first power over their minds, and love and friendship in riper years to hold it: for the time must come, when they will be past the rod and correction; and then, if the love of you make them not obedient and dutiful; if the love of virtue and reputation keep them not in laudable courses; I ask, what hold will you have upon them, to turn them to it? Indeed, fear of having a scanty portion, if they displease you, may make them slaves to your estate; but they will be nevertheless ill and wicked in private, and that restraint will not last always. Every man must some time or other be trusted to himself, and his own conduct; and he that is a good, a virtuous, and able man, must be made so within. And therefore, what he is to receive from education, what is to sway and influence his life, must be something put into him betimes: habits woven into the very principles of his nature; and not a counterfeit

carriage, and dissembled outside, put on by fear, only to avoid the present anger of a father, who perhaps may disinherit him.

43. This being laid down in general, as the course ought to be taken, it is fit we come now to consider the parts of the discipline to be used, a little more particularly. I have spoken so much of carrying a strict hand over children, that perhaps I shall be suspected of not considering enough what is due to their tender age and constitutions. But that opinion will vanish, when you have heard me a little farther. For I am very apt to think, that great severity of punishment does but very little good; nay, great harm in education: and I believe it will be found, that, *caeteris paribus,* those children who have been most chastised, seldom make the best men. All that I have hitherto contended for, is, that whatsoever rigour is necessary, it is more to be used, the younger children are; and, having by a due application wrought its effect, it is to be relaxed, and changed into a milder sort of government.

44. A compliance, and suppleness of their wills, being by a steady hand introduced by parents, before children have memories to retain the beginnings of it, will seem natural to them, and work afterwards in them, as if it were so; preventing all occasions of struggling, or repining. The only care is, that it be begun early, and inflexibly kept to, till awe and respect be grown familiar, and there appears not the least reluctancy in the submission and ready obedience of their minds. When this reverence is once thus established, (which it must be early, or else it will cost pains and blows to recover it, and the more, the longer it is deferred) it is by it, mixed still with as much indulgence as they made not an ill use of, and not by beating, chiding, or other servile punishments, they are for the future to be governed, as they grow up to more understanding.

45. That this is so, will be easily allowed, when it is but considered what is to be aimed at, in an ingenuous education; and upon what it turns.

(1.) He that has not a mastery over his inclinations, he that knows not how to resist the importunity of present pleasure or pain, for the sake of what reason tells him is fit to be done, wants the true principle of virtue and industry; and is in danger of never being good for anything. This temper, therefore, so contrary to unguided nature, is to be got betimes; and this habit, as the true foundation of future ability and happiness, is to be wrought into the mind, as early as may be, even from the first dawnings of any knowledge or apprehension in children; and so to be confirmed in them, by all the care and ways imaginable, by those who have the oversight of their education.

46. (2.) On the other side, if the mind be curbed, and humbled too much in children; if their spirits be abased and broken much, by too strict a hand over them; they lose all their vigour and industry, and are in a worse state than the former. For extravagant young fellows, that have liveliness and spirit, come sometimes to be set right, and so make able and great men: but dejected minds, timorous and tame, and low spirits, are hardly ever to be raised, and very seldom attain to anything. To avoid the danger that is on either hand is the great art: and he that has found a way how to keep up a child's spirit, easy, active, and free; and yet, at the same time, to restrain him from many things he

has a mind to, and to draw him to things that are uneasy to him; he, I say, that knows how to reconcile these seeming contradictions, has, in my opinion, got the true secret of education.

47. The usual lazy and short way by chastisement, and the rod, which is the only instrument of government that tutors generally know, or ever think of, is the most unfit of any to be used in education; because it tends to both those mischiefs; which as we have shown, are the Scylla and Charybdis, which, on the one hand or the other, ruin all that miscarry.

48. (1.) This kind of punishment contributes not at all to the mastery of our natural propensity to indulge corporal and present pleasure and to avoid pain at any rate; but rather encourages it; and thereby strengthens that in us, which is the root, from whence spring all vicious actions and the irregularities of life. From what other motive, but of sensual pleasure, and pain, does a child act, who drudges at his book against his inclination, or abstains from eating unwholesome fruit, that he takes pleasure in, only out of fear of whipping? He in this only prefers the greater corporal pleasure, or avoids the greater corporal pain. And what is it to govern his actions, and direct his conduct, by such motives as these? what is it, I say, but to cherish that principle in him, which it is our business to root out and destroy? And therefore I cannot think any correction useful to a child, where the shame of suffering for having done amiss does not work more upon him than the pain.

49. (2.) This sort of correction naturally breeds an aversion to that which it is the tutor's business to create a liking to. How obvious is it to observe, that children come to hate things which were at first acceptable to them, when they find themselves whipped, and chided, and teased about them? And it is not to be wondered at in them; when grown men would not be able to be reconciled to anything by such ways. Who is there that would not be disgusted with any innocent recreation, in itself indifferent to him, if he should with blows, or ill language, be hauled to it, when he had no mind? or be constantly so treated, for some circumstances in his application to it? This is natural to be so. Offensive circumstances ordinarily infect innocent things, which they are joined with: and the very sight of a cup, wherein anyone uses to take nauseous physic, turns his stomach; so that nothing will relish well out of it, though the cup be ever so clean, and well-shaped, and of the richest materials.

50. (3.) Such a sort of slavish discipline makes a slavish temper. The child submits, and dissembles obedience, whilst the fear of the rod hangs over him; but when that is removed, and, by being out of sight, he can promise himself impunity, he gives the greater scope to his natural inclination; which by this way is not at all altered, but on the contrary heightened and increased in him; and after such restraint, breaks out usually with the more violence. Or,

51. (4.) If severity carried to the highest pitch does prevail, and works a cure upon the present unruly distemper, it is often bringing in the room of it worse and more dangerous disease, by breaking the mind; and then, in the place of a disorderly young fellow, you have a low-spirited moped creature: who, however with his unnatural sobriety he may please silly people, who

commend tame inactive children, because they make no noise, nor give them any trouble; yet, at last, will probably prove as uncomfortable a thing to his friends, as he will be, all his life, an useless thing to himself and others.

52. Beating then, and all other sorts of slavish and corporal punishments, are not the discipline fit to be used in the education of those who would have wise, good, and ingenuous men; and therefore very rarely to be applied, and that only on great occasions, and cases of extremity. On the other side, to flatter children by rewards of things that are pleasant to them, is as carefully to be avoided. He that will give to his son apples, or sugar-plums, or what else of this kind he is most delighted with, to make him learn his book, does but authorise his love of pleasure, and cocker up that dangerous propensity, which he ought by all means to subdue and stifle in him. You can never hope to teach him to master it, whilst you compound for the check you give his inclination in one place, by the satisfaction you propose to it in another. To make a good, a wise, and a virtuous man, it is fit he should learn to cross his appetite, and deny his inclination to riches, finery, or pleasing his palate, &c. whenever his reason advises the contrary, and his duty requires it. But when you draw him to do anything that is fit, by the offer of money; or reward the pains of learning his book, by the pleasure of a luscious morsel; when you promise him a lace-cravat, or a fine new suit, upon performance of some of his little tasks; what do you, by proposing these as rewards, but allow them to be the good things he should aim at, and thereby encourage his longing for them, and accustom him to place his happiness in them? Thus people, to prevail with children to be industrious about their grammar, dancing, or some other such matter, of no great moment to the happiness or usefulness of their lives, by misapplied rewards and punishments, sacrifice their virtue, invert the order of their education, and teach them luxury, pride, or covetousness, &c. For in this way, flattering those wrong inclinations, which they should restrain and suppress, they lay the foundations of those future vices, which cannot be avoided, but by curbing our desires and accustoming them early to submit to reason. . . .

54. But if you take away the rod on one hand, and these little encouragements, which they are taken with, on the other; how then (will you say) shall children be governed? Remove hope and fear, and there is an end of all discipline. I grant, that good and evil, reward and punishment, are the only motives to a rational creature; these are the spur and reins, whereby all mankind are set on work and guided, and therefore they are to be made use of to children too. For I advise their parents and governors always to carry this in their minds, that children are to be treated as rational creatures. . . .

56. The rewards and punishments then whereby we should keep children in order are quite of another kind; and of that force, that when we can get them once to work, the business, I think, is done, and the difficulty is over. Esteem and disgrace are, of all others, the most powerful incentives to the mind, when once it is brought to relish them. If you can once get into children a love of credit, and an apprehension of shame and disgrace, you have put into them the true principle, which will constantly work, and incline them to the right. But it will be asked, How shall this be done?

I confess, it does not, at first appearance, want some difficulty; but yet I think it worth our while to seek the ways (and practise them when found) to attain this, which I look on as the great secret of education.

57. First, children (earlier perhaps than we think) are very sensible of praise and commendation. They find a pleasure in being esteemed and valued, especially by their parents, and those whom they depend on. If therefore the father caress and commend them, when they do well; show a cold and neglectful countenance to them upon doing ill; and this accompanied by a like carriage of the mother, and all others that are about them; it will in a little time make them sensible of the difference: and this, if constantly observed, I doubt not but will of itself work more than threats or blows, which lose their force, when once grown common, and are of no use when shame does not attend them; and therefore are to be forborn, and never to be used, but in the case hereafter mentioned, when it is brought to extremity.

58. But, secondly, to make the sense of esteem or disgrace sink the deeper, and be of the more weight, other agreeable or disagreeable things should constantly accompany these different states; not as particular rewards and punishments of this or that particular action, but as necessarily belonging to, and constantly attending one, who by his carriage has brought himself into a state of disgrace or commendation. By which way of treating them, children may as much as possible be brought to conceive, that those that are commended and in esteem for doing well, will necessarily be beloved and cherished by everybody, and have all other good things as a consequence of it; and, on the other side, when anyone by miscarriage falls into dis-esteem, and cares not to preserve his credit, he will unavoidably fall under neglect and contempt: and, in that state, the want of whatever might satisfy or delight him, will follow. In this way the objects of their desires are made assisting to virtue; when a settled experience from the beginning teaches children, that the things they delight in, belong to, and are to be enjoyed by those only, who are in a state of reputation. If by these means you can come once to shame them out of their faults, (for besides that, I would willingly have no punishment) and make them in love with the pleasure of being well thought on, you may turn them as you please, and they will be in love with all the ways of virtue. . . .

63. But if a right course be taken with children, there will not be so much need of the application of the common reward and punishments, as we imagined, and as the general practice has established. For all their innocent folly, playing, and childish actions, are to be left perfectly free and unrestrained, as far as they can consist with the respect due to those that are present; and that with the greatest allowance. If these faults of their age, rather than of the children themselves, were, as they should be, left only to time, and imitation, and riper years to cure, children would escape a great deal of misapplied and useless correction; which either fails to overpower the natural disposition of their childhood, and so, by an ineffectual familiarity, makes correction in other necessary cases of less use; or else if it be of force to restrain the natural gaiety of that age, it serves only to spoil the temper both of body and mind. If the noise and bustle of their play prove at any time inconvenient, or unsuitable to the

place or company they are in, (which can only be where their parents are) a look or a word from the father or mother, if they have established the authority they should, will be enough either to remove, or quiet them for that time. But this gamesome humour, which is wisely adapted by nature to their age and temper, should rather be encouraged, to keep up their spirits, and improve their strength and health, than curbed or restrained: and the chief art is to make all that they have to do, sport and play too.

64. And here give me leave to take notice of one thing I think a fault in the ordinary method of education; and that is, the charging of children's memories, upon all occasions, with rules and precepts, which they often do not understand, and are constantly as soon forgot as given. If it be some action you would have done, or done otherwise; whenever they forget, or do it awkwardly, make them do it over and over again, till they are perfect: whereby you will get these two advantages: first, to see whether it be an action they can do, or is fit to be expected of them. For sometimes children are bid to do things, which, upon trial, they are found not able to do; and had need be taught and exercised in, before they are required to do them. But it is much easier for a tutor to command, than to teach. Secondly, another thing got by it will be this, that by repeating the same action, till it be grown habitual in them, the performance will not depend on memory, or reflection, the concomitant of prudence and age, and not of childhood; but will be natural in them. Thus, bowing to a gentleman when he salutes him, and looking in his face when he speaks to him, is by constant use as natural to a well-bred man, as breathing; it requires no thought, no reflection. Having this way cured in your child any fault, it is cured for ever: and thus, one by one, you may weed them out all, and plant what habits you please.

65. I have seen parents so heap rules on their children, that it was impossible for the poor little ones to remember a tenth part of them, much less to observe them. However, they were either by words or blows corrected for the breach of those multiplied and often very impertinent precepts. Whence it naturally followed, that the children minded not what was said to them; when it was evident to them, that no attention they were capable of, was sufficient to preserve them from transgression, and the rebukes which followed it.

Let therefore your rules to your son be as few as is possible, and rather fewer than more than seem absolutely necessary. For if you burden him with many rules, one of these two things must necessarily follow, that either he must be very often punished, which will be of ill consequence, by making punishment too frequent and familiar; or else you must let the transgressions of some of your rules go unpunished, whereby they will of course grow contemptible, and your authority become cheap to him. Make but few laws but see they be well observed, when once made. Few years require but few laws; and as his age increases, when one rule is by practice well established, you may add another.

66. But pray remember, children are not to be taught by rules, which will be always slipping out of their memories. What you think necessary for them to do, settle in them by an indispensable practice, as often as the occasion re-

turns; and, if it be possible, make occasions. This will beget habits in them, which, being once established, operate of themselves easily and naturally, without the assistance of the memory. But here let me give two cautions: 1. The one is, that you keep them to the practice of what you would have grow into a habit in them, by kind words and gentle admonitions, rather as minding them of what they forget, than by harsh rebukes and chiding, as if they were wilfully guilty. Secondly, another thing you are to take care of, is, not to endeavour to settle too many habits at once, lest by a variety you confound them, and so perfect none. When constant custom has made any one thing easy and natural to them, and they practise it without reflection, you may then go on to another.

This method of teaching children by a repeated practice, and the same action done over and over again, under the eye and direction of the tutor, till they have got the habit of doing it well, and not by relying on rules trusted to their memories; has so many advantages, which way soever we consider it, that I cannot but wonder (if ill customs could be wondered at in anything) how it could possibly be so much neglected. I shall name one more that comes now in my way. By this method we shall see, whether what is required of him be adapted to his capacity, and any way suited to the child's natural genius and constitution: for that too must be considered in a right education. We must not hope wholly to change their original tempers, nor make the gay pensive and grave, nor the melancholy sportive, without spoiling them. God has stamped certain characters upon men's minds, which, like their shapes, may perhaps be a little mended; but can hardly be totally altered and transformed into the contrary.

He therefore, that is about children, should well study their natures and aptitudes, and see, by often trials, what turn they easily take, and what becomes them; observe what their native stock is, how it may be improved, and what it is fit for: he should consider what they want, whether they be capable of having it wrought into them by industry, and incorporated there by practice; and whether it be worthwhile to endeavour it. For, in many cases, all that we can do, or should aim at, is, to make the best of what nature has given; to prevent the vices and faults to which such a constitution is most inclined, and give it all the advantages it is capable of. Every one's natural genius should be carried as far as it could; but to attempt the putting another upon him; will be but labour in vain; and what is so plaistered on will at best sit but untowardly, and have always hanging to it the ungracefulness of constraint and affectation. . . .

71. . . . I must here take the liberty to mind parents of this one thing, viz. that he that will have his son have a respect for him and his orders, must himself have a great reverence for his son. *"Maxima debetur pueris reverentia."* You must do nothing before him, which you would not have him imitate. If anything escape you, which you would have pass for a fault in him, he will be sure to shelter himself under your example, and shelter himself so, as that it will not be easy to come at him to correct it in him the right way. If you punish him for what he sees you practise yourself, he will not think that severity to proceed from kindness in you, or carefulness to amend a fault in him; but will be apt to interpret it the peevishness and arbitrary imperiousness of a father, who, with-

out any ground for it, would deny his son the liberty and pleasures he takes himself. Or if you assume to yourself the liberty you have taken, as a privilege belonging to riper years, to which a child must not aspire, you do but add new force to your example, and recommend the action the more powerfully to him. For you must always remember, that children affect to be men earlier than is thought: and they love breeches, not for their cut, or ease, but because the having them is a mark or a step towards manhood. What I say of the father's carriage before his children, must extend itself to all those who have any authority over them, or for whom he would have them have any respect. . . .

73. (1.) None of the things they are to learn should ever be made a burden to them, or imposed on them as a task. Whatever is so proposed presently becomes irksome: the mind takes an aversion to it, though before it were a thing of delight or indifferency. Let a child be but ordered to whip his top at a certain time every day, whether he has or has not a mind to it; let this be but required of him as a duty, wherein he must spend so many hours morning and afternoon, and see whether he will not soon be weary of any play at this rate. Is it not so with grown men? What they do cheerfully of themselves, do they not presently grow sick of, and can no more endure, as soon as they find it is expected of them as a duty? Children have as much a mind to show that they are free that their own good actions come from themselves, that they are absolute and independent, as any of the proudest of you grown men, think of them as you please.

74. (2.) As a consequence of this, they should seldom be put about doing even those things you have got an inclination in them to, but when they have a mind and disposition to it. He that loves reading, writing, music, &c. finds yet in himself certain seasons wherein those things have no relish to him: and, if at that time he forces himself to it, he only pothers and wearies himself to no purpose. So it is with children. This change of temper should be carefully observed in them, and the favourable seasons of aptitude and inclination be heedfully laid hold of: and if they are not often enough forward to themselves, a good disposition should be talked into them, before they be set upon anything. . . .

81. It will perhaps be wondered, that I mention reasoning with children: and yet I cannot but think that the true way of dealing with them. They understand it as early as they do language; and, if I misobserve not, they love to be treated as rational creatures sooner than is imagined. It is a pride should be cherished in them, and, as much as can be, made the greatest instrument to turn them by.

But when I talk of reasoning, I do not intend any other but such as is suited to the child's capacity and apprehension. Nobody can think a boy of three or seven years old should be argued with as a grown man. Long discourses, and philosophical reasonings, at best amaze and confound, but do not instruct, children. When I say, therefore, that they must be treated as rational creatures, I mean, that you should make them sensible, by the mildness of your carriage, and the composure, even in your correction of them, that what you do is reasonable in you, and useful and necessary for them; and that it is not out of caprice, passion, or fancy, that you command or forbid them anything.

This they are capable of understanding; and there is no virtue they should be excited to, nor fault they should be kept from, which I do not think they may be convinced of: but it must be by such reasons as their age and understanding are capable of, and those proposed always in very few and plain words. The foundations on which several duties are built, and the fountains of right and wrong, from which they spring, are not, perhaps, easily to be let into the minds of grown men, not used to abstract their thoughts from common received opinions. Much less are children capable of reasonings from remote principles. They cannot conceive the force of long deductions: the reasons that move them must be obvious, and level to their thoughts, and such as may (if I may so say) be felt and touched. But yet, if their age, temper, and inclinations, be considered, they will never want such motives as may be sufficient to convince them. If there be no other more particular, yet these will always be intelligible, and of force, to deter them from any fault fit to be taken notice of in them, viz. that it will be a discredit and disgrace to them, and displease you. . . .

95. . . . [A] father will do well, as his son grows up, and is capable of it, to talk familiarly with him; nay, ask his advice, and consult with him, about those things wherein he has any knowledge or understanding. By this the father will gain two things, both of great moment. The one is, that it will put serious considerations into his son's thoughts, better than any rules or advices he can give him. The sooner you treat him as a man, the sooner he will begin to be one: and if you admit him into serious discourses sometimes with you, you will insensibly raise his mind above the usual amusements of youth, and those trifling occupations which it is commonly wasted in. For it is easy to observe, that many young men continue longer in the thought and conversation of schoolboys, than otherwise they would, because their parents keep them at that distance, and in that low rank, by all their carriage to them. . . .

118. Curiosity in children . . . is but an appetite after knowledge, and therefore ought to be encouraged in them, not only as a good sign, but as the great instrument nature has provided, to remove that ignorance they were born with, and which without this busy inquisitiveness will make them dull and useless creatures. The ways to encourage it, and keep it active and busy, are, I suppose, these following:

(1.) Not to check or discountenance any inquiries he shall make, nor suffer them to be laughed at; but to answer all his questions, and explain the matters he desires to know, so as to make them as much intelligible to him, as suits the capacity of his age and knowledge. But confound not his understanding with explications or notions that are above it, or with the variety or number of things that are not to his present purpose. Mark what it is his mind aims at in the question, and not what words he expresses it in: and, when you have informed and satisfied him in that, you shall see how his thoughts will enlarge themselves, and how by fit answers he may be led on farther than perhaps you could imagine. For knowledge is grateful to the understanding, as light to the eyes: children are pleased and delighted with it exceedingly, especially if they see that their inquiries are regarded, and that their desire of knowing is encouraged and commended. And I doubt not but one great reason, why many children abandon themselves wholly to silly sports, and trifle away all their time insipidly, is, because they have found their curiosity baulked, and their inquiries neglected. But had they been treated with more kindness and respect, and their questions answered, as they should, to their satisfaction, I doubt not but they would have taken more pleasure in learning, and improving their knowledge, wherein there would be still newness and variety, which is what they are delighted with, than in returning over and over to the same play and play things.

119. (2.) To this serious answering their questions, and informing their understandings in what they desire, as if it were a matter that needed it, should be added some peculiar ways of commendation. Let others, whom they esteem, be told before their faces of the knowledge they have in such and such things; and since we are all, even from our cradles, vain and proud creatures, let their vanity be flattered with things that will do them good; and let their pride set them on work on something which may turn to their advantage. Upon this ground you shall find, that there cannot be a greater spur to the attaining what you would have the elder learn and know himself, than to set him upon teaching it to his younger brothers and sisters.

120. (3.) As children's inquiries are not to be slighted, so also great care is to be taken, that they never receive deceitful and illuding answers. They easily perceive when they are slighted or deceived, and quickly learn the trick of neglect, dissimulation, and falsehood, which they observe others to make use of. We are not to intrench upon truth in any conversation, but least of all with children; since, if we play false with them, we not only deceive their expectation, and hinder their knowledge, but corrupt their innocence, and teach them the worst of vices. They are travellers newly arrived in a strange country, of which they know nothing: we should therefore make conscience not to mislead them. And though their questions seem sometimes not very material, yet they should be seriously answered; for however they may appear to us (to whom they are long since known) inquiries not worth the making, they are of moment to those who are wholly ignorant. Children are strangers to all we are acquainted with; and all the things they meet with, are at first unknown to them, as they once were to us: and happy are they who meet with civil people, that will comply with their ignorance, and help them to get out of it. . . .

133. This is what I have thought concerning the general method of educating a young gentleman; which, though I am apt to suppose may have some influence on the whole course of his education, yet I am far from imagining it contains all those particulars which his growing years, or peculiar temper, may require. But this being premised in general, we shall, in the next place, descend to a more particular consideration of the several parts of his education.

134. That which every gentleman (that takes any care of his education) desires for his son, besides the estate he leaves him, is contained (I suppose) in these four things, virtue, wisdom, breeding, and learning. . . .

135. I place virtue as the first and most necessary of those endowments that belong to a man or a gentleman, as absolutely requisite to make him valued and beloved by others, acceptable or tolerable to himself. Without that, I think, he will be happy neither in this, nor the other world. . . .

140. Wisdom I take, in the popular acceptation, for a man's managing his business ably, and with foresight, in this world. . . . To accustom a child to have true notions of things, and not to be satisfied till he has them; to raise his mind to great and worthy thoughts; and to keep him at a distance from falsehood, and cunning, which has always a broad mixture of falsehood in it; is the fittest preparation of a child for wisdom. The rest, which is to be learned from time, experience, and observation, and an acquaintance with men, their tempers and designs, is not to be expected in the ignorance and inadvertency of childhood, or the inconsiderate heat and unwariness of youth: all that can be done towards it, during this unripe age, is, as I have said, to accustom them to truth and sincerity; to a submission to reason; and, as much as may be, to reflection on their own actions.

141. The next good quality belonging to a gentleman, is good-breeding. There are two sorts of ill-breeding; the one, a sheepish bashfulness; and the other, a misbecoming negligence and disrespect in our carriage; both which are avoided, by duly observing this one rule, Not to think meanly of ourselves, and not to think meanly of others. . . .

147. You will wonder, perhaps, that I put learning last, especially if I tell you I think it the least part. This may seem strange in the mouth of a bookish man: and this making usually the chief, if not only bustle and stir about children, this being almost that alone which is thought on, when people talk of education, makes it the greater paradox. When I consider what ado is made about a little Latin and Greek, how many years are spent in it, and what a noise and business it makes to no purpose, I can hardly forbear thinking, that the parents of children still live in fear of the schoolmaster's rod, which they look on as the only instrument of education; as if a language or two were its whole business. How else is it possible, that a child should be chained to the oar seven, eight, or ten of the best years of his life, to get a language or two, which I think might be had at a great deal cheaper rate of pains and time, and be learned almost in playing?

Forgive me, therefore, if I say, I cannot with patience think, that a young gentleman should be put into the herd, and be driven with a whip and scourge, as if he were to run the gauntlet through the several classes, *"ad capiendum ingenii cultum."* "What then, say you, would you not have him write and read? Shall he be more ignorant than the clerk of our parish, who takes Hopkins and Sternhold for the best poets in the world, whom yet he makes worse than they are, by his ill reading?" Not so, not so fast, I beseech you. Reading, and writing, and learning, I allow to be necessary, but yet not the chief business. I imagine you would think him a very foolish fellow, that should not value a virtuous, or a wise man, infinitely before a great scholar. Not but that I think learning a great help to both, in well disposed minds; but yet it must be confessed also, that in others not so disposed, it helps them only to be the more foolish, or worse men. . . .

148. When he can talk, it is time he should begin to learn to read. But as to this, give me leave here to inculcate again what is very apt to be forgotten, viz. that a great care is to be taken, that it be never made as a business to him, nor

he look on it as a task. We naturally, as I said, even from our cradles, love liberty, and have therefore an aversion to many things, for no other reason, but because they are enjoined us. I have always had a fancy, that learning might be made a play and recreation to children; and that they might be brought to desire to be taught, if it were proposed to them as a thing of honour, credit, delight, and recreation, or as a reward for doing something else, and if they were never chided or corrected for the neglect of it. That which confirms me in this opinion is, that amongst the Portuguese, it is so much a fashion and emulation amongst their children to learn to read and write, that they cannot hinder them from it: they will learn it one from another, and are as intent on it as if it were forbid them. I remember, that being at a friend's house, whose younger son, a child in coats, was not easily brought to his book (being taught to read at home by his mother); I advised to try another way than requiring it of him as his duty. We therefore, in a discourse on purpose amongst ourselves, in his hearing, but without taking any notice of him, declared, that it was the privilege and advantage of heirs and elder brothers, to be scholars; that this made them fine gentlemen, and beloved by everybody: and that for younger brothers, it was a favour to admit them to breeding; to be taught to read and write was more than came to their share; they might be ignorant bumpkins and clowns, if they pleased. This so wrought upon the child, that afterwards he desired to be taught; would come himself to his mother to learn; and would not let his maid be quiet, till she heard him his lesson. I doubt not but some way like this might be taken with other children; and, when their tempers are found, some thoughts be instilled into them, that might set them upon desiring of learning themselves, and make them seek it, as another sort of play or recreation. But then, as I said before, it must never be imposed as a task, nor made a trouble to them. . . .

167. . . . . There is yet a farther reason, why masters and teachers should raise no difficulties to their scholars; but, on the contrary, should smooth their way, and readily help them forwards, where they find them stop. Children's minds are narrow and weak, and usually susceptible but of one thought at once. Whatever is in a child's head, fills it for the time, especially if set on with any passion. It should therefore be the skill and art of the teacher, to clear their heads of all other thoughts, whilst they are learning of anything, the better to make room for what he would instil into them, that it may be received with attention and application, without which it leaves no impression. The natural temper of children disposes their minds to wander. Novelty alone takes them; whatever that presents, they are presently eager to have a taste of, and are as soon satiated with it. They quickly grow weary of the same thing, and so have almost their whole delight in change and variety. It is a contradiction to the natural state of childhood, for them to fix their fleeting thoughts. Whether this be owing to the temper of their brains, or the quickness or instability of their animal spirits, over which the mind has not yet got a full command; this is visible, that it is a pain to children to keep their thoughts steady to anything. A lasting continued attention is one of the hardest tasks can be imposed on them: and therefore, he that requires their application, should endeavour to make

what he proposes as grateful and agreeable as possible; at least, he ought to take care not to join any displeasing or frightful idea with it. If they come not to their books with some kind of liking and relish, it is no wonder their thoughts should be perpetually shifting from what disgusts them, and seek better entertainment in more pleasing objects, after which they will unavoidably be gadding.

It is, I know, the usual method of tutors, to endeavour to procure attention in their scholars, and to fix their minds to the business in hand, by rebukes and corrections, if they find them ever so little wandering. But such treatment is sure to produce the quite contrary effect. Passionate words or blows from the tutor fill the child's mind with terror and affrightment, which immediately takes it wholly up, and leaves no room for other impressions. I believe there is nobody, that reads this, but may recollect, what disorder hasty or imperious words from his parents or teachers have caused in his thoughts; how for the time it has turned his brains, so that he scarce knew what was said by, or to him: he presently lost the sight of what he was upon; his mind was filled with disorder and confusion, and in that state was no longer capable of attention to anything else.

It is true, parents and governors ought to settle and establish their authority, by an awe over the minds of those under their tuition; and to rule them by that: but when they have got an ascendant over them, they should use it with great moderation, and not make themselves such scarecrows, that their scholars should always tremble in their sight. Such an austerity may make their government easy to themselves but of very little use to their pupils. It is impossible children should learn anything, whilst their thoughts are possessed and disturbed with any passion, especially fear, which makes the strongest impression on their yet tender and weak spirits. Keep the mind in an easy calm temper, when you would have it receive your instructions, or any increase of knowledge. It is as impossible to draw fair and regular characters on a trembling mind, as on a shaking paper.

The great skill of a teacher is to get and keep the attention of his scholar: whilst he has that, he is sure to advance as fast as the learner's abilities will carry him; and without that, all his bustle and pother will be to little or no purpose. To attain this, he should make the child comprehend (as much as may be) the usefulness of what he teaches him; and let him see, by what he has learned, that he can do something which he could not do before; something which gives him some power and real advantage above others, who are ignorant of it. To this he should add sweetness in all his instructions; and by a certain tenderness in his whole carriage, make the child sensible that he loves him, and designs nothing but his good; the only way to beget love in the child, which will make him hearken to his lessons, and relish what he teaches him.

Nothing but obstinacy should meet with any imperiousness or rough usage. All other faults should be corrected with a gentle hand; and kind encouraging words will work better and more effectually upon a willing mind, and even prevent a good deal of that perverseness, which rough and imperious usage often produces in well-disposed and generous minds. It is true, obstinacy and wilful neglects must be mastered, even though it costs blows to do it: but I am apt to think perverseness in the pupils is often the effect of forwardness in the tutor; and that most children would seldom have deserved blows, if needless and misapplied roughness had not taught them ill-nature, and given them an aversion to their teacher, and all that comes from him.

Inadvertency, forgetfulness, unsteadiness, and wandering of thought, are the natural faults of childhood: and therefore, when they are not observed to be wilful, are to be mentioned softly, and gained upon by time. If every slip of this kind produces anger and rating, the occasions of rebuke and corrections will return so often, that the tutor will be a constant terror and uneasiness to his pupils; which one thing is enough to hinder their profiting by his lessons, and to defeat all his methods of instruction.

Let the awe he has got upon their minds be so tempered with the constant marks of tenderness and good will, that affection may spur them to their duty, and make them find a pleasure in complying with his dictates. This will bring them with satisfaction to their tutor; make them hearken to him, as to one who is their friend, that cherishes them, and takes pains for their good; this will keep their thoughts easy and free, whilst they are with him, the only temper wherein the mind is capable of receiving new information, and of admitting into itself those impressions, which if not taken and retained, all that they and their teacher do together is lost labour; there is much uneasiness, and little learning. . . .

177. But under whose care soever a child is put to be taught, during the tender and flexible years of his life, this is certain, it should be one who thinks Latin and language the least part of education; one, who knowing how much virtue, and a well-tempered soul, is to be preferred to any sort of learning or language, makes it his chief business to form the mind of his scholars, and give that a right disposition: which, if once got, though all the rest should be neglected, would, in due time, produce all the rest; and which if it be not got, and settled, so as to keep out ill and vicious habits, languages and sciences, and all the other accomplishments of education, will be to no purpose, but to make the worse or more dangerous man. . . .

216. Though I am now come to a conclusion of what obvious remarks have suggested to me concerning education, I would not have it thought, that I look on it as a just treatise on this subject. There are a thousand other things that may need consideration; especially if one should take in the various tempers, different inclinations, and particular defaults, that are to be found in children; and prescribe proper remedies. The variety is so great, that it would require a volume; nor would that reach it. Each man's mind has some peculiarity, as well as his face, that distinguishes him from all others; and there are possibly scarce two children, who can be conducted by exactly the same method. Besides that, I think a prince, a nobleman, and an ordinary gentleman's son, should have different ways of breeding. But having had here only some general views, in reference to the main end and aims in education, and those designed for a gentleman's son, whom, being then very little, I considered only as white paper, or wax, to be moulded and fashioned as one pleases;

I have touched little more than those heads, which I judged necessary for the breeding of a young gentleman of his condition in general; and have now published these my occasional thoughts, with this hope, that, though this be far from being a complete treatise on this subject, or such as that everyone may find what will just fit his child in it; yet it may give some small light to those, whose concern for their dear little ones makes them so irregularly bold, that they dare venture to consult their own reason, in the education of their children, rather than wholly to rely upon old custom.

4

Jean Jacques Rousseau

In his *Emile* the Swiss-French philosopher Jean Jacques Rousseau (1712–1778) presents a remarkable number of powerful ideas. The book's insight into the distinctive character of a child's mind, its insistence that a child be treated as a valued person, and its stress on the importance of motivating a student to want to learn combine to make this work a landmark in the history of educational thought.

Rousseau's style of writing is vivid and seemingly easy to comprehend; yet some of his ideas may be difficult to make consistent. For example, he urges that children should be given "absolutely no orders of any kind" but in the same paragraph insists that "refusals be irrevocable."

The most serious challenge in defending Rousseau's overall position is to make coherent his central claim that nature provides the goals of education. For what is meant by the claim that a particular course of action is "natural"? According to the most obvious sense of that term, any human action is natural, since it is not miraculous but according to the laws of nature.

Rousseau was not the first thinker to try to utilize the notion of the "natural" as a justification for a social policy. Plato argued that each person ought to be occupied with the one task "natural" to that individual, although how the choice of this task was to be determined is unclear. And Aristotle, in one of his less sublime moments, defended slavery on the grounds that it was "nature's intention" for this institution to exist, although how he discovered this "intention" remains a mystery. A similar problem may beset Rousseau's claim that men and women ought not have the same education, since they are essentially different in character and temperament.

In any case, Rousseau's *Emile* remains one of the most influential books in philosophy of education and continues to provide a rich source of wisdom about teaching and learning.

Emile*
BOOK I

Everything is good as it comes from the hands of the Maker of the world but degenerates once it gets into the hands of man. Man makes one land yield the products of another, disregards differences of climates, elements and seasons, mutilates his dogs and horses, perverts and disfigures everything. Not content to leave anything as nature has made it, he must needs shape man himself to his notions, as he does the trees in his garden.

But under present conditions, human beings would be even worse than they are without this fashioning. A man left entirely to himself from birth would be the most misshapen of creatures. Prejudices, authority, necessity, example, the social institutions in which we are immersed, would crush out nature in him without putting anything in its place. He would fare like a shrub that has grown up by chance in the middle of a road, and got trampled underfoot by the passers-by.

Plants are fashioned by cultivation, men by education. We are born feeble and need strength; possessing nothing, we need assistance; beginning without intelligence, we need judgment. All that we lack at birth and need when grown up is given us by education. This education comes to us from nature, from men, or from things. The internal development of our faculties and organs is the education of nature. The use we learn to make of this development is the education of men. What comes to us from our experience of the things that affect us is the education of things. Each of us therefore is fashioned by three kinds of teachers. When their lessons are at variance the pupil is badly educated, and is never at peace with himself. When they coincide and lead to a common goal he goes straight to his mark and lives single-minded. Now, of these three educations the one due to nature is independent of us, and the one from things only depends on us to a limited extent. The education that comes from men is the only one within our control, and even that is doubtful. Who can hope to have the entire direction of the words and deeds of all the people around a child?

It is only by good luck that the goal can be reached. What is this goal? It is nature's own goal. Since the three educations must work together for a perfect result, the one that cannot be modified determines the course of the other two. But perhaps "nature" is too vague a word. We must try to fix its meaning. Nature, it has been said, is only habit. Is that really so? Are there not habits which are formed under pressure, leaving the original nature unchanged? One example is the habit of plants which have been forced away from the upright direction. When set free, the plant retains the bent forced upon it; but the sap has

*Reprinted by permission of the publisher from William Boyd, ed., *The Emile of Jean Jacques Rousseau: Selections* (New York: Teachers College Press, © 1962 by Teachers College, Columbia University. All rights reserved.), various selections.

not changed its first direction and any new growth the plant makes returns to the vertical. It is the same with human inclinations. So long as there is no change in conditions the inclinations due to habits, however unnatural, remain unchanged, but immediately the restraint is removed the habit vanishes and nature reasserts itself.

We are born capable of sensation and from birth are affected in diverse ways by the objects around us. As soon as we become conscious of our sensations we are inclined to seek or to avoid the objects which produce them: at first, because they are agreeable or disagreeable to us, later because we discover that they suit or do not suit us, and ultimately because of the judgments we pass on them by reference to the idea of happiness or perfection we get from reason. These inclinations extend and strengthen with the growth of sensibility and intelligence, but under the pressure of habit they are changed to some extent with our opinions. The inclinations before this change are what I call our nature. In my view everything ought to be in conformity with these original inclinations.

There would be no difficulty if our three educations were merely different. But what is to be done when they are at cross purposes? Consistency is plainly impossible when we seek to educate a man for others, instead of for himself. If we have to combat either nature or society, we must choose between making a man or making a citizen. We cannot make both. There is an inevitable conflict of aims, from which come two opposing forms of education: the one communal and public, the other individual and domestic.

To get a good idea of communal education, read Plato's *Republic*. It is not a political treatise, as those who merely judge books by their titles think. It is the finest treatise on education ever written. Communal education in this sense, however, does not and can not now exist. There are no longer any real fatherlands and therefore no real citizens. The words "fatherland" and "citizen" should be expunged from modern languages.

I do not regard the instruction given in those ridiculous establishments called colleges as "public," any more than the ordinary kind of education. This education makes for two opposite goals and reaches neither. The men it turns out are double-minded, seemingly concerned for others, but really only concerned for themselves. From this contradiction comes the conflict we never cease to experience in ourselves. We are drawn in different directions by nature and by man, and take a midway path that leads us nowhere. In this state of confusion we go through life and end up with our contradictions unsolved, never having been any good to ourselves or to other people.

There remains then domestic education, the education of nature. But how will a man who has been educated entirely for himself get on with other people? If there were any way of combining in a single person the twofold aim, and removing the contradictions of life, a great obstacle to happiness would be removed. But before passing judgment on this kind of man it would be necessary to follow his development and see him fully formed. It would be necessary, in word, to make the acquaintance of the natural man. This is the subject of our quest in this book.

What can be done to produce this very exceptional person? In point of fact all we have to do is to prevent anything being done. When it is only a matter of sailing against the wind it is enough to tack, but when the sea runs high and you want to stay where you are, you must throw out the anchor.

In the social order where all stations in life are fixed, every one needs to be brought up for his own station. The individual who leaves the place for which he has been trained is useless in any other. In Egypt, where the son was obliged to follow in his father's footsteps, education had at least an assured aim: in our country where social ranks are fixed, but the men in them are constantly changing, nobody knows whether he is doing his son a good or a bad turn when he educates him for his own rank.

In the natural order where all men are equal, manhood is the common vocation. One who is well educated for that will not do badly in the duties that pertain to it. The fact that my pupil is intended for the army, the church or the bar, does not greatly concern me. Before the vocation determined by his parents comes the call of nature to the life of human kind. Life is the business I would have him learn. When he leaves my hands, I admit he will not be a magistrate, or a soldier, or a priest. First and foremost, he will be a man. All that a man must be he will be when the need arises, as well as anyone else. Whatever the changes of fortune he will always be able to find a place for himself. . . .

A man of high rank once suggested that I should be his son's tutor. But having had experience already I knew myself unfit and I refused. Instead of the difficult task of educating a child, I now undertake the easier task of writing about it. To provide details and examples in illustration of my views and to avoid wandering off into airy speculations, I propose to set forth the education of Emile, an imaginary pupil, from birth to manhood. I take for granted that I am the right man for the duties in respect of age, health, knowledge and talents.

A tutor is not bound to his charge by the ties of nature as the father is, and so is entitled to choose his pupil, especially when as in this case he is providing a model for the education of other children. I assume that Emile is no genius, but a boy of ordinary ability: that he is the inhabitant of some temperate climate, since it is only in temperate climates that human beings develop completely; that he is rich, since it is only the rich who have need of the natural education that would fit them to live under all conditions; that he is to all intents and purposes an orphan, whose tutor having undertaken the parents' duties will also have their right to control all the circumstances of his upbringing; and, finally, that he is a vigorous, healthy, well-built child. . . .

We are born with a capacity for learning, but know nothing and distinguish nothing. The mind is cramped by imperfect half-formed organs and has not even the consciousness of its own existence. The movements, and cries of the new born child are purely mechanical, quite devoid of understanding and will.

Children's first sensations are wholly in the realm of feeling. They are only aware of pleasure and pain. With walking and grasp undeveloped, it takes a long time for them to construct the representative sensations which acquaint them with external objects; but even before these objects reach up to and depart from their eyes, if one may put it so, the recurrence of the sensations begins to subject them to the bondage of habit. You see their eyes always turning to the light and unconsciously taking the direction from which the light comes, so that you have to be careful to keep them facing the light in order to prevent them acquiring a squint or becoming cross-eyed. Similarly, they have to be accustomed quite early to darkness, or soon they will wail and cry if they find themselves in the dark. Food and sleep, if too precisely organised, come to be necessary at definite intervals, and soon the desire for them is due not to need but to habit. Or rather, habit adds a new need to that of nature. That is something to be avoided.

The only habit the child should be allowed to acquire is to contract none. He should not be carried on one arm more than the other or allowed to make use of one hand more than the other, or to want to eat, sleep or do things at definite hours; and he should be able to remain alone by night or day. Prepare in good time for the reign of freedom and the exercise of his powers, by allowing his body its natural habits and accustoming him always to be his own master and follow the dictates of his will as soon as he has a will of his own. . . .

BOOK II

. . . The more children can do for themselves the less help they need from other people. Added strength brings with it the sense needed for its direction. With the coming of self-consciousness at this second stage individual life really begins. Memory extends the sense of identity over all the moments of the child's existence. He becomes one and the same person, capable of happiness or sorrow. From this point on it is essential to regard him as a moral being. . . .

Your first duty is to be humane. Love childhood. Look with friendly eyes on its games, its pleasures, its amiable dispositions. Which of you does not sometimes look back regretfully on the age when laughter was ever on the lips and the heart free of care? Why steal from the little innocents the enjoyment of a time that passes all too quickly?

Already I hear the clamour of the false wisdom that regards the present as of no account and is for ever chasing a future which flees as we advance. This is the time to correct the evil inclinations of mankind, you reply. Suffering should be increased in childhood when it is least felt, to reduce it at the age of reason. But how do you know that all the fine lessons with which you oppress the feeble mind of the child will not do more harm than good? Can you prove that these bad tendencies you profess to be correcting are not due to your own misguided efforts rather than to nature?

If we are to keep in touch with reality we must never forget what befits our condition. Humanity has its place in the scheme of things. Childhood has its place in the scheme of human life. We must view the man as a man, and the child as a child. The best way to ensure human well-being is to give each person his place in life and keep him there, regulating the passions in accordance with the individual constitution. The rest depends on external factors without our control.

We can never know absolute good or evil. Everything in this life is mixed. We never experience a pure sentiment, or remain in the same state for two successive moments. Weal and woe are common to us all, but in differing measure. The happiest man is the one who suffers least: the most miserable the one who has least pleasure. Always the sufferings outweigh the enjoyments. The felicity of man here below is therefore a negative state, to be measured by the fewness of his ills. Every feeling of pain is inseparable from the desire to escape from it: every idea of pleasure inseparable from the desire for its enjoyment. Privation is implicit in desire, and all privations are painful. Consequently unhappiness consists in the excess of desire over power. A conscious being whose powers equalled his desires would be absolutely happy.

In what then does the human wisdom that leads to true happiness consist? Not simply in the diminution of desires, for if they fell below our power to achieve, part of our faculties would be unemployed and our entire being would not be satisfied. Neither does it consist in the extension of our faculties, for a disproportionate increase in our desires would only make us more miserable. True happiness comes with equality of power and will. The only man who gets his own way is the one who does not need another's help to get it: from which it follows that the supreme good is not authority, but freedom. The true freeman wants only what he can get, and does only what pleases him. This is my fundamental maxim. Apply it to childhood and all the rules of education follow.

There are two kinds of dependence: dependence on things, which is natural, and dependence on men, which is social. Dependence on things being nonmoral is not prejudicial to freedom and engenders no vices: dependence on men being capricious engenders them all. The only cure for this evil in society would be to put the law in place of the individual, and to arm the general will with a real power that made it superior to every individual will.

Keep the child in sole dependence on things and you will follow the natural order in the course of his education. Put only physical obstacles in the way of indiscreet wishes and let his punishments spring from his own actions. Without forbidding wrong-doing, be content to prevent it. Experience or impotence apart from anything else should take the place of law for him. Satisfy his desires, not because of his demands but because of his needs. He should have no consciousness of obedience when he acts, nor of mastery when someone acts for him. Let him experience liberty equally in his actions and in yours. ·

Be specially careful not to give the child empty formulae of politeness, to serve as magic words for subjecting his surroundings to his will and getting him what he wants at once. For my part I am less afraid of rudeness than of arrogance in Emile, and would rather have him say "Do this" as a request, than "Please" as a command. I am not concerned with the words he uses, but with what they imply.

Excessive severity and excessive indulgence are equally to be avoided. If you let children suffer you endanger health and life. If you are over-careful in shielding them from trouble of every kind you are laying up much unhappiness for the future: you are withdrawing them from the common lot of man, to which they must one day become subject in spite of you.

You will tell me that I am making the same mistake as those bad fathers whom I blamed for sacrificing their children's happiness for the sake of a distant time that may never come. That is not so, for the liberty I allow my pupil amply compensates for the slight hardships I let him experience. I see little scamps playing in the snow, blue and stiff with cold and scarcely able to move a finger. There is nothing to hinder them warming themselves, but they don't. If they were forced to come indoors they would feel the rigours of constraint a hundred times more than the cold. What then is there to complain about? Am I making the child unhappy by exposing him to hardships which he is quite willing to endure? I am doing him good at the present moment by leaving him free. I am doing him good in the future by arming him against inevitable evils. If he had to choose between being my pupil or yours, do you think he would hesitate for an instant?

The surest way to make your child unhappy is to accustom him to get everything he wants. With desire constantly increasing through easy satisfaction, lack of power will sooner or later force you to a refusal in spite of yourself, and the unwonted refusal will cause him deeper annoyance than the mere lack of what he desires. First he will want the stick in your hand, then the bird that flies past, then the star that shines above him. Everything he sees he will want: and unless you were God you could never hope to satisfy him. How could such a child possibly be happy? Happy! He is a despot, at once the meanest of slaves and the most wretched of creatures. Let us get back to the primitive way. Nature made children to be loved and helped, not to be obeyed and feared. Is there in the world a being more feeble and unhappy, more at the mercy of his environment, more in need of pity and protection than a child? Surely then there is nothing more offensive or more unseemly than the sight of a dictatorial headstrong child, issuing orders to those around him and assuming the tone of a master to people without whom he would perish.

On the other hand, it should be obvious that with the many restrictions imposed on children by their own weakness it is barbarous for us to add subjection to our caprices to the natural subjection, and take from them such limited liberty as they possess. Social servitude will come with the age of reason. Why anticipate it by a domestic servitude? Let one moment of life be free from this yoke which nature has not imposed, and leave the child to the enjoyment of his natural liberty.

I come back to practice. I have already said that what your child gets he should get because he needs it, not because he asks for it, and that he should never act from obedience but only from necessity. For this reason, the words "obey" and "command" must be banished from his vocabulary, still more the words "duty" and "obligation"; but "force," "necessity," "weakness" and "constraint" should be emphasised. It is impossible to form any idea of moral facts or social relations before the age of reason. Consequently the use of terms which express such ideas should as far as possible be avoided, for fear the child comes to attach to these words false ideas which cannot or will not be eradicated at a later time.

"Reason with children" was Locke's chief maxim. It is the one most popular today, but it does not seem to me justified by success. For my part I do not see any children more stupid than those who have been much reasoned with. Of all the human faculties, reason which may be said to be compounded of all the rest develops most slowly and with greatest difficulty. Yet it is reason that people want to use in the development of the first faculties. A reasonable man is the masterwork of a good education: and we actually pretend to be educating children by means of reason! That is beginning at the end. If children appreciated reason they would not need to be educated.

Instead of appealing to reason, say to the child: "You must not do that!" "Why not?" "Because it is wrong." "Why is it wrong?" "Because it is forbidden." "Why is it forbidden?" "Because it is wrong." That is the inevitable circle. To distinguish right from wrong and appreciate the reason for the duties of man is beyond a child's powers.

Nature wants children to be children before they are men. If we deliberately depart from this order we shall get premature fruits which are neither ripe nor well flavoured and which soon decay. We shall have youthful sages and grown up children. Childhood has ways of seeing, thinking and feeling peculiar to itself: nothing can be more foolish than to seek to substitute our ways for them. I should as soon expect a child of ten to be five feet in height as to be possessed of judgment.

Treat your pupil according to his age. Begin by putting him in his place and keep him in it so firmly that he will not think of leaving it. Then he will practice the most important lesson of wisdom before he knows what wisdom is. Give him absolutely no orders of any kind. Do not even let him imagine that you claim any authority over him. Let him only know that he is weak and you are strong, and that therefore he is at your mercy. Quite early let him feel the heavy yoke which nature imposes on man, the yoke of the necessity in things as opposed to human caprice. If there is anything he should not do, do not forbid him, but prevent him without explanation or reasoning. Whatever you give, give at the first word without prayers or entreaty, and above all without conditions. Give with pleasure, refuse with regret, but let your refusals be irrevocable. Your "No" once uttered must be a wall of brass which the child will stop trying to batter down once he has exhausted his strength on it five or six times.

It is strange that all the time people have been bringing up children nobody has thought of any instruments for their direction but emulation, jealousy, envy, vanity, greed or base fear; most dangerous passions all of them, sure to corrupt the soul. Foolish teachers think they are working wonders when they are simply making the children wicked in the attempt to teach them about goodness. Then they announce gravely: such is man. Yes, such is the man you have made. All the instruments have been tried but one, and that as it happens is the only one that can succeed: well regulated liberty.

Avoid verbal lessons with your pupil. The only kind of lesson he should get is that of experience. Never inflict any punishment, for he does not know what it is to be at fault. Being devoid of all morality in his actions he can do nothing morally wrong, nothing that deserves either punishment or reprimand.

Let us lay it down as an incontestable principle that the first impulses of nature are always right. There is no original perversity in the human heart. Of every vice we can say how it entered and whence it came. The only passion natural to man is self-love, or self-esteem in a broad sense. This self-esteem has no necessary reference to other people. In so far as it relates to ourselves it is good and useful. It only becomes good or bad in the social application we make of it. Until reason, which is the guide of self-esteem, makes its appearance, the child should not do anything because he is seen or heard by other people, but only do what nature demands of him. Then he will do nothing but what is right.

I do not mean to say that he will never do any mischief: that he will never hurt himself, for example, or break a valuable bit of furniture. He might do a great deal that was bad without being bad, because the wrong action depends on harmful intention and that he will never have. When children are left free to blunder it is better to remove everything that would make blundering costly, and not leave anything fragile and precious within reach. Their room should be furnished with plain solid furniture, without mirrors, china, or ornaments. My Emile whom I am bringing up in the country will have nothing in his room to distinguish it from that of a peasant. If in spite of your precautions the child manages to upset things and break some useful articles, do not punish or scold him for your own negligence. Do not even let him guess that he has annoyed you. Behave as if the furniture had got broken of itself. Consider you have done very well if you can avoid saying anything. . . .

May I set forth at this point the most important and the most useful rule in all education? It is not to save time but to waste it. The most dangerous period in human life is that between birth and the age of twelve. This is the age when errors and vices sprout, before there is any instrument for their destruction. When the instrument is available the roots have gone too deep to be extracted. The mind should remain inactive till it has all its faculties.

It follows from this that the first education should be purely negative. It consists not in teaching virtue and truth, but in preserving the heart from vice and the mind from error. If you could do nothing and let nothing be done, so that your pupil came to the age of twelve strong and healthy but unable to distinguish his right hand from his left, the eyes of his understanding would be open to reason from your very first lessons. In the absence of both prejudices and habits there would be nothing in him to oppose the effects of your teaching and care.

Do the opposite of what is usually done and you will almost always be right. Fathers and teachers, anxious to make a learned doctor instead of a child, correct, reprove, flatter, threaten, instruct, reason. There is a better way. Be reasonable and do not reason with your pupil. It is a mistake to try to get him to approve of things he dislikes. To bring reason into what is disagreeable at this stage will only discredit it. Exercise body, senses, powers, but keep the mind inactive as long as possible. Let childhood ripen in children.

The practical value of this method is confirmed by consideration of the distinctive genius of the child. Each mind has a form of its own in conformity with which it must be directed. If you are a wise man you will observe your pupil carefully before saying a word to him. In the first instance leave his essential character full liberty to manifest itself, in order to get a better view of his whole personality.

But where are we to place this child of ours when we are bringing him up like an automaton unaffected by anything outside himself? Must we keep him up in the moon or in some desert island? Are we to separate him from all human beings? Will he not see other children of his own age? Will he not see his relatives, his neighbours, his nurse, his lackey, even his tutor, who will assuredly be no angel? This is a very substantial objection. I have never pretended that it was easy to make education natural. Perhaps the difficulties are insurmountable. I do not say that anyone will reach the goal I have set, but I do say that the one who comes nearest will succeed best.

Remember that before you dare undertake the making of a man you must be a man yourself. While the child is as yet without knowledge of the world there is still time to make sure that everything around him is proper for him to see. To ensure this you must make yourself worthy of the respect and love of everybody, so that all will seek to please you. You will not be the child's master unless you are master of everything that surrounds him. This is another reason for bringing Emile up in the country, far from the filthy morals of the towns. The glitter of town life is seductive and corrupting while the gross vices of country people are more likely to repel than to seduce. In a village the tutor will be in much better control of the objects he wants the child to see. If he is helpful to the people, they will all be eager to oblige him and appear to his pupil as if they were in reality what the master would like them to be. If they do not correct their vices, they will at any rate refrain from scandalous behaviour, and that is all that is wanted for our purpose.

Be simple and hold yourself in check, you zealous teachers. Never be in a hurry to act. So far as you can, refrain from a good instruction for fear of giving a bad one. Since you cannot prevent the child learning from the examples set by others, confine your care to impressing these examples on his mind in the form which suits him best. The impetuous passions have a great effect on the child who witnesses them. Anger is so noisy in its expression that it cannot but be noticed by any one near. Here is obviously a chance for a pedagogue to concoct a fine discourse. But no fine discourses for you: not a word. Leave the child to come to you. Astounded by the sight of an angry man he will be sure to ask questions. Your answer is simple. It is suggested by the very things that have struck the senses. He sees an inflamed countenance, flashing eyes, threatening gestures; he hears cries: all signs that something is wrong with the body. Tell him quietly: 'The poor man is ill, he has an attack of fever.' Such an idea if given at the proper time will have as salutary effects as the most long-winded discourse, and it will have useful applications later on. On this way of thinking you are entitled, if the necessity arises, to treat a rebellious child as an invalid. You can confine him to his room, perhaps send him to bed, put him on a diet, and so make him afraid of his budding vices without him ever regarding the severity you are perhaps forced to use for their cure as a punishment. And should it happen that in a moment of heat you lose your own composure and moderation do not try to hide your faults. Just say to him frankly with a tender reproach: 'You have made me ill.'

My plan is not to go into details, but only to set forth general principles and give examples in difficult cases. I do not think it is possible to bring up a child to the age of twelve in society without giving him some idea of the relations of man to man and the moral aspects of human conduct. The best one can do is to postpone these necessary notions as long as possible, and when they can be no longer postponed to limit them to the immediate requirement.

Our first duties are to ourselves. Self is the centre of the primitive sentiments. The natural impulses all relate in the first instance to our preservation and well-being. Hence the first sentiment of justice does not come to us from what we owe others, but from what others owe us. It is another of the blunders of the ordinary education to talk to children about their duties, and say nothing about their rights. This takes them beyond their comprehension and their interest.

The first idea a child should have given him is not that of liberty but of property. To get that he must possess something of his own. To tell him that he owns his clothes, his furniture, his toys, means nothing to him. Though he uses them he does not know why or how they are his. He must be taken back to the origin of property.

The easiest way for him to learn about property is through the work he does in the garden in imitation of the gardener. He plants beans and when they come up they 'belong' to him. To explain what that term means I make him feel that he has put his time, his work, his effort, himself into them. Then one day he finds his beans dug up by Robert the gardener. The ground 'belongs' to the gardener and he must come to an arrangement with the man before he can raise beans again. The destructive child has to learn his lesson in another way. He breaks the windows of his room, Let the wind blow on him night and day and do not worry about him catching cold. It is better for him to catch cold than to be a fool. If he goes on breaking windows shut him up in a dark room without windows. The time will come when he has learned what property means and he is willing to respect other people's belongings.

We are now in the moral world and the door is open to vice. With conventions and duties come deceit and lying. As soon as we can do what we ought not to do, we seek to hide our misdeeds. With the failure to prevent evildoing the question of punishment arises. On fact there is never any need to inflict punishment as such on children. It should always come to them as the natural consequence of their bad conduct. In the case of lying, for example, you need not punish them because they have lied, but so arrange that if they lie they will not be believed even when they speak the truth, and will be accused of bad things they have not done.

Actually children's lies are all the work of their teachers. They try to teach them to tell the truth and in doing so teach them to lie. As for those of us who only give our pupils lessons of a practical kind and prefer them to be good rather than clever, we never demand the truth from them for fear they should hide it, and we never exact any promise lest they be tempted to break it. If something wrong has been done in my absence and I do not know the culprit, I take care not to accuse Emile or to ask: 'Was it you?' Nothing could be more indiscreet than such a question, especially if the child is guilty. If he thinks you know he has done wrong you will seem to be trying to trap him and the idea will turn him against you. If he thinks you do not know he will ask: 'Why should I reveal my fault?' and the imprudent question will be a temptation to lying.

What has been said about lying applies in many respects to all the other duties prescribed for children. To make them pious you take them to church where they are bored. You make them gabble prayers till they look forward to the happy time when they will no longer pray to God. You make them give alms to inspire charity, as if almsgiving were a matter for children only. Drop these pretences, teachers. Be virtuous and good yourselves, and the examples you set will impress themselves on your pupils' memories, and in due season will enter their hearts. . . .

I have now brought my pupils through the land of the sensations right up to the bounds of childish reason. The first step beyond this should take him towards manhood. But before entering on this new stage let us cast our eyes backward for a moment on the one we have traversed. Each age and state of life has its own proper perfection, its own distinctive maturity. People sometimes speak about a complete man. Let us think rather of a complete child. This vision will be new for us and perhaps not less agreeable.

When I picture to myself a boy of ten or twelve, healthy, strong and well built for his age, only pleasant thoughts arise in me, whether for his present or for his future. I see him bright, eager, vigorous, care-free, completely absorbed in the present, rejoicing in abounding vitality. I see him in the years ahead using senses, mind and power as they develop from day to day. I view him as a child and he pleases me. I think of him as a man and he pleases me still more. His warm blood seems to heat my own. I feel as if I were living in his life and am rejuvenated by his vivacity.

The clock strikes and all is changed. In an instant his eye grows dull and his merriment disappears. No more mirth, no more games! A severe, hard-faced man takes him by the hand, says gravely, "Come away, sir," and leads him off. In the room they enter I get a glimpse of books. Books! What a cheerless equipment for his age. As he is dragged away in silence, he casts a regretful look around him. His eyes are swollen with tears he dare not shed, his heart heavy with sighs he dare not utter.

Come, my happy pupil, and console us for the departure of the wretched boy. Here comes Emile, and at his approach I have a thrill of joy in which I see he shares. It is his friend and comrade, the companion of his games to whom he comes. His person, his bearing, his countenance reveal assurance and contentment. Health glows in his face. His firm step gives him an air of vigour. His complexion is refined without being effeminate; sun and wind have put on it the honourable imprint of his sex. His eyes are still unlighted by the fires of sentiment and have all their native serenity. His manner is open and free without the least insolence or vanity.

His ideas are limited but precise. If he knows nothing by heart, he knows a great deal by experience. If he is not as good a reader in books as other children, he reads better in the book of nature. His mind is not in his tongue but in his head. He has less memory but more judgment. He only knows one language, but he understands what he says; and if he does not talk as well as other children he can do things better than they can.

Habit, routine and custom mean nothing to him. What he did yesterday has no effect on what he does today. He never follows a fixed rule and never accepts authority or example. He only does or says what seems good to himself. For this reason you must not expect stock speeches or studied manners from him but just the faithful expression of his ideas and the conduct that comes from his inclinations.

You will find in him a few moral notions relating to his own situation, but not being an active member of society he has none relating to manhood. Talk to him about liberty, property and even convention, and he may understand you thus far. But speak to him about duty and obedience, and he will not know what you mean. Command him to do something, and he will pay no heed. But say to him: "If you will do me this favour, I will do the same for you another time"; and immediately he will hasten to oblige. For his part, if he needs any help he will ask the first person he meets as a matter of course. If you grant his request he will not thank you, but will feel that he has contracted a debt. If you refuse, he will neither complain nor insist. He will only say: "It could not be done." He does not rebel against necessity once he recognises it.

Work and play are all the same to him. His games are his occupations: he is not aware of any difference. He goes into everything he does with a pleasing interest and freedom. It is indeed a charming spectacle to see a nice boy of this age with open smiling countenance, doing the most serious things in his play or profoundly occupied with the most frivolous amusements.

Emile has lived a child's life and has arrived at the maturity of childhood, without any sacrifice of happiness in the achievement of his own perfection. He has acquired all the reason possible for his age, and in doing so has been as free and as happy as his nature allowed him to be. If by chance the fatal scythe were to cut down the flower of our hopes we would not have to bewail at the same time his life and his death, nor add to our griefs the memory of those we caused him. We would say that at any rate he had enjoyed his childhood and that nothing we had done had deprived him of what nature gave.

BOOK III

The whole course of life up to adolescence is a time of weakness, but there is one point during this first age of man at which strength exceeds the demands made on it by needs, and the growing creature though still absolutely weak becomes relatively strong. With needs incompletely developed, his powers more than suffice. As a man he would be very feeble: as a child he is very strong. This is the third stage of early life which for lack of a better word I continue to call childhood. It is not yet the age of puberty, but adolescence draws near.

At twelve or thirteen the child's powers develop much more rapidly than his needs. The sex passions, the most violent and terrible of all, have not yet awakened. He is indifferent to the rigours of weather and seasons, and braves them light-heartedly. His growing body heat takes the place of clothing. Appetite is his sauce, and everything nourishing tastes good. When he is tired he stretches himself out on the ground and goes to sleep. He is not troubled by imaginary wants. What people think does not trouble him. Not only is he self-sufficient but his strength goes beyond his requirements. . . .

Nevertheless, it will probably be necessary to give him a little guidance. But let it be very little, and avoid the appearance of it. If he goes wrong, do not correct his errors. Say nothing till he sees them and corrects them himself; or at most, arrange some practical situation which will make him realise things personally. If he never made mistakes he would never learn properly. In any case, the important thing is not that he should know the topography of the country, but that he should be able to get his information for himself. It does not matter greatly whether he has maps in his head, provided he knows what they represent and has a clear idea of the art of their construction. . . .

It is not a question of teaching him the sciences, but of giving him a taste for them, and methods of acquiring them when this taste is better developed. This is most certainly a fundamental principle in all good education. . . .

With the child's advance in intelligence other considerations compel greater care in the choice of his occupations. As soon as he comes to know himself well enough to understand what constitutes happiness for him and can judge what is fitting and what is not, he is in a position to appreciate the difference between work and play, and to regard play as relaxation from work. Thereafter matters of real utility may enter into his studies and lead him to apply himself more diligently than he did to mere amusements. The law of necessity, always operative, soon teaches man to do what he does not like, in order to avoid evils he would like still less. Such is the practice of foresight; and from foresight, well or ill directed, comes all the wisdom or all the unhappiness of mankind.

When children foresee their needs their intelligence has made real progress. They begin to know the value of time. For this reason, it is important to accustom them to employ their time on objects of an obvious utility that are within their understanding. All that pertains to the moral order and to social usage should not be put before them yet, because it does not mean anything for them. Why do you want to set a child to the studies of an age he may never reach, to the detriment of studies suited for the present? But you will ask: 'Will there be time for him to learn what he ought to know when the occasion for its use arises?' That I do not know. What I do know is that it is impossible for him to learn it sooner. Our real teachers are experience and feeling, and no one ever appreciates what is proper to manhood till he enters into its situations. A child knows that he is destined to become a man. Such of the ideas of adult life as are within his comprehension are occasions of instruction for him, but he ought to be kept in absolute ignorance of all the rest. This whole book is one long demonstration of this educational principle.

As soon as we have managed to give our pupil some idea of what the word 'utility' means, we have another strong hold on him. This word makes a deep impression on him, provided it has meaning for him on his own age level and he can see its bearing on his present well being. 'What is the good of that?' Henceforth this is the sacred question, the decisive question between him and me, in all the situations of our life. This is my infallible response to all his questions, and it serves to check the multitude of foolish queries with which children constantly bother people. Note what a powerful instrument I am putting into your hands for dealing with your pupil. Since he does not know the reason of anything, you can reduce him to silence at will while you with your knowledge and experience can show him the use of all you put before him. But make no mistake about it: when you ask him this question you are teaching him to put it to you in his turn. You can be sure that in future he will never fail to ask about anything you tell him: 'What is the good of it?'

I do not like explanatory speeches. Young people pay little attention to them and rarely remember them. Give them facts. I cannot say often enough, that we allow too great power to words. With our babbling education we only make babblers.

Suppose, when I am studying with my pupil the course of the sun and how to find our direction, he suddenly stops me to ask what good purpose all this serves. What a fine discourse I could give him—especially if people were listening in to our conversation—about the use of travel, the advantages of commerce, the special products of different regions, the customs of different peoples, the use of the calendar, the reckoning of the seasons for agriculture, the art of navigation. Politics, natural history, astronomy, even ethics and the law of nations, might enter into my explanation so as to give my pupil a great idea of all these subjects and a great desire to learn them. But not a single idea of all this would the boy understand. Unless he feared that he would be bothering me, he would ask what was the use of taking one's bearings. Actually our Emile, brought up in the country and accustomed to get ideas the hard way, would not listen to a single word of all this. At the first sentence he did not understand he would run off and leave me to perorate by myself. We must look for a more ordinary solution. My display of science is of no use to him.

When Emile wants to learn what use it is to know the position of the forest north of Montmorency, I put him off and next morning take him for a walk before breakfast. We get lost and the more we wander the more tired and hungry we become. We sit down to consider how we can get out. Crying is no use. 'Let us see your watch. What time is it?' 'It is noon,' says Emile, 'and I am so hungry.' At twelve o'clock the day before, he is reminded, we were observing the position of the forest from Montmorency. 'Did we not say that the forest was . . . ?' 'North of Montmorency,' says Emile, 'So Montmorency lies. . . .' 'South of the forest.' But we know how to find the north at midday. 'Yes,' says

Emile, 'by the direction of the shadows,' and comes to the conclusion that if we go the opposite way from the shadows we will find the town. And this we do. It is evident that astronomy is of some use after all. . . .

I hate books. They only teach us to talk about what we do not know. It is said that Hermes engraved the elements of science on pillars for fear his discoveries might perish in a deluge. If he had impressed them firmly on the human brain, they would have been kept safe there by tradition.

Is there no way of bringing together all the lessons scattered through a multitude of books and grouping them together round some common object which, even at this age, might be easy to see, interesting to follow and thought-provoking? If it were possible to invent a situation in which all the natural needs of mankind were made obvious to the mind of a child, and the ways of providing for these needs made equally clear, the simple lifelike picture of this condition of things would give the child's imagination its first training.

Eager philosopher, I see your own imagination lighting up. Do not trouble yourself. This situation has been found, and with all respect to you has been described better than you could do it, at any rate with greater truth and simplicity. Since it is essential that there should be books, there happens to be one book which in my opinion furnishes the most satisfactory treatise on natural education. This is the first book my Emile will read. For a long time it will constitute his entire library, and will always occupy an honoured place in it. It will be the text on which all our talks on the natural sciences will form a commentary. It will serve as a touchstone for our judgment as we progress, and so long as our taste remains unspoiled, it will continue to give us pleasure. What is this marvellous book? Is it Aristotle? Or Pliny? Or Buffon? Oh no, it is *Robinson Crusoe*.

Robinson Crusoe alone on his island, without the help of his fellows and the tools of the various arts, yet managing to procure food and safety, and even a measure of well-being: here is something of interest for every age, capable of being made attractive to children in a thousand ways. This condition, I admit, is not that of social man, and probably it is not to be that of Emile, but he should use it in the evaluation of all other conditions. The surest way for him to rise above prejudices and to bring his own judgments into line with the true relations of things is to put himself at the point of view of a solitary man, and to judge everything as this man would with reference to its real utility.

Rid of all its lumber, this novel, beginning with the shipwreck of Robinson near his island and concluding with the arrival of the ship that is to take him away, will furnish Emile with both amusement and instruction during the period of life under consideration. I want his head to be turned by it, and to have him busy himself unceasingly with his castle, his goats and his plantations. I want him to learn, not from books but from experience, all the things he would need to know in such a situation. I want him to think he is Robinson and imagine himself clothed in skins, with a large hat, a large sabre and all the grotesque equipment of the character, even to the umbrella he will not need. I want him to be concerned about the measures he would take if any one thing happened to be lacking, scrutinising his hero's conduct to see whether anything has been omitted or could be done better. You may be sure that he will plan a house for himself like Crusoe's. This is the veritable castle in Spain of this blessed age, when all that is required for happiness is freedom and the necessaries of life.

What an opportunity there is in this phantasy for a skilful grown-up who knows how to awaken it and use it to advantage. The child, eager to build a storehouse for his island will be more zealous to learn than the master to teach. He will concentrate on everything that is of use for the purpose. You will no longer have to direct him, only to hold him back. For the rest, let us hasten to establish him on this island while he is able to find complete happiness on it, for the day draws near when he will no longer want to live alone, and when Friday's company will not content him.

The practice of the natural arts for which a single man is sufficient leads to the pursuit of the industrial arts which call for the co-operation of many hands. The former can be practised by solitaries and savages, but the latter can only come into being in the society which they make necessary. So long as there is only physical need each man is self-sufficient. It is the introduction of luxuries that makes the sharing and differentiation of labour essential. . . .

Your main endeavour should be to keep away from your pupil all the notions of social relations which are beyond his comprehension; but when the interrelation of knowledge forces you to show him the mutual dependence of men, avoid the moral aspects and direct his attention to industry and the mechanical arts which make them useful to each other. As you take him from one workshop to another, never let him see any kind of work without putting his hand to it, and never let him leave till he knows perfectly the reason for all that he has observed. With that in view, set him an example by working yourself in the different occupations. To make him a master become an apprentice. You can be sure that he will learn more from an hour's work than he would remember after a day's explanations. . . .

Reader, do not give too much thought to the bodily activity and the skill of hand of our pupil. Consider rather the direction we are giving to his childish curiosities. Consider his senses, his inventive mind, his foresight. Consider the good head he will have. He will want to know all about everything he sees and does, and will take nothing for granted. He will refuse to learn anything until he acquires the knowledge that is implied in it. When he sees a spring made he will want to know how the steel was got from the mine. If he sees the pieces of a box put together, he will want to know how the tree was cut. When he is using a tool himself he will not fail to say of the tool he uses: "If I did not have this tool, how would I make one like it, or manage without it?"

At the beginning of this period of life we have taken advantage of the fact that our strength greatly exceeds our needs, to get away beyond ourselves. We have soared into the heavens and have surveyed the earth. We have studied the laws of nature. In a word, we have traversed the whole of our island. Now we come back gradually to our own dwelling. What is there for us to do when we have completed the study of our surroundings? We must convert them as much as we can to our own purposes. Up to this point, we have provided ourselves with all kinds of instruments without knowing which of them we will need. It may be that those which are of no use to us may be of service to other people and that we in turn may need theirs. In this way we will all find ourselves gaining by these exchanges. For this we must know the mutual needs of men; what each of us has to give and to get. Suppose there are ten men, each with ten kinds of needs, each applying himself to ten different kinds of work to provide for the necessities of life. The ten, because of differences of gift and talent, are likely to be less apt at some tasks than others, and all will be badly served when each does everything. But make a society of these ten, and let each man apply himself for his own benefit and that of the other nine to the kind of work that suits him best. Each one will profit by the talents of the others as if he personally had them all, and at the same time grow more perfect in his own line of work by constant practice. So it will come that the whole ten are perfectly provided for and will still have something left for others. This is the obvious basis of all our social institutions.

In this way the ideas of social relations take shape in the child's mind little by little, even before he becomes an active member of society himself. Emile sees that in order to have things for his own use he must have some he can exchange with other people. It is easy to lead him to feel the need for such exchanges and put himself in a position to profit by them.

As soon as he knows what life is, my first concern will be to teach him to preserve it. Up to this point I have ignored differences of station, rank or fortune, and I shall say little more about them in what follows, because man is the same in all stations. The rich man's stomach is no bigger than the poor man's, and his digestion no better. The master's arms are no longer and no stronger than the slave's. A "great" man is no greater than a man of the people. Natural needs being everywhere alike, the means of satisfying them should likewise be equal. Fit man's education to what man really is. Do you not see that if you try to fit him exclusively for one way of life you make him useless for every other? You put your trust in the existing social order and do not take into account the fact that that order is subject to inevitable revolutions, and that you can neither foresee nor prevent the revolution that may affect your children. . . .

Here is our child, ready to cease being a child and to enter on an individual life. More than ever he feels the necessity which binds him to things. After training his body and his senses, we have trained his mind and his judgment. In short, we have combined the use of his limbs with that of his faculties. We have made him an efficient thinking being and nothing further remains for us in the production of a complete man but to make him a loving, sensitive being: in fact, to perfect reason through sentiment. But before entering on this new order of things let us look back over the one we are leaving, and see where we have reached.

To begin with, our pupil had only sensations, now he has ideas: he had only feelings, now he judges; for from the comparison of several sensations, whether successive or simultaneous, and the judgment passed on them, there comes a sort of mixed or complex sensation which I call an idea. It is the particular way of forming ideas that gives its character to the human mind. A solid mind forms its ideas on real relations: a superficial one is content with appearances. Greater or less aptitude in the comparison of ideas and the discovery of relations is what makes the difference in the mental capacity of different people.

In sensation, judgment is purely passive—we feel what we feel: in perception or idea, it is active—it connects, compares, determines relations. It is never the sensation that is wrong but the judgment passed on it. The child says about the ice cream that it burns. That is a right sensation but a wrong judgment. So with the experiences of those who see a mirror for the first time, or enter a cellar at different times of the year, or dip a warm or cold hand into lukewarm water, or see the clouds passing over the moon as if they were stationary, or think the stick immersed in water is broken. All our mistakes in these cases come from judgment. Unfortunately social man is dependent on a great many things about which he has to judge. He must therefore be taught to reason correctly.

I will be told that in training the child to judge, I am departing from nature. I do not think so. Nature chooses her instruments, and makes use of them not according to opinion but according to necessity. There is a great difference between natural man living in nature and natural man living in the social state. Emile is not a savage to be banished to the deserts: he is a savage made to live in a town. He must know how to get a living in towns, and how to get on with their inhabitants, and to live with them, if not to live like them.

The best way of learning to judge correctly is to simplify our sense experiences as much as possible. To do this we must learn to check the reports of each sense by itself, over and above the check from the other senses. Then each sensation will become an idea, and this idea will always conform to the truth. This is the kind of acquirement I have tried to secure in this third stage of childhood.

Emile, who has been compelled to learn for himself and use his reason, has a limited knowledge, but the knowledge he has is his own, none of it half-known. Among the small number of things he really knows the most important is that there is much he does not know which he may one day come to know, much more that other people know that he will never know, and an infinity of things that nobody will ever know. He has a universal mind, not because of what he knows but from his faculty for acquiring knowledge: a mind open, intelligent, responsive, and (as Montaigne says) if not instructed, capable of being instructed. I am content if he knows the "wherefore" of all he does, and the "why" of all he believes.

The only knowledge Emile has at this stage is in the sphere of natural and physical facts. He does not even know the name of history, nor what metaphysics and ethics are. He knows the essential relations between man and things, but none of the moral relations between man and man. He has little ability to form general ideas or abstractions. He sees the qualities common to certain bodies without reasoning about the qualities in themselves. He knows abstract space by means of geometrical figures, and abstract quantity by means of algebraic symbols. These figures and signs are the basis of the abstractions, on which his senses rest. He does not seek to know things in themselves, but through the relations which interest him. He only judges external facts by their relation to himself, but this judgment of his is sound. Nothing fantastic or conventional enters into it. He sets most store on what is useful for him, and as he never departs from this method of evaluation, he is not swayed by accepted opinion.

Emile is hard working, temperate, patient, stable and courageous. His imagination, still unstimulated, does not exaggerate dangers. Few evils affect him and he can endure suffering calmly because he has learned not to fight against fate. As for death, he does not yet know what it is, but being accustomed to submit unresistingly to the laws of nature, he will die if he must without a struggle. To live a free man and hold human affairs lightly is the best way to prepare for death. In a word, Emile has every personal virtue. To add the social virtues he only needs to know the relations which call them into being. That knowledge his mind is now quite ready to receive.

He still thinks of himself without regard to others and is quite satisfied that others should give no thought to him. He asks nothing from other people and does not believe that he owes anything to them. Thus far he stands alone in human society. He is self-dependent and is better entitled to be so than any other person, since he is all that a child could be at his age. He has no mistaken ideas and no vices, other than those that nobody can avoid. He has a healthy body, agile limbs, a true mind free from prejudice, a free heart devoid of passion. Self-esteem, the first and most natural of all the passions, has still to awaken in him. Without disturbing anybody's peace he has lived happy, contented and free within the bounds of nature. Do you think that a child who has reached his fifteenth year like this has wasted his childhood?

BOOK IV

We are born twice over; the first time for existence, the second for life; once as human beings and later as men or as women. Up to puberty, children of the two sexes have nothing obvious to distinguish them. They are similar in features, in figure, in complexion, in voice. Girls are children, boys are children. The same name suffices for beings so much alike.

But man is not meant to remain a child for ever. At the time prescribed by nature he passes out of his childhood. As the fretting of the sea precedes the distant storm, this disturbing change is announced by the murmur of nascent passions. A change of mood, frequent tantrums, a constant unease of mind make the child hard to manage. He no longer listens to his master's voice. He is a lion in a fever. He mistrusts his guide and is averse to control.

With the moral signs of changing mood go patent physical changes. His countenance develops and takes on the imprint of a definite character. The soft slight down on his cheeks grows darker and firmer. His voice breaks, or rather, gets lost. He is neither child nor man, and he speaks like neither. His eyes, organs of the soul, which have hitherto said nothing, find language and expression as they light up with a new fire. He is becoming conscious that they can tell too much and he is learning to lower them and blush. He is disturbed for no reason whatever.

This is the second birth of which I spoke. Now is the time that man really enters into life and finds nothing alien to him. So far his guardian's responsibility has been child's play: it is only now that his task comes to have real importance. This stage at which ordinary educations end is just that when ours should begin.

The passions are the chief instruments for our preservation. The child's first sentiment is self-love, the only passion that is born with man. The second, which is derived from it, is the love he has for the people he sees ready to help him, and from this develops a kindly feeling for mankind. But with fresh needs and growing dependence on others comes the consciousness of social relations and with it the sense of duties and preferences. It is at this point that the child may become domineering, jealous, deceitful, vindictive. Self-love being concerned only with ourselves is content when our real needs are satisfied, but self-esteem which involves comparisons with other people never is and never can be content because it makes the impossible demand that others should prefer us to themselves. That is how it comes that the gentle kindly passions issue from self-love, while hate and anger spring from self-esteem. Great care and skill are required to prevent the human heart being depraved by the new needs of social life.

The proper study of man is that of his relationships. So long as he is aware of himself only as a physical being he should study himself in his relations with things. That is the task of childhood. When he comes to consciousness of himself as a moral being he should study himself in his relations with his fellows. This is the occupation of his whole life, beginning at the point we have now reached. . . .

Here it is important to take the opposite course from the one we have been following so far, and let the young man learn from other people's experience rather than his own. I would have you choose a young man's associates so that he may think well of those who live with him, and at the same time I would have you teach him to know the world so well that he may think ill of all that goes on in it. You want him to know and feel that man is naturally good, and to judge his neighbour by himself: equally, you want him to see how society corrupts men and to find in their prejudices the source of all their vices. This method, I have to admit, has its drawbacks and it is not easy to put into practice. If a young man is set to observe men too early and too close up, he will take a hateful pleasure in interpreting everything as badness and fail to see anything good in what is really good. Soon the general perversity will serve him as an excuse rather than as a warning, and he will say that if this is what man is, he himself has no wish to be different.

To get over this obstacle and bring him to an understanding of the human heart without risk of spoiling himself I would show him men in other times and places, in such a way that he can look on the scene as an outsider.

This is the time for history. By means of it he will read the hearts of men without the lessons of philosophy, and look on them as a mere spectator without prejudice and without passion: judging them, but neither their accomplice nor their accuser.

Unfortunately this study has dangers and drawbacks of various kinds. It is difficult to put one's self at a point of view from which to judge one's fellows fairly. One of the great vices of history is the portrayal of men by what is bad in them rather than by what is good. It is from revolutions and catastrophes that it derives its interest. So long as a nation grows and prospers in the calm of peaceful government, history has nothing to say about it. It only begins to tell about nations when they are no longer self-sufficient and have got mixed up in their neighbours' affairs. It only records their story when they enter on their decline. Our historians all begin where they ought to finish. Only bad men achieve fame: the good are either forgotten or held up to ridicule. Like philosophy, history always slanders mankind.

Moreover, the facts described in history never give an exact picture of what actually happened. They change form in the historian's head. They get moulded by his interests and take on the hue of his prejudices. Who can put the reader at the precise point where an event can be seen just as it took place? Ignorance or partisanship distorts everything. Without even altering a single feature a quite different face can be put on events by a broader or a narrower view of the relevant circumstances. How often a tree more or less, a rock to the right or the left, a cloud of dust blown up by the wind, have decided the outcome of a battle without anybody being aware of it! But that does not prevent the historian telling you the causes of defeat or victory with as much assurance as if he had been everywhere himself. In any case, what do the facts matter when the reason for them is unknown? And what lessons can I draw from an event when I am ignorant of the real cause of it? The historian gives me an explanation, but it is his own invention. And is not criticism itself, of which there is so much talk, only an art of guessing, the art of choosing among various lies the one most like the truth?

I will be told that historical precision is of less consequence than the truth about men and manners. So long as the human heart is well depicted, it will be said, it does not greatly matter whether events are accurately narrated or not. That is right, if the pictures are drawn close enough to nature. If, however, most of them are coloured by the historian's imagination, we are back again to the difficulty we set out to avoid, and are allowing writers an authority which has been denied the teacher. If my pupil is only to see pictures of fancy, I prefer to have them traced by my own hand. They will at least be those best suited for him.

The worst historians for a young man are those who pass judgment. Give him the facts and let him judge for himself. That is how he will learn to know men. If he is always guided by some author's judgment, he only sees through another's eyes: when he lacks these eyes he cannot see. . . .

To all these considerations must be added the fact that history is more concerned with actions than with men. It takes men at certain chosen moments when they are in full dress. It only depicts the public man when he is prepared to be seen, and does not follow him into the intimacies of friendship and private life. It is the coat rather than the person that is portrayed.

I would much rather have the study of human nature begin with the reading of the life story of individual men. In these stories the historian gets on the track of the man, and there is no escape from his scrutiny. . . .

It is true that the genius of nations, or of men in association, is very different from the character of man as an individual; and the knowledge of human nature got without examination of the form it assumes in the multitude, would be very imperfect. But it is no less true that it is necessary to begin with the study of man in order to form a judgment about men, and that one who had a complete knowledge of the dispositions of the constituent individuals might be able to foresee their joint effects in the body politic. . . .

One step more and we reach the goal. Self-esteem is a useful instrument but it has its dangers. Often it wounds the hand that employs it and rarely does good without also doing evil. Emile, comparing himself with other human beings and finding himself very fortunately situated, will be tempted to give credit to his own reason for the work of his guardian, and to attribute to his own merit the effects of his good fortune. He will say: "I am wise, and men are foolish." This is the error most to be feared, because it is the one hardest to eradicate. If choice had to be made I do not know whether I would not prefer the illusion of prejudice to the illusion of pride.

There is no remedy for vanity but experience. It is doubtful indeed if it can be cured at all; but at any rate its growth may be checked when it appears. Do not waste your time on fine arguments and try to convince an adolescent that he is a man like other men and subject to the same weaknesses. Make him feel it for himself, or he will never learn it. Once again, I have to make an exception to my own rules, by deliberately exposing my pupil to the mischances which may prove to him that he is no wiser than the rest of us. I will let flatterers get the better of him. If fools were to entice him into some extravagance or other I would let him run the risk. I will allow him to be duped by card sharpers, and leave him to be swindled by them. The only snares from which I would guard him with special care would be those of prostitutes. Actually Emile would not be readily tempted in these ways. It should be kept in mind that my constant plan is to take things at their worst. I try in the first place to prevent the vice, and then I assume its existence in order to show how it can be remedied.

The time for faults is the time for fables. Censure of an offender under cover of a fiction gives instruction without offence. The young man learns in this way that the moral of the tale is not a lie, from the truth that finds application in his own case. The child who has never been deceived by flattery sees no point in the fable of *The Fox and the Crow*, but the silly person who has been gulled by a flatterer understands perfectly what a fool the crow was. From a fact he draws a moral, and the experience which would speedily have been forgotten is engraved in his mind by the fable. There is no moral knowledge which cannot be acquired either through the experience of other people or of ourselves. Where the experience is too dangerous for the young man to get it at first hand, the lesson can be drawn from history. When the test has no serious consequences it is good for him to be exposed to it and to have the particular cases known to him summed up as maxims. I do not mean, however, that these maxims should be expounded or even stated. The moral at the end of most fables is badly conceived. Before I put the inimitable fables of La Fontaine into the hands of a young man I would cut out all the conclusions in which he takes the trouble to explain what he had just said so clearly and agreeably. If your pupil does not understand the fable without the explanation, you can be sure that he will not understand it in any case. Only men can learn from fables and now is the time for Emile to begin.

When I see young people confined to the speculative studies at the most active time of life and then cast suddenly into the world of affairs without the least experience, I find it as contrary to reason as to nature and am not at all surprised that so few people manage their lives well. By some strange perversity we are taught all sorts of useless things, but nothing is done about the art of conduct. We are supposed to be getting trained for society but are taught as if each one of us were going to live a life of contemplation in a solitary cell. You think you are preparing children for life when you teach them certain bodily contortions and meaningless strings of words. I also have been a teacher of the art of conduct. I have taught my Emile to live his own life, and more than that to earn his own bread. But that is not enough. To live in the world one must get on with people and know how to get a hold on them. It is necessary also to be able to estimate the action and reaction of individual interests in civil society and so forecast events as to be rarely at fault in one's enterprises.

It is by doing good that we become good. I know of no surer way. Keep your pupil occupied with all the good deeds within his power. Let him help poor people with money and with service, and get justice for the oppressed. Active benevolence will lead him to reconcile the quarrels of his comrades and to be concerned about the sufferings of the afflicted. By putting his kindly feelings into action in this way and drawing his own conclusions from the outcome of his efforts, he will get a great deal of useful knowledge. In addition to college lore he will acquire the still more important ability of applying his knowledge to the purposes of life.

My readers, I foresee, will be surprised to see me take my pupil through the whole of the early years without mentioning religion. At fifteen he was not aware that he had a soul, and perhaps at eighteen it is not yet time for him to learn. For if he learns sooner than is necessary he runs the risk of never knowing.

My picture of hopeless stupidity is a pedant teaching the catechism to children. If I wanted to make a child dull I would compel him to explain what he says when he repeats his catechism. It may be objected that since most of the Christian doctrines are mysteries it would be necessary for the proper understanding of them to wait, not merely till the child becomes a man but till the man is no more. To that I reply, in the first place, that there are mysteries man can neither conceive nor believe and that I see no purpose in teaching them to children unless it be to teach them to lie. I say, further, that to admit there are mysteries one must understand that they are incomprehensible, and that this is an idea which is quite beyond children. For an age when all is mystery, there can be no mysteries, properly so-called.

Let us be on guard against presenting the truth to those unable to comprehend it. The effect of that is to substitute error for truth. It would be better to have no idea of the Divine Being than to have ideas that are mean, fantastic and unworthy. 'I would rather people believed there was no Plutarch in the world,' says the good Plutarch, 'than that it should be said that he was unjust, envious, jealous, and such a tyrant that he exacts more than can be performed.'

The worst thing about the distorted images of the Deity imprinted on children's minds, is that they endure all their lives, so that even when they grow up their God is still the God of their childhood. Every child who believes in God is an idolater, or rather he thinks of God in human shape. Once the imagination has seen God, it is very seldom that the understanding conceives Him. I once met in Switzerland a good pious mother who was so convinced of this that she would not teach her son religion in his early years, for fear he might be content with this crude instruction and neglect a better when he came to the age of reason. This child never heard God spoken about save with devotion and reverence, and he was silenced when he tried to speak of Him, on the ground that the subject was too great and too sublime for him. This reserve roused his curiosity, and his pride made him look forward to the time when he would know the mystery so carefully hidden from him. The less that was said about God the more he thought of Him. The child saw God everywhere. My own fear is that this air of mystery might excite a young man's imagination overmuch and turn his head so that he would become a fanatic rather than a believer.

But there is no fear of anything like that happening with my Emile. He always refuses to pay any attention to everything beyond his grasp and hears with indifference things he does not understand. When he does begin to be troubled by these great questions, it will not be because they have been put before him, but because the natural progress of his intelligence is taking his inquiries in that direction.

At this point I see a difficulty ahead: a difficulty all the greater because it is due less to the facts of the situation than to the cowardice of those who are afraid to face up to it. Let us at least be bold enough to state the problem. A child has to be brought up in his father's religion, and always gets ample proof that this religion, whatever it is, is the only true one, and all the others are absurd and ridiculous. In matters of religion more than in any other opinion triumphs. What then are we, who profess to cast off the yoke of opinion and seek to be independent of authority, to do about this? We do not wish to teach our Emile anything which he could not learn for himself in any country. In what religion are we to bring him up? With which sect is the man of nature to be connected? The answer it seems to me is very simple. We will not make him join this sect or that, but put him in the position to choose the one to which he himself is led by the best use of his reason. . . .

So long as we take no account of the authority of man or the prejudices of the country of our birth and educate according to nature, the light of reason by itself can lead us no further than to natural religion: and to that I confine myself with Emile. If he is to have another religion I have no longer the right to be his guide. The choice is his alone.

We are working in concert with nature. While she is forming the physical man we are seeking to form the moral man; but the two do not progress at the same rate. The body is already strong and sturdy while the soul remains dull and feeble, and in spite of all that human skill can do the temperament is always ahead of the reason. So far as we have gone our main endeavour has been to hold back the one side and bring on the other so that as far as possible the man we are training may be at one with himself. In developing his nature we have controlled his sensibility by cultivating the reason. By taking him to the essence of things we have saved him from the domination of the senses. It has been easy to lead him from the study of nature to the search for its Author.

In doing this we have gained a fresh hold on our pupil. It is only now that he has come to have a real interest in being good and doing good, whether anyone sees him or not and without the compulsion of law; and is concerned to be on right terms with God and do his duty whatever the cost. He has learned to cherish virtue not merely for the love of social order (which for all of us is subordinate to the love of self) but for the love of the Author of his being which enters into his self-love, so that in the end he may enjoy the lasting happiness which peace of conscience and the contemplation of God promise him in another life after he has made good use of the present life. . . .

Let us now look at Emile as he enters into society, not to become a leader but to become acquainted with it and to find his mate. Whatever the rank into which he may be born, whatever the society he enters, his first appearance will be simple and unpretentious. He neither has nor desires the qualities that make an immediate impression. He sets too little store by the opinions of men to be concerned about their prejudices, and is not concerned to have people esteem him till they know him. His way of presenting himself is neither modest nor conceited, but just natural and sincere. He knows neither constraint nor concealment. He is the same in company as when he is alone. He speaks little, because he has no desire to attract notice. For the same reason he only speaks about things that are of practical value, being too well informed ever to be a babbler. Far from despising the ways of other people, he conforms quite readily to them: not for the sake of appearing versed in the conventions or affecting fashionable airs, but simply to avoid notice. He is never more at his ease than when nobody is paying him any attention.

When he studies the ways of men in society as he formerly studied their passions in history, he will often have occasion to reflect on the things that gratify or offend the human heart. This will lead him to philosophise on the principles of taste, and this is the study that is most fitting for this period of life.

There is no need to go far for a definition of taste. Taste is simply the faculty of judging what pleases or displeases the greatest number of people. This does not mean that there are more people of taste than others. For though the majority judge sanely about any particular thing, there are few who possess this sanity about everything. Taste is like beauty. Though the most general tastes put together make good taste, there are not many people of taste, just as beauty is constituted by an assemblage of the most common traits and yet there are few beautiful persons.

We are not concerned here with the things we like because they are useful, or dislike because they are harmful. Taste has nothing to do with the necessities of life: it applies to things which are indifferent to us or at most have the interest that goes with our amusements. This is what makes decisions of taste so difficult and seemingly so arbitrary. I should add that taste has local rules which make it dependent in very many ways on region, custom, government and institutions, as well as other rules relating to age, sex and character. That is why there can be no disputing about tastes.

Taste is natural to all men, but all do not possess it in equal measure. The degree of taste we may have depends on native sensibility: the form it takes under cultivation depends on the social groups in which we have lived. In the first place, it is necessary to live in numerous social groups and make many comparisons. In the second place, these must be groups for amusement and leisure, for in those that have to do with practical affairs it is interest and not pleasure that has to be considered. In the third place, there must not be too great inequality in the group and the tyranny of opinion must not be excessive: otherwise fashion stifles taste and people no longer desire what pleases but what gives distinction.

This matter of taste is one to which Emile cannot be indifferent in his present enquiries. The knowledge of what may be agreeable or disagreeable to men is essential to one who has need of them, and no less to one who wants to be useful to them. It is important to please people if you want to serve them. . . .

To keep his taste pure and healthy I will . . . arrange to have useful conversations with him, and by directing the talk to topics that please him I will make these conversations both amusing and instructive. Now is the time to read agreeable books, and to teach him to analyse speech and appreciate all the beauties of eloquence and diction. Contrary to the general belief, there is little to be gained from the study of languages for themselves; but the study of languages leads to the study of the general principles of grammar. It is necessary to know Latin to get a proper knowledge of French. To learn the rules of the art of speech we must study and compare the two languages.

There is moreover a certain simplicity of taste that goes to the heart, which is to be found only in the writings of the ancients. In oratory, in poetry, in every kind of literature, the pupil will find them, as in history, abundant in matter and sober in judgment. In contrast with this our authors talk much and say little. To be always accepting their judgment as right is not the way to acquire a judgment of our own. . . .

Generally speaking Emile will have more liking for the writings of the ancients than our own, for the good reason that coming first they are nearer nature and their genius is more distinctive. Whatever may be said to the contrary the human reason shows no advance. What is gained in one direction is lost in another. All minds start from the same point, and the time spent in learning what others think is so much time lost for learning to think for ourselves. As time goes on there is more acquired knowledge and less vigour of mind.

It is not for the study of morals but of taste that I take Emile to the theatre, for it is there above all that taste reveals itself to thinking people. "Give no thought to moral precepts," I will say to him: "it is not here that you will learn them." The theatre is not intended to give truth but to humour and amuse. Nowhere can the art of pleasing men and touching the human heart be so well learned. The study of drama leads to the study of poetry: their object is the same. If Emile has even a glimmering of taste for poetry he will cultivate Greek, Latin and Italian—the languages of the poets—with great pleasure. The study of them will give him unlimited entertainment, and will profit him all the more on that account. They will bring him delight at an age and in circumstances when the heart finds charm in every kind of beauty. Imagine on the one hand my Emile, and, on the other, some young college scamp, reading the Fourth Book of the *Aeneid,* or Tibullus, or Plato's *Banquet.* What a difference there is: the heart of the one stirred to its depth by something that does not impress the other at all. Stop the reading, young man: you are too greatly moved. I want you to find pleasure in the language of love, but not to be carried away by it. Be a man of feeling, but also a wise man. Actually, it is of no consequence whether Emile succeeds in the dead languages, in literature, in poetry or not. It would not matter greatly if he were ignorant of them all. His education is not really concerned with such diversions.

My main object in teaching him to feel and love beauty in every form is to fix his affections and his tastes on it and prevent his natural appetites from deteriorating so that he comes to look for the means of happiness in his wealth instead of finding it within himself. As I have said elsewhere, taste is simply the art of appreciating the little things, but since the pleasure of life depends on a multitude of little things such concern is not unimportant. It is by means of them that we come to enrich our lives with the good things at our disposal. . . .

BOOK V

We have reached the last act in the drama of youth but the denouement has still to come.

It is not good for man to be alone. Emile is now a man. We must give him the mate we have promised him. The mate is Sophie. Once we know what kind of a person she is, we will know better where to find her and we will be able to complete our task.

Sophie should be as typically woman as Emile is man. She must possess all the characteristics of humanity and of womanhood which she needs for playing her part in the physical and the moral order. Let us begin by considering in what respects her sex and ours agree and differ.

In everything that does not relate to sex the woman is as the man: they are alike in organs, needs and capacities. In whatever way we look at them the difference is only one of less or more. In everything that relates to sex there are correspondences and differences. The difficulty is to determine what in their constitution is due to sex and what is not. All we know with certainty is that the common features are due to the species and the differences to sex. From this twofold point of view we find so many likenesses and so many contrasts that we cannot but marvel that nature has been able to create two beings so much alike with constitutions so different.

The sameness and the difference cannot but have an effect on mentality. This is borne out by experience and shows the futility of discussions about sex superiorities and inequalities. A perfect man and a perfect woman should no more resemble each other in mind than in countenance: and perfection does not admit of degrees. . . .

Plato in his *Republic* gives women the same physical training as men. That is what might be expected. Having made an end of private families in his state and not knowing what to do with the women, he found himself compelled to make men of them. That wonderful genius provided for everything in his plans, and went out of his way to meet an objection that nobody was likely to make, while missing the real objection. I am not speaking about the so-called community of wives, so often charged against him by people who have not read him. What I refer to is the social promiscuity which ignored the differences of sex by giving men and women the same occupations, and sacrificed the sweetest sentiments of nature to the artificial sentiment of loyalty which could not exist without them. He did not realise that the bonds of convention always develop from some natural attachment: that the love one has for his neighbours is the basis of his devotion to the state; that the heart is linked with the great fatherland through the little fatherland of the home; that it is the good son, the good husband, the good father, that makes the good citizen.

Once it has been shown that men and women are essentially different in character and temperament, it follows that they ought not to have the same education. In accordance with the direction of nature they ought to co-operate in action, but not to do the same things. To complete the attempt we have been making to form the man of nature, we must now go on to consider how the fitting mate for him is to be formed.

If you want right guidance, always follow the leadings of nature. Everything that characterises sex should be respected as established by nature. Men's pride leads them astray when, comparing women with themselves, they say, as they are continually doing, that women have this or that defect, which is absent in men. What would be defects in men are good qualities in women, which are necessary to make things go on well. Women on their side never stop complaining that we men make coquettes of them and keep amusing them with trifles in order to maintain our ascendency. What a foolish idea! When have men ever had to do with the education of girls? Who prevents the mothers bringing up their daughters as they please? Are we men to blame if girls please us by their beauty and attract us by the art they have learned from their mothers? Well, try to educate them like men. They will be quite willing. But the more they resemble men the less will be their power over men, and the greater their own subjection.

The faculties common to the sexes are not equally shared between them; but take them all in all, they are well balanced. The more womanly a woman is, the better. Whenever she exercises her own proper powers she gains by it: when she tries to usurp ours she becomes our inferior. Believe me, wise mother, it is a mistake to bring up your daughter to be like a good man. Make her a good woman, and you can be sure that she will be worth more for herself and for us. This does not mean that she should be brought up in utter ignorance and confined to domestic tasks. A man does not want to make his companion a servant and deprive himself of the peculiar charms of her company. That is quite against the teaching of nature, which has endowed women with quick pleasing minds. Nature means them to think, to judge, to love, to know and to cultivate the mind as well as the countenance. This is the equipment nature has given them to compensate for their lack of strength and enable them to direct the strength of men.

As I see it, the special functions of women, their inclinations and their duties, combine to suggest the kind of education they require. Men and women are made for each other but they differ in the measure of their dependence on each other. We could get on better without women than women could get on without us. To play their part in life they must have our willing help, and for that they must earn our esteem. By the very law of nature women are at the mercy of men's judgments both for themselves and for their children. It is not enough that they should be estimable: they must be esteemed. It is not enough that they should be beautiful: they must be pleasing. It is not enough that they should be wise: their wisdom must be recognised. Their honour does not rest on their conduct but on their reputation. Hence the kind of education they get should be the very opposite of men's in this respect. Public opinion is the tomb of a man's virtue but the throne of a woman's.

On the good constitution of the mothers depends that of the children and the early education of men is in their hands. On women too depend the morals, the passions, the tastes, the pleasures, aye and the happiness of men. For this reason their education must be wholly directed to their relations with men. To give them pleasure, to be useful to them, to win their love and esteem, to train them in their childhood, to care for them when they grow up, to give them counsel and consolation, to make life sweet and agreeable for them: these are the tasks of women in all times for which they should be trained from childhood. . . .

Let us now look at the picture of Sophie which has been put before Emile, the image he has of the woman who can make him happy.

Sophie is well born and has a good natural disposition. She has a feeling heart which sometimes makes her imagination difficult to control. Her mind is acute rather than precise: her temper easy but variable; her person ordinary but pleasing. Her countenance gives indication of a soul—with truth. Some girls have good qualities she lacks and others have the qualities she possesses in fuller measure; but none has these qualities better combined in a happy character. Without being very striking, she interests and charms, and it is difficult to say why. . . .

One morning when they had not seen each other for two days I went into Emile's room with a letter in my hand. Looking at him fixedly, I said: 'What would you do if someone were to inform you that Sophie is dead?' He gave a loud cry, sprang up and struck his hands, and without a word looked at me with haggard eyes. 'Reassure yourself,' I said; 'she is alive and well, and we are expected tonight. Let us go for a short stroll and we can talk things over. We must be happy, dear Emile,' I said. 'Happiness is the end of every sentient being. It is the first desire impressed on us by nature and the only one that never leaves us. But where is happiness to be found? Nobody knows. Everybody seeks it: nobody finds it. All through life we pursue it, but die without attaining it. If you want to live happily fix your heart on the beauty that never perishes. Let your desires be limited by your condition in life and put your duties before your inclinations. Extend the law of necessity into the sphere of morals and learn to lose whatever can be taken from you, and to rise above the chances of life. Then you will be happy in spite of fortune and wise in spite of passion. In the good things that are most fragile you will find a pleasure that nothing can disturb. They will not possess you but you will possess them; and you will discover that in this passing world man only enjoys what he is ready to give up. You will not have the illusion of imaginary pleasures, it is true, but neither will you suffer the sorrows that attend them. When you no longer attach an undue importance to life you will pass your own life untroubled and come to the end of it without fear. Others, terror-stricken, may believe that when death comes they will cease to be. You, being aware of the nothingness of this life, will know that the real life is just beginning.'

Emile listened with anxious attention. He foresaw the hard discipline to which I had it in mind to subject him. 'What must I do?' he asked, with eyes downcast. 'You must leave Sophie. Sophie is not yet eighteen and you are barely twenty-two. This is the age for love but not for marriage. You are too young to be the father and mother of a family. Do you not know how premature motherhood can weaken the constitution, ruin the health and shorten the life of young women? When mother and child are both growing and the substance needed for the growth of each of them has to be shared between the two, neither get what nature meant them to get. As for yourself, have you given proper thought to the duties you undertake when you become a husband and a father? When you become the head of a family you become a member of the state. Do you know what that involves? You have studied the duties of a man but do you know what the duties of a citizen are? Do you know what is meant by "government," "laws," "country"? Do you know the price that has to be paid for life and the causes for which you must be ready to die? Before entering the civil order seek to realise and understand what is your proper place in it.'

Emile stood silent for a moment, then looked at me steadily: 'When do we start?' he said. 'In a week's time,' I replied. Sophie I consoled and reassured. Let her keep faith with him as he would with her, and I swear that they will be married in two years' time. . . .

The question is much discussed whether it is good for young people to travel. A better way of putting it would be to ask whether it is enough for an educated man to know only his own countrymen. For my part I am firmly convinced that anyone who only knows the people among whom he lives does not know mankind. But even admitting the utility of travel, does it follow that it is good for everybody? Far from it. It is only good for the few people who are strong enough in themselves to listen to the voice of error and not let themselves be seduced, and see examples of vice and not be led astray. Travel develops the natural bent and makes a man either good or bad. More come back bad than good because more start off with an inclination to badness. But those who are well born and have a good nature which has been well trained, those who travel with a definite purpose of learning, all come back better than they went away. That applies to my Emile.

Everything done rationally should have its rules. This holds good for travel, considered as a part of education. To travel merely for the sake of travelling is to wander about like a vagabond. Even to travel for instruction is too vague a matter. A journey without some definite aim is of no use. I would give a young man an obvious interest in learning, and this interest (if well chosen) would in turn fix the nature of the instruction. After he has considered his physical relations with the world and his moral relations with other men, it remains for him to consider his civic relations with his compatriots. For this he must study the nature of government in general, then the different forms of government, and finally the particular government under which he has been born, in order to know whether it is the one suited for him. By a right which nothing can annul, every man when he reaches his majority and becomes his own master is entitled to renounce the contract by which he is bound to the community and leave the country of his birth. It is only by staying on in that country after coming to the age of reason that he is judged to confirm tacitly the engagement made by his ancestors. Yet the place of his birth being a gift of nature, he gives up something of his own if he renounces it.

Here is what I would say to Emile. 'Up to this time you have not been your own master but have lived under my direction. You are coming to the age when the law allows you the control of your property and makes you master of your person. You have in mind establishing a household of your own, and that is as it should be: it is one of the duties of a man. But before you marry you must know what kind of man you want to be, how you mean to spend your life, what measures you are going to take to ensure a living for yourself and your family. Are you willing to depend on men you despise? Are you willing to have your fortune and your social position determined by civil relations which will subject you for all time to the discretion of other people?' Next, I would describe to him all the different ways of turning his possessions to account in commerce, in public office, in finance, and show him that in every case his position would be precarious and dependent. There is another way of employing his time and himself, I would tell him. You can join the army and hire yourself out at a very high rate to go and kill people who never did you any harm. But far from making you independent of other resources, this job only makes them more necessary for you.

It may be surmised that none of these occupations will be greatly to Emile's taste. 'Do you think I have forgotten the games of my childhood,' he will say to me. 'Have I lost my arms? Has my strength failed? Can I no longer work? All the property I want is a little farm in some corner of the world. My only ambition will be to work it and live free from worry. With Sophie and my land I will be rich.' 'You speak of your own land, dear Emile. But where are you going to find it? In what corner of the earth can you say: "I am my own master and master of the ground I occupy?" There are places where a man can become rich: none where he can spend his life without riches. Nowhere is it possible to live a free and independent life, doing ill to no one, fearing ill from no one. Your plan, Emile, is a fine one and an honourable one, and it would certainly bring you happiness. Let us do our best to realise it. I have a proposal to make. Let us devote the two years till you are due to return to Sophie to looking for a place of refuge somewhere in Europe where you can live happily with your family, secure from danger. If we succeed you will have found the happiness which is sought in vain by so many others. If we do not succeed, you will be cured of an illusion. You will console yourself for an unavoidable evil, and submit to the law of necessity.'

The time has come to draw to an end. We must bring Emile back to Sophie. We have spent almost two years going through some of the great states of Europe and many of the small ones. We have learned two or three of the chief languages. We have seen the unusual things in natural history, government, arts and men. Emile, consumed with impatience, calls my attention to the fact that the time is nearly up. Then I say to him: 'Well, my friend, you remember the main object of our travels. What conclusions have you reached after all your observations?' Unless I have been wrong in my method he will answer something like this: 'What conclusion? To remain the kind of person you have trained me to be, and not to add by my own will any bonds to those which nature and the laws have put on me. The more I examine the work of men in their institutions, the more I see that in seeking independence they make themselves slaves. To avoid being carried away by the torrent of things they form a thousand attachments: then when they try to take a step forward they are surprised to find themselves being held back. It seems to me that the way to become free is just to do nothing, and give up trying to be free. You yourself, master, have made me free by teaching me to yield to necessity. What matters the fortune left me by my parents? I will begin by not depending on it. If I am allowed I will keep it: if it is taken from me I will not let myself be carried away with it. Rich or poor I will be free. What does my earthly condition matter? Wherever there are men I am among brothers: where there are none I have still my own home. If my belongings enslave me I will give them up without hesitation. I can work for my living. Whatever time death comes I will defy it. Having accepted things as they are I will never need to struggle against destiny. There is one and only one chain I shall always wear, and in that I will glory. Give me Sophie, and I am free.'

'My dear Emile,' I reply, 'I am very pleased to hear you speak like a man. Before you set out on your travels I knew what the outcome would be. I knew that when you made acquaintance with our institutions you would not be tempted to put greater confidence in them than they deserve. Men vainly aspire to freedom under safeguard of the laws. Liberty is not to be found in any form of government. It is in the heart of the free man. He takes it with him everywhere. If I were to speak to you about the duties of citizenship you would perhaps ask me "Where is my country?" and think you had confounded me. You would be wrong, however. You must not say: "What does it matter to me where I live?" It does matter that you should be where you can fulfil all your duties as a man, and one of these duties is to be loyal to the place of your birth. Your fellow-countrymen protected you in childhood. They are entitled to your love when you become a man. You should live among them, or wherever you can be most useful to them. For that, I am not urging you to go and reside in a big town. On the contrary, one of the examples good men can give to others is that of a patriarchal life in the country. That was the first life of man, and still the finest and most natural to those with unspoiled hearts.' I like to think how Emile and Sophie in their simple retreat may spread benefits around them, putting fresh life into the country and reviving the worn-out spirits of unfortunate villagers. . . .

At last I see approaching the most delightful day in Emile's life and the happiest in mine. I see the crown set on my labours. The goodly couple are united in an indissoluble bond. Their lips utter and their hearts confirm enduring vows. They are wedded.

'My children,' I say to them as I take them both by the hand, 'it is three years since I saw the beginnings of the ardent love that makes you happy today. It has gone on growing steadily, and I see from your eyes that now it has reached its greatest intensity. After this it can only decline.' My readers can imagine the indignant vows of Emile, and the scornful air with which Sophie withdraws her hand from mine, and the protesting glances of mutual adoration they exchange. I let them have their way, and then I proceed. 'I have often thought that if it were possible to prolong the happiness of love in marriage we would have a heaven on earth. Would you like me to tell you what in my belief is the only way to secure that?' They look at each other with a mocking smile. 'It is simple and easy,' I continue. 'It is to go on being lovers after you are married.' 'That will not be hard for us,' says Emile, laughing at my secret. 'Perhaps harder than you think,' I reply. 'Knots which are too tightly drawn break. That is what happens to the marriage tie when too great a strain is put on it. The faithfulness required of a married couple is the most sacred of all obligations but the power it gives one partner over the other is too great. Constraint and love go ill together, and the pleasures of marriage are not to be had on demand. It is impossible to make a duty of tender affection and to treat the sweetest pledges of love as a right. What right there is comes from mutual desire: nature knows no other. Neither belongs to the other except by his or her own good will. Both must remain master of their persons and their caresses.

'When Emile became your husband, Sophie, he became your head and by the will of nature you owe him obedience. But when the wife is like you it is good for the husband to be guided by her: that is also the law of nature and it gives you as much authority over his heart as his sex gives him over your person. Make yourself dear to him by your favours and respected by your refusals. On these terms you will get his confidence; he will listen to your advice and settle nothing without consulting you. After love has lasted a considerable time a sweet habit takes its place, and the attraction of confidence succeeds the transports of passion. When you cease to be Emile's mistress you will be his wife and sweetheart and the mother of his children, and you will enjoy the closest intimacy. Remember that if your husband lives happily with you, you will be a happy woman.'

'Dear Emile,' I say to the young husband, 'all through life a man has need of a counsellor and guide. Up to the present I have tried to fulfil that duty to you. At this point my lengthy task comes to an end and another takes it over. Today I abdicate the authority you have allowed me. From this time on, Sophie is your tutor.'

Gradually the first rapture calms down and leaves them to experience in peace the delights of their new state. Happy lovers, worthy spouses! How often I am enraptured as I contemplate my work in them, and my heart beats quicker. How often I take their hands in mine, blessing Providence and uttering heartfelt sighs; and they in their turn are affected and share my transports. If happiness is to be found anywhere in earth, it is to be found in the retreat where we live.

Some months later Emile comes into my room and embraces me. 'Master,' he says, 'congratulate your boy. He hopes soon to have the honour to be a father. There will be new cares for us and for you. I do not mean to let you bring up the son as you have brought up the father. God forbid that a task so sweet and holy should fall to any one but me. But remain the teacher of the young teachers. Advise and direct us, and we will be ready to learn. I will have need of you as long as I live. I need you more than ever now that the tasks of my manhood are beginning. You have completed your own tasks. Lead me to imitate you, and enjoy your well-earned rest.'

5

Immanuel Kant

Despite the immense influence of the German philosopher Immanuel Kant (1724–1804) on the history of philosophy, his writings in education have been curiously neglected. This situation is unfortunate, since his work contains many points of vital importance.

Kant believes that "the greatest and most difficult problem to which man can devote himself is the problem of education." He claims that it is through education that human nature can be constantly improved. He points out that students may either be "trained" or "enlightened." Animals are trained; children should be taught to think. Kant also emphasizes the importance of experimentation in education, the advantages of public education, and the principle that "the best way to understand is to do."

Since Kant's views on ethics are so widely studied, it is of special interest to consider his views on moral education. His rule that no child should be shown special preference, that all should be treated with equal respect, is related to his basic moral principle that each human being is an end, whose existence has in itself absolute worth. Kant's emphasis on the importance of "maxims" in teaching a child morality is related to Kant's overall ethical position, according to which the moral worth of an action depends on the principle on which it is based rather than the actual consequences of performing the action. And Kant's claim that the primary aim of moral education is the formation of character derives from the premise of his moral philosophy, according to which nothing can be regarded as good without qualification except a good will, whose constitution, Kant says, is character. These examples all serve as a reminder of the close relationship between a thinker's ethical and educational views.

Thoughts on Education*
CHAPTER 1
INTRODUCTION

1. Man is the only being who needs education. For by education we must understand nurture (the tending and feeding of the child), discipline, and teaching, together with culture. According to this, man is in succession infant (requiring nursing), child (requiring discipline), and scholar (requiring teaching).

2. Animals use their powers, as soon as they are possessed of them, according to a regular plan—that is, in a way not harmful to themselves.

It is indeed wonderful, for instance, that young swallows, when newly hatched and still blind, are careful not to defile their nests.

Animals therefore need no nurture, but at the most, food, warmth, and guidance, or a kind of protection. It is true, most animals need feeding, but they do not require nurture. For by nurture we mean the tender care and attention which parents must bestow upon their children, so as to prevent them from using their powers in a way which would be harmful to themselves. For instance, should an animal cry when it comes into the world, as children do, it would surely become a prey to wolves and other wild animals, which would gather round, attracted by its cry.

3. Discipline changes animal nature into human nature. Animals are by their instinct all that they ever can be; some other reason has provided everything for them at the outset. But man needs a reason of his own. Having no instinct, he has to work out a plan of conduct for himself. Since, however, he is not able to do this all at once, but comes into the world undeveloped, others have to do it for him.

4. All the natural endowments of mankind must be developed little by little out of man himself, through his own effort.

One generation educates the next. The first beginnings of this process of educating may be looked for either in a rude and unformed, or in a fully developed condition of man. If we assume the latter to have come first, man must at all events afterwards have degenerated and lapsed into barbarism.

It is discipline, which prevents man from being turned aside by his animal impulses from humanity, his appointed end. Discipline, for instance, must restrain him from venturing wildly and rashly into danger. Discipline, thus, is merely negative, its action being to counteract man's natural unruliness. The positive part of education is instruction.

Unruliness consists in independence of law. By discipline men are placed in subjection to the laws of mankind, and brought to feel their constraint. This, however, must be accomplished early. Children, for instance, are first sent to school, not so much with the object of their learning something, but rather that

*The translation is by Annette Churton.

they may become used to sitting still and doing exactly as they are told. And this to the end that in later life they should not wish to put actually and instantly into practice anything that strikes them.

5. The love of freedom is naturally so strong in man, that when once he has grown accustomed to freedom, he will sacrifice everything for its sake. For this very reason discipline must be brought into play very early; for when this has not been done, it is difficult to alter character later in life. Undisciplined men are apt to follow every caprice.

We see this also among savage nations, who, though they may discharge functions for some time like Europeans, yet can never become accustomed to European manners. With them, however, it is not the noble love of freedom which Rousseau and others imagine, but a kind of barbarism—the animal, so to speak, not having yet developed its human nature. Men should therefore accustom themselves early to yield to the commands of reason, for if a man be allowed to follow his own will in his youth, without opposition, a certain lawlessness will cling to him throughout his life. And it is no advantage to such a man that in his youth he has been spared through an over-abundance of motherly tenderness, for later on all the more will he have to face opposition from all sides, and constantly receive rebuffs, as soon as he enters into the business of the world. . . .

7. Man can only become man by education. He is merely what education makes of him. It is noticeable that man is only educated by man—that is, by men who have themselves been educated. Hence with some people it is want of discipline and instruction on their own part, which makes them in turn unfit educators of their pupils. Were some being of higher nature than man to undertake our education, we should then be able to see what man might become. It is, however, difficult for us accurately to estimate man's natural capabilities, since some things are imparted to man by education, while other things are only developed by education. Were it possible, by the help of those in high rank, and through the united forces of many people, to make an experiment on this question, we might even by this means be able to gain some information as to the degree of eminence which it is possible for man to attain. But it is as important to the speculative mind, as it is sad to one who loves his fellow-men, to see how those in high rank generally care only for their own concerns, and take no part in the important experiments of education, which bring our nature one step nearer to perfection.

There is no one who, having been neglected in his youth, can come to years of discretion without knowing whether the defect lies in discipline or culture (for so we may call instruction). The uncultivated man is crude, the undisciplined is unruly. Neglect of discipline is a greater evil than neglect of culture, for this last can be remedied later in life, but unruliness cannot be done away with, and a mistake in discipline can never be repaired. It may be that education will be constantly improved, and that each succeeding generation will advance one step towards the perfecting of mankind; for with education is involved the great secret of the perfection of human nature. It is only now that something may be done in this direction, since for the first time people have begun to judge rightly, and un-

derstand clearly, what actually belongs to a good education. It is delightful to realise that through education human nature will be continually improved, and
brought to such a condition as is worthy of the nature of man. This opens out to
us the prospect of a happier human race in the future.

8. The prospect of a *theory of education* is a glorious ideal, and it matters
little if we are not able to realise it at once. Only we must not look upon the
idea as chimerical, nor decry it as a beautiful dream, notwithstanding the difficulties that stand in the way of its realisation.

An idea is nothing else than the conception of a perfection which has not
yet been experienced. For instance, the idea of a perfect republic governed by
principles of justice—is such an idea impossible, because it has not yet been
experienced?

Our idea must in the first place be correct, and then, notwithstanding all
the hindrances that still stand in the way of its realisation, it is not at all impossible. Suppose, for instance, lying to become universal, would truth-speaking
on that account become nothing but a whim? And the idea of an education
which will develop all man's natural gifts is certainly a true one.

9. Under the present educational system man does not fully attain to the
object of his being; for in what various ways men live! Uniformity can only result when all men act according to the same principles, which principles
would have to become with them a second nature. What we can do is to work
out a scheme of education better suited to further its objects, and hand down
to posterity directions as to how this scheme may be carried into practice, so
that they might be able to realise it gradually. . . .

10. There are many germs lying undeveloped in man. It is for us to make
these germs grow, by *developing his natural gifts* in their due proportion, and to
see that he fulfils his destiny. Animals accomplish this for themselves unconsciously. Man must strive to attain it, but this he cannot do if he has not even a
conception as to the object of his existence. For the individual it is absolutely
impossible to attain this object. Let us suppose the first parents to have been
fully developed, and see how they educate their children. These first parents
set their children an example, which the children imitate and in this way develop some of their own natural gifts. All their gifts cannot, however, be developed in this way, for it all depends on occasional circumstances what examples
children see. In times past men had no conception of the perfection to which
human nature might attain—even now we have not a very clear idea of the
matter. This much, however, is certain: that no individual man, no matter what
degree of culture may be reached by his pupils, can insure their attaining their
destiny. To succeed in this, not the work of a few individuals only is necessary,
but that of the whole human race.

11. Education is an *art* which can only become perfect through the practice of many generations. Each generation, provided with the knowledge of the
foregoing one, is able more and more to bring about an education which shall
develop man's natural gifts in their due proportion and in relation to their end,
and thus advance the whole human race towards its destiny. Providence has

willed, that man shall bring forth for himself the good that lies hidden in his nature, and has spoken, as it were, thus to man: "Go forth into the world! I have equipped thee with every tendency towards the good. Thy part let it be to develop those tendencies. Thy happiness and unhappiness depend upon thyself alone."

12. Man must develop his tendency towards *the good*. Providence has not placed goodness ready formed in him, but merely as a tendency and without the distinction of moral law. Man's duty is to improve himself; to cultivate his mind; and, when he finds himself going astray, to bring the moral law to bear upon himself. Upon reflection we shall find this very difficult. Hence the greatest and most difficult problem to which man can devote himself is the problem of education. For insight depends on education, and education in its turn depends on insight. It follows therefore that education can only advance by slow degrees, and a true conception of the method of education can only arise when one generation transmits to the next its stores of experience and knowledge, each generation adding something of its own before transmitting them to the following. . . .

14. Since the development of man's natural gifts does not take place of itself, all education is an art. Nature has placed no instinct in him for that purpose. The *origin* as well as the *carrying out* of this art is either *mechanical* and without plan, ruled by given circumstances, or it involves the exercise of *judgment*. The art of education is only then mechanical, when on chance occasions we learn by experience whether anything is useful or harmful to man. All education which is merely mechanical must carry with it many mistakes and deficiencies, because it has no sure principle to work upon. If education is to develop human nature so that it may attain the object of its being, it must involve the exercise of judgment. Educated parents are examples which children use for their guidance. If, however, the children are to progress beyond their parents, education must become a study, otherwise we can hope for nothing from it, and one man whose education has been spoilt will only repeat his own mistakes in trying to educate others. The mechanism of education must be changed into a science, and one generation may have to pull down what another had built up.

15. One *principle of education* which those men especially who form educational schemes should keep before their eyes is this—children ought to be educated, not for the present, but for a possibly improved condition of man in the future; that is, in a manner which is adapted to the *idea of humanity* and the whole destiny of man. This principle is of great importance. Parents usually educate their children merely in such a manner that, however bad the world may be, they may adapt themselves to its present conditions. But they ought to give them an education so much better than this, that a better condition of things may thereby be brought about in the future. . . .

18. Through education, then, man must be made—

First, subject to *discipline*; by which we must understand that influence which is always restraining our animal nature from getting the better of our manhood, either in the individual as such, or in man as a member of society. Discipline, then, is merely restraining unruliness.

Secondly, education must also supply men with *culture*. This includes information and instruction. It is culture which brings out ability. Ability is the possession of a faculty which is capable of being adapted to various ends. Ability, therefore, does not determine any ends, but leaves that to circumstances as they arise afterwards.

Some accomplishments are essentially good for everybody—reading and writing, for instance; others, merely in the pursuit of certain objects, such as music, which we pursue in order to make ourselves liked. Indeed, the various purposes to which ability may be put are almost endless.

Thirdly, education must also supply a person with *discretion*, so that he may be able to conduct himself in society, that he may be liked, and that he may gain influence. For this a kind of culture is necessary which we call *refinement*. The latter requires manners, courtesy, and a kind of discretion which will enable him to use all men for his own ends. . . .

Fourthly, *moral training* must form a part of education. It is not enough that a man shall be fitted for any end, but his disposition must be so trained that he shall choose none but good ends—good ends being those which are necessarily approved by everyone, and which may at the same time be the aim of everyone.

19. Man may be either broken in, trained, and mechanically taught, or he may be really enlightened. Horses and dogs are broken in; and man, too, may be broken in.

It is, however, not enough that children should be merely broken in; for it is of greater importance that they shall learn to *think*. By learning to think, man comes to act according to fixed principles and not at random. Thus we see that a real education implies a great deal. But as a rule, in our private education *the fourth and most important point is still too much neglected,* children being for the most part educated in such a way that moral training is left to the Church. And yet how important it is that children should learn from their youth up to detest vice!—not merely on the ground that God has forbidden it, but because vice is detestable in itself. If children do not learn this early, they are very likely to think that, if only God had not forbidden it, there would be no harm in practising wickedness, and that it would otherwise be allowed, and that therefore He would probably make an exception now and then. But God is the most holy being, and wills only what is good, and desires that we may love virtue for its own sake, and not merely because He requires it. . . .

27. In the first period of childhood the child must learn submission and positive obedience. In the next stage he should be allowed to think for himself, and to enjoy a certain amount of freedom, although still obliged to follow certain rules. In the first period there is a mechanical, in the second a moral constraint.

28. The child's submission is either *positive* or *negative. Positive* in that he is obliged to do what he is told, because he cannot judge for himself, and the faculty of imitation is still strong in him; or *negative,* in that he is obliged to do

what others wish him to do, if he wishes others to do him a good turn. In the former case, the consequence of not obeying is punishment; in the latter, the fact that people do not comply with his wishes. He is in this case, though capable of thinking for himself, dependent on others with regard to his own pleasure.

29. One of the greatest problems of education is how to unite submission to the necessary *restraint* with the child's capability of exercising his *freewill*—for restraint is necessary. How am I to develop the sense of freedom in spite of the restraint? I am to accustom my pupil to endure a restraint of his freedom, and at the same time I am to guide him to use his freedom aright. Without this all education is merely mechanical, and the child, when his education is over, will never be able to make a proper use of his freedom. He should be made to feel early the inevitable opposition of society, that he may learn how difficult it is to support himself, to endure privation, and to acquire those things which are necessary to make him independent.

30. Here we must observe the following:—First, we must allow the child from his earliest childhood perfect liberty in every respect (except on those occasions when he might hurt himself—as, for instance, when he clutches at a knife), provided that in acting so he does not interfere with the liberty of others. For instance, as soon as he screams or is too boisterously happy, he annoys others.

Secondly, he must be shown that he can only attain his own ends by allowing others to attain theirs. For instance, should he be disobedient, or refuse to learn his lessons, he ought to be refused any treat he may have been looking forward to.

Thirdly, we must prove to him that restraint is only laid upon him that he may learn in time to use his liberty aright, and that his mind is being cultivated so that one day he may be free; that is, independent of the help of others. This is the last thing a child will come to understand. It is much later in life that children realise such facts as that they will afterwards have to support themselves; for they imagine that they can always go on as they are in their parents' house, and that food and drink will always be provided for them without any trouble on their part. . . .

[W]e see the advantage of public education in that under such a system, we learn to measure our powers with those of others, and to know the limits imposed upon us by the rights of others. Thus we can have no preference shown us, because we meet with opposition everywhere, and we can only make our mark and obtain an advantage over others by real merit. Public education is the best school for future citizens. . . .

31. Education is either *physical* or "practical." One part of physical education is that which man has in common with animals, namely, feeding and tending. "Practical" or *moral* training is that which teaches a man how to live as a free being. (We call anything *"practical"* which has reference to freedom.) This is the education of a personal character, of a free being, who is able to maintain himself, and to take his proper place in society, keeping at the same time a proper sense of his own individuality.

32. This *"practical"* education consists, then, of three parts:—

(a) The *ordinary curriculum of the school*, where the child's general ability is developed—the work of the schoolmaster.

(b) Instruction in the practical matters of life—to act with wisdom and discretion—the work of the private tutor or governess.

(c) The training of moral character.

Men need the training of school-teaching or instruction to develop the ability necessary to success in the various vocations of life. School-teaching bestows upon each member an individual value of his own.

Next, by learning the lesson of discretion in the practical matters of life, he is educated as a citizen, and becomes of value to his fellow-citizens, learning both how to accommodate himself to their society and also how to profit by it.

Lastly, moral training imparts to man a value with regard to the whole human race.

33. Of these three divisions of education school-teaching comes *first* in order of time; for a child's abilities must first be developed and trained, otherwise he is incapable of gaining knowledge in the practical matters of life. Discretion is the faculty of using our abilities aright.

Moral training, in as far as it is based upon fundamental principles which a man must himself comprehend, comes last in order of time. In so far, however, as it is based on common sense merely, it must be taken into account from the beginning, at the same time with physical training; for if moral training be omitted, many faults will take root in the child, against which all influences of education at a later stage will be powerless. As to ability and the general knowledge of life, everything must depend entirely upon the age of the pupil. Let a child be clever after the manner of children; let him be shrewd and good-natured in a childish way, but not cunning like a man. The latter is as unsuitable for a child as a childish mind is for a grown-up person.

CHAPTER II
PHYSICAL EDUCATION

47. With regard to the training of character—which we may indeed call also, in a certain sense, physical culture—we must chiefly bear in mind that *discipline* should not be slavish. For a child ought always to be conscious of his freedom, but always in such a way as not to interfere with the liberty of others—in which case he must be met with opposition. Many parents refuse their children everything they ask, in order that they may exercise their patience, but in doing so they require from their children more patience than they have themselves. This is cruel. One ought rather to give a child as much as will agree with him, and then tell him "that is enough"; but this decision must be absolutely final. No attention should ever be given to a child when he cries for anything, and children's wishes should never be complied with if they try to extort something by crying; but if they ask properly, it should be given them, provided it is for their good. By this the child will also become accustomed to

being open-minded; and since he does not annoy anyone by his crying, everybody will be friendly towards him.

Providence seems indeed to have given children happy, winning ways, in order that they may gain people's hearts. Nothing does children more harm than to exercise a vexatious and slavish discipline over them with a view to breaking their self-will. . . .

50. No better than this vexatious system of bringing up children is that of perpetually *playing with* and *caressing* the child; this makes him self-willed and deceitful, and by betraying to him their weakness, parents lose the necessary respect in the eyes of the child. If, on the other hand, he is so trained that he gets nothing by crying for it, he will be frank without being bold, and modest without being timid. *Boldness,* or, what is almost the same thing, *insolence,* is insufferable. There are many men whose constant insolence has given them such an expression that their very look leads one to expect rudeness from them, while you have only to look at others to see at once that they are incapable of being rude to anyone. Now we can always be frank in our demeanour, provided our frankness be united with a certain kindness. . . .

54. The *will* of children . . . must not be broken, but merely bent in such a way that it may yield to natural obstacles. At the beginning, it is true, the child must obey blindly. It is unnatural that a child should command by his crying, and that the strong should obey the weak. Children should never, even in their earliest childhood, be humoured because they cry, nor allowed to extort anything by crying. Parents often make a mistake in this, and then, wishing to undo the result of their over-indulgence, they deny their children in later life whatever they ask for. It is, however, very wrong to refuse them without cause what they may naturally expect from the kindness of their parents, merely for the sake of opposing them, and that they, being the weaker, should be made to feel the superior power of their parents.

55. To grant children their wishes is to *spoil* them; to thwart them purposely is an utterly *wrong way of bringing them up.* The former generally happens as long as they are the playthings of their parents, and especially during the time when they are beginning to talk. By spoiling a child, however, very great harm is done, affecting its whole life. Those who thwart the wishes of children prevent them (and must necessarily prevent them) at the same time from showing their anger; but their inward rage will be all the stronger, for children have not yet learned to control themselves.

The following rules should accordingly be observed with children from their earliest days:—When they cry, and we have reason to believe they are hurt, we should go to their help. On the other hand, when they cry simply from temper, they should be left alone. And this way of dealing with them should be continued as they grow older. In this case the opposition the child meets with is quite natural, and, properly speaking, merely negative, consisting simply in his not being indulged. Many children, on the other hand, get all they want from their parents by persistent asking. If children are allowed to get whatever they want by crying, they become ill-tempered; while if they are allowed to get whatever they want by asking, their characters are weakened.

Should there, then, be no important reason to the contrary, a child's request should be granted; should there be a reason to the contrary, it should not be granted, no matter how often the request is repeated. A refusal should always be final. This will shortly have the effect of making its repetition unnecessary.

56. Supposing—what is of extremely rare occurrence—that a child should be naturally inclined to be *stubborn*, it is best to deal with him in this way:—If he refuses to do anything to please us, we must refuse to do anything to please him.

Breaking a child's will makes him a slave, while natural opposition makes him docile. . . .

CHAPTER IV
CULTIVATION OF THE MIND

63. We come now to the *cultivation of the mind*, which also we may call, in a certain sense, physical. . . .

This physical cultivation of the mind, however, must be distinguished from moral training, in that it aims only at nature, while moral training aims at freedom. A man may be highly cultivated physically, he may have a well-cultivated mind; but if he lacks moral culture, he will be a wicked man. . . .

65. Various plans of education have been drawn up by different people, in order to discover the best methods—a most praiseworthy undertaking. One among others suggests that children should be allowed to *learn everything as it were in play*. . . . This is an utterly preposterous notion. A child must play, must have his hours of recreation; but he must also learn to work. It is a good thing, doubtless, to exercise skill, as it is to cultivate the mind, but these two kinds of culture should have their separate hours. Moreover, it is a great misfortune for man that he is by nature so inclined to inaction. The longer a man gives way to this inclination, the more difficult will he find it to make up his mind to work.

66. In *work* the occupation is not pleasant in itself, but it is undertaken for the sake of the end in view. In *games*, on the other hand, the occupation is pleasant in itself without having any other end in view. When we go for a walk, we do so for the sake of the walk, and therefore the further we go the pleasanter it is; while when we go to a certain place, our object is the company which we shall find there, or something else, and therefore we shall naturally choose the shortest way. The same thing happens in card games. It is really extraordinary how reasonable men can sit by the hour and shuffle cards. It is not, it seems, so easy for men to leave off being children. For how is this a better game than the children's game of ball? It is true that grown men do not care to ride hobby-horses, but they ride other hobbies.

67. It is of the greatest importance that children should learn to work. Man is the only animal who is obliged to work. He must go through a long apprenticeship before he can enjoy anything for his own sustenance. The question whether Heaven would not have shown us greater kindness by supplying all our wants without the necessity of work on our part must certainly be an-

swered in the negative, for man needs occupation, even occupation that involves a certain amount of restraint. Just as false a notion is it that if Adam and Eve had only remained in Paradise they would have done nothing there but sit together singing pastoral songs and admiring the beauty of Nature. Were this so, they would have been tormented with *ennui*, just as much as other people in the same position.

Men ought to be occupied in such a way that, filled with the idea of the end which they have before their eyes, they are not conscious of themselves, and the best rest for them is the rest which follows work. In the same way a child must become accustomed to work, and where can the inclination to work be cultivated so well as at school? School is a place of compulsory culture. It is very bad for a child to learn to look upon everything as play. He must, it is true, have his time for recreation, but he must also have his time for work. Even though the child does not at once understand the use of this restraint, later in life he will recognise its value. It would be merely training the child to bad habits of inquisitiveness were one always to answer his questions: "What is the use of this?" or, "What is the use of that?" Education must be compulsory, but it need not therefore be slavish.

68. With regard to the *"free"* cultivation of the *mental faculties*, we must remember that this cultivation is going on constantly. It really deals with the superior faculties. The inferior faculties must be cultivated along with them, but only with a view to the superior; for instance, the intelligence with a view to the understanding—the principal rule that we should follow being that no mental faculty is to be cultivated by itself, but always in relation to others; for instance, the imagination to the advantage of the understanding.

The inferior faculties have no value in themselves; for instance, a man who has a good memory, but no judgment. Such a man is merely a walking dictionary. These beasts of burden of Parnassus are of some use, however, for if they cannot do anything useful themselves they at least furnish material out of which others may produce something good. Intelligence divorced from judgment produces nothing but foolishness. Understanding is the knowledge of the general. Judgment is the application of the general to the particular. Reason is the power of understanding the connection between the general and the particular. This free culture runs its course from childhood onwards till the time that the young man is released from all education. When a young man, for instance, quotes a general rule, we may make him quote examples drawn from history or fable in which this rule is disguised, passages from the poets where it is expressed, and thus encourage him to exercise both his intelligence and his memory, &c.

69. The maxim *Tantum scimus, quantum memoria tenemus*[1] is quite true—hence it is very necessary to cultivate the memory. Things are so constituted that the understanding first follows the mental impression, and the memory must preserve this impression. So it is, for instance, in languages. We learn them either by the formal method of committing them to memory or by conversation—this last being the best method for modern languages. The learning of words is really necessary, but the best plan is for the youth to learn words as

he comes across them in the author he is reading. The youth should have a certain set task. In the same way geography is best learnt mechanically. What is learnt in a mechanical way is best retained by the memory, and in a great many cases this way is indeed very useful. The proper mechanism for the study of history has yet to be found. An attempt has been made in this direction consisting of a system of tables, but the result has not been very satisfactory. History, however, is an excellent means of exercising the understanding in judging rightly. Learning by heart is very necessary, but doing it merely for the sake of exercising the memory is of no use educationally—for instance, the learning of a speech by heart. At all events, it only serves to encourage forwardness. Besides this, declamation is only proper for grown-up men. The same may be said of all those things which we learn merely for some future examination or with a view to *futuram oblivionem*.[2] The memory should only be occupied with such things as are important to be retained, and which will be of service to us in real life. Novel-reading is the worst thing for children, since they can make no further use of it, and it merely affords them entertainment for the moment. Novel-reading weakens the memory. For it would be ridiculous to remember novels in order to relate them to others. Therefore all novels should be taken away from children. Whilst reading them they weave, as it were, an inner romance of their own, rearranging the circumstances for themselves; their fancy is thus imprisoned, but there is no exercise of thought.

Distractions must never be allowed, least of all in school, for the result will be a certain propensity in that direction which might soon grow into a habit. Even the finest talents may be wasted when once a man is subject to distraction. Although children are inattentive at their games, they soon recall their attention. We may notice, however, that they are most distracted when they are thinking of some mischief, for then they are contriving either how to hide it, or else how to repair the evil done. They then only half hear anything, give wrong answers, and know nothing about what they are reading, &c.

70. The memory must be cultivated early, but we must be careful to cultivate the understanding at the same time.

The memory is cultivated (i) by learning the names which are met with in tales, (ii) by reading and writing. But as to reading, children should practise it with the head, without depending on the spelling. (iii) By languages, which children should first learn by hearing, before they read anything.

Then a well-constructed so-called *orbis pictus* will prove very useful. We might begin with botany, mineralogy, and natural history in general. In order to make sketches of these objects, drawing and modelling will have to be learned, and for this some knowledge of mathematics is necessary. The first lessons in science will most advantageously be directed to the study of geography, mathematical as well as physical. Tales of travel, illustrated by pictures and maps, will lead on to political geography. From the present condition of the earth's surface we go back to its earlier condition, and this leads us to ancient geography, ancient history, and so on.

But in teaching children we must seek insensibly to unite knowledge with the carrying out of that knowledge into practice. Of all the sciences, mathematics seems to be the one that best fulfils this. Further, knowledge and speech (ease in speaking, fluency, eloquence) must be united. The child, however, must learn also to distinguish clearly between knowledge and mere opinion and belief. Thus we prepare the way for a right understanding, and a *right*—not a *refined* or *delicate*—taste. This taste must at first be that of the senses, especially the eyes, but ultimately of ideas.

71. It is necessary to have rules for everything which is intended to cultivate the understanding. It is very useful mentally to separate the rules, that the understanding may proceed not merely mechanically, but with the consciousness of following a rule.

It is also very useful to bring these rules into a set form, and thus commit them to memory. If we keep the rule in our memory, though we forget its application, we shall soon find our way again.

Here the question arises whether the rules shall first be studied *in abstracto,* and whether they ought to be studied after they have been applied, or whether the rule and its application should be studied side by side. This last is the only advisable course; otherwise the application of the rule is very uncertain till the rule itself is learned.

But from time to time the rules must also be arranged in classes, for it is difficult to keep them in memory when they are not associated together. Consequently in learning languages the study of grammar must always, to a certain extent, come first.

72. We must now give a systematic idea of the whole aim of education, and the means of obtaining it.

I. *The general cultivation of the mental faculties, as distinguished from the cultivation of particular mental faculties.*—This aims at skill and perfection, and has not for its object the imparting of any particular knowledge, but the general strengthening of the mental faculties.

This culture is either (a) *physical*—here everything depends upon exercise and discipline, without the child needing to learn any "maxims"; it is passive for the pupil, who has only to follow the guidance of others—or (b) it is moral. This depends not upon discipline, but upon "maxims." All will be spoilt if moral training rests upon examples, threats, punishments, and so on. It would then be merely discipline. We must see that the child does right on account of his own "maxims," and not merely from habit; and not only that he does right, but that he does it because it is right. For the whole moral value of actions consists in "maxims" concerning the good.

Physical education, then, is distinguished from moral in the former being passive, while the latter is active, for the child. He should always understand the principle of an action, and its relation to the idea of duty.

73. II. *The cultivation of particular mental faculties.*—This includes the cultivation of the faculty of cognition, of the senses, the imagination, memory, power of attention, and intelligence—in a word, the inferior powers of the understanding.

Of the cultivation of the senses—eyesight, for instance—we have already spoken. As to the cultivation of the imagination, the following is to be noticed:—Children generally have a very lively imagination, which does not need to be expanded or made more intense by the reading of fairy tales. It needs rather to be curbed and brought under rule, but at the same time should not be left quite unoccupied. There is something in maps which attracts everybody, even the smallest children. When they are tired of everything else, they will still learn something by means of maps. And this is a good amusement for children, for here their imagination is not allowed to rove, since it must, as it were, confine itself to certain figures. We might really begin with geography in teaching children. Figures of animals, plants, and so on, might be added at the same time; these will make the study of geography more lively. History, however, would probably have to come later on.

With regard to the power of attention, we may remark that this faculty needs general strengthening. The power of rigidly fixing our thoughts upon one object is not so much a talent as a weakness of our mind, which in this case is inflexible, and does not allow itself to be applied at pleasure. But distraction is the enemy of all education. Memory depends upon our attention.

74. As regards the cultivation of the *superior mental faculties,* this includes the cultivation of the understanding, judgment, and reason. The understanding may at first be cultivated, in a certain way, passively also, either by quoting examples which prove the rules, or, on the contrary, by discovering rules for particular cases. The judgment shows us what use to make of the understanding. Understanding is necessary in order that we may understand what we learn or say, and that we may not repeat anything without understanding it. How many people hear and read things which they do not understand, though they believe them! Of that kind are both images and real things.

It is through reason that we get an insight into principles. But we must remember that we are speaking here of a reason which still needs guidance. Hence the child should not be encouraged to be always reasoning, nor should we indulge in reasoning in the presence of children, about things which surpass their conception.

We are not dealing here with speculative reason, but only with reflection upon actual occurrences, according to their causes and effects. It is in its arrangement and working a practical reason.

75. The best way of cultivating the mental faculties is to *do ourselves* all that we wish to accomplish; for instance, by carrying out into practice the grammatical rule which we have learnt. We understand a map best when we are able to draw it out for ourselves. The best way to understand is to do. That which we learn most thoroughly, and remember the best, is what we have in a way taught ourselves. There are but few men, however, who are capable of doing this. They are called self-taught.

76. In the culture of *reason* we must proceed according to the Socratic method. Socrates, who called himself the midwife of his hearers' knowledge, gives examples in his dialogues, which Plato has in a manner preserved for us, of the way in which, even in the case of grown-up people, ideas may be drawn forth from their own individual reason. In many respects children need not exercise their reason. They must not be allowed to argue about everything. It is

not necessary for them to know the principles of everything connected with their education; but when the question of duty arises, they should be made to understand those principles. But on the whole we should try to draw out their own ideas, founded on reason, rather than to introduce such ideas into their minds. The Socratic method should form, then, the rule for the catechetical method. True it is somewhat slow, and it is difficult to manage so that in drawing ideas out of one child the others shall also learn something. The mechanical method of catechising is also useful in some sciences; for instance, in the explanation of revealed religion. In universal religion, on the other hand, we must employ the Socratic method. As to what has to be learnt historically, the mechanical method of catechising is much to be commended.

CHAPTER V
MORAL CULTURE

77. *Moral culture* must be based upon "maxims," not upon discipline; the one prevents evil habits, the other trains the mind to think. We must see, then, that the child should accustom himself to act in accordance with "maxims," and not from certain ever-changing springs of action. Through discipline we form certain habits, moreover, the force of which becomes lessened in the course of years. The child should learn to act according to "maxims," the reasonableness of which he is able to see for himself. One can easily see that there is some difficulty in carrying out this principle with young children, and that moral culture demands a great deal of insight on the part of parents and teachers.

Supposing a child tells a lie, for instance, he ought not to be punished, but treated with contempt, and told that he will not be believed in the future, and the like. If you punish a child for being naughty, and reward him for being good, he will do right merely for the sake of the reward; and when he goes out into the world and finds that goodness is not always rewarded, nor wickedness always punished, he will grow into a man who only thinks about how he may get on in the world, and does right or wrong according as he finds either of advantage to himself.

78. "*Maxims*" ought to originate in the human being as such. In moral training we should seek early to infuse into children ideas as to what is right and wrong. If we wish to establish morality, we must abolish punishment. Morality is something so sacred and sublime that we must not degrade it by placing it in the same rank as discipline. The first endeavour in moral education is the formation of character. Character consists in readiness to act in accordance with "maxims." At first they are school "maxims," and later "maxims" of mankind. At first the child obeys rules. "Maxims" are also rules, but subjective rules. They proceed from the understanding of man. No infringement of school discipline must be allowed to go unpunished, although the punishment must always fit the offence.

79. If we wish to *form the characters* of children, it is of the greatest importance to point out to them a certain plan, and certain rules, in everything; and these must be strictly adhered to. For instance, they must have set times for sleep, for work, and for pleasure; and these times must be neither shortened nor lengthened. With indifferent matters children might be allowed to choose for themselves, but having once made a rule they must always follow it. We must, however, form in children the character of a child, and not the character of a citizen.

Unmethodical men are not to be relied on; it is difficult to understand them, and to know how far we are to trust them. It is true we often blame people who always act by rule—for instance, the man who does everything by the clock, having a fixed hour for every one of his actions—but we blame them often unreasonably, for this exactness, though it looks like pedantry, goes far towards helping the formation of character.

80. Above all things, obedience is an essential feature in the character of a child, especially of a school boy or girl. This obedience is twofold, including absolute obedience to his master's commands, and obedience to what he feels to be a good and reasonable will. Obedience may be the result of compulsion; it is then *absolute:* or it may arise out of confidence; it is then obedience of the second kind. This *voluntary* obedience is very important, but the former is also very necessary, for it prepares the child for the fulfilment of laws that he will have to obey later, as a citizen, even though he may not like them.

81. Children, then, must be subject to a certain law of *necessity*. This law, however, must be a general one—a rule which has to be kept constantly in view, especially in schools. The master must not show any predilection or preference for one child above others; for thus the law would cease to be general. As soon as a child sees that the other children are not all placed under the same rules as himself, he will at once become refractory.

82. One often hears it said that we should put everything before children in such a way that they shall do it from *inclination*. In some cases, it is true, this is all very well, but there is much besides which we must place before them as *duty*. And this will be of great use to them throughout their life. For in the paying of rates and taxes, in the work of the office, and in many other cases, we must be led, not by inclination, but by duty. Even though a child should not be able to see the reason of a duty, it is nevertheless better that certain things should be prescribed to him in this way; for, after all, a child will always be able to see that he has certain duties as a child, while it will be more difficult for him to see that he has certain duties as a human being. Were he able to understand this also—which, however, will only be possible in the course of years—his obedience would be still more perfect.

83. Every transgression of a command in a child is a want of obedience, and this brings *punishment* with it. Also, should a command be disobeyed through inattention, punishment is still necessary. This punishment is either *physical* or *moral*. It is *moral* when we do something derogatory to the child's longing to be honoured and loved (a longing which is an aid to moral training); for instance, when we humiliate the child by treating him coldly and dis-

tantly. This longing of children should, however, be cultivated as much as possible. Hence this kind of punishment is the best, since it is an aid to moral training—for instance, if a child tells a lie, a look of contempt is punishment enough, and punishment of a most appropriate kind.

Physical punishment consists either in refusing a child's requests or in the infliction of pain. The first is akin to moral punishment, and is of a negative kind. The second form must be used with caution, lest an *indoles servilis*[3] should be the result. It is of no use to give children rewards; this makes them selfish, and gives rise to an *indoles mercenaria.*[4]

84. Further, obedience is either that of the child or that of the *youth.* Disobedience is always followed by punishment. This is either a really *natural* punishment, which a man brings upon himself by his own behaviour—for instance, when a child gets ill from over-eating—and this kind of punishment is the best, since a man is subject to it throughout his life, and not merely during his childhood; or, on the other hand, the punishment is artificial. By taking into consideration the child's desire to be loved and respected, such punishments may be chosen as will have a lasting effect upon its character. Physical punishments must merely supplement the insufficiency of moral punishment. If moral punishment have no effect at all, and we have at last to resort to physical punishment, we shall find after all that no good character is formed in this way. At the beginning, however, physical restraint may serve to take the place of reflection.

85. Punishments inflicted with signs of *anger* are useless. Children then look upon the punishment simply as the result of anger, and upon themselves merely as the victims of that anger; and as a general rule punishment must be inflicted on children with great caution, that they may understand that its one aim is their improvement. . . . If physical punishment is often repeated, it makes a child stubborn; and if parents punish their children for obstinacy, they often become all the more obstinate. Besides, it is not always the worst men who are obstinate, and they will often yield easily to kind remonstrance.

86. The obedience of the growing *youth* must be distinguished from the obedience of the *child.* The former consists in submission to rules of duty. To do something for the sake of duty means obeying reason. It is in vain to speak to children of duty. They look upon it in the end as something which if not fulfilled will be followed by the rod. A child may be guided by mere instinct. As he grows up, however, the idea of duty must come in. Also the idea of shame should not be made use of with children, but only with those who have left childhood for youth. For it cannot exist with them till the idea of honour has first taken root.

87. The second principal feature in the formation of a child's character is *truthfulness.* This is the foundation and very essence of character. A man who tells lies has no character, and if he has any good in him it is merely the result of a certain kind of temperament. Some children have an inclination towards lying, and this frequently for no other reason than that they have a lively imagination. It is the father's business to see that they are broken of this habit, for mothers generally look upon it as a matter of little or no importance, even

finding in it a flattering proof of the cleverness and ability of their children. This is the time to make use of the sense of shame, for the child in this case will understand it well. The blush of shame betrays us when we lie, but it is not always a proof of it, for we often blush at the shamelessness of others who accuse us of guilt. On no condition must we punish children to force the truth from them, unless their telling a lie immediately results in some mischief; *then* they may be punished for that mischief. The withdrawal of respect is the only fit punishment for lying.

Punishments may be divided into *negative* and *positive* punishments. The first may be applied to laziness or viciousness; for instance, lying, disobedience. Positive punishment may be applied to acts of spitefulness. But above all things we must take care never to bear children a grudge.

88. A third feature in the child's character is *sociableness*. He must form friendships with other children, and not be always by himself. Some teachers, it is true, are opposed to these friendships in schools, but this is a great mistake. Children ought to prepare themselves for the sweetest enjoyment of life.

If a teacher allows himself to prefer one child to another, it must be on account of its character, and not for the sake of any talents the child may possess; otherwise jealousy will arise, which is opposed to friendship.

Children ought to be open-hearted and cheerful in their looks as the sun. A joyful heart alone is able to find its happiness in the good. A religion which makes people gloomy is a false religion; for we should serve God with a joyful heart, and not of constraint.

Children should sometimes be released from the narrow constraint of school, otherwise their natural joyousness will soon be quenched. When the child is set free he soon recovers his natural elasticity. Those games in which children, enjoying perfect freedom, are ever trying to outdo one another, will serve this purpose best, and they will soon make their minds bright and cheerful again.

89. Many people imagine that the years of their youth are the pleasantest and best of their lives; but it is not really so. They are the most troublesome; for we are then under strict discipline, can seldom choose our own friends, and still more seldom can we have our freedom. As Horace says: *Multa tulit, fecitque puer, sudavit et alsit.*[5]

90. Children should only be taught those things which are suited to their age. Many parents are pleased with the precocity of their offspring; but as a rule, nothing will come of such children. A child should be clever, but only as a child. He should not ape the manners of his elders. For a child to provide himself with moral sentences proper to manhood is to go quite beyond his province and to become merely an imitator. He ought to have merely the understanding of a child, and not seek to display it too early. A precocious child will never become a man of insight and clear understanding. It is just as much out of place for a child to follow all the fashions of the time, to curl his hair, wear ruffles, and even carry a snuff-box. He will thus acquire affected manners not becoming to a child. Polite society is a burden to him, and he entirely lacks a man's heart. For that very reason we must set ourselves early to fight against

all signs of vanity in a child; or, rather, we must give him no occasion to become vain. This easily happens by people prattling before children, telling them how beautiful they are, and how well this or that dress becomes them, and promising them some finery or other as a reward. Finery is not suitable for children. They must accept their neat and simple clothes as necessaries merely.

At the same time the parents must not set great store by their own clothes, nor admire themselves; for here, as everywhere, example is all-powerful, and either strengthens or destroys good precepts.

CHAPTER VI
PRACTICAL EDUCATION

91. Practical education includes (1) skill, (2) discretion, and (3) morality.

With regard to *skill*, we must see that it is thorough, and not superficial. We must not pretend to know things which we afterwards cannot accomplish. Skill must be characterised by thoroughness, and this thoroughness should gradually become a habit. Thoroughness is an essential element in the formation of a man's character, while skill is necessary for talent.

92. As regards *discretion*, it consists in the art of turning our skill to account; that is, of using our fellow-men for our own ends. For this several things are necessary. Properly speaking, it is the last quality attained by man, but it ranks second in importance.

In order that a child may acquire prudence, he must learn to disguise his feelings and to be reserved, while at the same time he learns to read the character of others. It is chiefly with regard to his own character that he must cultivate reserve. Decorum is the art of outward behaviour, and this is an art that we must possess. It is difficult to read the characters of others, but we must learn to do this without losing our own reserve. For this end a kind of dissembling is necessary; that is to say, we have to hide our faults and keep up that outward appearance. This is not necessarily deceit, and is sometimes allowable, *although* it does border closely on insincerity.

Dissimulation, however, is but a desperate expedient. To be prudent it is necessary that we should not lose our temper; on the other hand, we should not be too apathetic. A man should be brave without being violent—two qualities which are quite distinct. A brave man is one who is desirous of exercising his will. This desire necessitates control of the passions. Discretion is a matter of temperament.

93. *Morality* is a matter of character. *Sustine et abstine,*[6] such is the preparation for a wise moderation. The first step towards the formation of a good character is to put our passions on one side. We must take care that our desires and inclinations do not become passions, by learning to go without those things that are denied to us. *Sustine* implies endure and accustom thyself to endure. Courage and a certain bent of mind towards it are necessary for renunciation. We ought to accustom ourselves to opposition, the refusal of our requests, and so on.

'Sympathy' is a matter of temperament. Children, however, ought to be prevented from contracting the habit of a sentimental maudlin sympathy. 'Sympathy' is really sensitiveness, and belongs only to characters of delicate feeling. It is distinct from compassion, and it is an evil, consisting as it does merely in lamenting over a thing. It is a good thing to give children some pocket-money of their own, that they may help the needy; and in this way we should see if they are really compassionate or not. But if they are only charitable with their parents' money, we have no such test.

The saying *Festina lente* expresses constant activity, by which we must hasten to learn a great deal—that is, *festina*. But we must also learn thoroughly, and this needs time; that is, *lente.* The question here arises whether it is better to know a great many things in a superficial way or a few things thoroughly. It is better to know but little, and that little thoroughly, than to know a great deal and that superficially; for one becomes aware of the shallowness of superficial knowledge later on. But the child does not know as yet in what condition he may be with regard to requiring this or that branch of knowledge: it is best, therefore, that he should know something thoroughly of all, otherwise he will but deceive and dazzle others by his superficially acquired knowledge.

94. Our ultimate aim is the formation of *character.* Character consists in the firm purpose to accomplish something, and then also in the actual accomplishing of it. *Vir propositi tenax,*[7] said Horace, and this is a good character. For instance, if a man makes a promise, he must keep it, however inconvenient it may be to himself; for a man who makes a resolution and fails to keep it will have no more confidence in himself. Suppose, for example, that a man resolves to rise early every morning that he may study, or do something or other, or take a walk—and excuses himself in spring because the mornings are still too cold, and rising early might injure his health, and in summer because it is well to allow himself to sleep, and sleep is pleasant—thus he puts off his resolution from day to day, until he ends in having no confidence in himself.

Those things which are contrary to morality must be excluded from such resolutions. The character of a wicked man is evil; but then, in this case, we do not call it 'character' any longer, but obstinacy; and yet there is still a certain satisfaction to find such a man holding fast to his resolutions and carrying them out, though it would be much better if he showed the same persistency in good things.

Those who delay to fulfil their resolutions will do but little in life. We cannot expect much good to come of so-called future conversion. The sudden conversion of a man who has led a vicious life cannot possibly be enduring, in that it would be nothing short of a miracle to expect a man who has lived in such a way suddenly to assume the well-conducted life of a man who has always had good and upright thoughts. For the same reason we can expect no good to come from pilgrimages, mortifications, and fastings; for it is difficult to see how such customs can, all at once, make a virtuous man out of a vicious one. How can it make a man more upright, or improve him in any way, to fast by day and to feast at night; to impose a penance upon his body, which can in no way help towards improving his mind?

95. *To form the foundation of moral character in children,* we must observe the following:—

We must place before them the duties they have to perform, as far as possible, by examples and rules. The duties which a child has to fulfil are only the common duties towards himself and towards others. These duties must be the natural outcome of the kind of question involved. We have thus to consider more closely:—

(1) *The child's duties towards himself.*—These do not consist in putting on fine clothes, in having sumptuous dinners, and so on, although his food should be good and his clothing neat. They do not consist in seeking to satisfy his cravings and inclinations; for, on the contrary, he ought to be very temperate and abstemious. But they consist in his being conscious that man possesses a certain dignity, which ennobles him above all other creatures, and that it is his duty so to act as not to violate in his own person this dignity of mankind. We are acting contrary to the dignity of man, for instance, when we give way to drink, or commit unnatural sins, or practise all kinds of irregularities, and so on, all of which place man far below the animals. Further, to be cringing in one's behaviour to others; to be always paying compliments, in order by such undignified conduct to ingratiate ourselves, as we assume—all this is against the dignity of man.

We can easily find opportunities for making children conscious of the dignity of man, even in their own persons. For instance, in the case of uncleanliness, which is at least unbecoming to mankind. But it is really through lying that a child degrades himself below the dignity of man, since lying presupposes the power of thinking and of communicating one's thoughts to others. Lying makes a man the object of common contempt, and is a means of robbing him of the respect for and trust in himself that every man should have.

(2) *The child's duties towards others.*—A child should learn early to reverence and respect the rights of others, and we must be careful to see that this reverence is realised in his actions. For instance, were a child to meet another poorer child and to push him rudely away, or to hit him, and so on, we must not say to the aggressor, 'Don't do that, you will hurt him; you should have pity, he is a poor child,' and so on. But we must treat him in the same haughty manner, because his conduct is against the rights of man. Children have as yet no idea, properly speaking, of generosity. We may, for instance, notice that when a child is told by his parents to share his slice of bread-and-butter with another, without being promised a second slice, the child either refuses to obey, or obeys unwillingly. It is, besides, useless to talk to a child of generosity, as it is not yet in his power to be generous.

96. Many writers . . . have either quite omitted, or explained falsely, that chapter of morality which teaches *our duties towards ourselves.* Our duties towards ourselves consist, as has been already said, in guarding, each in our own person, the dignity of mankind. A man will only reproach himself if he has the idea of mankind before his eyes. In this idea he finds an original, with which he compares himself. But when years increase, then is the critical period in which the idea of the dignity of man alone will suffice to keep the young

man in bounds. But the youth must have some timely hints which will help him to know what he is to approve and what to mistrust.

97. Almost all our schools are lacking in something which would nevertheless greatly tend to the formation of uprightness in children—namely, a *catechism of right conduct.* This should contain, in a popular form, everyday questions of right and wrong. For instance, a man has a certain debt to pay today, but he sees another man in sore need, and, moved with pity, gives him the money which belongs of right to his creditor. Is this right or wrong?

It is wrong, for we must be free from obligation before we can be generous. When we give alms, we do a meritorious act; but in paying our debts, we do what we are bound to do.

Again, can a lie ever be justified by necessity? No, there is no single instance in which a lie can be justified. If this rule were not strictly adhered to, children especially would take the smallest excuse for a necessity, and would very often allow themselves to tell lies. If there were a book of this kind, an hour might very profitably be spent daily in studying it, so that children might learn and take to heart lessons on right conduct—that apple of God's eye upon earth.

98. As to the *obligation of benevolence,* it is not an absolute obligation. We must arouse the sympathies of children, not so much to feel for the sorrows of others as to a sense of their duty to help them. Children ought not to be full of feeling, but they should be full of the idea of duty. Many people, indeed, become hard-hearted, where once they were pitiful, because they have so often been deceived. It is in vain to point out to children the meritorious side of actions. Religious teachers often make the mistake of representing acts of benevolence as meritorious, without seeing that all we can do for God is just to do what we are bound to do; and in doing good to the poor, we are only doing our duty. For the inequality of man arises only from accidental circumstances—if I possess wealth, to what do I owe it but to the laying hold of circumstances favourable to me or to my predecessors?—while our consideration of the whole remains ever the same.

99. We only excite envy in a child by telling him to compare his own worth with the worth of others. He ought rather to compare himself with a concept of his reason. For humility is really nothing else than the comparing of our own worth with the standard of moral perfection. Thus, for instance, the Christian religion makes people humble, not by preaching humility, but by teaching them to compare themselves with the highest pattern of perfection. It is very absurd to see humility in depreciating ourselves. 'See how such and such a child behaves himself!' An exclamation of this kind produces only a very ignoble mode of thinking; for if a man estimates his own worth by the worth of others, he either tries to elevate himself above others or to detract from another's worth. But this last is envy. We then only seek to impute faults to others, in order that we may compare favourably with them. Thus the spirit of emulation, wrongly applied, only arouses envy. Emulation may occasionally be used to good purpose, as when we tell a child, in order to convince him of the possibility of performing a certain task, that others could easily do it. We

must on no account allow one child to humiliate another. We must seek to avoid every form of pride which is founded upon superiority of fortune. At the same time we must seek to cultivate frankness in the child. This is an unassuming confidence in himself, the possession of which places him in a position to exhibit his talents in a becoming manner. This self-confidence is to be distinguished from insolence, which is really indifference to the judgment of others.

100. All the cravings of men are either formal (relating to freedom and power), or material (set upon a certain object)—that is to say, either cravings of imagination or enjoyment—or, finally, cravings for the continuation of these two things as elements of happiness. Cravings of the first kind are the lust of honour (ambition), the lust of power, and the lust of possession. Those of the second kind are sexual indulgence (voluptuousness), enjoyment of good things (good living), or the enjoyment of social intercourse (love of amusement).

Cravings of the third kind, finally, are love of life, love of health, and love of ease (freedom from care as regards the future).

Vices are either those of malice, baseness, or narrow-mindedness.

To the first belong envy, ingratitude, and joy at the misfortune of others. To the second kind belong injustice, unfaithfulness (deceitfulness), dissoluteness—and this in the squandering of wealth as well as of health (intemperance) and of honour.

Vices of the third kind are those of unkindness, niggardliness, and idleness (effeminacy).

101. *Virtues* are either virtues of merit or merely of obligation or of innocence.

To the first belong magnanimity (shown in self-conquest in times of anger or when tempted to ease and the lust of possession), benevolence, and self-command.

To the second belong honesty, propriety, peaceableness; and to the third, finally, belong honourableness, modesty, and content.

102. But is man by nature morally good or bad? He is neither, for he is not by nature a moral being. He only becomes a moral being when his reason has developed ideas of duty and law. One may say, however, that he has a natural inclination to every vice, for he has inclinations and instincts which would urge him one way, while his reason would drive him in another. He can only become morally good by means of virtue—that is to say, by self-restraint— though he may be innocent as long as his vicious inclinations lie dormant.

Vices, for the most part, arise in this way, that civilisation does violence to Nature; and yet our destiny as human beings is to emerge from our natural state as animals. Perfect art becomes second nature.

103. Everything in education depends upon establishing correct principles, and leading children to understand and accept them. They must learn to substitute abhorrence for what is revolting and absurd, for hatred; the fear of their own conscience, for the fear of man and divine punishment; self-respect and inward dignity, for the opinions of men; the inner value of actions, for words and mere impulses; understanding, for feeling; and joyousness and piety with good humour, for a morose, timid, and gloomy devotion.

But above all things we must keep children from esteeming the *merita for-tunae*[8] too highly.

104. In looking at the education of children with regard to *religion,* the first question which arises is whether it is practicable to impart religious ideas to children early in life. On this point much has been written in educational works. Religious ideas always imply a theology; and how can young people be taught theology when they do not yet know themselves, much less the world? Is the youth who as yet knows nothing of duty in the condition to comprehend an immediate duty towards God? This much is certain—that, could it be brought about that children should never witness a single act of veneration to God, never even hear the name of God spoken, it might then be the right order of things to teach them first about ends and aims, and of what concerns mankind; to sharpen their judgment; to instruct them in the *order and beauty of the works of Nature;* then add a wider knowledge of the structure of the universe; and then only might be revealed to them for the first time the idea of a Supreme Being—a Law-giver. But since this mode of proceeding is impossible, according to the present condition of society, and we cannot prevent children from hearing the name of God and seeing tokens of man's devotion to Him; if we were to teach them something about God only when they are grown up, the result would be either indifference or false ideas—for instance, terror of God's power. Since, then, it is to be feared that such ideas might find a dwelling-place in the child's imagination, to avoid it we should seek early to impart religious ideas to the child. But this instruction must not be merely the work of memory and imitation; the way chosen must be always in accordance with Nature. Children will understand—without abstract ideas of duty, of obligations, of good and bad conduct—that there is a law of duty which is not the same as ease, utility, or other considerations of the kind, but something universal, which is not governed by the caprice of men. The teacher himself, however, must form this idea.

At first we must ascribe everything to Nature, and afterwards Nature herself to God; showing at first, for instance, how everything is disposed for the preservation of the species and their equilibrium, but at the same time with consideration in the long run for man, that he may attain happiness.

The idea of God might first be taught by analogy with that of a father under whose care we are placed, and in this way we may with advantage point out to the child the unity of men as represented by one family.

105. What, then, is *religion?* Religion is the law in us, in so far as it derives emphasis from a Law-giver and a Judge above us. It is morality applied to the knowledge of God. If religion is not united to morality, it becomes merely an endeavour to win favour. Hymn-singing, prayers, and church-going should only give men fresh strength, fresh courage to advance; or they should be the utterance of a heart inspired with the idea of duty. They are but preparations for good works, and not the works themselves; and the only real way in which we may please God is by our becoming better men.

In teaching a child we must first begin with the law which is in him. A vi-cious man is contemptible to himself, and this contempt is inborn, and does not arise in the first instance because God has forbidden vice; for it does not necessarily follow that the law-giver is the author of the law. A prince, for instance, may forbid stealing in his country without being called the original prohibitor of theft. From this, man learns to understand that it is a good life alone which makes him worthy of happiness. The divine law must at the same time be recognised as Nature's law, for it is not arbitrary. Hence religion belongs to all morality.

We must not, however, begin with theology. The religion which is founded merely on theology can never contain anything of morality. Hence we derive no other feelings from it but fear on the one hand, and hope of reward on the other, and this produces merely a superstitious cult. Morality, then, must come first and theology follow; and that is religion.

106. The law that is within us we call conscience. Conscience, properly speaking, is the application of our actions to this law. The reproaches of conscience would be without effect, if we did not regard it as the representative of God, who, while He has raised up a tribunal over us, has also established a judgment-seat within us. If religion is not added to moral conscientiousness, it is of no effect. Religion without moral conscientiousness is a service of superstition. People will serve God by praising Him and reverencing His power and wisdom, without thinking how to fulfil the divine law; nay, even without knowing and searching out His power, wisdom, and so on. These hymn-singings are an opiate for the conscience of such people, and a pillow upon which it may quietly slumber.

107. Children cannot comprehend all *religious ideas*, notwithstanding there are some which we ought to teach them; these, however, must be more negative than positive. It is of no use whatever to let children recite formulae; it only produces a misconception of piety. The true way of honouring God consists in acting in accordance with His will, and this is what we must teach children to do. We must see to it that the name of God is not so often taken in vain, and this by ourselves as well as by children. If we use it in congratulating our friends—even with pious intent—this also is a misuse of the holy name. The idea of God ought to fill people with reverence every time they hear His name spoken. And it should be pronounced but seldom and never lightly. The child must learn to feel reverence towards God, as the Lord of life and of the whole world; further, as one who cares for men, and lastly as their Judge. We are told of Newton that he never pronounced the name of God without pausing for a while and meditating upon it.

108. Through an explanation which unites the ideas of *God* and of *duty* the child learns the better to respect the divine care for creatures, and will thus be kept from an inclination towards destruction and cruelty, which we so often see in the torture of small animals. At the same time we should teach the child to discover good in evil. For instance, beasts of prey and insects are patterns of cleanliness and diligence; so, too, evil men are a warning to follow the law; and birds, by waylaying worms, protect the garden; and so on.

109. We must, then, give children some idea of the Supreme Being, in order that when they see others praying, and so on, they may know to whom

they are praying, and why. But these ideas must be few in number, and, as has been said, merely negative. We must begin to impart them from early youth, being careful at the same time that they do not esteem men according to their religious observances, for, in spite of the diversity of religions, religion is everywhere the same. . . .

Notes

1. We know just so much as we remember.
2. Future forgetfulness.
3. A slavish disposition.
4. The disposition of a hireling.
5. The lad who hopes to win the race has borne and done much; he has endured extremes of heat and cold.
6. Endure and abstain.
7. A man who keeps steadfast to his purpose.
8. Strokes of luck.

6

John Stuart Mill

The British philosopher John Stuart Mill (1806–1873) did not write a book devoted to the philosophy of education, but the extended lecture he delivered at the University of St. Andrews in 1867 presents both his ideal of a liberal education suitable for university students and his justification for each of the subjects he recommends for inclusion in the curriculum.

He explains that a liberal education does not train individuals for their trades but is intended to enable persons to be reflective members of their society, carrying out their professions and all other civic duties with intelligence and broad perspective. As he puts it, if we are "capable and sensible" people, we are able to be "capable and sensible lawyers or physicians."

He stresses the danger of concentrating on one subject to the exclusion of all others, claiming that such an approach will "narrow and pervert the mind," leading to "a general prejudice, common to all narrow specialists, against large views, from an incapacity to take in and appreciate the grounds of them."

As an antidote to such intellectual tunnel vision, Mill urges that students should learn something of "all the great subjects of human interest," including logic, mathematics, the sciences, social sciences, history, philosophy, literature, and the arts. The knowledge thus acquired will serve as "intellectual capital," to be expended whenever needed to help make increased sense of human affairs.

Mill was an ardent defender of representative democracy, whose success depends most importantly on a well-educated citizenry. Here is another example of how political philosophy affects philosophy of education.

Inaugural Address
at Saint Andrews

In complying with the custom which prescribes that the person whom you have called by your suffrages to the honorary presidency of your University should embody in an Address a few thoughts on the subjects which most nearly concern a seat of liberal education, let me begin by saying, that this usage appears to me highly commendable. Education, in its larger sense, is one of the most inexhaustible of all topics. Though there is hardly any subject on which so much has been written, by so many of the wisest men, it is as fresh to those who come to it with a fresh mind, a mind not hopelessly filled full with other people's conclusions, as it was to the first explorers of it; and notwithstanding the great mass of excellent things which have been said respecting it, no thoughtful person finds any lack of things both great and small still waiting to be said, or waiting to be developed and followed out to their consequences. Education, moreover, is one of the subjects which most essentially require to be considered by various minds, and from a variety of points of view. For, of all many-sided subjects, it is the one which has the greatest number of sides. Not only does it include whatever we do for ourselves, and whatever is done for us by others, for the express purpose of bringing us somewhat nearer to the perfection of our nature; it does more: in its largest acceptation, it comprehends even the indirect effects produced on character and on the human faculties, by things of which the direct purposes are quite different; by laws, by forms of government, by the industrial arts, by modes of social life; nay, even by physical facts not dependent on human will; by climate, soil, and local position. Whatever helps to shape the human being—to make the individual what he is, or hinder him from being what he is not—is part of his education. And a very bad education it often is, requiring all that can be done by cultivated intelligence and will, to counteract its tendencies. To take an obvious instance: the niggardliness of Nature in some places, by engrossing the whole energies of the human being in the mere preservation of life, and her over-bounty in others, affording a sort of brutish subsistence on too easy terms, with hardly any exertion of the human faculties, are both hostile to the spontaneous growth and development of the mind; and it is at those two extremes of the scale that we find human societies in the state of most unmitigated savagery. I shall confine myself, however, to education in the narrower sense; the culture which each generation purposely gives to those who are to be its successors, in order to qualify them for at least keeping up, and if possible for raising, the level of improvement which has been attained. Nearly all here present are daily occupied either in receiving or in giving this sort of education; and the part of it which most concerns you at present is that in which you are yourselves engaged—the stage of education which is the appointed business of a national University.

The proper function of a University in national education is tolerably well understood. At least there is a tolerably general agreement about what a University is not. It is not a place of professional education. Universities are not intended to teach the knowledge required to fit men for some special mode of gaining their livelihood. Their object is not to make skilful lawyers, or physicians, or engineers, but capable and cultivated human beings. It is very right that there should be public facilities for the study of professions. It is well that there should be Schools of Law, and of Medicine, and it would be well if there were schools of engineering, and the industrial arts. The countries which have such institutions are greatly the better for them; and there is something to be said for having them in the same localities, and under the same general superintendence, as the establishments devoted to education properly so called. But these things are no part of what every generation owes to the next, as that on which its civilization and worth will principally depend. They are needed only by a comparatively few, who are under the strongest private inducements to acquire them by their own efforts; and even those few do not require them until after their education, in the ordinary sense, has been completed. Whether those whose speciality they are, will learn them as a branch of intelligence or as a mere trade, and whether, having learned them, they will make a wise and conscientious use of them or the reverse, depends less on the manner in which they are taught their profession, than upon what sort of minds they bring to it— what kind of intelligence, and of conscience, the general system of education has developed in them. Men are men before they are lawyers, or physicians, or merchants, or manufacturers; and if you make them capable and sensible men, they will make themselves capable and sensible lawyers or physicians. What professional men should carry away with them from a University, is not professional knowledge, but that which should direct the use of their professional knowledge, and bring the light of general culture to illuminate the technicalities of a special pursuit. Men may be competent lawyers without general education, but it depends on general education to make them philosophic lawyers—who demand, and are capable of apprehending, principles, instead of merely cramming their memory with details. And so of all other useful pursuits, mechanical included. Education makes a man a more intelligent shoemaker, if that be his occupation, but not by teaching him how to make shoes; it does so by the mental exercise it gives, and the habits it impresses.

This, then, is what a mathematician would call the higher limit of University education: its province ends where education, ceasing to be general, branches off into departments adapted to the individual's destination in life. The lower limit is more difficult to define. A University is not concerned with elementary instruction: the pupil is supposed to have acquired that before coming here. But where does elementary instruction end, and the higher studies begin? Some have given a very wide extension to the idea of elementary instruction. According to them, it is not the office of a University to give instruction in single branches of knowledge from the commencement. What the pupil should be taught here (they think), is to methodize his knowledge: to look at every separate part of it in its relation to the other parts, and to the whole; combining the partial glimpses which he has obtained of the field of human knowledge at different points, into a general map, if I may so speak, of the entire region; observing how all knowledge is connected, how we ascend to one branch by means of another, how the higher modifies the lower, and the lower helps us to understand the higher; how every existing reality is a compound of many properties, of which each science or distinct mode of study reveals but a small part, but the whole of which must be included to enable us to know it truly as a fact in Nature, and not as a mere abstraction.

This last stage of general education, destined to give the pupil a comprehensive and connected view of the things which he has already learned separately, includes a philosophic study of the Methods of the sciences; the modes in which the human intellect proceeds from the known to the unknown. We must be taught to generalize our conception of the resources which the human mind possesses for the exploration of nature; to understand how man discovers the real facts of the world, and by what tests he can judge whether he has really found them. And doubtless this is the crown and consummation of a liberal education: but before we restrict a University to this highest department of instruction—before we confine it to teaching, not knowledge, but the philosophy of knowledge—we must be assured that the knowledge itself has been acquired elsewhere. Those who take this view of the function of a University are not wrong in thinking that the schools, as distinguished from the Universities, ought to be adequate to teaching every branch of general instruction required by youth, so far as it can be studied apart from the rest. But where are such schools to be found? Since science assumed its modern character, nowhere; and in these islands less even than elsewhere. This ancient kingdom, thanks to its great religious reformers, had the inestimable advantage, denied to its southern sister, of excellent parish schools, which gave, really and not in pretence, a considerable amount of valuable literary instruction to the bulk of the population, two centuries earlier than in any other country. But schools of a still higher description have been, even in Scotland, so few and inadequate, that the Universities have had to perform largely the functions which ought to be performed by schools; receiving students at an early age, and undertaking not only the work for which the schools should have prepared them, but much of the preparation itself. Every Scottish University is not a University only, but a High School, to supply the deficiency of other schools. And if the English Universities do not do the same, it is not because the same need does not exist, but because it is disregarded. Youths come to the Scottish Universities ignorant, and are there taught. The majority of those who come to the English Universities come still more ignorant, and ignorant they go away.

In point of fact, therefore, the office of a Scottish University comprises the whole of a liberal education, from the foundations upwards. And the scheme of your Universities has, almost from the beginning, really aimed at including the whole, both in depth and in breadth. You have not, as the English Universities so long did, confined all the stress of your teaching, all your real effort to teach, within the limits of two subjects, the classical languages and mathematics. You did not wait till the last few years to establish a Natural Science and a Moral Science Tripos. Instruction in both those departments was organized long ago; and your teachers of those subjects have not been nominal professors, who did not lecture: some of the greatest names in physical and in moral science have taught in your Universities, and by their teaching contributed to form some of the most distinguished intellects of the last and present centuries. To comment upon the course of education at the Scottish Universities is to pass in review every essential department of general culture. The best use, then, which I am able to make of the present occasion, is to offer a few remarks on each of those departments, considered in its relation to human cultivation at large; adverting to the nature of the claims which each has to a place in liberal education; in what special manner they each conduce to the improvement of the individual mind and the benefit of the race; and how they all conspire to the common end, the strengthening, exalting, purifying, and beautifying of our common nature, and the fitting out of mankind with the necessary mental implements for the work they have to perform through life.

Let me first say a few words on the great controversy of the present day with regard to the higher education, the difference which most broadly divides educational reformers and conservatives; the vexed question between the ancient languages, and the modern sciences and arts; whether general education should be classical—let me use a wider expression, and say literary—or scientific. A dispute as endlessly, and often as fruitlessly agitated as that old controversy which it resembles, made memorable by the names of Swift and Sir William Temple in England, and Fontenelle in France—the contest for superiority between the ancients and the moderns. This question, whether we should be taught the classics or the sciences, seems to me, I confess, very like a dispute whether painters should cultivate drawing or coloring, or, to use a more homely illustration, whether a tailor should make coats or trousers. I can only reply by the question, Why not both? Can anything deserve the name of a good education which does not include literature and science too? If there were no more to be said than that scientific education teaches us to think, and literary education to express our thoughts, do we not require both? and is not anyone a poor, maimed, lopsided fragment of humanity who is deficient in either? We are not obliged to ask ourselves whether it is more important to know the languages or the sciences. Short as life is, and shorter still as we make it by the time we waste on things which are neither business, nor meditation, nor pleasure, we are not so badly off that our scholars need be ignorant of the laws and properties of the world they live in, or our scientific men destitute of poetic feeling and artistic cultivation. I am amazed at the limited conception which many educational reformers have formed to themselves of a human being's power of acquisition. The study of science, they truly say, is indispensable: our present education neglects it: there is truth in this too, though it is not all truth: and they think it impossible to find room for the studies which they desire to encourage, but by turning out, at least from general education, those which are now chiefly cultivated. How absurd, they say, that the whole of boyhood should be taken up in acquiring an imperfect knowledge of two dead languages. Absurd indeed: but is the human mind's capacity to learn, measured by that of Eton and Westminster to teach? I should prefer to see these reformers pointing their attacks against the shameful inefficiency of the schools, public and private, which pretend to teach these two languages and do not. I should like to hear them denounce the wretched methods of teaching, and the criminal idleness and supineness, which waste the entire boyhood of the pupils without really giving to most of them more than a smattering, if even that, of the only kind of knowledge which is even pretended to be cared for. Let us try what conscientious and intelligent teaching can do, before we presume to decide what cannot be done.

Scotland has on the whole, in this respect, been considerably more fortunate than England. Scotch youths have never found it impossible to leave school or the University having learned somewhat of other things besides Greek and Latin; and why? Because Greek and Latin have been better taught. A beginning of classical instruction has all along been made in the common schools; and the common schools of Scotland, like her Universities, have never been the mere shams that the English Universities were during the last century, and the greater part of the English classical schools still are. The only tolerable Latin Grammars for school purposes that I know of, which had been produced in these islands until very lately, were written by Scotchmen. Reason, indeed, is beginning to find its way by gradual infiltration even into English schools, and to maintain a contest, though as yet a very unequal one, against routine. A few practical reformers of school tuition, of whom Arnold was the most eminent, have made a beginning of amendment in many things; but reforms, worthy of the name, are always slow, and reform even of governments and churches is not so slow as that of schools, for there is the great preliminary difficulty of fashioning the instruments; of teaching the teachers. If all the improvements in the mode of teaching languages which are already sanctioned by experience, were adopted into our classical schools, we should soon cease to hear of Latin and Greek as studies which must engross the school years, and render impossible any other acquirements. If a boy learned Greek and Latin on the same principle on which a mere child learns with such ease and rapidity any modern language, namely, by acquiring some familiarity with the vocabulary by practice and repetition, before being troubled with grammatical rules,—those rules being acquired with tenfold greater facility when the cases to which they apply are already familiar to the mind,—an average schoolboy, long before the age at which schooling terminates, would be able to read fluently and with intelligent interest any ordinary Latin or Greek author in prose or verse, would have a competent knowledge of the grammatical structure of both languages, and have had time besides for an ample amount of scientific instruction. I might go much farther; but I am as unwilling to speak out all that I think practicable in this matter, as George Stephenson was about railways, when he calculated the average speed of a train at ten miles an hour, because if he had estimated it higher, the practical men would have turned a deaf ear to him, as that most unsafe character in their estimation, an enthusiast and a visionary. The results have shown, in that case, who was the real practical man. What the results would show in the other case, I will not attempt to anticipate. But I will say confidently, that if the two classical languages were properly taught, there would be no need whatever for ejecting them from the school course, in order to have sufficient time for everything else that need be included therein.

Let me say a few words more on this strangely limited estimate of what it is possible for human beings to learn, resting on a tacit assumption that they are already as efficiently taught as they ever can be. So narrow a conception not only vitiates our idea of education, but actually, if we receive it, darkens our anticipations as to the future progress of mankind. For if the inexorable conditions of human life make it useless for one man to attempt to know more than one thing, what is to become of the human intellect as facts accumulate? In every generation, and now more rapidly than ever, the things which it is necessary that somebody should know are more and more multiplied. Every department of knowledge becomes so loaded with details, that one who endeavors to know it with minute accuracy, must confine himself to a smaller and smaller portion of the whole extent: every science and art must be cut up into subdivisions, until each man's portion, the district which he thoroughly knows, bears about the same ratio to the whole range of useful knowledge that the art of putting on a pin's head does to the field of human industry. Now, if, in order to know that little completely, it is necessary to remain wholly ignorant of all the rest, what will soon be the worth of a man, for any human purpose except his own infinitesimal fraction of human wants and requirements? His state will be even worse than that of simple ignorance. Experience proves that there is no one study or pursuit, which, practised to the exclusion of all others, does not narrow and pervert the mind; breeding in it a class of prejudices special to that pursuit, besides a general prejudice, common to all narrow specialities, against large views, from an incapacity to take in and appreciate the grounds of them. We should have to expect that human nature would be more and more dwarfed, and unfitted for great things, by its very proficiency in small ones. But matters are not so bad with us: there is no ground for so dreary an anticipation. It is not the utmost limit of human acquirement to know only one thing, but to combine a minute knowledge of one or a few things with a general knowledge of many things. By a general knowledge I do not mean a few vague impressions. An eminent man, one of whose writings is part of the course of this University, Archbishop Whately, has well discriminated between a general knowledge and a superficial knowledge. To have a general knowledge of a subject is to know only its leading truths, but to know these not superficially but thoroughly, so as to have a true conception of the subject in its great features; leaving the minor details to those who require them for the purposes of their special pursuit. There is no incompatibility between knowing a wide range of subjects up to this point, and some one subject with the completeness required by those who make it their principal occupation. It is this combination which gives an enlightened public: a body of cultivated intellects, each taught by its attainments in its own province what real knowledge is, and knowing enough of other subjects to be able to discern who are those that know them better. The amount of knowledge is not to be lightly estimated, which qualifies us for judging to whom we may have recourse for more. The elements of the more important studies being widely diffused, those who have reached the higher summits find a public capable of appreciating their superiority, and prepared to follow their lead. It is thus, too, that minds are formed capable of guiding and improving public opinion on the greater concerns of practical life. Government and civil society are the most complicated of all subjects accessible to the human mind; and he who would deal competently with them as a thinker, and not as a blind follower of a party, requires not only a general knowledge of the leading facts of life, both moral and material, but an understanding exercised and disciplined in the principles and rules of sound thinking, up to a point which neither the experience of life, nor any one science or branch of knowledge, affords. Let us understand, then, that it should be our aim in learning, not merely to know the one thing which is to be our principal occupation, as well as it can be known, but to do this and also to know something of all the great subjects of human interest; taking care to know that something accurately; marking well the dividing line between what we know accurately and what we do not; and remembering that our object should be to obtain a true view of nature and life in their broad outline, and that it is idle to throw away time upon the details of anything which is to form no part of the occupation of our practical energies.

It by no means follows, however, that every useful branch of general, as distinct from professional, knowledge, should be included in the curriculum of school or University studies. There are things which are better learned out of school, or when the school years, and even those usually passed in a Scottish University, are over. I do not agree with those reformers who would give a regular and prominent place in the school or University course to modern languages. This is not because I attach small importance to the knowledge of them. No one can in our age be esteemed a well-instructed person who is not familiar with at least the French language, so as to read French books with ease; and there is great use in cultivating a familiarity with German. But living languages are so much more easily acquired by intercourse with those who use them in daily life; a few months in the country itself, if properly employed, go so much farther than as many years of school lessons; that it is really waste of time for those to whom that easier mode is attainable, to labor at them with no help but that of books and masters: and it will in time be made attainable, through international schools and colleges, to many more than at present. Universities do enough to facilitate the study of modern languages, if they give a mastery over that ancient language which is the foundation of most of them, and the possession of which makes it easier to learn four or five of the continental languages than it is to learn one of them without it. Again, it has always seemed to me a great absurdity that history and geography should be taught in schools; except in elementary schools for the children of the laboring classes, whose subsequent access to books is limited. Who ever really learned history and geography except by private reading? and what an utter failure a system of education must be, if it has not given the pupil a sufficient taste for reading to seek for himself those most attractive and easily intelligible of all kinds of knowledge! Besides, such history and geography as can be taught in schools exercise none of the faculties of the intelligence except the memory. A University is indeed the place where the student should be introduced to the Philosophy of History; where professors who not merely know the facts, but have exercised their minds on them, should initiate him into the causes and explanations, so far as within our reach, of the past life of mankind in its principal features. Historical criticism also—the tests of historical truth—are a subject to which his attention may well be drawn in this stage of his education. But of the mere facts of history, as commonly accepted, what educated youth of any mental activity does not learn as much as is necessary, if he is simply turned loose into an historical library? What he needs on this, and on most other matters of common information, is, not that he should be taught it in boyhood, but that abundance of books should be accessible to him.

The only languages, then, and the only literature, to which I would allow a place in the ordinary curriculum, are those of the Greeks and Romans; and to these I would preserve the position in it which they at present occupy. That position is justified, by the great value, in education, of knowing well some other cultivated language and literature than one's own, and by the peculiar value of those particular languages and literatures.

There is one purely intellectual benefit from a knowledge of languages, which I am specially desirous to dwell on. Those who have seriously reflected on the causes of human error, have been deeply impressed with the tendency of mankind to mistake words for things. Without entering into the metaphysics of the subject, we know how common it is to use words glibly and with apparent propriety, and to accept them confidently when used by others, without ever having had any distinct conception of the things denoted by them. To quote again from Archbishop Whately, it is the habit of mankind to mistake familiarity for accurate knowledge. As we seldom think of asking the meaning of what we see every day, so when our ears are used to the sound of a word or a phrase, we do not suspect that it conveys no clear idea to our minds, and that we should have the utmost difficulty in defining it, or expressing, in any other words, what we think we understand by it. Now, it is obvious in what manner this bad habit tends to be corrected by the practice of translating with accuracy from one language to another, and hunting out the meanings expressed in a vocabulary with which we have not grown familiar by early and constant use. I hardly know any greater proof of the extraordinary genius of the Greeks, than that they were able to make such brilliant achievements in abstract thought, knowing, as they generally did, no language but their own. But the Greeks did not escape the effects of this deficiency. Their greatest intellects, those who laid the foundation of philosophy and of all our intellectual culture, Plato and Aristotle, are continually led away by words; mistaking the accidents of language for real relations in nature, and supposing that things which have the same name in the Greek tongue must be the same in their own essence. There is a well-known saying of Hobbes, the far-reaching significance of which you will more and more appreciate in proportion to the growth of your own intellect: "Words are the counters of wise men, but the money of fools." With the wise man a word stands for the fact which it represents; to the fool it is itself the fact. To carry on Hobbes's metaphor, the counter is far more likely to be taken for merely what it is, by those who are in the habit of using many different kinds of counters. But, besides the advantage of possessing another cultivated language, there is a further consideration equally important. Without knowing the language of a people, we never really know their thoughts, their feelings, and their type of character: and unless we do possess this knowledge, of some other people than ourselves, we remain, to the hour of our death, with our intellects only half expanded. Look at a youth who has never been out of his family circle: he never dreams of any other opinions or ways of thinking than those he has been bred up in; or, if he has heard of any such, attributes them to some moral defect, or inferiority of nature or education. If his family are Tory, he cannot conceive the possibility of being a Liberal; if Liberal, of being a Tory. What the notions and habits of a single family are to a boy who has had no intercourse beyond it, the notions and habits of his own country are to him who is ignorant of every other. Those notions and habits are to him human nature itself; whatever varies from them is an unaccountable aberration which he cannot mentally realize: the idea that any other ways can be right, or as near an approach to right as some of his own, is inconceivable to him. This does not merely close his eyes to the many things which every country still has to learn from others: it hinders every country from reaching the improvement which it could otherwise attain by itself. We are not likely to correct any of our opinions or mend any of our ways, unless we begin by conceiving that they are capable of amendment: but merely to know that foreigners think differently from ourselves, without understanding why they do so, or what they really do think, does but confirm us in our self-conceit, and connect our national vanity with the preservation of our own peculiarities. Improvement consists in bringing our opinions into nearer agreement with facts; and we shall not be likely to do this while we look at facts only through glasses colored by those very opinions. But since we cannot divest ourselves of preconceived notions, there is no known means of eliminating their influence but by frequently using the differently colored glasses of other people: and those of other nations, as the most different, are the best.

But if it is so useful, on this account, to know the language and literature of any other cultivated and civilized people, the most valuable of all to us in this respect are the languages and literature of the ancients. No nations of modern and civilized Europe are so unlike one another, as the Greeks and Romans are unlike all of us; yet without being, as some remote Orientals are, so totally dissimilar, that the labor of a life is required to enable us to understand them. Were this the only gain to be derived from a knowledge of the ancients, it would already place the study of them in a high rank among enlightening and liberalizing pursuits. It is of no use saying that we may know them through modern writings. We may know something of them in that way; which is much better than knowing nothing. But modern books do not teach us ancient thought; they teach us some modern writer's notion of ancient thought. Modern books do not show us the Greeks and Romans; they tell us some modern writer's opinions about the Greeks and Romans. Translations are scarcely better. When we want really to know what a person thinks or says, we seek it at first hand from himself. We do not trust to another person's impression of his meaning, given in another person's words; we refer to his own. Much more is it necessary to do so when his words are in one language, and those of his reporter in another. Modern phraseology never conveys the exact meaning of a Greek writer; it cannot do so, except by a diffuse explanatory circumlocution which no translator dares use. We must be able, in a certain degree, to think in Greek, if we would represent to ourselves how a Greek thought; and this not only in the abstruse region of metaphysics, but about the political, religious, and even domestic concerns of life. I will mention a further aspect of this question, which, though I have not the merit of originating it, I do not remember to have seen noticed in any book. There is no part of our knowledge which it is more useful to obtain at first hand—to go to the fountain head for—than our knowledge of history. Yet this, in most cases, we hardly ever do. Our conception of the past is not drawn from its own records, but from books written about it, containing not the facts, but a view of the facts which has shaped itself in the mind of somebody of our own or a very recent time. Such books are very instructive and valuable; they help us to understand history, to interpret history, to draw just conclusions from it; at the worst, they set us the example of trying to do all this; but they are not themselves history. The knowledge they give is upon trust, and even when they have done their best, it is not only incomplete, but partial, because confined to what a few modern writers have seen in the materials, and have thought worth picking out from among them. How little we learn of our own ancestors from Hume, or Hallam, or Macaulay, compared with what we know if we add to what these tell us, even a little reading of contemporary authors and documents! The most recent historians are so well aware of this, that they fill their pages with extracts from the original materials, feeling that these extracts are the real history, and their comments and thread of narrative are only helps towards understanding it. Now, it is part of the great worth to us of our Greek and Latin studies, that in them we do read history in the original sources. We are in actual contact with contemporary minds; we are not dependent on hearsay; we have something by which we can test and check the representations and theories of modern historians. It may be asked, Why then not study the original materials of modern history? I answer, It is highly desirable to do so; and let me remark by the way, that even this requires a dead language; nearly all the documents prior to the Reformation, and many subsequent to it, being written in Latin. But the exploration of these documents, though a most useful pursuit, cannot be a branch of education. Not to speak of their vast extent, and the fragmentary nature of each, the strongest reason is, that in learning the spirit of our own past ages, until a comparatively recent period, from contemporary writers, we learn hardly anything else. Those authors, with a few exceptions, are little worth reading on their own account. While, in studying the great writers of antiquity, we are not only learning to understand the ancient mind, but laying in a stock of wise thought and observation, still valuable to ourselves; and at the same time making ourselves familiar with a number of the most perfect and finished literary compositions which the human mind has produced—compositions which, from the altered conditions of human life, are likely to be seldom paralleled, in their sustained excellence, by the times to come.

Even as mere languages, no modern European language is so valuable a discipline to the intellect as those of Greece and Rome, on account of their regular and complicated structure. Consider for a moment what grammar is. It is the most elementary part of logic. It is the beginning of the analysis of the thinking process. The principles and rules of grammar are the means by which the forms of language are made to correspond with the universal forms of thought. The distinctions between the various parts of speech, between the cases of nouns, the moods and tenses of verbs, the functions of particles, are distinctions in thought, not merely in words. Single nouns and verbs express objects and events, many of which can be cognized by the senses: but the modes of putting nouns and verbs together, express the relations of objects and events, which can be cognized only by the intellect; and each different mode corresponds to a different relation. The structure of every sentence is a lesson in logic. The various rules of syntax oblige us to distinguish between the subject and predicate of a proposition, between the agent, the action, and the thing acted upon; to mark when an idea is intended to modify or qualify, or merely to unite with, some other idea; what assertions are categorical, what only conditional; whether the intention is to express similarity or contrast, to make a plurality of assertions conjunctively or disjunctively; what portions of a sentence, though grammatically complete within themselves, are mere members or subordinate parts of the assertion made by the entire sentence. Such things form the subject-matter of universal grammar; and the languages which teach it best are those which have the most definite rules, and which provide distinct forms for the greatest number of distinctions in thought, so that if we fail to attend precisely and accurately to any of these, we cannot avoid committing a solecism in language. In these qualities the classical languages have an incomparable superiority over every modern language, and over all languages, dead or living, which have a literature worth being generally studied.

But the superiority of the literature itself, for purposes of education, is still more marked and decisive. Even in the substantial value of the matter of which it is the vehicle, it is very far from having been superseded. The discoveries of the ancients in science have been greatly surpassed, and as much of them as is still valuable loses nothing by being incorporated in modern treatises: but what does not so well admit of being transferred bodily, and has been very imperfectly carried off even piecemeal, is the treasure which they accumulated of what may be called the wisdom of life; the rich store of experience of human nature and conduct, which the acute and observing minds of those ages, aided in their observations by the greater simplicity of manners and life, consigned to their writings, and most of which retains all its value. The speeches in Thucydides; the Rhetoric, Ethics, and Politics of Aristotle; the Dialogues of Plato; the Orations of Demosthenes; the Satires, and especially the Epistles of Horace; all the writings of Tacitus; the great work of Quintilian, a repertory of the best thoughts of the ancient world on all subjects connected with education; and, in a less formal manner, all that is left to us of the ancient historians, orators, philosophers, and even dramatists, are replete with remarks and maxims of singular good sense and penetration, applicable both to political and to private life: and the actual truths we find in them are even surpassed in value by the encouragement and help they give us in the pursuit of truth. Human invention has never produced anything so valuable, in the way both of stimulation and of discipline to the inquiring intellect, as the dialectics of the ancients, of which many of the works of Aristotle illustrate the theory, and those of Plato exhibit the practice. No modern writings come near to these, in teaching, both by precept and example, the way to investigate truth, on those subjects, so vastly important to us, which remain matters of controversy, from the difficulty or impossibility of bringing them to a directly experimental test. To question all things; never to turn away from any difficulty; to accept no doctrine either from ourselves or from other people without a rigid scrutiny by negative criticism, letting no fallacy, or incoherence, or confusion of thought, slip by unperceived; above all, to insist upon having the meaning of a word clearly understood before using it, and the meaning of a proposition before assenting to it; these are the lessons we learn from the ancient dialecticians. With all this vigorous management of the negative element, they inspire no scepticism about the reality of truth, or indifference to its pursuit. The noblest enthusiasm, both for the search after truth and for applying it to its highest uses, pervades these writers, Aristotle no less than Plato, though Plato has incomparably the greater power of imparting those feelings to others. In cultivating, therefore, the ancient languages as our best literary education, we are all the while laying an admirable foundation for ethical and philosophical culture. In purely literary excellence—in perfection of form—the pre-eminence of the ancients is not disputed. In every department which they attempted,—and they attempted almost all,—their composition, like their sculpture, has been to the greatest modern artists an example, to be looked up to with hopeless admiration, but of inappreciable value as a light on high, guiding their own endeavors. In prose and in poetry, in epic, lyric, or dramatic, as in historical, philosophical, and oratorical art, the pinnacle on which they stand is equally eminent. I am now speaking of the form, the artistic perfection of treatment; for, as regards substance, I consider modern poetry to be superior to ancient, in the same manner, though in a less degree, as modern science: it enters deeper into nature. The feelings of the modern mind are more various, more complex and manifold, that those of the ancients ever were. The modern mind is, what the ancient mind was not, brooding and self-conscious; and its meditative self-consciousness has discovered depths in the human soul which the Greeks and Romans did not dream of, and would not have understood. But what they had got to express, they expressed in a manner which few even of the greatest moderns have seriously attempted to rival. It must be remembered that they had more time, and that they wrote chiefly for a select class, possessed of leisure. To us who write in a hurry for people who read in a hurry, the attempt to give an equal degree of finish would be loss of time. But to be familiar with perfect models is not the less important to us because the element in which we work precludes even the effort to equal them. They show us at least what excellence is, and make us desire it, and strive to get as near to it as is within our reach. And this is the value to us of the ancient writers, all the more emphatically, because their excellence does not admit of being copied, or directly imitated. It does not consist in a trick which can be learned, but in the perfect adaptation of means to ends. The secret of the style of the great Greek and Roman authors is, that it is the perfection of good sense. In the first place, they never use a word without a meaning, or a word which adds nothing to the meaning. They always (to begin with) had a meaning; they knew what they wanted to say; and their whole purpose was to say it with the highest degree of exactness and completeness, and bring it home to the mind with the greatest possible clearness and vividness. It never entered into their thoughts to conceive of a piece of writing as beautiful in itself, abstractedly from what it had to express: its beauty must all be subservient to the most perfect expression of the sense. The *curiosa felicitas* which their critics ascribed in a pre-eminent degree to Horace, expresses the standard at which they all aimed. Their style is exactly described by Swift's definition, "the right words in the right places." Look at an oration of Demosthenes; there is nothing in it which calls attention to itself as style at all: it is only after a close examination we perceive that every word is what it should be, and where it should be, to lead the hearer smoothly and imperceptibly into the state of mind which the orator wishes to produce. The perfection of the workmanship is only visible in the total absence of any blemish or fault, and of anything which checks the flow of thought and feeling, anything which even momentarily distracts the mind from the main purpose. But then (as has been well said) it was not the object of Demosthenes to make the Athenians cry out, "What a splendid speaker!" but to make them say, "Let us march against Philip!" It was only in the decline of ancient literature that ornament began to be cultivated merely as ornament. In the time of its maturity, not the merest epithet was put in because it was thought beautiful in itself; nor even for a merely descriptive purpose, for epithets purely descriptive were one of the corruptions of style which abound in Lucan, for example: the word had no business there unless it brought out some feature which was wanted, and helped to place the object in the light which the purpose of the composition required. These conditions being complied with, then indeed the intrinsic beauty of the means used was a source of additional effect, of which it behooved them to avail themselves, like rhythm and melody of versification. But these great writers knew that ornament for the sake of ornament, ornament which attracts attention to itself, and shines by its own beauties, only does so by calling off the mind from the main object, and thus not only interferes with the higher purpose of human discourse, which ought, and generally professes, to have some matter to communicate, apart from the mere excitement of the moment, but also spoils the perfection of the composition as a piece of fine art, by destroying the unity of effect. This, then, is the first great lesson in composition to be learned from the classical authors. The second is, not to be prolix. In a single paragraph, Thucydides can give a clear and vivid representation of a battle, such as a reader who has once taken it into his mind can seldom forget. The

most powerful and affecting piece of narrative perhaps in all historical literature, is the account of the Sicilian catastrophe in his seventh book; yet how few
pages does it fill! The ancients were concise, because of the extreme pains they
took with their compositions; almost all moderns are prolix, because they do
not. The great ancients could express a thought so perfectly in a few words or
sentences, that they did not need to add any more: the moderns, because they
cannot bring it out clearly and completely at once, return again and again,
heaping sentence upon sentence, each adding a little more elucidation, in
hopes that, though no single sentence expresses the full meaning, the whole together may give a sufficient notion of it. In this respect I am afraid we are
growing worse, instead of better, for want of time and patience, and from the
necessity we are in of addressing almost all writings to a busy and imperfectly
prepared public. The demands of modern life are such, the work to be done,
the mass to be worked upon, are so vast, that those who have anything particular to say—who have, as the phrase goes, any message to deliver—cannot afford to devote their time to the production of masterpieces. But they would do
far worse than they do, if there had never been masterpieces, or if they had
never known them. Early familiarity with the perfect makes our most imperfect production far less bad than it otherwise would be. To have a high standard of excellence often makes the whole difference of rendering our work
good when it would otherwise be mediocre.

For all these reasons I think it important to retain these two languages
and literatures in the place they occupy, as a part of liberal education, that is, of
the education of all who are not obliged by their circumstances to discontinue
their scholastic studies at a very early age. But the same reasons which vindi-
cate the place of classical studies in general education, show also the proper
limitation of them. They should be carried as far as is sufficient to enable the
pupil, in after life, to read the great works of ancient literature with ease. Those
who have leisure and inclination to make scholarship, or ancient history, or
general philology, their pursuit, of course require much more; but there is no
room for more in general education. The laborious idleness in which the
schooltime is wasted away in the English classical schools deserves the sever-
est reprehension. To what purpose should the most precious years of early life
be irreparably squandered in learning to write bad Latin and Greek verses? I
do not see that we are much the better even for those who end by writing good
ones. I am often tempted to ask the favorites of nature and fortune, whether all
the serious and important work of the world is done, that their time and energy can be spared for these *nugae difficiles.* I am not blind to the utility of composing in a language, as a means of learning it accurately. I hardly know any
other means equally effectual. But why should not prose composition suffice?
What need is there of original composition at all? if that can be called original
which unfortunate school-boys, without any thoughts to express, hammer out
on compulsion from mere memory, acquiring the pernicious habit which a
teacher should consider it one of his first duties to repress—that of merely
stringing together borrowed phrases? The exercise in composition, most suitable to the requirements of learners, is that most valuable one, of retranslating

from translated passages of a good author: and to this might be added, what still exists in many Continental places of education, occasional practice in talking Latin. There would be something to be said for the time spent in the manufacture of verses, if such practice were necessary for the enjoyment of ancient poetry; though it would be better to lose that enjoyment than to purchase it at so extravagant a price. But the beauties of a great poet would be a far poorer thing than they are, if they only impressed us through a knowledge of the technicalities of his art. The poet needed those technicalities: they are not necessary to us. They are essential for criticising a poem, but not for enjoying it. All that is wanted is sufficient familiarity with the language, for its meaning to reach us without any sense of effort, and clothed with the associations on which the poet counted for producing his effect. Whoever has this familiarity, and a practised ear, can have as keen a relish of the music of Virgil and Horace, as of Gray, or Burns, or Shelley, though he know not the metrical rules of a common Sapphic or Alcaic. I do not say that these rules ought not to be taught, but I would have a class apart for them, and would make the appropriate exercises an optional, not a compulsory part of the school teaching.

Much more might be said respecting classical instruction, and literary cultivation in general, as a part of liberal education. But it is time to speak of the uses of scientific instruction; or rather its indispensable necessity, for it is recommended by every consideration which pleads for any high order of intellectual education at all.

The most obvious part of the value of scientific instruction—the mere information that it gives—speaks for itself. We are born into a world which we have not made; a world whose phenomena take place according to fixed laws, of which we do not bring any knowledge into the world with us. In such a world we are appointed to live, and in it all our work is to be done. Our whole working power depends on knowing the laws of the world—in other words, the properties of the things which we have to work with, and to work among, and to work upon. We may and do rely, for the greater part of this knowledge, on the few who in each department make its acquisition their main business in life. But unless an elementary knowledge of scientific truths is diffused among the public, they never know what is certain and what is not, or who are entitled to speak with authority and who are not: and they either have no faith at all in the testimony of science, or are the ready dupes of charlatans and impostors. They alternate between ignorant distrust, and blind, often misplaced, confidence. Besides, who is there who would not wish to understand the meaning of the common physical facts that take place under his eye? Who would not wish to know why a pump raises water, why a lever moves heavy weights, why it is hot at the tropics and cold at the poles, why the moon is sometimes dark and sometimes bright, what is the cause of the tides? Do we not feel that he who is totally ignorant of these things, let him be ever so skilled in a special profession, is not an educated man, but an ignoramus? It is surely no small part of education to put us in intelligent possession of the most important and most universally interesting facts of the universe, so that the world which surrounds us may not be a sealed book to us, uninteresting because unintelligible.

This, however, is but the simplest and most obvious part of the utility of science, and the part which, if neglected in youth, may be the most easily made up for afterwards. It is more important to understand the value of scientific instruction as a training and disciplining process, to fit the intellect for the proper work of a human being. Facts are the materials of our knowledge, but the mind itself is the instrument; and it is easier to acquire facts, than to judge what they prove, and how, through the facts which we know, to get to those which we want to know.

The most incessant occupation of the human intellect throughout life is the ascertainment of truth. We are always needing to know what is actually true about something or other. It is not given to us all to discover great general truths that are a light to all men and to future generations; though with a better general education the number of those who could do so would be far greater than it is. But we all require the ability to judge between the conflicting opinions which are offered to us as vital truths; to choose what doctrines we will receive in the matter of religion, for example; to judge whether we ought to be Tories, Whigs, or Radicals, or to what length it is our duty to go with each; to form a rational conviction on great questions of legislation and internal policy, and on the manner in which our country should behave to dependencies and to foreign nations. And the need we have of knowing how to discriminate truth, is not confined to the larger truths. All through life it is our most pressing interest to find out the truth about all the matters we are concerned with. If we are farmers we want to find what will truly improve our soil; if merchants, what will truly influence the markets of our commodities; if judges, or jurymen, or advocates, who it was that truly did an unlawful act, or to whom a disputed right truly belongs. Every time we have to make a new resolution or alter an old one, in any situation in life, we shall go wrong unless we know the truth about the facts on which our resolution depends. Now, however different these searchers for truth may look, and however unlike they really are in their subject-matter, the methods of getting at truth, and the tests of truth, are in all cases much the same. There are but two roads by which truth can be discovered—observation and reasoning; observation, of course, including experiment. We all observe, and we all reason, and therefore, more or less successfully, we all ascertain truths: but most of us do it very ill, and could not get on at all were we not able to fall back on others who do it better. If we could not do it in any degree, we should be mere instruments in the hands of those who could: they would be able to reduce us to slavery. Then how shall we best learn to do this? By being shown the way in which it has already been successfully done. The process by which truth is attained, reasoning and observation, have been carried to their greatest known perfection in the physical sciences. As classical literature furnishes the most perfect types of the art of expression, so do the physical sciences those of the art of thinking. Mathematics, and its application to astronomy and natural philosophy, are the most complete example of the discovery of truths by reasoning; experimental science, of their discovery by direct observation. In all these cases we know that we can trust the operation, because the conclusions to which it has led have been found true by subsequent trial. It is by the study of these, then, that we may hope to qualify ourselves for distinguishing truth, in cases where there do not exist the same ready means of verification.

In what consists the principal and most characteristic difference between one human intellect and another? In their ability to judge correctly of evidence. Our direct perceptions of truth are so limited,—we know so few things by immediate intuition, or, as it used to be called, by simple apprehension,—that we depend, for almost all our valuable knowledge, on evidence external to itself; and most of us are very unsafe hands at estimating evidence, where an appeal cannot be made to actual eyesight. The intellectual part of our education has nothing more important to do than to correct or mitigate this almost universal infirmity—this summary and substance of nearly all purely intellectual weakness. To do this with effect needs all the resources which the most perfect system of intellectual training can command. Those resources, as every teacher knows, are but of three kinds: first, models; secondly, rules; thirdly, appropriate practice. The models of the art of estimating evidence are furnished by science; the rules are suggested by science; and the study of science is the most fundamental portion of the practice.

Take, in the first instance, mathematics. It is chiefly from mathematics we realize the fact that there actually is a road to truth by means of reasoning; that anything real, and which will be found true when tried, can be arrived at by a mere operation of the mind. The flagrant abuse of mere reasoning in the days of the schoolmen, when men argued confidently to supposed facts of outward nature without properly establishing their premises, or checking the conclusions by observation, created a prejudice in the modern, and especially in the English mind, against deductive reasoning altogether, as a mode of investigation. The prejudice lasted long, and was upheld by the misunderstood authority of Lord Bacon; until the prodigious applications of mathematics to physical science—to the discovery of the laws of external nature—slowly and tardily restored the reasoning process to the place which belongs to it as a source of real knowledge. Mathematics, pure and applied, are still the great conclusive example of what can be done by reasoning. Mathematics also habituates us to several of the principal precautions for the safety of the process. Our first studies in geometry teach us two invaluable lessons. One is, to lay down at the beginning, in express and clear terms, all the premises from which we intend to reason. The other is, to keep every step in the reasoning distinct and separate from all the other steps, and to make each step safe before proceeding to another; expressly stating to ourselves, at every joint in the reasoning, what new premise we there introduce. It is not necessary that we should do this at all times, in all our reasonings. But we must be always able and ready to do it. If the validity of our argument is denied, or if we doubt it ourselves, that is the way to check it. In this way we are often enabled to detect at once the exact place where paralogism or confusion get in: and after sufficient practice we may be able to keep them out from the beginning. It is to mathematics, again, that we owe our first notion of a connected body of truth; truths which grow out of one another, and hang together so that each implies all the rest; that no one of them can be questioned without contradicting another or others, until in the end it appears that no part of the system can be false unless the whole is so. Pure mathematics first gave us this conception; applied mathematics extends it to the realm of physical nature. Applied mathematics shows us that not only the truths of abstract number and extension, but the external facts of the universe, which we apprehend by our senses, form, at least in a large part of all nature, a web similarly held together. We are able, by reasoning from a few fundamental truths, to explain and predict the phenomena of material objects: and what is still more remarkable, the fundamental truths were themselves found out by reasoning; for they are not such as are obvious to the senses, but had to be inferred by a mathematical process from a mass of minute details, which alone came within the direct reach of human observation. When Newton, in this manner, discovered the laws of the solar system, he created, for all posterity, the true idea of science. He gave the most perfect example we are ever likely to have, of that union of reasoning and observation, which by means of facts that can be directly observed, ascends to laws which govern multitudes of other facts—laws which not only explain and account for what we see, but give us assurance beforehand of much that we do not see, much that we never could have found out by observation, though, having been found out, it is always verified by the result.

While mathematics, and the mathematical sciences, supply us with a typical example of the ascertainment of truth by reasoning,—those physical sciences which are not mathematical, such as chemistry, and purely experimental physics, show us in equal perfection the other mode of arriving at certain truth, by observation, in its most accurate form—that of experiment. The value of mathematics in a logical point of view is an old topic with mathematicians, and has even been insisted on so exclusively as to provoke a counter-exaggeration, of which a well-known essay by Sir William Hamilton is an example: but the logical value of experimental science is comparatively a new subject; yet there is no intellectual discipline more important than that which the experimental sciences afford. Their whole occupation consists in doing well, what all of us, during the whole of life, are engaged in doing, for the most part badly. All men do not affect to be reasoners, but all profess, and really attempt, to draw inferences from experience: yet hardly anyone, who has not been a student of the physical sciences, sets out with any just idea of what the process of interpreting experience really is. If a fact has occurred once or oftener, and another fact has followed it, people think they have got an experiment, and are well on the road towards showing that the one fact is the cause of the other. If they did but know the immense amount of precaution necessary to a scientific experiment; with what sedulous care the accompanying circumstances are contrived and varied, so as to exclude every agency but that which is the subject of the experiment—or, when disturbing agencies cannot be excluded, the minute accuracy with which their influence is calculated and allowed for, in order that the residue may contain nothing but what is due to the one agency under examination; if these things were attended to, people would be much less easily satisfied that their opinions have the evidence of experience; many popular notions and generalizations which are in all mouths, would be thought a great deal less certain than they are supposed to be; but we should begin to lay the foundation of really experimental knowledge on things which are now the subjects of mere vague discussion, where one side finds as much to say and says it as confidently as another, and each person's opinion is less determined by evidence than by his accidental interest or prepossession. In politics, for instance, it is evident to whoever comes to the study from that of the experimental sciences, that no political conclusions of any value for practice can be arrived at by direct experience. Such specific experience as we can have serves only to verify, and even that insufficiently, the conclusions of reasoning. Take any active force you please in politics; take the liberties of England, or free trade: how should we know that either of these things conduced to prosperity, if we could discern no tendency in the things themselves to produce it? If we had only the evidence of what is called our experience, such prosperity as we enjoy might be owing to a hundred other causes, and might have been obstructed, not promoted, by these. All true political science is, in one sense of the phrase, *à priori*, being deduced from the tendencies of things— tendencies known either through our general experience of human nature, or as the result of an analysis of the course of history, considered as a progressive evolution. It requires, therefore, the union of induction and deduction, and the mind that is equal to it must have been well disciplined in both. But familiarity with scientific experiment at least does the useful service of inspiring a wholesome scepticism about the conclusions which the mere surface of experience suggests.

The study, on the one hand, of mathematics and its applications, on the other, of experimental science, prepares us for the principal business of the intellect, by the practice of it in the most characteristic cases, and by familiarity with the most perfect and successful models of it. But in great things as in small, examples and models are not sufficient: we want rules as well. Familiarity with the correct use of a language in conversation and writing does not make rules of grammar unnecessary; nor does the amplest knowledge of sciences of reasoning and experiment dispense with rules of logic. We may have heard correct reasonings and seen skilful experiments all our lives—we shall not learn by mere imitation to do the like, unless we pay careful attention to how it is done. It is much easier in these abstract matters, than in purely mechanical ones, to mistake bad work for good. To mark out the difference between them is the province of logic. Logic lays down the general principles and laws of the search after truth; the conditions which, whether recognized or not, must actually have been observed if the mind has done its work rightly. Logic is the intellectual complement of mathematics and physics. Those sciences give the practice, of which Logic is the theory. It declares the principles, rules, and precepts, of which they exemplify the observance.

The science of Logic has two parts; ratiocinative and inductive logic. The one helps to keep us right in reasoning from premises, the other in concluding from observation. Ratiocinative logic is much older than inductive, because reasoning in the narrower sense of the word is an easier process than induction, and the science which works by mere reasoning, pure mathematics, had been carried to a considerable height while the sciences of observation were still in the purely empirical period. The principles of ratiocination, therefore, were the earliest understood and systematized, and the logic of ratiocination is even now suitable to an earlier stage in education than that of induction. The principles of induction cannot be properly understood without some previous study of the inductive sciences; but the logic of reasoning, which was already carried to a high degree of perfection by Aristotle, does not absolutely require even a knowledge of mathematics, but can be sufficiently exemplified and illustrated from the practice of daily life.

Of Logic I venture to say, even if limited to that of mere ratiocination, the theory of names, propositions, and the syllogism, that there is no part of intellectual education which is of greater value, or whose place can so ill be supplied by anything else. Its uses, it is true, are chiefly negative; its function is, not so much to teach us to go right, as to keep us from going wrong. But in the operations of the intellect it is so much easier to go wrong than right; it is so utterly impossible for even the most vigorous mind to keep itself in the path but by maintaining a vigilant watch against all deviations, and noting all the byways by which it is possible to go astray—that the chief difference between one reasoner and another consists in their less or greater liability to be misled. Logic points out all the possible ways in which, starting from true premises, we may draw false conclusions. By its analysis of the reasoning process, and the forms it supplies for stating and setting forth our reasonings, it enables us to guard the points at which a fallacy is in danger of slipping in, or to lay our fingers upon the place where it has slipped in. When I consider how very simple the theory of reasoning is, and how short a time is sufficient for acquiring a thorough knowledge of its principles and rules, and even considerable expertness in applying them, I can find no excuse for omission to study it on the part of anyone who aspires to succeed in any intellectual pursuit. Logic is the great disperser of hazy and confused thinking: it clears up the fogs which hide from us our own ignorance, and make us believe that we understand a subject when we do not. We must not be led away by talk about inarticulate giants who do great deeds without knowing how, and see into the most recondite truths without any of the ordinary helps, and without being able to explain to other people how they reach their conclusions, nor consequently to convince any other people of the truth of them. There may be such men, as there are deaf and dumb persons who do clever things; but for all that, speech and hearing are faculties by no means to be dispensed with. If you want to know whether you are thinking rightly, put your thoughts into words. In the very attempt to do this you will find yourselves, consciously or unconsciously, using logical forms. Logic compels us to throw our meaning into distinct propositions, and our reasonings into distinct steps. It makes us conscious of all the implied assumptions on which we are proceeding, and which, if not true, vitiate the entire process. It makes us aware what extent of doctrine we commit ourselves to by any course of reasoning, and obliges us to look the implied premises in the face, and make up our minds whether we can stand to them. It makes our opinions consistent with themselves and with one another, and forces us to think clearly, even when it cannot make us think correctly. It is true that error may be consistent and systematic as well as truth; but this is not the common case. It is no small advantage to see clearly the principles and consequences involved in our opinions, and which we must either accept, or else abandon those opinions. We are much nearer to finding truth when we search for it in broad daylight. Error, pursued rigorously to all that is implied in it, seldom fails to get detected by coming into collision with some known and admitted fact.

You will find abundance of people to tell you that logic is no help to thought, and that people cannot be taught to think by rules. Undoubtedly rules by themselves, without practice, go but a little way in teaching anything. But if the practice of thinking is not improved by rules, I venture to say it is the only difficult thing done by human beings that is not so. A man learns to saw wood principally by practice, but there are rules for doing it, grounded on the nature of the operation, and if he is not taught the rules, he will not saw well until he has discovered them for himself. Wherever there is a right way and a wrong, there must be a difference between them, and it must be possible to find out what the difference is; and when found out and expressed in words, it is a rule for the operation. If anyone is inclined to disparage rules, I say to him, try to learn anything which there are rules for, without knowing the rules, and see how you succeed. To those who think lightly of the school logic, I say, take the trouble to learn it. You will easily do so in a few weeks, and you will see whether it is of no use to you in making your mind clear, and keeping you from stumbling in the dark over the most outrageous fallacies. Nobody, I believe, who has really learned it, and who goes on using his mind, is insensible to its benefits, unless he started with a prejudice, or, like some eminent English and Scottish thinkers of the past century, is under the influence of a reaction against the exaggerated pretensions made by the schoolmen, not so much in behalf of logic as of the reasoning process itself. Still more highly must the use of logic be estimated, if we include in it, as we ought to do, the principles and rules of Induction as well as of Ratiocination. As the one logic guards us against bad deduction, so does the other against bad generalization, which is a still more universal error. If men easily err in arguing from one general proposition to another, still more easily do they go wrong in interpreting the observations made by themselves and others. There is nothing in which an untrained mind shows itself more hopelessly incapable, than in drawing the proper general conclusions from its own experience. And even trained minds, when all their training is on a special subject, and does not extend to the general principles of induction, are only kept right when there are ready opportunities of verifying their inferences by facts. Able scientific men, when they venture upon subjects in which they have no facts to check them, are often found drawing conclusions or making generalizations from their experimental knowledge, such as any sound theory of induction would show to be utterly unwarranted. So true is it that practice alone, even of a good kind, is not sufficient without principles and rules. Lord Bacon had the great merit of seeing that rules were necessary, and conceiving, to a very considerable extent, their true character. The defects of his conception were such as were inevitable while the inductive sciences were only in the earliest stage of their progress, and the highest efforts of the human mind in that direction had not yet been made. Inadequate as the Baconian view of induction was, and rapidly as the practice outgrew it, it is only within a generation or two that any considerable improvement has been made in the theory; very much through the impulse given by two of the many distinguished men who have adorned the Scottish Universities—Dugald Stewart and Brown.

I have given a very incomplete and summary view of the educational benefits derived from instruction in the more perfect sciences, and in the rules for the proper use of the intellectual faculties which the practice of those sciences has suggested. There are other sciences, which are in a more backward state, and tax the whole powers of the mind in its mature years, yet a beginning of which may be beneficially made in university studies, while a tincture of them is valuable even to those who are never likely to proceed farther. The first is physiology; the science of the laws of organic and animal life, and especially of the structure and functions of the human body. It would be absurd to pretend that a profound knowledge of this difficult subject can be acquired in youth, or as a part of general education. Yet an acquaintance with its leading truths is one of those acquirements which ought not to be the exclusive property of a particular profession. The value of such knowledge for daily uses has been made familiar to us all by the sanitary discussions of late years. There is hardly one among us who may not, in some position of authority, be required to form an opinion and take part in public action on sanitary subjects. And the importance of understanding the true conditions of health and disease—of knowing how to acquire and preserve that healthy habit of body which the most tedious and costly medical treatment so often fails to restore when once lost—should secure a place in general education for the principal maxims of hygiene, and some of those even of practical medicine. For those who aim at high intellectual cultivation, the study of physiology has still greater recommendations, and is, in the present state of advancement of the higher studies, a real necessity. The practice which it gives in the study of nature is such as no other physical science affords in the same kind, and is the best introduction to the difficult questions of politics and social life. Scientific education, apart from professional objects, is but a preparation for judging rightly of Man, and of his requirements and interests. But to this final pursuit, which has been called *par excellence* the proper study of mankind, physiology is the most serviceable of the sciences, because it is the nearest. Its subject is already Man: the same complex and manifold being, whose properties are not independent of circumstance, and immovable from age to age, like those of the ellipse and hyperbola, or of sulphur and phosphorus, but are infinitely various, indefinitely modifiable by art or accident, graduating by the nicest shades into one another, and reacting upon one another in a thousand ways, so that they are seldom capable of being isolated and observed separately. With the difficulties of the study of a being so constituted, the physiologist, and he alone among scientific inquirers, is already familiar. Take what view we will of man as a spiritual being, one part of his nature is far more like another than either of them is like anything else. In the organic world we study nature under disadvantages very similar to those which affect the study of moral and political phenomena: our means of making experiments are almost as limited, while the extreme complexity of the facts makes the conclusions of general reasoning unusually precarious, on account of the vast number of circumstances that conspire to determine every result. Yet, in spite of these obstacles, it is found possible in physiology to arrive at a considerable number of well-ascertained and important truths. This, therefore, is an excellent school in which to study the means of overcoming similar difficulties elsewhere. It is in physiology, too, that we are first introduced to some of the conceptions which play the greatest part in the moral and social sciences, but which do not occur at all in those of inorganic nature; as, for instance, the idea of predisposition, and of predisposing causes, as distinguished from exciting causes. The operation of all moral forces is immensely influenced by predisposition: without that element, it is impossible to explain the commonest facts of history and social life. Physiology is also the first science in which we recognize the influence of habit—the tendency of something to happen again merely because it has happened before. From physiology, too, we get our clearest notion of what is meant by development or evolution. The growth of a plant or animal from the first germ is the typical specimen of a phenomenon which rules through the whole course of the history of man and society—increase of function, through expansion and differentiation of structure by internal forces. I cannot enter into the subject at greater length; it is enough if I throw out hints which may be germs of further thought in yourselves. Those who aim at high intellectual achievements may be assured that no part of their time will be less wasted, than that which they employ in becoming familiar with the methods and with the main conceptions of the science of organization and life.

Physiology, at its upper extremity, touches on Psychology, or the Philosophy of Mind: and without raising any disputed questions about the limits between Matter and Spirit, the nerves and brain are admitted to have so intimate a connection with the mental operations, that the student of the last cannot dispense with a considerable knowledge of the first. The value of psychology itself need hardly be expatiated upon in a Scottish University; for it has always been there studied with brilliant success. Almost everything which has been contributed from these islands towards its advancement since Locke and Berkeley, has until very lately, and much of it even in the present generation, proceeded from Scottish authors and Scottish professors. Psychology, in truth, is simply the knowledge of the laws of human nature. If there is anything that deserves to be studied by man, it is his own nature and that of his fellow-men: and if it is worth studying at all, it is worth studying scientifically, so as to reach the fundamental laws which underlie and govern all the rest. With regard to the suitableness of this subject for general education, a distinction must be made. There are certain observed laws of our thoughts and of our feelings which rest upon experimental evidence, and, once seized, are a clew to the interpretation of much that we are conscious of in ourselves, and observe in one another. Such, for example, are the laws of association. Psychology, so far as it consists of such laws,—I speak of the laws themselves, not of their disputed applications,—is as positive and certain a science as chemistry, and fit to be taught as such. When, however, we pass beyond the bounds of these admitted truths, to questions which are still in controversy among the different philosophical schools—how far the higher operations of the mind can be explained by association, how far we must admit other primary principles—what faculties of the mind are simple, what complex, and what is the composition of the latter—above all, when we embark upon the sea of metaphysics properly so called, and inquire, for instance, whether time and space are real existences, as is our spontaneous impression, or forms of our sensitive faculty, as is maintained by Kant, or complex ideas generated by association; whether matter and spirit are conceptions merely relative to our faculties, or facts existing *per se*, and in the latter case, what is the nature and limit of our knowledge of them; whether the will of man is free or determined by causes, and what is the real difference between the two doctrines; matters on which the most thinking men, and those who have given most study to the subjects, are still divided; it is neither to be expected nor desired that those who do not specially devote themselves to the higher departments of speculation should employ much of their time in attempting to get to the bottom of these questions. But it is a part of liberal education to know that such controversies exist, and, in a general way, what has been said on both sides of them. It is instructive to know the failures of the human intellect as well as its successes, its imperfect as well as its perfect attainments; to be aware of the open questions, as well as of those which have been definitively resolved. A very summary view of these disputed matters may suffice for the many; but a system of education is not intended solely for the many; it has to kindle the aspirations and aid the efforts of those who are destined to stand forth as thinkers above the multitude: and for these there is hardly to be found any discipline comparable to that which these metaphysical controversies afford. For they are essentially questions about the estimation of evidence; about the ultimate grounds of belief; the conditions required to justify our most familiar and intimate convictions; and the real meaning and import of words and phrases which we have used from infancy as if we understood all about them, which are even at the foundation of human language, yet of which no one except a metaphysician has rendered to himself a complete account. Whatever philosophical opinions the study of these questions may lead us to adopt, no one ever came out of the discussion of them without increased vigor of understanding, an increased demand for precision of thought and language, and a more careful and exact appreciation of the nature of proof. There never was any sharpener of the intellectual faculties superior to the Berkeleian controversy. There is even now no reading more profitable to students—confining myself to writers in our own language, and notwithstanding that so many of their speculations are already obsolete—than Hobbes and Locke, Reid and Stewart, Hume, Hartley, and Brown; on condition that these great thinkers are not read passively, as masters to be followed, but actively, as supplying materials and incentives to thought. To come to our own contemporaries, he who has mastered Sir William Hamilton and your own lamented Ferrier as distinguished representatives of one of the two great schools of philosophy, and an eminent Professor in a neighboring University, Professor Bain, probably the greatest living authority in the other, has gained a practice in the most searching methods of philosophic investigation applied to the most arduous subjects, which is no inadequate preparation for any intellectual difficulties that he is ever likely to be called on to resolve.

In this brief outline of a complete scientific education, I have said nothing about direct instruction in that which it is the chief of all the ends of intellectual education to qualify us for—the exercise of thought on the great interests of mankind as moral and social beings—ethics and politics, in the largest sense. These things are not, in the existing state of human knowledge, the subject of a science, generally admitted and accepted. Politics cannot be learned once for all, from a text-book, or the instructions of a master. What we require to be taught on that subject, is to be our own teachers. It is a subject on which we have no masters to follow; each must explore for himself, and exercise an independent judgment. Scientific politics do not consist in having a set of conclusions ready made, to be applied everywhere indiscriminately, but in setting the mind to work in a scientific spirit to discover in each instance the truths applicable to the given case. And this, at present, scarcely any two persons do in the same way. Education is not entitled, on this subject, to recommend any set of opinions as resting on the authority of established science. But it can supply the student with materials for his own mind, and helps to use them. It can make him acquainted with the best speculations on the subject, taken from different points of view; none of which will be found complete, while each embodies some considerations really relevant, really requiring to be taken into the account. Education may also introduce us to the principal facts which have a direct bearing on the subject, namely, the different modes or stages of civilization that have been found among mankind, and the characteristic properties of each. This is the true purpose of historical studies, as prosecuted in a University. The leading facts of ancient and modern history should be known by the student from his private reading: if that knowledge be wanting, it cannot possibly be supplied here. What a Professor of History has to teach, is the meaning of those facts. His office is to help the student in collecting from history what are the main differences between human beings, and between the institutions of society, at one time or place and at another; in picturing to himself human life and the human conception of life, as they were at the different stages of human development; in distinguishing between what is the same in all ages and what is progressive, and forming some incipient conception of the causes and laws of progress. All these things are as yet very imperfectly understood even by the most philosophic inquirers, and are quite unfit to be taught dogmatically. The object is to lead the student to attend to them; to make him take interest in history not as a mere narrative, but as a chain of causes and effects still unwinding itself before his eyes, and full of momentous consequences to himself and his descendants; the unfolding of a great epic or dramatic action, to terminate in the happiness or misery, the elevation or degradation, of the human race; an unremitting conflict between good and evil powers, of which every act done by any of us, insignificant as we are, forms one of the incidents; a conflict in which even the smallest of us cannot escape from taking part, in which whoever does not help the right side is helping the wrong, and for our share in which, whether it be greater or smaller, and let its actual consequences be visible or in the main invisible, no one of us can escape the responsibility. Though education cannot arm and equip its pupils for this fight with any complete philosophy either of politics or of history, there is much positive instruction that it can give them, having a direct bearing on the duties of citizenship. They should be taught the outlines of the civil and political institutions of their own country, and in a more general way, of the more advanced of the other civilized nations. Those branches of politics, or of the laws of social life, in which there exists a collection of facts or thoughts sufficiently shifted and methodized to form the beginning of a science, should be taught *ex professo*. Among the chief of these is Political Economy; the sources and conditions of wealth and material prosperity for aggregate bodies of human beings. This study approaches nearer to the rank of a science, in the sense in which we apply that name to the physical sciences, than anything else connected with politics yet does. I need not enlarge on the important lessons which it affords for the guidance of life, and for the estimation of laws and institutions, or on the necessity of knowing all that it can teach in order to have true views of the course of human affairs, or form plans for their improvement which will stand actual trial. The same persons who cry down Logic will generally warn you against Political Economy. It is unfeeling, they will tell you. It recognizes unpleasant facts. For my part, the most unfeeling thing I know of is the law of gravitation: it breaks the neck of the best and most amiable person without scruple, if he forgets for a single moment to give heed to it. The winds and waves too are very unfeeling. Would you advise those who go to sea to deny the winds and waves—or to make use of them, and find the means of guarding against their dangers? My advice to you is to study the great writers on Political Economy, and hold firmly by whatever in them you find true; and depend upon it that if you are not selfish or hardhearted already, Political Economy will not make you so. Of no less importance than Political Economy is the study of what is called Jurisprudence; the general principles of law; the social necessities which laws are required to meet; the features common to all systems of law, and the differences between them; the requisites of good legislation, the proper mode of constructing a legal system, and the best constitution of courts of justice and modes of legal procedure. These things are not only the chief part of the business of government, but the vital concern of every citizen; and their improvement affords a wide scope for the energies of any duly prepared mind, ambitious of contributing towards the better condition of the human race. For this, too, admirable helps have been provided by writers of our own or of a very recent time. At the head of them stands Bentham, undoubtedly the greatest master who ever devoted the labor of a life to let in light on the subject of law, and who is the more intelligible to nonprofessional persons, because, as his way is, he builds up the subject from its foundation in the facts of human life, and shows, by careful consideration of ends and means, what law might and ought to be, in deplorable contrast with what it is. Other enlightened jurists have followed with contributions of two kinds, as the type of which I may take two works, equally admirable in their respective times. Mr. Austin, in his Lectures on Jurisprudence, takes for his basis the Roman law, the most elaborately consistent legal system which history has shown us in actual operation, and that which the greatest number of accomplished minds have employed themselves in harmonizing. From this he singles out the principles and distinctions which are of general applicability, and employs the powers and resources of a most precise and analytic mind to give to those principles and distinctions a philosophic basis, grounded in the universal reason of mankind, and not in mere technical convenience. Mr. Maine, in his treatise on Ancient Law in its relations to Modern Thought, shows from the history of law, and from what is known of the primitive institutions of mankind, the origin of much that has lasted till now, and has a firm footing both in the laws and in the ideas of modern times; showing that many of these things never originated in reason, but are relics of the institutions of barbarous society, modified more or less by civilization, but kept standing by the persistency of ideas which were the offspring of those barbarous institutions, and have survived their parent. The path opened by Mr. Maine has been followed up by others, with additional illustrations of the influence of obsolete ideas on modern institutions, and of obsolete institutions on modern ideas; an action and reaction which perpetuate, in many of the greatest concerns, a mitigated barbarism; things being continually accepted as dictates of nature and necessities of life, which, if we knew all, we should see to have originated in artificial arrangements of society, long since abandoned and condemned.

To these studies I would add International Law; which I decidedly think should be taught in all Universities, and should form part of all liberal education. The need of it is far from being limited to diplomatists and lawyers: it extends to every citizen. What is called the Law of Nations is not properly law, but a part of ethics; a set of moral rules, accepted as authoritative by civilized states. It is true that these rules neither are nor ought to be of eternal obligation, but do and must vary more or less from age to age, as the consciences of nations become more enlightened and the exigencies of political society undergo change. But the rules mostly were at their origin, and still are, an application of the maxims of honesty and humanity to the intercourse of states. They were introduced by the moral sentiments of mankind, or by their sense of the general interest, to mitigate the crimes and sufferings of a state of war, and to restrain governments and nations from unjust or dishonest conduct towards one another in time of peace. Since every country stands in numerous and various relations with the other countries of the world, and many, our own among the number, exercise actual authority over some of these, a knowledge of the established rules of international morality is essential to the duty of every nation, and therefore of every person in it who helps to make up the nation, and whose voice and feeling form a part of what is called public opinion. Let not any one pacify his conscience by the delusion that he can do no harm if he takes no part, and forms no opinion. Bad men need nothing more to compass their ends, than that good men should look on and do nothing. He is not a good man who, without a protest, allows wrong to be committed in his name, and with the means which he helps to supply, because he will not trouble himself to use his mind on the subject. It depends on the habit of attending to and looking into public transactions, and on the degree of information and solid judgment respecting them that exists in the community, whether the conduct of the nation as a nation, both within itself and towards others, shall be selfish, corrupt, and tyrannical, or rational and enlightened, just and noble.

Of these more advanced studies, only a small commencement can be made at schools and Universities; but even this is of the highest value, by awakening an interest in the subjects, by conquering the first difficulties, and inuring the mind to the kind of exertion which the studies require, by implanting a desire to make further progress, and directing the student to the best tracks and the best helps. So far as these branches of knowledge have been acquired, we have learned, or been put into the way of learning, our duty, and our work in life. Knowing it, however, is but half the work of education; it still remains, that what we know, we shall be willing and determined to put in practice. Nevertheless, to know the truth is already a great way towards disposing us to act upon it. What we see clearly and apprehend keenly, we have a natural desire to act out. "To see the best, and yet the worst pursue," is a possible but not a common state of mind; those who follow the wrong have generally first taken care to be voluntarily ignorant of the right. They have silenced their conscience, but they are not knowingly disobeying it. If you take an average human mind while still young, before the objects it has chosen in life have given it a turn in any bad direction, you will generally find it desiring what is good, right, and for the benefit of all; and if that season is properly used to implant the knowledge and give the training which shall render rectitude of judgment more habitual than sophistry, a serious barrier will have been erected against the inroads of selfishness and falsehood. Still, it is a very imperfect education which trains the intelligence only, but not the will. No one can dispense with an education directed expressly to the moral as well as the intellectual part of his being. Such education, so far as it is direct, is either moral or religious; and these may either be treated as distinct, or as different aspects of the same thing. The subject we are now considering is not education as a whole, but scholastic education, and we must keep in view the inevitable limitations of what schools and Universities can do. It is beyond their power to educate morally or religiously. Moral and religious education consists in training the feelings and the daily habits; and these are, in the main, beyond the sphere and inaccessible to the control of public education. It is the home, the family, which gives us the moral or religious education we really receive: and this is completed, and modified, sometimes for the better, often for the worse, by society, and the opinions and feelings with which we are there surrounded. The moral or religious influence which a University can exercise, consists less in any express teaching, than in the pervading tone of the place. Whatever it teaches, it should teach as penetrated by a sense of duty; it should present all

knowledge as chiefly a means to worthiness of life, given for the double purpose of making each of us practically useful to his fellow-creatures, and of elevating the character of the species itself; exalting and dignifying our nature.
There is nothing which spreads more contagiously from teacher to pupil than
elevation of sentiment: often and often have students caught from the living
influence of a professor a contempt for mean and selfish objects, and a noble
ambition to leave the world better than they found it, which they have carried
with them throughout life. In these respects, teachers of every kind have natural and peculiar means of doing with effect what everyone who mixes with
his fellow-beings, or addresses himself to them in any character, should feel
bound to do to the extent of his capacity and opportunities. What is special to a
University on these subjects belongs chiefly, like the rest of its work, to the intellectual department. A University exists for the purpose of laying open to
each succeeding generation, as far as the conditions of the case admit, the accumulated treasure of the thoughts of mankind. As an indispensable part of this,
it has to make known to them what mankind at large, their own country, and
the best and wisest individual men, have thought on the great subjects of
morals and religion. There should be, and there is in most Universities, professorial instruction in moral philosophy; but I could wish that this instruction
were of a somewhat different type from what is ordinarily met with. I could
wish that it were more expository, less polemical, and above all less dogmatic.
The learner should be made acquainted with the principal systems of moral
philosophy which have existed and been practically operative among
mankind, and should hear what there is to be said for each: the Aristotelian,
the Epicurean, the Stoic, the Judaic, the Christian in the various modes of its interpretation, which differ almost as much from one another as the teachings of
those earlier schools. He should be made familiar with the different standards
of right and wrong which have been taken as the basis of ethics; general utility,
natural justice, natural rights, a moral sense, principles of practical reason, and
the rest. Among all these, it is not so much the teacher's business to take a side,
and fight stoutly for some one against the rest, as it is to direct them all towards the establishment and preservation of the rules of conduct most advantageous to mankind. There is not one of these systems which has not its good
side; not one from which there is not something to be learned by the votaries of
the others; not one which is not suggested by a keen, though it may not always
be a clear, perception of some important truths, which are the prop of the system, and the neglect or undervaluing of which in other systems, is their characteristic infirmity. A system which may be as a whole erroneous, is still valuable, until it has forced upon mankind a sufficient attention to the portion of
truth which suggested it. The ethical teacher does his part best, when he points
out how each system may be strengthened even on its own basis, by taking
into more complete account the truths which other systems have realized more
fully and made more prominent. I do not mean that he should encourage an
essentially sceptical eclecticism. While placing every system in the best aspect
it admits of, and endeavoring to draw from all of them the most salutary consequences compatible with their nature, I would by no means debar him from

enforcing by his best arguments his own preference for some one of the number. They cannot be all true; though those which are false as theories may contain particular truths, indispensable to the completeness of the true theory. But on this subject, even more than on any of those I have previously mentioned, it is not the teacher's business to impose his own judgment, but to inform and discipline that of his pupil.

And this same clew, if we keep hold of it, will guide us through the labyrinth of conflicting thought into which we enter when we touch the great question of the relation of education to religion. As I have already said, the only really effective religious education is the parental—that of home and childhood. All that social and public education has in its power to do, further than by a general pervading tone of reverence and duty, amounts to little more than the information which it can give; but this is extremely valuable. I shall not enter into the question which has been debated with so much vehemence in the last and present generation, whether religion ought to be taught at all in Universities and public schools, seeing that religion is the subject of all others on which men's opinions are most widely at variance. On neither side of this controversy do the disputants seem to me to have sufficiently freed their minds from the old notion of education, that it consists in the dogmatic inculcation from authority, of what the teacher deems true. Why should it be impossible, that information of the greatest value, on subjects connected with religion, should be brought before the student's mind; that he should be made acquainted with so important a part of the national thought, and of the intellectual labors of past generations, as those relating to religion, without being taught dogmatically the doctrines of any church or sect? Christianity being an historical religion, the sort of religious instruction which seems to me most appropriate to a University is the study of ecclesiastical history. If teaching, even on matters of scientific certainty, should aim quite as much at showing how the results are arrived at, as at teaching the results themselves, far more, then, should this be the case on subjects where there is the widest diversity of opinion among men of equal ability, and who have taken equal pains to arrive at the truth. This diversity should of itself be a warning to a conscientious teacher that he has no right to impose his opinion authoritatively upon a youthful mind. His teaching should not be in the spirit of dogmatism, but in that of inquiry. The pupil should not be addressed as if his religion has been chosen for him, but as one who will have to choose it for himself. The various Churches, established and unestablished, are quite competent to the task which is peculiarly theirs—that of teaching each its own doctrines, as far as necessary, to its own rising generation. The proper business of a University is different; not to tell us from authority what we ought to believe, and make us accept the belief as a duty, but to give us information and training, and help us to form our own belief in a manner worthy of intelligent beings, who seek for truth at all hazards, and demand to know all the difficulties, in order that they may be better qualified to find, or recognize, the most satisfactory mode of resolving them. The vast importance of these questions—the great results as regards the conduct of our lives, which depend upon our choosing one belief or another—are the strongest reasons why we should not trust our judgment when it has been formed in ignorance of the evidence, and why we should not consent to be restricted to a one-sided teaching, which informs us of what a particular teacher or association of teachers receive as true doctrine and sound argument, but of nothing more.

I do not affirm that a University, if it represses free thought and inquiry, must be altogether a failure, for the freest thinkers have often been trained in the most slavish seminaries of learning. The great Christian reformers were taught in Roman Catholic Universities; the sceptical philosophers of France were mostly educated by the Jesuits. The human mind is sometimes impelled all the more violently in one direction, by an over-zealous and demonstrative attempt to drag it in the opposite. But this is not what Universities are appointed for—to drive men from them, even into good, by excess of evil. A University ought to be a place of free speculation. The more diligently it does its duty in all other respects, the more certain it is to be that. The old English Universities, in the present generation, are doing better work than they have done within human memory in teaching the ordinary studies of their curriculum; and one of the consequences has been, that whereas they formerly seemed to exist mainly for the repression of independent thought, and the chaining up of the individual intellect and conscience, they are now the great foci of free and manly inquiry, to the higher and professional classes, south of the Tweed. The ruling minds of those ancient seminaries have at last remembered that to place themselves in hostility to the free use of the understanding, is to abdicate their own best privilege, that of guiding it. A modest deference, at least provisional, to the united authority of the specially instructed, is becoming in a youthful and imperfectly formed mind; but when there is no united authority—when the specially instructed are so divided and scattered that almost any opinion can boast of some high authority, and no opinion whatever can claim all; when, therefore, it can never be deemed extremely improbable that one who uses his mind freely may see reason to change his first opinion; then, whatever you do, keep, at all risks, your minds open: do not barter away your freedom of thought. Those of you who are destined for the clerical profession are, no doubt, so far held to a certain number of doctrines, that, if they ceased to believe them, they would not be justified in remaining in a position in which they would be required to teach insincerely. But use your influence to make those doctrines as few as possible. It is not right that men should be bribed to hold out against conviction—to shut their ears against objections, or, if the objections penetrate, to continue professing full and unfaltering belief when their confidence is already shaken. Neither is it right that, if men honestly profess to have changed some of their religious opinions, their honesty should as a matter of course exclude them from taking a part for which they may be admirably qualified, in the spiritual instruction of the nation. The tendency of the age, on both sides of the ancient Border, is towards the relaxation of formularies, and a less rigid construction of articles. This very circumstance, by making the limits of orthodoxy less definite, and obliging everyone to draw the line for himself, is an embarrassment to consciences. But I hold entirely with those clergymen who elect to remain in the national church, so long as they are able to accept its articles and confessions in any sense or with any interpretation consistent with common honesty, whether it be the generally received interpretation or not. If all were to desert the church who put a large and liberal construction on its terms of communion, or who would wish to see those terms widened, the national provision for religious teaching and worship would be left utterly to those who take the narrowest, the most literal, and purely textual view of the formularies; who, though by no means necessarily bigots for their allies, and who, however great their merits may be,—and they are often very great,—yet, if the church is improvable, are not the most likely persons to improve it. Therefore, if it were not an impertinence in me to tender advice in such a matter, I should say, let all who conscientiously can, remain in the church. A church is far more easily improved from within than from without. Almost all the illustrious reformers of religion began by being clergymen; but they did not think that their profession as clergymen was inconsistent with being reformers. They mostly indeed ended their days outside the churches in which they were born; but it was because the churches, in an evil hour for themselves, cast them out. They did not think it any business of theirs to withdraw. They thought they had a better right to remain in the fold, than those had who expelled them.

I have now said what I had to say on the two kinds of education which the system of schools and Universities is intended to promote—intellectual education and moral education; knowledge and the training of the knowing faculty, conscience and that of the moral faculty. These are the two main ingredients of human culture; but they do not exhaust the whole of it. There is a third division, which, if subordinate, and owing allegiance to the two others, is barely inferior to them, and not less needful to the completeness of the human being; I mean the aesthetic branch; the culture which comes through poetry and art, and may be described as the education of the feelings, and the cultivation of the beautiful. This department of things deserves to be regarded in a far more serious light than is the custom of these countries. It is only of late, and chiefly by a superficial imitation of foreigners, that we have begun to use the word Art by itself, and to speak of Art as we speak of Science, or Government, or Religion: we used to talk of the Arts, and more specifically of the Fine Arts: and even by them were vulgarly meant only two forms of art, Painting and Sculpture, the two which as a people we cared least about—which were regarded even by the more cultivated among us as little more than branches of domestic ornamentation, a kind of elegant upholstery. The very words "Fine Arts" called up a notion of frivolity, of great pains expended on a rather trifling object—on something which differed from the cheaper and commoner arts of producing pretty things, mainly by being more difficult, and by giving fops an opportunity of pluming themselves on caring for it, and on being able to talk about it. This estimate extended in no small degree, though not altogether, even to poetry, the queen of arts, but, in Great Britain, hardly included under the name. It cannot exactly be said that poetry was little thought of; we were proud of our Shakespeare and Milton, and in one period at least of our history, that of Queen Anne, it was a high literary distinction to be a poet; but poetry was hardly looked upon in any serious light, or as having much value except as an amusement or excitement, the superiority of which over others principally consisted in being that of a more refined order of minds. Yet the celebrated saying of Fletcher of Saltoun, "Let who will make the laws of a people if I write their songs," might have taught us how great an instrument for acting on the human mind we were undervaluing. It would be difficult for anybody to imagine that "Rule Britannia," for example, or "Scots wha hae," had no permanent influence on the higher region of human character: some of Moore's songs have done more for Ireland than all Grattan's speeches: and songs are far from being the highest or most impressive form of poetry. On these subjects, the mode of thinking and feeling of other countries was not only not intelligible, but not credible, to an average Englishman.

To find Art ranking on a complete equality, in theory at least, with Philosophy, Learning, and Science—as holding an equally important place among the agents of civilization and among the elements of the worth of humanity; to find even painting and sculpture treated as great social powers, and the art of a country as a feature, in its character and condition, little inferior in importance to either its religion or its government; all this only did not amaze and puzzle Englishmen, because it was too strange for them to be able to realize it, or, in truth, to believe it possible: and the radical difference of feeling on this matter between the British people and those of France, Germany, and the Continent generally, is one among the causes of that extraordinary inability to understand one another, which exists between England and the rest of Europe, while it does not exist to anything like the same degree between one nation of Continental Europe and another. It may be traced to the two influences which have chiefly shaped the British character since the days of the Stuarts: commercial money-getting business, and religious Puritanism. Business, demanding the whole of the faculties, and whether pursued from duty or the love of gain, regarding as a loss of time whatever does not conduce directly to the end; Puritanism, which, looking upon every feeling of human nature, except fear and reverence for God, as a snare, if not as partaking of sin, looked coldly, if not disapprovingly, on the cultivation of the sentiments. Different causes have produced different effects in the Continental nations; among whom it is even now observable that virtue and goodness are generally for the most part an affair of the sentiments, while with us they are almost exclusively an affair of duty. Accordingly, the kind of advantage which we have had over many other countries in point of morals—I am not sure that we are not losing it—has consisted in greater tenderness of conscience. In this we have had on the whole a real superiority, though one principally negative; for conscience is with most men a power chiefly in the way of restraint—a power which acts rather in staying our hands from any great wickedness, than by the direction it gives to the general course of our desires and sentiments. One of the commonest types of character among us is that of a man all whose ambition is self-regarding; who has no higher purpose in life than to enrich or raise in the world himself and his family; who never dreams of making the good of his fellow-creatures or of his country an habitual object, further than giving away, annually or from time to time, certain sums in charity; but who has a conscience sincerely alive to whatever is generally considered wrong, and would scruple to use any very illegitimate means for attaining his self-interested objects. While it will often happen in other countries that men whose feelings and whose active energies point strongly in an unselfish direction, who have the love of their country, of human improvement, of human freedom, even of virtue, in great strength, and of whose thoughts and activity a large share is devoted to disinterested objects, will yet, in the pursuit of these or of any other objects that they strongly desire, permit themselves to do wrong things which the other man, though intrinsically, and taking the whole of his character, farther removed from what a human being ought to be, could not bring himself to commit. It is of no use to debate which of these two states of mind is the best, or rather the least bad. It is quite possible to cultivate the conscience and the sentiments too. Nothing hinders us from so training a man that he will not, even for a disinterested purpose, violate the moral law, and also feeding and encouraging those high feelings, on which we mainly rely for lifting men above low and sordid objects, and giving them a higher conception of what constitutes success in life. If we wish men to practise virtue, it is worth while trying to make them love virtue, and feel it an object in itself, and not a tax paid for leave to pursue other objects. It is worth training them to feel, not only actual wrong or actual meanness, but the absence of noble aims and endeavors, as not merely blamable but also degrading; to have a feeling of the miserable smallness of mere self in the face of this great universe, of the collective mass of our fellow-creatures, in the face of past history and of the indefinite future— the poorness and insignificance of human life if it is to be all spent in making things comfortable for ourselves and our kin, and raising ourselves and them a step or two on the social ladder.

Thus feeling, we learn to respect ourselves only so far as we feel capable of nobler objects: and if unfortunately those by whom we are surrounded do not share our aspirations, perhaps disapprove the conduct to which we are prompted by them—to sustain ourselves by the ideal sympathy of the great characters in history, or even in fiction, and by the contemplation of an idealized posterity: shall I add, of ideal perfection embodied in a Divine Being? Now, of this elevated tone of mind the great source of inspiration is poetry, and all literature so far as it is poetical and artistic. We may imbibe exalted feelings from Plato, or Demosthenes, or Tacitus, but it is in so far as those great men are not solely philosophers, or orators, or historians, but poets and artists. Nor is it only loftiness, only the heroic feelings, that are bred by poetic cultivation. Its power is as great in calming the soul as in elevating it—in fostering the milder emotions, as the more exalted. It brings home to us all those aspects of life which take hold of our nature on its unselfish side, and lead us to identify our joy and grief with the good or ill of the system of which we form a part; and all those solemn or pensive feelings, which, without having any direct application to conduct, incline us to take life seriously, and predispose us to the reception of anything which comes before us in the shape of duty. Who does not feel a better man after a course of Dante, or of Wordsworth, or, I will add, of Lucretius or the Georgics, or after brooding over Gray's Elegy, or Shelley's Hymn to Intellectual Beauty? I have spoken of poetry, but all the other modes of art produce similar effects in their degree. The races and nations whose senses are naturally finer and their sensuous perceptions more exercised than ours, receive the same kind of impressions from painting and sculpture; and many of the more delicately organized among themselves do the same. All the arts of expression tend to keep alive and in activity the feelings they express. Do you think that the great Italian painters would have filled the place they did in the European mind, would have been universally ranked among the greatest men of their time, if their productions had done nothing for it but to serve as the decoration of a public hall or a private *salon?* Their Nativities and Crucifixions, their glorious Madonnas and Saints, were to their susceptible Southern countrymen the great school not only of devotional, but of all the elevated and all the imaginative feelings. We colder Northerns may approach to a conception of this function of art when we listen to an oratorio of Handel, or give ourselves up to the emotions excited by a Gothic cathedral. Even apart from any specific emotional expression, the mere contemplation of beauty of a high order produces in no small degree this elevating effect on the character. The power of natural scenery addresses itself to the same region of human nature which corresponds to Art. There are few capable of feeling the sublimer order of natural beauty, such as your own Highlands and other mountain regions afford, who are not, at least temporarily, raised by it above the littlenesses of humanity, and made to feel the puerility of the petty objects which set men's interests at variance, contrasted with the nobler pleasures which all might share. To whatever avocations we may be called in life, let us never quash these susceptibilities within us, but carefully seek the opportunities of maintaining them in exercise. The more prosaic our ordinary duties, the more necessary it is to keep up the tone of our minds by frequent visits to that higher region of thought and feeling, in which every work seems dignified in proportion to the ends for which, and the spirit in which, it is done; where we learn, while eagerly seizing every opportunity of exercising higher faculties and performing higher duties, to regard all useful and honest work as a public function, which may be ennobled by the mode of performing it—which has not properly any other nobility than what that gives—and which, if ever so humble, is never mean but when it is meanly done, and when the motives from which it is done are mean motives.

There is, besides, a natural affinity between goodness and the cultivation of the Beautiful, when it is real cultivation, and not a mere unguided instinct. He who has learned what beauty is, if he be of a virtuous character, will desire to realize it in his own life—will keep before himself a type of perfect beauty in human character, to light his attempts at self-culture. There is a true meaning in the saying of Goethe, though liable to be misunderstood and perverted, that the Beautiful is greater than the Good; for it includes the Good, and adds something to it: it is the Good made perfect, and fitted with all the collateral perfections which make it a finished and completed thing. Now, this sense of perfection, which would make us demand from every creation of man the very utmost that it ought to give, and render us intolerant of the smallest fault in ourselves or in anything we do, is one of the results of Art cultivation. No other human productions come so near to perfection as works of pure Art. In all other things, we are, and may reasonably be, satisfied if the degree of excellence is as great as the object immediately in view seems to us to be worth: but in Art, the perfection is itself the object. If I were to define Art, I should be inclined to call it, the endeavor after perfection in execution. If we meet with even a piece of mechanical work which bears the marks of being done in this spirit—which is done as if the workman loved it, and tried to make it as good as possible, though something less good would have answered the purpose for which it was ostensibly made—we say that he has worked like an artist. Art, when really cultivated, and not merely practised empirically, maintains, what it first gave the conception of, an ideal Beauty, to be eternally aimed at, though surpassing what can be actually attained; and by this idea it trains us never to be completely satisfied with imperfection in what we ourselves do and are: to idealize, as much as possible, every work we do, and most of all, our own characters and lives.

And now, having travelled with you over the whole range of the materials and training which a University supplies as a preparation for the higher uses of life, it is almost needless to add any exhortation to you to profit by the gift. Now is your opportunity for gaining a degree of insight into subjects larger and far more ennobling than the minutiae of a business or a profession, and for acquiring a facility of using your minds on all that concerns the higher interests of man, which you will carry with you into the occupations of active life, and which will prevent even the short intervals of time which that may leave you, from being altogether lost for noble purposes. Having once conquered the first difficulties, the only ones of which the irksomeness surpasses the interest; having turned the point beyond which what was once a task becomes a pleasure; in even the busiest after-life, the higher powers of your mind will make progress imperceptibly, by the spontaneous exercise of your thoughts, and by the lessons you will know how to learn from daily experience. So, at least, it will be if in your earlier studies you have fixed your eyes upon the ultimate end from which those studies take their chief value—that of making you more effective combatants in the great fight which never ceases to rage between Good and Evil, and more equal to coping with the ever new problems which the changing course of human nature and human society present to be resolved. Aims like these commonly retain the footing which they have once established in the mind; and their presence in our thoughts keeps our higher faculties in exercise, and makes us consider the acquirements and powers which we store up at any time of our lives, as a mental capital, to be freely expended in helping forward any mode which presents itself of making mankind in any respect wiser or better, or placing any portion of human affairs on a more sensible and rational footing than its existing one. There is not one of us who may not qualify himself so to improve the average amount of opportunities, as to leave his fellow-creatures some little the better for the use he has known how to make of his intellect. To make this little greater, let us strive to keep ourselves acquainted with the best thoughts that are brought forth by the original minds of the age; that we may know what movements stand most in need of our aid, and that, as far as depends on us, the good seed may not fall on a rock, and perish without reaching the soil in which it might have germinated and flourished. You are to be a part of the public who are to welcome, encourage, and help forward the future intellectual benefactors of humanity; and you are, if possible, to furnish your contingent to the number of those benefactors. Nor let anyone be discouraged by what may seem, in moments of despondency, the lack of time and of opportunity. Those who know how to employ opportunities will often find that they can create them: and what we achieve depends less on the amount of time we possess, than on the use we make of our time. You and your like are the hope and resource of your country in the coming generation. All great things which that generation is destined to do, have to be done by some like you; several will assuredly be done by persons for whom society has done much less, to whom it has given far less preparation, than those whom I am now addressing. I do not attempt to instigate you by the prospect of direct rewards, either earthly or heavenly; the less we think about being rewarded in either way, the better for us. But there is one reward which will not fail you, and which may be called disinterested, because it is not a consequence, but it is inherent in the very fact of deserving it; the deeper and more varied interest you will feel in life: which will give it tenfold its value, and a value which will last to the end. All merely personal objects grow less valuable as we advance in life: this not only endures, but increases.

7

Alfred North Whitehead

Alfred North Whitehead (1861–1947) never wrote a comprehensive work in philosophy of education, but he occasionally delivered lectures concerned with educational policy. These incisive talks are collected in his book *The Aims of Education and Other Essays.*

Whitehead and Dewey were contemporaries, and their ideas are in some notable respects similar. Like Dewey, Whitehead stresses the importance of utilizing knowledge, the need to interest students in their work, and the dangers of undiscriminating discipline.

But to what extent are Whitehead's emphases on the concept of "style" and the theory of "The Rhythm of Education" consistent with Dewey's position? The two thinkers display different approaches, which are partially accounted for by their different social and academic backgrounds. Whitehead, an Englishman, was educated and taught at Cambridge University. Dewey was born in Vermont and educated at the University of Vermont. He taught high school in Pennsylvania before embarking on his career in graduate education.

Among Whitehead's compelling thoughts is that "one secret of a successful teacher is that he has formulated quite clearly in his mind what the pupil has got to know in precise fashion." An inexperienced teacher often hesitates to present material in an easily understandable fashion for fear that doing so may rob students of their initiative or creativity. Such a teacher soon learns that the presentation of material in a disorganized, confusing manner results in disorganized, confused students. As Whitehead notes, "a certain ruthless definiteness is essential in education."

One further point should be emphasized. Whitehead expresses the view that "A merely well-informed man is the most useless bore on God's earth." He does not say, nor does he believe, that information is useless. Whitehead was himself one of the best-informed persons of his time.

The Aims of Education and Other Essays*
CHAPTER I
THE AIMS OF EDUCATION

Culture is activity of thought, and receptiveness to beauty and humane feeling. Scraps of information have nothing to do with it. A merely well-informed man is the most useless bore on God's earth. What we should aim at producing is men who possess both culture and expert knowledge in some special direction. Their expert knowledge will give them the ground to start from, and their culture will lead them as deep as philosophy and as high as art. We have to remember that the valuable intellectual development is self-development, and that it mostly takes place between the ages of sixteen and thirty. As to training, the most important part is given by mothers before the age of twelve. A saying due to Archbishop Temple illustrates my meaning. Surprise was expressed at the success in after-life of a man, who as a boy at Rugby had been somewhat undistinguished. He answered, "It is not what they are at eighteen, it is what they become afterwards that matters."

In training a child to activity of thought, above all things we must beware of what I will call "inert ideas"—that is to say, ideas that are merely received into the mind without being utilized, or tested, or thrown into fresh combinations.

In the history of education, the most striking phenomenon is that schools of learning, which at one epoch are alive with a ferment of genius, in a succeeding generation exhibit merely pedantry and routine. The reason is, that they are overladen with inert ideas. Education with inert ideas is not only useless: it is, above all things, harmful—*Corruptio optimi, pessima*. Except at rare intervals of intellectual ferment, education in the past has been radically infected with inert ideas. That is the reason why uneducated clever women, who have seen much of the world, are in middle life so much the most cultured part of the community. They have been saved from this horrible burden of inert ideas. Every intellectual revolution which has ever stirred humanity into greatness has been a passionate protest against inert ideas. Then, alas, with pathetic ignorance of human psychology, it has proceeded by some educational scheme to bind humanity afresh with inert ideas of its own fashioning.

Let us now ask how in our system of education we are to guard against this mental dryrot. We enunciate two educational commandments, "Do not teach too many subjects," and again, "What you teach, teach thoroughly."

The result of teaching small parts of a large number of subjects is the passive reception of disconnected ideas, not illumined with any spark of vitality. Let the main ideas which are introduced into a child's education be few and

---

important, and let them be thrown into every combination possible. The child should make them his own, and should understand their application here and now in the circumstances of his actual life. From the very beginning of his education, the child should experience the joy of discovery. The discovery which he has to make, is that general ideas give an understanding of that stream of events which pours through his life, which is his life. By understanding I mean more than a mere logical analysis, though that is included. I mean "understanding" in the sense in which it is used in the French proverb, "To understand all, is to forgive all." Pedants sneer at an education which is useful. But if education is not useful, what is it? Is it a talent, to be hidden away in a napkin? Of course, education should be useful, whatever your aim in life. It was useful to Saint Augustine and it was useful to Napoleon. It is useful, because understanding is useful.

I pass lightly over that understanding which should be given by the literary side of education. Nor do I wish to be supposed to pronounce on the relative merits of a classical or a modern curriculum. I would only remark that the understanding which we want is an understanding of an insistent present. The only use of a knowledge of the past is to equip us for the present. No more deadly harm can be done to young minds than by depreciation of the present. The present contains all that there is. It is holy ground; for it is the past, and it is the future. At the same time it must be observed that an age is no less past if it existed two hundred years ago than if it existed two thousand years ago. Do not be deceived by the pedantry of dates. The ages of Shakespeare and of Molière are no less past than are the ages of Sophocles and of Virgil. The communion of saints is a great and inspiring assemblage, but it has only one possible hall of meeting, and that is, the present; and the mere lapse of time through which any particular group of saints must travel to reach that meeting-place, makes very little difference.

Passing now to the scientific and logical side of education, we remember that here also ideas which are not utilized are positively harmful. By utilizing an idea, I mean relating it to that stream, compounded of sense perceptions, feelings, hopes, desires, and of mental activities adjusting thought to thought, which forms our life. I can imagine a set of beings which might fortify their souls by passively reviewing disconnected ideas. Humanity is not built that way—except perhaps some editors of newspapers.

In scientific training the first thing to do with an idea is to prove it. But allow me for one moment to extend the meaning of "prove"; I mean—to prove its worth. Now an idea is not worth much unless the propositions in which it is embodied are true. Accordingly an essential part of the proof of an idea is the proof, either by experiment or by logic, of the truth of the propositions. But it is not essential that this proof of the truth should constitute the first introduction to the idea. After all, its assertion by the authority of respectable teachers is sufficient evidence to begin with. In our first contact with a set of propositions, we commence by appreciating their importance. That is what we all do in after-life. We do not attempt, in the strict sense, to prove or to disprove anything, unless its importance makes it worthy of that honour. These two processes of proof, in the narrow sense, and of appreciation, do not require a rigid separation in time. Both can be proceeded with nearly concurrently. But in so far as either process must have the priority, it should be that of appreciation by use.

Furthermore, we should not endeavour to use propositions in isolation. Emphatically I do not mean, a neat little set of experiments to illustrate Proposition I and then the proof of Proposition I, a neat little set of experiments to illustrate Proposition II and then the proof of Proposition II, and so on to the end of the book. Nothing could be more boring. Interrelated truths are utilized *en bloc,* and the various propositions are employed in any order, and with any reiteration. Choose some important applications of your theoretical subject; and study them concurrently with the systematic theoretical exposition. Keep the theoretical exposition short and simple, but let it be strict and rigid so far as it goes. It should not be too long for it to be easily known with thoroughness and accuracy. The consequences of a plethora of half-digested theoretical knowledge are deplorable. Also the theory should not be muddled up with the practice. The child should have no doubt when it is proving and when it is utilizing. My point is that what is proved should be utilized, and that what is utilized should—so far as is practicable—be proved. I am far from asserting that proof and utilization are the same thing.

At this point of my discourse, I can most directly carry forward my argument in the outward form of a digression. We are only just realizing that the art and science of education require a genius and a study of their own; and that this genius and this science are more than a bare knowledge of some branch of science or of literature. This truth was partially perceived in the past generation; and headmasters, somewhat crudely, were apt to supersede learning in their colleagues by requiring left-hand bowling and a taste for football. But culture is more than cricket, and more than football, and more than extent of knowledge.

Education is the acquisition of the art of the utilization of knowledge. This is an art very difficult to impart. Whenever a textbook is written of real educational worth, you may be quite certain that some reviewer will say that it will be difficult to teach from it. Of course it will be difficult to teach from it. If it were easy, the book ought to be burned; for it cannot be educational. In education, as elsewhere, the broad primrose path leads to a nasty place. . . .

We now return to my previous point, that theoretical ideas should always find important applications within the pupil's curriculum. This is not an easy doctrine to apply, but a very hard one. It contains within itself the problem of keeping knowledge alive, of preventing it from becoming inert, which is the central problem of all education.

The best procedure will depend on several factors, none of which can be neglected, namely, the genius of the teacher, the intellectual type of the pupils, their prospects in life, the opportunities offered by the immediate surroundings of the school, and allied factors of this sort. It is for this reason that the uniform external examination is so deadly. We do not denounce it because we are cranks, and like denouncing established things. We are not so childish. Also, of course, such examinations have their use in testing slackness. Our reason of dislike is very definite and very practical. It kills the best part of culture. When you analyze in the light of experience the central task of education, you find that its successful accomplishment depends on a delicate adjustment of many variable factors. The reason is that we are dealing with human minds, and not with dead matter. The evocation of curiosity, of judgment, of the power of mastering a complicated tangle of circumstances, the use of theory in giving foresight in special cases—all these powers are not be be imparted by a set rule embodied in one schedule of examination subjects.

I appeal to you, as practical teachers. With good discipline, it is always possible to pump into the minds of a class a certain quantity of inert knowledge. You take a textbook and make them learn it. So far, so good. The child then knows how to solve a quadratic equation. But what is the point of teaching a child to solve a quadratic equation? There is a traditional answer to this question. It runs thus: The mind is an instrument, you first sharpen it, and then use it; the acquisition of the power of solving a quadratic equation is part of the process of sharpening the mind. Now there is just enough truth in this answer to have made it live through the ages. But for all its half-truth, it embodies a radical error which bids fair to stifle the genius of the modern world. I do not know who was first responsible for this analogy of the mind to a dead instrument. For aught I know, it may have been one of the seven wise men of Greece, or a committee of the whole lot of them. Whoever was the originator, there can be no doubt of the authority which it has acquired by the continuous approval bestowed upon it by eminent persons. But whatever its weight of authority, whatever the high approval which it can quote, I have no hesitation in denouncing it as one of the most fatal, erroneous, and dangerous conceptions ever introduced into the theory of education. The mind is never passive; it is a perpetual activity, delicate, receptive, responsive to stimulus. You cannot postpone its life until you have sharpened it. Whatever interest attaches to your subject-matter must be evoked here and now; whatever powers you are strengthening in the pupil, must be exercised here and now; whatever possibilities of mental life your teaching should impart, must be exhibited here and now. That is the golden rule of education, and a very difficult rule to follow.

The difficulty is just this: the apprehension of general ideas, intellectual habits of mind, and pleasurable interest in mental achievement can be evoked by no form of words however accurately adjusted. All practical teachers know that education is a patient process of the mastery of details, minute by minute, hour by hour, day by day. There is no royal road to learning through an airy path of brilliant generalizations. There is a proverb about the difficulty of seeing the wood because of the trees. That difficulty is exactly the point which I am enforcing. The problem of education is to make the pupil see the wood by means of the trees.

The solution which I am urging, is to eradicate the fatal disconnection of subjects which kills the vitality of our modern curriculum. There is only one subject-matter for education, and that is Life in all its manifestations. Instead of this single unity, we offer children—Algebra, from which nothing follows; Geometry, from which nothing follows; Science, from which nothing follows;

History, from which nothing follows; a Couple of Languages, never mastered; and lastly, most dreary of all, Literature, represented by plays of Shakespeare, with philological notes and short analyses of plot and character to be in substance committed to memory. Can such a list be said to represent Life, as it is known in the midst of the living of it? The best that can be said of it is, that it is a rapid table of contents which a deity might run over in his mind while he was thinking of creating a world, and has not yet determined how to put it together. . . .

Fortunately, the specialist side of education presents an easier problem than does the provision of a general culture. For this there are many reasons. One is that many of the principles of procedure to be observed are the same in both cases, and it is unnecessary to recapitulate. Another reason is that specialist training takes place—or should take place—at a more advanced stage of the pupil's course, and thus there is easier material to work upon. But undoubtedly the chief reason is that the specialist study is normally a study of peculiar interest to the student. He is studying it because, for some reason, he wants to know it. This makes all the difference. The general culture is designed to foster an activity of mind; the specialist course utilizes this activity. But it does not do to lay too much stress on these neat antitheses. As we have already seen, in the general course foci of special interest will arise; and similarly in the special study, the external connections of the subject drag thought outwards.

Again, there is not one course of study which merely gives general culture, and another which gives special knowledge. The subjects pursued for the sake of a general education are special subjects specially studied; and, on the other hand, one of the ways of encouraging general mental activity is to foster a special devotion. You may not divide the seamless coat of learning. What education has to impart is an intimate sense for the power of ideas, for the beauty of ideas, and for the structure of ideas, together with a particular body of knowledge which has peculiar reference to the life of the being possessing it.

The appreciation of the structure of ideas is that side of a cultured mind which can only grow under the influence of a special study. I mean that eye for the whole chess-board, for the bearing of one set of ideas on another. Nothing but a special study can give any appreciation for the exact formulation of general ideas, for their relations when formulated, for their service in the comprehension of life. A mind so disciplined should be both more abstract and more concrete. It has been trained in the comprehension of abstract thought and in the analysis of facts.

Finally, there should grow the most austere of all mental qualities; I mean the sense for style. It is an aesthetic sense, based on admiration for the direct attainment of a foreseen end, simply and without waste. Style in art, style in literature, style in science, style in logic, style in practical execution have fundamentally the same aesthetic qualities, namely, attainment and restraint. The love of a subject in itself and for itself, where it is not the sleepy pleasure of pacing a mental quarter-deck, is the love of style as manifested in that study.

Here we are brought back to the position from which we started, the utility of education. Style, in its finest sense, is the last acquirement of the educated mind; it is also the most useful. It pervades the whole being. The administrator with a sense for style hates waste; the engineer with a sense for style economizes his material; the artisan with a sense for style prefers good work. Style is the ultimate morality of mind.

But above style, and above knowledge, there is something, a vague shape like fate above the Greek gods. That something is Power. Style is the fashioning of power, the restraining of power. But, after all, the power of attainment of the desired end is fundamental. The first thing is to get there. Do not bother about your style, but solve your problem, justify the ways of God to man, administer your province, or do whatever else is set before you.

Where, then, does style help? In this, with style the end is attained without side issues, without raising undesirable inflammations. With style you attain your end and nothing but your end. With style the effect of your activity is calculable, and foresight is the last gift of gods to men. With style your power is increased, for your mind is not distracted with irrelevancies, and you are more likely to attain your object. Now style is the exclusive privilege of the expert. Whoever heard of the style of an amateur painter, of the style of an amateur poet? Style is always the product of specialist study, the peculiar contribution of specialism to culture.

English education in its present phase suffers from a lack of definite aim, and from an external machinery which kills its vitality. Hitherto in this address I have been considering the aims which should govern education. In this respect England halts between two opinions. It has not decided whether to produce amateurs or experts. The profound change in the world which the nineteenth century has produced is that the growth of knowledge has given foresight. The amateur is essentially a man with appreciation and with immense versatility in mastering a given routine. But he lacks the foresight which comes from special knowledge. The object of this address is to suggest how to produce the expert without loss of the essential virtues of the amateur. . . .

When one considers in its length and in its breadth the importance of this question of the education of a nation's young, the broken lives, the defeated hopes, the national failures, which result from the frivolous inertia with which it is treated, it is difficult to restrain within oneself a savage rage. In the conditions of modern life the rule is absolute, the race which does not value trained intelligence is doomed. Not all your heroism, not all your social charm, not all your wit, not all your victories on land or at sea, can move back the finger of fate. Today we maintain ourselves. Tomorrow science will have moved forward yet one more step, and there will be no appeal from the judgment which will then be pronounced on the uneducated.

We can be content with no less than the old summary of educational ideal which has been current at any time from the dawn of our civilization. The essence of education is that it be religious.

Pray, what is religious education?

A religious education is an education which inculcates duty and reverence. Duty arises from our potential control over the course of events. Where attainable knowledge could have changed the issue, ignorance has the guilt of vice. And the foundation of reverence is this perception, that the present holds within itself the complete sum of existence, backwards and forwards, that whole amplitude of time, which is eternity.

CHAPTER III
THE RHYTHMIC CLAIMS OF FREEDOM AND DISCIPLINE

. . . The antithesis in education between freedom and discipline is not so sharp as a logical analysis of the meanings of the terms might lead us to imagine. The pupil's mind is a growing organism. On the one hand, it is not a box to be ruthlessly packed with alien ideas: and, on the other hand, the ordered acquirement of knowledge is the natural food for a developing intelligence. Accordingly, it should be the aim of an ideally constructed education that the discipline should be the voluntary issue of free choice, and that the freedom should gain an enrichment of possibility as the issue of discipline. The two principles, freedom and discipline, are not antagonists, but should be so adjusted in the child's life that they correspond to a natural sway, to and fro, of the developing personality. It is this adaptation of freedom and discipline to the natural sway of development that I have elsewhere called The Rhythm of Education. I am convinced that much disappointing failure in the past has been due to neglect of attention to the importance of this rhythm. My main position is that the dominant note of education at its beginning and at its end is freedom, but that there is an intermediate stage of discipline with freedom in subordination: Furthermore, that there is not one unique threefold cycle of freedom, discipline, and freedom; but that all mental development is composed of such cycles, and of cycles of such cycles. Such a cycle is a unit cell, or brick; and the complete stage of growth is an organic structure of such cells. In analyzing any one such cell, I call the first period of freedom the "stage of Romance," the intermediate period of discipline I call the "stage of Precision," and the final period of freedom is the "stage of Generalization."

Let me now explain myself in more detail. There can be no mental development without interest. Interest is the *sine qua non* for attention and apprehension. You may endeavour to excite interest by means of birch rods, or you may coax it by the incitement of pleasurable activity. But without interest there will be no progress. Now the natural mode by which living organisms are excited towards suitable self-development is enjoyment. The infant is lured to adapt itself to its environment by its love of its mother and its nurse; we eat because we like a good dinner: we subdue the forces of nature because we have been lured to discovery by an insatiable curiosity: we enjoy exercise: and we enjoy the unchristian passion of hating our dangerous enemies. Undoubtedly pain is one subordinate means of arousing an organism to action. But it only supervenes on the failure of pleasure. Joy is the normal healthy spur for the *élan vital*. I am not maintaining that we can safely abandon ourselves to the allurement of the greater immediate joys. What I do mean is that we should seek to arrange the development of character along a path of natural activity, in itself pleasurable. The subordinate stiffening of discipline must be directed to secure some long-time good; although an adequate object must not be too far below the horizon, if the necessary interest is to be retained.

The second preliminary point which I wish to make, is the unimportance—indeed the evil—of barren knowledge. The importance of knowledge lies in its use, in our active mastery of it—that is to say, it lies in wisdom. It is a convention to speak of mere knowledge, apart from wisdom, as of itself imparting a peculiar dignity to its possessor. I do not share in this reverence for knowledge as such. It all depends on who has the knowledge and what he does with it. That knowledge which adds greatness to character is knowledge so handled as to transform every phase of immediate experience. It is in respect to the activity of knowledge that an over-vigorous discipline in education is so harmful. The habit of active thought, with freshness, can only be generated by adequate freedom. Undiscriminating discipline defeats its own object by dulling the mind. If you have much to do with the young as they emerge from school and from the university, you soon note the dulled minds of those whose education has consisted in the acquirement of inert knowledge. Also the deplorable tone of English society in respect to learning is a tribute to our educational failure. Furthermore, this overhaste to impart mere knowledge defeats itself. The human mind rejects knowledge imparted in this way. The craving for expansion, for activity, inherent in youth is disgusted by a dry imposition of disciplined knowledge. The discipline, when it comes, should satisfy a natural craving for the wisdom which adds value to bare experience.

But let us now examine more closely the rhythm of these natural cravings of the human intelligence. The first procedure of the mind in a new environment is a somewhat discursive activity amid a welter of ideas and experience. It is a process of discovery, a process of becoming used to curious thoughts, of shaping questions, of seeking for answers, of devising new experiences, of noticing what happens as the result of new ventures. This general process is both natural and of absorbing interest. We must often have noticed children between the ages of eight and thirteen absorbed in its ferment. It is dominated by wonder, and cursed be the dullard who destroys wonder. Now undoubtedly this stage of development requires help, and even discipline. The environment within which the mind is working must be carefully selected. It must, of course, be chosen to suit the child's stage of growth, and must be adapted to individual needs. In a sense it is an imposition from without; but in a deeper sense it answers to the call of life within the child. In the teacher's consciousness the child has been sent to his telescope to look at the stars, in the child's consciousness he has been given free access to the glory of the heavens. Unless, working somewhere, however obscurely, even in the dullest child, there is this transfiguration of imposed routine, the child's nature will refuse to assimilate the alien material. It must never be forgotten that education is not a process of packing articles in a trunk. Such a simile is entirely inapplicable. It is, of course, a process completely of its own peculiar genus. Its nearest analogue is the assimilation of food by a living organism: and we all know how necessary to health is palatable food under suitable conditions. When you have put your boots in a trunk, they will stay there till you take them out again; but this is not at all the case if you feed a child with the wrong food.

This initial stage of romance requires guidance in another way. After all the child is the heir to long ages of civilisation, and it is absurd to let him wander in the intellectual maze of men in the Glacial Epoch. Accordingly, a certain pointing out of important facts, and of simplifying ideas, and of usual names, really strengthens the natural impetus of the pupil. In no part of education can you do without discipline or can you do without freedom; but in the stage of romance the emphasis must always be on freedom, to allow the child to see for itself and to act for itself. My point is that a block in the assimilation of ideas inevitably arises when a discipline of precision is imposed before a stage of romance has run its course in the growing mind. There is no comprehension apart from romance. It is my strong belief that the cause of so much failure in the past has been due to the lack of careful study of the due place of romance. Without the adventure of romance, at the best you get inert knowledge without initiative, and at the worst you get contempt of ideas—without knowledge.

But when this stage of romance has been properly guided another craving grows. The freshness of inexperience has worn off; there is general knowledge of the groundwork of fact and theory: and, above all, there has been plenty of independent browsing amid first-hand experiences, involving adventures of thought and of action. The enlightenment which comes from precise knowledge can now be understood. It corresponds to the obvious requirements of common sense, and deals with familiar material. Now is the time for pushing on, for knowing the subject exactly, and for retaining in the memory its salient features. This is the stage of precision. This stage is the sole stage of learning in the traditional scheme of education, either at school or university. You had to learn your subject, and there was nothing more to be said on the topic of education. The result of such an undue extension of a most necessary period of development was the production of a plentiful array of dunces, and of a few scholars whose natural interest had survived the car of Juggernaut. There is, indeed, always the temptation to teach pupils a little more of fact and of precise theory than at that stage they are fitted to assimilate. If only they could, it would be so useful. We—I am talking of schoolmasters and of university dons—are apt to forget that we are only subordinate elements in the education of a grown man; and that, in their own good time, in later life our pupils will learn for themselves. The phenomena of growth cannot be hurried beyond certain very narrow limits. But an unskilful practitioner can easily damage a sensitive organism. Yet, when all has been said in the way of caution, there is such a thing as pushing on, of getting to know the fundamental details and the main exact generalisations, and of acquiring an easy mastery of technique. There is no getting away from the fact that things have been found out, and that to be effective in the modern world you must have a store of definite acquirement of the best practice. To write poetry you must study metre; and to build bridges you must be learned in the strength of material. Even the Hebrew prophets had learned to write, probably in those days requiring no mean effort. The untutored art of genius is—in the words of the Prayer Book—a vain thing, fondly invented.

During the stage of precision, romance is the background. The stage is dominated by the inescapable fact that there are right ways and wrong ways, and definite truths to be known. But romance is not dead, and it is the art of teaching to foster it amidst definite application to appointed task. It must be fostered for one reason, because romance is after all a necessary ingredient of that balanced wisdom which is the goal to be attained. But there is another reason: The organism will not absorb the fruits of the task unless its powers of apprehension are kept fresh by romance. The real point is to discover in practice that exact balance between freedom and discipline which will give the greatest rate of progress over the things to be known. I do not believe that there is any abstract formula which will give information applicable to all subjects, to all types of pupils, or to each individual pupil; except indeed the formula of rhythmic sway which I have been insisting on, namely, that in the earlier stage the progress requires that the emphasis be laid on freedom, and that in the later middle stage the emphasis be laid on the definite acquirement of allotted tasks. I freely admit that if the stage of romance has been properly managed, the discipline of the second stage is much less apparent, that the children know how to go about their work, want to make a good job of it, and can be safely trusted with the details. Furthermore, I hold that the only discipline, important for its own sake, is self-discipline, and that this can only be acquired by a wide use of freedom. But yet—so many are the delicate points to be considered in education—it is necessary in life to have acquired the habit of cheerfully undertaking imposed tasks. The conditions can be satisfied if the tasks correspond to the natural cravings of the pupil at his stage of progress, if they keep his powers at full stretch, and if they attain an obviously sensible result, and if reasonable freedom is allowed in the mode of execution.

The difficulty of speaking about the way a skilful teacher will keep romance alive in his pupils arises from the fact that what takes a long time to describe, takes a short time to do. The beauty of a passage of Virgil may be rendered by insisting on beauty of verbal enunciation, taking no longer than prosy utterance. The emphasis on the beauty of a mathematical argument, in its marshalling of general considerations to unravel complex fact, is the speediest mode of procedure. The responsibility of the teacher at this stage is immense. To speak the truth, except in the rare case of genius in the teacher, I do not think that it is impossible to take a whole class very far along the road of precision without some dulling of the interest. It is the unfortunate dilemma that initiative and training are both necessary, and that training is apt to kill initiative.

But this admission is not to condone a brutal ignorance of methods of mitigating this untoward fact. It is not a theoretical necessity, but arises because perfect tact is unattainable in the treatment of each individual case. In the past the methods employed assassinated interest; we are discussing how to reduce the evil to its smallest dimensions. I merely utter the warning that education is a difficult problem, to be solved by no one simple formula.

In this connection there is, however, one practical consideration which is largely neglected. The territory of romantic interest is large, ill-defined, and not to be controlled by any explicit boundary. It depends on the chance flashes of insight. But the area of precise knowledge, as exacted in any general educational system, can be, and should be, definitely determined. If you make it too wide you will kill interest and defeat your own object: if you make it too narrow your pupils will lack effective grip. Surely, in every subject in each type of curriculum, the precise knowledge required should be determined after the most anxious inquiry. This does not now seem to be the case in any effective way. For example, in the classical studies of boys destined for a scientific career—a class of pupils in whom I am greatly interested—What is the Latin vocabulary which they ought definitely to know? Also what are the grammatical rules and constructions which they ought to have mastered? Why not determine these once and for all, and then bend every exercise to impress just these on the memory, and to understand their derivatives, both in Latin and also in French and English. Then, as to other constructions and words which occur in the reading of texts, supply full information in the easiest manner. A certain ruthless definiteness is essential in education. I am sure that one secret of a successful teacher is that he has formulated quite clearly in his mind what the pupil has got to know in precise fashion. He will then cease from half-hearted attempts to worry his pupils with memorising a lot of irrelevant stuff of inferior importance. The secret of success is pace, and the secret of pace is concentration. But, in respect to precise knowledge, the watchword is pace, pace, pace. Get your knowledge quickly, and then use it. If you can use it, you will retain it.

We have now come to the third stage of the rhythmic cycle, the stage of generalisation. There is here a reaction towards romance. Something definite is now known; aptitudes have been acquired; and general rules and laws are clearly apprehended both in their formulation and their detailed exemplification. The pupil now wants to use his new weapons. He is an effective individual, and it is effects that he wants to produce. He relapses into the discursive adventures of the romantic stage, with the advantage that his mind is now a disciplined regiment instead of a rabble. In this sense, education should begin in research and end in research. After all, the whole affair is merely a preparation for battling with the immediate experiences of life, a preparation by which to qualify each immediate moment with relevant ideas and appropriate actions. An education which does not begin by evoking initiative and end by encouraging it must be wrong. For its whole aim is the production of active wisdom.

In my own work at universities I have been much struck by the paralysis of thought induced in pupils by the aimless accumulation of precise knowledge, inert and unutilised. It should be the chief aim of a university professor to exhibit himself in his own true character—that is, as an ignorant man thinking, actively utilising his small share of knowledge. In a sense, knowledge shrinks as wisdom grows: for details are swallowed up in principles. The details of knowledge which are important will be picked up *ad hoc* in each avocation of life, but the habit of the active utilisation of well-understood principles is the final possession of wisdom. The stage of precision is the stage of growing into the apprehension of principles by the acquisition of a precise knowledge of details. The stage of generalisations is the stage of shedding details in favour of the active application of principles, the details retreating into subconscious habits. We don't go about explicitly retaining in our own minds that two and two make four, though once we had to learn it by heart. We trust to habit for our elementary arithmetic. But the essence of this stage is the emergence from the comparative passivity of being trained into the active freedom of application. Of course, during this stage, precise knowledge will grow, and more actively than ever before, because the mind has experienced the power of definiteness, and responds to the acquisition of general truth, and of richness of illustration. But the growth of knowledge becomes progressively unconscious, as being an incident derived from some active adventure of thought.

So much for the three stages of the rhythmic unit of development. In a general way the whole period of education is dominated by this threefold rhythm. Till the age of thirteen or fourteen there is the romantic stage, from fourteen to eighteen the stage of precision, and from eighteen to two and twenty the stage of generalisation. But these are only average characters, tinging the mode of development as a whole. I do not think that any pupil completes his stages simultaneously in all subjects. For example, I should plead that while language is initiating its stage of precision in the way of acquisition of vocabulary and of grammar, science should be in its full romantic stage. The romantic stage of language begins in infancy with the acquisition of speech, so that it passes early towards a stage of precision; while science is a late comer. Accordingly a precise inculcation of science at an early age wipes out initiative and interest, and destroys any chance of the topic having any richness of content in the child's apprehension. Thus, the romantic stage of science should persist for years after the precise study of language has commenced.

There are minor eddies, each in itself a threefold cycle, running its course in each day, in each week, and in each term. There is the general apprehension of some topic in its vague possibilities, the mastery of the relevant details, and finally the putting of the whole subject together in the light of the relevant knowledge. Unless the pupils are continually sustained by the evocation of interest, the acquirement of technique, and the excitement of success, they can never make progress, and will certainly lose heart. Speaking generally, during the last thirty years the schools of England have been sending up to the universities a disheartened crowd of young folk, inoculated against any outbreak of intellectual zeal. The universities have seconded the efforts of the schools and emphasised the failure. Accordingly, the cheerful gaiety of the young turns to other topics, and thus educated England is not hospitable to ideas. When we can point to some great achievement of our nation—let us hope that it may be something other than a war—which has been won in the classroom of our schools, and not in their playing-fields, then we may feel content with our modes of education. . . .

8

John Dewey

The American philosopher John Dewey (1859–1952) is the only thinker who has constructed a philosophy of education comparable in scope and depth to that of Plato. While Plato's educational philosophy rests on his belief in aristocracy and the power of pure reason, Dewey's educational philosophy rests on his belief in democracy and the power of scientific method.

A democratic society, according to Dewey is one "which makes provision for participation in the good of all its members on equal terms and which secures flexible readjustment of its institutions through interaction of the different forms of associated life." Dewey's view is that the class society outlined in *The Republic* results in the subordination of individuality. What Plato failed to note is that "each individual constitutes his own class."

Dewey considers scientific method to consist in "observation, reflection, and testing . . . deliberately adopted to secure a settled, assured subject matter." The essence of his position is that utilization of this method is effective not only in science but also in all aspects of life. "Science is experience becoming rational," and rationality or reasonableness has proved to be the most reliable method of reaching the truth, no matter what the field of inquiry. What Plato overlooked is that "there is no such thing as genuine knowledge and fruitful understanding except as the offspring of *doing*" and that "knowledge furnishes the means of understanding . . . what is to be done." In short, one acquires knowledge by intelligent action, and the possession of knowledge enables one to act more intelligently.

Dewey's insights into the educational process are so numerous and subtle that it is difficult to summarize them adequately. It is important, however, to warn the reader that Dewey's ideas have often been misinterpreted, and views are attributed to him that are the opposite of those he explicitly espouses.

Dewey, it is said, defended the idea that children should not be disciplined and should be left free to do whatever they choose. His actual view, which he stated on numerous occasions, is that "it is . . . fatal . . . to permit capricious or discontinuous action in the name of spontaneous self-expression."

Dewey is also accused of defending the view that subject matter should be taught only for its future practical value and not its present intrinsic value. But as Dewey wrote, "it is true of arithmetic, as it is of poetry that . . . it ought to be good to be appreciated on its own account—just as an enjoyable experience. . . .

Every subject at some phase of its development should possess, what is for the individual concerned with it, an aesthetic quality."

The first work reprinted here, *The Child and the Curriculum*, is a 1902 monograph in which Dewey presents the essentials of his position. The succeeding group of selections come from his masterpiece of fourteen years later, *Democracy and Education*. Dewey wrote the short work *Experience and Education* when he was nearly eighty years old. It contains a remarkably clear and concise presentation of his philosophy of education, and a careful reading should help to forestall future misinterpretations of his thought.

The Child and the Curriculum*

Profound differences in theory are never gratuitous or invented. They grow out of conflicting elements in a genuine problem—a problem which is genuine just because the elements, taken as they stand, are conflicting. Any significant problem involves conditions that for the moment contradict each other. Solution comes only by getting away from the meaning of terms that is already fixed upon and coming to see the conditions from another point of view, and hence in a fresh light. But this reconstruction means travail of thought. Easier than thinking with surrender of already formed ideas and detachment from facts already learned, is just to stick by what is already said, looking about for something with which to buttress it against attack.

Thus sects arise; schools of opinion. Each selects that set of conditions that appeal to it; and then erects them into a complete and independent truth, instead of treating them as a factor in a problem, needing adjustment.

The fundamental factors in the educative process are an immature, undeveloped being; and certain social aims, meanings, values incarnate in the matured experience of the adult. The educative process is the due interaction of these forces. Such a conception of each in relation to the other as facilitates completest and freest interaction is the essence of educational theory.

But here comes the effort of thought. It is easier to see the conditions in their separateness, to insist upon one at the expense of the other, to make antagonists of them, than to discover a reality to which each belongs. The easy thing is to seize upon something in the nature of the child, or upon something in the developed consciousness of the adult, and insist upon *that* as the key to the whole problem. When this happens a really serious practical problem—that of interaction—is transformed into an unreal, and hence insoluble, theoretic problem. Instead of seeing the educative steadily and as a whole, we see conflicting terms. We get the case of the child *vs.* the curriculum; of the individual nature *vs.* social culture. Below all other divisions in pedagogic opinion lies this opposition.

The child lives in a somewhat narrow world of personal contacts. Things hardly come within his experience unless they touch, intimately and obviously, his own well-being, or that of his family and friends. His world is a world of persons with their personal interests, rather than a realm of facts and laws. Not truth, in the sense of conformity to external fact, but affection and sympathy, is its keynote. As against this, the course of study met in the school presents material stretching back indefinitely in time, and extending outward indefinitely into space. The child is taken out of his familiar physical environment, hardly more than a square mile or so in area, into the wide world—yes, and even to the bounds of the solar system. His little span of personal memory and tradition is overlaid with the long centuries of the history of all peoples.

*Reprinted by permission of Southern Illinois University Press.

Again, the child's life is an integral, a total one. He passes quickly and readily from one topic to another, as from one spot to another, but is not conscious of transition or break. There is no conscious isolation, hardly conscious distinction. The things that occupy him are held together by the unity of the personal and social interests which his life carries along. Whatever is uppermost in his mind constitutes to him, for the time being, the whole universe. That universe is fluid and fluent; its contents dissolve and re-form with amazing rapidity. But, after all, it is the child's own world. It has the unity and completeness of his own life. He goes to school, and various studies divide and fractionize the world for him. Geography selects, it abstracts and analyzes one set of facts, and from one particular point of view. Arithmetic is another division, grammar another department, and so on indefinitely.

Again, in school each of these subjects is classified. Facts are torn away from their original place in experience and rearranged with reference to some general principle. Classification is not a matter of child experience; things do not come to the individual pigeon-holed. The vital ties of affection, the connecting bonds of activity, hold together the variety of his personal experiences. The adult mind is so familiar with the notion of logically ordered facts that it does not recognize—it cannot realize—the amount of separating and reformulating which the facts of direct experience have to undergo before they can appear as a "study," or branch of learning. A principle, for the intellect, has had to be distinguished and defined; facts have had to be interpreted in relation to this principle, not as they are in themselves. They have had to be regathered about a new centre which is wholly abstract and ideal. All this means a development of a special intellectual interest. It means ability to view facts impartially and objectively; that is, without reference to their place and meaning in one's own experience. It means capacity to analyze and to synthesize. It means highly matured intellectual habits and the command of a definite technique and apparatus of scientific inquiry. The studies as classified are the product, in a word, of the science of the ages, not of the experience of the child.

These apparent deviations and differences between child and curriculum might be almost indefinitely widened. But we have here sufficiently fundamental divergences: first, the narrow but personal world of the child against the impersonal but infinitely extended world of space and time; second, the unity, the single whole-heartedness of the child's life, and the specializations and divisions of the curriculum; third, an abstract principle of logical classification and arrangement, and the practical and emotional bonds of child life.

From these elements of conflict grow up different educational sects. One school fixes its attention upon the importance of the subject-matter of the curriculum as compared with the contents of the child's own experience. It is as if they said: Is life petty, narrow, and crude? Then studies reveal the great, wide universe with all its fullness and complexity of meaning. Is the life of the child egoistic, self-centered, impulsive? Then in these studies is found an objective universe of truth, law, and order. Is his experience confused, vague, uncertain, at the mercy of the moment's caprice and circumstance? Then studies introduce a world arranged on the basis of eternal and general truth; a world where all is measured and defined. Hence the moral: ignore and minimize the child's individual peculiarities, whims, and experiences. They are what we need to get away from. They are to be obscured or eliminated. As educators our work is precisely to substitute for these superficial and casual affairs stable and well-ordered realities; and these are found in studies and lessons.

Subdivide each topic into studies; each study into lessons; each lesson into specific facts and formulae. Let the child proceed step by step to master each one of these separate parts, and at last he will have covered the entire ground. The road which looks so long when viewed in its entirety, is easily traveled, considered as a series of particular steps. Thus emphasis is put upon the logical subdivisions and consecutions of the subject-matter. Problems of instruction are problems of procuring texts giving logical parts and sequences, and of presenting these portions in class in a similar definite and graded way. Subject-matter furnishes the end, and it determines method. The child is simply the immature being who is to be matured; he is the superficial being who is to be deepened; his is narrow experience which is to be widened. It is his to receive, to accept. His part is fulfilled when he is ductile and docile.

Not so, says the other sect. The child is the starting-point, the centre, and the end. His development, his growth, is the ideal. It alone furnishes the standard. To the growth of the child all studies are subservient; they are instruments valued as they serve the needs of growth. Personality, character, is more than subject-matter. Not knowledge or information, but self-realization, is the goal. To possess all the world of knowledge and lose one's own self is as awful a fate in education as in religion. Moreover, subject-matter never can be got into the child from without. Learning is active. It involves reaching out of the mind. It involves organic assimilation starting from within. Literally, we must take our stand with the child and our departure from him. It is he and not the subject-matter which determines both quality and quantity of learning.

The only significant method is the method of the mind as it reaches out and assimilates. Subject-matter is but spiritual food, possible nutritive material. It cannot digest itself; it cannot of its own accord turn into bone and muscle and blood. The source of whatever is dead, mechanical, and formal in schools is found precisely in the subordination of the life and experience of the child to the curriculum. It is because of this that "study" has become a synonym for what is irksome, and a lesson identical with a task.

This fundamental opposition of child and curriculum set up by these two modes of doctrine can be duplicated in a series of other terms. "Discipline" is the watchword of those who magnify the course of study; "interest" that of those who blazon "The Child" upon their banner. The standpoint of the former is logical; that of the latter psychological. The first emphasizes the necessity of adequate training and scholarship on the part of the teacher; the latter that of need of sympathy with the child, and knowledge of his natural instincts. "Guidance and control" are the catchwords of one school; "freedom and initiative" of the other. Law is asserted here; spontaneity proclaimed there. The old, the conservation of what has been achieved in the pain and toil of the ages, is dear to the one; the new, change, progress, wins the affection of the other. Inertness and routine, chaos and anarchism, are accusations bandied back and forth. Neglect of the sacred authority of duty is charged by one side, only to be met by counter-charges of suppression of individuality through tyrannical despotism.

Such oppositions are rarely carried to their logical conclusion. Common sense recoils at the extreme character of these results. They are left to theorists, while common sense vibrates back and forward in a maze of inconsistent compromise. The need of getting theory and practical common sense into closer connection suggests a return to our original thesis: that we have here conditions which are necessarily related to each other in the educative process, since this is precisely one of interaction and adjustment.

What, then, is the problem? It is just to get rid of the prejudicial notion that there is some gap in kind (as distinct from degree) between the child's experience and the various forms of subject-matter that make up the course of study. From the side of the child, it is a question of seeing how his experience already contains within itself elements—facts and truths—of just the same sort as those entering into the formulated study; and, what is of more importance, of how it contains within itself the attitudes, the motives, and the interests which have operated in developing and organizing the subject-matter to the plane which it now occupies. From the side of the studies, it is a question of interpreting them as outgrowths of forces operating in the child's life, and of discovering the steps that intervene between the child's present experience and their richer maturity.

Abandon the notion of subject-matter as something fixed and ready-made in itself, outside the child's experience; cease thinking of the child's experience as also something hard and fast; see it as something fluent, embryonic, vital; and we realize that the child and the curriculum are simply two limits which define a single process. Just as two points define a straight line, so the present standpoint of the child and the facts and truths of studies define instruction. It is continuous reconstruction, moving from the child's present experience out into that represented by the organized bodies of truth that we call studies.

On the face of it, the various studies, arithmetic, geography, language, botany, etc., are themselves experience—they are that of the race. They embody the cumulative outcome of the efforts, the strivings, and successes of the human race generation after generation. They present this, not as a mere accumulation, not as a miscellaneous heap of separate bits of experience, but in some organized and systematized way—that is, as reflectively formulated.

Hence, the facts and truths that enter into the child's present experience, and those contained in the subject-matter of studies, are the initial and final terms of one reality. To oppose one to the other is to oppose the infancy and maturity of the same growing life; it is to set the moving tendency and the final result of the same process over against each other; it is to hold that the nature and the destiny of the child war with each other.

If such be the case, the problem of the relation of the child and the curriculum presents itself in this guise: Of what use, educationally speaking, is it to be able to see the end in the beginning? How does it assist us in dealing with the early stages of growth to be able to anticipate its later phases? The studies, as we have agreed, represent the possibilities of development inherent in the child's immediate crude experience. But, after all, they are not parts of that present and immediate life. Why, then, or how, make account of them?

Asking such a question suggests its own answer. To see the outcome is to know in what direction the present experience is moving, provided it move normally and soundly. The far-away point, which is of no significance to us simply as far away, becomes of huge importance the moment we take it as defining a present direction of movement. Taken in this way it is of no remote and distant result to be achieved, but a guiding method in dealing with the present. The systematized and defined experience of the adult mind, in other words, is of value to us in interpreting the child's life as it immediately shows itself, and in passing on to guidance or direction.

Let us look for a moment at these two ideas: interpretation and guidance. The child's present experience is in no way self-explanatory. It is not final, but transitional. It is nothing complete in itself, but just a sign or index of certain growth-tendencies. As long as we confine our gaze to what the child here and now puts forth, we are confused and misled. We cannot read its meaning. Extreme depreciations of the child morally and intellectually, and sentimental idealizations of him, have their root in a common fallacy. Both spring from taking stages of a growth or movement as something cut off and fixed. The first fails to see the promise contained in feelings and deeds which, taken by themselves, are unpromising and repellant; the second fails to see that even the most pleasing and beautiful exhibitions are but signs, and that they begin to spoil and rot the moment they are treated as achievements.

What we need is something which will enable us to interpret, to appraise, the elements in the child's present puttings forth and fallings away, his exhibitions of power and weakness, in the light of some larger growth-process in which they have their place. Only in this way can we discriminate. If we isolate the child's present inclinations, purposes, and experiences from the place they occupy and the part they have to perform in a developing experience, all stand upon the same level; all alike are equally good and equally bad. But in the movement of life different elements stand upon different planes of value. Some of the child's deeds are symptoms of a waning tendency; they are survivals in functioning of an organ which has done its part and is passing out of vital use. To give positive attention to such qualities is to arrest development upon a lower level. It is systematically to maintain a rudimentary phase of growth. Other activities are signs of a culminating power and interest; to them applies the maxim of striking while the iron is hot. As regards them, it is perhaps a matter of now or never. Selected, utilized, emphasized, they may mark a turning-point for good in the child's whole career; neglected, an opportunity goes, never to be recalled. Other acts and feelings are prophetic; they represent the dawning of flickering light that will shine steadily only in the far future. As regards them there is little at present to do but give them fair and full chance, waiting for the future for definite direction.

Just as, upon the whole, it was the weakness of the "old education" that it made invidious comparisons between the immaturity of the child and the maturity of the adult, regarding the former as something to be got away from as soon as possible and as much as possible; so it is the danger of the "new education" that it regard the child's present powers and interests as something finally significant in themselves. In truth, his learnings and achievements are fluid and moving. They change from day to day and from hour to hour.

It will do harm if child-study leave in the popular mind the impression that a child of a given age has a positive equipment of purposes and interests to be cultivated just as they stand. Interests in reality are but attitudes toward possible experiences; they are not achievements; their worth is in the leverage they afford, not in the accomplishment they represent. To take the phenomena presented at a given age as in any way self-explanatory or self-contained is inevitably to result in indulgence and spoiling. Any power, whether of child or adult, is indulged when it is taken on its given and present level in consciousness. Its genuine meaning is in the propulsion it affords toward a higher level. It is just something to do with. Appealing to the interest upon the present plane means excitation; it means playing with a power so as continually to stir it up without directing it toward definite achievement. Continuous initiation, continuous starting of activities that do not arrive, is, for all practical purposes, as bad as the continual repression of initiative in conformity with supposed interests of some more perfect thought or will. It is as if the child were forever tasting and never eating; always having his palate tickled upon the emotional side, but never getting the organic satisfaction that comes only with digestion of food and transformation of it into working power.

As against such a view, the subject-matter of science and history and art serves to reveal the real child to us. We do not know the meaning either of his tendencies or of his performances excepting as we take them as germinating seed, or opening bud, of some fruit to be borne. The whole world of visual nature is all too small an answer to the problem of the meaning of the child's instinct for light and form. The entire science of physics is none too much to interpret adequately to us what is involved in some simple demand of the child for explanation of some casual change that has attracted his attention. The art of Rafael or of Corot is none too much to enable us to value the impulses stirring in the child when he draws and daubs.

So much for the use of the subject-matter in interpretation. Its further employment in direction or guidance is but an expansion of the same thought. To interpret the fact is to see it in its vital movement, to see it in its relation to growth. But to view it as a part of a normal growth is to secure the basis for guiding it. Guidance is not external imposition. *It is freeing the life-process for its own most adequate fulfillment.* What was said about disregard of the child's present experience because of its remoteness from mature experience; and of the sentimental idealization of the child's naïve caprices and performances, may be repeated here with slightly altered phrase. There are those who see no alternative between forcing the child from without, or leaving him entirely alone. Seeing no alternative, some choose one mode, some another. Both fall into the same fundamental error. Both fail to see that development is a definite process, having its own law which can be fulfilled only when adequate and normal conditions are provided. Really to interpret the child's present crude impulses in counting, measuring, and arranging things in rhythmic series, involves mathematical scholarship—a knowledge of the mathematical formulae and relations which have, in the history of the race, grown out of just such crude beginnings. To see the whole history of development which intervenes between these two terms is simply to see what step the child needs to take just here and now; to what use he needs to put his blind impulse in order that it may get clarity and gain force.

If, once more, the "old education" tended to ignore the dynamic quality, the developing force inherent in the child's present experience, and therefore to assume that direction and control were just matters of arbitrarily putting the child in a given path and compelling him to walk there, the "new education" is in danger of taking the idea of development in altogether too formal and empty a way. The child is expected to "develop" this or that fact or truth out of his own mind. He is told to think things out, or work things out for himself, without being supplied any of the environing conditions which are requisite to start and guide thought. Nothing can be developed from nothing; nothing but the crude can be developed out of the crude—and this is what surely happens when we throw the child back upon his achieved self as a finality, and invite him to spin new truths of nature or of conduct out of that. It is certainly as futile to expect a child to evolve a universe out of his own mere mind as it is for a philosopher to attempt that task. Development does not mean just getting something out of the mind. It is a development of experience and into experience that is really wanted. And this is impossible save as just that educative medium is provided which will enable the powers and interests that have been selected as valuable to function. They must operate, and how they operate will depend almost entirely upon the stimuli which surround them, and the material upon which they exercise themselves. The problem of direction is thus the problem of selecting appropriate stimuli for instincts and impulses which it is desired to employ in the gaining of new experience. What new experiences are desirable, and thus what stimuli are needed, it is impossible to tell except as there is some comprehension of the development which is aimed at; except, in a word, as the adult knowledge is drawn upon as revealing the possible career open to the child.

It may be of use to distinguish and to relate to each other the logical and the psychological aspects of experience—the former standing for subject-matter in itself, the latter for it in relation to the child. A psychological statement of experience follows its actual growth; it is historic; it notes steps actually taken, the uncertain and tortuous, as well as the efficient and successful. The logical point of view, on the other hand, assumes that the development has reached a certain positive stage of fulfillment. It neglects the process and considers the outcome. It summarizes and arranges, and thus separates the achieved results from the actual steps by which they were forthcoming in the first instance. We may compare the difference between the logical and the psychological to the difference between the notes which an explorer makes in a new country, blazing a trail and finding his way along as best he may, and the finished map that is constructed after the country has been thoroughly explored. The two are mutually dependent. Without the more or less accidental and devious paths traced by the explorer there would be no facts which could be utilized in the making of the complete and related chart. But no one would get the benefit of the explorer's trip if it was not compared and checked up with similar wanderings undertaken by others; unless the new geographical facts learned, the streams crossed, the mountains climbed, etc., were viewed, not as mere incidents in the journey of the particular traveler, but (quite apart from the individual explorer's life) in relation to other similar facts already known. The map orders individual experiences, connecting them with one another irrespective of the local and temporal circumstances and accidents of their original discovery.

Of what use is this formulated statement of experience? Of what use is the map?

Well, we may first tell what the map is not. The map is not a substitute for a personal experience. The map does not take the place of an actual journey. The logically formulated material of a science or branch of learning, of a study, is no substitute for the having of individual experiences. The mathematical formula for a falling body does not take the place of personal contact and immediate individual experience with the falling thing. But the map, a summary, an arranged and orderly view of previous experiences, serves as a guide to future experience; it gives direction; it facilitates control; it economizes effort, preventing useless wandering, and pointing out the paths which lead most quickly and most certainly to a desired result. Through the map every new traveler may get for his own journey the benefits of the results of others' explorations without the waste of energy and loss of time involved in their wanderings—wanderings which he himself would be obliged to repeat were it not for just the assistance of the objective and generalized record of their performances. That which we call a science or study puts the net product of past experience in the form which makes it most available for the future. It represents a capitalization which may at once be turned to interest. It economizes the workings of the mind in every way. Memory is less taxed because the facts are grouped together about some common principle, instead of being connected solely with the varying incidents of their original discovery. Observation is assisted; we know what to look for and where to look. It is the difference between looking for a needle in a haystack, and searching for a given paper in a well-arranged cabinet. Reasoning is directed, because there is a certain general path or line laid out along which ideas naturally march, instead of moving from one chance association to another.

There is, then, nothing final about a logical rendering of experience. Its value is not contained in itself; its significance is that of standpoint, outlook, method. It intervenes between the more casual, tentative, and round-about experiences of the past, and more controlled and orderly experiences of the future. It gives past experience in that net form which renders it most available and most significant, most fecund for future experience. The abstractions, generalizations, and classifications which it introduces all have prospective meaning.

The formulated result is then not to be opposed to the process of growth. The logical is not set over against the psychological. The surveyed and arranged result occupies a critical position in the process of growth. It marks a turning-point. It shows how we may get the benefit of past effort in controlling future endeavor. In the largest sense the logical standpoint is itself psychological; it has its meaning as a point in the development of experience, and its justification is in its functioning in the future growth which it insures.

Hence the need of reinstating into experience the subject-matter of the studies, or branches of learning. It must be restored to the experience from which it has been abstracted. It needs to be *psychologized;* turned over, translated into the immediate and individual experiencing within which it has its origin and significance.

Every study or subject thus has two aspects: one for the scientist as a scientist; the other for the teacher as a teacher. These two aspects are in no sense opposed or conflicting. But neither are they immediately identical. For the scientist, the subject-matter represents simply a given body of truth to be employed in locating new problems, instituting new researches, and carrying them through to a verified outcome. To him the subject-matter of the science is self-contained. He refers various portions of it to each other; he connects new facts with it. He is not, as a scientist, called upon to travel outside its particular bounds; if he does, it is only to get more facts of the same general sort. The problem of the teacher is a different one. As a teacher he is not concerned with adding new facts to the science he teaches; in propounding new hypotheses or in verifying them. He is concerned with the subject-matter of the science as *representing a given stage and phase of the development of experience.* His problem is that of inducing a vital and personal experiencing. Hence, what concerns him, as teacher, is the ways in which that subject may become a part of experience; what there is in the child's present that is usable with reference to it; how such elements are to be used; how his own knowledge of the subject-matter may assist in interpreting the child's needs and doings, and determine the medium in which the child should be placed in order that his growth may be properly directed. He is concerned, not with the subject-matter as such, but with the subject-matter as a related factor in a total and growing experience. Thus to see it is to psychologize it.

It is the failure to keep in mind the double aspect of subject-matter which causes the curriculum and child to be set over against each other as described in our early pages. The subject-matter, just as it is for the scientist, has no direct relationship to the child's present experience. It stands outside of it. The danger here is not a merely theoretical one. We are practically threatened on all sides. Text-book and teacher vie with each other in presenting to the child the subject-matter as it stands to the specialist. Such modification and revision as it undergoes are a mere elimination of certain scientific difficulties, and the general reduction to a lower intellectual level. The material is not translated into life-terms, but is directly offered as a substitute for, or an external annex to, the child's present life.

Three typical evils result: In the first place, the lack of any organic connection with what the child has already seen and felt and loved makes the material purely formal and symbolic. There is a sense in which it is impossible to value too highly the formal and the symbolic. The genuine form, the real symbol, serve as methods in the holding and discovery of truth. They are tools by which the individual pushes out most surely and widely into unexplored areas. They are means by which he brings to bear whatever of reality he has succeeded in gaining in past searchings. But this happens only when the symbol really symbolizes—when it stands for and sums up in shorthand actual experiences which the individual has already gone through. A symbol which is induced from without, which has not been led up to in preliminary activities, is, as we say, a *bare* or *mere* symbol; it is dead and barren. Now, any fact, whether of arithmetic, or geography, or grammar, which is not led up to and into out of something which has previously occupied a significant position in the child's life for its own sake, is forced into this position. It is not a reality, but just the sign of a reality which *might* be experienced if certain conditions were fulfilled. But the abrupt presentation of the fact as something known by others, and requiring only to be studied and learned by the child, rules out such conditions of fulfillment. It condemns the fact to be a hieroglyph: it would mean something if one only had the key. The clue being lacking, it remains an idle curiosity, to fret and obstruct the mind, a dead weight to burden it.

The second evil in this external presentation is lack of motivation. There are not only no facts or truths which have been previously felt as such with which to appropriate and assimilate the new, but there is no craving, no need, no demand. When the subject-matter has been psychologized, that is, viewed as an outgrowth of present tendencies and activities, it is easy to locate in the present some obstacle, intellectual, practical, or ethical, which can be handled more adequately if the truth in question be mastered. This need supplies motive for the learning. An end which is the child's own carries him on to possess the means of its accomplishment. But when material is directly supplied in the form of a lesson to be learned as a lesson, the connecting links of need and aim are conspicuous for their absence. What we mean by the mechanical and dead in instruction is a result of this lack of motivation. The organic and vital mean interaction—they mean play of mental demand and material supply.

The third evil is that even the most scientific matter, arranged in most logical fashion, loses this quality, when presented in external, ready-made fashion, by the time it gets to the child. It has to undergo some modification in order to shut out some phases too hard to grasp, and to reduce some of the attendant difficulties. What happens? Those things which are most significant to the scientific man, and most valuable in the logic of actual inquiry and classification, drop out. The really thought-provoking character is obscured, and the organizing function disappears. Or, as we commonly say, the child's reasoning powers, the faculty of abstraction and generalization, are not adequately developed. So the subject-matter is evacuated of its logical value, and, though it is what it is only from the logical standpoint, is presented as stuff only for "memory." This is the contradiction: the child gets the advantage neither of the adult logical formulation, nor of his own native competencies of apprehension and response. Hence the logic of the child is hampered and mortified, and we are almost fortunate if he does not get actual non-science, flat and common-place residua of what was gaining scientific vitality a generation or two ago—degenerate reminiscence of what someone else once formulated on the basis of the experience that some further person had, once upon a time, experienced.

The train of evils does not cease. It is all too common for opposed erroneous theories to play straight into each other's hands. Psychological considerations may be slurred or shoved one side; they cannot be crowded out. Put out of the door, they come back through the window. Somehow and somewhere motive must be appealed to, connection must be established between the mind and its material. There is no question of getting along without this bond of connection; the only question is whether it be such as grows out of the material itself in relation to the mind, or be imported and hitched on from some outside source. If the subject-matter of the lessons be such as to have an appropriate place within the expanding consciousness of the child, if it grows out of his own past doings, thinkings, and sufferings, and grows into application in further achievements and receptivities, then no device or trick of method has to be resorted to in order to enlist "interest." The psychologized *is* of interest—that is, it is placed in the whole of conscious life so that it shares the worth of that life. But the externally presented material, that, conceived and generated in standpoints and attitudes remote from the child, and developed in motives alien to him, has no such place of its own. Hence the recourse to adventitious leverage to push it in, to factitious drill to drive it in, to artificial bribe to lure it in.

Three aspects of this recourse to outside ways for giving the subject-matter some psychological meaning may be worth mentioning. Familiarity breeds contempt, but it also breeds something like affection. We get used to the chains we wear, and we miss them when removed. 'Tis an old story that through custom we finally embrace what at first wore a hideous mien. Unpleasant, because meaningless, activities may get agreeable if long enough persisted in. *It is possible for the mind to develop interest in a routine or mechanical procedure, if conditions are continually supplied which demand that mode of operation and preclude any other sort.* I frequently hear dulling devices and empty exercises defended and extolled because "the children take such an 'interest' in them." Yes, that is the worst of it; the mind, shut out from worthy employ and missing the taste of adequate performance, comes down to the level of that which is left to it to know and do, and perforce takes an interest in a cabined and cramped experience. To find satisfaction in its own exercise is the normal law of mind, and if large and meaningful business for the mind be denied, it tries to content itself with the formal movements that remain to it—and too often succeeds, save in those cases of more intense activity which cannot accommodate themselves, and that make up the unruly and *déclassé* of our school product. An interest in the formal apprehension of symbols and in their memorized reproduction becomes in many pupils a substitute for the original and vital interest in reality; and all because, the subject-matter of the course of study being out of relation to the concrete mind of the individual, some substitute bond to hold it in some kind of working relation to the mind must be discovered and elaborated.

The second substitute for living motivation in the subject-matter is that of contrast-effects; the material of the lesson is rendered interesting, if not in itself, at least in contrast with some alternative experience. To learn the lesson is more interesting than to take a scolding, be held up to general ridicule, stay after school, receive degradingly low marks, or fail to be promoted. And very much of what goes by the name of "discipline," and prides itself upon opposing the doctrines of a soft pedagogy and upon upholding the banner of effort and duty, is nothing more or less than just this appeal to "interest" in its obverse aspect—to fear, to dislike of various kinds of physical, social, and personal pain. The subject-matter does not appeal; it cannot appeal; it lacks origin and bearing in a growing experience. So the appeal is to the thousand and one outside and irrelevant agencies which may serve to throw, by sheer rebuff and rebound, the mind back upon the material from which it is constantly wandering.

Human nature being what it is, however, it tends to seek its motivation in the agreeable rather than in the disagreeable, in direct pleasure rather than in alternative pain. And so has come up the modern theory and practice of the "interesting," in the false sense of that term. The material is still left; so far as its own characteristics are concerned, just material externally selected and formulated. It is still just so much geography and arithmetic and grammar study; not so much potentiality of child-experience with regard to language, earth, and numbered and measured reality. Hence the difficulty of bringing the mind to bear upon it; hence its repulsiveness; the tendency for attention to wander; for other acts and images to crowd in and expel the lesson. The legitimate way out is to transform the material; to psychologize it—that is, once more, to take it and to develop it within the range and scope of the child's life. But it is easier and simpler to leave it as it is, and then by trick of method to *arouse* interest, to *make* it *interesting*; to cover it with sugar-coating; to conceal its barrenness by intermediate and unrelated material; and finally, as it were, to get the child to swallow and digest the unpalatable morsel while he is enjoying tasting something quite different. But alas for the analogy! Mental assimilation is a matter of consciousness; and if the attention has not been playing upon the actual material, that has not been apprehended, nor worked into faculty.

How, then, stands the case of Child *vs*. Curriculum? What shall the verdict be? The radical fallacy in the original pleadings with which we set out is the supposition that we have no choice save either to leave the child to his own unguided spontaneity or to inspire direction upon him from without. Action is response; it is adaptation, adjustment. There is no such thing as sheer self-activity possible—because all activity takes place in a medium, in a situation, and with reference to its conditions. But, again, no such thing as imposition of truth from without, as insertion of truth from without, is possible. All depends upon the activity which the mind itself undergoes in responding to what is presented from without. Now, the value of the formulated wealth of knowledge that makes up the course of study is that it may enable the educator to *determine the environment of the child,* and thus by indirection to direct. Its primary value, its primary indication, is for the teacher, not for the child. It says to the teacher: Such and such are the capacities, the fulfillments, in truth and beauty and behavior, open to these children. Now see to it that day by day the conditions are such that *their own activities* move inevitably in this direction, toward such culmination of themselves. Let the child's nature fulfill its own destiny, revealed to you in whatever of science and art and industry the world now holds as its own.

The case is of Child. It is his present powers which are to assert themselves; his present capacities which are to be exercised; his present attitudes which are to be realized. But save as the teacher knows, knows wisely and thoroughly, the race-experience which is embodied in that thing we call the Curriculum, the teacher knows neither what the present power, capacity, or attitude is, nor yet how it is to be asserted, exercised, and realized.

Democracy and Education*
7. THE DEMOCRATIC CONCEPTION IN EDUCATION

For the most part, save incidentally, we have hitherto been concerned with education as it may exist in any social group. We have now to make explicit the differences in the spirit, material, and method of education as it operates in different types of community life. To say that education is a social function, securing direction and development in the immature through their participation in the life of the group to which they belong, is to say in effect that education will vary with the quality of life which prevails in a group. Particularly is it true that a society which not only changes but which has the ideal of such change as will improve it, will have different standards and methods of education from one which aims simply at the perpetuation of its own customs. To make the general ideas set forth applicable to our own educational practice, it is, therefore, necessary to come to closer quarters with the nature of present social life.

1. The Implications of Human Association

Society is one word, but many things. Men associate together in all kinds of ways and for all kinds of purposes. One man is concerned in a multitude of di-

---

*Reprinted by permission of Southern Illinois University Press.

verse groups, in which his associates may be quite different. It often seems as if they had nothing in common except that they are modes of associated life. Within every larger social organization there are numerous minor groups: not only political subdivisions, but industrial, scientific, religious, associations. There are political parties with differing aims, social sets, cliques, gangs, corporations, partnerships, groups bound closely together by ties of blood, and so in endless variety. In many modern states, and in some ancient, there is great diversity of populations, of varying languages, religions, moral codes, and traditions. From this standpoint, many a minor political unit, one of our large cities, for example, is a congeries of loosely associated societies, rather than an inclusive and permeating community of action and thought.[1]

The terms society, community, are thus ambiguous. They have both a eulogistic or normative sense, and a descriptive sense; a meaning *de jure* and a meaning *de facto*. In social philosophy, the former connotation is almost always uppermost. Society is conceived as one by its very nature. The qualities which accompany this unity, praiseworthy community of purpose and welfare, loyalty to public ends, mutuality of sympathy, are emphasized. But when we look at the facts which the term *denotes* instead of confining our attention to its intrinsic *connotation,* we find not unity, but a plurality of societies, good and bad. Men banded together in a criminal conspiracy, business aggregations that prey upon the public while serving it, political machines held together by the interest of plunder, are included. If it is said that such organizations are not societies because they do not meet the ideal requirements of the notion of society, the answer, in part, is that the conception of society is then made so "ideal" as to be of no use, having no reference to facts; and in part, that each of these organizations, no matter how opposed to the interests of other groups, has something of the praiseworthy qualities of "Society" which hold it together. There is honor among thieves, and a band of robbers has a common interest as respects its members. Gangs are marked by fraternal feeling, and narrow cliques by intense loyalty to their own codes. Family life may be marked by exclusiveness, suspicion, and jealousy as to those without, and yet be a model of amity and mutual aid within. Any education given by a group tends to socialize its members, but the quality and value of the socialization depends upon the habits and aims of the group.

Hence, once more, the need of a measure for the worth of any given mode of social life. In seeking this measure, we have to avoid two extremes. We cannot set up, out of our heads, something we regard as an ideal society. We must base our conception upon societies which actually exist, in order to have any assurance that our ideal is a practicable one. But, as we have just seen, the ideal cannot simply repeat the traits which are actually found. The problem is to extract the desirable traits of forms of community life which actually exist, and employ them to criticize undesirable features and suggest improvement. Now in any social group whatever, even in a gang of thieves, we find some interest held in common, and we find a certain amount of interaction and cooperative intercourse with other groups. From these two traits we derive our standard. How numerous and varied are the interests which are consciously shared? How full and free is the interplay with other forms of association? If we apply these considerations to, say, a criminal band, we find that the ties which consciously hold the members together are few in number, reducible almost to a common interest in plunder; and that they are of such a nature as to isolate the group from other groups with respect to give and take of the values of life. Hence, the education such a society gives is partial and distorted. If we take, on the other hand, the kind of family life which illustrates the standard, we find that there are material, intellectual, aesthetic interests in which all participate and that the progress of one member has worth for the experience of other members—it is readily communicable—and that the family is not an isolated whole, but enters intimately into relationships with business groups, with schools, with all the agencies of culture, as well as with other similar groups, and that it plays a due part in the political organization and in return receives support from it. In short, there are many interests consciously communicated and shared; and there are varied and free points of contact with other modes of association.

I. Let us apply the first element in this criterion to a despotically governed state. It is not true there is no common interest in such an organization between governed and governors. The authorities in command must make some appeal to the native activities of the subjects, must call some of their powers into play. Talleyrand said that a government could do everything with bayonets except sit on them. This cynical declaration is at least a recognition that the bond of union is not merely one of coercive force. It may be said, however, that the activities appealed to are themselves unworthy and degrading—that such a government calls into functioning activity simply capacity for fear. In a way, this statement is true. But it overlooks the fact that fear need not be an undesirable factor in experience. Caution, circumspection, prudence, desire to foresee future events so as to avert what is harmful, these desirable traits are as much a product of calling the impulse of fear into play as is cowardice and abject submission. The real difficulty is that the appeal to fear is *isolated*. In evoking dread and hope of specific tangible reward—say comfort and ease—many other capacities are left untouched. Or rather, they are affected, but in such a way as to pervert them. Instead of operating on their own account they are reduced to mere servants of attaining pleasure and avoiding pain.

This is equivalent to saying that there is no extensive number of common interests; there is no free play back and forth among the members of the social group. Stimulation and response are exceedingly one-sided. In order to have a large number of values in common, all the members of the group must have an equable opportunity to receive and to take from others. There must be a large variety of shared undertakings and experiences. Otherwise, the influences which educate some into masters, educate others into slaves. And the experience of each party loses in meaning, when the free interchange of varying modes of life-experience is arrested. A separation into a privileged and a subject-class prevents social endosmosis. The evils thereby affecting the superior class are less material and less perceptible, but equally real. Their culture tends to be sterile, to be turned back to feed on itself; their art becomes a showy display and artifical; their wealth luxurious; their knowledge over-specialized; their manners fastidious rather than humane.

Lack of the free and equitable intercourse which springs from a variety of shared interests makes intellectual stimulation unbalanced. Diversity of stimulation means novelty, and novelty means challenge to thought. The more activity is restricted to a few definite lines—as it is when there are rigid class lines preventing adequate interplay of experiences—the more action tends to become routine on the part of the class at a disadvantage, and capricious, aimless, and explosive on the part of the class having the materially fortunate position. Plato defined a slave as one who accepts from another the purposes which control his conduct. This condition obtains even where there is no slavery in the legal sense. It is found wherever men are engaged in activity which is socially serviceable, but whose service they do not understand and have no personal interest in. Much is said about scientific management of work. It is a narrow view which restricts the science which secures efficiency of operation to movements of the muscles. The chief opportunity for science is the discovery of the relations of a man to his work—including his relations to others who take part—which will enlist his intelligent interest in what he is doing. Efficiency in production often demands division of labor. But it is reduced to a mechanical routine unless workers see the technical, intellectual, and social relationships involved in what they do, and engage in their work because of the motivation furnished by such perceptions. The tendency to reduce such things as efficiency of activity and scientific management to purely technical externals is evidence of the one-sided stimulation of thought given to those in control of industry—those who supply its aims. Because of their lack of all-round and well-balanced social interest, there is not sufficient stimulus for attention to the human factors and relationships in industry. Intelligence is narrowed to the factors concerned with technical production and marketing of goods. No doubt, a very acute and intense intelligence in these narrow lines can be developed, but the failure to take into account the significant social factors means none the less an absence of mind, and a corresponding distortion of emotional life.

II. This illustration (whose point is to be extended to all associations lacking reciprocity of interest) brings us to our second point. The isolation and exclusiveness of a gang or clique brings its antisocial spirit into relief. But this same spirit is found wherever one group has interests "of its own" which shut it out from full interaction with other groups, so that its prevailing purpose is the protection of what it has got, instead of reorganization and progress through wider relationships. It marks nations in their isolation from one another; families which seclude their domestic concerns as if they had no connection with a larger life; schools when separated from the interest of home and community; the divisions of rich and poor; learned and unlearned. The essential point is that isolation makes for rigidity and formal institutionalizing of life, for static and selfish ideals within the group. That savage tribes regard aliens and enemies as synonymous is not accidental. It springs from the fact that they have identified their experience with rigid adherence to their past customs. On such a basis it is wholly logical to fear intercourse with others, for such contact might dissolve custom. It would certainly occasion reconstruction. It is a commonplace that an alert and expanding mental life depends upon an enlarging range of contact with the physical environment. But the principle applies even more significantly to the field where we are apt to ignore it—the sphere of social contacts.

Every expansive era in the history of mankind has coincided with the operation of factors which have tended to eliminate distance between peoples and classes previously hemmed off from one another. Even the alleged benefits of war, so far as more than alleged, spring from the fact that conflict of peoples at least enforces intercourse between them and thus accidentally enables them to learn from one another, and thereby to expand their horizons. Travel, economic and commercial tendencies, have at present gone far to break down external barriers; to bring peoples and classes into closer and more perceptible connection with one another. It remains for the most part to secure the intellectual and emotional significance of this physical annihilation of space.

2. The Democratic Ideal

The two elements in our criterion both point to democracy. The first signifies not only more numerous and more varied points of shared common interest, but greater reliance upon the recognition of mutual interests as a factor in social control. The second means not only freer interaction between social groups (once isolated so far as intention could keep up a separation) but change in social habit—its continuous readjustment through meeting the new situations produced by varied intercourse. And these two traits are precisely what characterize the democratically constituted society.

Upon the educational side, we note first that the realization of a form of social life in which interests are mutually interpenetrating, and where progress, or readjustment, is an important consideration, makes a democratic community more interested than other communities have cause to be in deliberate and systematic education. The devotion of democracy to education is a familiar fact. The superficial explanation is that a government resting upon popular suffrage cannot be successful unless those who elect and who obey their governors are educated. Since a democratic society repudiates the principle of external authority, it must find a substitute in voluntary disposition and interest; these can be created only by education. But there is a deeper explanation. A democracy is more than a form of government; it is primarily a mode of associated living, of conjoint communicated experience. The extension in space of the number of individuals who participate in an interest so that each has to refer his own action to that of others, and to consider the action of others to give point and direction to his own, is equivalent to the breaking down of those barriers of class, race, and national territory which kept men from perceiving the full import of their activity. These more numerous and more varied points of contact denote a greater diversity of stimuli to which an individual has to respond; they consequently put a premium on variation in his action.

They secure a liberation of powers which remain suppressed as long as the incitations to action are partial, as they must be in a group which in its exclusiveness shuts out many interests.

The widening of the area of shared concerns, and the liberation of a greater diversity of personal capacities which characterize a democracy, are not of course the product of deliberation and conscious effort. On the contrary, they were caused by the development of modes of manufacture and commerce, travel, migration, and intercommunication which flowed from the command of science over natural energy. But after greater individualization on one hand, and a broader community of interest on the other have come into existence, it is a matter of deliberate effort to sustain and extend them. Obviously a society to which stratification into separate classes would be fatal, must see to it that intellectual opportunities are accessible to all on equable and easy terms. A society marked off into classes need be specially attentive only to the education of its ruling elements. A society which is mobile, which is full of channels for the distribution of a change occurring anywhere, must see to it that its members are educated to personal initiative and adaptability. Otherwise, they will be overwhelmed by the changes in which they are caught and whose significance or connections they do not perceive. The result will be a confusion in which a few will appropriate to themselves the results of the blind and externally directed activities of others.

3. The Platonic Educational Philosophy

Subsequent chapters will be devoted to making explicit the implications of the democratic ideas in education. In the remaining portions of this chapter, we shall consider the educational theories which have been evolved in three epochs when the social import of education was especially conspicuous. The first one to be considered is that of Plato. No one could better express than did he the fact that a society is stably organized when each individual is doing that for which he has aptitude by nature in such a way as to be useful to others (or to contribute to the whole to which he belongs); and that it is the business of education to discover these aptitudes and progressively to train them for social use. Much which has been said so far is borrowed from what Plato first consciously taught the world. But conditions which he could not intellectually control led him to restrict these ideas in their application. He never got any conception of the indefinite plurality of activities which may characterize an individual and a social group, and consequently limited his view to a limited number of *classes* of capacities and of social arrangements.

Plato's starting point is that the organization of society depends ultimately upon knowledge of the end of existence. If we do not know its end, we shall be at the mercy of accident and caprice. Unless we know the end, the good, we shall have no criterion for rationally deciding what the possibilities are which should be promoted, nor how social arrangements are to be ordered. We shall have no conception of the proper limits and distribution of activities—what he called justice—as a trait of both individual and social organization. But how is the knowledge of the final and permanent good to be achieved? In dealing with this question we come upon the seemingly insuperable obstacle that such knowledge is not possible save in a just and harmonious social order. Everywhere else the mind is distracted and misled by false valuations and false perspectives. A disorganized and factional society sets up a number of different models and standards. Under such conditions it is impossible for the individual to attain consistency of mind. Only a complete whole is fully self-consistent. A society which rests upon the supremacy of some factor over another irrespective of its rational or proportionate claims, inevitably leads thought astray. It puts a premium on certain things and slurs over others, and creates a mind whose seeming unity is forced and distorted. Education proceeds ultimately from the patterns furnished by institutions, customs, and laws. Only in a just state will these be such as to give the right education; and only those who have rightly trained minds will be able to recognize the end, and ordering principle of things. We seem to be caught in a hopeless circle. However, Plato suggested a way out. A few men, philosophers or lovers of wisdom—or truth—may by study learn at least in outline the proper patterns of true existence. If a powerful ruler should form a state after these patterns, then its regulations could be preserved. An education could be given which would sift individuals, discovering what they were good for, and supplying a method of assigning each to the work in life for which his nature fits him. Each doing his own part, and never transgressing, the order and unity of the whole would be maintained.

It would be impossible to find in any scheme of philosophic thought a more adequate recognition on one hand of the educational significance of social arrangements and, on the other, of the dependence of those arrangements upon the means used to educate the young. It would be impossible to find a deeper sense of the function of education in discovering and developing personal capacities, and training them so that they would connect with the activities of others. Yet the society in which the theory was propounded was so undemocratic that Plato could not work out a solution for the problem whose terms he clearly saw.

While he affirmed with emphasis that the place of the individual in society should not be determined by birth or wealth or any conventional status, but by his own nature as discovered in the process of education, he had no perception of the uniqueness of individuals. For him they fall by nature into classes, and into a very small number of classes at that. Consequently the testing and sifting function of education only shows to which one of three classes an individual belongs. There being no recognition that each individual constitutes his own class, there could be no recognition of the infinite diversity of active tendencies and combinations of tendencies of which an individual is capable. There were only three types of faculties or powers in the individual's constitution. Hence education would soon reach a static limit in each class, for only diversity makes change and progress.

In some individuals, appetites naturally dominate; they are assigned to the laboring and trading class, which expresses and supplies human wants.

Others reveal, upon education, that over and above appetites, they have a generous, outgoing, assertively courageous disposition. They become the citizen-subjects of the state; its defenders in war; its internal guardians in peace. But their limit is fixed by their lack of reason, which is a capacity to grasp the universal. Those who possess this are capable of the highest kind of education, and become in time the legislators of the state—for laws are the universals which control the particulars of experience. Thus it is not true that in intent, Plato subordinated the individual to the social whole. But it is true that lacking the perception of the uniqueness of every individual, his incommensurability with others, and consequently not recognizing that a society might change and yet be stable, his doctrine of limited powers and classes came in net effect to the idea of the subordination of individuality.

We cannot better Plato's conviction that an individual is happy and society well organized when each individual engages in those activities for which he has a natural equipment, nor his conviction that it is the primary office of education to discover this equipment to its possessor and train him for its effective use. But progress in knowledge has made us aware of the superficiality of Plato's lumping of individuals and their original powers into a few sharply marked-off classes; it has taught us that original capacities are indefinitely numerous and variable. It is but the other side of this fact to say that in the degree in which society has become democratic, social organization means utilization of the specific and variable qualities of individuals, not stratification by classes. Although his educational philosophy was revolutionary, it was none the less in bondage to static ideals. He thought that change or alteration was evidence of lawless flux; that true reality was unchangeable. Hence while he would radically change the existing state of society, his aim was to construct a state in which change would subsequently have no place. The final end of life is fixed; given a state framed with this end in view, not even minor details are to be altered. Though they might not be inherently important, yet if permitted they would inure the minds of men to the idea of change, and hence be dissolving and anarchic. The breakdown of his philosophy is made apparent in the fact that he could not trust to gradual improvements in education to bring about a better society which should then improve education, and so on indefinitely. Correct education could not come into existence until an ideal state existed, and after that education would be devoted simply to its conservation. For the existence of this state he was obliged to trust to some happy accident by which philosophic wisdom should happen to coincide with possession of ruling power in the state.

4. The "Individualistic" Ideal of the Eighteenth Century

In the eighteenth-century philosophy we find ourselves in a very different circle of ideas. "Nature" still means something antithetical to existing social organization; Plato exercised a great influence upon Rousseau. But the voice of nature now speaks for the diversity of individual talent and for the need of free development of individuality in all its variety. Education in accord with nature furnishes the goal and the method of instruction and discipline. Moreover, the native or original endowment was conceived, in extreme cases, as nonsocial or even as antisocial. Social arrangements were thought of as mere external expedients by which these nonsocial individuals might secure a greater amount of private happiness for themselves.

Nevertheless, these statements convey only an inadequate idea of the true significance of the movement. In reality its chief interest was in progress and in social progress. The seeming antisocial philosophy was a somewhat transparent mask for an impetus toward a wider and freer society—towards cosmopolitanism. The positive ideal was humanity. In membership in humanity, as distinct from a state, man's capacities would be liberated; while in existing political organizations his powers were hampered and distorted to meet the requirements and selfish interests of the rulers of the state. The doctrine of extreme individualism was but the counterpart, the obverse, of ideals of the indefinite perfectibility of man and of a social organization having a scope as wide as humanity. The emancipated individual was to become the organ and agent of a comprehensive and progressive society.

The heralds of this gospel were acutely conscious of the evils of the social estate in which they found themselves. They attributed these evils to the limitations imposed upon the free powers of man. Such limitation was both distorting and corrupting. Their impassioned devotion to emancipation of life from external restrictions which operated to the exclusive advantage of the class to whom a past feudal system consigned power, found intellectual formulation in a worship of nature. To give "nature" full swing was to replace an artificial, corrupt, and inequitable social order by a new and better kingdom of humanity. Unrestrained faith in Nature as both a model and a working power was strengthened by the advances of natural science. Inquiry freed from prejudice and artificial restraints of church and state had revealed that the world is a scene of law. The Newtonian solar system, which expressed the reign of natural law, was a scene of wonderful harmony, where every force balanced with every other. Natural law would accomplish the same result in human relations, if men would only get rid of the artificial man-imposed coercive restrictions.

Education in accord with nature was thought to be the first step in insuring this more social society. It was plainly seen that economic and political limitations were ultimately dependent upon limitations of thought and feeling. The first step in freeing men from external chains was to emancipate them from the internal chains of false beliefs and ideals. What was called social life, existing institutions, were too false and corrupt to be entrusted with this work. How could it be expected to undertake it when the undertaking meant its own destruction? "Nature" must then be the power to which the enterprise was to be left. Even the extreme sensationalistic theory of knowledge which was current derived itself from this conception. To insist that mind is originally passive and empty was one way of glorifying the possibilities of education. If the mind was a wax tablet to be written upon by objects, there were no limits to the possibility of education by means of the natural environment. And since the natural world of objects is a scene of harmonious "truth," this education would infallibly produce minds filled with the truth.

5. Education as National and as Social

As soon as the first enthusiasm for freedom waned, the weakness of the theory upon the constructive side became obvious. Merely to leave everything to nature was, after all, but to negate the very idea of education; it was to trust to the accidents of circumstance. Not only was some method required but also some positive organ, some administrative agency for carrying on the process of instruction. The "complete and harmonious development of all powers," having as its social counterpart an enlightened and progressive humanity, required definite organization for its realization. Private individuals here and there could proclaim the gospel; they could not execute the work. A Pestalozzi could try experiments and exhort philanthropically inclined persons having wealth and power to follow his example. But even Pestalozzi saw that any effective pursuit of the new educational ideal required the support of the state. The realization of the new education destined to produce a new society was, after all, dependent upon the activities of existing states. The movement for the democratic idea inevitably became a movement for publicly conducted and administered schools.

So far as Europe was concerned, the historic situation identified the movement for a state-supported education with the nationalistic movement in political life—a fact of incalculable significance for subsequent movements. Under the influence of German thought in particular, education became a civic function and the civic function was identified with the realization of the ideal of the national state. The "state" was substituted for humanity; cosmopolitanism gave way to nationalism. To form the citizen, not the "man," became the aim of education. The historic situation to which reference is made is the after-effects of the Napoleonic conquests, especially in Germany. The German states felt (and subsequent events demonstrate the correctness of the belief) that systematic attention to education was the best means of recovering and maintaining their political integrity and power. Externally they were weak and divided. Under the leadership of Prussian statesmen they made this condition a stimulus to the development of an extensive and thoroughly grounded system of public education.

This change in practice necessarily brought about a change in theory. The individualistic theory receded into the background. The state furnished not only the instrumentalities of public education but also its goal. When the actual practice was such that the school system, from the elementary grades through the university faculties, supplied the patriotic citizen and soldier and the future state official and administrator and furnished the means for military, industrial, and political defense and expansion, it was impossible for theory not to emphasize the aim of social efficiency. And with the immense importance attached to the nationalistic state, surrounded by other competing and more or less hostile states, it was equally impossible to interpret social efficiency in terms of a vague cosmopolitan humanitarianism. Since the maintenance of a particular national sovereignty required subordination of individuals to the superior interests of the state both in military defense and in struggles for international supremacy in commerce, social efficiency was understood to imply a like subordination. The educational process was taken to be one of disciplinary training rather than of personal development. Since, however, the ideal of culture as complete development of personality persisted, educational philosophy attempted a reconciliation of the two ideas. The reconciliation took the form of the conception of the "organic" character of the state. The individual in his isolation is nothing; only in and through an absorption of the aims and meaning of organized institutions does he attain true personality. What appears to be his subordination to political authority and the demand for sacrifice of himself to the commands of his superiors is in reality but making his own the objective reason manifested in the state—the only way in which he can become truly rational. The notion of development which we have seen to be characteristic of institutional idealism (as in the Hegelian philosophy) was just such a deliberate effort to combine the two ideas of complete realization of personality and thoroughgoing "disciplinary" subordination to existing institutions.

The extent of the transformation of educational philosophy which occurred in Germany in the generation occupied by the struggle against Napoleon for national independence, may be gathered from Kant, who well expresses the earlier individual-cosmopolitan ideal. In his treatise on Pedagogics, consisting of lectures given in the later years of the eighteenth century, he defines education as the process by which man becomes man. Mankind begins its history submerged in nature—not as Man who is a creature of reason, while nature furnishes only instinct and appetite. Nature offers simply the germs which education is to develop and perfect. The peculiarity of truly human life is that man has to create himself by his own voluntary efforts; he has to make himself a truly moral, rational, and free being. This creative effort is carried on by the educational activities of slow generations. Its acceleration depends upon men consciously striving to educate their successors not for the existing state of affairs but so as to make possible a future better humanity. But there is the great difficulty. Each generation is inclined to educate its young so as to get along in the present world instead of with a view to the proper end of education: the promotion of the best possible realization of humanity as humanity. Parents educate their children so that they may get on; princes educate their subjects as instruments of their own purposes.

Who, then, shall conduct education so that humanity may improve? We must depend upon the efforts of enlightened men in their private capacity. "All culture begins with private men and spreads outward from them. Simply through the efforts of persons of enlarged inclinations, who are capable of grasping the ideal of a future better condition, is the gradual approximation of human nature to its end possible. . . . Rulers are simply interested in such training as will make their subjects better tools for their own intentions." Even the subsidy by rulers of privately conducted schools must be carefully safeguarded. For the rulers' interest in the welfare of their own nation instead of in what is best for humanity, will make them, if they give money for the schools, wish to draw their plans. We have in this view an express statement of the points characteristic of the eighteenth-century individualistic cosmopolitanism. The full development of private personality is identified with the aims of humanity as a whole and with the idea of progress. In addition we have an explicit fear of the hampering influence of a state-conducted and state-regulated education upon the attainment of these ideas. But in less than two decades after this time, Kant's philosophic successors, Fichte and Hegel, elaborated the idea that the chief function of the state is educational; that in particular the regeneration of Germany is to be accomplished by an education carried on in the interests of the state, and that the private individual is of necessity an egoistic, irrational being, enslaved to his appetites and to circumstances unless he submits voluntarily to the educative discipline of state institutions and laws. In this spirit, Germany was the first country to undertake a public, universal, and compulsory system of education extending from the primary school through the university, and to submit to jealous state regulation and supervision all private educational enterprises.

Two results should stand out from this brief historical survey. The first is that such terms as the individual and the social conceptions of education are quite meaningless taken at large, or apart from their context. Plato had the ideal of an education which should equate individual realization and social coherency and stability. His situation forced his ideal into the notion of a society organized in stratified classes, losing the individual in the class. The eighteenth-century educational philosophy was highly individualistic in form, but this form was inspired by a noble and generous social ideal: that of a society organized to include humanity, and providing for the indefinite perfectibility of mankind. The idealistic philosophy of Germany in the early nineteenth century endeavored again to equate the ideals of a free and complete development of cultured personality with social discipline and political subordination. It made the national state an intermediary between the realization of private personality on one side and of humanity on the other. Consequently, it is equally possible to state its animating principle with equal truth either in the classic terms of "harmonious development of all the powers of personality" or in the more recent terminology of "social efficiency." All this reenforces the statement which opens this chapter: The conception of education as a social process and function has no definite meaning until we define the kind of society we have in mind.

These considerations pave the way for our second conclusion. One of the fundamental problems of education in and for a democratic society is set by the conflict of a nationalistic and a wider social aim. The earlier cosmopolitan and "humanitarian" conception suffered both from vagueness and from lack of definite organs of execution and agencies of administration. In Europe, in the Continental states particularly, the new idea of the importance of education for human welfare and progress was captured by national interests and harnessed to do a work whose social aim was definitely narrow and exclusive.

The social aim of education and its national aim were identified, and the result was a marked obscuring of the meaning of a social aim.

This confusion corresponds to the existing situation of human intercourse. On the one hand, science, commerce, and art transcend national boundaries. They are largely international in quality and method. They involve interdependencies and cooperation among the peoples inhabiting different countries. At the same time, the idea of national sovereignty has never been as accentuated in politics as it is at the present time. Each nation lives in a state of suppressed hostility and incipient war with its neighbors. Each is supposed to be the supreme judge of its own interests, and it is assumed as matter of course that each has interests which are exclusively its own. To question this is to question the very idea of national sovereignty which is assumed to be basic to political practice and political science. This contradiction (for it is nothing less) between the wider sphere of associated and mutually helpful social life and the narrower sphere of exclusive and hence potentially hostile pursuits and purposes, exacts of educational theory a clearer conception of the meaning of "social" as a function and test of education than has yet been attained.

Is it possible for an educational system to be conducted by a national state and yet the full social ends of the educative process not be restricted, constrained, and corrupted? Internally, the question has to face the tendencies, due to present economic conditions, which split society into classes some of which are made merely tools for the higher culture of others. Externally, the question is concerned with the reconciliation of national loyalty, of patriotism, with superior devotion to the things which unite men in common ends, irrespective of national political boundaries. Neither phase of the problem can be worked out by merely negative means. It is not enough to see to it that education is not actively used as an instrument to make easier the exploitation of one class by another. School facilities must be secured of such amplitude and efficiency as will in fact and not simply in name discount the effects of economic inequalities, and secure to all the wards of the nation equality of equipment for their future careers. Accomplishment of this end demands not only adequate administrative provision of school facilities, and such supplementation of family resources as will enable youth to take advantage of them, but also such modification of traditional ideals of culture, traditional subjects of study and traditional methods of teaching and discipline as will retain all the youth under educational influences until they are equipped to be masters of their own economic and social careers. The ideal may seem remote of execution, but the democratic ideal of education is a farcical yet tragic delusion except as the ideal more and more dominates our public system of education.

The same principle has application on the side of the considerations which concern the relations of one nation to another. It is not enough to teach the horrors of war and to avoid everything which would stimulate international jealousy and animosity. The emphasis must be put upon whatever binds people together in cooperative human pursuits and results, apart from geographical limitations. The secondary and provisional character of national sovereignty in respect to the fuller, freer, and more fruitful association and intercourse of all human beings with one another must be instilled as a working disposition of mind. If these applications seem to be remote from a consideration of the philosophy of education, the impression shows that the meaning of the idea of education previously developed has not been adequately grasped. This conclusion is bound up with the very idea of education as a freeing of individual capacity in a progressive growth directed to social aims. Otherwise a democratic criterion of education can only be inconsistently applied.

Summary

Since education is a social process, and there are many kinds of societies, a criterion for educational criticism and construction implies a *particular* social ideal. The two points selected by which to measure the worth of a form of social life are the extent in which the interests of a group are shared by all its members, and the fullness and freedom with which it interacts with other groups. An undesirable society, in other words, is one which internally and externally sets up barriers to free intercourse and communication of experience. A society which makes provision for participation in its good of all its members on equal terms and which secures flexible readjustment of its institutions through interaction of the different forms of associated life is in so far democratic. Such a society must have a type of education which gives individuals a personal interest in social relationships and control, and the habits of mind which secure social changes without introducing disorder.

Three typical historic philosophies of education were considered from this point of view. The Platonic was found to have an ideal formally quite similar to that stated, but which was compromised in its working out by making a class rather than an individual the social unit. The so-called individualism of the eighteenth-century enlightenment was found to involve the notion of a society as broad as humanity, of whose progress the individual was to be the organ. But it lacked any agency for securing the development of its ideal as was evidenced in its falling back upon Nature. The institutional idealistic philosophies of the nineteenth century supplied this lack by making the national state the agency, but in so doing narrowed the conception of the social aim to those who were members of the same political unit, and reintroduced the idea of the subordination of the individual to the institution.

8. AIMS IN EDUCATION

1. The Nature of an Aim

The account of education given in our earlier chapters virtually anticipated the results reached in a discussion of the purport of education in a democratic community. For it assumed that the aim of education is to enable individuals to continue their education—or that the object and reward of learning is continued capacity for growth. Now this idea cannot be applied to *all* the members of a society except where intercourse of man with man is mutual, and except where there is adequate provision for the reconstruction of social habits and institutions by means of wide stimulation arising from equitably distributed interests. And this means a democratic society. In our search for aims in education, we are not concerned, therefore, with finding an end outside of the educative process to which education is subordinate. Our whole conception forbids. We are rather concerned with the contrast which exists when aims belong within the process in which they operate and when they are set up from without. And the latter state of affairs must obtain when social relationships are not equitably balanced. For in that case, some portions of the whole social group will find their aims determined by an external dictation; their aims will not arise from the free growth of their own experience, and their nominal aims will be means to more ulterior ends of others rather than truly their own.

Our first question is to define the nature of an aim so far as it falls within an activity, instead of being furnished from without. We approach the definition by a contrast of mere *results* with *ends*. Any exhibition of energy has results. The wind blows about the sands of the desert; the position of the grains is changed. Here is a result, an effect, but not an *end*. For there is nothing in the outcome which completes or fulfills what went before it. There is mere spatial redistribution. One state of affairs is just as good as any other. Consequently there is no basis upon which to select an earlier state of affairs as a beginning, a later as an end, and to consider what intervenes as a process of transformation and realization.

Consider for example the activities of bees in contrast with the changes in the sands when the wind blows them about. The results of the bees' actions may be called ends not because they are designed or consciously intended, but because they are true terminations or completions of what has preceded. When the bees gather pollen and make wax and build cells, each step prepares the way for the next. When cells are built, the queen lays eggs in them; when eggs are laid, they are sealed and bees brood them and keep them at a temperature required to hatch them. When they are hatched, bees feed the young till they can take care of themselves. Now we are so familiar with such facts, that we are apt to dismiss them on the ground that life and instinct are a kind of miraculous thing anyway. Thus we fail to note what the essential characteristic of the event is; namely, the significance of the temporal place and order of each element; the way each prior event leads into its successor while the successor takes up what is furnished and utilizes it for some other stage, until we arrive at the end, which, as it were, summarizes and finishes off the process.

Since aims relate always to results, the first thing to look to when it is a question of aims, is whether the work assigned possesses intrinsic continuity. Or is it a mere serial aggregate of acts, first doing one thing and then another? To talk about an educational aim when approximately each act of a pupil is dictated by the teacher, when the only order in the sequence of his acts is that which comes from the assignment of lessons and the giving of directions by another, is to talk nonsense. It is equally fatal to an aim to permit capricious or discontinuous action in the name of spontaneous self-expression. An aim implies an orderly and ordered activity, one in which the order consists in the progressive completing of a process. Given an activity having a time span and cumulative growth within the time succession, an aim means foresight in advance of the end or possible termination. If bees anticipated the consequences of their activity, if they perceived their end in imaginative foresight, they would have the primary element in an aim. Hence it is nonsense to talk about the aim of education—or any other undertaking—where conditions do not permit of foresight of results, and do not stimulate a person to look ahead to see what the outcome of a given activity is to be.

In the next place the aim as a foreseen end gives direction to the activity; it is not an idle view of a mere spectator, but influences the steps taken to reach the end. The foresight functions in three ways. In the first place, it involves careful observation of the given conditions to see what are the means available for reaching the end, and to discover the hindrances in the way. In the second place, it suggests the proper order or sequence in the use of means. It facilitates an economical selection and arrangement. In the third place, it makes choice of alternatives possible. If we can predict the outcome of acting this way or that, we can then compare the value of the two courses of action; we can pass judgment upon their relative desirability. If we know that stagnant water breeds mosquitoes and that they are likely to carry disease, we can, disliking that anticipated result, take steps to avert it. Since we do not anticipate results as mere intellectual onlookers, but as persons concerned in the outcome, we are partakers in the process which produces the result. We intervene to bring about this result or that.

Of course these three points are closely connected with one another. We can definitely foresee results only as we make careful scrutiny of present conditions, and the importance of the outcome supplies the motive for observations. The more adequate our observations, the more varied is the scene of conditions and obstructions that presents itself, and the more numerous are the alternatives between which choice may be made. In turn, the more numerous the recognized possibilities of the situation, or alternatives of action, the more meaning does the chosen activity possess, and the more flexibly controllable is it. Where only a single outcome has been thought of, the mind has nothing else to think of; the meaning attaching to the act is limited. One only steams ahead toward the mark. Sometimes such a narrow course may be effective. But if unexpected difficulties offer themselves, one has not as many resources at command as if he had chosen the same line of action after a broader survey of the possibilities of the field. He cannot make needed readjustments readily.

The net conclusion is that acting with an aim is all one with acting intelligently. To foresee a terminus of an act is to have a basis upon which to observe, to select, and to order objects and our own capacities. To do these things means to have a mind—for mind is precisely intentional purposeful activity controlled by perception of facts and their relationships to one another. To have a mind to do a thing is to foresee a future possibility; it is to have a plan for its accomplishment; it is to note the means which make the plan capable of execution and the obstructions in the way,—or, if it is really a *mind* to do the thing and not a vague aspiration—it is to have a plan which takes account of resources and difficulties. Mind is capacity to refer present conditions to future results, and future consequences to present conditions. And these traits are just what is meant by having an aim or a purpose. A man is stupid or blind or un-intelligent—lacking in mind—just in the degree in which in any activity he does not know what he is about, namely, the probable consequences of his acts. A man is imperfectly intelligent when he contents himself with looser guesses about the outcome than is needful, just taking a chance with his luck, or when he forms plans apart from study of the actual conditions, including his own capacities. Such relative absence of mind means to make our feelings the measure of what is to happen. To be intelligent we must "stop, look, listen" in making the plan of an activity.

To identify acting with an aim and intelligent activity is enough to show its value—its function in experience. We are only too given to making an entity out of the abstract noun "consciousness." We forget that it comes from the adjective "conscious." To be conscious is to be aware of what we are about; conscious signifies the deliberate, observant, planning traits of activity. Consciousness is nothing which we have which gazes idly on the scene around one or which has impressions made upon it by physical things; it is a name for the purposeful quality of an activity, for the fact that it is directed by an aim. Put the other way about, to have an aim is to act with meaning, not like an automatic machine; it is to *mean* to do something and to perceive the meaning of things in the light of that intent.

2. The Criteria of Good Aims

We may apply the results of our discussion to a consideration of the criteria involved in a correct establishing of aims. (1) The aim set up must be an out-growth of existing conditions. It must be based upon a consideration of what is already going on; upon the resources and difficulties of the situation. Theories about the proper end of our activities—educational and moral theories—often violate this principle. They assume ends lying *outside* our activities; ends foreign to the concrete make-up of the situation; ends which issue from some outside source. Then the problem is to bring our activities to bear upon the realization of these externally supplied ends. They are something for which we *ought* to act. In any case such "aims" limit intelligence; they are not the expression of mind in foresight, observation, and choice of the better among alternative possibilities. They limit intelligence because, given ready-made, they must be imposed by some authority external to intelligence, leaving to the latter nothing but a mechanical choice of means.

(2) We have spoken as if aims could be completely formed prior to the attempt to realize them. This impression must now be qualified. The aim as it first emerges is a mere tentative sketch. The act of striving to realize it tests its worth. If it suffices to direct activity successfully, nothing more is required, since its whole function is to set a mark in advance; and at times a mere hint may suffice. But usually—at least in complicated situations—acting upon it brings to light conditions which had been overlooked. This calls for revision of

the original aim; it has to be added to and subtracted from. An aim must, then, be *flexible*; it must be capable of alteration to meet circumstances. An end established externally to the process of action is always rigid. Being inserted or imposed from without, it is not supposed to have a working relationship to the concrete conditions of the situation. What happens in the course of action neither confirms, refutes, nor alters it. Such an end can only be insisted upon. The failure that results from its lack of adaptation is attributed simply to the perverseness of conditions, not to the fact that the end is not reasonable under the circumstances. The value of a legitimate aim, on the contrary, lies in the fact that we can use it to change conditions. It is a method for dealing with conditions so as to effect desirable alterations in them. A farmer who should passively accept things just as he finds them would make as great a mistake as he who framed his plans in complete disregard of what soil, climate, etc., permit. One of the evils of an abstract or remote external aim in education is that its very inapplicability in practice is likely to react into a haphazard snatching at immediate conditions. A good aim surveys the present state of experience of pupils, and forming a tentative plan of treatment, keeps the plan constantly in view and yet modifies it as conditions develop. The aim, in short, is experimental, and hence constantly growing as it is tested in action.

(3) The aim must always represent a freeing of activities. The term *end in view* is suggestive, for it puts before the mind the termination or conclusion of some process. The only way in which we can define an activity is by putting before ourselves the objects in which it terminates—as one's aim in shooting is the target. But we must remember that the *object* is only a mark or sign by which the mind specifies the *activity* one desires to carry out. Strictly speaking, not the target but *hitting* the target is the end in view; one *takes* aim by means of the target, but also by the sight on the gun. The different objects which are thought of are means of *directing* the activity. Thus one aims at, say, a rabbit; what he wants is to shoot straight: a certain kind of activity. Or, if it is the rabbit he wants, it is not the rabbit apart from his activity, but as a factor in activity; he wants to eat the rabbit, or to show it as evidence of his marksmanship— he wants to do something with it. The doing with the thing, not the thing in isolation, is his end. The object is but a phase of the active end,—continuing the activity successfully. This is what is meant by the phrase, used above, "freeing activity."

In contrast with fulfilling some process in order that activity may go on, stands the static character of an end which is imposed from without the activity. It is always conceived of as fixed; it is *something* to be attained and possessed. When one has such a notion, activity is a mere unavoidable means to something else; it is not significant or important on its own account. As compared with the end it is but a necessary evil; something which must be gone through before one can reach the object which is alone worthwhile. In other words, the external idea of the aim leads to a separation of means from end, while an end which grows up within an activity as plan for its direction is always both ends and means, the distinction being only one of convenience. Every means is a temporary end until we have attained it. Every end becomes a means of carrying activity further as soon as it is achieved. We call it end when it marks off the future direction of the activity in which we are engaged; means when it marks off the present direction. Every divorce of end from means diminishes by that much the significance of the activity and tends to reduce it to a drudgery from which one would escape if he could. A farmer has to use plants and animals to carry on his farming activities. It certainly makes a great difference to his life whether he is fond of them, or whether he regards them merely as means which he has to employ to get something else in which alone he is interested. In the former case, his entire course of activity is significant; each phase of it has its own value. He has the experience of realizing his end at every stage; the postponed aim, or end in view, being merely a sight ahead by which to keep his activity going fully and freely. For if he does not look ahead, he is more likely to find himself blocked. The aim is as definitely a *means* of action as is any other portion of an activity.

3. Applications in Education

There is nothing peculiar about educational aims. They are just like aims in any directed occupation. The educator, like the farmer, has certain things to do, certain resources with which to do, and certain obstacles with which to contend. The conditions with which the farmer deals, whether as obstacles or resources, have their own structure and operation independently of any purpose of his. Seeds sprout, rain falls, the sun shines, insects devour, blight comes, the seasons change. His aim is simply to utilize these various conditions; to make his activities and their energies work together, instead of against one another. It would be absurd if the farmer set up a purpose of farming, without any reference to these conditions of soil, climate, characteristics of plant growth, etc. His purpose is simply a foresight of the consequences of his energies connected with those of the things about him, a foresight used to direct his movements from day to day. Foresight of possible consequences leads to more careful and extensive observation of the nature and performances of the things he had to do with, and to laying out a plan—that is, of a certain order in the acts to be performed.

It is the same with the educator, whether parent or teacher. It is as absurd for the latter to set up their "own" aims as the proper objects of the growth of the children as it would be for the farmer to set up an ideal of farming irrespective of conditions. Aims mean acceptance of responsibility for the observations, anticipations, and arrangements required in carrying on a function—whether farming or educating. Any aim is of value so far as it assists observation, choice, and planning in carrying on activity from moment to moment and hour to hour; if it gets in the way of the individual's own common sense (as it will surely do if imposed from without or accepted on authority) it does harm.

And it is well to remind ourselves that education as such has no aims. Only persons, parents, and teachers, etc., have aims, not an abstract idea like education. And consequently their purposes are indefinitely varied, differing with different children, changing as children grow and with the growth of experience on the part of the one who teaches. Even the most valid aims which can be put in words will, as words, do more harm than good unless one recognizes that they are not aims, but rather suggestions to educators as to how to observe, how to look ahead, and how to choose in liberating and directing the energies of the concrete situations in which they find themselves. As a recent writer has said: "To lead this boy to read Scott's novels instead of old Sleuth's stories; to teach this girl to sew; to root out the habit of bullying from John's make up; to prepare this class to study medicine,—these are samples of the millions of aims we have actually before us in the concrete work of education."

Bearing these qualifications in mind, we shall proceed to state some of the characteristics found in all good educational aims. (1) An educational aim must be founded upon the intrinsic activities and needs (including original instincts and acquired habits) of the given individual to be educated. The tendency of such an aim as preparation is, as we have seen, to omit existing powers, and find the aim in some remote accomplishment or responsibility. In general, there is a disposition to take considerations which are dear to the hearts of adults and set them up as ends irrespective of the capacities of those educated. There is also an inclination to propound aims which are so uniform as to neglect the specific powers and requirements of an individual, forgetting that all learning is something which happens to an individual at a given time and place. The larger range of perception of the adult is of great value in observing the abilities and weaknesses of the young, in deciding what they may amount to. Thus the artistic capacities of the adult exhibit what certain tendencies of the child are capable of; if we did not have the adult achievements we should be without assurance as to the significance of the drawing, reproducing, modeling, coloring activities of childhood. So if it were not for adult language, we should not be able to see the import of the babbling impulses of infancy. But it is one thing to use adult accomplishments as a context in which to place and survey the doings of childhood and youth; it is quite another to set them up as a fixed aim without regard to the concrete activities of those educated.

(2) An aim must be capable of translation into a method of cooperating with the activities of those undergoing instruction. It must suggest the kind of environment needed to liberate and to organize *their* capacities. Unless it lends itself to the construction of specific procedures, and unless these procedures test, correct, and amplify the aims, the latter is worthless. Instead of helping the specific task of teaching, it prevents the use of ordinary judgment in observing and sizing up the situation. It operates to exclude recognition of everything except what squares up with the fixed end in view. Every rigid aim just because it is rigidly given seems to render it unnecessary to give careful attention to concrete conditions. Since it *must* apply anyhow, what is the use of noting details which do not count?

The vice of externally imposed ends has deep roots. Teachers receive them from superior authorities; these authorities accept them from what is current in the community. The teachers impose them upon children. As a first consequence, the intelligence of the teacher is not free; it is confined to receiving the aims laid down from above. Too rarely is the individual teacher so free from the dictation of authoritative supervisor, textbook on methods, prescribed course of study, etc., that he can let his mind come to close quarters with the pupil's mind and the subject matter. This distrust of the teacher's experience is then reflected in lack of confidence in the responses of pupils. The latter receive their aims through a double or treble external imposition, and are constantly confused by the conflict between the aims which are natural to their own experience at the time and those in which they are taught to acquiesce. Until the democratic criterion of the intrinsic significance of every growing experience is recognized, we shall be intellectually confused by the demand for adaptation to external aims.

(3) Educators have to be on their guard against ends that are alleged to be general and ultimate. Every activity, however specific, is, of course, general in its ramified connections, for it leads out indefinitely into other things. So far as a general idea makes us more alive to these connections, it cannot be too general. But "general" also means "abstract," or detached from all specific context. And such abstractness means remoteness, and throws us back, once more, upon teaching and learning as mere means of getting ready for an end disconnected from the means. That education is literally and all the time its own reward means that no alleged study or discipline is educative unless it is worthwhile in its own immediate having. A truly general aim broadens the outlook; it stimulates one to take more consequences (connections) into account. This means a wider and more flexible observation of means. The more interacting forces, for example, the farmer takes into account, the more varied will be his immediate resources. He will see a greater number of possible starting places, and a greater number of ways of getting at what he wants to do. The fuller one's conception of possible future achievements, the less his present activity is tied down to a small number of alternatives. If one knew enough, one could start almost anywhere and sustain his activities continuously and fruitfully.

Understanding then the term general or comprehensive aim simply in the sense of a broad survey of the field of present activities, we shall take up some of the larger ends which have currency in the educational theories of the day, and consider what light they throw upon the immediate concrete and diversified aims which are always the educator's real concern. We premise (as indeed immediately follows from what has been said) that there is no need of making a choice among them or regarding them as competitors. When we come to act in a tangible way we have to select or choose a particular act at a particular time, but any number of comprehensive ends may exist without competition, since they mean simply different ways of looking at the same scene. One cannot climb a number of different mountains simultaneously, but the views had when different mountains are ascended supplement one another: they do not set up incompatible, competing worlds. Or, putting the matter in a slightly different way, one statement of an end may suggest certain questions and observations, and another statement another set of questions, calling for other observations. Then the more general ends we have, the better.

One statement will emphasize what another slurs over. What a plurality of hypotheses does for the scientific investigator, a plurality of stated aims may do for the instructor.

Summary

An aim denotes the result of any natural process brought to consciousness and made a factor in determining present observation and choice of ways of acting. It signifies that an activity has become intelligent. Specifically it means foresight of the alternative consequences attendant upon acting in a given situation in different ways, and the use of what is anticipated to direct observation and experiment. A true aim is thus opposed at every point to an aim which is imposed upon a process of action from without. The latter is fixed and rigid; it is not a stimulus to intelligence in the given situation, but is an externally dictated order to do such and such things. Instead of connecting directly with present activities, it is remote, divorced from the means by which it is to be reached. Instead of suggesting a freer and better balanced activity, it is a limit set to activity. In education, the currency of these externally imposed aims is responsible for the emphasis put upon the notion of preparation for a remote future and for rendering the work of both teacher and pupil mechanical and slavish.

12. THINKING IN EDUCATION

1. The Essentials of Method

No one doubts, theoretically, the importance of fostering in school good habits of thinking. But apart from the fact that the acknowledgment is not so great in practice as in theory, there is not adequate theoretical recognition that all which the school can or need do for pupils, so far as their *minds* are concerned (that is, leaving out certain specialized muscular abilities), is to develop their ability to think. The parceling out of instruction among various ends such as acquisition of skill (in reading, spelling, writing, drawing, reciting); acquiring information (in history and geography), *and* training of thinking is a measure of the ineffective way in which we accomplish all three. Thinking which is not connected with increase of efficiency in action, and with learning more about ourselves and the world in which we live, has something the matter with it just as thought. . . . And skill obtained apart from thinking is not connected with any sense of the purposes for which it is to be used. It consequently leaves a man at the mercy of his routine habits and of the authoritative control of others, who know what they are about and who are not especially scrupulous as to their means of achievement. And information severed from thoughtful action is dead, a mind-crushing load. Since it simulates knowledge and thereby develops the poison of conceit, it is a most powerful obstacle to further growth in the grace of intelligence. The sole direct path to enduring improvement in the methods of instruction and learning consists in centering upon the conditions which exact, promote, and test thinking. Thinking *is* the method of intelligent learning, of learning that employs and rewards mind. We speak, legitimately enough, about the method of thinking, but the important thing to bear in mind about method is that thinking is method, the method of intelligent experience in the course which it takes.

I. The initial stage of that developing experience which is called thinking is *experience*. This remark may sound like a silly truism. It ought to be one; but unfortunately it is not. On the contrary, thinking is often regarded both in philosophic theory and in educational practice as something cut off from experience, and capable of being cultivated in isolation. In fact, the inherent limitations of experience are often urged as the sufficient ground for attention to thinking. Experience is then thought to be confined to the senses and appetites; to a mere material world, while thinking proceeds from a higher faculty (of reason), and is occupied with spiritual or at least literary things. So, oftentimes, a sharp distinction is made between pure mathematics as a peculiarly fit subject matter of thought (since it has nothing to do with physical existences) and applied mathematics, which has utilitarian but not mental value.

Speaking generally, the fundamental fallacy in methods of instruction lies in supposing that experience on the part of pupils may be assumed. What is here insisted upon is the necessity of an actual empirical situation as the initiating phase of thought. Experience is here taken as previously defined: trying to do something and having the thing perceptibly do something to one in return. The fallacy consists in supposing that we can begin with ready-made subject matter of arithmetic, or geography, or whatever, irrespective of some direct personal experience of a situation. Even the kindergarten and Montessori techniques are so anxious to get at intellectual distinctions, without "waste of time," that they tend to ignore—or reduce—the immediate crude handling of the familiar material of experience, and to introduce pupils at once to material which expresses the intellectual distinctions which adults have made. But the first stage of contact with any new material, at whatever age of maturity, must inevitably be of the trial and error sort. An individual must actually try, in play or work, to do something with material in carrying out his own impulsive activity, and then note the interaction of his energy and that of the material employed. This is what happens when a child at first begins to build with blocks, and it is equally what happens when a scientific man in his laboratory begins to experiment with unfamilar objects.

Hence the first approach to any subject in school, if thought is to be aroused and not words acquired, should be as unscholastic as possible. To realize what an experience, or empirical situation, means, we have to call to mind the sort of situation that presents itself outside of school; the sort of occupations that interest and engage activity in ordinary life. And careful inspection of methods which are permanently successful in formal education, whether in arithmetic or learning to read, or studying geography, or learning physics or a foreign language, will reveal that they depend for their efficiency upon the fact that they go back to the type of the situation which causes reflection out of school in ordinary life. They give the pupils something to do, not something to learn; and the doing is of such a nature as to demand thinking, or the intentional noting of connections; learning naturally results.

That the situation should be of such a nature as to arouse thinking means of course that it should suggest something to do which is not either routine or capricious—something, in other words, presenting what is new (and hence uncertain or problematic) and yet sufficiently connected with existing habits to call out an effective response. An effective response means one which accomplishes a perceptible result, in distinction from a purely haphazard activity, where the consequences cannot be mentally connected with what is done. The most significant question which can be asked, accordingly, about any situation or experience proposed to induce learning is what quality of problem it involves.

At first thought, it might seem as if usual school methods measured well up to the standard here set. The giving of problems, the putting of questions, the assigning of tasks, the magnifying of difficulties, is a large part of school work. But it is indispensable to discriminate between genuine and simulated or mock problems. The following questions may aid in making such discrimination. (*a*) Is there anything *but* a problem? Does the question naturally suggest itself within some situation of personal experience? Or is it an aloof thing, a problem only for the purposes of conveying instruction in some school topic? Is it the sort of trying that would arouse observation and engage experimentation outside of school? (*b*) Is it the pupil's own problem, or is it the teacher's or textbook's problem, made a problem for the pupil only because he cannot get the required mark or be promoted or win the teacher's approval, unless he deals with it? Obviously, these two questions overlap. They are two ways of getting at the same point: Is the experience a personal thing of such a nature as inherently to stimulate and direct observation of the connections involved, and to lead to inference and its testing? Or is it imposed from without, and is the pupil's problem simply to meet the external requirement?

Such questions may give us pause in deciding upon the extent to which current practices are adapted to develop reflective habits. The physical equipment and arrangements of the average schoolroom are hostile to the existence of real situations of experience. What is there similar to the conditions of everyday life which will generate difficulties? Almost everything testifies to the great premium put upon listening, reading, and the reproduction of what is told and read. It is hardly possible to overstate the contrast between such conditions and the situations of active contact with things and persons in the home, on the playground, in fulfilling of ordinary responsibilities of life. Much of it is not even comparable with the questions which may arise in the mind of a boy or girl in conversing with others or in reading books outside of the school. No one has ever explained why children are so full of questions outside of the school (so that they pester grown-up persons if they get any encouragement), and the conspicuous absence of display of curiosity about the subject matter of school lessons. Reflection on this striking contrast will throw light upon the question of how far customary school conditions supply a context of experience in which problems naturally suggest themselves. No amount of improvement in the personal technique of the instructor will wholly remedy this state of things. There must be more actual material, more *stuff,* more appliances, and more opportunities for doing things, before the gap can be overcome. And where children are engaged in doing things and in discussing what arises in the course of their doing, it is found, even with comparatively indifferent modes of instruction, that children's inquiries are spontaneous and numerous, and the proposals of solution advanced, varied, and ingenious.

As a consequence of the absence of the materials and occupations which generate real problems, the pupil's problems are not his; or, rather, they are his *only as* a pupil, not as a human being. Hence the lamentable waste in carrying over such expertness as is achieved in dealing with them to the affairs of life beyond the schoolroom. A pupil has a problem, but it is the problem of meeting the peculiar requirements set by the teacher. His problem becomes that of finding out what the teacher wants, what will satisfy the teacher in recitation and examination and outward deportment. Relationship to subject matter is no longer direct. The occasions and material of thought are not found in the arithmetic or the history or geography itself, but in skillfully adapting that material to the teacher's requirements. The pupil studies, but unconsciously to himself the objects of his study are the conventions and standards of the school system and school authority, not the nominal "studies." The thinking thus evoked is artificially one-sided at the best. At its worst, the problem of the pupil is not how to meet the requirements of school life, but how to *seem* to meet them—or, how to come near enough to meeting them to slide along without an undue amount of friction. The type of judgment formed by these devices is not a desirable addition to character. If these statements give too highly colored a picture of usual school methods, the exaggeration may at least serve to illustrate the point: the need of active pursuits, involving the use of material to accomplish purposes, if there are to be situations which normally generate problems occasioning thoughtful inquiry.

II. There must be *data* at command to supply the considerations required in dealing with the specific difficulty which has presented itself. Teachers following a "developing" method sometimes tell children to think things out for themselves as if they could spin them out of their own heads. The material of thinking is not thoughts, but actions, facts, events, and the relations of things. In other words, to think effectively one must have had, or now have, experiences which will furnish him resources for coping with the difficulty at hand. A difficulty is an indispensable stimulus to thinking, but not all difficulties call out thinking. Sometimes they overwhelm and submerge and discourage. The perplexing situation must be sufficiently like situations which have already been dealt with so that pupils will have some control of the means of handling it. A large part of the art of instruction lies in making the difficulty of new problems large enough to challenge thought, and small enough so that, in addition to the confusion naturally attending the novel elements, there shall be luminous familiar spots from which helpful suggestions may spring.

In one sense, it is a matter of indifference by what psychological means the subject matter for reflection is provided. Memory, observation, reading, communication, are all avenues for supplying data. The relative proportion to be obtained from each is a matter of the specific features of the particular problem in hand. It is foolish to insist upon observation of objects presented to the senses if the student is so familiar with the objects that he could just as well recall the facts independently. It is possible to induce undue and crippling dependence upon sense-presentations. No one can carry around with him a museum of all the things whose properties will assist the conduct of thought. A well-trained mind is one that has a maximum of resources behind it, so to speak, and that is accustomed to go over its past experiences to see what they yield. On the other hand, a quality or relation of even a familiar object may previously have been passed over, and be just the fact that is helpful in dealing with the question. In this case direct observation is called for. The same principle applies to the use to be made of observation on one hand and of reading and "telling" on the other. Direct observation is naturally more vivid and vital. But it has its limitations; and in any case it is a necessary part of education that one should acquire the ability to supplement the narrowness of his immediately personal experiences by utilizing the experiences of others. Excessive reliance upon others for data (whether got from reading or listening) is to be depreciated. Most objectionable of all is the probability that others, the book or the teacher, will supply solutions ready-made, instead of giving material that the student has to adapt and apply to the question in hand for himself.

There is no inconsistency in saying that in schools there is usually both too much and too little information supplied by others. The accumulation and acquisition of information for purposes of reproduction in recitation and examination is made too much of. "Knowledge," in the sense of information, means the working capital, the indispensable resources, of further inquiry; of finding out, or learning, more things. Frequently it is treated as an end itself, and then the goal becomes to heap it up and display it when called for. This static, cold-storage ideal of knowledge is inimical to educative development. It not only lets occasions for thinking go unused, but it swamps thinking. No one could construct a house on ground cluttered with miscellaneous junk. Pupils who have stored their "minds" with all kinds of material which they have never put to intellectual uses are sure to be hampered when they try to think. They have no practice in selecting what is appropriate, and no criterion to go by; everything is on the same dead static level. On the other hand, it is quite open to question whether, if information actually functioned in experience through use in application to the student's own purposes, there would not be need of more varied resources in books, pictures, and talks than are usually at command.

III. The correlate in thinking of facts, data, knowledge already acquired, is suggestions, inferences, conjectured meanings, suppositions, tentative explanations:—*ideas,* in short. Careful observation and recollection determine what is given, what is already there, and hence assured. They cannot furnish what is lacking. They define, clarify, and locate the question; they cannot supply its answer. Projection, invention, ingenuity, devising come in for that purpose. The data *arouse* suggestions, and only by reference to the specific data can we pass upon the appropriateness of the suggestions. But the suggestions run beyond what is, as yet, actually *given* in experience. They forecast possible results, things *to* do, not facts (things already done). Inference is always an invasion of the unknown, a leap from the known.

In this sense, a thought (what a thing suggests but is not as it is presented) is creative,—an incursion into the novel. It involves some inventiveness. What is suggested must, indeed, be familiar in *some* context; the novelty, the inventive devising, clings to the new light in which it is seen, the different use to which it is put. When Newton thought of his theory of gravitation, the creative aspect of his thought was not found in its materials. They were familiar; many of them commonplaces—sun, moon, planets, weight, distance, mass, square of numbers. These were not original ideas; they were established facts. His originality lay in the *use* to which these familiar acquaintances were put by introduction into an unfamiliar context. The same is true of every striking scientific discovery, every great invention, every admirable artistic production. Only silly folk identify creative originality with the extraordinary and fanciful; others recognize that its measure lies in putting everyday things to uses which had not occurred to others. The operation is novel, not the materials out of which it is constructed.

The educational conclusion which follows is that *all* thinking is original in a projection of considerations which have not been previously apprehended. The child of three who discovers what can be done with blocks, or of six who finds out what he can make by putting five cents and five cents together, is really a discoverer, even though everybody else in the world knows it. There is a genuine increment of experience; not another item mechanically added on, but enrichment by a new quality. The charm which the spontaneity of little children has for sympathetic observers is due to perception of this intellectual originality. The joy which children themselves experience is the joy of intellectual constructiveness—of creativeness, if the word may be used without misunderstanding.

The educational moral I am chiefly concerned to draw is not, however, that teachers would find their own work less of a grind and strain if school conditions favored learning in the sense of discovery and not in that of storing away what others pour into them; nor that it would be possible to give even children and youth the delights of personal intellectual productiveness—true and important as are these things. It is that no thought, no idea, can possibly be conveyed as an idea from one person to another. When it is told, it is, to the one to whom it is told, another given fact, not an idea. The communication may stimulate the other person to realize the question for himself and to think out a like idea, or it may smother his intellectual interest and suppress his dawning effort at thought. But what he *directly* gets cannot be an idea. Only by wrestling with the conditions of the problem at first hand, seeking and finding his own way out, does he think. When the parent or teacher has provided the conditions which stimulate thinking and has taken a sympathetic attitude toward the activities of the learner by entering into a common or conjoint experience, all has been done which a second party can do to instigate learning. The rest lies with the one directly concerned. If he cannot devise his own solution (not of course in isolation, but in correspondence with the teacher and other pupils) and find his own way out he will not learn, not even if he can recite some correct answer with one hundred per cent accuracy. We can and do supply ready-made "ideas" by the thousand; we do not usually take much pains to see that the one learning engages in significant situations where his own activities generate, support, and clinch ideas—that is, perceived meanings or connections. This does not mean that the teacher is to stand off and look on; the alternative to furnishing ready-made subject matter and listening to the accuracy with which it is reproduced is not quiescence, but participation, sharing, in an activity. In such shared activity, the teacher is a learner, and the learner is, without knowing it, a teacher—and upon the whole, the less consciousness there is, on either side, of either giving or receiving instruction, the better.

IV. Ideas, as we have seen, whether they be humble guesses or dignified theories, are anticipations of possible solutions. They are anticipations of some continuity or connection of an activity and a consequence which has not as yet shown itself. They are therefore tested by the operation of acting upon them. They are to guide and organize further observations, recollections, and experiments. They are intermediate in learning, not final. All educational reformers, as we have had occasion to remark, are given to attacking the passivity of traditional education. They have opposed pouring in from without, and absorbing like a sponge; they have attacked drilling in material as into hard and resisting rock. But it is not easy to secure conditions which will make the getting of an idea identical with having an experience which widens and makes more precise our contact with the environment. Activity, even self-activity, is too easily thought of as something merely mental, cooped up within the head, or finding expression only through the vocal organs.

While the need of application of ideas gained in study is acknowledged by all the more successful methods of instruction, the exercises in application are sometimes treated as devices for *fixing* what has already been learned and for getting greater practical skill in its manipulation. These results are genuine and not to be despised. But practice in applying what has been gained in study ought primarily to have an intellectual quality. As we have already seen, thoughts just as thoughts are incomplete. At best they are tentative; they are suggestions, indications. They are standpoints and methods for dealing with situations of experience. Till they are applied in these situations they lack full point and reality. Only application tests them, and only testing confers full meaning and a sense of their reality. Short of use made of them, they tend to segregate into a peculiar world of their own. It may be seriously questioned whether the philosophies . . . which isolate mind and set it over against the world did not have their origin in the fact that the reflective or theoretical class of men elaborated a large stock of ideas which social conditions did not allow them to act upon and test. Consequently men were thrown back into their own thoughts as ends in themselves.

However this may be, there can be no doubt that a peculiar artificiality attaches to much of what is learned in schools. It can hardly be said that many students consciously think of the subject matter as unreal; but it assuredly does not possess for them the kind of reality which the subject matter of their vital experiences possesses. They learn not to expect that sort of reality of it; they become habituated to treating it as having reality for the purposes of recitations, lessons, and examinations. That it should remain inert for the experiences of daily life is more or less a matter of course. The bad effects are twofold. Ordinary experience does not receive the enrichment which it should; it is not fertilized by school learning. And the attitudes which spring from getting used to and accepting half-understood and ill-digested material weaken vigor and efficiency of thought.

If we have dwelt especially on the negative side, it is for the sake of suggesting positive measures adapted to the effectual development of thought. Where schools are equipped with laboratories, shops, and gardens, where dramatizations, plays, and games are freely used, opportunities exist for reproducing situations of life, and for acquiring and applying information and ideas in the carrying forward of progressive experiences. Ideas are not segregated, they do not form an isolated island. They animate and enrich the ordinary course of life. Information is vitalized by its function; by the place it occupies in direction of action.

The phrase "opportunities exist" is used purposely. They may not be taken advantage of; it is possible to employ manual and constructive activities in a physical way, as means of getting just bodily skill; or they may be used almost exclusively for "utilitarian," i.e., pecuniary, ends. But the disposition on the part of upholders of "cultural" education to assume that such activities are merely physical or professional in quality, is itself a product of the philosophies which isolate mind from direction of the course of experience and hence from action upon and with things. When the "mental" is regarded as a self-contained separate realm, a counterpart fate befalls bodily activity and movements. They are regarded as at the best mere external annexes to mind. They may be necessary for the satisfaction of bodily needs and the attainment of external decency and comfort, but they do not occupy a necessary place in mind nor enact an indispensable role in the completion of thought. Hence they have no place in a liberal education—i.e., one which is concerned with the interests of intelligence. If they come in at all, it is as a concession to the material needs of the masses. That they should be allowed to invade the education of the élite is unspeakable. This conclusion follows irresistibly from the isolated conception of mind, but by the same logic it disappears when we perceive what mind really is—namely, the purposive and directive factor in the development of experience.

While it is desirable that all educational institutions should be equipped so as to give students an opportunity for acquiring and testing ideas and information in active pursuits typifying important social situations, it will, doubtless, be a long time before all of them are thus furnished. But this state of affairs does not afford instructors an excuse for folding their hands and persisting in methods which segregate school knowledge. Every recitation in every subject gives an opportunity for establishing cross connections between the subject matter of the lesson and the wider and more direct experiences of everyday life. Classroom instruction falls into three kinds. The least desirable treats each lesson as an independent whole. It does not put upon the student the responsibility of finding points of contact between it and other lessons in the same subject, or other subjects of study. Wiser teachers see to it that the student is systematically led to utilize his earlier lessons to help understand the present one, and also to use the present to throw additional light upon what has already been acquired. Results are better, but school subject matter is still isolated. Save by accident, out-of-school experience is left in its crude and comparatively irreflective state. It is not subject to the refining and expanding influences of the more accurate and comprehensive material of direct instruction. The latter is not motivated and impregnated with a sense of reality by being intermingled with the realities of everyday life. The best type of teaching bears in mind the desirability of affecting this interconnection. It puts the student in the habitual attitude of finding points of contact and mutual bearings.

Summary

Processes of instruction are unified in the degree in which they centre in the production of good habits of thinking. While we may speak, without error, of the method of thought, the important thing is that thinking is the method of an educative experience. The essentials of method are therefore identical with the essentials of reflection. They are first that the pupil have a genuine situation of experience—that there be a continuous activity in which he is interested for its own sake; secondly, that a genuine problem develop within this situation as a stimulus to thought; third, that he possess the information and make the observations needed to deal with it; fourth, that suggested solutions occur to him which he shall be responsible for developing in an orderly way; fifth, that he have opportunity and occasion to test his ideas by application, to make their meaning clear and to discover for himself their validity.

18. EDUCATIONAL VALUES

2. The Valuation of Studies

The theory of educational values involves not only an account of the nature of appreciation as fixing the measure of subsequent valuations, but an account of the specific directions in which these valuations occur. To value means primarily to prize, to esteem; but secondarily it means to apprize, to estimate. It means, that is, the act of cherishing something, holding it dear, and also the act of passing judgment upon the nature and amount of its value as compared with something else. To value in the latter sense is to valuate or evaluate. The distinction coincides with that sometimes made between intrinsic and instrumental values. Intrinsic values are not objects of judgment, they cannot (as intrinsic) be compared, or regarded as greater and less, better or worse. They are invaluable; and if a thing is invaluable, it is neither more nor less so than any other invaluable. But occasions present themselves when it is necessary to choose, when we must let one thing go in order to take another. This establishes an order of preference, a greater and less, better and worse. Things judged or passed upon have to be estimated in relation to some third thing, some further end. With respect to that, they are means, or instrumental values.

We may imagine a man who at one time thoroughly enjoys converse with his friends, at another the hearing of a symphony; at another the eating of his meals; at another the reading of a book; at another the earning of money, and so on. As an appreciative realization, each of these is an intrinsic value. It occupies a particular place in life; it serves its own end, which cannot be supplied by a substitute. There is no question of comparative value, and hence none of valuation. Each is the specific good which it is, and that is all that can be said. In its own place, none is a means to anything beyond itself. But there may arise a situation in which they compete or conflict, in which a choice has to be made. Now comparison comes in. Since a choice has to be made, we want to know the respective claims of each competitor. What is to be said for it? What does it offer in comparison with, as balanced over against, some other possibility? Raising these questions means that a particular good is no longer an end in itself, an intrinsic good. For if it were, its claims would be incomparable, imperative. The question is now as to its status as a means of realizing something else, which is then the invaluable of *that* situation. If a man has just eaten, or if he is well fed generally and the opportunity to hear music is a rarity, he will probably prefer the music to eating. In the given situation that will render the greater contribution. If he is starving, or if he is satiated with music for the time being, he will naturally judge food to have the greater worth. In the abstract or at large, apart from the needs of a particular situation in which choice has to be made, there is no such thing as degrees or order of value.

Certain conclusions follow with respect to educational values. We cannot establish a hierarchy of values among studies. It is futile to attempt to arrange them in an order, beginning with one having least worth and going on to that of maximum value. In so far as any study has a unique or irreplaceable function in experience, in so far as it marks a characteristic enrichment of life, its worth is intrinsic or incomparable. Since education is not a means to living, but is identical with the operation of living a life which is fruitful and inherently significant, the only ultimate value which can be set up is just the process of living itself. And this is not an end to which studies and activities are subordinate means; it is the whole of which they are ingredients. And what has been said about appreciation means that every study in one of its aspects ought to have just such ultimate significance. It is as true of arithmetic as it is of poetry that in some place and at some time it ought to be a good to be appreciated on its own account—just as an enjoyable experience, in short. If it is not, then when the time and place come for it to be used as a means of instrumentality, it will be in just that much handicapped. Never having been realized or appreciated for itself, one will miss something of its capacity as a resource for other ends.

It equally follows that when we compare studies as to their values, that is, treat them as means to something beyond themselves, that which controls their proper valuation is found in the specific situation in which they are to be used. The way to enable a student to apprehend the instrumental value of arithmetic is not to lecture him upon the benefit it will be to him in some remote and uncertain future, but to let him discover that success in something he is interested in doing depends upon ability to use number.

It also follows that the attempt to distribute distinct sorts of value among different studies is a misguided one, in spite of the amount of time recently devoted to the undertaking. Science for example may have *any* kind of value, depending upon the situation into which it enters as a means. To some the value of science may be military; it may be an instrument in strengthening means of offense or defense; it may be technological, a tool for engineering; or it may be commercial—an aid in the successful conduct of business; under other conditions, its worth may be philanthropic—the service it renders in relieving human suffering; or again it may be quite conventional—of value in establishing one's social status as an "educated" person. As matter of fact, science serves all these purposes, and it would be an arbitrary task to try to fix upon one of them as its "real" end. All that we can be sure of educationally is that science should be taught so as to be an end in itself in the lives of students— something worth while on account of its own unique intrinsic contribution to the experience of life. Primarily it must have "appreciation value." If we take something which seems to be at the opposite pole, like poetry, the same sort of statement applies. It may be that, at the present time, its chief value is the contribution it makes to the enjoyment of leisure. But that may represent a degenerate condition rather than anything necessary. Poetry has historically been allied with religion and morals; it has served the purpose of penetrating the mysterious depths of things. It has had an enormous patriotic value. Homer to the Greeks was a Bible, a textbook of morals, a history, and a national inspiration. In any case, it may be said that an education which does not succeed in making poetry a resource in the business of life as well as in its leisure, has something the matter with it—or else the poetry is artificial poetry.

The same considerations apply to the value of a study or a topic of a study with reference to its motivating force. Those responsible for planning and teaching the course of study should have grounds for thinking that the studies and topics included furnish both direct increments to the enriching of lives of the pupils and also materials which they can put to use in other concerns of direct interest. Since the curriculum is always getting loaded down with purely inherited traditional matter and with subjects which represent mainly the energy of some influential person or group of persons in behalf of something dear to them, it requires constant inspection, criticism, and revision to make sure it is accomplishing its purpose. Then there is always the probability that it represents the values of adults rather than those of children and youth, or those of pupils a generation ago rather than those of the present day. Hence a further need for a critical outlook and survey. But these considerations do not mean that for a subject to have motivating value to a pupil (whether intrinsic or instrumental) is the same thing as for him to be aware of the value, or to be able to tell what the study is good for.

In the first place, as long as any topic makes an immediate appeal, it is not necessary to ask what it is good for. This is a question which can be asked only about instrumental values. Some goods are not good *for* anything; they are just goods. Any other notion leads to an absurdity. For we cannot stop asking the question about an instrumental good, one whose value lies in its being good *for* something, unless there is at some point something intrinsically good, good for itself. To a hungry, healthy child, food is a good of the situation; we do not have to bring him to consciousness of the ends subserved by food in order to supply a motive to eat. The food in connection with his appetite *is* a motive. The same thing holds of mentally eager pupils with respect to many topics. Neither they nor the teacher could possibly foretell with any exactness the purposes learning is to accomplish in the future; nor as long as the eagerness continues is it advisable to try to specify particular goods which are to come of it. The proof of a good is found in the fact that the pupil responds; his response *is* use. His response to the material shows that the subject functions in his life. It is unsound to urge that, say, Latin has a value *per se* in the abstract, just as a study, as a sufficient justification for teaching it. But it is equally absurd to argue that unless teacher or pupil can point out some definite assignable future use to which it is to be put, it lacks justifying value. When pupils are genuinely concerned in learning Latin, that is of itself proof that it possesses value. The most which one is entitled to ask in such cases is whether in view of the shortness of time, there are not other things of intrinsic value which in addition have greater instrumental value.

This brings us to the matter of instrumental values—topics studied because of some end beyond themselves. If a child is ill and his appetite does not lead him to eat when food is presented, or if his appetite is perverted so that he prefers candy to meat and vegetables, conscious reference to results is indicated. He needs to be made conscious of consequences as a justification of the positive or negative value of certain objects. Or the state of things may be normal enough, and yet an individual not be moved by some matter because he does not grasp how his attainment of some intrinsic good depends upon active concern with what is presented. In such cases, it is obviously the part of wisdom to establish consciousness of connection. In general what is desirable is that a topic be presented in such a way that it either have an immediate value, and require no justification, or else be perceived to be a means of achieving something of intrinsic value. An instrumental value then has the intrinsic value of being a means to an end.

It may be questioned whether some of the present pedagogical interest in the matter of values of studies is not either excessive or else too narrow. Sometimes it appears to be a labored effort to furnish an apologetic for topics which no longer operate to any purpose, direct or indirect, in the lives of pupils. At other times, the reaction against useless lumber seems to have gone to the extent of supposing that no subject or topic should be taught unless some quite definite future utility can be pointed out by those making the course of study or by the pupil himself, unmindful of the fact that life is its own excuse for being; and that definite utilities which can be pointed out are themselves justified only because they increase the experienced content of life itself.

26. THEORIES OF MORALS

3. Intelligence and Character

A noteworthy paradox often accompanies discussions of morals. On the one hand, there is an identification of the moral with the rational. Reason is set up as a faculty from which proceed ultimate moral intuitions, and sometimes, as in the Kantian theory, it is said to supply the only proper moral motive. On the other hand, the value of concrete, everyday intelligence is constantly underestimated, and even deliberately depreciated. Morals is often thought to be an affair with which ordinary knowledge has nothing to do. Moral knowledge is thought to be a thing apart, and conscience is thought of as something radically different from consciousness. This separation, if valid, is of especial significance for education. Moral education in school is practically hopeless when we set up the development of character as a supreme end, and at the same time treat the acquiring of knowledge and the development of understanding, which of necessity occupy the chief part of school time, as having nothing to do with character. On such a basis, moral education is inevitably reduced to some kind of catechetical instruction, or lessons about morals. Lessons "about morals" signify as matter of course lessons in what other people think about virtues and duties. It amounts to something only in the degree in which pupils happen to be already animated by a sympathetic and dignified regard for the sentiments of others. Without such a regard, it has no more influence on character than information about the mountains of Asia; with a service regard, it increases dependence upon others, and throws upon those in authority the responsibility for conduct. As a matter of fact, direct instruction in morals has been effective only in social groups where it was a part of the authoritative control of the many by the few. Not the teaching as such but the reenforcement of it by the whole régime of which it was an incident made it effective. To attempt to get similar results from lessons about morals in a democratic society is to rely upon sentimental magic.

At the other end of the scale stands the Socratic-Platonic teaching which identifies knowledge and virtue—which holds that no man does evil knowingly but only because of ignorance of the good. This doctrine is commonly attacked on the ground that nothing is more common than for a man to know the good and yet do the bad: not knowledge, but habituation or practice, and motive are what is required. Aristotle, in fact, at once attacked the Platonic teaching on the ground that moral virtue is like an art, such as medicine: the experienced practitioner is better than a man who has theoretical knowledge but no practical experience of disease and remedies. The issue turns, however, upon what is meant by knowledge. Aristotle's objection ignored the gist of Plato's teaching to the effect that man could not attain a theoretical insight into the good except as he had passed through years of practical habituation and strenuous discipline. Knowledge of the good was not a thing to be got either from books or from others, but was achieved through a prolonged education. It was the final and culminating grace of a mature experience of life. Irrespective of Plato's position, it is easy to perceive that the term knowledge is used to denote things as far apart as intimate and vital personal realization,—a conviction gained and tested in experience,—and a second-handed, largely symbolic, recognition that persons in general believe so and so—a devitalized remote information. That the latter does not guarantee conduct, that it does not profoundly affect character, goes without saying. But if knowledge means something of the same sort as our conviction gained by trying and testing that sugar is sweet and quinine bitter, the case stands otherwise. Every time a man sits on a chair rather than on a stove, carries an umbrella when it rains, consults a doctor when ill—or in short performs any of the thousand acts which make up his daily life, he proves that knowledge of a certain kind finds direct issue in conduct. There is every reason to suppose that the same sort of knowledge of good has a like expression; in fact "good" is an empty term unless it includes the satisfactions experienced in such situations as those mentioned. Knowledge that other persons are supposed to know something might lead one to act so as to win the approbation others attach to certain actions, or at least so as to give others the impression that one agrees with them; there is no reason why it should lead to personal initiative and loyalty in behalf of the beliefs attributed to them.

It is not necessary, accordingly, to dispute about the proper meaning of the term knowledge. It is enough for educational purposes to note the different qualities covered by the one name, to realize that it is knowledge gained at first hand through the exigencies of experience which affects conduct in significant ways. If a pupil learns things from books simply in connection with school lessons and for the sake of reciting what he has learned when called upon, then knowledge will have effect upon *some* conduct—namely upon that of reproducing statements at the demand of others. There is nothing surprising that such "knowledge" should not have much influence in the life out of school. But this is not a reason for making a divorce between knowledge and conduct, but for holding in low esteem this kind of knowledge. The same thing may be said of knowledge which relates merely to an isolated and technical speciality; it modifies action but only in its own narrow line. In truth, the problem of moral education in the schools is one with the problem of securing knowledge—the knowledge connected with the system of impulses and habits. For the use to which any known fact is put depends upon its connections. The knowledge of dynamite of a safecracker may be identical in verbal form with that of a chemist; in fact, it is different, for it is knit into connection with different aims and habits, and thus has a different import.

Our prior discussion of subject matter as proceeding from direct activity having an immediate aim, to the enlargement of meaning found in geography and history, and then to scientifically organized knowledge, was based upon the idea of maintaining a vital connection between knowledge and activity.

What is learned and employed in an occupation having an aim and involving cooperation with others is moral knowledge, whether consciously so regarded or not. For it builds up a social interest and confers the intelligence needed to make that interest effective in practice. Just because the studies of the curriculum represent standard factors in social life, they are organs of initiation into social values. As mere school studies, their acquisition has only a technical worth. Acquired under conditions where their social significance is realized, they feed moral interest and develop moral insight. Moreover, the qualities of mind discussed under the topic of method of learning are all of them intrinsically moral qualities. Open-mindedness, single-mindedness, sincerity, breadth of outlook, thoroughness, assumption of responsibility for developing the consequences of ideas which are accepted, are moral traits. The habit of identifying moral characteristics with external conformity to authoritative prescriptions may lead us to ignore the ethical value of these intellectual attitudes, but the same habit tends to reduce morals to a dead and machine-like routine. Consequently while such an attitude has moral results, the results are morally undesirable—above all in a democratic society where so much depends upon personal disposition.

4. The Social and the Moral

All of the separations which we have been criticizing—and which the idea of education set forth in the previous chapters is designed to avoid—spring from taking morals too narrowly,—giving them, on one side, a sentimental goody-goody turn without reference to effective ability to do what is socially needed, and, on the other side, overemphasizing convention and tradition so as to limit morals to a list of definitely stated acts. As a matter of fact, morals are as broad as acts which concern our relationships with others. And potentially this includes all our acts, even though their social bearing may not be thought of at the time of performance. For every act, by the principle of habit, modifies disposition—it sets up a certain kind of inclination and desire. And it is impossible to tell when the habit thus strengthened may have a direct and perceptible influence on our association with others. Certain traits of character have such an obvious connection with our social relationships that we call them "moral" in an emphatic sense—truthfulness, honesty, chastity, amiability, etc. But this only means that they are, as compared with some other attitudes, central:— that they carry other attitudes with them. They are moral in an emphatic sense not because they are isolated and exclusive, but because they are so intimately connected with thousands of other attitudes which we do not explicitly recognize—which perhaps we have not even names for. To call them virtues in their isolation is like taking the skeleton for the living body. The bones are certainly important, but their importance lies in the fact that they support other organs of the body in such a way to make them capable of integrated effective activity. And the same is true of the qualities of character which we specifically designate virtues. Morals concern nothing less than the whole character, and the whole character is identical with the man in all his concrete makeup and manifestations. To possess virtue does not signify to have cultivated a few nameable and exclusive traits; it means to be fully and adequately what one is capable of becoming through association with others in all the offices of life.

The moral and the social quality of conduct are, in the last analysis, identical with each other. It is then but to restate explicitly the import of our earlier chapters regarding the social function of education to say that the measure of the worth of the administration, curriculum, and methods of instruction of the school is the extent to which they are animated by a social spirit. And the great danger which threatens school work is the absence of conditions which make possible a permeating social spirit; this is the great enemy of effective moral training. For this spirit can be actively present only when certain conditions are met.

(*i*) In the first place, the school must itself be a community life in all which that implies. Social perceptions and interests can be developed only in a genuinely social medium—one where there is give and take in the building up on a common experience. Informational statements about things can be acquired in relative isolation by anyone who previously has had enough intercourse with others to have learned language. But realization of the *meaning* of the linguistic signs is quite another matter. That involves a context of work and play in association with others. The plea which has been made for education through continued constructive activities in this book rests upon the fact they afford an opportunity for a social atmosphere. In place of a school set apart from life as a place for learning lessons, we have a miniature social group in which study and growth are incidents of present shared experience. Playgrounds, shops, workrooms, laboratories not only direct the natural active tendencies of youth, but they involve intercourse, communication, and cooperation,—all extending the perception of connections.

(*ii*) The learning in school should be continuous with that out of school. There should be a free interplay between the two. This is possible only when there are numerous points of contact between the social interests of the one and of the other. A school is conceivable in which there should be a spirit of companionship and shared activity, but where its social life would no more represent or typify that of the world beyond the school walls than that of a monastery. Social concern and understanding would be developed, but they would not be available outside; they would not carry over. The proverbial separation of town and gown, the cultivation of academic seclusion, operate in this direction. So does such adherence to the culture of the past as generates a reminiscent social spirit, for this makes an individual feel more at home in the life of other days than in his own. A professedly cultural education is peculiarly exposed to this danger. An idealized past becomes the refuge and solace of the spirit; present-day concerns are found sordid, and unworthy of attention. But as a rule, the absence of a social environment in connection with which learning is a need and a reward is the chief reason for the isolation of the school; and this isolation renders school knowledge inapplicable to life and so infertile in character.

A narrow and moralistic view of morals is responsible for the failure to recognize that all the aims and values which are desirable in education are themselves moral. Discipline, natural development, culture, social efficiency, are moral traits—marks of a person who is a worthy member of that society which it is the business of education to further. There is an old saying to the effect that it is not enough for a man to be good; he must be good for something. The something for which a man must be good is capacity to live as a social member so that what he gets from living with others balances with what he contributes. What he gets and gives as a human being, a being with desires, emotions, and ideas, is not external possessions, but a widening and deepening of conscious life—a more intense, disciplined, and expanding realization of meanings. What he *materially* receives and gives is at most opportunities and means for the evolution of conscious life. Otherwise, it is neither giving nor taking, but a shifting about of the position of things in space, like the stirring of water and sand with a stick. Discipline, culture, social efficiency, personal refinement, improvement of character are but phases of the growth of capacity nobly to share in such a balanced experience. And education is not a mere means to such a life. Education is such a life. To maintain capacity for such education is the essence of morals. For conscious life is a continual beginning afresh.

Notes

1. There is a much neglected strain in Rousseau tending intellectually in this direction. He opposed the existing state of affairs on the ground that it formed *neither* the citizen nor the man. Under existing conditions, he preferred to try for the latter rather than for the former. But there are many sayings of his which point to the formation of the citizen as ideally the higher, and which indicate that his own endeavor, as embodied in *Emile,* was simply the best makeshift the corruption of the times permitted him to sketch.

Experience and Education*
PREFACE

All social movements involve conflicts which are reflected intellectually in controversies. It would not be a sign of health if such an important social interest as education were not also an arena of struggles, practical and theoretical. But for theory, at least for the theory that forms a philosophy of education, the

---

*Reprinted by permission of Southern Illinois University Press.

practical conflicts and the controversies that are conducted upon the level of these conflicts, only set a problem. It is the business of an intelligent theory of education to ascertain the causes for the conflicts that exist and then, instead of taking one side or the other, to indicate a plan of operations proceeding from a level deeper and more inclusive than is represented by the practices and ideas of the contending parties.

This formulation of the business of the philosophy of education does not mean that the latter should attempt to bring about a compromise between opposed schools of thought, to find a *via media*, nor yet make an eclectic combination of points picked out hither and yon from all schools. It means the necessity of the introduction of a new order of conceptions leading to new modes of practice. It is for this reason that it is so difficult to develop a philosophy of education, the moment tradition and custom are departed from. It is for this reason that the conduct of schools, based upon a new order of conceptions, is so much more difficult than is the management of schools which walk in beaten paths. Hence, every movement in the direction of a new order of ideas and of activities directed by them calls out, sooner or later, a return to what appear to be simpler and more fundamental ideas and practices of the past—as is exemplified at present in education in the attempt to revive the principles of ancient Greece and of the middle ages.

It is in this context that I have suggested at the close of this little volume that those who are looking ahead to a new movement in education, adapted to the existing need for a new social order, should think in terms of Education itself rather than in terms of some 'ism about education, even such an 'ism as "progressivism." For in spite of itself any movement that thinks and acts in terms of an 'ism becomes so involved in reaction against other 'isms that it is unwittingly controlled by them. For it then forms its principles by reaction against them instead of by a comprehensive constructive survey of actual needs, problems, and possibilities. Whatever value is possessed by the essay presented in this little volume resides in its attempt to call attention to the larger and deeper issues of Education so as to suggest their proper frame of reference.

1. TRADITIONAL *VS.* PROGRESSIVE EDUCATION

Mankind likes to think in terms of extreme opposites. It is given to formulating its beliefs in terms of *Either-Ors*, between which it recognizes no intermediate possibilities. When forced to recognize that the extremes cannot be acted upon, it is still inclined to hold that they are all right in theory but that when it comes to practical matters circumstances compel us to compromise. Educational philosophy is no exception. The history of educational theory is marked by opposition between the idea that education is development from within and that it is formation from without; that it is based upon natural endowments and that education is a process of overcoming natural inclination and substituting in its place habits acquired under external pressure.

At present, the opposition, so far as practical affairs of the school are concerned, tends to take the form of contrast between traditional and progressive education. If the underlying ideas of the former are formulated broadly, without the qualifications required for accurate statement, they are found to be about as follows: The subject-matter of education consists of bodies of information and of skills that have been worked out in the past; therefore, the chief business of the school is to transmit them to the new generation. In the past, there have also been developed standards and rules of conduct; moral training consists in forming habits of action in conformity with these rules and standards. Finally, the general pattern of school organization (by which I mean the relations of pupils to one another and to the teachers) constitutes the school a kind of institution sharply marked off from other social institutions. Call up in imagination the ordinary schoolroom, its time-schedules, schemes of classification, of examination and promotion, of rules of order, and I think you will grasp what is meant by "pattern of organization." If then you contrast this scene with what goes on in the family, for example, you will appreciate what is meant by the school being a kind of institution sharply marked off from any other form of social organization.

The three characteristics just mentioned fix the aims and methods of instruction and discipline. The main purpose or objective is to prepare the young for future responsibilities and for success in life, by means of acquisition of the organized bodies of information and prepared forms of skill which comprehend the material of instruction. Since the subject-matter as well as standards of proper conduct are handed down from the past, the attitude of pupils must, upon the whole, be one of docility, receptivity, and obedience. Books, especially textbooks, are the chief representatives of the lore and wisdom of the past, while teachers are the organs through which pupils are brought into effective connection with the material. Teachers are the agents through which knowledge and skills are communicated and rules of conduct enforced.

I have not made this brief summary for the purpose of criticizing the underlying philosophy. The rise of what is called new education and progressive schools is of itself a product of discontent with traditional education. In effect it is a criticism of the latter. When the implied criticism is made explicit it reads somewhat as follows: The traditional scheme is, in essence, one of imposition from above and from outside. It imposes adult standards, subject-matter, and methods upon those who are only growing slowly toward maturity. The gap is so great that the required subject-matter, the methods of learning and of behaving are foreign to the existing capacities of the young. They are beyond the reach of the experience the young learners already possess. Consequently, they must be imposed; even though good teachers will use devices of art to cover up the imposition so as to relieve it of obviously brutal features.

But the gulf between the mature or adult products and the experience and abilities of the young is so wide that the very situation forbids much active participation by pupils in the development of what is taught. Theirs is to do—and learn, as it was the part of the six hundred to do and die. Learning here means acquisition of what already is incorporated in books and in the heads of the elders. Moreover, that which is taught is thought of as essentially static. It is taught as a finished product, with little regard either to the ways in which it was originally built up or to changes that will surely occur in the future. It is to a large extent the cultural product of societies that assumed the future would be much like the past, and yet it is used as educational food in a society where change is the rule, not the exception.

If one attempts to formulate the philosophy of education implicit in the practices of the newer education, we may, I think, discover certain common principles amid the variety of progressive schools now existing. To imposition from above is opposed expression and cultivation of individuality; to external discipline is opposed free activity; to learning from texts and teachers, learning through experience; to acquisition of isolated skills and techniques by drill, is opposed acquisition of them as means of attaining ends which make direct vital appeal; to preparation for a more or less remote future is opposed making the most of the opportunities of present life; to static aims and materials is opposed acquaintance with a changing world.

Now, all principles by themselves are abstract. They become concrete only in the consequences which result from their application. Just because the principles set forth are so fundamental and far-reaching, everything depends upon the interpretation given them as they are put into practice in the school and the home. It is at this point that the reference made earlier to *Either-Or* philosophies becomes peculiarly pertinent. The general philosophy of the new education may be sound, and yet the difference in abstract principles will not decide the way in which the moral and intellectual preference involved shall be worked out in practice. There is always the danger in a new movement that in rejecting the aims and methods of that which it would supplant, it may develop its principles negatively rather than positively and constructively. Then it takes its clew in practice from that which is rejected instead of from the constructive development of its own philosophy.

I take it that the fundamental unity of the newer philosophy is found in the idea that there is an intimate and necessary relation between the processes of actual experience and education. If this be true, then a positive and constructive development of its own basic idea depends upon having a correct idea of experience. Take, for example, the question of organized subject-matter—which will be discussed in some detail later. The problem for progressive education is: What is the place and meaning of subject-matter and or organization *within* experience? How does subject-matter function? Is there anything inherent in experience which tends towards progressive organization of its contents? What results follow when the materials of experience are not progressively organized? A philosophy which proceeds on the basis of rejection, of sheer opposition, will neglect these questions. It will tend to suppose that because the old education was based on ready-made organization, therefore it suffices to reject the principle of organization *in toto*, instead of striving to discover what it means and how it is to be attained on the basis of experience. We might go through all the points of difference between the new and the old education and reach similar conclusions. When external control is rejected, the problem becomes that of finding the factors of control that are inherent within experience. When external authority is rejected, it does not follow that all authority should be rejected, but rather that there is need to search for a more effective source of authority. Because the older education imposed the knowledge, methods, and the rules of conduct of the mature person upon the young, it does not follow, except upon the basis of the extreme *Either-Or* philosophy, that the knowledge and skill of the mature person has no directive value for the experience of the immature. On the contrary, basing education upon personal experience may mean more multiplied and more intimate contacts between the mature and the immature than ever existed in the traditional school, and consequently more, rather than less, guidance by others. The problem, then, is: how these contacts can be established without violating the principle of learning through personal experience. The solution of this problem requires a well thought-out philosophy of the social factors that operate in the constitution of individual experience.

What is indicated in the foregoing remarks is that the general principles of the new education do not of themselves solve any of the problems of the actual or practical conduct and management of progressive schools. Rather, they set new problems which have to be worked out on the basis of a new philosophy of experience. The problems are not even recognized, to say nothing of being solved, when it is assumed that it suffices to reject the ideas and practices of the old education and then go to the opposite extreme. Yet I am sure that you will appreciate what is meant when I say that many of the newer schools tend to make little or nothing of organized subject-matter of study; to proceed as if any form of direction and guidance by adults were an invasion of individual freedom, and as if the idea that education should be concerned with the present and future meant that acquaintance with the past has little or no role to play in education. Without pressing these defects to the point of exaggeration, they at least illustrate what is meant by a theory and practice of education which proceeds negatively or by reaction against what has been current in education rather than by a positive and constructive development of purposes, methods, and subject-matter on the foundation of a theory of experience and its educational potentialities.

It is not too much to say that an educational philosophy which professes to be based on the idea of freedom may become as dogmatic as ever was the traditional education which is reacted against. For any theory and set of practices is dogmatic which is not based upon critical examination of its own underlying principles. Let us say that the new education emphasizes the freedom of the learner. Very well. A problem is now set. What does freedom mean and what are the conditions under which it is capable of realization? Let us say that the kind of external imposition which was so common in the traditional school limited rather than promoted the intellectual and moral development of the young. Again, very well. Recognition of this serious defect sets a problem. Just what is the role of the teacher and of books in promoting the educational development of the immature? Admit that traditional education employed as the subject-matter for study facts and ideas so bound up with the past as to give little help in dealing with the issues of the present and future. Very well. Now we have the problem of discovering the connection which actually exists *within* experience between the achievements of the past and the issues of the present. We have the problem of ascertaining how acquaintance with the past may be translated into a potent instrumentality for dealing effectively with the future. We may reject knowledge of the past as the *end* of education and thereby only emphasize its importance as a *means*. When we do that we have a problem that is new in the story of education: How shall the young become acquainted with the past in such a way that the acquaintance is a potent agent in appreciation of the living present?

2. THE NEED OF A THEORY OF EXPERIENCE

In short, the point I am making is that rejection of the philosophy and practice of traditional education sets a new type of difficult educational problem for those who believe in the new type of education. We shall operate blindly and in confusion until we recognize this fact; until we thoroughly appreciate that departure from the old solves no problems. What is said in the following pages is, accordingly, intended to indicate some of the main problems with which the newer education is confronted and to suggest the main lines along which their solution is to be sought. I assume that amid all uncertainties there is one permanent frame of reference: namely, the organic connection between education and personal experience; or, that the new philosophy of education is committed to some kind of empirical and experimental philosophy. But experience and experiment are not self-explanatory ideas. Rather, their meaning is part of the problem to be explored. To know the meaning of empiricism we need to understand what experience is.

The belief that all genuine education comes about through experience does not mean that all experiences are genuinely or equally educative. Experience and education cannot be directly equated to each other. For some experiences are mis-educative. Any experience is mis-educative that has the effect of arresting or distorting the growth of further experience. An experience may be such as to engender callousness; it may produce lack of sensitivity and of responsiveness. Then the possibilities of having richer experience in the future are restricted. Again, a given experience may increase a person's automatic skill in a particular direction and yet tend to land him in a groove or rut; the effect again is to narrow the field of further experience. An experience may be immediately enjoyable and yet promote the formation of a slack and careless attitude; this attitude then operates to modify the quality of subsequent experiences so as to prevent a person from getting out of them what they have to give. Again, experiences may be so disconnected from one another that, while each is agreeable or even exciting in itself, they are not linked cumulatively to one another. Energy is then dissipated and a person becomes scatter-brained. Each experience may be lively, vivid, and "interesting," and yet their disconnectedness may artificially generate dispersive, disintegrated, centrifugal habits. The consequence of formation of such habits is inability to control future experiences. They are then taken, either by way of enjoyment or of discontent and revolt, just as they come. Under such circumstances, it is idle to talk of self-control.

Traditional education offers a plethora of examples of experiences of the kinds just mentioned. It is a great mistake to suppose, even tacitly, that the traditional schoolroom was not a place in which pupils had experiences. Yet this is tacitly assumed when progressive education as a plan of learning by experience is placed in sharp opposition to the old. The proper line of attack is that the experiences which were had, by pupils and teachers alike, were largely of a wrong kind. How many students, for example, were rendered callous to ideas, and how many lost the impetus to learn because of the way in which learning was experienced by them? How many acquired special skills by means of automatic drill so that their power of judgment and capacity to act intelligently in new situations was limited? How many came to associate the learning process with ennui and boredom? How many found what they did learn so foreign to the situations of life outside the school as to give them no power of control over the latter? How many came to associate books with dull drudgery, so that they were "conditioned" to all but flashy reading matter?

If I ask these questions, it is not for the sake of wholesale condemnation of the old education. It is for quite another purpose. It is to emphasize the fact, first, that young people in traditional schools do have experiences; and, secondly, that the trouble is not the absence of experiences, but their defective and wrong character—wrong and defective from the standpoint of connection with further experience. The positive side of this point is even more important in connection with progressive education. It is not enough to insist upon the necessity of experience, nor even of activity in experience. Everything depends upon the *quality* of the experience which is had. The quality of any experience has two aspects. There is an immediate aspect of agreeableness or disagreeableness, and there is its influence upon later experiences. The first is obvious and easy to judge. The *effect* of an experience is not borne on its face. It sets a problem to the educator. It is his business to arrange for the kind of experiences which, while they do not repel the student, but rather engage his activities are, nevertheless, more than immediately enjoyable since they promote having desirable future experiences. Just as no man lives or dies to himself, so no experience lives and dies to itself. Wholly independent of desire or intent, every experience lives on in further experiences. Hence the central problem of an education based upon experience is to select the kind of present experiences that live fruitfully and creatively in subsequent experiences.

Later, I shall discuss in more detail the principle of the continuity of experience or what may be called the experiential continuum. Here I wish simply to emphasize the importance of this principle for the philosophy of educative experience. A philosophy of education, like any theory, has to be stated in words, in symbols. But so far as it is more than verbal it is a plan for conducting education. Like any plan, it must be framed with reference to what is to be done and how it is to be done. The more definitely and sincerely it is held that education is a development within, by, and for experience, the more important it is that there shall be clear conceptions of what experience is. Unless experience is so conceived that the result is a plan for deciding upon subject-matter, upon methods of instruction and discipline, and upon material equipment and social organization of the school, it is wholly in the air. It is reduced to a form of words which may be emotionally stirring but for which any other set of words might equally well be substituted unless they indicate operations to be initiated and executed. Just because traditional education was a matter of routine in which the plans and programs were handed down from the past, it does not follow that progressive education is a matter of planless improvisation.

The traditional school could get along without any consistently developed philosophy of education. About all it required in that line was a set of abstract words like culture, discipline, our great cultural heritage, etc., actual guidance being derived not from them but from custom and established routines. Just because progressive schools cannot rely upon established traditions and institutional habits, they must either proceed more or less haphazardly or be directed by ideas which, when they are made articulate and coherent, form a philosophy of education. Revolt against the kind of organization characteristic of the traditional school constitutes a demand for a kind of organization based upon ideas. I think that only slight acquaintance with the history of education is needed to prove that educational reformers and innovators alone have felt the need for a philosophy of education. Those who adhered to the established system needed merely a few fine-sounding words to justify existing practices. The real work was done by habits which were so fixed as to be institutional. The lesson for progressive education is that it requires in an urgent degree, a degree more pressing than was incumbent upon former innovators, a philosophy of education based upon a philosophy of experience.

I remarked incidentally that the philosophy in question is, to paraphrase the saying of Lincoln about democracy, one of education of, by, and for experience. No one of these words, *of, by,* or *for,* names anything which is self-evident. Each of them is a challenge to discover and put into operation a principle of order and organization which follows from understanding what educative experience signifies.

It is, accordingly, a much more difficult task to work out the kind of materials, of methods, and of social relationships that are appropriate to the new education than is the case with traditional education. I think many of the difficulties experienced in the conduct of progressive schools and many of the criticisms leveled against them arise from this source. The difficulties are aggravated and the criticisms are increased when it is supposed that the new education is somehow easier than the old. This belief is, I imagine, more or less current. Perhaps it illustrates again the *Either-Or* philosophy, springing from the idea that about all which is required is *not* to do what is done in traditional schools.

I admit gladly that the new education is *simpler* in principle than the old. It is in harmony with principles of growth, while there is very much which is artificial in the old selection and arrangement of subjects and methods, and artificiality always leads to unnecessary complexity. But the easy and the simple are not identical. To discover what is really simple and to act upon the discovery is an exceedingly difficult task. After the artificial and complex is once institutionally established and ingrained in custom and routine, it is easier to walk in the paths that have been beaten than it is, after taking a new point of view, to work out what is practically involved in the new point of view. The old Ptolemaic astronomical system was more complicated with its cycles and epicycles than the Copernican system. But until organization of actual astronomical phenomena on the ground of the latter principle had been effected the easiest course was to follow the line of least resistance provided by the old intellectual habit. So we come back to the idea that a coherent *theory* of experience, affording positive direction to selection and organization of appropriate educational methods and materials, is required by the attempt to give new direction to the work of the schools. The process is a slow and arduous one. It is a matter of growth, and there are many obstacles which tend to obstruct growth and to deflect it into wrong lines.

I shall have something to say later about organization. All that is needed, perhaps, at this point is to say that we must escape from the tendency to think of organization in terms of the *kind* of organization, whether of content (or subject-matter), or of methods and social relations, that mark traditional education. I think that a good deal of the current opposition to the idea of organization is due to the fact that it is so hard to get away from the picture of the studies of the old school. The moment "organization" is mentioned imagination goes almost automatically to the kind of organization that is familiar, and in revolting against that we are led to shrink from the very idea of any organization. On the other hand, educational reactionaries, who are now gathering force, use the absence of adequate intellectual and moral organization in the newer type of school as proof not only of the need of organization, but to identify any and every kind of organization with that instituted before the rise of experimental science. Failure to develop a conception of organization upon the empirical and experimental basis gives reactionaries a too easy victory. But the fact that the empirical sciences now offer the best type of intellectual organization which can be found in any field shows that there is no reason why we, who call ourselves empiricists, should be "pushovers" in the matter of order and organization.

3. CRITERIA OF EXPERIENCE

If there is any truth in what has been said about the need of forming a theory of experience in order that education may be intelligently conducted upon the basis of experience, it is clear that the next thing in order in this discussion is to present the principles that are most significant in framing this theory. I shall not, therefore, apologize for engaging in a certain amount of philosophical analysis, which otherwise might be out of place. I may, however, reassure you to some degree by saying that this analysis is not an end in itself but is engaged in for the sake of obtaining criteria to be applied later in discussion of a number of concrete and, to most persons, more interesting issues.

I have already mentioned what I called the category of continuity, or the experiential continuum. This principle is involved, as I pointed out, in every attempt to discriminate between experiences that are worth while education-ally and those that are not. It may seem superfluous to argue that this discrimi-nation is necessary not only in criticizing the traditional type of education but also in initiating and conducting a different type. Nevertheless, it is advisable to pursue for a little while the idea that it is necessary. One may safely assume, I suppose, that one thing which has recommended the progressive movement is that it seems more in accord with the democratic ideal to which our people is committed than do the procedures of the traditional school, since the latter have so much of the autocratic about them. Another thing which has con-tributed to its favorable reception is that its methods are humane in compari-son with the harshness so often attending the policies of the traditional school.

The question I would raise concerns why we prefer democratic and hu-mane arrangements to those which are autocratic and harsh. And by "why," I mean the *reason* for preferring them, not just the *causes* which lead us to the preference. One *cause* may be that we have been taught not only in the schools but by the press, the pulpit, the platform, and our laws and law-making bodies that democracy is the best of all social institutions. We may have so assimilated this idea from our surroundings that it has become an habitual part of our mental and moral make-up. But similar causes have led other persons in dif-ferent surroundings to widely varying conclusions—to prefer fascism, for ex-ample. The cause for our preference is not the same thing as the reason why we *should* prefer it.

It is not my purpose here to go in detail into the reason. But I would ask a single question: Can we find any reason that does not ultimately come down to the belief that democratic social arrangements promote a better quality of human experience, one which is more widely accessible and enjoyed, than do nondemocratic and anti-democratic forms of social life? Does not the principle of regard for individual freedom and for decency and kindliness of human re-lations come back in the end to the conviction that these things are tributary to a higher quality of experience on the part of a greater number than are meth-ods of repression and coercion or force? Is it not the reason for our preference that we believe that mutual consultation and convictions reached through per-suasion, make possible a better quality of experience than can otherwise be provided on any wide scale?

If the answer to these questions is in the affirmative (and personally I do not see how we can justify our preference for democracy and humanity on any other ground), the ultimate reason for hospitality to progressive education, be-cause of its reliance upon and use of humane methods and its kinship to democracy, goes back to the fact that discrimination is made between the in-herent values of different experiences. So I come back to the principle of conti-nuity of experience as a criterion of discrimination.

At bottom, this principle rests upon the fact of habit, when *habit* is interpreted biologically. The basic characteristic of habit is that every experience enacted and undergone modifies the one who acts and undergoes, while this modification affects, whether we wish it or not, the quality of subsequent experiences. For it is a somewhat different person who enters into them. The principle of habit so understood obviously goes deeper than the ordinary conception of *a* habit as a more or less fixed way of doing things, although it includes the latter as one of its special cases. It covers the formation of attitudes, attitudes that are emotional and intellectual; it covers our basic sensitivities and ways of meeting and responding to all the conditions which we meet in living. From this point of view, the principle of continuity of experience means that every experience both takes up something from those which have gone before and modifies in some way the quality of those which come after. As the poet states it,

> . . . all experience is an arch wherethro'
> Gleams that untravell'd world, whose margin fades
> Forever and forever when I move.

So far, however, we have no ground for discrimination among experiences. For the principle is of universal application. There is *some* kind of continuity in every case. It is when we note the different forms in which continuity of experience operates that we get the basis of discriminating among experiences. I may illustrate what is meant by an objection which has been brought against an idea which I once put forth—namely, that the educative process can be identified with growth when that is understood in terms of the active participle, *growing.*

Growth, or growing as developing, not only physically but intellectually and morally, is one exemplification of the principle of continuity. The objection made is that growth might take many different directions: a man, for example, who starts out on a career of burglary may grow in that direction, and by practice may grow into a highly expert burglar. Hence it is argued that "growth" is not enough; we must also specify the direction in which growth takes place, the end towards which it tends. Before, however, we decide that the objection is conclusive we must analyze the case a little further.

That a man may grow in efficiency as a burglar, as a gangster, or as a corrupt politician, cannot be doubted. But from the standpoint of growth as education and education as growth the question is whether growth in this direction promotes or retards growth in general. Does this form of growth create conditions for further growth, or does it set up conditions that shut off the person who has grown in this particular direction from the occasions, stimuli, and opportunities for continuing growth in new directions? What is the effect of growth in a special direction upon the attitudes and habits which alone open up avenues for development in other lines? I shall leave you to answer these questions, saying simply that when and *only* when development in a particular line conduces to continuing growth does it answer to the criterion of education as growing. For the conception is one that must find universal and not specialized limited application.

I return now to the question of continuity as a criterion by which to discriminate between experiences which are educative and those which are miseducative. As we have seen, there is some kind of continuity in any case since every experience affects for better or worse the attitudes which help decide the quality of further experiences, by setting up certain preference and aversion, and making it easier or harder to act for this or that end. Moreover, every experience influences in some degree the objective conditions under which further experiences are had. For example, a child who learns to speak has a new facility and new desire. But he has also widened the external conditions of subsequent learning. When he learns to read, he similarly opens up a new environment. If a person decides to become a teacher, lawyer, physician, or stockbroker, when he executes his intention he thereby necessarily determines to some extent the environment in which he will act in the future. He has rendered himself more sensitive and responsive to certain conditions, and relatively immune to those things about him that would have been stimuli if he had made another choice.

But, while the principle of continuity applies in some way in every case, the quality of the present experience influences the *way* in which the principle applies. We speak of spoiling a child and of the spoilt child. The effect of overindulging a child is a continuing one. It sets up an attitude which operates as an automatic demand that persons and objects cater to his desires and caprices in the future. It makes him seek the kind of situation that will enable him to do what he feels like doing at the time. It renders him averse to and comparatively incompetent in situations which require effort and perseverance in overcoming obstacles. There is no paradox in the fact that the principle of the continuity of experience may operate so as to leave a person arrested on a low plane of development, in a way which limits later capacity for growth.

On the other hand, if an experience arouses curiosity, strengthens initiative, and sets up desires and purposes that are sufficiently intense to carry a person over dead places in the future, continuity works in a very different way. Every experience is a moving force. Its value can be judged only on the ground of what it moves toward and into. The greater maturity of experience which should belong to the adult as educator puts him in a position to evaluate each experience of the young in a way in which the one having the less mature experience cannot do. It is then the business of the educator to see in what direction an experience is heading. There is no point in his being more mature if, instead of using his greater insight to help organize the conditions of the experience of the immature, he throws away his insight. Failure to take the moving force of an experience into account so as to judge and direct it on the ground of what it is moving into means disloyalty to the principle of experience itself. The disloyalty operates in two directions. The educator is false to the understanding that he should have obtained from his own past experience. He is also unfaithful to the fact that all human experience is ultimately social: that it involves contact and communication. The mature person, to put it in moral terms, has no right to withhold from the young on given occasions whatever capacity for sympathetic understanding his own experience has given him.

No sooner, however, are such things said than there is a tendency to react to the other extreme and take what has been said as a plea for some sort of disguised imposition from outside. It is worth while, accordingly, to say something about the way in which the adult can exercise the wisdom his own wider experience gives him without imposing a merely external control. On one side, it is his business to be on the alert to see what attitudes and habitual tendencies are being created. In this direction he must, if he is an educator, be able to judge what attitudes are actually conducive to continued growth and what are detrimental. He must, in addition, have that sympathetic understanding of individuals as individuals which gives him an idea of what is actually going on in the minds of those who are learning. It is, among other things, the need for these abilities on the part of the parent and teacher which makes a system of education based upon living experience a more difficult affair to conduct successfully than it is to follow the patterns of traditional education.

But there is another aspect of the matter. Experience does not go on simply inside a person. It does go on there, for it influences the formation of attitudes of desire and purpose. But this is not the whole of the story. Every genuine experience has an active side which changes in some degree the objective conditions under which experiences are had. The difference between civilization and savagery, to take an example on a large scale, is found in the degree in which previous experiences have changed the objective conditions under which subsequent experiences take place. The existence of roads, of means of rapid movement and transportation, tools, implements, furniture, electric light and power, are illustrations. Destroy the external conditions of present civilized experience, and for a time our experience would relapse into that of barbaric peoples.

In a word, we live from birth to death in a world of persons and things which in large measure is what it is because of what has been done and transmitted from previous human activities. When this fact is ignored, experience is treated as if it were something which goes on exclusively inside an individual's body and mind. It ought not to be necessary to say that experience does not occur in a vacuum. There are sources outside an individual which give rise to experience. It is constantly fed from these springs. No one would question that a child in a slum tenement has a different experience from that of a child in a cultured home; that the country lad has a different kind of experience from the city boy, or a boy on the seashore one different from the lad who is brought up on inland prairies. Ordinarily we take such facts for granted as too commonplace to record. But when their educational import is recognized, they indicate the second way in which the educator can direct the experience of the young without engaging in imposition. A primary responsibility of educators is that they not only be aware of the general principle of the shaping of actual experience by environing conditions, but that they also recognize in the concrete what surroundings are conducive to having experiences that lead to growth. Above all, they should know how to utilize the surroundings, physical and social, that exist so as to extract from them all that they have to contribute to building up experiences that are worth while.

Traditional education did not have to face this problem; it could systematically dodge this responsibility. The school environment of desks, blackboards, a small school yard, was supposed to suffice. There was no demand that the teacher should become intimately acquainted with the conditions of the local community, physical, historical, economic, occupational, etc., in order to utilize them as educational resources. A system of education based upon the necessary connection of education with experience must, on the contrary, if faithful to its principle, take these things constantly into account. This tax upon the educator is another reason why progressive education is more difficult to carry on than was ever the traditional system.

It is possible to frame schemes of education that pretty systematically subordinate objective conditions to those which reside in the individuals being educated. This happens whenever the place and function of the teacher, of books, of apparatus and equipment, of everything which represents the products of the more mature experience of elders, is systematically subordinated to the immediate inclinations and feelings of the young. Every theory which assumes that importance can be attached to these objective factors only at the expense of imposing external control and of limiting the freedom of individuals rests finally upon the notion that experience is truly experience only when objective conditions are subordinated to what goes on within the individuals having the experience.

I do not mean that it is supposed that objective conditions can be shut out. It is recognized that they must enter in: so much concession is made to the inescapable fact that we live in a world of things and persons. But I think that observation of what goes on in some families and some schools would disclose that some parents and some teachers are acting upon the idea of *subordinating* objective conditions to internal ones. In that case, it is assumed not only that the latter are primary, which in one sense they are, but that just as they temporarily exist they fix the whole educational process.

Let me illustrate from the case of an infant. The needs of a baby for food, rest, and activity are certainly primary and decisive in one respect. Nourishment must be provided; provision must be made for comfortable sleep, and so on. But these facts do not mean that a parent shall feed the baby at any time when the baby is cross or irritable, that there shall not be a program of regular hours of feeding and sleeping, etc. The wise mother takes account of the needs of the infant but not in a way which dispenses with her own responsibility for regulating the objective conditions under which the needs are satisfied. And if she is a wise mother in this respect, she draws upon past experiences of experts as well as her own for the light that these shed upon what experiences are in general most conducive to the normal development of infants. Instead of these conditions being subordinated to the immediate internal condition of the baby, they are definitely ordered so that a particular kind of *interaction* with these immediate internal states may be brought about.

The word "interaction," which has just been used, expresses the second chief principle for interpreting an experience in its educational function and force. It assigns equal rights to both factors in experience—objective and internal conditions. Any normal experience is an interplay of these two sets of conditions. Taken together, or in their interaction, they form what we call a *situation*. The trouble with traditional education was not that it emphasized the external conditions that enter into the control of the experiences but that it paid so little attention to the internal factors which also decide what kind of experience is had. It violated the principle of interaction from one side. But this violation is no reason why the new education should violate the principle from the other side—except upon the basis of the extreme *Either-Or* educational philosophy which has been mentioned.

The illustration drawn from the need for regulation of the objective conditions of a baby's development indicates, first, that the parent has responsibility for arranging the conditions under which an infant's experience of food, sleep, etc., occurs, and, secondly, that the responsibility is fulfilled by utilizing the funded experience of the past, as this is represented, say, by the advice of competent physicians and others who have made a special study of normal physical growth. Does it limit the freedom of the mother when she uses the body of knowledge thus provided to regulate the objective conditions of nourishment and sleep? Or does the enlargement of her intelligence in fulfilling her parental function widen her freedom? Doubtless if a fetish were made of the advice and directions so that they came to be inflexible dictates to be followed under every possible condition, then restriction of freedom of both parent and child would occur. But this restriction would also be a limitation of the intelligence that is exercised in personal judgment.

In what respect does regulation of objective conditions limit the freedom of the baby? Some limitation is certainly placed upon its immediate movements and inclinations when it is put in its crib, at a time when it wants to continue playing, or does not get food at the moment it would like it, or when it isn't picked up and dandled when it cries for attention. Restriction also occurs when mother or nurse snatches a child away from an open fire into which it is about to fall. I shall have more to say later about freedom. Here it is enough to ask whether freedom is to be thought of and adjudged on the basis of relatively momentary incidents or whether its meaning is found in the continuity of developing experience.

The statement that individuals live in a world means, in the concrete, that they live in a series of situations. And when it is said that they live *in* these situations, the meaning of the word "in" is different from its meaning when it is said that pennies are "in" a pocket or paint is "in" a can. It means, once more, that interaction is going on between an individual and objects and other persons. The conceptions of *situation* and of *interaction* are inseparable from each other. An experience is always what it is because of a transaction taking place between an individual and what, at the time, constitutes his environment, whether the latter consists of persons with whom he is talking about some topic or event, the subject talked about being also a part of the situation; or the toys with which he is playing; the book he is reading (in which his environing conditions at the time may be England or ancient Greece or an imaginary region); or the materials of an experiment he is performing. The environment, in other words, is whatever conditions interact with personal needs, desires, purposes, and capacities to create the experience which is had. Even when a person builds a castle in the air he is interacting with the objects which he constructs in fancy.

The two principles of continuity and interaction are not separate from each other. They intercept and unite. They are, so to speak, the longitudinal and lateral aspects of experience. Different situations succeed one another. But because of the principle of continuity something is carried over from the earlier to the later ones. As an individual passes from one situation to another, his world, his environment, expands or contracts. He does not find himself living in another world but in a different part or aspect of one and the same world. What he has learned in the way of knowledge and skill in one situation becomes an instrument of understanding and dealing effectively with the situations which follow. The process goes on as long as life and learning continue. Otherwise the course of experience is disorderly, since the individual factor that enters into making an experience is split. A divided world, a world whose parts and aspects do not hang together, is at once a sign and a cause of a divided personality. When the splitting-up reaches a certain point we call the person insane. A fully integrated personality, on the other hand, exists only when successive experiences are integrated with one another. It can be built up only as a world of related objects is constructed.

Continuity and interaction in their active union with each other provide the measure of the educative significance and value of an experience. The immediate and direct concern of an educator is then with the situations in which interaction takes place. The individual, who enters as a factor into it, is what he is at a given time. It is the other factor, that of objective conditions, which lies to some extent within the possibility of regulation by the educator. As has already been noted, the phrase "objective conditions" covers a wide range. It includes what is done by the educator and the way in which it is done, not only words spoken but the tone of voice in which they are spoken. It includes equipment, books, apparatus, toys, games played. It includes the materials with which an individual interacts, and, most important of all, the total *social* set-up of the situations in which a person is engaged.

When it is said that the objective conditions are those which are within the power of the educator to regulate, it is meant, of course, that his ability to influence directly the experience of others and thereby the education they obtain places upon him the duty of determining that environment which will interact with the existing capacities and needs of those taught to create a worthwhile experience. The trouble with traditional education was not that educators took upon themselves the responsibility for providing an environment. The trouble was that they did not consider the other factor in creating an experience; namely, the powers and purposes of those taught. It was assumed that a certain set of conditions was intrinsically desirable, apart from its ability to evoke a certain quality of response in individuals. This lack of mutual adaptation made the process of teaching and learning accidental. Those to whom the provided conditions were suitable managed to learn. Others got on as best they could. Responsibility for selecting objective conditions carries with it, then, the responsibility for understanding the needs and capacities of the individuals who are learning at a given time. It is not enough that certain materials and methods have proved effective with other individuals at other times. There must be a reason for thinking that they will function in generating an experience that has educative quality with particular individuals at a particular time.

It is no reflection upon the nutritive quality of beefsteak that it is not fed to infants. It is not an invidious reflection upon trigonometry that we do not teach it in the first or fifth grade of school. It is not the subject *per se* that is educative or that is conducive to growth. There is no subject that is in and of itself, or without regard to the stage of growth attained by the learner, such that inherent educational value can be attributed to it. Failure to take into account adaptation to the needs and capacities of individuals was the source of the idea that certain subjects and certain methods are intrinsically cultural or intrinsically good for mental discipline. There is no such thing as educational value in the abstract. The notion that some subjects and methods and that acquaintance with certain facts and truths possess educational value in and of themselves is the reason why traditional education reduced the material of education so largely to a diet of predigested materials. According to this notion, it was enough to regulate the quantity and difficulty of the material provided, in a scheme of quantitative grading, from month to month and from year to year. Otherwise a pupil was expected to take it in the doses that were prescribed from without. If the pupil left it instead of taking it, if he engaged in physical truancy, or in the mental truancy of mind-wandering and finally built up an emotional revulsion against the subject, he was held to be at fault. No question was raised as to whether the trouble might not lie in the subject-matter or in the way in which it was offered. The principle of interaction makes it clear that failure of adaptation of material to needs and capacities of individuals may cause an experience to be non-educative quite as much as failure of an individual to adapt himself to the material.

The principle of continuity in its educational application means, nevertheless, that the future has to be taken into account at every stage of the educational process. This idea is easily misunderstood and is badly distorted in traditional education. Its assumption is, that by acquiring certain skills and by learning certain subjects which would be needed later (perhaps in college or perhaps in adult life) pupils are as a matter of course made ready for the needs and circumstances of the future. Now "preparation" is a treacherous idea. In a certain sense every experience should do something to prepare a person for later experiences of a deeper and more expansive quality. That is the very meaning of growth, continuity, reconstruction of experience. But it is a mistake to suppose that the mere acquisition of a certain amount of arithmetic, geography, history, etc., which is taught and studied because it may be useful at some time in the future, has this effect, and it is a mistake to suppose that acquisition of skills in reading and figuring will automatically constitute preparation for their right and effective use under conditions very unlike those in which they were acquired.

Almost everyone has had occasion to look back upon his school days and wonder what has become of the knowledge he was supposed to have amassed during his years of schooling, and why it is that the technical skills he acquired have to be learned over again in changed form in order to stand him in good stead. Indeed, he is lucky who does not find that in order to make progress, in order to go ahead intellectually, he does not have to unlearn much of what he learned in school. These questions cannot be disposed of by saying that the subjects were not actually learned, for they were learned at least sufficiently to enable a pupil to pass examinations in them. One trouble is that the subject-matter in question was learned in isolation; it was put, as it were, in a water-tight compartment. When the question is asked, then, what has become of it, where has it gone to, the right answer is that it is still there in the special compartment in which it was originally stowed away. If exactly the same conditions recurred as those under which it was acquired, it would also recur and be available. But it was segregated when it was acquired and hence is so disconnected from the rest of experience that it is not available under the actual conditions of life. It is contrary to the laws of experience that learning of this kind, no matter how thoroughly engrained at the time, should give genuine preparation.

Nor does failure in preparation end at this point. Perhaps the greatest of all pedagogical fallacies is the notion that a person learns only the particular thing he is studying at the time. Collateral learning in the way of formation of enduring attitudes, of likes and dislikes, may be and often is much more important than the spelling lesson or lesson in geography or history that is learned. For these attitudes are fundamentally what count in the future. The most important attitude that can be formed is that of desire to go on learning. If impetus in this direction is weakened instead of being intensified, something much more than mere lack of preparation takes place. The pupil is actually robbed of native capacities which otherwise would enable him to cope with the circumstances that he meets in the course of his life. We often see persons who have had little schooling and in whose case the absence of set schooling proves to be a positive asset. They have at least retained their native common sense and power of judgment, and its exercise in the actual conditions of living has given them the precious gift of ability to learn from the experiences they have. What avail is it to win prescribed amounts of information about geography and history, to win ability to read and write, if in the process the individual loses his own soul: loses his appreciation of things worth while, of the values to which these things are relative; if he loses desire to apply what he has learned and, above all, loses the ability to extract meaning from his future experiences as they occur?

What, then, is the true meaning of preparation in the educational scheme? In the first place, it means that a person, young or old, gets out of his present experience all that there is in it for him at the time in which he has it. When preparation is made the controlling end, then the potentialities of the present are sacrificed to a supposititious future. When this happens, the actual preparation for the future is missed or distorted. The ideal of using the present simply to get ready for the future contradicts itself. It omits, and even shuts out, the very conditions by which a person can be prepared for his future. We always live at the time we live and not at some other time, and only by extracting at each present time the full meaning of each present experience are we prepared for doing the same thing in the future. This is the only preparation which in the long run amounts to anything.

All this means that attentive care must be devoted to the conditions which give each present experience a worth while meaning. Instead of inferring that it doesn't make much difference what the present experience is as long as it is enjoyed, the conclusion is the exact opposite. Here is another matter where it is easy to react from one extreme to the other. Because traditional schools tended to sacrifice the present to a remote and more or less unknown future, therefore it comes to be believed that the educator has little responsibility for the kind of present experiences the young undergo. But the relation of the present and the future is not an *Either-Or* affair. The present affects the future anyway. The persons who should have some idea of the connection between the two are those who have achieved maturity. Accordingly, upon them devolves the responsibility for instituting the conditions for the kind of present experience which has a favorable effect upon the future. Education as growth or maturity should be an ever-present process.

4. SOCIAL CONTROL

I have said that educational plans and projects, seeing education in terms of life-experience, are thereby committed to framing and adopting an intelligent theory or, if you please, philosophy of experience. Otherwise they are at the mercy of every intellectual breeze that happens to blow. I have tried to illustrate the need for such a theory by calling attention to two principles which are fundamental in the constitution of experience: the principles of interaction and of continuity. If, then, I am asked why I have spent so much time on expounding a rather abstract philosophy, it is because practical attempts to develop schools based upon the idea that education is found in life-experience are bound to exhibit inconsistencies and confusions unless they are guided by some conception of what experience is, and what marks off educative experience from non-educative and mis-educative experience. I now come to a group of actual educational questions the discussion of which will, I hope, provide topics and material that are more concrete than the discussion up to this point.

The two principles of continuity and interaction as criteria of the value of experience are so intimately connected that it is not easy to tell just what special educational problem to take up first. Even the convenient division into problems of subject-matter or studies and of methods of teaching and learning is likely to fail us in selection and organization of topics to discuss. Consequently, the beginning and sequence of topics is somewhat arbitrary. I shall commence, however, with the old question of individual freedom and social control and pass on to the questions that grow naturally out of it.

It is often well in considering educational problems to get a start by temporarily ignoring the school and thinking of other human situations. I take it that no one would deny that the ordinary good citizen is as a matter of fact subject to a great deal of social control and that a considerable part of this control is not felt to involve restriction of personal freedom. Even the theoretical anarchist, whose philosophy commits him to the idea that state or government control is an unmitigated evil, believes that with abolition of the political state other forms of social control would operate: indeed, his opposition to governmental regulation springs from his belief that other and to him more normal modes of control would operate with abolition of the state.

Without taking up this extreme position, let us note some examples of social control that operate in everyday life, and then look for the principle underlying them. Let us begin with the young people themselves. Children at recess or after school play games, from tag and one-old-cat to baseball and football. The games involve rules, and these rules order their conduct. The games do not go on haphazardly or by a succession of improvisations. Without rules there is no game. If disputes arise there is an umpire to appeal to, or discussion and a kind of arbitration are means to a decision; otherwise the game is broken up and comes to an end.

There are certain fairly obvious controlling features of such situations to which I want to call attention. The first is that the rules are a part of the game. They are not outside of it. No rules, then no game; different rules, then a different game. As long as the game goes on with a reasonable smoothness, the players do not feel that they are submitting to external imposition but that they are playing the game. In the second place an individual may at times feel that a decision isn't fair and he may even get angry. But he is not objecting to a rule but to what he claims is a violation of it, to some one-sided and unfair action. In the third place, the rules, and hence the conduct of the game, are fairly standardized. There are recognized ways of counting out, of selection of sides, as well as for positions to be taken, movements to be made, etc. These rules have the sanction of tradition and precedent. Those playing the game have seen, perhaps, professional matches and they want to emulate their elders. An element that is conventional is pretty strong. Usually, a group of youngsters change the rules by which they play only when the adult group to which they look for models have themselves made a change in the rules, while the change made by the elders is at least supposed to conduce to making the game more skillful or more interesting to spectators.

Now, the general conclusion I would draw is that control of individual actions is effected by the whole situation in which individuals are involved, in which they share and of which they are cooperative or interacting parts. For even in a competitive game there is a certain kind of participation, of sharing in a common experience. Stated the other way around, those who take part do not feel that they are bossed by an individual person or are being subjected to the will of some outside superior person. When violent disputes do arise, it is usually on the alleged ground that the umpire or some person on the other side is being unfair; in other words, that in such cases some individual is trying to impose his individual will on someone else.

It may seem to be putting too heavy a load upon a single case to argue that this instance illustrates the general principle of social control of individuals without the violation of freedom. But if the matter were followed out through a number of cases, I think the conclusion that this particular instance does illustrate a general principle would be justified. Games are generally competitive. If we took instances of cooperative activities in which all members of a group take part, as for example in well-ordered family life in which there is mutual confidence, the point would be even clearer. In all such cases it is not the will or desire of any one person which establishes order but the moving spirit of the whole group. The control is social, but individuals are parts of a community, not outside of it.

I do not mean by this that there are no occasions upon which the authority of, say, the parent does not have to intervene and exercise fairly direct control. But I do say that, in the first place, the number of these occasions is slight in comparison with the number of those in which the control is exercised by situations in which all take part. And what is even more important, the authority in question when exercised in a well-regulated household or other community group is not a manifestation of merely personal will; the parent or teacher exercises it as the representative and agent of the interests of the group as a whole. With respect to the first point, in a well-ordered school the main reliance for control of this and that individual is upon the activities carried on and upon the situations in which these activities are maintained. The teacher reduces to a minimum the occasions in which he or she has to exercise authority in a personal way. When it is necessary, in the second place, to speak and act firmly, it is done in behalf of the interest of the group, not as an exhibition of personal power. This makes the difference between action which is arbitrary and that which is just and fair.

Moreover, it is not necessary that the difference should be formulated in words, by either teacher or the young, in order to be felt in experience. The number of children who do not feel the difference (even if they cannot articulate it and reduce it to an intellectual principle) between action that is motivated by personal power and desire to dictate and action that is fair, because in the interest of all, is small. I should even be willing to say that upon the whole children are more sensitive to the signs and symptoms of this difference than are adults. Children learn the difference when playing with one another. They are willing, often too willing if anything, to take suggestions from one child and let him be a leader if his conduct adds to the experienced value of what they are doing, while they resent the attempt at dictation. Then they often withdraw and when asked why, say that it is because so-and-so "is too bossy."

I do not wish to refer to the traditional school in ways which set up a caricature in lieu of a picture. But I think it is fair to say that one reason the personal commands of the teacher so often played an undue role and a reason why the order which existed was so much a matter of sheer obedience to the will of an adult was because the situation almost forced it upon the teacher. The school was not a group or community held together by participation in common activities. Consequently, the normal, proper conditions of control were lacking. Their absence was made up for, and to a considerable extent had to be made up for, by the direct intervention of the teacher, who, as the saying went, "*kept* order." He kept it because order was in the teacher's keeping, instead of residing in the shared work being done.

The conclusion is that in what are called the new schools, the primary source of social control resides in the very nature of the work done as a social enterprise in which all individuals have an opportunity to contribute and to which all feel a responsibility. Most children are naturally "sociable." Isolation is even more irksome to them than to adults. A genuine community life has its ground in this natural sociability. But community life does not organize itself in an enduring way purely spontaneously. It requires thought and planning ahead. The educator is responsible for a knowledge of individuals and for a knowledge of subject-matter that will enable activities to be selected which lend themselves to social organization, an organization in which all individuals have an opportunity to contribute something, and in which the activities in which all participate are the chief carrier of control.

I am not romantic enough about the young to suppose that every pupil will respond or that any child of normally strong impulses will respond on every occasion. There are likely to be some who, when they come to school, are already victims of injurious conditions outside of the school and who have become so passive and unduly docile that they fail to contribute. There will be others who, because of previous experience, are bumptious and unruly and perhaps downright rebellious. But it is certain that the general principle of social control cannot be predicated upon such cases. It is also true that no general rule can be laid down for dealing with such cases. The teacher has to deal with them individually. They fall into general classes, but no two are exactly alike. The educator has to discover as best he or she can the causes for the recalcitrant attitudes. He or she cannot, if the educational process is to go on, make it a question of pitting one will against another in order to see which is strongest, nor yet allow the unruly and non-participating pupils to stand permanently in the way of the educative activities of others. Exclusion perhaps is the only available measure at a given juncture, but it is no solution. For it may strengthen the very causes which have brought about the undesirable anti-social attitude, such as desire for attention or to show off.

Exceptions rarely prove a rule or give a clew to what the rule should be. I would not, therefore, attach too much importance to these exceptional cases, although it is true at present that progressive schools are likely often to have more than their fair share of these cases, since parents may send children to such schools as a last resort. I do not think weakness in control when it is found in progressive schools arises in any event from these exceptional cases. It is much more likely to arise from failure to arrange in advance for the kind of work (by which I mean all kinds of activities engaged in) which will create situations that of themselves tend to exercise control over what this, that, and the other pupil does and how he does it. This failure most often goes back to lack of sufficiently thoughtful planning in advance. The causes for such lack are varied. The one which is peculiarly important to mention in this connection is the idea that such advanced planning is unnecessary and even that it is inherently hostile to the legitimate freedom of those being instructed.

Now, of course, it is quite possible to have preparatory planning by the teacher done in such a rigid and intellectually inflexible fashion that it does result in adult imposition, which is none the less external because executed with tact and the semblance of respect for individual freedom. But this kind of planning does not follow inherently from the principle involved. I do not know what the greater maturity of the teacher and the teacher's greater knowledge of the world, of subject-matters and of individuals, is for unless the teacher can arrange conditions that are conducive to community activity and to organization which exercises control over individual impulses by the mere fact that all are engaged in communal projects. Because the kind of advance planning heretofore engaged in has been so routine as to leave little room for the free play of individual thinking or for contributions due to distinctive individual experience, it does not follow that all planning must be rejected. On the contrary, there is incumbent upon the educator the duty of instituting a much more intelligent, and consequently more difficult, kind of planning. He must survey the capacities and needs of the particular set of individuals with whom he is dealing and must at the same time arrange the conditions which provide the subject-matter or content for experiences that satisfy these needs and develop these capacities. The planning must be flexible enough to permit free play for individuality of experience and yet firm enough to give direction towards continuous development of power.

The present occasion is a suitable one to say something about the province and office of the teacher. The principle that development of experience comes about through interaction means that education is essentially a social process. This quality is realized in the degree in which individuals form a community group. It is absurd to exclude the teacher from membership in the group. As the most mature member of the group he has a peculiar responsibility for the conduct of the interactions and intercommunications which are the very life of the group as a community. That children are individuals whose freedom should be respected while the more mature person should have no freedom as an individual is an idea too absurd to require refutation. The tendency to exclude the teacher from a positive and leading share in the direction of the activities of the community of which he is a member is another instance of reaction from one extreme to another. When pupils were a class rather than a social group, the teacher necessarily acted largely from the outside, not as a director of processes of exchange in which all had a share. When education is based upon experience and educative experience is seen to be a social process, the situation changes radically. The teacher loses the position of external boss or dictator but takes on that of leader of group activities.

In discussing the conduct of games as an example of normal social control, reference was made to the presence of a standardized conventional factor. The counterpart of this factor in school life is found in the question of manners, especially of good manners in the manifestations of politeness and courtesy. The more we know about customs in different parts of the world at different times in the history of mankind, the more we learn how much manners differ from place to place and time to time. This fact proves that there is a large conventional factor involved. But there is no group at any time or place which does not have some code of manners as, for example, with respect to proper ways of greeting other persons. The particular form a convention takes has nothing fixed and absolute about it. But the existence of some form of convention is not itself a convention. It is a uniform attendant of all social relationships. At the very least, it is the oil which prevents or reduces friction.

It is possible, of course, for these social forms to become, as we say, "mere formalities." They may become merely outward show with no meaning behind them. But the avoidance of empty ritualistic forms of social intercourse does not mean the rejection of every formal element. It rather indicates the need for development of forms of intercourse that are inherently appropriate to social situations. Visitors to some progressive schools are shocked by the lack of manners they come across. One who knows the situation better is aware that to some extent their absence is due to the eager interest of children to go on with what they are doing. In their eagerness they may, for example, bump into each other and into visitors with no word of apology. One might say that that this condition is better than a display of merely external punctilio accompanying intellectual and emotional lack of interest in school work. But it also represents a failure in education, a failure to learn one of the most important lessons of life, that of mutual accommodation and adaptation. Education is going on in a one-sided way, for attitudes and habits are in process of formation that stand in the way of the future learning that springs from easy and ready contact and communication with others.

5. THE NATURE OF FREEDOM

At the risk of repeating what has been often said by me I want to say something about the other side of the problem of social control, namely, the nature of freedom. The only freedom that is of enduring importance is freedom of intelligence, that is to say, freedom of observation and of judgment exercised in behalf of purposes that are intrinsically worth while. The commonest mistake made about freedom is, I think, to identify it with freedom of movement, or with the external or physical side of activity. Now, this external and physical side of activity cannot be separated from the internal side of activity; from freedom of thought, desire, and purpose. The limitation that was put upon outward action by the fixed arrangements of the typical traditional schoolroom, with its fixed rows of desks and its military regimen of pupils who were permitted to move only at certain fixed signals, put a great restriction upon intellectual and moral freedom. Strait-jacket and chain-gang procedures had to be done away with if there was to be a chance for growth of individuals in the intellectual springs of freedom without which there is no assurance of genuine and continued normal growth.

But the fact still remains that an increased measure of freedom of outer movement is a *means,* not an end. The educational problem is not solved when this aspect of freedom is obtained. Everything then depends, so far as education is concerned, upon what is done with this added liberty. What end does it serve? What consequences flow from it? Let me speak first of the advantages which reside potentially in increase of outward freedom. In the first place, without its existence it is practically impossible for a teacher to gain knowledge of the individuals with whom he is concerned. Enforced quiet and acquiescence prevent pupils from disclosing their real natures. They enforce artificial uniformity. They put seeming before being. They place a premium upon preserving the outward appearance of attention, decorum, and obedience. And everyone who is acquainted with schools in which this system prevailed well knows that thoughts, imaginations, desires, and sly activities ran their own unchecked course behind this façade. They were disclosed to the teacher only when some untoward act led to their detection. One has only to contrast this highly artificial situation with normal human relations outside the schoolroom, say in a well-conducted home, to appreciate how fatal it is to the teacher's acquaintance with and understanding of the individuals who are, supposedly, being educated. Yet without this insight there is only an accidental chance that the material of study and the methods used in instruction will so come home to an individual that his development of mind and character is actually directed. There is a vicious circle. Mechanical uniformity of studies and methods creates a kind of uniform immobility and this reacts to perpetuate uniformity of studies and of recitations, while behind this enforced uniformity individual tendencies operate in irregular and more or less forbidden ways.

The other important advantage of increased outward freedom is found in the very nature of the learning process. That the older methods set a premium upon passivity and receptivity has been pointed out. Physical quiescence puts a tremendous premium upon these traits. The only escape from them in the standardized school is an activity which is irregular and perhaps disobedient. There cannot be complete quietude in a laboratory or workshop. The non-social character of the traditional school is seen in the fact that it erected silence into one of its prime virtues. There is, of course, such a thing as intense intellectual activity without overt bodily activity. But capacity for such intellectual activity marks a comparatively late achievement when it is continued for a long period. There should be brief intervals of time for quiet reflection provided for even the young. But they are periods of genuine reflection only when they follow after times of more overt action and are used to organize what has been gained in periods of activity in which the hands and other parts of the body beside the brain are used. Freedom of movement is also important as a means of maintaining normal physical and mental health. We have still to learn from the example of the Greeks who saw clearly the relation between a sound body and a sound mind. But in all the respects mentioned freedom of outward action is a means to freedom of judgment and of power to carry deliberately chosen ends into execution. The amount of external freedom which is needed varies from individual to individual. It naturally tends to decrease with increasing maturity, though its complete absence prevents even a mature individual from having the contacts which will provide him with new materials upon which his intelligence may exercise itself. The amount and the quality of this kind of free activity as a means of growth is a problem that must engage the thought of the educator at every stage of development.

There can be no greater mistake, however, than to treat such freedom as an end in itself. It then tends to be destructive of the shared cooperative activities which are the normal source of order. But, on the other hand, it turns freedom which should be positive into something negative. For freedom from restriction, the negative side, is to be prized only as a means to a freedom which is power: power to frame purposes, to judge wisely, to evaluate desires by the consequences which will result from acting upon them; power to select and order means to carry chosen ends into operation.

Natural impulses and desires constitute in any case the starting point. But there is no intellectual growth without some reconstruction, some remaking, of impulses and desires in the form in which they first show themselves. This remaking involves inhibition of impulse in its first estate. The alternative to externally imposed inhibition is inhibition through an individual's own reflection and judgment. The old phrase "stop and think" is sound psychology. For thinking is stoppage of the immediate manifestation of impulse until that impulse has been brought into connection with other possible tendencies to action so that a more comprehensive and coherent plan of activity is formed. Some of the other tendencies to action lead to use of eye, ear, and hand to observe objective conditions; others result in recall of what has happened in the past. Thinking is thus a postponement of immediate action, while it effects internal control of impulse through a union of observation and memory, this union being the heart of reflection. What has been said explains the meaning of the well-worn phrase "self-control." The ideal aim of education is creation of power of self-control. But the mere removal of external control is no guarantee for the production of self-control. It is easy to jump out of the frying-pan into the fire. It is easy, in other words, to escape one form of external control only to find oneself in another and more dangerous form of external control. Impulses and desires that are not ordered by intelligence are under the control of accidental circumstances. It may be a loss rather than a gain to escape from the control of another person only to find one's conduct dictated by immediate whim and caprice; that is, at the mercy of impulses into whose formation intelligent judgment has not entered. A person whose conduct is controlled in this way has at most only the illusion of freedom. Actually he is directed by forces over which he has no command.

6. THE MEANING OF PURPOSE

It is, then, a sound instinct which identifies freedom with power to frame purposes and to execute or carry into effect purposes so framed. Such freedom is in turn identical with self-control; for the formation of purposes and the organization of means to execute them are the work of intelligence. Plato once defined a slave as the person who executes the purposes of another, and, as has just been said, a person is also a slave who is enslaved to his own blind desires. There is, I think, no point in the philosophy of progressive education which is sounder than its emphasis upon the importance of the participation of the learner in the formation of the purposes which direct his activities in the learning process, just as there is no defect in traditional education greater than its failure to secure the active cooperation of the pupil in construction of the purposes involved in his studying. But the meaning of purposes and ends is not self-evident and self-explanatory. The more their educational importance is emphasized, the more important it is to understand what a purpose is; how it arises and how it functions in experience.

A genuine purpose always starts with an impulse. Obstruction of the immediate execution of an impulse converts it into a desire. Nevertheless neither impulse nor desire is itself a purpose. A purpose is an end-view. That is, it involves foresight of the consequences which will result from acting upon impulse. Foresight of consequences involves the operation of intelligence. It demands, in the first place, observation of objective conditions and circumstances. For impulse and desire produce consequences not by themselves alone but through their interaction or cooperation with surrounding conditions. The impulse for such a simple action as walking is executed only in active conjunction with the ground on which one stands. Under ordinary circumstances, we do not have to pay much attention to the ground. In a ticklish situation we have to observe very carefully just what the conditions are, as in climbing a steep and rough mountain where no trail has been laid out. Exercise of observation is, then, one condition of transformation of impulse into a purpose. As in the sign by a railway crossing, we have to stop, look, listen.

But observation alone is not enough. We have to understand the *significance* of what we see, hear, and touch. This significance consists of the consequences that will result when what is seen is acted upon. A baby may *see* the brightness of a flame and be attracted thereby to reach for it. The significance of the flame is then not its brightness but its power to burn, as the consequence that will result from touching it. We can be aware of consequences only because of previous experiences. In cases that are familiar because of many prior experiences we do not have to stop to remember just what those experiences were. A flame comes to signify light and heat without our having expressly to think of previous experiences of heat and burning. But in unfamiliar cases, we cannot tell just what the consequences of observed conditions will be unless we go over past experiences in our mind, unless we reflect upon them and by seeing what is similar in them to those now present, go on to form a judgment of what may be expected in the present situation.

The formation of purposes is, then, a rather complex intellectual operation. It involves (1) observation of surrounding conditions; (2) knowledge of what has happened in similar situations in the past, a knowledge obtained partly by recollection and partly from the information, advice, and warning of those who have had a wider experience; and (3) judgment which puts together what is observed and what is recalled to see what they signify. A purpose differs from an original impulse and desire through its translation into a plan and method of action based upon foresight of the consequences of acting under given observed conditions in a certain way. "If wishes were horses, beggars would ride." Desire for something may be intense. It may be so strong as to override estimation of the consequences that will follow acting upon it. Such occurrences do not provide the model for education. The crucial educational problem is that of procuring the postponement of immediate action upon desire until observation and judgment have intervened. Unless I am mistaken, this point is definitely relevant to the conduct of progressive schools. Overemphasis upon activity as an end, instead of upon *intelligent* activity, leads to identification of freedom with immediate execution of impulses and desires. This identification is justified by a confusion of impulse with purpose; although, as has just been said, there is no purpose unless overt action is postponed until there is foresight of the consequences of carrying the impulse into execution—a foresight that is impossible without observation, information, and judgment. Mere foresight, even if it takes the form of accurate prediction, is not, of course, enough. The intellectual anticipation, the idea of consequences, must blend with desire and impulse to acquire moving force. It then gives direction to what otherwise is blind, while desire gives ideas impetus and momentum. An idea then becomes a plan in and for an activity to be carried out. Suppose a man has a desire to secure a new home, say by building a house. No matter how strong his desire, it cannot be directly executed. The man must form an idea of what kind of house he wants, including the number and arrangement of rooms, etc. He has to draw a plan, and have blue prints and specifications made. All this might be an idle amusement for spare time unless he also took stock of his resources. He must consider the relation of his funds and available credit to the execution of the plan. He has to investigate available sites, their price, their nearness to his place of business, to a congenial neighborhood, to school facilities, and so on and so on. All of the things reckoned with: his ability to pay, size and needs of family, possible locations, etc., etc., are objective facts. They are no part of the original desire. But they have to be viewed and judged in order that a desire may be converted into a purpose and a purpose into a plan of action.

All of us have desires, all at least who have not become so pathological that they are completely apathetic. These desires are the ultimate moving springs of action. A professional businessman wishes to succeed in his career; a general wishes to win the battle; a parent to have a comfortable home for his family, and to educate his children, and so on indefinitely. The intensity of the desire measures the strength of the efforts that will be put forth. But the wishes are empty castles in the air unless they are translated into the means by which they may be realized. The question of *how soon* or of means takes the place of a projected imaginative end, and, since means are objective, they have to be studied and understood if a genuine purpose is to be formed.

Traditional education tended to ignore the importance of personal impulse and desire as moving springs. But this is no reason why progressive education should identify impulse and desire with purpose and thereby pass lightly over the need for careful observation, for wide range of information, and for judgment if students are to share in the formation of the purposes which activate them. In an *educational* scheme, the occurrence of a desire and impulse is not the final end. It is an occasion and a demand for the formation of a plan and method of activity. Such a plan, to repeat, can be formed only by study of conditions and by securing all relevant information.

The teacher's business is to see that the occasion is taken advantage of. Since freedom resides in the operations of intelligent observation and judgment by which a purpose is developed, guidance given by the teacher to the exercise of the pupil's intelligence is an aid to freedom, not a restriction upon it. Sometimes teachers seem to be afraid even to make suggestions to the members of a group as to what they should do. I have heard of cases in which children are surrounded with objects and materials and then left entirely to themselves, the teacher being loath to suggest even what might be done with the materials lest freedom be infringed upon. Why, then, even supply materials, since they are a source of some suggestion or other? But what is more important is that the suggestion upon which pupils act must in any case come from somewhere. It is impossible to understand why a suggestion from one who has a larger experience and a wider horizon should not be at least as valid as a suggestion arising from some more or less accidental source.

It is possible of course to abuse the office, and to force the activity of the young into channels which express the teacher's purpose rather than that of the pupils. But the way to avoid this danger is not for the adult to withdraw entirely. The way is, first, for the teacher to be intelligently aware of the capacities, needs, and past experiences of those under instruction, and, secondly, to allow the suggestion made to develop into a plan and project by means of the further suggestions contributed and organized into a whole by the members of the group. The plan, in other words, is a cooperative enterprise, not a dictation. The teacher's suggestion is not a mold for a cast-iron result but is a starting point to be developed into a plan through contributions from the experience of all engaged in the learning process. The development occurs through reciprocal give-and-take, the teacher taking but not being afraid also to give. The essential point is that the purpose grow and take shape through the process of social intelligence.

7. PROGRESSIVE ORGANIZATION OF SUBJECT-MATTER

Allusion has been made in passing a number of times to objective conditions involved in experience and to their function in promoting or failing to promote the enriched growth of further experience. By implication, these objective conditions, whether those of observation, of memory, of information procured from others, or of imagination, have been identified with the subject-matter of study and learning; or, speaking more generally, with the stuff of the course of study. Nothing, however, has been said explicitly so far about subject-matter as such. That topic will now be discussed. One consideration stands out clearly when education is conceived in terms of experience. Anything which can be called a study, whether arithmetic, history, geography, or one of the natural sciences, must be derived from materials which at the outset fall within the scope of ordinary life-experience. In this respect the newer education contrasts sharply with procedures which start with facts and truths that are outside the range of the experience of those taught, and which, therefore, have the problem of discovering ways and means of bringing them within experience. Undoubtedly one chief cause for the great success of newer methods in early elementary education has been its observance of the contrary principle.

But finding the material for learning within experience is only the first step. The next step is the progressive development of what is already experienced into a fuller and richer and also more organized form, a form that gradually approximates that in which subject-matter is presented to the skilled, mature person. That this change is possible without departing from the organic connection of education with experience is shown by the fact that this change takes place outside of the school and apart from formal education. The infant, for example, begins with an environment of objects that is very restricted in space and time. That environment steadily expands by the momentum inherent in experience itself without aid from scholastic instruction. As the infant learns to reach, creep, walk, and talk, the intrinsic subject-matter of its experience widens and deepens. It comes into connection with new objects and events which call out new powers, while the exercise of these powers refines and enlarges the content of its experience. Life-space and life-durations are expanded. The environment, the world of experience, constantly grows larger and, so to speak, thicker. The educator who receives the child at the end of this period has to find ways for doing consciously and deliberately what "nature" accomplishes in the earlier years.

It is hardly necessary to insist upon the first of the two conditions which have been specified. It is a cardinal precept of the newer school of education that the beginning of instruction shall be made with the experience learners already have; that this experience and the capacities that have been developed during its course provide the starting point for all further learning. I am not so sure that the other condition, that of orderly development toward expansion and organization of subject-matter through growth of experience, receives as much attention. Yet the principle of continuity of educative experience requires that equal thought and attention be given to solution of this aspect of the educational problem. Undoubtedly this phase of the problem is more difficult than the other. Those who deal with the preschool child, with the kindergarten child, and with the boy and girl of the early primary years do not have much difficulty in determining the range of past experience or in finding activities that connect in vital ways with it. With older children both factors of the problem offer increased difficulties to the educator. It is harder to find out the background of the experience of individuals and harder to find out just how the subject-matters already contained in that experience shall be directed so as to lead out to larger and better organized fields.

It is a mistake to suppose that the principle of the leading on of experience to something different is adequately satisfied simply by giving pupils some new experiences any more than it is by seeing to it that they have greater skill and ease in dealing with things with which they are already familiar. It is also essential that the new objects and events be related intellectually to those of earlier experiences, and this means that there be some advance made in conscious articulation of facts and ideas. It thus becomes the office of the educator to select those things within the range of existing experience that have the promise and potentiality of presenting new problems which by stimulating new ways of observation and judgment will expand the area of further experience. He must constantly regard what is always won not as a fixed possession but as an agency and instrumentality for opening new fields which make new demands upon existing powers of observation and of intelligent use of memory. Connectedness in growth must be his constant watchword.

The educator more than the member of any other profession is concerned to have a long look ahead. The physician may feel his job done when he has restored a patient to health. He has undoubtedly the obligation of advising him how to live so as to avoid similar troubles in the future. But, after all, the conduct of his life is his own affair, not the physician's; and what is more important for the present point is that as far as the physician does occupy himself with instruction and advice as to the future of his patient he takes upon himself the function of an educator. The lawyer is occupied with winning a suit for his client or getting the latter out of some complication into which he has got himself. If it goes beyond the case presented to him he too becomes an educator. The educator by the very nature of his work is obliged to see his present work in terms of what it accomplishes, or fails to accomplish, for a future whose objects are linked with those of the present.

Here, again, the problem for the progressive educator is more difficult than for the teacher in the traditional school. The latter had indeed to look ahead. But unless his personality and enthusiasm took him beyond the limits that hedged in the traditional school, he could content himself with thinking of the next examination period or the promotion to the next class. He could envisage the future in terms of factors that lay within the requirements of the school system as that conventionally existed. There is incumbent upon the teacher who links education and actual experience together a more serious and a harder business. He must be aware of the potentialities for leading students into new fields which belong to experiences already had, and must use this knowledge as his criterion for selection and arrangement of the conditions that influence their present experience.

Because the studies of the traditional school consisted of subject-matter that was selected and arranged on the basis of the judgment of adults as to what would be useful for the young sometime in the future, the material to be learned was settled upon outside the present life-experience of the learner. In consequence, it had to do with the past; it was such as had proved useful to men in past ages. By reaction to an opposite extreme, as unfortunate as it was probably natural under the circumstances, the sound idea that education should derive its materials from present experience and should enable the learner to cope with the problems of the present and future has often been converted into the idea that progressive schools can to a very large extent ignore the past. If the present could be cut off from the past, this conclusion would be sound. But the achievements of the past provide the only means at command for understanding the present. Just as the individual has to draw in memory upon his own past to understand the conditions in which he individually finds himself, so the issues and problems of present *social* life are in such intimate and direct connection with the past that students cannot be prepared to understand either these problems or the best way of dealing with them without delving into their roots in the past. In other words, the sound principle that the objectives of learning are in the future and its immediate materials are in present experience can be carried into effect only in the degree that present experience is stretched, as it were, backward. It can expand into the future only as it is also enlarged to take in the past.

If time permitted, discussion of the political and economic issues which the present generation will be compelled to face in the future would render this general statement definite and concrete. The nature of the issues cannot be understood save as we know how they came about. The institutions and customs that exist in the present and that give rise to present social ills and dislocations did not arise overnight. They have a long history behind them. Attempt to deal with them simply on the basis of what is obvious in the present is bound to result in adoption of superficial measures which in the end will only render existing problems more acute and more difficult to solve. Policies framed simply upon the ground of knowledge of the present cut off from the past is the counterpart of heedless carelessness in individual conduct. The way out of scholastic systems that made the past an end in itself is to make acquaintance with the past a *means* of understanding the present. Until this problem is worked out, the present clash of educational ideas and practices will continue. On the one hand, there will be reactionaries that claim that the main, if not the sole, business of education is transmission of the cultural heritage. On the other hand, there will be those who hold that we should ignore the past and deal only with the present and future.

That up to the present time the weakest point in progressive schools is in the matter of selection and organization of intellectual subject-matter is, I think, inevitable under the circumstances. It is as inevitable as it is right and proper that they should break loose from the cut and dried material which formed the staple of the old education. In addition, the field of experience is very wide and it varies in its contents from place to place and from time to time. A single course of studies for all progressive schools is out of the question; it would mean abandoning the fundamental principle of connection with life-experiences. Moreover, progressive schools are new. They have had hardly more than a generation in which to develop. A certain amount of uncertainty and of laxity in choice and organization of subject-matter is, therefore, what was to be expected. It is no ground for fundamental criticism or complaint.

It is a ground for legitimate criticism, however, when the ongoing movement of progressive education fails to recognize that the problem of selection and organization of subject-matter for study and learning is fundamental. Improvisation that takes advantage of special occasions prevents teaching and learning from being stereotyped and dead. But the basic material of study cannot be picked up in a cursory manner. Occasions which are not and cannot be foreseen are bound to arise wherever there is intellectual freedom. They should be utilized. But there is a decided difference between using them in the development of a continuing line of activity and trusting to them to provide the chief material of learning.

Unless a given experience leads out into a field previously unfamiliar no problems arise, while problems are the stimulus to thinking. That the conditions found in present experience should be used as sources of problems is a characteristic which differentiates education based upon experience from traditional education. For in the latter, problems were set from outside. Nonetheless, growth depends upon the presence of difficulty to be overcome by the exercise of intelligence. Once more, it is part of the educator's responsibility to see equally to two things: First, that the problem grows out of the conditions of the experience being had in the present, and that it is within the range of the capacity of students; and, secondly, that it is such that it arouses in the learner an active quest for information and for production of new ideas. The new facts and new ideas thus obtained become the ground for further experiences in which new problems are presented. The process is a continuous spiral. The inescapable linkage of the present with the past is a principle whose application is not restricted to a study of history. Take natural science, for example. Contemporary social life is what it is in very large measure because of the results of application of physical science. The experience of every child and youth, in the country and the city, is what it is in its present actuality because of appliances which utilize electricity, heat, and chemical processes. A child does not eat a meal that does not involve in its preparation and assimilation chemical and physiological principles. He does not read by artificial light or take a ride in a motor car or on a train without coming into contact with operations and processes which science has engendered.

It is a sound educational principle that students should be introduced to scientific subject-matter and be initiated into its facts and laws through acquaintance with everyday social applications. Adherence to this method is not only the most direct avenue to understanding of science itself but as the pupils grow more mature it is also the surest road to the understanding of the economic and industrial problems of present society. For they are the products to a very large extent of the application of science in production and distribution of commodities and services, while the latter processes are the most important factor in determining the present relations of human beings and social groups to one another. It is absurd, then, to argue that processes similar to those studied in laboratories and institutes of research are not a part of the daily life-experience of the young and hence do not come within the scope of education based upon experience. That the immature cannot study scientific facts and principles in the way in which mature experts study them goes without saying. But this fact, instead of exempting the educator from responsibility for using present experiences so that learners may gradually be led, through extraction of facts and laws, to experience of a scientific order, sets one of his main problems.

For if it is true that existing experience in detail and also on a wide scale is what it is because of the application of science, first, to processes of production and distribution of goods and services, and then to the relations which human beings sustain socially to one another, it is impossible to obtain an understanding of present social forces (without which they cannot be mastered and directed) apart from an education which leads learners into knowledge of the very same facts and principles which in their final organization constitute the sciences. Nor does the importance of the principle that learners should be led to acquaintance with scientific subject-matter cease with the insight thereby given into present social issues. The methods of science also point the way to the measures and policies by means of which a better social order can be brought into existence. The applications of science which have produced in large measure the social conditions which now exist do not exhaust the possible field of their application. For so far science has been applied more or less casually and under the influence of ends, such as private advantage and power, which are a heritage from the institutions of a prescientific age.

We are told almost daily and from many sources that it is impossible for human beings to direct their common life intelligently. We are told, on one hand, that the complexity of human relations, domestic and international, and on the other hand, the fact that human beings are so largely creatures of emotion and habit, make impossible large-scale social planning and direction by intelligence. This view would be more credible if any systematic effort, beginning with early education and carried on through the continuous study and learning of the young, had ever been undertaken with a view to making the method of intelligence, exemplified in science, supreme in education. There is nothing in the inherent nature of habit that prevents intelligent method from becoming itself habitual; and there is nothing in the nature of emotion to prevent the development of intense emotional allegiance to the method.

The case of science is here employed as an illustration of progressive selection of subject-matter resident in present experience towards organization: an organization which is free, not externally imposed, because it is in accord with the growth of experience itself. The utilization of subject-matter found in the present life-experience of the learner towards science is perhaps the best illustration that can be found of the basic principle of using existing experience as the means of carrying learners on to a wider, more refined, and better organized environing world, physical and human, than is found in the experiences from which educative growth sets out. Hogben's recent work, *Mathematics for the Million*, shows how mathematics, if it is treated as a mirror of civilization and as a main agency in its progress, can contribute to the desired goal as surely as can the physical sciences. The underlying ideal in any case is that of progressive organization of knowledge. It is with reference to organization of knowledge that we are likely to find *Either-Or* philosophies most acutely active. In practice, if not in so many words, it is often held that since traditional education rested upon a conception of organization of knowledge that was almost completely contemptuous of living present experience, therefore education based upon living experience should be contemptuous of the organization of facts and ideas.

When a moment ago I called this organization an *ideal,* I meant, on the negative side, that the educator cannot start with knowledge already organized and proceed to ladle it out in doses. But as an ideal the active process of organizing facts and ideas is an ever-present educational process. No experience is educative that does not tend both to knowledge of more facts and entertaining of more ideas and to a better, a more orderly, arrangement of them. It is not true that organization is a principle foreign to experience. Otherwise experience would be so dispersive as to be chaotic. The experience of young children centres about persons and the home. Disturbance of the normal order of relationships in the family is now known by psychiatrists to be a fertile source of later mental and emotional troubles—a fact which testifies to the reality of this kind of organization. One of the great advances in early school education, in the kindergarten and early grades, is that it preserves the social and human centre of the organization of experience, instead of the older violent shift of the centre of gravity. But one of the outstanding problems of education, as of music, is modulation. In the case of education, modulation means movement from a social and human centre toward a more objective intellectual scheme of organization, always bearing in mind, however, that intellectual organization is not an end in itself but is the means by which social relations, distinctively human ties and bonds, may be understood and more intelligently ordered.

When education is based in theory and practice upon experience, it goes without saying that the organized subject-matter of the adult and the specialist cannot provide the starting point. Nevertheless, it represents the goal toward which education should continuously move. It is hardly necessary to say that one of the most fundamental principles of the scientific organization of knowledge is the principle of cause-and-effect. The way in which this principle is grasped and formulated by the scientific specialist is certainly very different from the way in which it can be approached in the experience of the young. But neither the relation nor grasp of its meaning is foreign to the experience of even the young child. When a child two or three years of age learns not to approach a flame too closely and yet to draw near enough a stove to get its warmth he is grasping and using the causal relation. There is no intelligent activity that does not conform to the requirements of the relation, and it is intelligent in the degree in which it is not only conformed to but consciously borne in mind.

In the earlier forms of experience the causal relation does not offer itself in the abstract but in the form of the relation of means employed to ends attained; of the relation of means and consequences. Growth in judgment and understanding is essentially growth in ability to form purposes and to select and arrange means for their realization. The most elementary experiences of the young are filled with cases of the means-consequence relation. There is not a meal cooked nor a source of illumination employed that does not exemplify this relation. The trouble with education is not the absence of situations in which the causal relation is exemplified in the relation of means and consequences. Failure to utilize the situations so as to lead the learner on to grasp the relation in the given cases of experience is, however, only too common. The logician gives the names "analysis and synthesis" to the operations by which means are selected and organized in relation to a purpose.

This principle determines the ultimate foundation for the utilization of *activities* in school. Nothing can be more absurd educationally than to make a plea for a variety of active occupations in the school while decrying the need for progressive organization of information and ideas. Intelligent activity is distinguished from aimless activity by the fact that it involves selection of means—analysis—out of the variety of conditions that are present, and their arrangement—synthesis—to reach an intended aim or purpose. That the more immature the learner is, the simpler must be the ends held in view and the more rudimentary the means employed, is obvious. But the principle of organization of activity in terms of some perception of the relation of consequences to means applies even with the very young. Otherwise an activity ceases to be educative because it is blind. With increased maturity, the problem of interrelation of means becomes more urgent. In the degree in which intelligent observation is transferred from the relation of means to ends to the more complex question of the relation of means to one another, the idea of cause and effect becomes prominent and explicit. The final justification of shops, kitchens, and so on in the school is not just that they afford opportunity for activity, but that they provide opportunity for the *kind* of activity or for the acquisition of mechanical skills which leads students to attend to the relation of means and ends, and then to consideration of the way things interact with one another to produce definite effects. It is the same in principle as the ground for laboratories in scientific research.

Unless the problem of intellectual organization can be worked out on the ground of experience, reaction is sure to occur toward externally imposed methods of organization. There are signs of this reaction already in evidence. We are told that our schools, old and new, are failing in the main task. They do not develop, it is said, the capacity for critical discrimination and the ability to reason. The ability to think is smothered, we are told, by accumulation of miscellaneous ill-digested information, and by the attempt to acquire forms of skill which will be immediately useful in the business and commercial world. We are told that these evils spring from the influence of science and from the magnification of present requirements at the expense of the tested cultural heritage from the past. It is argued that science and its methods must be subordinated; that we must return to the logic of ultimate first principles expressed in the logic of Aristotle and St. Thomas, in order that the young may have sure anchorage in their intellectual and moral life, and not be at the mercy of every passing breeze that blows.

If the method of science had ever been consistently and continuously applied throughout the day-by-day work of the school in all subjects, I should be more impressed by this emotional appeal than I am. I see at bottom but two alternatives between which education must choose if it is not to drift aimlessly. One of them is expressed by the attempt to induce educators to return to the intellectual methods and ideals that arose centuries before scientific method was developed. The appeal may be temporarily successful in a period when general insecurity, emotional and intellectual as well as economic, is rife. For under these conditions the desire to lean on fixed authority is active. Nevertheless, it is so out of touch with all the conditions of modern life that I believe it is folly to seek salvation in this direction. The other alternative is systematic utilization of scientific method as the pattern and ideal of intelligent exploration and exploitation of the potentialities inherent in experience.

The problem involved comes home with peculiar force to progressive schools. Failure to give constant attention to development of the intellectual content of experiences and to obtain ever-increasing organization of facts and ideas may in the end merely strengthen the tendency toward a reactionary return to intellectual and moral authoritarianism. The present is not the time nor place for a disquisition upon scientific method. But certain features of it are so closely connected with any educational scheme based upon experience that they should be noted.

In the first place, the experimental method of science attaches more importance, not less, to ideas as ideas than do other methods. There is no such thing as experiment in the scientific sense unless action is directed by some leading idea. The fact that the ideas employed are hypotheses, not final truths, is the reason why ideas are more jealously guarded and tested in science than anywhere else. The moment they are taken to be first truths in themselves there ceases to be any reason for scrupulous examination of them. As fixed truths they must be accepted and that is the end of the matter. But as hypotheses, they must be continuously tested and revised, a requirement that demands they be accurately formulated.

In the second place, ideas or hypotheses are tested by the consequences which they produce when they are acted upon. This fact means that the consequences of action must be carefully and discriminatingly observed. Activity that is not checked by observation of what follows from it may be temporarily enjoyed. But intellectually it leads nowhere. It does not provide knowledge about the situations in which action occurs nor does it lead to clarification and expansion of ideas.

In the third place, the method of intelligence manifested in the experimental method demands keeping track of ideas, activities, and observed consequences. Keeping track is a matter of reflective review and summarizing, in which there is both discrimination and record of the significant features of a developing experience. To reflect is to look back over what has been done so as to extract the net meanings which are the capital stock for intelligent dealing with further experiences. It is the heart of intellectual organization and of the disciplined mind.

I have been forced to speak in general and often abstract language. But what has been said is organically connected with the requirement that experiences in order to be educative must lead out into an expanding world of subject-matter, a subject-matter of facts or information and of ideas. This condition is satisfied only as the educator views teaching and learning as a continuous process of reconstruction of experience. This condition in turn can be satisfied only as the educator has a long look ahead, and views every present experience as a moving force in influencing what future experiences will be. I am aware that the emphasis I have placed upon scientific method may be misleading, for it may result only in calling up the special technique of laboratory research as that is conducted by specialists. But the meaning of the emphasis placed upon scientific method has little to do with specialized techniques. It means that scientific method is the only authentic means at our command for getting at the significance of our everyday experiences of the world in which we live. It means that scientific method provides a working pattern of the way in which and the conditions under which experiences are used to lead ever onward and outward. Adaptation of the method to individuals of various degrees of maturity is a problem for the educator, and the constant factors in the problem are the formation of ideas, acting upon ideas, observation of the conditions which result, and organization of facts and ideas for future use. Neither the ideas, nor the activities, nor the observations, nor the organization are the same for a person six years old as they are for one twelve or eighteen years old, to say nothing of the adult scientist. But at every level there is an expanding development of experience if experience is educative in effect. Consequently, whatever the level of experience, we have no choice but either to operate in accord with the pattern it provides or else to neglect the place of intelligence in the development and control of a living and moving experience.

8. EXPERIENCE—THE MEANS AND GOAL OF EDUCATION

In what I have said I have taken for granted the soundness of the principle that education in order to accomplish its ends both for the individual learner and for society must be based upon experience—which is always the actual life-experience of some individual. I have not argued for the acceptance of this principle nor attempted to justify it. Conservatives as well as radicals in education are profoundly discontented with the present educational situation taken as a whole. There is at least this much agreement among intelligent persons of both schools of educational thought. The educational system must move one way or another, either backward to the intellectual and moral standards of a pre-scientific age or forward to ever greater utilization of scientific method in the development of the possibilities of growing, expanding experience. I have but endeavored to point out some of the conditions which must be satisfactorily fulfilled if education takes the latter course.

For I am so confident of the potentialities of education when it is treated as intelligently directed development of the possibilities inherent in ordinary experience that I do not feel it necessary to criticize here the other route nor to advance arguments in favor of taking the route of experience. The only ground for anticipating failure in taking this path resides to my mind in the danger that experience and the experimental method will not be adequately conceived. There is no discipline in the world so severe as the discipline of experience subjected to the tests of intelligent development and direction. Hence the only ground I can see for even a temporary reaction against the standards, aims, and methods of the newer education is the failure of educators who professedly adopt them to be faithful to them in practice. As I have emphasized more than once, the road of the new education is not an easier one to follow than the old road but a more strenuous and difficult one. It will remain so until it has attained its majority and that attainment will require many years of serious cooperative work on the part of its adherents. The greatest danger that attends its future is, I believe, the idea that it is an easy way to follow, so easy that its course may be improvised, if not in an impromptu fashion, at least almost from day to day or from week to week. It is for this reason that instead of extolling its principles, I have confined myself to showing certain conditions which must be fulfilled if it is to have the successful career which by right belongs to it.

I have used frequently in what precedes the words "progressive" and "new" education. I do not wish to close, however, without recording my firm belief that the fundamental issue is not of new versus old education nor of progressive against traditional education but a question of what anything whatever must be to be worthy of the name *education*. I am not, I hope and believe, in favor of any ends or any methods simply because the name progressive may be applied to them. The basic question concerns the nature of education with no qualifying adjectives prefixed. What we want and need is education pure and simple, and we shall make surer and faster progress when we devote ourselves to finding out just what education is and what conditions have to be satisfied in order that education may be a reality and not a name or a slogan. It is for this reason alone that I have emphasized the need for a sound philosophy of experience.

PART II

Contemporary Issues

Contemporary thought in philosophy of education, much of it built on the work of the major educational philosophers from Plato to Dewey, involves a variety of subject matters and methodologies. Part II focuses on three areas of wide concern: schools, teaching, and curriculum. Each section includes readings that reflect a diversity of philosophical approaches.

The first section starts with A. S. Neill's skeptical challenge to traditional classroom structures, followed by Kieran Egan's rejoinder to the sort of program Neill espouses. Michael Walzer explores the role of schools within a society committed to egalitarian principles, and Amy Gutmann considers how different political systems imply different approaches to schooling. Her commitment to democracy and democratic education is shared by Israel Scheffler, who emphasizes the importance of a democracy's providing its citizens with an appropriate moral education.

The second section opens with Paul H. Hirst's analysis of the concept of teaching. The proper relationship between teacher and student is discussed from the perspectives of a traditional Christian thinker, Jacques Maritain; a Third World educator, Paulo Freire; and a feminist theorist, Nel Noddings. Understanding the moral development of children, a critical aspect of teaching them, is the focus of the selection by Gareth Matthews.

The third section begins with Sidney Hook's defense of a liberal arts curriculum. Jane Roland Martin weighs the principles that should guide curricular change, and Maxine Greene suggests how reforms in the curriculum should reflect our social heterogeneity. Richard Rorty develops some curricular implications of recent European thought, and John R. Searle assesses the strengths and weaknesses of opposing sides in the current curricular controversies of higher education. Theodore de Bary's concluding essay brings together many of the themes in this section by illustrating the ways in which thoughtful curricular development that takes account of a multiplicity of cultural traditions can help us to achieve appropriate educational goals.

A

Schools

9 Summerhill*

A. S. Neill

A. S. Neill (1883–1973) was an English educational reformer who founded Summerhill, a school based on the principle that students ought to be given the widest possible latitude in choosing their own ways of living and learning. Interest in such "open education," as it later became known, spread in the United States during the late 1960s.

THE IDEA OF SUMMERHILL

This is a story of a modern school—Summerhill.

Summerhill was founded in the year 1921. The school is situated within the village of Leiston, in Suffolk, England, and is about one hundred miles from London.

Just a word about Summerhill pupils. Some children come to Summerhill at the age of five years, and others as late as fifteen. The children generally remain at the school until they are sixteen years old. We generally have about twenty-five boys and twenty girls.

The children are divided into three age groups: The youngest range from five to seven, the intermediates from eight to ten, and the oldest from eleven to fifteen.

Generally we have a fairly large sprinkling of children from foreign countries. At the present time (1960) we have five Scandinavians, one Hollander, one German and one American.

The children are housed by age groups with a house mother for each group. The intermediates sleep in a stone building, the seniors sleep in huts. Only one or two older pupils have rooms for themselves. The boys live two or three or four to a room, and so do the girls. The pupils do not have to stand room inspection and no one picks up after them. They are left free. No one tells them what to wear: they put on any kind of costume they want to at any time.

Newspapers call it a *Go-as-you-please School* and imply that it is a gathering of wild primitives who know no law and have no manners.

It seems necessary, therefore, for me to write the story of Summerhill as honestly as I can. That I write with a bias is natural; yet I shall try to show the demerits of Summerhill as well as its merits. Its merits will be the merits of healthy, free children whose lives are unspoiled by fear and hate.

Obviously, a school that makes active children sit at desks studying mostly useless subjects is a bad school. It is a good school only for those who believe in *such* a school, for those uncreative citizens who want docile, uncreative children who will fit into a civilization whose standard of success is money.

---

*From *Summerhill* by permission of A. P. Watt Ltd. on behalf of Ena Neill and Zoe Readhead.

Summerhill began as an experimental school. It is no longer such; it is now a demonstration school, for it demonstrates that freedom works.

When my first wife and I began the school, we had one main idea: *to make the school fit the child*—instead of making the child fit the school.

I had taught in ordinary schools for many years. I knew the other way well. I knew it was all wrong. It was wrong because it was based on an adult conception of what a child should be and of how a child should learn. The other way dated from the days when psychology was still an unknown science.

Well, we set out to make a school in which we should allow children freedom to be themselves. In order to do this, we had to renounce all discipline, all direction, all suggestion, all moral training, all religious instruction. We have been called brave, but it did not require courage. All it required was what we had—a complete belief in the child as a good, not an evil, being. For almost forty years, this belief in the goodness of the child has never wavered; it rather has become a final faith.

My view is that a child is innately wise and realistic. If left to himself without adult suggestion of any kind, he will develop as far as he is capable of developing. Logically, Summerhill is a place in which people who have the innate ability and wish to be scholars will be scholars; while those who are only fit to sweep the streets will sweep the streets. But we have not produced a street cleaner so far. Nor do I write this snobbishly, for I would rather see a school produce a happy street cleaner than a neurotic scholar.

What is Summerhill like? Well, for one thing, lessons are optional. Children can go to them or stay away from them—for years if they want to. There *is* a timetable—but only for the teachers.

The children have classes usually according to their age, but sometimes according to their interests. We have no new methods of teaching, because we do not consider that teaching in itself matters very much. Whether a school has or has not a special method for teaching long division is of no significance, for long division is of no importance except to those who *want* to learn it. And the child who *wants* to learn long division *will* learn it no matter how it is taught.

Children who come to Summerhill as kindergarteners attend lessons from the beginning of their stay; but pupils from other schools vow that they will never attend any beastly lessons again at any time. They play and cycle and get in people's way, but they fight shy of lessons. This sometimes goes on for months. The recovery time is proportionate to the hatred their last school gave them. Our record case was a girl from a convent. She loafed for three years. The average period of recovery from lesson aversion is three months.

Strangers to this idea of freedom will be wondering what sort of madhouse it is where children play all day if they want to. Many an adult says, "If I had been sent to a school like that, I'd never have done a thing." Others say, "Such children will feel themselves heavily handicapped when they have to compete against children who have been made to learn."

I think of Jack who left us at the age of seventeen to go into an engineering factory. One day, the managing director sent for him.

"You are the lad from Summerhill," he said. "I'm curious to know how such an education appears to you now that you are mixing with lads from the old schools. Suppose you had to choose again, would you go to Eton or Summerhill?"

"Oh, Summerhill, of course," replied Jack.

"But what does it offer that the other schools don't offer?"

Jack scratched his head. "I dunno," he said slowly; "I think it gives you a feeling of complete self-confidence."

"Yes," said the manager dryly, "I noticed it when you came into the room."

"Lord," laughed Jack, "I'm sorry if I gave you that impression."

"I liked it," said the director. "Most men when I call them into the office fidget about and look uncomfortable. You came in as my equal. By the way, what department did you say you would like to transfer to?"

This story shows that learning in itself is not as important as personality and character. Jack failed in his university exams because he hated book learning. But his lack of knowledge about *Lamb's Essays* or the French language did not handicap him in life. He is now a successful engineer.

All the same, there is a lot of learning in Summerhill. Perhaps a group of our twelve-year-olds could not compete with a class of equal age in handwriting or spelling or fractions. But in an examination requiring originality, our lot would beat the others hollow.

We have no class examinations in the school, but sometimes I set an exam for fun. The following questions appeared in one such paper:

> Where are the following:—Madrid, Thursday Island, yesterday, love, democracy, hate, my pocket screwdriver (alas, there was no helpful answer to that one).

> Give meanings for the following: (the number shows how many are expected for each)—Hand (3) . . . only two got the third right—the standard of measure for a horse. Brass (4) . . . metal, cheek, top army officers, department of an orchestra. Translate Hamlet's To-be-or-not-to-be speech into Summerhillese.

These questions are obviously not intended to be serious, and the children enjoy them thoroughly. Newcomers, on the whole, do not rise to the answering standard of pupils who have become acclimatized to the school. Not that they have less brain power, but rather because they have become so accustomed to work in a serious groove that any light touch puzzles them.

This is the play side of our teaching. In all classes much work is done. If, for some reason, a teacher cannot take his class on the appointed day, there is usually much disappointment for the pupils.

David, aged nine, had to be isolated for whooping cough. He cried bitterly. "I'll miss Roger's lesson in geography," he protested. David had been in the school practically from birth, and he had definite and final ideas about the necessity of having his lessons given to him. David is now a lecturer in mathematics at London University.

A few years ago someone at a General School Meeting (at which all school rules are voted by the entire school, each pupil and each staff member having one vote) proposed that a certain culprit should be punished by being banished from lessons for a week. The other children protested on the ground that the punishment was too severe.

My staff and I have a hearty hatred of all examinations. To us, the university exams are anathema. But we cannot refuse to teach children the required subjects. Obviously, as long as the exams are in existence, they are our master. Hence, the Summerhill staff is always qualified to teach to the set standard.

Not that many children want to take these exams; only those going to the university do so. And such children do not seem to find it especially hard to tackle these exams. They generally begin to work for them seriously at the age of fourteen, and they do the work in about three years. Of course they don't always pass at the first try. The more important fact is that they try again.

Summerhill is possibly the happiest school in the world. We have no truants and seldom a case of homesickness. We very rarely have fights—quarrels, of course, but seldom have I seen a stand-up fight like the ones we used to have as boys. I seldom hear a child cry, because children when free have much less hate to express than children who are downtrodden. Hate breeds hate, and love breeds love. Love means approving of children, and that is essential in any school. You can't be on the side of children if you punish them and storm at them. Summerhill is a school in which the child knows that he is approved of.

Mind you, we are not above and beyond human foibles. I spent weeks planting potatoes one spring, and when I found eight plants pulled up in June, I made a big fuss. Yet there was a difference between my fuss and that of an authoritarian. My fuss was about potatoes, but the fuss an authoritarian would have made would have dragged in the question of morality—right and wrong. I did not say that it was wrong to steal my spuds; I did not make it a matter of good and evil—I made it a matter of *my spuds*. They were *my* spuds and they should have been left alone. I hope I am making the distinction clear.

Let me put it another way. To the children, I am no authority to be feared. I am their equal, and the row I kick up about my spuds has no more significance to them than the row a boy may kick up about his punctured bicycle tire. It is quite safe to have a row with a child when you are equals.

Now some will say: "That's all bunk. There can't be equality. Neill is the boss; he is bigger and wiser." That is indeed true. I am the boss, and if the house caught fire the children would run to me. They know that I am bigger and more knowledgeable, but that does not matter when I meet them on their own ground, the potato patch, so to speak.

When Billy, aged five, told me to get out of his birthday party because I hadn't been invited, I went at once without hesitation—just as Billy gets out of my room when I don't want his company. It is not easy to describe this relationship between teacher and child, but every visitor to Summerhill knows what I mean when I say that the relationship is ideal. One sees it in the attitude to the staff in general. Rudd, the chemistry man, is Derek. Other members of the staff are known as Harry, and Ulla, and Pam. I am Neill, and the cook is Esther.

In Summerhill, everyone has equal rights. No one is allowed to walk on my grand piano, and I am not allowed to borrow a boy's cycle without his permission. At a General School Meeting, the vote of a child of six counts for as much as my vote does.

But, says the knowing one, in practice of course the voices of the grownups count. Doesn't the child of six wait to see how you vote before he raises his hand? I wish he sometimes would, for too many of my proposals are beaten. Free children are not easily influenced; the absence of fear accounts for this phenomenon. Indeed, the absence of fear is the finest thing that can happen to a child.

Our children do not fear our staff. One of the school rules is that after ten o'clock at night there shall be quietness on the upper corridor. One night, about eleven, a pillow fight was going on, and I left my desk, where I was writing, to protest against the row. As I got upstairs, there was a scurrying of feet and the corridor was empty and quiet. Suddenly I heard a disappointed voice say, "Humph, it's only Neill," and the fun began again at once. When I explained that I was trying to write a book downstairs, they showed concern and at once agreed to chuck the noise. Their scurrying came from the suspicion that their bedtime officer (one of their own age) was on track.

I emphasize the importance of this absence of fear of adults. A child of nine will come and tell me he has broken a window with a ball. He tells me, because he isn't afraid of arousing wrath or moral indignation. He may have to pay for the window, but he doesn't have to fear being lectured or being punished.

There was a time some years back when the School Government resigned, and no one would stand for election. I seized the opportunity of putting up a notice: "In the absence of a government, I herewith declare myself Dictator. Heil Neill!" Soon there were mutterings. In the afternoon Vivien, aged six, came to me and said, "Neill, I've broken a window in the gym."

I waved him away. "Don't bother me with little things like that," I said, and he went.

A little later he came back and said he had broken two windows. By this time I was curious, and asked him what the great idea was.

"I don't like dictators," he said, "and I don't like going without my grub." (I discovered later that the opposition to dictatorship had tried to take itself out on the cook, who promptly shut up the kitchen and went home.)

"Well," I asked, "what are you going to do about it?"

"Break more windows," he said doggedly.

"Carry on," I said, and he carried on.

When he returned, he announced that he had broken seventeen windows. "But mind," he said earnestly, "I'm going to pay for them."

"How?"

"Out of my pocket money. How long will it take me?"

I did a rapid calculation. "About ten years," I said.

He looked glum for a minute; then I saw his face light up. "Gee," he cried, "I don't have to pay for them at all."

"But what about the private property rule?" I asked. "The windows are my private property."

"I know that but there isn't any private property rule now. There isn't any government, and the government makes the rules."

It may have been my expression that made him add, "But all the same I'll pay for them."

But he didn't have to pay for them. Lecturing in London shortly afterward, I told the story; and at the end of my talk, a young man came up and handed me a pound note "to pay for the young devil's windows." Two years later, Vivien was still telling people of his windows and of the man who paid for them. "He must have been a terrible fool, because he never even saw me."

Children make contact with strangers more easily when fear is unknown to them. English reserve is, at bottom, really fear; and that is why the most reserved are those who have the most wealth. The fact that Summerhill children are so exceptionally friendly to visitors and strangers is a source of pride to me and my staff.

We must confess, however, that many of our visitors are people of interest to the children. The kind of visitor most unwelcome to them is the teacher, especially the earnest teacher, who wants to see their drawing and written work. The most welcome visitor is the one who has good tales to tell—of adventure and travel or, best of all, of aviation. A boxer or a good tennis player is surrounded at once, but visitors who spout theory are left severely alone.

The most frequent remark that visitors make is that they cannot tell who is staff and who is pupil. It is true: the feeling of unity is that strong when children are approved of. There is no deference to a teacher as a teacher. Staff and pupils have the same food and have to obey the same community laws. The children would resent any special privileges given to the staff.

When I used to give the staff a talk on psychology every week, there was a muttering that it wasn't fair. I changed the plan and made the talks open to everyone over twelve. Every Tuesday night, my room is filled with eager youngsters who not only listen but give their opinions freely. Among the subjects the children have asked me to talk about have been these: The Inferiority Complex, The Psychology of Stealing, The Psychology of the Gangster, The Psychology of Humor, Why Did Man Become a Moralist?, Masturbation, Crowd Psychology. It is obvious that such children will go out into life with a broad clear knowledge of themselves and others.

The most frequent question asked by Summerhill visitors is, "Won't the child turn round and blame the school for not making him learn arithmetic or music?" The answer is that young Freddy Beethoven and young Tommy Einstein will refuse to be kept away from their respective spheres.

The function of the child is to live his own life—not the life that his anxious parents think he should live, nor a life according to the purpose of the educator who thinks he knows what is best. All this interference and guidance on the part of adults only produces a generation of robots.

You cannot *make* children learn music or anything else without to some degree converting them into will-less adults. You fashion them into accepters of the *status quo*—a good thing for a society that needs obedient sitters at dreary desks, standers in shops, mechanical catchers of the 8:30 suburban train—a society, in short, that is carried on the shabby shoulders of the scared little man—the scared-to-death conformist.

SUMMERHILL EDUCATION VS. STANDARD EDUCATION

I hold that the aim of life is to find happiness, which means to find interest. Education should be a preparation for life. Our culture has not been very successful. Our education, politics, and economics lead to war. Our medicines have not done away with disease. Our religion has not abolished usury and robbery. Our boasted humanitarianism still allows public opinion to approve of the barbaric sport of hunting. The advances of the age are advances in mechanism—in radio and television, in electronics, in jet planes. New world wars threaten, for the world's social conscience is still primitive.

If we feel like questioning today, we can pose a few awkward questions. Why does man seem to have many more diseases than animals have? Why does man hate and kill in war when animals do not? Why does cancer increase? Why are there so many suicides? So many insane sex crimes? Why the hate that is anti-Semitism? Why Negro hating and lynching? Why backbiting and spite? Why is sex obscene and a leering joke? Why is being a bastard a social disgrace? Why the continuance of religions that have long ago lost their love and hope and charity? Why, a thousand whys about our vaunted state of civilized eminence!

I ask these questions because I am by profession a teacher, one who deals with the young. I ask these questions because those so often asked by teachers are the unimportant ones, the ones about school subjects. I ask what earthly good can come out of discussions about French or ancient history or what not when these subjects don't matter a jot compared to the larger question of life's natural fulfillment—of man's inner happiness.

How much of our education is real doing, real self-expression? Handwork is too often the making of a pin tray under the eye of an expert. Even the Montessori system, well-known as a system of directed play, is an artificial way of making the child learn by doing. It has nothing creative about it.

In the home, the child is always being taught. In almost every home, there is always at least one ungrown-up grownup who rushes to show Tommy how his new engine works. There is always someone to lift the baby up on a chair when baby wants to examine something on the wall. Every time we show Tommy how his engine works we are stealing from that child the joy of life—the joy of discovery—the joy of overcoming an obstacle. Worse! We make that child come to believe that he is inferior, and must depend on help.

Parents are slow in realizing how unimportant the learning side of school is. Children, like adults, learn what they want to learn. All prize-giving and marks and exams sidetrack proper personality development. Only pedants claim that learning from books is education.

Books are the least important apparatus in a school. All that any child needs is the three R's; the rest should be tools and clay and sports and theater and paint and freedom.

Most of the school work that adolescents do is simply a waste of time, of energy, of patience. It robs youth of its right to play and play and play; it puts old heads on young shoulders.

When I lecture to students at teacher training colleges and universities, I am often shocked at the ungrownupness of these lads and lasses stuffed with useless knowledge. They know a lot; they shine in dialectics; they can quote the classics—but in their outlook on life many of them are infants. For they have been taught *to know,* but have not been allowed *to feel.* These students are friendly, pleasant, eager, but something is lacking—the emotional factor, the power to subordinate thinking to feeling. I talk to these of a world they have missed and go on missing. Their textbooks do not deal with human character, or with love, or with freedom, or with self-determination. And so the system goes on, aiming only at standards of book learning—goes on separating the head from the heart.

It is time that we were challenging the school's notion of work. It is taken for granted that every child should learn mathematics, history, geography, some science, a little art, and certainly literature. It is time we realized that the average young child is not much interested in any of these subjects.

I prove this with every new pupil. When told that the school is free, every new pupil cries, "Hurrah! You won't catch me doing dull arithmetic and things!"

I am not decrying learning. But learning should come after play. And learning should not be deliberately seasoned with play to make it palatable.

Learning is important—but not to everyone. Nijinsky could not pass his school exams in St. Petersburg, and he could not enter the State Ballet without passing those exams. He simply could not learn school subjects—his mind was elsewhere. They faked an exam for him, giving him the answers with the papers—so a biography says. What a loss to the world if Nijinsky had had to really pass those exams!

Creators learn what they want to learn in order to have the tools that their originality and genius demand. We do not know how much creation is killed in the classroom with its emphasis on learning.

I have seen a girl weep nightly over her geometry. Her mother wanted her to go to the university, but the girl's whole soul was artistic. I was delighted when I heard that she had failed her college entrance exams for the seventh time. Possibly, the mother would now allow her to go on the stage as she longed to do.

Some time ago, I met a girl of fourteen in Copenhagen who had spent three years in Summerhill and had spoken perfect English here. "I suppose you are at the top of your class in English," I said.

She grimaced ruefully. "No. I'm at the bottom of my class, because I don't know English grammar," she said. I think that disclosure is about the best commentary on what adults consider education.

Indifferent scholars who, under discipline, scrape through college or university and become unimaginative teachers, mediocre doctors, and incompetent lawyers would possibly be good mechanics or excellent bricklayers or first-rate policemen.

We have found that the boy who cannot or will not learn to read until he is, say, fifteen is always a boy with a mechanical bent who later on becomes a good engineer or electrician. I should not dare dogmatize about girls who never go to lessons, especially to mathematics and physics. Often such girls spend much time with needlework, and some, later on in life, take up dress-making and designing. It is an absurd curriculum that makes a prospective dressmaker study quadratic equations or Boyle's Law.

Caldwell Cook wrote a book called *The Play Way*, in which he told how he taught English by means of play. It was a fascinating book, full of good things, yet I think it was only a new way of bolstering the theory that learning is of the utmost importance. Cook held that learning was so important that the pill should be sugared with play. This notion that unless a child is learning something the child is wasting his time is nothing less than a curse—a curse that blinds thousands of teachers and most school inspectors. Fifty years ago the watchword was "Learn through doing." Today the watchword is "Learn through playing." Play is thus used only as a means to an end, but to what good end I do not really know.

If a teacher sees children playing with mud, and he thereupon improves the shining moment by holding forth about river-bank erosion, what end has he in view? What child cares about river erosion? Many so-called educators be-lieve that it does not matter what a child learns as long as he is *taught* some-thing. And, of course, with schools as they are—just mass-production facto-ries—what can a teacher do but teach something and come to believe that teaching, in itself, matters most of all?

When I lecture to a group of teachers, I commence by saying that I am not going to speak about school subjects or discipline or classes. For an hour my audience listens in rapt silence; and after the sincere applause, the chairman announces that I am ready to answer questions. At least three-quarters of the questions deal with subjects and teaching.

I do not tell this in any superior way. I tell it sadly to show how the class-room walls and the prisonlike buildings narrow the teacher's outlook, and pre-vent him from seeing the true essentials of education. His work deals with the part of a child that is above the neck; and perforce, the emotional, vital part of the child is foreign territory to him.

I wish I could see a bigger movement of rebellion among our younger teachers. Higher education and university degrees do not make a scrap of dif-ference in confronting the evils of society. A learned neurotic is not any differ-ent than an unlearned neurotic.

In all countries, capitalist, socialist, or communist, elaborate schools are built to educate the young. But all the wonderful labs and workshops do noth-ing to help John or Peter or Ivan surmount the emotional damage and the so-cial evils bred by the pressure on him from his parents, his schoolteachers, and the pressure of the coercive quality of our civilization.

10   Open Education: Open to What?*

Kieran Egan

The author is Professor of Education at Simon Fraser University. In this essay he assesses "open education," a concept, popularized in the 1960s, whose origins go back at least to Rousseau. What sorts of openness are involved and which educational purposes they serve are key questions at issue.

1

'Open education' suggests, by metaphorical extension, a removal of obstacles so that the benefits of education are available to everyone. We think of open doors; the barrier no longer hinders movement forwards, the things beyond are not hidden, and one may pass through easily and freely. In the case of education, openness is to those things that make the experience of being human as good and as rich as possible, so that all our children might have life and have it more abundantly.

Much of the literature on open education is best understood as a reaction to traditional forms of schooling, which are described as heavily academic, pre-packaged, sterile, the purveyors of a hallowed and ossified body of content being concerned with drip-feeding it to resisting children who see no value in it *per se* and no example of its enriching the lives of those who are purveying it. Open education is concerned to remove the obstacles which this bad kind of schooling has put in the way of children. Much of the literature on open education describes how these obstacles should be removed, and deals with a vast array of issues from loving children to the kinds of classroom furnishings that will best promote 'opening' the world to the child and the child to the world.

A general characterization of open education must include a family of variously related elements: individualization; freedom for children to explore; provision of rich environments for learning; children encouraged to plan their own activities; interdisciplinary inquiry; flexible scheduling; open areas; cooperative work; talking and play; children's interests determining activities; flexible groupings; non-didactic teacher—rather, a facilitator of learning; children encouraged to learn by experience.

Underlying these characteristics there is a pervading sense of optimism. Open education is optimistic, in the traditional sense, in its assessment of human nature, believing that children's curiosity will lead them naturally towards things of educational value, so that if each child's interests are allowed to determine his or her activities in school, they—better than any externally imposed scheme—will lead to the best education for that child. This optimism is also expressed in the belief that the benefits of education are not genetically restricted to an élite. The past restriction of the best educational benefits to an

---

*From *The Philosophy of Open Education*, 1975, by permission of Routledge and Kegan Paul.

élite is seen as due rather to its social privileges and the allotment of disproportionate resources to its educational advantage.

A further element underlying, and often surfacing in, open education literature is an almost chiliastic vision of change; a sense that the pace of change
is so fast, and accelerating, that traditional knowledge and training provide entirely insufficient tools for children to deal with the world in which they are
going to be adults.

These characteristics of open education account for its emphasis on procedural, formal, methodological concerns. Nothing in particular follows from
these characteristics about the *content* of an open school curriculum. There is
an overriding emphasis on process as against content. If open education is
seen as some kind of process, however, it makes sense to ask towards what it is
proceeding—open to what? More generally, what are the educational aims of
open education?

This is a difficult question to approach, because an important part of the
aim is the process itself. That is, the lives of children are not seen as simply instrumental—appropriately to be sacrificed to some final product—but as important in themselves here and now, and one central aim of open education is
to make the here and now of children in schools better. One result, then, is the
'humanizing' and civilizing of those schools that are influenced by open education. This represents a movement of considerable social importance, but as
an educational movement it is restricted almost exclusively to the *conditions* in
which education may take place. Similarly, the heavy emphasis on procedures
lacking specification of what body of skills and content should be mastered,
means that the results of the expressed ideals of open education are not so
much educated people, in the traditional sense, as people in whom the *conditions* for becoming educated are ideal.

Clearly, the assumption in open education is that each child will master a
body of skills and content and become, in the traditional sense, educated. But
what particular skills and content will be mastered, it is argued, are better determined by the individual child's interests and developing curiosity than by
criteria derived from values meaningful to an older generation brought up in a
world very different from that which the child will know.

But while the child's developing mind may provide the primary criteria
for appropriate activities, it clearly develops through a dialectical interaction
with the natural, social, and cultural worlds. Some criteria for educating must,
therefore, be derived from a sense of what it is best for children to learn in
order to encourage their individual development so that they will properly understand and appreciate those worlds. The following section, then, tries to
identify those aims of open education that are concerned not with the process
or conditions of educating but with the ideal product of that process.

2

References to the aims of open education in terms of some product tend to be
very general. Typically, there are statements about fulfilling the child's poten-

tial; producing people with highly developed thinking skills properly prepared for social participation and exploration of reality; harmoniously developing the whole person; self-actualization. If one searches for an explicit and precise description of the ideal product of open education, one will be disappointed. But this is not to say that open education programs lack clarity and precision. How is the content of these programs determined?

The elements identified in the previous section are, of course, important. Optimism that children's interests will determine what is of best educational value leads to creating a classroom environment that will encourage them to choose their activities for themselves. The chiliastic vision of change leads away from specifying content towards teaching *how* to think flexibly and productively. And perhaps even more influential is the clear image of what open education is reacting against: if there are rigid rows of desks, open up the room; if there is competition, let there be cooperation; if there is excessive emphasis on the cognitive, give attention to the affective.

These elements, however, do not reveal what content open education most values as aids to the developing child's mind. Either they refer to the conditions in which education takes place or they provide only negative principles. What are the positive principles that determine, for example, what particular things are to be made available for children to choose from? What education principles are implied by the range of experiences provided? Or, put more generally, how does open education distinguish an educational from any other kind of experience?

Again, it is difficult to find a clear answer. If anything, the question is rejected as a hangover from traditional, and improper, compartmentalizing of experience, or it is met with the response that *all* experiences are educational—whether walking in the woods, learning Greek, or living in a family. The open school curriculum, then, is open to expansion in all directions, encompassing the whole world and the whole range of human experience.

Such a response is clearly consistent with those elements of open education so far considered, yet it only serves to shift the focus of the same question, which becomes reformulated as: what criteria determine what experiences are educationally more valuable than others? (This is not to ask for a static list of activities, but rather for principles whereby, for example, the facilitative role of the teacher is to operate, or the limits of appropriate classroom activities are determined.)

Again, it is not possible to find such criteria clearly enunciated. Open education does not have any clear means of ranking kinds of experiences on some hierarchy of educational value. It rejects the idea that some kind of yardstick outside the individual child may be applied to assess the educational value of his experiences. The relative value of activities is seen almost entirely in terms of their relevance to the child's needs.

So the focus of the question must be adjusted again: how is the educational relevance of one experience distinguished from that of another? By reference to the needs of the developing child. And how is the relative importance of different needs determined? By reference to the empirical results of, say, Piaget and the sensitivity of the teacher. But Piaget tells us only about the structures of conceptual development, and gives few clues for determining the relative value of educational experiences except in the vaguest and most general sense. Being sensitive to the needs of children provides no principles to guide us in satisfying competing needs. (Also an important part of educating involves what may be called developing needs. That is, no one *needs* to be able to appreciate Beethoven's music, but we would usually consider it desirable that a need for such beauty be developed. Simple sensitivity to needs already present in the child provides no means for deciding which of the infinite variety of potential needs should be encouraged.)

Open education literature, then, avoids questions about criteria that could determine what things in the natural, social, and cultural worlds are more or less important for children to learn, and responsibility for answering such questions is placed on the child. The child's interests and needs are the overriding determiners of the educational value of experiences, activities, and learning.[1]

Given the theory of open education, it would be difficult to answer the question that Boswell asked Dr. Johnson when they were talking about education on Tuesday, July 26, 1763, in London. What, he wanted to know, was the best thing to teach children first? He was assuming a curriculum of content, composed of what one thinks it is important that children should learn about the world. A curriculum of content, in this traditional sense, could not be composed from principles derived from open education literature. This is entirely consistent with all the beliefs, assumptions, and arguments of open education. Internal consistency, however, while a necessary condition for a sensible educational theory, is far from a sufficient condition.

We may thus ask, despite its internal consistency, is open education educationally sensible? To answer this question we should consider some of the problems that arise for an educational movement which lacks effective criteria for determining the relative educational value of things in the world apart from the interests of children.[2]

3

Open education lacks or is weak in self-critical referents; it lacks clear means for judging its own success or failure as an educational movement. As the overriding principles are procedural, *whatever* happens when these procedures are operating has to be success. If the schooling process conforms to the ideals of openness, then *whatever* results is unassailable on educational grounds; because the concept of education has been reduced to applying those elements that we have considered above. Proponents of open education have an effective defense against criticism from outside, but must pay a heavy price for such security; they are defenseless against themselves and theoretically helpless when disagreements emerge among them.[3]

They are defenseless against themselves because their facilitating guidance is limited to that range of things that they have themselves found rewarding; they have no grounds on which to appeal beyond these to that wider tradition of what western man has found of persisting value. Ideally individual open school teachers have absorbed a range of these experiences, but they will be more or less limited. Thus, lacking the reasons traditional school teachers have for referring constantly, and often no doubt ineffectually, to a range of experiences beyond their own, open education teachers must close off educational possibilities for children and tend inevitably towards provincialism. Also, of course, no comparisons of educational effectiveness can be made between competing theories, because there are no results by which they can be compared that are more important than the process itself.

A further problem follows from the conclusion that open school programs derive their clarity largely from an image of what they are reacting against. The lack of criteria apart from children's needs and interests for deciding appropriate content means that open education tends both to be unduly influenced by traditional schooling practices and to confuse what it is reacting against with elements only contingently associated.

One of the characteristics of the traditional curriculum has been a body of knowledge that students are to be exposed to, regardless of their interest in it. Let us take, for example, knowledge about the Italian Renaissance. The stereotype of 'teaching the Renaissance' that open school teachers react against involves following a curriculum guide, having the students learn the names and dates of various artists, and showing perhaps some slides or posters of their work. No access is provided to the languages of Renaissance art and the teacher's passions are clearly unengaged by its products. It is taught because it is in the curriculum guide, and has always been considered 'important.'

Appreciation of the most sophisticated arts has, on the whole, been restricted to an élite few fortunate enough to have a disproportionate amount of time, energy, and talent expended on giving them access to these most refined products of the human mind. But fourteenth- and fifteenth-century Florence, we are told, is irrelevant to the needs of 'ghetto' children.[4] And, given that most open school teachers, like their traditional counterparts, also lack the kind of education that would enable them properly to read the languages of the Renaissance arts, Florence in its glory is irrelevant also to them. No enthusiasm on their part will persuade children that the effort of mastering the difficult access is worthwhile. Thus, the Renaissance will remain 'irrelevant to the needs' of nearly all children. The difference between the traditional school teacher and the open school teacher, in this case, is that the former will go through the largely vacuous motions anyway and the latter will instead do something perceived as more relevant to the children's needs.

The problem for open education, however, lies in the tendency to associate benefits enjoyed by a privileged class with the élitist class-system that provides those benefits. Thus, a movement which, in some of its rhetoric, asserts the aim of opening access to the best benefits of education to all children often, in practice, closes off those benefits because they are associated with a pernicious social system. The extreme of this, evident in a disturbing amount of open education literature, is anti-intellectualism, an acceptance of ignorance of the cultural world as part of an 'educational' program.

Traditional school teachers often face dilemmas due to conflicting criteria—their theory of an ideal product and their desire to engage the child's interests. For example, a teacher may believe, on good grounds, that children in the early years of primary school learn languages more easily than at any later period. The teacher may also believe it is desirable that adults should be able to read and appreciate Aeschylus and Ovid. To do this it is necessary to learn Greek and Latin. Acquiring facility in Greek and Latin is difficult, and certainly does not interest a typical seven-year-old child. Nor do Aeschylus or Ovid interest a seven-year-old child. The traditional school teacher faces a dilemma, generally stated as: certain desirable educational ends cannot be achieved without very difficult work that is largely meaningless at the time and involves much tedium, yet their achievement is well worth the effort. The open school teacher faces no such dilemma. Either her enthusiasm for Aeschylus and Greek is so infectious that the children become interested in learning the language, in which case Greek may be taught, or the children do not become interested in learning Greek, or lose interest in it after a while, in which case Greek and Aeschylus are irrelevant to the child's interests.

It is far from clear that a theoretical justification for avoiding such dilemmas is educationally desirable. The problem arises again from the lack of criteria for establishing the importance or relevance of anything apart from a student's interest in it. Aeschylus may seem a small loss to those who have never read him, but more generally if the interest elicited is the main criterion for the relevance of any activity, experiences will tend to be considered educationally valuable only to the degree that they are engaging. The exhilaration of a mountain sunrise is thus judged for educational value *vis-à-vis* a Greek grammar lesson on the grounds of their engagingness as experiences. In this way, the concept of education is opened up enormously and loses the relative precision it has had traditionally when it has been attached to a more or less clearly specified body of skills and content and kinds of activities.

Similarly, the concept of learning is expanded and generalized beyond the limits of traditional educational language. From relative restriction, it too has been enlarged to encompass all experience. It has become generalized towards whatever common thing is shared in 'learning' from a mountain sunrise and a Greek grammar lesson. It has expanded almost to mean 'remembering.' The lack of criteria drawn from an ideal product means that there is no defense against measuring education and learning in terms of those experiences that are the most engaging and memorable. As these experiences will have effects that will be evident in behavior, the quality of education now becomes measurable in terms of degrees of behavioral change. Thus an encounter session in which someone's basic values are undermined becomes necessarily a valuable educational experience.

While open education is dominated by well-meaning people, this opening up of educational concepts may seem useful for the expanded activity it permits in educational institutions. But it is well to be aware that it is based on a theory of education that lacks any significant defense against the techniques of religious conversion, the manipulation of immature emotions, ideologizing, and so on. If we open up concepts, it is good to be aware of the full range of what they are opened up to.

Above are just a couple of examples of the dangers that may follow from a theoretical structure in which educational aims are almost exclusively procedural. The philosopher's defense has been to point out that the needs and interests of children can be used as procedural criteria but not as *educational* criteria. Pointing this out, however, seems a trivial semantic shuffle in the face of a mass movement whose theoretical structure has altered the semantic rules and the meaning of the vocabulary elements.

I have considered some of the dangers inherent in a reactionary educational movement that effectively lacks criteria of educational value derived from a sense of what things in the world are more and less important for children to learn, regardless of their immediate interests. I have so far concentrated on ideas that lead to differences from traditional schooling. Finally I want to consider what I think is the most powerful motivator of the open education movement, and these ideas it shares with what it is reacting against.

4

The stereotype of traditional education that open education literature presents, while to some degree a bogeyman created by the myth of oppression, only too truly reflects a substantial proportion of current teaching. According to the stereotype, traditional teachers derive their guiding principles exclusively from their image of an ideal product, which is some centuries out of date, and entirely ignore the present child's interests and natural development. This is almost too kind. There is no such guiding light for these traditional teachers who, at the best, see their ideal product in terms of a profession or job or, amorphously, as a 'useful member of society.' In other words, no image of an ideal *educated* person provides criteria for activities in such traditional classrooms. Such an ideal might once have been implicit in designing the curriculum that is still more or less followed, but it has long since decayed. These conservative teachers are now guided by unquestioned custom. They perform reflex genuflections before a set of names, dates, and ideas that do not significantly enliven their own lives but which they vaguely believe will enable students to be decent and useful citizens. The stereotypical traditional education, then, quite as much as open education lacks a living vision of an educational product to guide practice.

Given this, I want to argue that the *educational* differences between open education and its conservative counterpart are trivial. Why, then, the virulence of the debate? Because their concerns have moved from educational questions to ideological ones. Sensitivity in the debate is directed increasingly towards ideological nuances and is less and less able to handle educational issues. Some of the major manifestos of open education explicitly state their political purpose to use schools to effect specific social changes. This, of course, is nothing new—what is new is the vacuum of *educational* thought in which the protagonists argue about the function and role of educational institutions and the education of children.

Clearly, we have failed to find the non-procedural educational criteria that determine the content both of open school curricula and that of their conservative counterparts because these criteria are ideological. Neither one has an image of an educated person as a product; both take an ideological position and aim primarily to produce people dedicated to specific social and political ends.

Dr. Johnson's response to Boswell on that July morning was:[5]

> there is no matter what you teach them first, any more than what leg you shall put in your breeches first. Sir, you may stand disputing which is best to put in first, but in the meantime your backside is bare. Sir, while you stand considering which of two things you should teach your child first, another boy has learnt 'em both.

It is only too obvious at present that while the ideological dispute about schools and their uses continues, our educational backside is bare indeed. And, as the overriding criteria for both open education and its conservative counterpart are drawn from other than educational aims, it seems appropriate to conclude that neither should properly be considered an educational movement.[6]

While the move towards ideology might account for the virulence of much current 'educational' debate, however, it does not account for the success of open education as a mass movement. The reason for this, I think, is not because it reacts against conservative and ossified schooling but because it goes a crucial step further in the same direction. The move towards ideology is simply the other face of the move away from considering content in education. Open education's present dynamism may derive from its having taken the radical step of providing a rationale, however thin, for not having to take responsibility for curriculum content at all.

This retreat from content has been progressing at an increasing rate through the last half century, particularly, and most rapidly, in North America. It is clearly a response to very general cultural and social developments. It is too simple just to call it a failure of nerve, but that takes us towards it. Involvement in devastating wars and the complexity of social change seem to have stunned that sense of confidence that is the foundation of a civilization, giving strength to its two great enemies, fear and ignorance.

Johnson was unafraid to specify that children should learn and the order in which they should learn things, but people in recent decades have become increasingly afraid. Just as we are what we eat, we are also what we know. The recent failure of nerve consists in not daring to specify what knowledge is important. The rationale for not daring is the rapid rate of change, but this is a weak excuse except for those who are eager to avoid the hard and persisting questions of education.

Facing these questions constantly—for instance, *what* and *how* should we teach children for the best?—and reassessing our responses in the light of changing circumstances is a necessary part of a theory of education. If open education claims to be a movement of any educational significance it will have to face the question of content in a way that it has so far shirked in favor of easy ideologizing.

Our education system is designed to initiate children into western civilization and its intellectual adventure. Central to this civilization, as the word suggests, is civility, and harmony in the development of mind and body. Teachers who are ignorant of western civilization and the nature of its intellectual adventure are in a weak position for initiating children. They are, among other things, prey to any mindless Utopian fad and accompanying jargon that comes near them. Their ignorance of the western tradition prevents them from understanding why it is of value and so they communicate no sense of its value in their teaching. Students, consequently, suffer from being ideologized, not educated. Much student frustration and alienation seems to stem from ignorance about a world they cannot control or affect because they know next to nothing about how it got this way or what it is all about. Like the 'facilitators' who ideologized them, they know all the answers without having understood the questions.

Notes

1. Each individual teacher does, more or less informally, apply such criteria in distinguishing between experiences and activities. Children's search for subtle cues as to how they should behave means that the facilitative role of the open school teacher provides very clear and compelling guidance. My concern here, however, is with the explicit theory of open education and the guidance it offers for practice.
2. Certain 'relevant' things, like reading, writing, learning about communities, etc., are prescribed presumably because of the unlikelihood of an illiterate child entirely ignorant about the world surviving easily and being happy in society. But my concern is with how 'relevance' is determined for rather less basic content as well.
3. This problem has proved fatal to many 'free schools.' In those cases the overriding value was 'freedom,' and the concept of education tended to become reduced to whatever happened when students were given certain 'freedoms.' Because there were thus no grounds on which to measure success or failure apart from the degree or kinds of freedoms provided, the inescapable failures of some of the 'free schools'—*felt* by everyone connected with them—were not open to discussion or correction on rational grounds. Personal vituperation or escape were the only recourses available to staff and students alike, with the consequent collapse of the institutions.
4. I mention 'ghetto' children, firstly because such a statement seems self-evident to most proponents of open education, and secondly because much of the dynamic of the open education movement has come from the heroic and inspiring work a number of teachers have done in revising curricula to make schooling in some way sensible to some of these children in extremely poor social conditions. The appropriateness of this work for ghetto children has been extended by argument to schools and situations in which it seems not at all appropriate. The sense of relevance has been preserved by abuses of language that assert similarities (for example, 'students are niggers') and the acceptance of an oppressors/oppressed myth that obscures far more than it clarifies, but does allow many middle-class teachers

to adopt the role of the oppressed and thus relinquish responsibility for a range of educational decisions.

5. *Boswell's London Journal, 1762–1763,* ed. Frederick A. Pottle, McGraw-Hill, 1950, p. 323. Interpreting this in the light of Bruner's assertion that one can teach anything to a child at any age in some intellectually honest way, it seems unobjectionable.

6. This is not to say that social or political concerns might not be more important than educational ones. It is to say that we are not in a situation where desirable social ends and education are incompatible, and so educational institutions should operate with educational principles as overriding.

11   Spheres of Justice*

Michael Walzer

The author is Professor of Social Science at the Institute for Advanced Study in Princeton, New Jersey. In this chapter he explores how a democracy's commitment to equality should be exemplified in its system of schooling. Among the controversial issues he explores are educational vouchers, talent tracking, and school busing.

THE IMPORTANCE OF SCHOOLS

Every human society educates its children, its new and future members. Education expresses what is, perhaps, our deepest wish: to continue, to go on, to persist in the face of time. It is a program for social survival. And so it is always relative to the society for which it is designed. The purpose of education, according to Aristotle, is to reproduce in each generation the "type of character" that will sustain the constitution: a particular character for a particular constitution.[1] But there are difficulties here. The members of society are unlikely to agree about what the constitution, in Aristotle's broad sense, actually is, or what it is becoming, or what it should be. Nor are they likely to agree about what character type will best sustain it or how that type might best be produced. In fact, the constitution will probably require more than one character type; the schools will not only have to train their students, they will also have to sort them out; and that is bound to be a controversial business.

Education is not, then, merely relative—or, its relativity doesn't tell us all we need to know about either its normative function or its actual effects. If it were true that the schools aways served to reproduce society as it is—the established hierarchies, the prevailing ideologies, the existing workforce—and did nothing more, it would make no sense to talk about a just distribution of educational goods. Distribution here would parallel distribution elsewhere; there would be no independent sphere and no internal logic. Something like this may well be true when there are no schools—when parents educate their own children or apprentice them in their future trades. Then social reproduction is direct and unmediated; the sorting-out process is carried on within the family with no need for communal intervention; and there exists no body of knowledge or intellectual discipline distinct from family chronicles and trade mysteries in terms of which the constitution can be interpreted, evaluated, argued about. But schools, teachers, and ideas create and fill an intermediate space. They provide a context, not the only one, but by far the most important one, for the development of critical understanding and for the production, as well as the reproduction, of social critics. This is a fact of life in all complex societies; even Marxist professors acknowledge (and conservative statements worry about) the relative autonomy of the schools.[2] But social criticism is the result of autonomy and doesn't help to explain it. What is most important is that schools, teachers, and ideas constitute a new set of social goods, conceived independently of other goods, and requiring, in turn, an independent set of distributive processes.

Teaching positions, student places, authority in the schools, grades and promotions, different sorts and levels of knowledge—all these have to be distributed, and the distributive patterns cannot simply mirror the patterns of the economy and the political order, because the goods in question are different goods. Of course, education is always supportive of some particular form of adult life, and the appeal from school to society, from a conception of educational justice to a conception of social justice, is always legitimate. But in making this appeal, we must also attend to the special character of the school, the teacher-student relationship, intellectual discipline generally. Relative autonomy is a function of what the educational process is and of the social goods that it involves as soon as it ceases to be direct and unmediated.

I want to stress the verb of being: what the educational process *is*. Justice has to do not only with the effects but also with the experience of education. The schools fill an intermediate space between family and society, and they also fill an intermediate time between infancy and adulthood. This is, no doubt, a space and a time for training and preparation, rehearsals, initiation ceremonies, "commencements," and so on; but the two also constitute a here-and-now that has its own importance. Education distributes to individuals not only their futures but their presents as well. Whenever there is space and time enough for such distributions, the educational process takes on a characteristic normative structure. I don't mean to describe anything like its "essence"; I simply want to suggest the most common conception of what it should be like. This is a conception that one finds in many different societies and the only one with which I shall be concerned. The adult world is represented, and its knowledge, traditions, and rituals are interpreted, by a corps of teachers who confront their students in a more or less enclosed community—what John

Dewey called a "special social environment."[3] The students are granted a partial moratorium from the demands of society and economy. The teachers, too, are protected from the immediate forms of external pressure. They teach the truths they understand, and the same truths, to all the students in front of them, and respond to questions as best they can, without regard to the students' social origins.

That's not, I suppose, the way things always, or even usually, work in practice. It is all too easy to provide a list of tyrannical intrusions on the educational community, to describe the precariousness of academic freedom, the dependence of teachers on patrons and officials, the privileges that upper-class students routinely command, and all the expectations, prejudices, habits of deference and authority that students and teachers alike carry with them into the schoolroom. But I shall assume the reality of the norm, for the most interesting and the hardest distributive questions arise only after that assumption has been made. Which children is it who are admitted into the enclosed communities? Who goes to school? And to what sort of school? (What is the strength of the enclosure?) To study what? For how long? With what other students?

I'm not going to say much about the distribution of teaching positions. Teaching is commonly conceived as an office, and so it is necessary to look for qualified people and to open to all citizens an equal chance to qualify. And teaching is a particular office; it calls for particular qualifications, whose precise character has to be debated by town councils, governing boards, and search committees. I should stress, however, that my general assumption—that schools constitute a special environment and have a certain normative structure—militates against the practice of leaving education to the old men and women of the larger community or rotating ordinary citizens through the faculties.[4] For all such practices undercut the mediating character of the educational process and tend to reproduce the more direct "passing on" of folk memories, traditions, and skills. Strictly speaking, the existence of schools is tied up with the existence of intellectual disciplines and so of a corps of men and women qualified in those disciplines.

The Aztec "House of the Young Men"

Consider for a moment—it is an exotic but not atypical example—the educational system of the Aztec Indians. In ancient Mexico, there were two sorts of school. One was called simply the "house of the young men" and was attended by the mass of male children. It offered instruction in "the bearing of arms, arts and crafts, history and tradition, and ordinary religious observance"; and it seems to have been presided over by ordinary citizens, chosen from among the more experienced warriors, who "carried on in special quarters instruction given in a simpler day by the old men of the clan."[5] A very different sort of education was provided for the children of the élite (and for some selected children of plebian families)—more austere, more rigorous, and more intellectual, too. In special schools attached to monasteries and temples, "all the knowledge of time and the country was taught: reading and writing in the pictographic characters, divination, chronology, poetry, and rhetoric." Now the teachers came from the priestly class, "chosen without any regard to their family, but only to their morals, their practices, their knowledge of doctrine and the purity of their lives."[6] We don't know how the children were chosen; in principle, at least, similar qualities were probably required, for it was from these schools that the priests themselves came. Though an élite education demanded sacrifice and self-discipline, it seems likely that school places were eagerly sought, particularly by ambitious plebes. In any case, I assume the existence of schools of this second kind; without them, distributive questions hardly arise.

One could argue that the "house of the young men" was also an intermediate institution. Aztec girls, unless they were trained as priestesses, mostly stayed at home and learned the womanly arts from the old women of the family. But these are two examples of the same thing: social reproduction in its direct form. The girls would henceforth remain at home, while the boys would band together to fight endless wars with neighboring cities and tribes. Nor would the selection of a few old women to teach the traditional folkways in a "house of the young women" have constituted an autonomous educational process. For that we must have teachers trained and tested in the "knowledge of doctrine." Assume now that there are such teachers. Whom should they teach?

BASIC SCHOOLING: AUTONOMY AND EQUALITY

The mass of children can be divided, for purposes of education, in a number of ways. The simplest and most common division, of which most educational programs well into modern times have been nothing but variations, has this form: mediated education for the few, direct education for the many. This is the way men and women in their conventional roles—rulers and ruled, priests and laymen, upper classes and plebeian classes—have historically been distinguished. And, I suppose, reproduced, though it is important to say again that mediated education is always likely to turn out skeptics and adventurers alongside its more standard products. In any case, schools have mostly been élite institutions, dominated by birth and blood, or wealth, or gender, or hierarchical rank, and dominating in turn, over religious and political office. But this fact has little to do with their internal character; and, indeed, there is no easy way of enforcing the necessary distinctions from within the educational community. Here, let's say, is a body of doctrine having to do with government. To whom should it be taught? The established rulers claim the doctrine for themselves and their children. But unless children are naturally divided into rulers and ruled, it would seem, from the standpoint of the teachers, that the doctrine should be taught to anyone who presents himself and is capable of learning it. "If there were one class in the state," wrote Aristotle, "surpassing all others as much as gods and heroes are supposed to surpass mankind," then the teachers might plausibly direct their attention to that class alone. "But that is a difficult assumption to make, and we have nothing in actual life like the gulf between kings and subjects which the writer Scylax describes as existing in India."[7] Except in Scylax's India, then, no children can rightly be excluded from the enclosed community where the doctrine of government is taught. The same thing is true of other doctrines; nor does it require a philosopher to understand this.

Hillel on the Roof

An old Jewish folktale describes the great Talmudic sage as an impoverished young man who wanted to study at one of the Jerusalem academies. He earned money by chopping wood, but barely enough money to keep himself alive, let alone pay the admission fees for the lectures. One cold winter night, when he had no money at all, Hillel climbed to the roof of the school building and listened through the skylight. Exhausted, he fell asleep and was soon covered with snow. The next morning, the assembled scholars saw the sleeping figure blocking the light. When they realized what he had been doing, they immediately admitted him to the academy, waiving the fees. It didn't matter that he was ill dressed, pennyless, a recent immigrant from Babylonia, his family unknown. He was so obviously a student.[8]

The story depends for its force upon a set of assumptions about how schooling should be distributed. It is not a complete set; one couldn't derive an educational system from this sort of folk wisdom. But here is an understanding of the community of teachers and students that has no place for social distinctions. If the teachers see a likely student, they take him. At least, that is the way legendary, and therefore ideal, teachers behave; they ask none of the conventional questions about wealth and status. One could almost certainly find legends, and actual biographies, similar to the Hillel story in other cultures. Many Chinese officials, for example, began their careers as poor farm boys taken in by a village teacher.[9] Is that the way teachers were supposed to behave? I don't know the answer in the case of China, but we are still inclined today, I think, to accept the moral of the Hillel story. "To serve educational needs, without regard to the vulgar irrelevancies of class and income," wrote R. H. Tawney, "is a part of the teacher's honor."[10] When schools are exclusive, it is because they have been captured by a social élite, not because they are schools.

But it is only the democratic state (or church or synagogue) that insists upon *inclusive* schools, where future citizens can be prepared for political (or religious) life. Now distribution is determined by what the school is for and not simply by what it is, by the social meaning of war or work or worship—or of citizenship, which commonly includes all of these. I don't mean that democracy requires democratic schools; Athens got along well enough without them. But if there is a body of knowledge that citizens must grasp, or think they must grasp, so as to play their parts, then they have to go to school; and then all of them have to go to school. Thus Aristotle, in opposition to the practices of his own city: "the system of education in a state must . . . be one and the same for all, and the provision of this system must be a matter of public action."[11] This is a simple equality in the sphere of education; and while simplicity is soon lost—for no educational system can ever be "the same for all"—it nevertheless fixes the policies of the democratic school. The simple equality of students is relative to the simple equality of citizens: one person/one vote, one child/one place in the educational system. We can think of educational equality as a form of welfare provision, where all children, conceived as future citizens, have the same need to know, and where the ideal of membership is best served if they are all taught the same things. Their education cannot be allowed to hang on the social standing or the economic capacity of their parents. (It remains a question whether it should hang on the moral and political convictions of their parents, for democratic citizens may well disagree about what their children need to know; I shall come back to this point.)

Simple equality is connected to need: all future citizens need an education. Seen from within the school, of course, need is by no means the sole criterion for the distribution of knowledge. Interest and capacity are at least as important—as the Hillel story suggests. Indeed, the teacher-student relationship seems to rest, above all, on these latter two. Teachers look for students, students look for teachers, who share their interests; and then they work together until the students have learned what they wanted to know or have gone as far as they can. Nevertheless, democratic need is by no means a political imposition on the schools. Advocates of democracy rightly claim that all children have an interest in the government of the state and a capacity to understand it. They meet the crucial requirements. But it is also true that children don't take an interest to the same degree, and that they don't have the same capacity to understand. Hence, as soon as they are inside the school, they can hardly help but begin to distinguish themselves.

How a school responds to these distinctions depends very much on its purposes and its curriculum. If the teachers are committed to the basic disciplines necessary for democratic politics, they will try to establish a shared knowledge among their students and to raise them to something like the same level. The aim is not to repress differences but rather to postpone them, so that children learn to be citizens first—workers, managers, merchants, and professionals only afterward. Everyone studies the subjects that citizens need to know. Schooling ceases to be the monopoly of the few; it no longer automatically commands rank and office.[12] For there is no privileged access to citizenship, no way of getting more of it, or getting it faster, by doing better at school. Schooling guarantees nothing and exchanges for very little, but it provides the common currency of political and social life. Isn't this a plausible account at least of basic education? Teaching children to read is, after all, an egalitarian business, even if teaching literary criticism (say) is not. The goal of the reading teacher is not to provide equal chances but to achieve equal results. Like the democratic theorist, he assumes that all his students have an interest and are able to learn. He doesn't try to make it equally possible for students to read; he tries to engage them in reading and *teach them to read*. Perhaps they should have equal chances to become literary critics, to hold professorships, publish articles, attack other people's books, but reading they should have simply; they should be readers (even if reading buys no privileges). Here the democratic commitment of the larger community is not so much reflected as matched and enhanced by the democratic practice of the school, once children are in school.

The Japanese Example

The match is all the more likely under contemporary conditions, the more autonomous a school is within the larger community. For the pressure to enlarge upon the natural distinctions that already exist among the students, to search out and mark off the future leaders of the country, comes almost entirely from the outside. In a valuable study of the development of educational equality in Japan in the years since the Second World War, William Cummings has argued that schools can provide a genuinely common education only if they are protected from corporate and governmental intrusion. Conversely, if they are protected, schools are likely to have egalitarian effects even in a capitalistic society.[13] Assume, as I have been doing, the existence of more or less enclosed educational communities, and a certain sort of equality follows for every group of students face to face with a teacher. Add to this that every child goes to school, that there is a common curriculum, and that the enclosure is strong, and then the sphere of education is likely to be a highly egalitarian place.

But only for the students: students and teachers are not equals; indeed, the authority of teachers is necessary to the equality of students. The teachers are the guardians of the enclosure. In the Japanese case, Cummings argues, the crucial condition of educational equality has been the relative strength of the teachers' union.[14] It is, to be sure, a special feature of the case that this is a socialist union. But then, socialists, or people calling themselves socialists, have produced very different kinds of school. What has made for equality in Japan is that the union has been led by its ideology to resist the (inegalitarian) pressures of government officials, pressed themselves by the élite of corporate managers. The schools have been shaped less by socialist theory than by the natural results of that resistance—that is, the day-to-day practice of autonomy. Here are independent teachers, a body of knowledge, and students who need to know. What follows? I will quote and comment upon some of Cumming's conclusions.

1. "The schools are organically organized with a minimum of internal differentiation. . . . At the primary level there are no specialty teachers, and ability tracking is not practiced."[15] This simply enacts Aristotle's maxim for democratic schools: "Training for an end which is common should also itself be common."[16] Internal differentiation in the early grades is a sign of a weak school (or of teachers uncertain of their vocation), surrendering to the tyranny of race or class.
2. Teachers "try to bring all the students up [to a common standard] by creating a positive situation in which all [of them] receive rewards . . . by adjusting the classroom pace to the learning rates of students, and by relying on students to tutor each other."[17] It can't be said that the brighter children are held back by such procedures. Student-teaching is a form of recogni-

tion; and it is also a learning experience for the "teacher" as well as the student, an experience of real value for democratic politics. *Learn, then teach* is the practice of a strong school, capable of enlisting students in its central enterprise. The effect is to "minimize the incidence of exceptionally low achievers."

3. "The . . . curriculum is demanding, geared to the learning rate of the better-than-average student."[18] Another sign of strong schools and ambitious teachers. It is often said that the decision to educate everyone necessarily leads to a lowering of standards. But this is true only if the schools are weak, incapable of resisting the pressures of a hierarchical society. I include among these pressures not only the demands of business leaders for minimally educated and contented workers but also the apathy and indifference of many parents trapped at the lower levels of the hierarchy—and the arrogance of many other parents established at the upper levels. These groups, too, are socially reproductive, and democratic education is likely to succeed only insofar as it draws their children into its own enclosure. It may be an important feature of the Japanese case, then, that "students spend far more hours at school than do their counterparts in most other advanced societies."

4. "The relative equality of cognitive performance moderates the propensity of children to rank each other. . . . Instead, the children are disposed to see themselves as working together to master the curriculum."[19] This disposition may be further enhanced by the fact that all students—and teachers, too—share in the cleaning and repair of the school. There are virtually no maintenance personnel in Japanese schools: the educational community is self-contained, consisting only of teachers and students. "The maintenance of the school is everyone's responsibility."[20] The shared learning and the shared working point alike to a world of citizens rather than to a division of labor. And so they discourage the comparisons that the division of labor, at least in its conventional forms, endlessly provokes.

I have omitted various complicating features of Cummings's analysis that are not immediately relevant here. My purpose has been to suggest the effects of normative schooling under democratic conditions. These effects can be summed up very simply. Everyone is taught the basic knowledge necessary for an active citizenship, and the great majority of students learn it. The experience of learning is itself democratic, bring its own rewards of mutuality and camaraderie as well as of individual achievement. It is possible, of course, to gather children into schools for the sole purpose of not educating them there or of teaching them nothing more than a bare literacy. Then education, by the default of the schools, is in effect unmediated and is carried on in the family or on the streets; or it is mediated by television, the movies, and the music industry, and the schools are nothing but a (literal) holding operation until children are old enough to work. Schools of this sort may well have walls to keep the children in, but they have no walls to keep society and economy out. They are hollow buildings, not centers of autonomous learning; and then some alternative is necessary to train, not the citizens, but the managers and professionals of the next generation—thus reproducing in a new form the old distinction between direct and mediated education and maintaining the basic structure of a class society. But the distribution of educational goods within autonomous schools will make for equality.

SPECIALIZED SCHOOLS

Democratic education begins with simple equality: common work for a common end. Education is distributed equally to every child—or, more accurately, every child is helped to master the same body of knowledge. That doesn't mean that every child is treated in exactly the same way as every other child. Praise is plentifully distributed in Japanese schools, for example, but it is not equally distributed to all the children. Some of the children regularly play the part of student-teachers; some of them are always students. Backward and apathetic children probably receive a disproportionate share of the teachers' attention. What holds them all together is the strong school and the core curriculum.

But simple equality is entirely inappropriate as soon as the core has been grasped and the common end achieved. After that, education must be shaped to the interests and capacities of individual students. And the schools themselves must be more receptive to the particular requirements of the workaday world. Bernard Shaw has suggested that at this point schools should simply be dispensed with—precisely because they can no longer fix common goals for all their students. He identifies schooling with simple equality:

> When a child has learnt its social creed and catechism and can read, write, reckon, and use its hands: in short, when it is qualified to make its way about in modern cities and do ordinary useful work, it had better be left to find out for itself what is good for it in the direction of higher cultivation. If it is a Newton or a Shakespeare, it will learn the calculus or the art of the theater without having them shoved down its throat: all that is necessary is that it should have access to books, teachers, and theaters. If its mind does not want to be highly cultivated, its mind should be left alone on the grounds that its mind knows what is good for it.[21]

This is Shaw's version of "deschooling." Unlike the version advocated by Ivan Illich in the 1970s, it builds upon years of prior schoolwork, and so is not foolish.[22] Shaw is probably right to argue that young men and women should be allowed to sort themselves out and make their way in the world without official certification. We have come to overemphasize the importance, not of schooling itself, but of schooling indefinitely extended. The effect is to rob the economy of its only legitimate proletariat, the proletariat of the young, and to make promotion up the ranks more difficult than it need be for real proletarians.

But it is not at all clear just how long it takes to learn one's "social catechism" or what knowledge is included in knowing one's way around a modern city. Something more than street knowledge, certainly, else schooling would be unnecessary from the beginning. Nor would it be satisfactory from a democratic standpoint if some children moved quickly onto the streets while the parents of the others purchased a further education that gave them access to privileged places in the city. For this reason, every advance in the school-leaving age has been a victory for equality. At some point, however, that must cease to be true, for it can't be the case that a single life course is equally appropriate for all children. With regard to the course represented by the schools, the opposite claim is more plausible: there will never be a political community of equal citizens if schoolwork is the only path to adult responsibility. For some children, beyond a certain age, school is a kind of prison (but they have done nothing to deserve imprisonment!), endured because of legal requirements or for the sake of a diploma. Surely these children should be set free and then helped to learn the work they want to do on the job. Equal citizenship requires a common schooling—its precise length a matter for political debate; but it does not require a uniform educational career.

What about young men and women who want to continue in school for the sake, say, of a general and liberal education? We might most simply provide for them by maintaining open enrollments beyond the school-leaving age: do away with grading, permit no failures, and sort people out, if that is necessary, only at the end of the process. Students would study whatever they were interested in learning, and would continue to study until their interest in this or that subject (or in studying) was exhausted. Then they would do something else. But interests are at least potentially infinite; and on a certain view of human life, one should study as long as one has breath. There is little likelihood that the political community could raise the necessary money for an education of this sort, and no reason to suppose that the people who give up studying are morally required to support those who continue. Medieval monks and Talmudic sages were indeed supported by the work of ordinary men and women, and that may well have been a good thing. Such support is not morally required, however, not in a society like ours, not even if the chance to become a monk or a sage or the contemporary equivalent were equally available to everyone.

But if the community underwrites the general education of some of its citizens, as we do today for college students, then it has to do so for any of them who are interested—not only in colleges but also, as Tawney has argued, "in the midst of the routine of their working lives." Tawney, who devoted many years to the Workers' Educational Association, is entirely right to insist that higher education of this sort should not be available solely on the basis of "a career of continuous school attendance from five to eighteen."[23] One can imagine a great variety of schools and courses, catering to students of different ages and educational histories, run at national and local levels, attached to unions, professional associations, factories, museums, old-age homes, and so on. In these settings, to be sure, schooling shades off into other, less formal sorts of teaching and learning. The "enclosed community" loses its physical reality, becomes a metaphor for critical distance. But insofar as we are distribut-

ing school places (the "college of hard knocks" has always had open enroll-
ment), I don't think we should give up the idea of the enclosure or yield any
more distance than we have to. The only extension of basic education appropriate to a democracy is one that provides real opportunities, real intellectual
freedom, not just for some students conventionally gathered together, but for
all the others, too.

I cannot specify any particular level of support for this provision. Here
again, there is room for democratic debate. Nor is it the case, as some educational radicals have argued, that democracy itself is impossible without a public program of continuing education.[24] Democracy is in danger only if such a
program is organized undemocratically, not if it isn't organized at all. As with
monks and sages, so with ordinary citizens: it is a good thing if they are able to
study indefinitely, without a professional purpose, for the sake of what
Tawney calls "a reasonable and humane conduct of life"; but the only point
critical for the theory of justice is that this sort of study not be the exclusive
privilege of a few people, picked out by state officials through a system of examinations. To study the "humane conduct of life," no one needs to qualify.

The case is different, however, with regard to specialized or professional
training. Here interest alone cannot serve as a distributive criterion; nor can interest and capacity serve: there are too many interested and capable people.
Perhaps, in the best of all possible worlds, we would educate all such people
for as long as they were educable. This, it might be said, is the only standard
intrinsic to the idea of education—as if capable men and women were empty
vessels that ought to be filled to the brim. But this is to conceive of an education abstracted from every particular body of knowledge and from every system of professional practice. Specialized schooling doesn't just go on and on
until the student has learned everything he can possibly learn; it stops when
he has learned something, when he is acquainted with the state of knowledge
in a field. We will plausibly look in advance for some assurance that he can
learn that much and learn it well. And if we have only a limited amount of
money to spend, or if there are only a limited number of places requiring that
particular training, we will plausibly look for some assurance that he can learn
it especially well.

Educating citizens is a matter of communal provision, a kind of welfare. I
would suggest that we commonly conceive of a more specialized education as
a kind of office. Students must qualify for it. They qualify, presumably, by
some display of interest and capacity; but these two yield nothing like a right
to a specialized education, for the necessary specializations are a matter for
communal decision, and so is the number of places available in the specialized
schools. Students have the same right that citizens generally have with regard
to office holding: that they be given equal consideration in the awarding of the
available places. And students have this additional right: that insofar as they
are prepared for office holding in the public schools, they should, so far as possible, be equally prepared.

The education of a gentleman, wrote John Milton, should fit the children
who receive it "to perform justly, skillfully, magnanimously, all the offices both

private and public of peace and war."[25] In a modern democratic state, citizens take on the prerogatives and obligations of gentility, but their education prepares them only to be voters and soldiers or (perhaps) presidents and generals, but not to advise presidents about the dangers of nuclear technology, not to advise generals about the risks of this or that strategic plan, not to prescribe medicines, design buildings, teach the next generation, and so on. These specialized offices require a further education. The political community will want to make sure that its leaders—and its ordinary members, too—get the best possible advice and service. And the corps of teachers has a parallel interest in the most apt students. Hence the need for a selection process aimed at locating within the set of future citizens a subset of future "experts." The standard form of this process is not difficult to discover: the universal civil service examination . . . is simply introduced into the schools. But this makes for deep strains in the fabric of a democratic education.

The more successful basic schooling is, the more apt the body of future citizens is, the more intense is the competition for advanced places in the educational system, and the deeper is the frustration of those children who fail to qualify.[26] Established élites are then likely to demand earlier and earlier selection, so that the schoolwork of the unselected is turned into a training in passivity and resignation. Teachers in strong schools will resist this demand, and so will the children—or, better, the parents of the children will resist, insofar as they are politically alert and capable. Indeed, equality of consideration would seem to require such resistance, for children learn at different rates and awaken intellectually at different ages. Any once-and-for-all selection process is certain to be unfair to some students; it will also be unfair to young people who have stopped studying and gone to work. And so there must be procedures for reconsideration and, more important, for lateral as well as upward movement into the specialized schools.

Assuming a limited number of places, however, these procedures will only multiply the number of ultimately frustrated candidates. There is no avoiding that, but it is morally disastrous only if the competition is not for school places and educational chances so much as it is for the status, power, and wealth conventionally joined to professional standing. The schools, however, need have nothing to do with this trinity of advantage. No feature of the educational process requires the link between higher education and hierarchical rank. Nor is there any reason to think that the most apt students would give up their educations were that link broken and future office holders paid, say, "workmen's wages." Some students, certainly, will make better engineers, surgeons, nuclear physicists, and so on, than their fellows will. It remains the task of the specialized schools to find these students, give them some sense of what they can do, and set them on their way. Specialized education is necessarily a monopoly of the talented or, at least, of those students most capable at any given moment of deploying their talents. But this is a legitimate monopoly. Schools cannot avoid differentiating among their students, advancing some and turning others away; but the differences they discover and enforce should be intrinsic to the work, not to the status of the work. They should have to do with achievement, not with the economic and political rewards of achievement; they should be inwardly focused, matters of praise and pride within the schools and then within the profession, but of uncertain standing in the larger world. Of uncertain standing: for achievement may still carry with it, given a little luck, not wealth and power but authority and prestige. I am describing not schools for saints but only centers of learning rather more insulated than at present from the business of "making it."

George Orwell's Schooldays

It might help at this point to consider a negative example; and in the vast literature on schools and schooling, there is no more perfectly negative example than Orwell's account of the English prep school that he attended in the 1910s. Some questions have been raised about the accuracy of the account, but on the points most relevant here we can, I think, assume its truth.[27] Orwell's "Crossgates" was designed to prepare students for admission to schools like Harrow and Eton, where England's upper civil servants and leading professional men were trained. A prep school is by definition not an autonomous center of learning, but Crossgates's dependency was doubled by the fact that it was not only an educational but also a commercial enterprise—and a rather precarious one at that. So the owners and the teachers shaped their work to the requirements of Harrow and Eton, on the one hand, and to the prejudices and ambitions of the parents of their pupils, on the other. The first of these external forces gave form to the curriculum. "Your job," wrote Orwell, "was to learn exactly those things that would give an examiner the impression that you knew more than you did know, and as far as possible to avoid burdening your brain with anything else. Subjects which lacked examination-value . . . were almost completely neglected." The second determined the government of the school and the character of social relations within it. "All the very rich boys were more or less undisguisedly favored. . . . I doubt that Sims [the Master] ever caned any boy whose father's income was much above 2000 pounds a year."[28] So the class system was reproduced—naïvely by the boys, with calculation by the masters.

These external forces—the élite public schools and the paying parents—did not always work to the same end. Crossgates had to provide some serious academic training, and its success in doing so had to be displayed, if it was to attract students. Hence it needed not only rich boys but bright ones, too. And since the parents most able to pay did not necessarily produce the children most likely to do well on the exams, the owners of Crossgates invested money in a small number of non-paying or reduced tuition students, looking for a return in the form of academic prestige. Orwell was one of these students. "If I had 'gone off,' as promising boys sometimes do, I imagine [Sims] would have got rid of me swiftly. As it was, I won him two scholarships when the time came, and no doubt he made full use of them in his prospectuses."[29] So, in the profoundly anti-intellectual setting of the prep school, there existed a few potential intellectuals, uneasy, intermittently grateful and sullen, occasionally rebellious. Tolerated for their brains, they were subjected to a hundred petty humiliations designed to teach them what the other boys took for granted: that no one really counted unless he was rich, and that the greatest virtue was not to earn money but simply to have it. Orwell was invited to qualify for educational advancement and then for bureaucratic or professional office—but only within a system where the highest qualifications were hereditary. Though wealthy parents were, in effect, buying advantages for their children, the children were taught to claim those advantages as a matter of right. They were not taught much else. Crossgates, as Orwell described it, is a perfect illustration of the tyranny of wealth and class over learning.

I suspect that any prep school, conceived as a commercial venture, will be the instrument of tyranny—indeed, of these particular tyrannies. For the market can never be a closed environment; it is (and should be) a place where money counts. Hence, again, the importance of a common "prep" for all children in strong and independent schools. But how can one prevent parents from spending their money on a little extra preparation? Even if all parents had the same income, some of them would be more ready than others to use what they had for their children's education. And even if schools like Crossgates were abolished, legally banned, parents could still hire tutors for their children. Or, if parents were knowledgeable enough, they could tutor their children themselves: professionals and office holders passing on their instincts for survival and advance, the folkways of their class.

Short of separating children from their parents, there is no way of preventing this sort of thing. It can, however, play a greater or a lesser role in social life generally. Parental support for schools like Crossgates, for example, will vary with the steepness of the social hierarchy and with the number of access points to specialized training and official positions. Orwell was told that he would either do well on the exams or end up as a "little office-boy at forty pounds a year."[30] His fate was to be decided, with no chance of reprieve, at the age of twelve. If that is an accurate picture, then Crossgates looks almost like a sensible institution—oppressive perhaps, but not irrational. But suppose the picture were different. Suppose that the sneer with which one said, and the shiver with which one heard, that awful phrase "office-boy at forty pounds a year" were both of them inappropriate. Suppose that offices were differently organized from the way they were in 1910, so that "boys" could move up (or around) within them. Suppose that the public schools were one—but not the only—way of finding interesting and prestigious work to do. Then Crossgates might begin to appear as unattractive to parents as it was to many of the children. The "prep" would be less critical, the exam less frightening, and the space and time available for learning would be greatly enhanced. Even specialized schools require some freedom from social pressure if they are to do their work—hence a society organized to yield that freedom. Schools can never be entirely free; but if they are to be free at all, there must be constraints in other distributive spheres, constraints roughly of the sort I have already described, on what money can buy, for example, and on the extent and importance of office.

ASSOCIATION AND SEGREGATION

Basic education is a coercive business. At the lower levels, at least, schools are institutions that children must be required to attend:

>The whining school-boy, with his satchel,
>And shining morning face, creeping like snail
>Unwillingly to school

is a stock figure in many different cultures.[31] In Shakespeare's time, the will that drove the unwilling boy to school was a parental will; the state did not compel attendance. The education of children depended upon the wealth, ambition, and cultivation of their parents. That seems to us a wrongful dependency: first, because the community as a whole has an interest in education; and, second, because the children themselves are assumed to have an interest, though they may not understand it yet. Both these interests look to the future, to what children will be and to the work they will do, and not, or not simply, to what their parents are, or to how they stand in society, or to the wealth they hold. Communal provision best meets these interests; for it, too, is forward-looking, designed to enhance the competence of individuals and the integration of (future) citizens. But this is necessarily provision of a special sort, whose recipents are not enrolled but conscripted. Abolish the conscription, and children are thrown back, not—as advocates of "deschooling" like to suggest—upon their own resources but upon the resources of their parents.

Because they are conscripted, schoolchildren are like soldiers and prisoners, and they are unlike ordinary citizens who decide for themselves what they will do and with whom they will associate. But one should not make too much of either the resemblance or the difference.[32] Prisoners are sometimes "reformed," and the training that soldiers receive is sometimes useful in civilian life; but we would be lying to ourselves if we pretended that education was the chief purpose of prisons or armies. These institutions are shaped to the purposes of the community, not to those of the individuals who are dragged into them. Soldiers serve their country; prisoners "serve time." But schoolchildren in an important sense serve themselves. The distribution of prison places and, sometimes, of army places is a distribution of social bads, of pains and risks. But it isn't merely a pretence of adults that school places are social goods. Adults speak from their own experience when they say that, and they anticipate the views that children will one day hold. And, of course, the adults also remember that children in their after-school hours are free in ways that the adults themselves can only envy and never recapture.

Still, school attendance is compulsory; and because of that compulsion, it isn't only places that are distributed to children; children themselves are distributed among the available places. The public schools have no *a priori* existence; they must be constituted and their students assigned by a political decision. We require, then, a principle of association. Who goes to school with whom? This is a distributive question in two senses. It is distributive, first, because the content of the curriculum varies with the character of its recipients. If children are associated as future citizens, they will be taught the history and laws of their country. If they are associated as fellow believers in this or that religion, they will study ritual and theology. If they are associated as future workers, they will receive a "vocational" education; if as future professionals, an "academic" education. If bright students are brought together, they will be taught at one level; dull students, at another. The examples could be extended indefinitely to match the prevailing set of human differences and social distinctions. Even if we assume, as I have been doing, that children are associated as citizens and given a common education, it is still true that they can't all study together; they must be segregated into schools and classes. And how this is done remains a distributive question because, second, children are each others' resources: comrades and rivals, challenging one another, helping one another, forming what may well be the crucial friendships of their adult lives. The content of the curriculum is probably less important than the human environment within which it is taught. It is no surprise, then, that association and segregation are the most hotly contested issues in the sphere of education. Parents take a much livelier interest in the schoolmates than in the schoolbooks of their children. They are right to do so—and not only in the cynical sense that "whom you know matters more than what you know." Since so much of what we know we learn from our peers, whom and what always go together.

Randomness is the most obvious associative principle. If we were to bring children together without regard to the occupations and wealth of their parents, without regard to the political or religious commitments of their parents, and if, moreover, we were to bring them together in boarding schools, cut off from day-to-day contact with their parents, we might produce perfectly autonomous educational communities. The teacher would confront his students as if they were nothing but students, without a past and with an open future— whatever future their learning would make possible. This kind of association has occasionally been advocated by leftist groups in the name of (simple) equality, and it might well achieve that goal. Certainly, the opportunity to qualify for specialized training would be more equally distributed than under any alternative arrangement. But random association would represent a triumph not only for the school but also for the state. The child who is nothing but a student does not exist; he would have to be created; and this could only be achieved, I suspect, in a tyrannical society. Education, in any case, is more properly described as the training of particular persons, with identities, aspirations, lives of their own. This particularity is represented by the family, defended by parents. Autonomous schools are mediating institutions; they stand in a tension with parents (but not only with them). Abolish compulsory education, and one loses the tension; children become the mere subjects of their families and of the social hierarchy in which their families are implanted. Abolish the family, and the tension is lost again; children become the mere subjects of the state.

The crucial distributive problem in the sphere of education is to make children commoners of learning without destroying what is uncommon about them, their social as well as their genetic particularity. I shall argue that there is, given certain social conditions, a preferred solution to this problem, a form of complex equality that best fits the normative model of the school, on the one hand, and the requirements of democratic politics, on the other. But there is no unique solution. The character of a mediating institution can be determined only by reference to the social forces between which it mediates. A balance must always be struck, different in different times and places.

In discussing some of the possibilities, I shall draw my examples from the contemporary United States, a society considerably more heterogeneous than either Orwell's England or post-Second World War Japan. Here, more clearly than anywhere else, the requirements of basic education and equality of consideration come up against the facts of ethnic, religious, and racial pluralism, and the problems of association and segregation take an especially acute form. I want to stress in advance, however, that these problems also have a general form. Marxist writers have sometimes suggested that the advent of communism would bring an end to all differences rooted in race and religion. Maybe so. But even communist parents will not share a single philosophy of education (whatever else they share). They will disagree over what sorts of school are best for the community at large or for their own children, and so it will remain a question whether children whose parents have different educational philosophies should attend the same schools. In fact, that is a question today, though it is overshadowed by less intellectual differences.

If we stand inside the school, what associative principles seem most appropriate? What reasons do we have for bringing this particular group of children together? Except for a literal incapacity to learn, there are no reasons for exclusion that have to do with the school as a school. Reasons for inclusion are correlative with academic subjects. Specialized schools bring together qualified students, with special interests and capacities. In the case of basic education, the reason for bringing students together is need (we assume interest and capacity). What is crucial here is the need of every child to grow up within this democratic community and take his place as a competent citizen. Hence the schools should aim at a pattern of association anticipating that of adult men and women in a democracy. This is the principle that best fits the schools' central purpose, but it is a very general principle. It excludes randomness, for we can be sure that adults will not (by definition and in any community) associate randomly, without regard to their interests, occupations, blood relationships, and so on. But beyond that, there are a number of associative patterns and institutional forms that at least seem compatible with the education of democratic citizens.

Private Schools and Educational Vouchers

Neither compulsory education nor a common curriculum requires that all children go to the same sorts of school or that all schools stand in the same relation to the political community. It is a feature of American liberalism that educational entrepreneurs, like-minded parents, and religious organizations are all allowed to sponsor private schools. Here the associative principle is probably best described as parental interest and ideology—though these must be taken to include an interest in social standing and an ideology of social class. The claim is that parents should be able to get what they want, exactly what they want, for their children. This doesn't necessarily eliminate the mediating role of the school, for the state can still license private schools and set common curricular requirements. Nor do parents always want for their children exactly what they themselves can provide. Perhaps they are socially or intellectually or even religiously ambitious: eager that the children become more prominent, more sophisticated, or more devout than their parents are. And the teachers in many private schools have (what Orwell's teachers clearly lacked) a strong sense of corporate identity and intellectual mission. In any case, don't adults associate in exactly this way, on the basis of their social class or religious commitment (or their ideas about how to educate their children)?

But private schools are expensive, and so parents are not equally capable of associating their children as they please. This inequality seems wrong, especially if the associations are thought to be beneficial: why should children be denied such benefits simply because of the accident of their birth? With public support, the supposed benefits could be much more widely distributed. This is the thrust of the "voucher plan," a proposal that tax money available for educational purposes be turned over to parents in the form of vouchers that could be spent on the open market.[33] To absorb these vouchers, all sorts of new schools would be founded, catering to the full range of parental interests and ideologies. Some schools would still cater to class interests, requiring tuition payments over and above the voucher and so assuring wealthy parents that their children need associate only or chiefly with their social kind. But I will leave this point aside (there is an easy legislative remedy). What is more important is that the voucher plan would guarantee that children go to school with other children whose parents, at least, were very much like their own.

The voucher plan is a pluralist proposal, but it suggests a pluralism of a peculiar sort. For while the plan may well strengthen traditional organizations like the Catholic Church, the unit for which it is specifically designed is the organization of like-minded parents. It points toward, and would help to create, a society in which there was no strong geographic base or customary loyalty but, rather, a large and changing variety of ideological groups—or better, of groups of consumers brought together by the market. Citizens would be highly mobile, rootless, moving easily from one association to another. Their moves would be their choices, and so they would avoid the endless arguments and compromises of democratic politics whose participants are more or less permanently bound together. Citizens with vouchers in their hands could, in Albert Hirschman's terms, always choose "exit" over "voice."[34]

I doubt that there could possibly exist among such citizens a sufficient community of ideas and feelings to sustain the voucher plan—which is, after all, still a form of communal provision. Even a minimal welfare state requires deeper and stronger relationships. In any case, the actual experience that children would have in schools freely chosen by their parents hardly anticipates rootlessness and easy mobility. For most children, parental choice almost certainly means less diversity, less tension, less opportunity for personal change than they would find in schools to which they were politically assigned. Their schools would be more like their homes. Perhaps such an arrangement predicts their own future choices, but it hardly predicts the full range of their contacts, working relationships, and political alliances in a democratic society. Parental choice might cut across ethnic and racial lines in a way that political assignments sometimes don't. But even that is uncertain since ethnicity and race would surely be, as they are today, two of the principles around which private schools were organized. And even if these were acceptable principles, so long as they weren't the only ones, in a pluralist society, it has to be stressed that for particular children they would be the only ones.

The voucher plan assumes the activism of parents, not in the community at large but narrowly, on behalf of their own children. But its greatest danger, I think, is that it would expose many children to a combination of entrepreneurial ruthlessness and parental indifference. Even concerned parents are, after all, often busy elsewhere. And then children can be defended only by agents of the state, governmental inspectors enforcing a general code. Indeed, state agents may still have work to do even if parents are active and involved. For the community has an interest in the education of children, and so do the children, which neither parents nor entrepreneurs adequately represent. But that interest must be publicly debated and given specific form. That is the work of democratic assemblies, parties, movements, clubs, and so on. And it is the pattern of association necessary for this work that basic education must anticipate. Private schools don't do that. The communal provision of educational goods, then, has to take a more public form—else it won't contribute to the training of citizens. I don't think that there is any need for a frontal assault on parental choice, so long as its chief effect is to provide ideological diversity on the margins of a predominantly public system. In principle, educational goods should not be up for purchase, but the purchase is tolerable if it doesn't carry with it (as it still does, for example, in Britain today) enormous social advantages. Here, as in other areas of communal provision, the stronger the public system, the easier one can be about the uses of money alongside it. Nor is there much reason to worry about those private schools that provide specialized education, so long as scholarships are widely available, and so long as there are alternative routes to public and private office. A voucher plan for specialized schooling and on-the-job training would make a lot of sense. But this would not serve to associate children in accordance with parental preference; it would allow them to follow their own preferences.

TALENT TRACKS

The career open to talents is a principle dear to American liberalism, and it has often been argued that schools should be shaped to the requirements of that career. Children who can move along quickly should be allowed to do so, while the work of slower students should be adjusted to the pace of their learning. Both groups will be happier, so the argument goes; and within each the children will find their authentic and future friends—and, indeed, their likely spouses. In later life, they will continue to associate with people of roughly similar intelligence. Parents who think their children especially bright tend to favor this sort of segregation, partly so that the children make the "right" contacts, partly so that they are not bored in school, partly in the belief that intelligence reinforced is even more intelligent. Just for this reason, however, there is often a counterdemand—that bright children be distributed throughout the school so as to stimulate and reinforce the others. This looks like using the bright students as a resource for the less bright, treating the former as means rather than as ends, much as we treat able-bodied young men when we conscript them to defend ordinary citizens. But such treatment seems wrong in the case of students, whose education is supposed to serve their own interests as well as those of the community. Whether distributing the bright students constitutes using them, however, depends upon what one takes as the natural starting point of their conscription. If the starting point is everyday residence and play, for example, then it is the segregation of the bright students that can plausibly be criticized: it looks now like a willful impoverishment of the educational experience of the others.

At the height of the Cold War, immediately after the Soviet Union sent its first rocket into space, tracking was advocated as a kind of national defense: the early recruitment of scientists and technicians, trained men and women whom we needed, or thought we needed, in large numbers. If the community that one wants to defend is a democracy, however, no form of recruitment can precede the "recruitment" of citizens. Certainly, citizens today require an education in modern science; without that, they will hardly be prepared for "all the offices both private and public of peace and war." And presumably this education will inspire some of them to pursue one or another scientific specialization; if many such people are required, additional inducements can be offered. There is no need, however, to pick out the future specialists early on, give them their proper names, as it were, before the others have had their chance at inspiration. To do so is simply to acknowledge defeat before the "recruitment" of citizens has half begun—and it will be resisted, as the Japanese example suggests, in strong schools, especially at the primary level.

Nor is it true that the tracks anticipate, though they may help to form, the associative patterns of adult citizens. The adult world is not segregated by intelligence. All sorts of work relationships, up and down the status hierarchy, require mixing; and, more important, democratic politics requires it. One could not conceivably organize a democratic society without bringing together people of every degree and kind of talent and lack of talent—not only in cities and towns but also in parties and movements (not to speak of bureaucracies and armies). The fact that people tend to marry at their intellectual level is of marginal interest, for public education in a democratic society is only incidentally a training for marriage or for private life generally. If there were no public life, or if democratic politics were radically devalued, then tracking by talent would be easier to defend.

More limited uses of segregation are permissible, however, even among future citizens. There are educational reasons for separating out children who are having special difficulties with mathematics, for example, or with a second language. But there are neither educational nor social reasons for making such distinctions across the board, creating a two-class system within the schools or creating radically different sorts of schools for different sorts of students. When this is done, and especially when it is done early in the educational process, it is not the associations of citizens that are being anticipated, but the class system in roughly its present form. Children are brought together chiefly on the basis of their pre-school socialization and home environments. It is a denial of the school's enclosure. In the United States today, this denial is likely to produce a hierarchy not only of social classes but also of racial groups. Inequality is doubled; and the doubling, as we have reason to know, is especially dangerous for democratic politics.

Integration and School Busing

We will not avoid racial segregation, however, by associating children on the basis of residence and play; for in the United States today, children of different races rarely live and play together. Nor do they receive a common education. These facts don't arise most importantly from differences in the amount of money spent on their schooling or in the quality of the teaching or the content of the curriculum; they have their origins in the social character and the expectations of the children themselves. In ghetto and slum schools, children are prepared, and prepare one another, for ghetto and slum life. The enclosure is never strong enough to protect them from themselves and from their immediate environment. They are labeled, and taught to label one another, by their social location. The only way to change all this, it is often said, is to shift the location, to separate schools from neighborhoods. This can be done by moving ghetto and slum children out of their local schools or by moving other children in. Either way, it is the associational pattern that is being changed.

The goal is the integration of future citizens, but it's not easy to say exactly what new patterns that goal requires. Logic presses us toward a public system where the social composition of every school would be exactly the same—not random but proportional association. Different sorts of children would be mixed in the same ratio in every school within a given area, the ratio varying from area to area with the overall character of the population. But how are we to identify the appropriate areas? And how are we to sort out the children: by race alone, or by religion, or ethnic group, or social class? A perfect proportionality would seem to require areas incorporating the largest possible range of groups and then the most detailed sorting out of members. But the federal judges who decided such questions in the 1970s focused their attention on established political units (cities and towns) and on racial integration alone. "In Boston," Judge William Garrity declared in a decision requiring extensive intracity busing, "the public school population is approximately two-thirds white and one-third black; ideally, every school would have the same proportions."[35] No doubt, there are good reasons for stopping at that point, but it is worth emphasizing that the principle of proportional association would require much more elaborate arrangements.

On the other hand, no form of proportional association anticipates the choices of democratic citizens. Consider, for example, the argument of many black activists in and around the civil rights movement. Even in a political community free of every taint of racism, they insisted, most black Americans would choose to live together, shaping their own neighborhoods and controlling local institutions. The only way to anticipate that pattern is to establish local control now. If the schools were run by black professionals and supported by black parents, the ghetto would cease to be a place of discouragement and defeat.[36] What equality requires, on this view, is that the association of black children with other black children carries with it the same mutual reinforcement as the association of white children with other white children. To opt for proportionality is to admit that such reinforcement is impossible—and to do so (again) before there has been any serious effort to make it work.

This is a powerful argument, but it faces in America today a major difficulty. The residential segregation of black Americans is very different from that of other groups: a great deal more thoroughgoing and a great deal less voluntary. It doesn't anticipate pluralism so much as it anticipates separatism. It isn't the pattern that we would expect to find among democratic citizens. Under such conditions, local control is likely to defeat the purposes of educational mediation. Given a political victory for the local activists, schooling will become a means of enforcing some very strong version of group identity, much as it is in the public schools of a new nation-state.[37] Children will be educated for an ideological rather than an actual citizenship. There is no reason for the larger community to pay for an education of that sort. But how far can we deviate from it while still respecting the associations that blacks would form even in a fully democratic community? Equally important, how far can we deviate from it while still respecting the associations that other people have already formed? I don't know exactly how to draw the line, but I am inclined to think that strict proportionality draws it badly.

I assume a pluralist society: so long as adults associate freely, they will shape diverse communities and cultures within the larger political community. They will certainly do this in a country of immigrants, but they will do it elsewhere, too. And then the education of children has to be group-dependent—at least in the sense that the particularity of the group, represented concretely by the family, is one of the poles between which the schools mediate. But the other pole is the larger community, represented concretely by the state, which rests upon the cooperation and mutual involvement of all the groups. So the schools, while they respect pluralism, must also work to bring children together in ways that hold open possibilities for cooperation. This is all the more important when the pluralist pattern is involuntary and distorted. It is not necessary that all schools be identical in social composition; it is necessary that different sorts of children encounter one another within them.

This necessity sometimes requires what is called (by those who oppose it) "forced busing"—as if public education must for some reason dispense with public transportation. The phrase is in any case unfair, since all school assignments are compulsory in character. So, for that matter, is schooling itself: forced reading and forced arithmetic. It may still be true that busing programs designed to meet the requirements of strict proportionality represent a more overt kind of coercion, a more direct disruption of everyday living patterns, than is desirable. The American experience suggests, moreover, that schools integrated by bringing together children who live entirely apart are unlikely to become integrated schools. Even strong schools may fail when they are forced to cope with social conflicts generated on the outside (and continually reinforced from the outside). On the other hand, it is clear that state officials have imposed racial separatism even when actual living arrangements called for, or at least allowed for, different associational patterns. This kind of imposition requires repair, and repair may now require busing. It would be foolish to rule it out. One would also hope for a more direct assault upon tyrannical distributions in the spheres of housing and employment—which no educational arrangement can possibly repair.

Neighborhood Schools

In principle, as I have already argued, neighborhoods have no admissions policies. Whether they are shaped originally by individuals and families who cluster together or by administrative decisions, highway placement, land speculation, industrial development, subway and bus routes, and so on, they will come in time, barring the use of force, to include a heterogeneous population— "not a selection, but rather a specimen of life as a whole," or at least of national life as a whole. A neighborhood school, then, does not—or not for long—serve a group of people who have chosen one another as neighbors. But insofar as different groups come to regard a school as their own, its existence may serve to heighten feelings of community. This was one of the purposes of the public school from its inception: each school was to be a little melting pot, and neighborliness was the first of its products, on the way, as it were, to citizenship. It was assumed that school districts geographically drawn would be socially mixed, and that the children who came together in the classroom would come from very different class and ethnic backgrounds. Because of protective covenants, zoning laws, and gerrymandered school districts, this was never consistently true across any particular city or town; I'm not sure whether it is more or less true now than it used to be. With regard to racial mixing, however, the evidence is clear: neighborhood schools keep black and white children apart. For this reason, the associative principle of neighborhood has come under harsh criticism.

It is, nevertheless, the preferred principle. For politics is always territorially based; and the neighborhood (or the borough, town, township, "end" of town: the contiguous set of neighborhoods) is historically the first, and still the most immediate and obvious, base for democratic politics. People are most likely to be knowledgeable and concerned, active and effective, when they are close to home, among friends and familiar enemies. The democratic school, then, should be an enclosure within a neighborhood: a special environment within a known world, where children are brought together as students exactly as they will one day come together as citizens. In this setting, the school most easily realizes its mediating role. On the one hand, children go to schools that their parents are likely to understand and support. On the other hand, political decisions about the schools are made by a diverse group of parents and non-parents, within limits set by the state. And these decisions are carried out by teachers educated (mostly) outside the neighborhood and professionally as well as politically responsible. It is an arrangement made for conflict—and, in fact, school politics in the United States has probably been the most lively and engaging kind of politics. Few parents are ever entirely satisfied by its outcomes, and children are almost certain to find a world at school different from the one they know at home. The school is simultaneously a "house of the young men and women" and a place with its own characteristic intellectual discipline.

Parents often try to defeat this discipline, and the corps of teachers is not always strong enough to maintain it. The actual distribution of schooling is shaped in significant ways by local political struggles over the size and the everyday government of the school district, the allocation of funds, the search for new teachers, the precise content of the curriculum, and so on. Neighborhood schools will never be the same across different neighborhoods. Hence the simple equality of one child/one place in the educational system makes for only a part of the story of justice in education. But I think it is fair to say that when neighborhoods are open (when racial or ethnic identity is not dominant over membership and place), and when every neighborhood has its own strong school, then justice has been done. The children are equals within a complex set of distributive arrangements. They receive a common education, even if there is some variation in the curriculum (and in the ways teachers stress or elide this or that area within the curriculum) from place to place. The cohesiveness of the faculty and the cooperative or critical zeal of the parents will vary, too; but these are variations intrinsic to the character of a democratic school, inevitable features of complex equality.

The same thing can be said of the patterns of student association. Some school districts will be more heterogeneous than others; some contacts across groups, more tense than others. The boundary conflicts endemic to a pluralist society will be faced in every school, but sometimes in a milder, sometimes in a more acute, form. It requires extraordinary ideological zeal or great priggishness to insist that they be faced in their most acute form everywhere and all the time. One could, indeed, arrange for that, but only by a radical use of state power. Now, the state has much to do with regard to education. It requires school attendance, establishes the general character of the curriculum, polices the certification process. But if the schools are to have any inward strength at all, there must be limits on the state's activity—limits fixed by the integrity of academic subjects, by the professionalism of teachers, by the principle of equal consideration—and by an associative pattern that anticipates democratic politics but is not dominated by the powers-that-be or the reigning ideologies. Just as success in the Cold War was never a reason for doing anything more than improving the quality and attractiveness of the specialized schools, so the goal of an integrated society was never a reason for going beyond the remedies required to end willful segregation. Any more radical subordination of schooling to political purpose undermines the strength of the school, the success of its mediation, and then the value of schooling as a social good. Ultimately, it makes for less, not greater, equality when students and teachers are subject to the tyranny of politics.

Notes

1. Aristotle, *The Politics,* 1337a. trans. Ernest Barker (Oxford, 1948), p. 390.
2. See Samuel Bowles and Herbert Gintis, *Schooling in Capitalist America* (New York, 1976), p. 12.
3. John Dewey, *Democracy and Education* (New York, 1961), pp. 18–22.
4. Cf. Rousseau's proposals in *The Government of Poland,* trans. Willmoore Kendall (Indianapolis, 1972), p. 20: "Above all, do not make the mistake of turning teaching into a career." That seems to me exactly wrong.
5. G. C. Vaillant, *The Aztecs of Mexico* (Harmondsworth, England, 1950), p. 117.
6. Jacques Soustelle, *The Daily Life of the Aztecs,* trans. Patrick O'Brian (Harmondsworth, England, 1964), pp. 178, 175, respectively.
7. Aristotle, *The Politics,* 1332b [1], p. 370.
8. The story is retold in Aaron H. Blumenthal, *If I Am Only for Myself: The Story of Hillel* (n. p1., 1974), pp. 2–3.
9. See the appendix ("Selected Cases . . .") to Ping-Ti Ho, *The Ladder of Success in Imperial China: Aspects of Social Mobility, 1368–1911* (New York, 1962), pp. 267–318.
10. R. H. Tawney, *The Radical Tradition* (New York, 1964), p. 69.
11. Aristotle, *The Politics* 1332b [1], p. 370.
12. Hence it is commonly argued that the value of, say, a high school education is "debased" as it is more widely distributed; see the useful discussion by David K. Cohen and Barbara Neufeld, "The Failure of High Schools and the Progress of Education," in *Daedalus,* Summer 1981, p. 79 and generally.
13. William Cummings, *Education and Equality in Japan* (Princeton, 1980), pp. 4–5.
14. Ibid., p. 273.
15. Ibid., p. 274; see also p. 154.
16. Aristotle, *The Politics* 1337a [1], p. 127.
17. Cummings, *Japan* [13], p. 274; see also p. 127.
18. Ibid., p. 275.
19. Ibid.
20. Ibid., p. 117.
21. Bernard Shaw, *The Intelligent Woman's Guide to Socialism, Capitalism, Sovietism, and Fascism* (Harmondsworth, England, 1937), pp. 436–37.
22. See Ivan Illich, *Deschooling Society* (New York, 1972), who has nothing to say about how elementary education would be carried out in a "deschooled" society.
23. Tawney, *Radical Tradition* [10], pp. 79–80, 83.
24. See David Page, "Against Higher Education for Some," in *Education for Democracy,* ed. David Rubinstein and Colin Stoneman (2nd ed., Harmondsworth, England, 1972), pp. 227–28.

25. John Milton, "Of Education," in *Complete Prose Works of John Milton*, vol. II, ed. Ernest Sirluck (New Haven, 1959), p. 379.
26. See the discussion in Cummings, *Japan* [13], chap. 8, of the growing numbers of Japanese children competing for university positions.
27. Bernard Crick, *George Orwell: A Life* (Boston, 1980), chap. 2, reviews the evidence.
28. George Orwell, "Such, Such Were the Joys, " in *The Collected Essays, Journalism, and Letters of George Orwell*, ed. Sonia Orwell and Ian Angus (New York, 1968), vol. III, p. 336.
29. Ibid., p. 343.
30. Ibid., p. 340.
31. William Shakespeare, *As You Like It*, II:5.
32. See Michael Foucault's account of the "carceral continuum," which includes prisons, asylums, armies, factories, and schools, in *Discipline and Punish: The Birth of the Prison*, trans. Alan Sheridan (New York, 1979), pp. 293–308. Foucault makes too much of the resemblance.
33. John E. Coons and Stephen D. Sugarman, *Education by Choice: The Case for Family Control* (Berkeley, 1978).
34. Albert O. Hirschman, *Exit, Voice, and Loyalty: Responses to Decline in Firms, Organizations, and States* (Cambridge, Mass., 1970).
35. See the critical discussion of the Garrity decision and "statistical parity" in general, in Nathan Glazer, *Affirmative Discrimination: Ethnic Inequality and Public Policy* (New York, 1975), pp. 65–66.
36. Congress of Racial Equality (CORE), "A Proposal for Community School Districts" (1970) in *The Great School Bus Controversy*, ed. Nicolaus Mills (New York, 1973), pp. 311–21.
37. This is especially clear when the local activists speak a "foreign" language; see Noel Epstein, *Language, Ethnicity, and the Schools* (Institute for Educational Leadership, Washington, D.C., 1977).

12   Democratic Education*

Amy Gutmann

The author is Professor of Politics at Princeton University. In this essay she critically examines three theories of the role of education within a society, in particular, those drawn from the writings of Plato, Locke, and Mill. She finds none entirely satisfying and develops an alternative especially suited to promote the ideals of a democratic community.

"We are born weak, we need strength; helpless, we need aid; foolish we need reason. All that we lack at birth, that we need when we come to man's estate, is the gift of education." So broadly understood as what we learn "from nature, from men, and from things,"[1] the gift of education may make us who we are, but is not ours to give. Like Rousseau, we therefore direct our concern to that portion of education most amenable to our influence: the conscious efforts of men and women to inform the intellect and to shape the character of less educated people. And we naturally begin by asking what the purposes of human education should be—what kind of people should human education seek to create?

Perhaps the most commonly articulated answer is relativistic. "The citizens of a state should always be educated to suit the constitution of their state," Aristotle argued.[2] "The laws of education must be relative to the principles of government,"[3] Montesquieu agreed, as did Durkheim and several more contemporary social theorists.

Many moralists react unfavorably to the mere mention of relativism because they associate it with the view, properly called "subjectivism," that claims morality to be nothing more than personal opinion. Aristotle, Montesquieu, and Durkheim reject subjectivism for the far more defensible view that the deepest, shared moral commitments of a society—its "constitution" in Aristotelian terms or "political principles" in Montesquieu's more modern sense—serve as the standard for determining the justice of its educational practices. Conservatism is the moral hazard of this form of relativism. Does justice demand that citizens be educated to suit the constitution of their society if that constitution supports cruelty and injustice? The strongest formulation of educational relativism suggests not, or at least not necessarily. Education must be guided by the *principles,* not the practices, of a regime. Educational relativism is conservative not in the narrow sense of maintaining the status quo, but in the broad sense of supporting existing social ideals.

The problem of reinforcing cruelty and injustice through education arises only in the event that the principles (not the practices) of a society support cruelty and injustice. This problem may be rare, but it is not merely hypothetical. Some societies—slave societies of the past and South Africa today, for example—probably rest on racist principles. Any credible form of educational relativism must either find critical principles within even the most thoroughly racist societies or recognize limits to the principles that are justifiable by a society's internal understandings.[4] When societies or the most powerful groups within them transgress those limits by, for example, committing themselves to racist principles, revolution or civil war becomes a precondition of moral education.

Many unjust societies, however, are not morally dedicated to cruelty or injustice. Marxist principles, for example, provide ample grounds for Soviet dissidents to condemn virtually all the practices of Soviet regimes that strike many Americans as cruel or unjust. On the regime's interpretation of Marxism, criticism may become impossible. But "the education of a citizen in the spirit of his constitution does not consist in his doing the actions in which the partisans of oligarchy, or the adherents of democracy, delight. It consists in his doing the actions by which an oligarchy, or a democracy, will be enabled to survive."[5]

Relativism, according to Aristotle's formulation, does not require us to accept the moral interpretation of the ruling class as the morally ruling interpretation.

But what interpretation should rule? How do we determine the principles of a particular society, or its constitution, in Aristotle's sense? This question poses a greater challenge to relativism than the charge of conservatism once one recognizes that the "members of a society are unlikely to agree about what the constitution, in Aristotle's broad sense, actually is, or what it is becoming, or what it should be. Nor are they likely to agree about what character type will best sustain it or how that type might best be produced."[6] If this is the case, then believing in educational relativism is compatible with believing in any one of a wide range of incompatible interpretations of educational justice. So whether or not we accept the basic tenet of educational relativism (that citizens should be educated according to the political principles of their society), we must use some form of philosophical analysis to defend a set of principles or to determine which set of principles and whose interpretation of them ought to rule. The controversy over relativism—or at least educational relativism—is best set aside if we are to make any progress in analyzing the purposes of education.

The form of analysis that follows might best be called dialectical, although I hesitate to call it such.[7] It begins by evaluating the most commonly held theories concerning educational purposes, authorities, and distributions, not simply for the sake of criticism but to develop a better theory, which integrates the strengths while avoiding the weaknesses of the standard views. The method will not satisfy strict foundationalists, who believe that any defensible political theory must begin by discovering some unquestionable or self-evident starting point, and build from the ground up (so to speak). I fear that even were I to discover such a starting point, I could not possibly build enough upon it to speak about educational issues of any political moment before this book, or my life, ended. The fear of foundationalists is the reverse, of course: that so much moral talk about politics and education is indefensible because it does not refer back to basic principles. Yet my dialectical method is not without foundations in this sense: it enables me to defend an internally consistent and intuitively acceptable set of basic premises and principles, basic at least with respect to our society.

An important advantage of this method over strict foundationalism is that one can arrive at a democratic theory of education without first defending a conception of human nature upon which theories of education are typically constructed. The fallacy of relying on deductions from axioms of human nature is that most of the politically significant features of human character are products of our education. If education is what gives us our distinctive character, then we cannot determine the purposes of education by invoking an a priori theory of human nature. "Nature" may set the bounds beyond which a society cannot accomplish its educational purposes. But the constraints of nature surely leave societies a vast choice among competing educational purposes. Education may aim to *perfect* human nature by developing its potentialities, to *deflect* it into serving socially useful purposes, or to *defeat* it by repressing those inclinations that are socially destructive.[8] We can choose among and give content to these aims only by developing a normative theory of what the educational purposes of our society should be.

We have inherited not one but several such normative theories, which compete for our allegiance and account for many of our social disagreements as well as our personal uncertainties concerning the purposes of education. Three of the most distinct and distinguished of these theories can be drawn from interpretations of Plato, John Locke, and John Stuart Mill.[9] I call them (for reasons that will become apparent) the theories of the *family state,* the *state of families,* and the *state of individuals.* Despite their differences, each treats questions of education (its purposes, distributions, and authorities) as part of a principled *political* theory. That is the tradition within which I work, although I reject—or at least modify—the principles suggested by each of these theories in favor of a more democratic theory, which (I argue) supplies a more adequate ground for determining educational purposes, authority, and the distribution of educational goods for our society.

THE FAMILY STATE

Can we speak meaningfully about a good education without knowing what a just society and a virtuous person are? Socrates poses this challenge to the Sophists in the *Protagoras.* Like most of Socrates's questions, it has remained unanswered after twenty-five centuries. But it is still worth re-asking.

In his critique of the Sophists and in the *Republic,* Plato suggests that we cannot speak about a good education without knowing what justice and virtue really are, rather than what a society assumes that they are by virtue of their shared social understandings. Justice, Socrates suggests, is the concurrent realization of individual and social good. Since the good life for individuals entails contributing to the social good, there is no necessary conflict between what is good for us and what is good for our society—provided our society is just. The defining feature of the family state is that it claims exclusive educational authority as a means of establishing a harmony—one might say, a constitutive relation—between individual and social good based on knowledge. Defenders of the family state expect to create a level of like-mindedness and camaraderie among citizens that most of us expect to find only within families (and now perhaps not even there).[10] The purpose of education in the family state is to cultivate that unity by teaching all educable children what the (sole) good life is for them and by inculcating in them a desire to pursue the good life above all inferior ones. Citizens of a well-ordered family state learn that they cannot realize their own good except by contributing to the social good, and they are also educated to desire only what is good for themselves and their society.

One need not accept Plato's view of natural human inequality to take seriously his theoretical defense of the family state. Once we discount this view, we can find in Plato the most cogent defense of the view that state authority over education is necessary for establishing a harmony between individual virtue and social justice. Unless children learn to associate their own good with the social good, a peaceful and prosperous society will be impossible. Unless the social good that they are taught is worthy of pursuit, they will grow to be unfulfilled and dissatisfied with the society that miseducated them. All states that claim less than absolute authority over the education of children will therefore degenerate out of internal disharmony.

It is important to emphasize that Plato's family state provides no support for any educational authority that teaches children a way of life that cannot be rationally defended as morally superior to other ways of life. The state may not argue simply: "Because we wish to achieve social harmony, we shall indoctrinate all children to believe that *our* way of life is best." A reasonable response then would surely be: "But why should you have the authority to impose *your* way of thinking on the next generation? Why shouldn't I have the authority to impose *my* way?" And, of course, there will be many other reasonable people whose reponses will be the same, but whose conceptions of the good life will be at odds with both mine and that of the state's educational authorities. On the Platonic argument, it is essential to the justice of the state's educational claims that its conception of the good life for every person be the *right* one.

Before pursuing the Platonic argument, we might consider a non-Platonic form of the family state, where educational authority is based not on the state's greater wisdom but on its status as the "political" parent of all its citizens. When the Laws and the Constitution of Athens speak to Socrates in the *Crito* of his duty to obey, they claim not that they are right but that they have a right to rule him: "Did we not give you life in the first place? Was it not through us that your father married your mother and begot you? . . . [S]ince you have been born and brought up and educated, can you deny, in the first place, that you were our child and servant, both you and your ancestors?"[11] The advantage of resting the authority of the family state on parental imagery is obvious: the state need not claim greater wisdom; it need only claim that it begot, brought up, and educated its citizens. This imagery is suggestive in some situations, but its moral force is doubtful as a defense of a state's right to educate—or to rule more generally—in disregard of the best interests or the moral convictions of its citizens. Because a family state is at best the *artificial* parent of its citizens, it must create the conditions under which citizens are bound to honor and obey it. The moral force of parental imagery in politics (as suggested by Socrates's subsequent arguments in the *Crito* concerning the freedom available to Athenian citizens) varies either with the degree to which the wisdom of a state exceeds that of its citizens or with the fit between the goods pursued by a state and those valued by its citizens.[12] A state that lacks wisdom or that rules against the moral convictions of most citizens cannot credibly claim parental status. Not even natural parents, moreover, may properly assert an absolute right to educate their children. I argue this later against the state of families, but need not pursue it here because citizens, after all, are not children, and states are at most metaphorical, not real, parents of their citizens.

The Platonic family state therefore rightly rejects the relativism of the non-Platonic family state, which would ground education on the mere opinions of state authorities, as readily as it rejects the subjectivism of Sophists, which defines a good education as one that simply satisfies the preferences of students. States that assume a parental role to educate according to false opinion are no better than Sophists who assume a professorial role to teach children virtue without knowing what virtue is. Indeed, sophistical states are worse because they wield more power.

But the Platonic family state has its own problems. The most obvious one is the difficulty of determining the best constitution for any society and the correct conception of the good for any person. Although this is a very serious problem, I shall not pursue it because it is not necessarily decisive for my argument.[13] After all, neither do we know that a single conception of justice and the good *cannot* be discovered. Even if discovery is improbable, the possibility of discovering something so valuable may justify subordinating other values to the search—perhaps even the freedoms of individuals to pursue what they believe to be a good life and to support what they believe to be a good society. Unless we can establish the value of these freedoms, we shall lack a sufficient moral argument against the claims of the family state. An argument based solely on skepticism about the possibility of discovering virtue and justice is not only inadequate but dangerous, because skepticism can also be used to defeat the claim that personal and political freedoms are valuable human goods.

The more telling criticism of the family state proceeds by accepting the possibility that someone sufficiently wise and conscientious might discover the good. She would then try to convince the rest of us that she had discovered *the* good, not just another contestable theory of the good, and the good for *us*, not just the good appropriate to some other people. It's possible that a few of us—an unusually open-minded or uncommitted few—might be convinced, but most of us (as Plato realized) would not; and we would refuse to relinquish all authority over the education of our children to the philosopher-queen (or the state).

In order to create a just family state, the philosopher therefore must wipe the social slate clean by exiling "all those in the city who happen to be older than ten; and taking over their children, . . . rear them—far away from those dispositions they now have from their parents. . . ."[14] That is an exorbitantly high price to pay for realizing a just society. Socrates himself on behalf of the philosopher recoils from the idea, suggesting that "he won't be willing to mind the political things . . . in his fatherland unless some divine chance coincidentally comes to pass."[15]

This objection to the family state is not a purely practical one—pointing to the impossibility of realizing a just society in an unjust world. Even if the philosopher-queen is right in claiming that a certain kind of life is objectively good, she is wrong in assuming that the objectively good is good for those of us who are too old or too miseducated to identify the objectively good with what is good for our own lives. "That may be the best life to which people—educated from birth in the proper manner—can aspire," we might admit, "but it's not the good life for *us*. And don't we have a claim to living a life that is good for us?" The objectively good life, defined as the life that is best for people who are rightly educated from birth, need not be the good life, or even the closest approximation of the good life, for people who have been wrongly educated. Could my personal identity be sustained were someone to succeed in imposing upon me (perhaps through brainwashing) the consciousness and life suitable to the contemporary equivalent of a Platonic guardian? Suppose that a life devoted to the *polis* but deprived of a family and private property is objectively better than any I would choose for myself. The question of personal identity still remains: Can I live this life while still retaining my own identity? People who know me well will strongly suspect that the answer is "no," even if they cannot offer a theory of personal identity that would confirm their suspicions. If we would have to be stripped of our personal identities to become Platonic guardians, then the best life for *us* is less than the objectively best on Platonic grounds.

What about a state that lets us live our less-than-objectively good lives, but that insists on educating our children so they will not face the same dilemma or create the same problem for the next generation of citizens? Here a significant variant of the previous problem arises: "Don't we also have a claim to try to perpetuate the way of life that seems good to us within our families? After all, an essential part of *our* good life is imparting an understanding of our values to our children." We can say something similar about our good as citizens: "Don't we also have a claim to participate in shaping the basic structure of our society? After all, an essential part of our good is the freedom to share in shaping the society that in turn influences our very evaluation of a family and the degree to which different kinds of families flourish." The Platonic perspective refuses to recognize the force of these claims about *our* good. Yet these claims constitute the most forceful challenge to the philosopher-queen's claim to have discovered the good for us, even if she has discovered what is objectively good for our children. The cycle of imperfection must continue,[16] not merely because the costs of realizing the family state are too great, but because our good must be counted in any claim about what constitutes a just society for us and our children.[17] Our good might conceivably be overridden by the prospects of achieving the objectively good life for our children, but the objectively good is likely to be the fully operative good only for a society of orphaned infants.

If she is perfectly wise, the philosopher-queen must moderate her claims. Perhaps she may claim to know what is good for our children, but surely she may not claim the right to impose that good on them without taking our good, both as parents and as citizens, into account. If we now relax the rather absurd assumption that we can find a perfectly wise philosopher-queen, we shall want some assurance from even the wisest educational authority that our good as parents and as citizens, and not just the good of our children, will be considered in designing the educational system for our society. The only acceptable form of assurance is for parents and citizens both to have a significant share of educational authority.

If one begins with a society whose members all already agree about what is good (say, an entire society of Old Order Amish), then the moral dilemmas of personal identity and transformation costs may never arise. Unlike some contemporary theorists who in their criticisms of liberalism implicitly support a family state, Plato faces up to its more troubling implications. Part of Platonic wisdom is not to assume away the problems of founding a family state, but to recognize that the process of creating social agreement on the good comes at a very high price, and to wonder whether the price is worth paying.

Yet Plato ultimately fails to recognize the moral implication of the fact that our attachments to (and disagreements over) the good run so deep, into our earliest education. Even if there is an objective ideal of the good for an imaginary society created out of orphaned infants, our good is relative to our education and the choices we are capable of making for ourselves, our children, and our communities. The objectively good life for us, we might say, must be a life that can fulfill us according to our best moral lights. This, I think, is the truth in educational relativism.[18] As long as we differ not just in our opinions but in our moral convictions about the good life, the state's educational role cannot be defined as realizing *the* good life, objectively defined, for each of its citizens. Neither can educational authorities simply claim that a good education is whatever in their opinion is best for the state.

The family state attempts to constrain our choices among ways of life and educational purposes in a way that is incompatible with our identity as parents and citizens. In its unsuccessful attempt to do so, it successfully demonstrates that we cannot ground our conception of a good education merely on personal or political preferences. Plato presents a forceful case for resting educational authority exclusively with a centralized state, a case grounded on the principle that knowledge should be translated into political power. But even the Platonic case is not sufficiently strong to override the claims of parents and citizens to share in social reproduction, claims to which I return in defending a democratic state of education.

THE STATE OF FAMILIES

States that aspire to the moral unity of families underestimate the strength and deny the legitimacy of the parental impulse to pass values on to children. Radically opposed to the family state is the state of families, which places educational authority exclusively in the hands of parents, thereby permitting parents to predispose their children, through education, to choose a way of life consistent with their familial heritage. Theorists of the state of families typically justify placing educational authority in the hands of parents on grounds either of consequences or of rights. John Locke maintained that parents are the best protectors of their children's future interests. Some Catholic theologians, following Thomas Aquinas, claim that parents have a natural right to educational authority. Many modern-day defenders of the state of families maintain both, and add another argument: if the state is committed to the freedom of individuals, then it must cede educational authority to parents whose freedom includes the right to pass their own way of life on to their children.[19] Charles Fried, for example, argues that "the right to form one's child's values, one's child's life plan and the right to lavish attention on the child are extensions of the basic right not to be interfered with in doing these things for oneself."[20] Fried bases parental rights over children on "the facts of reproduction" and the absence of a societal right to make choices for children. Fried's denial of a societal right is based on the consequentialist judgment that parents can be relied upon to pursue the best interests of their children.

Although the appeal of the state of families is apparent upon recognizing the defects of a family state, none of these theoretical arguments justifies resting educational authority exclusively—or even primarily—in the hands of parents. It is one thing to recognize the right (and responsibility) of parents to educate their children as members of a family, quite another to claim that this right of familial education extends to a right of parents to insulate their children from exposure to ways of life or thinking that conflict with their own. The consequentialist argument is surely unconvincing: parents cannot be counted upon to equip their children with the intellectual skills necessary for rational deliberation. Some parents, such as the Old Order Amish in America, are morally committed to shielding their children from all knowledge that might lead them to doubt and all worldly influences that might weaken their religious beliefs.[21] Many other parents, less radical in their rejection of modern society, are committed to teaching their children religious and racial intolerance.

To criticize the state of families, however, it is not enough to demonstrate that the perspectives of these parents are *wrong*, for we can never realistically expect any educational authority to be infallible. The strongest argument against the state of families is that neither parents nor a centralized state have a right to exclusive authority over the education of children. Because children are members of both families and states, the educational authority of parents and of polities has to be partial to be justified. We appreciate the danger of permitting a centralized state to monopolize education largely for this reason. The similar danger of placing all authority in the hands of parents may be less widely appreciated, at least in the United States, because support for parental authority over education has been associated historically with Lockean liberalism. Because the Lockean state cedes adult citizens the freedom to choose their own good, many liberals (like Fried) assume that it must also cede parents the freedom to educate their children without state interference.[22] To the worry that parents might abuse their authority, many liberals invoke a secular variant of Locke's response:

> God hath woven into the Principles of Human Nature such a tenderness for their Off-spring, that there is little fear that Parents should use their power with too much rigour; the excess is seldom on the severe side, the strong byass of Nature drawing the other way.[23]

Other liberals, more critical of the state of families, call Locke's premise into question by citing the prevalence of physical child abuse in this country.

But one need not dispute Locke's claim about the direction and force of "Nature's byass" to conclude that parental instincts are an insufficient reason for resting educational authority exclusively in the family. The same principle that requires a state to grant adults personal and political freedom also commits it to assuring children an education that makes those freedoms both possible and meaningful in the future. A state makes choice possible by teaching its future citizens respect for opposing points of view and ways of life. It makes choice meaningful by equipping children with the intellectual skills necessary to evaluate ways of life different from that of their parents. History suggests that without state provision or regulation of education, children will be taught neither mutual respect among persons nor rational deliberation among ways of life. To save their children from future pain, especially the pain of eternal damnation, parents have historically shielded their children from diverse associations, convinced them that all other ways of life are sinful, and implicitly fostered (if not explicitly taught them) disrespect for people who are different. This spirit is inimical to the kind of liberal character that Locke argued that parents should teach their children.[24] The end—moral freedom—that Locke recommends in his *Essay on Education* requires us to question the means—exclusive parental authority—that Locke defends in the *Second Treatise,* once we can assume (as Locke could not) the political possibility of dividing educational authority between families and the state.

This argument against exclusive parental authority depends neither upon parental ignorance nor upon irrationality. From the perspective of individual parents who desire above all to perpetuate their particular way of life, teaching disrespect for differing ways of life need not be irrational even if the outcome turns out to be undesirable. For many deeply religious parents, mutual respect is a public good (in the strict economic sense). As long as they have reason to believe that their religion will continue to be respected, they need not worry about teaching their children to respect other religions. But even if they can foresee a serious threat to their religion in the future, they still have no reason to believe that they can solve (or even ameliorate) the problem by teaching their children to respect the disrespectful.

American history provides an informative example. Many public schools in the mid-nineteenth century were, to say the least, disrespectful of Catholicism. Catholic children who attended these schools were often humiliated, sometimes whipped for refusing to read the King James version of the Bible. Imagine that instead of becoming more respectful, public schools had been abolished, and states had subsidized parents to send their children to the private school of their choice. Protestant parents would have sent their children to Protestant schools, Catholic parents to Catholic schools. The Protestant majority would have continued to educate their children to be disrespectful if not intolerant of Catholics. The religious prejudices of Protestant parents would have been visited on their children, and the social, economic, and political effects of those prejudices would have persisted, probably with considerably less public protest, to this very day. There may be little reason today for Catholic parents to worry that privatizing schools will reinstitutionalize bigotry against

Catholics, at least in the short run. But one reason that Catholics need not worry is that a state of families today would be built on the moral capital created over almost a century by a public school system. That moral capital is just now being created for blacks and Hispanics, and even more well-established minorities might reasonably fear that returning to a state of families would eventually squander the moral capital created by public schooling.

Like most collective goods, the "costs" of mutual respect among citizens may have to be imposed on everyone to avoid the free-rider problem. But this virtue is a cost only to parents who do not accept its intrinsic moral worth. The state of families can overcome the free-rider problem by violating its basic premise of parental supremacy in education and requiring all parents to let schools teach their children mutual respect. For children who are not yet free (in any case) to make their own choices, teaching the lesson of mutual respect is not a cost. It is both an instrumental good and a good worth valuing on its own account. Teaching mutual respect is instrumental to assuring all children the freedom to choose in the future. It is a good in itself to all citizens who are not yet committed to a way of life that precludes respect for other ways of life.

The state of families mistakenly conflates the welfare of children with the freedom of parents when it assumes that the welfare of children is best defined or secured by the freedom of parents. But the state of families rightly recognizes, as the family state does not, the value of parental freedom, at least to the extent that such freedom does not interfere with the interests of children in becoming mutually respectful citizens of a society that sustains family life. There is no simple solution to the tension between the freedom of parents and the welfare of children. The state may not grant parents absolute authority over their children's education in the name of individual freedom, nor may it claim exclusive educational authority in the name of communal solidarity. That there is no *simple* solution, however, should not deter us from searching for a better solution than that offered by either the family state or the state of families.

The attractions of the state of families are apparent to most Americans: by letting parents educate their own children as they see fit, the state avoids all the political battles that rage over the content of public education. The state of families also appears to foster pluralism by permitting many ways of life to be perpetuated in its midst. But both these attractions are only superficial in a society where many parents would teach racism, for example, in the absence of political pressure to do otherwise. States that abdicate all educational authority to parents sacrifice their most effective and justifiable instrument for securing mutual respect among their citizens.

The "pluralism" commonly identified with the state of families is superficial because its internal variety serves as little more than an ornament for onlookers. Pluralism is an important political value insofar as social diversity enriches our lives by expanding our understanding of differing ways of life. To reap the benefits of social diversity, children must be exposed to ways of life different from their parents and—in the course of their exposure—must embrace certain values, such as mutual respect among persons, that make social diversity both possible and desirable. There is no reason to assume that placing educational authority exclusively in the hands of parents is the best way of achieving these ends, and good reason to reject the claim that, regardless of the consequences for individual citizens or for society as a whole, parents have a natural right to exclusive educational authority over their children. Children are no more the property of their parents than they are the property of the state.

THE STATE OF INDIVIDUALS

"It is in the case of children," John Stuart Mill argued, "that misapplied notions of liberty are a real obstacle to the fulfillment by the State of its duties. One would almost think that a man's children were supposed to be literally, and not metaphorically, a part of himself, so jealous is opinion of the smallest interference of law with his absolute and exclusive control over them. . . ."[25] Having exposed the central flaw in the state of families, Mill defended a more liberal conception of education. "All attempts by the State to bias the conclusions of its citizens on disputed subjects are evil," Mill argued. Some contemporary liberals extend the logic of Mill's argument to defend what I call a state of individuals.[26] They criticize all educational authorities that threaten to bias the choices of children toward some disputed or controversial ways of life and away from others. Their ideal educational authority is one that maximizes future choice without prejudicing children towards any controversial conception of the good life. The state of individuals thus responds to the weakness of both the family state and the state of families by championing the dual goals of *opportunity* for choice and *neutrality* among conceptions of the good life. A just educational authority must not bias children's choices among good lives, but it must provide every child with an opportunity to choose freely and rationally among the widest range of lives.

If neutrality is what we value, then a child must be protected from all—or at least all controversial—social prejudices. Neither parents nor states are capable of fulfilling this educational ideal. Parents are unlikely (and unwilling) to resist a strong human impulse: the desire to pass some of their particular prejudices on to their children. And even the most liberal states are bound to subvert the neutrality principle: they will try, quite understandably, to teach children to appreciate the basic (but disputed) values and the dominant (but controversial) cultural prejudices that hold their society together.[27]

Recognizing the power of these parental and political impulses, some liberals look for an educational authority more impartial than parents or public officials—"experts" or professional educators—motivated solely, or at least predominantly, by the interests of children in learning and unconstrained by parental or political authority. I suspect that were professional educators ever to rule, they would convince everyone, albeit unintentionally, that liberal neutrality is an unlivable ideal. But as long as we focus our critical attention on the detrimental effects of parental and political prejudices, we are likely to overlook the limitations of the neutrality ideal, and the tension between it and the ideal of opportunity. Children may grow to have a greater range of choice (and to live more satisfying lives) if their education is biased by those values favored by their society. Bentham and Kant both recognized this. Kant defended—as one of four essential parts of a basic education—teaching children the kind of "discretion" associated with "refinement" of manners, which "changes according to the ever-changing tastes of different ages."[28] One of the primary aims of education, according to Bentham, was to secure for children "admission into and agreeable intercourse with good company."[29]

Contemporary liberal theorists often invoke the spirit of Bentham, Kant, or Mill to defend the ideal of neutrality, overlooking both its moral limitations and the subsequent qualifications that each of these theorists placed on the ideal. All sophisticated liberals recognize the practical limitation of neutrality as an educational ideal: it is, in its fullest form, unrealizable. But most fail to appreciate the value of our resistance to the ideal of unprejudiced individual freedom: the value of our desire to cultivate, and allow communities to cultivate, only a select range of choice for children, to prune and weed their desires and aspirations so they are likely to choose a worthy life and sustain a flourishing society when they mature and are free to choose for themselves. Bruce Ackerman argues:

> Such horticultural imagery has no place in a liberal theory of education. We have no right [and the state has no right] to look upon future citizens as if we were master gardeners who can tell the difference between a pernicious weed and a beautiful flower. A system of liberal education provides children with a sense of the very different lives that could be theirs.[30]

But what *kind* of sense do we want to provide? Of *which* very different lives? Ackerman, like all sensible liberals, recognizes that the capacity for rational choice requires that we place some prior limitations on children's choices. To have a rational sense of what we want to become, we need to know who we are; otherwise our choices will be endless and meaningless.[31] We learn to speak English rather than Urdu, not by choice, but by cultural determination.[32] And this cultural determination limits the range of our future choices, even if it does not uniquely determine who we become. Ackerman identifies this prior determination with the need for "cultural coherence," which he uses to justify the family and its nonneutral education. The need for cultural coherence, Ackerman argues, does not justify "adult pretensions to moral superiority."[33] Neither parents nor the state may shape the character of children on the grounds that they can distinguish between better and worse moral character, yet they may shape children's character for the sake of cultural coherence, or in order to maximize their future freedom of choice.

Why, one might ask, should parents and states be free to shape children's character and guide their choices for the sake of cultural coherence but not for the sake of their leading morally good lives? Sometimes the claim that we know better than children the difference between morally good and bad lives is not a pretension to moral superiority, but a reflection of our greater moral maturity. Why, then, should adults resist shaping children's character and guiding their choices on *moral* grounds?

The resistance of many contemporary liberals to one of our strongest moral impulses stems, I suspect, from formulating educational purposes and their justifications as a dichotomous choice.[34] Either we must educate children so that they are free to choose among the widest range of lives (given the constraints of cultural coherence) because freedom of choice is the paramount good, or we must educate children so that they will choose *the* life that we believe is best because leading a virtuous life is the paramount good. Let children define their own identity or define it for them. Give children liberty or give them virtue. Neither alternative is acceptable: we legitimately value education not just for the liberty but also for the virtue that it bestows on children; and the virtue that we value includes the ability to deliberate among competing conceptions of the good.

But precisely which virtues do "we" value? No set of virtues remains undisputed in the United States, or in any modern society that allows its members to dispute its dominant understandings. The problem in using education to bias children towards some conceptions of the good life and away from others stems not from pretense on the part of educators to moral superiority over children but from an assertion on their part to political authority over other citizens who reject their conception of virtue. Neutrality is no more acceptable a solution to this problem than the use of education to inculcate a nonneutral set of virtues. Neither choice—to teach or not to teach virtue—is uncontroversial. Neither avoids the problem of instituting an educational authority whose aims are not universally accepted among adult citizens. The decision not to teach virtue (or, more accurately, to teach only the virtues of free choice) faces opposition by citizens who can claim, quite reasonably, that freedom of choice is not the only, or even the primary, purpose of education. Why should these citizens be forced to defer to the view that children must be educated for freedom rather than for virtue? Liberals might reply that freedom is the *correct* end of education. This reply is inadequate, because being right is neither a necessary nor a sufficient condition for claiming the right to shape the character of future citizens.

Because the educational ideal of free choice commands no *special* political legitimacy, the state of individuals poses the same problem as the family state. Even if liberals could establish that, of all disputed aims of education, neutrality is singularly right, they would still have to establish why being right is a necessary or sufficient condition for ruling. The same argument that holds against the family state holds against the state of individuals: being right is not a necessary or sufficient condition because parents and citizens have a legitimate interest (independent of their "rightness") in passing some of their most salient values on to their children.

Proponents of the state of individuals might argue that they avoid the problem of the family state by offering a principled solution morally distinct from that of the family state: authorize only those authorities whose educational techniques maximize the future freedom of children. They try, as Ackerman does and I once did,[35] to justify pruning children's desires solely on liberal paternalistic grounds: by restricting the freedom of children when they are young, we increase it over their lifetimes. Although the liberal state is often contrasted to the family state, its end of individual freedom is subject to a similar challenge. Why must freedom be the sole end of education, given that most of us value things that conflict with freedom? We value, for example, the moral sensibility that enables us to discriminate between good and bad lives, and the character that inclines us to choose good rather than bad lives.[36] A well-cultivated moral character constrains choice among lives at least as much as it expands choice. Why prevent teachers from cultivating moral character by biasing the choices of children toward good lives and, if necessary, by constraining the range of lives that children are capable of choosing when they mature?

Liberals occasionally reply that the standard of freedom supports such moral education. When teachers or parents admonish children not to be lazy, for example, the implicit purpose of their admonition is to expand the future freedom of children by encouraging them to become the kind of people who have the greatest range of choice later in life.[37] This reply begs two crucial questions: Is such an admonition easier to justify because it furthers the freedom of children rather than cultivates a virtue? Is the aim of educating children for freedom as fully compatible with teaching them virtue as this example suggests?

The answer to each question, I suspect, is "no," because both educational ends—freedom and virtue—are controversial, and neither is inclusive. To establish a privileged place for freedom as *the* aim of education, liberals would have to demonstrate that freedom is the singular social good, a demonstration that cannot succeed in a society where citizens sometimes (one need not claim always) value virtue above freedom. Were freedom of choice an inclusive good such that teaching children to choose entailed teaching them virtue, then the debate between whether to educate for freedom or for virtue would be academic. It's not academic, because an education for freedom and for virtue part company in any society whose citizens are free not to act virtuously, yet it is at least as crucial to cultivate virtue in a free society as it is in one where citizens are constrained to act virtuously. The admonition not to be lazy may serve the cause of cultivating virtue rather than maximizing children's freedom in an affluent society that offers generous benefits to the unemployed, but why should it be any more suspect on this account? Neither aim of education is neutral, and each can exclude the other, at least in some instances. Assuming that some citizens value virtue, others freedom, and the two aims do not support identical pedagogical practices, the more liberal aim cannot claim a privileged political position. Educators need not be bound to maximize the future choices of children if freedom is not the only value.

By what standards, then, if any, are educators bound to teach? After criticizing the liberal paternalistic standard—constrain the present freedom of children only if necessary to maximize their future freedom—we are left with the problem of finding another standard that can justify a necessarily nonneutral education in the face of social disagreement concerning what constitutes the proper aim of education. Shifting the grounds of justification from future free-dom to some other substantive end—such as happiness, autonomy, intellectual excellence, salvation, or social welfare—only re-creates the same problem. None of these standards is sufficiently inclusive to solve the problem of justifi-cation in the face of dissent by citizens whose conception of the good life and the good society threatens to be undermined by the conception of a good (but necessarily nonneutral) education instituted by some (necessarily exclusive) educational authority.

Our task therefore is to find a more inclusive ground for justifying non-neutrality in education. We disagree over the relative value of freedom and virtue, the nature of the good life, and the elements of moral character. But our desire to search for a more inclusive ground presupposes a common commit-ment that is, broadly speaking, political. We are committed to collectively re-creating the society that we share. Although we are not collectively committed to any particular set of educational aims, we are committed to arriving at an agreement on our educational aims (an agreement that could take the form of justifying a diverse set of educational aims and authorities). The substance of this core commitment is conscious social reproduction. As citizens, we aspire to a set of educational practices and authorities of which the following can be said: these are the practices and authorities to which we, acting collectively as a society, have consciously agreed. It follows that a society that supports con-scious social reproduction must educate all educable children to be capable of participating in collectively shaping their society.

Conscious social reproduction, like any educational end, is not self-evi-dently correct or uncontroversial. But it is a minimally problematical end inso-far as it leaves maximum room for citizens collectively to shape education in their society. A society committed to conscious social reproduction has a com-pelling response to those adults who object to the form or the content of educa-tion on grounds that it indirectly subverts or directly conflicts with their moral values. "The virtues and moral character we are cultivating," the educational authorities can reply in the first instance, "are necessary to give children the chance collectively to shape their society. The kind of character you are asking us to cultivate would deprive children of that chance, the very chance that le-gitimates your own claim to educational authority." If the challenge is directed to the teaching of values that directly conflict with those of some citizens, then the response to dissenting adults can take the following form: "The values we are teaching are the product of a collective decision to which you were party. Insofar as that decision deprives no one of the opportunity to participate in fu-ture decisions, its outcome is legitimate, even if it is not correct."[38]

I have yet to elaborate and defend the democratic theory of education that would fully justify these responses, but assuming for the moment that this is the kind of defense that any nonneutral education demands, a substantial truth in the liberal educational ideal would remain: it would be an illegitimate pretension to educational authority on anyone's part to deprive any child of the capacities necessary for choice among good lives. The pretension would be illegitimate for two reasons. First: even if I know that my way of life is best, I cannot translate this claim into the claim that I have a right to impose my way of life on anyone else, even on my own child, at the cost of depriving her of the capacity to choose a good life. Second: many if not all of the capacities necessary for choice among good lives are also necessary for choice among good societies. A necessary (but not sufficient) condition of conscious social reproduction is that citizens have the capacity to deliberate among alternative ways of personal and political life. To put this point in more "liberal" language: a good life and a good society for self-reflective people require (respectively) individual and collective freedom of choice.

But neither a good life nor a good society require *maximizing* freedom of choice. Educational authorities may teach children that religious intolerance and racial bigotry (for example) are wrong without claiming that the justification for their nonneutrality is the future freedom of children. The justification for teaching these virtues is that they constitute the kind of character necessary to create a society committed to conscious social reproduction. We need not claim that this kind of society—a democracy—is justified "*sub specie aeternitatis*"[39] to defend its unique legitimacy for us. Most Americans are committed to sharing sovereignty with each other and almost all who are uncommitted are unwilling to live the kind of life that would result from their rejection of this fundamental democratic premise.

One might still wonder what accounts for the widespread appeal of the liberal ideal of neutrality if it is so mistaken. I suspect that its broad appeal rests on a healthy suspicion of claims to moral superiority among educators. The history of schooling in this country (and every other) is full of false claims by educational authorities to moral superiority. In the course of raising our children, we probably have made some ourselves. Reflecting on these rather frequent lapses, we may become suspicious of all such claims. No credible theory of education, however, supports all assertions of moral superiority or all moral distinctions that adults make in their role as educators. But neither can any credible theory deny the legitimacy of all such claims. A democratic theory of education, I later argue, requires us to challenge the propriety of some claims and distinctions: the claim, for example, that one race is inherently superior to another, or, to take a more controversial example, the claim that a woman's place is in the home. In admitting moral distinctions among lives and characters, we bear the burden of differentiating between legitimate and spurious moral distinctions. The state of individuals promises to relieve citizens of this burden by using education to free all children to make their own discriminations. Yet we have seen that accepting freedom as the goal of education does not provide an escape from the burden of choosing (on some grounds) among the many possible lives that children can be taught to appreciate.

Liberals who still insist on defending neutrality might give a more practical reason for admitting cultural prejudices but not moral discriminations into the educational process: it may be harder to agree collectively on moral discriminations than on cultural prejudices. Requiring that all children be taught English, for example, may at one time in American history have seemed to be less controversial than requiring that they all be taught religious toleration. In order to reach a collective moral agreement on the principles of schooling, on this argument, we must agree not to admit our moral disagreements into our public deliberations over educational means and ends.

Perhaps this argument was once soundly prudential, but its premise is surely very shaky today. If recent political battles over bilingualism are any evidence, teaching cultural prejudice is just as controversial as teaching moral principle, perhaps because our political principles are so closely tied to our cultural prejudices. But even if we grant the premise, the liberal neutrality position fares no better by this reasoning than what one might call the moralist position. To a moralist who believes that a primary purpose of education is to cultivate good character, a view that denies the justice of this educational purpose is just as controversial as a view that offers a direct challenge to the idea that a certain kind of character is good or bad. It makes more sense, on both prudential and democratic grounds, to admit the direct challenge and to take the chance that we might lose the political battle to teach religious toleration as a virtue, for example, rather than give up any chance that education will serve one of its primary purposes—cultivating the kind of character conducive to democratic sovereignty.

A DEMOCRATIC STATE OF EDUCATION

Cultivating character is a legitimate—indeed, an inevitable—function of education. And there are many kinds of moral character—each consistent with conscious social reproduction—that a democratic state may legitimately cultivate. Who should decide what kind of character to cultivate? I have examined and rejected three popular and philosophically forceful answers to this question. Theorists of the family state rest educational authority exclusively in the hands of a centralized state in a mistaken attempt to wed knowledge of the good life with political power. Theorists of the state of families place educational authority exclusively in the hands of parents, on the unfounded assumption that they have a natural right to such authority or that they will thereby maximize the welfare of their children. Theorists of the state of individuals refuse to rest educational authority in any hands without the assurance that the choices of children will not be prejudiced in favor of some ways of life and against others—an assurance that no educator can or should be expected to provide.

If my criticisms are correct, then these three theories are wrong. None provides an adequate foundation for educational authority. Yet each contains a partial truth. States, parents, and professional educators all have important roles to play in cultivating moral character. A democratic state of education recognizes that educational authority must be shared among parents, citizens, and professional educators even though such sharing does not guarantee that power will be wedded to knowledge, that parents can successfully pass their prejudices on to their children, or that education will be neutral among competing conceptions of the good life.

If a democratic state of education does not guarantee virtue based on knowledge, or the autonomy of families, or neutrality among ways of life, what is the value of its premise of shared educational authority? The broad distribution of educational authority among citizens, parents, and professional educators supports the core value of democracy: conscious social reproduction in its most inclusive form. Unlike a family state, a democratic state recognizes the value of parental education in perpetuating particular conceptions of the good life. Unlike a state of families, a democratic state recognizes the value of professional authority in enabling children to appreciate and to evaluate ways of life other than those favored by their families. Unlike a state of individuals, a democratic state recognizes the value of political education in predisposing children to accept those ways of life that are consistent with sharing the rights and responsibilities of citizenship in a democratic society. A democratic state is therefore committed to allocating educational authority in such a way as to provide its members with an education adequate to participating in democratic politics, to choosing among (a limited range of) good lives, and to sharing in the several subcommunities, such as families, that impart identity to the lives of its citizens.

A democratic state of education constrains choice among good lives not only out of necessity but out of a concern for civic virtue. Democratic states can acknowledge two reasons for permitting communities to use education to predispose children toward some ways of life and away from others. One reason is grounded on the value of moral freedom, a value not uniquely associated with democracy. All societies of self-reflective beings must admit the moral value of enabling their members to discern the difference between good and bad ways of life. Children do not learn to discern this difference on the basis of an education that strives for neutrality among ways of life. Children are not taught that bigotry is bad, for example, by offering it as one among many competing conceptions of the good life, and then subjecting it to criticism on grounds that bigots do not admit that other people's conceptions of the good are "equally" good. Children first become the kind of people who are repelled by bigotry, and then they feel the force of the reasons for their repulsion. The liberal reasons to reject bigotry are quite impotent in the absence of such sensibilities: they offer no compelling argument to people who feel no need to treat other people as equals and are willing to live with the consequences of their disrespect. To cultivate in children the character that feels the force of right reason is an essential purpose of education in any society.

The second, more specifically democratic, reason for supporting the non-neutral education of states and families is that the good of children includes not just freedom of choice, but also identification with and participation in the good of their family and the politics of their society. The need for cultural coherence does not fully capture this democratic value, because it would not be enough for a centralized state to choose a set of parents and a coherent cultural orientation at random for children. People, quite naturally, value the specific cultural and political orientations of their society and family more than those of others, even if they cannot provide objective reasons for their preferences.

The fact that these cultural orientations are theirs is an adequate (and generalizable) reason. Just as we love our (biological or adopted) children more than those of our friends because they are a part of *our* family, so we differentially value the cultural orientations of our country because it is *ours*. We need not claim moral superiority (or ownership) to say any of this. We need claim only that some ways of life are better than others *for us and our children* because these orientations impart meaning to and enrich the internal life of family and society. To focus exclusively on the value of freedom, or even on the value of moral freedom, neglects the value that parents and citizens may legitimately place on *partially* prejudicing the choices of children by their familial and political heritages.

In authorizing (but not requiring) democratic states and families within them to predispose children to particular ways of life, we integrate the insights of both the family state and the state of families into a democratic theory on education. But in doing so, we do not necessarily avoid the weakness of both theories in sanctioning the imposition of a noncritical consciousness on children. To avoid this weakness, a democratic state must aid children in developing the capacity to understand and to evaluate competing conceptions of the good life and the good society. The value of critical deliberation among good lives and good societies would be neglected by a society that inculcated in children uncritical acceptance of any particular way or ways of (personal and political) life. Children might then be taught to accept uncritically the set of beliefs, say, that supports the view that the only acceptable role for women is to serve men and to raise children. A society that inculcated such a sexist set of values would be undemocratic not because sexist values are wrong (although I have no doubt that they are, at least for our society), but because that society failed to secure any space for educating chidren to deliberate critically among a range of good lives and good societies. To integrate the value of critical deliberation among good lives, we must defend some principled limits on political and parental authority over education, limits that in practice require parents and states to cede some educational authority to professional educators.

One limit is that of *nonrepression*. The principle of nonrepression prevents the state, and any group within it, from using education to restrict rational deliberation of competing conceptions of the good life and the good society. Nonrepression is not a principle of negative freedom. It secures freedom from interference only to the extent that it forbids using education to restrict *rational* deliberation or consideration of different ways of life. Nonrepression is therefore compatible with the use of education to inculcate those character traits, such as honesty, religious toleration, and mutual respect for persons, that serve as foundations for rational deliberation of differing ways of life. Nor is nonrepression a principle of positive liberty, as commonly understood. Although it secures more than a freedom from interference, the "freedom to" that it secures is not a freedom to pursue the singularly correct way of personal or political life, but the freedom to deliberate rationally among different ways of life.[40] Rational deliberation should be secured, I have argued, not because it is neutral among all ways of life—even all decent ways of life. Rational deliberation makes some ways of life—such as that of the Old Order Amish—more difficult to pursue insofar as dedication to such lives depends upon resistance to rational deliberation. Rational deliberation remains the form of freedom most suitable to a democratic society in which adults must be free to deliberate and disagree but constrained to secure the intellectual grounds for deliberation and disagreement among children. Although nonrepression constitutes a limit on democratic authority, its defense thus derives from the primary value of democratic education. Because *conscious* social reproduction is the primary ideal of democratic education, communities must be prevented from using education to stifle rational deliberation of competing conceptions of the good life and the good society.

A second principled limit on legitimate democratic authority, which also follows from the primary value of democratic education, is *nondiscrimination*. For democratic education to support conscious *social* reproduction, all educable children must be educated. Nondiscrimination extends the logic of nonrepression, since states and families can be selectively repressive by excluding entire groups of children from schooling or by denying them an education conducive to deliberation among conceptions of the good life and the good society. Repression has commonly taken the more passive form of discrimination in schooling against racial minorities, girls, and other disfavored groups of children. The effect of discrimination is often to repress, at least temporarily, the capacity and even the desire of these groups to participate in the processes that structure choice among good lives. Nondiscrimination can thus be viewed as the distributional complement to nonrepression. In its most general application to education, nondiscrimination prevents the state, and all groups within it, from denying anyone an educational good on grounds irrelevant to the legitimate social purpose of that good. Applied to those forms of education necessary to prepare children for future citizenship (participation in conscious social reproduction), the nondiscrimination principle becomes a principle of nonexclusion. No educable child may be excluded from an education adequate to participating in the political processes that structure choice among good lives.

Why is a theory that accepts these two principled constraints on popular (and parental) sovereignty properly considered democratic? Democratic citizens are persons partially constituted by subcommunities (such as their family, their work, play, civic, and religious groups), yet free to choose a way of life compatible with their larger communal identity because no single subcommunity commands absolute authority over their education, and because the larger community has equipped them for deliberating and thereby participating in the democratic processes by which choice among good lives and the chance to pursue them are politically structured. The principles of nonrepression and nondiscrimination simultaneously support deliberative freedom and communal self-determination. The form of educational relativism acceptable under these principles is therefore democratic in a significant sense: all citizens must be educated so as to have a chance to share in self-consciously shaping the structure of their society. Democratic education is not neutral among conceptions of the good life, nor does its defense depend on a claim to neutrality. Democratic education is bound to restrict pursuit, although not conscious consideration, of ways of life dependent on the suppression of politically relevant knowledge. Democratic education supports choice among those ways of life that are compatible with conscious social reproduction.

Nondiscrimination requires that *all* educable children be educated adequately to participate as citizens in shaping the future structure of their society. Their democratic participation as adults, in turn, shapes the education of the next generation of children, within the constraints set by nondiscrimination and nonrepression. These principles permit families and other subcommunities to shape but not totally to determine their children's future choices, in part by preventing any single group from monopolizing educational authority and in part by permitting (indeed, obligating) professional educators to develop in children the deliberative capacity to evaluate competing conceptions of good lives and good societies. Democratic education thus appreciates the value of education as a means of creating (or re-creating) cohesive communities and of fostering deliberative choice without elevating either of these partial purposes to an absolute or overriding end.

Like the family state, a democratic state of education tries to teach virtue—not the virtue of the family state (power based upon knowledge), but what might best be called *democratic* virtue: the ability to deliberate, and hence to participate in conscious social reproduction. Like the state of families, a democratic state upholds a degree of parental authority over education, resisting the strong communitarian view that children are creatures of the state. But in recognizing that children are future citizens, the democratic state resists the view, implicit in the state of families, that children are creatures of their parents. Like the state of individuals, a democratic state defends a degree of professional authority over education—not on grounds of liberal neutrality, but to the extent necessary to provide children with the capacity to evaluate those ways of life most favored by parental and political authorities. . . .

Notes

1. Jean Jacques Rousseau, *Emile, or On Education,* trans. Barbara Foxley (New York: Everyman, 1972), p. 6.
2. *The Politics of Aristotle,* ed. and trans. Ernest Barker (London: Oxford University Press, 1958), p. 332 (1337a).
3. Montesquieu, *The Spirit of the Laws,* trans. Thomas Nugent (London, 1750), 1: 42. Cf. *The Writings of Benjamin Franklin,* ed. Albert H. Smyth (New York and London, 1905–1907), 10: 97–105; and Emile Durkheim, *Moral Education* (New York: Free Press, 1961), *passim.*
4. Even the most thoroughly racist societies typically generate internal criticism. Consider the interpretation of apartheid by the dissident Afrikaner, André Brink. Having characterized apartheid as "an extension of an entire value system, embracing all the territories of social experience, economics, philosophy, morality and above all religion," Brink argues that "the dissident is fighting to assert the most positive

and creative aspects of his heritage. . . . In summary, apartheid, as I see it, denied what is best in the Afrikaner himself. . . . What it denies is the Afrikaner's reverence for life, his romanticism, his sense of the mystical, his deep attachment to the earth, his generosity, his compassion. . . . The dissident struggles in the name of what the Afrikaner could and should have become *in the light of his own history. . . .*" André Brink, *Writing in a State of Siege: Essays on Politics and Literature* (New York: Summit Books, 1983), pp. 19–20. Emphasis added.

I set aside here the question of how relativism could develop the theoretical resources either to choose "what is best" within a culture or to set limits on the acceptance of internally generated principles. The democratic theory developed below provides a set of limits (in the constraints of nonrepression and nondiscrimination) consistent with, but not derivable from, relativism.

5. *The Politics of Aristotle,* p. 233 (1310a).
6. Michael Walzer, *Spheres of Justice* (New York: Basic Books, 1983), p. 197.
7. The reason for my hesitation is not that suggested by one of my high-school civics books, which defined dialectic as "the Communist manner of reasoning—a convenient substitute for standard logic." See Roger Swearingen, *The World of Communism* (New York: Houghton Mifflin, 1962), p. 247. Rather, I hesitate because the Aristotelian sense of the term has been all but lost in our ordinary language. Although the dialectical method cannot establish scientific knowledge (which must be based on truth, not just opinion), according to Aristotle, "dialectic is a process of criticism wherein lies the path to the principles of all inquiries." *Topica,* in *The Works of Aristotle,* trans. W. D. Ross, vol. 1 (Oxford: Oxford University Press, 1928), 101b3.
8. Robert Fullinwider suggested this trilogy to me.
9. It should go without saying that my aim in constructing these theories is not to offer an interpretation of Plato, Locke, and Mill that is faithful to their intentions or to the full range of their arguments. My aim is rather to *use* their theories to illuminate the principles underlying three of the most common and compelling political understandings of education in our society.
10. That we no longer assume (it may never have been accurate to do so) that families are "havens in a heartless world" does not prevent us from retaining the ideal of family life as a realm where parents and children identify their own good with the good of the whole. We are (perhaps increasingly) tempted to think along Platonic lines, however, that this identification is not sufficient to creating an ideal family life. A just division of work, of emotional support, and of the other rewards and burdens of family life between husband and wife may be another necessary part of our ideal. For better or for worse, the condition of familial justice may have become a prerequisite to achieving the condition of a harmonious identification of wills. Compare Michael J. Sandel, *Liberalism and the Limits of Justice* (New York: Cambridge University Press, 1982), pp. 33–34 and *passim.*
11. *Crito,* in *The Last Days of Socrates,* trans. Hugh Tredennick (Harmondsworth: Penguin Books, 1970), pp. 90–91 (50b–51c).
12. Ibid., pp. 92–93 (51c–52e).
13. See, for example, Karl Popper, *The Open Society and Its Enemies* (Princeton, N.J.: Princeton University Press, 1971), vol. 1, chs. 3 and 9, pp. 18–34, 157–68.
14. *The Republic of Plato,* trans. Allan Bloom (New York: Basic Books, 1968), p. 220 (541a).
15. Ibid., p. 274 (592a).
16. Alternately, one might argue: If the philosopher-queen could convince us that her claims are correct, then the cycle of imperfection need not continue. But the only contest in which she can be said to have convinced us (rather than to have manipu-

lated our views by taking advantage of her monopoly on political power) is democratic. The family state therefore must become democratic to be legitimate.

17. And, one might add, we can only know our good if our conception is uncoerced. Our conception must, to borrow a phrase from Bernard Williams, "grow from inside human life." The idea of an uncoerced conception of the good life, like the idea of an uncoerced social agreement on an ethical life, "implies free institutions, ones that allow not only for free inquiry but also for diversity of life and some ethical variety." See Bernard Williams, *Ethics and the Limits of Philosophy* (Cambridge, Mass.: Harvard University Press, 1985), pp. 172–73.

18. Cf. Bernard Williams, "The Truth in Relativism," in *Moral Luck* (New York: Cambridge University Press, 1981), pp. 132–43.

19. For the former justification, see Milton Freedman, *Capitalism and Freedom* (Chicago: University of Chicago Press, 1962), pp. 85–107; and John E. Coons and Stephen Sugarman, *Education by Choice: The Case for Family Control* (Berkeley: University of California Press, 1978). For the latter, see Thomas Aquinas, *Supplement Summa Theologica un Divini Illius Magistri of His Holiness Pope Pius XI*, and a 1936 encyclical of the Catholic Church, where Aquinas is quoted as saying: "The child is naturally something of the father, . . . so by natural right the child before reaching the age of reason, is under the father's care. Hence it would be contrary to natural justice if any disposition were made concerning [the child] against the will of the parents." (Quoted in Francis Schrag, "The Right to Educate," *School Review*, vol. 79, no. 3 [May 1971]: 363.) Article 41 of the Irish Constitution also "recognizes the Family as the natural primary and fundamental unit group of Society, and as a moral institution, possessing inalienable and imprescriptible rights, antecedent and superior to all positive law." (Quoted in Walter F. Murphy, "An Ordering of Constitutional Values," *Southern California Law Review*, vol. 53, no. 2 [January 1980]: 739.)

20. Charles Fried, *Right and Wrong* (Cambridge, Mass.: Harvard University Press, 1978), p. 152.

21. See *Wisconsin v. Yoder*, 406 U.S. 210–11.

22. The Lockean argument, therefore, does not depend for its force, as some critics have maintained, on the claim that children are the property of their parents, a claim that Locke himself rejected.

23. Locke, "The Second Treatise of Government," in *Two Treatises of Government*, intro. Peter Laslett (New York: Cambridge University Press, 1960), ch. 6, sec. 67, p. 355.

24. For an interpretation of Locke's understanding of liberal character, see Nathan Tarcov, *Locke's Education for Liberty* (Chicago: University of Chicago Press, 1984).

25. Mill, *On Liberty*, ch. 5, para. 12.

26. Mill himself suggested an educational policy often associated with the state of families: the government should "leave to parents to obtain the education where and how they pleased, and content itself with helping to pay the school fees of the poorer classes of children . . ." (*On Liberty*, ch. 5, para. 13). There are, however, two significant differences between Mill's defense of private schools and that of the state of families. (1) Mill's preference for private control of schools follows not from a principled defense of parental choice but from an empirical presumption that state control of schools leads to repression ("a despotism over the mind"). Since absolute parental control over education also threatens despotism over children's minds, it is as suspect on Millean grounds. (2) Perhaps for this reason, Mill severely limits the educational authority of parents by (among other things) a system of "public examinations, extending to all children and beginning at an early age." If a child fails the examination, Mill recommends that "the father, unless he has some

sufficient ground of excuse, might be subjected to a moderate fine, to be worked out, if necessary, by his labor. . . ." To insure neutrality, the knowledge tested by the examination should "be confined to facts and positive science exclusively" (ch. 5, para. 14).

27. I assume from here on the understanding that liberalism aims at neutrality only among disputed or controversial conceptions of the good. I therefore omit further use of the adjectives "disputed" or "controversial."

28. Kant, *Kant on Education*, p. 19.

29. Jeremy Bentham, *Chrestomathia* (1816), in *The Works of Jeremy Bentham* (Edinburgh, 1843), p. 10.

30. Ackerman, *Social Justice*, p. 139.

31. This is an insight common to critics of liberalism. See, e.g., Sandel, *Liberalism and the Limits of Justice*, esp. pp. 161–65, 168–83.

32. Ackerman, *Social Justice*, p. 141.

33. Ibid., p. 148.

34. The tendency to dichotomize our moral choices is not unique to advocates of liberal neutrality. What I call the "tyranny of dualisms" is also common to communitarian critics of liberalism. See my "Communitarian Critics of Liberalism," *Philosophy and Public Affairs*, vol. 14, no. 5 (Summer 1985): 316–20.

35. See Amy Gutmann, "Children, Paternalism and Education: A Liberal Argument," *Philosophy and Public Affairs*, vol. 9, no. 4 (Summer 1980): 338–58.

36. For an excellent account of moral freedom, see Susan Wolf, "Asymmetrical Freedom," *The Journal of Philosophy* (1980): 151–66.

37. Ackerman suggests this rationale in *Social Justice*, pp. 147–49.

38. If as a result of the decision, someone is deprived of the opportunity to participate in future decisions, or if the decisionmaking process is not truly collective, then this response is unwarranted. In the first instance (as I later classify), the content of the decision renders it repressive; in the second, the decisionmaking process is discriminatory.

39. Cf. Rawls, *A Theory of Justice*, p. 587.

40. For a conceptual analysis of freedom that fits my understanding of rational freedom, see Gerald C. MacCallum, Jr., "Negative and Positive Freedom," *Philosophical Review* 76 (1967): 312–34. Reprinted in Richard E. Flathman, ed., *Concepts in Social and Political Philosophy* (New York: Macmillan, 1973), pp. 294–308.

13   Moral Education and the Democratic Ideal*
Israel Scheffler

The author is Professor Emeritus of Philosophy at Harvard University. In this article, originally prepared as a background paper for a congressional committee's hearings on education, he considers the role of schools in promoting moral education in a democracy. He stresses the fundamental importance of developing the skills of critical thinking in students who will be expected to participate intelligently in the governance of their society.

INTRODUCTION

What should be the purpose and content of an educational system in a democratic society, in so far as it relates to moral concerns? This is a very large question, with many and diverse ramifications. Only its broadest aspects can here be treated, but a broad treatment, though it must ignore detail, may still be useful in orienting our thought and highlighting fundamental distinctions and priorities.

EDUCATION IN A DEMOCRACY

Commitment to the ideal of democracy as an organizing principle of society has radical and far-reaching consequences, not only for basic political and legal institutions, but also for the educational conceptions that guide the development of our children. All institutions, indeed, operate through the instrumentality of persons; social arrangements are 'mechanisms' only in a misleading metaphorical sense. In so far as education is considered broadly, as embracing all those processes through which a society's persons are developed, it is thus of fundamental import for all the institutions of society, without exception. A society committed to the democratic ideal is one that makes peculiarly difficult and challenging demands of its members; it accordingly also makes stringent demands of those processes through which its members are educated.

What is the democratic ideal, then, as a principle of social organization? It aims so to structure the arrangements of society as to rest them ultimately upon the freely given consent of its members. Such an aim requires the institutionalization of reasoned procedures for the critical and public review of policy; it demands that judgments of policy be viewed not as the fixed privilege of any class or élite but as the common task of all, and it requires the supplanting of arbitrary and violent alteration of policy with institutionally channeled change ordered by reasoned persuasion and informed consent.

The democratic ideal is that of an open and dynamic society: open, in that there is no antecedent social blueprint which is itself to be taken as a dogma immune to critical evaluation in the public forum; dynamic, in that its fundamental institutions are not designed to arrest change but to order and channel it by exposing it to public scrutiny and resting it ultimately upon the choices of its members. The democratic ideal is antithetical to the notion of a fixed class of rulers, with privileges resting upon social myths which it is forbidden to question. It envisions rather a society that sustains itself not by the indoctrination of myth, but by the reasoned choices of its citizens, who continue to favor it in the light of a critical scrutiny both of it and its alternatives.

Choice of the democratic ideal rests upon the hope that this ideal will be sustained and strengthened by critical and responsible inquiry into the truth about social matters. The democratic faith consists not in a dogma, but in a reasonable trust that unfettered inquiry and free choice will themselves be chosen, and chosen again, by free and informed men.

The demands made upon education in accord with the democratic ideal are stringent indeed; yet these demands are not ancillary but essential to it. As Ralph Barton Perry has said:[1]

> Education is not merely a boon conferred by democracy, but a condition of its survival and of its becoming that which is undertakes to be. Democracy is that form of social organization which most depends on personal character and moral autonomy. The members of a democratic society cannot be the wards of their betters; for there is no class of betters. . . . Democracy demands of every man what in other forms of social organization is demanded only of a segment of society. . . . Democratic education is therefore a peculiarly ambitious education. It does not educate men for prescribed places in life, shaping them to fit the requirements of a preexisting and rigid division of labor. Its idea is that the social system itself, which determines what places there are to fill, shall be created by the men who fill them. It is true that in order to live and to live effectively men must be adapted to their social environment, but only in order that they may in the long run adapt that environment to themselves. Men are not building materials to be fitted to a preestablished order, but are themselves the architects of order. They are not forced into Procrustean beds, but themselves design the beds in which they lie. Such figures of speech symbolize the underlying moral goal of democracy as a society in which the social whole justifies itself to its personal members.

To see how radical such a vision is in human history, we have only to reflect how differently education has been conceived. In traditional authoritarian societies education has typically been thought to be a process of perpetuating the received lore, considered to embody the central doctrines upon which human arrangements were based. These doctrines were to be inculcated through education; they were not to be questioned. Since, however, a division between the rulers and the ruled was fundamental in such societies, the education of governing élites was sharply differentiated from the training and opinion-formation reserved for the masses. Plato's *Republic,* the chief work of educational philosophy in our ancient literature, outlines an education for the rulers in a hierarchical utopia in which the rest of the members are to be deliberately nourished on myths. And an authoritative contemporary Soviet textbook on *Pedagogy* declares that, 'Education in the USSR is a weapon for strengthening the Soviet state and the building of a classless society . . . the work of the school is carried on by specially trained people who are guided by the state.'[2] The school was indeed defined by the party program of March 1919 as 'an instrument of the class struggle. It was not only to teach the general principles of communism but "to transmit the spiritual, organizational, and educative influence of the proletariat to the half- and nonproletarian strata of the working masses." '[3] In nondemocratic societies, education is two-faced: it is a weapon or an instrument for shaping the minds of the ruled in accord with the favored and dogmatic myth of the rulers; it is, however, for the latter, an induction into the prerogatives and arts of rule, including the arts of manipulating the opinions of the masses.

To choose the democratic ideal for society is wholly to reject the conception of education as an *instrument* of rule; it is to surrender the idea of shaping or molding the mind of the pupil. The function of education in a democracy is rather to liberate the mind, strengthen its critical powers, inform it with knowledge and the capacity for independent inquiry, engage its human sympathies, and illuminate its moral and practical choices. This function is, further, not to be limited to any given subclass of members, but to be extended, in so far as possible, to all citizens, since all are called upon to take part in processes of debate, criticism, choice, and co-operative effort upon which the common social structure depends. 'A democracy which educates for democracy is bound to regard all of its members as heirs who must so far as possible be qualified to enter into their birthright.'[4]

IMPLICATIONS FOR SCHOOLING

Education, in its broad sense, is more comprehensive than schooling, since it encompasses all those processes through which a society's members are developed. Indeed, all institutions influence the development of persons working within, or affected by, them. Institutions are complex structures of actions and expectations, and to live within their scope is to order one's own actions and expectations in a manner that is modified, directly or subtly, by that fact. Democratic institutions, in particular, requiring as they do the engagement and active concern of all citizens, constitute profoundly educative resources. It is important to note this fact in connection with our theme, for it suggests that formal agencies of schooling do not, and cannot, carry the whole burden of education in a democratic society, in particular moral and character education. All institutions have an educational side, no matter what their primary functions may be. The question of moral education in a democracy must accordingly be raised not only within the scope of the classroom, but also within the several realms of institutional conduct. Are political policies and arrangements genuinely open to rational scrutiny and public control? Do the courts and agencies of government operate fairly? What standards of service and integrity are prevalent in public offices? Does the level of political debate meet appropriate requirements of candor and logical argument? Do journalism and the mass media expose facts and alternatives, or appeal to fads and emotionalism? These and many other allied questions pertain to the status of moral education within a democratic society. To take them seriously is to recognize that moral education presents a challenge not only to the schools, but also to every other institution of society.

Yet the issue must certainly be raised specifically in connection with schools and schooling. What is the province of morality in the school, particularly the democratic school? Can morality conceivably be construed as a *sub-*

ject, consisting in a set of maxims of conduct, or an account of current mores, or a list of rules derived from some authoritative source? Is the function of moral education rather to ensure conformity to a certain code of behavior regulating the school? Is it, perhaps, to involve pupils in the activities of student organizations or in discussion of 'the problems of democracy'? Or, since morality pertains to the whole of what transpires in school, is the very notion of specific moral schooling altogether misguided?

These questions are very difficult, not only as matters of implementation, but also in theory. For it can hardly be said that there is firm agreement among moralists and educators as to the content and scope of morality. Yet the tradition of moral philosophy reveals a sense of morality as a comprehensive institution over and beyond particular moral codes, which seems to me especially consonant with the democratic ideal, and can, at least in outline, be profitably explored in the context of schooling. What is this sense?

It may perhaps be initially perceived by attention to the language of moral judgment. To say that an action is 'right,' or that some course 'ought' to be followed, is not simply to express one's taste or preference; it is also to make a claim. It is to convey that the judgment is backed by reasons, and it is further to invite discussions of such reasons. It is, finally, to suggest that these reasons will be found compelling when looked at impartially and objectively, that is to say, taking all relevant facts and interests into account and judging the matter as fairly as possible. To make a moral claim is, typically, to rule out the simple expression of feelings, the mere giving of commands, or the mere citation of authorities. It is to commit oneself, at least in principle, to the 'moral point of view,' that is, to the claim that one's recommended course has a point which can be clearly seen if one takes the trouble to survey the situation comprehensively, with impartial and sympathetic consideration of the interests at stake, and with respect for the persons involved in the issue. The details vary in different philosophical accounts, but the broad outlines are generally acknowledged by contemporary moral theorists.[5]

If morality can be thus described, as an institution, then it is clear that we err if we confuse our allegiance to any particular code with our commitment to this institution; we err in mistaking our prevalent code for the *moral point of view* itself. Of course, we typically hold our code to be justifiable from the moral point of view. However, if we are truly committed to the latter, we must allow the possibility that further consideration or new information or emergent human conditions may require revision in our code. The situation is perfectly analogous to the case of science education; we err if we confuse our allegiance to the current corpus of scientific doctrines with our commitment to scientific method. Of course we hold our current science to be justifiable by scientific method, but that very method itself commits us to hold contemporary doctrines fallible and revisable in the light of new arguments or new evidence that the future may bring to light. For scientific doctrines are not held simply as a matter of arbitrary preference; they are held for reasons. To affirm them is to invite all who are competent to survey these reasons and to judge the issues comprehensively and fairly on their merits.

Neither in the case of morality nor in that of science is it possible to convey the underlying *point of view* in the abstract. It would make no sense to say, 'Since our presently held science is likely to be revised for cause in the future, let us just teach scientific method and give up the teaching of content.' The content is important in and of itself, and as a basis for further development in the future. Moreover, one who knew nothing about specific materials of science in the concrete could have no conception of the import of an abstract and second-order scientific method. Nevertheless, it certainly does not follow that the method is of no consequence. On the contrary, to teach current science without any sense of the reasons that underlie it, and of the logical criteria by which it may itself be altered in the future, is to prevent its further intelligent development. Analogously, it makes no sense to say that we ought to teach the moral point of view in the abstract since our given practices are likely to call for change in the future. Given practices are indispensable, not only in organizing present energies, but in making future refinements and revisions possible. Moreover, one who had no concrete awareness of a given tradition of practice, who had no conception of what rule-governed conduct is, could hardly be expected to comprehend what the moral point of view might be, as a second-order vantage point on practice. Nevertheless, it does not follow that the latter vantage point is insignificant. Indeed, it is fundamental in so far as we hold our given practices to be reasonable, that is, justifiable in principle upon fair and comprehensive survey of the facts and interests involved.

There is, then, a strong analogy between the moral and the scientific points of view, and it is no accident that we speak of reasons in both cases. We can be reasonable in matters of practice as well as in matters of theory. We can make a fair assessment of the evidence bearing on a hypothesis of fact, as we can make a fair disposition of interests in conflict. In either case, we are called upon to overcome our initial tendencies to self-assertiveness and partiality by a more fundamental allegiance to standards of reasonable judgment comprehensible to all who are competent to investigate the issues. In forming such an allegiance, we commit ourselves to the theoretical possibility that we may need to revise our current beliefs and practices as a consequence of 'listening to reason.' We reject arbitrariness in principle, and accept the responsibility of critical justification of our current doctrines and rules of conduct.

It is evident, moreover, that there is a close connection between the general concept of *reasonableness*, underlying the moral and the scientific points of view, and the democratic ideal. For the latter demands the institutionalization of 'appeals to reason' in the sphere of social conduct. In requiring that social policy be subject to open and public review, and institutionally revisable in the light of such review, the democratic ideal rejects the rule of dogma and of arbitrary authority as the ultimate arbiter of social conduct. In fundamental allegiance to channels of open debate, public review, rational persuasion and orderly change, a democratic society in effect holds its own current practices open to revision in the future. For it considers these practices to be not self-evident, or guaranteed by some fixed and higher authority, or decidable exclusively by some privileged élite, but subject to rational criticism, that is, purporting to sustain themselves in the process of free exchange of reasons in an attempt to reach a fair and comprehensive judgment.

Here, it seems to me, is the central connection between moral, scientific, and democratic education, and it is this central connection that provides, in my opinion, the basic clue for school practice. For what it suggests is that the fundamental trait to be encouraged is that of reasonableness. To cultivate this trait is to liberate the mind from dogmatic adherence to prevalent ideological fashions, as well as from the dictates of authority. For the rational mind is encouraged to go behind such fashions and dictates and to ask for their justifications, whether the issue be factual or practical. In training our students to reason we train them to be critical. We encourage them to ask questions, to look for evidence, to seek and scrutinize alternatives, to be critical of their own ideas as well as those of others. This educational course precludes taking schooling as an instrument for shaping their minds to a preconceived idea. For if they seek reasons, it is their evaluation of such reasons that will determine what ideas they eventually accept.

Such a direction in schooling is fraught with risk, for it means entrusting our current conceptions to the judgment of our pupils. In exposing these conceptions to their rational evaluation we are inviting them to see for themselves whether our conceptions are adequate, proper, fair. Such a risk is central to scientific education, where we deliberately subject our current theories to the test of continuous evaluation by future generations of our student-scientists. It is central also to our moral code, *in so far as* we ourselves take the moral point of view toward this code. And, finally, it is central to the democratic commitment which holds social policies to be continually open to free and public review. In sum, rationality liberates, but there is no liberty without risk.

Let no one, however, suppose that the liberating of minds is equivalent to freeing them from discipline. *Laissez-faire* is not the opposite of dogma. To be reasonable is a difficult achievement. The habit of reasonableness is not an airy abstract entity that can be skimmed off the concrete body of thought and practice. Consider again the case of science: scientific method can be learned only in and through its corpus of current materials. Reasonableness in science is an aspect or dimension of scientific tradition, and the body of the tradition is indispensable as a base for grasping this dimension. Science needs to be taught in such a way as to bring out this dimension as a consequence, but the consequence cannot be taken neat. Analogously for the art of moral choice: the moral point of view is attained, if at all, by acquiring a tradition of practice, embodied in rules and habits of conduct. Without a preliminary immersion in such a tradition—an appreciation of the import of its rules, obligations, rights, and demands—the concept of choice of actions and rules for oneself can hardly be achieved. Yet the prevalent tradition of practice can itself be taught in such a way as to encourage the ultimate attainment of a superordinate and comprehensive moral point of view.

The challenge of moral education is the challenge to develop critical thought in the sphere of practice and it is continuous with the challenge to develop critical thought in all aspects and phases of schooling. Moral schooling is not, therefore, a thing apart, something to be embodied in a list of maxims, something to be reckoned as simply another subject, or another activity, curricular or extracurricular. It does, indeed, have to pervade the *whole* of the school experience.

Nor is it thereby implied that moral education ought to concern itself solely with the general structure of this experience, or with the effectiveness of the total 'learning environment' in forming the child's habits. The critical questions concern the *quality* of the environment: what is the *nature* of the particular school experience, comprising content as well as structure? Does it liberate the child in the long run, as he grows to adulthood? Does it encourage respect for persons, and for the arguments and reasons offered in personal exchanges? Does it open itself to questioning and discussion? Does it provide the child with fundamental schooling in the traditions of reason, and the arts that are embodied therein? Does it, for example, encourage the development of linguistic and mathematical abilities, the capacity to read a page and follow an argument? Does it provide an exposure to the range of historical experience and the realms of personal and social life embodied in literature, the law, and the social sciences? Does it also provide an exposure to particular domains of scientific work in which the canons of logical reasoning and evidential deliberation may begin to be appreciated? Does it afford opportunity for individual initiative in reflective inquiry and practical projects? Does it provide a stable personal milieu in which the dignity of others and the variation of opinion may be appreciated, but in which a common and overriding love for truth and fairness may begin to be seen as binding oneself and one's fellows in a universal human community?

If the answer is negative, it matters not how effective the environment is in shaping concrete results in conduct. For the point of moral education in a democracy is antithetical to mere shaping. It is rather to liberate.

Notes

1. Ralph Barton Perry, *Realms of Value,* Cambridge: Harvard University Press, 1954, pp. 431–2. Excerpt reprinted in I. Scheffler, ed., *Philosophy and Education,* 2nd ed., Boston: Allyn & Bacon, 1966, pp. 32 ff.
2. Cited in Introduction to George S. Counts and Nucia P. Lodge, eds. and translators, *I Want To Be Like Stalin: From the Russian Text on Pedagogy* (by B. P. Yesipov and N. K. Goncharov). New York: John Day, 1947, pp. 14, 18. (The materials cited are from the 3rd ed. of the *Pedagogy,* published in 1946.)
3. Frederic Lilge, "Lenin and the Politics of Education," *Slavic Review* (June 1968), Vol. XXVII. No. 2, p. 255.
4. Ralph Barton Perry, *op. cit.,* p. 432.
5. See, for example, Kurt Baier, *The Moral Point of View,* Ithaca: Cornell University Press, 1958; William K. Frankena, *Ethics,* Englewood Cliffs, N.J.: Prentice Hall, 1963, and R. S. Peters, *Ethics and Education,* Glenview, Ill.: Scott Foresman, 1967. Additional articles of interest may be found in Sect. V, 'Moral Education' and Sect. VI, 'Education, Religion, and Politics,' in I. Scheffler, ed., *Philosophy and Education.*

B

Teaching

14   What Is Teaching?*

Paul H. Hirst

> The author is Professor of Education at the University of Cambridge. His aim in
> this essay is not to offer advice for the improvement of teaching but rather to ana-
> lyze the concept of teaching itself. Such conceptual analysis was the hallmark of
> analytic philosophy prior to the early 1970s, when it began to broaden into a con-
> sideration of the applications of theory to practical issues in ethics, social philoso-
> phy, and philosophy of education.

The question with which this paper is concerned is simply 'What is teaching?'
How do we distinguish teaching from other activities? This is, I think, a very
important question for at least four reasons. First, a lot of new educational
methods are now widely canvassed in which the significance of teaching is far
from clear. Repeatedly one finds an almost exclusive emphasis on certain activities of the pupils, say those of inquiry, discovery, and play, not on the activities
of the teacher. In the discussion of such methods it seems to me there is much
misunderstanding of what teaching is and therefore of what it involves, and
this not infrequently leads to a very distorted view of the whole educational
situation. Secondly, people are now aware of a range of activities, some of them
thought to be morally undesirable, whose relation to teaching is by no means
clear: activities like indoctrinating, preaching, advertising, and propagandiz-
ing. There are many terms that are as it were in the same logical band as 'teaching', and we are I think rightly getting more sensitive as to whether or not the
activities these terms label ought to go on in school. If we can get clearer about
the nature of teaching it will surely help us to see the character of these other
processes and their interconnections. Similar problems are raised by the use of
teaching machines and other devices, not to mention sleep-teaching.

Thirdly, we are clearly in need of a great deal of carefully controlled empirical research on the effectiveness of different teaching methods. But without
the clearest concept of what teaching is, it is impossible to find appropriate be-
havioural criteria whereby to assess what goes on in the classroom. Most
teaching methods new and old are advocated or defended on little more than
hunch or personal prejudice. What we need to know are some relevant empirical facts, but these we cannot find if we are uncertain how to identify cases of
teaching anyway. And finally, being clear about what teaching is matters vitally because how teachers understand teaching very much affects what they
actually do in the classroom. If it is the case that our activities depend on how
we ourselves see them, what we believe about them, then if we have crazy,
fuzzy ideas about teaching, we will be likely to do crazy and fuzzy things in its
name. One of the most important things for a teacher is surely to be clear about
the nature of the central activity in which he is professionally involved. And if

*From the *Journal of Curriculum Studies*, vol. 3, no. 1 (May, 1971), pp. 5–18, by permission of Taylor
& Francis and the author.

that is true for teachers in general, it is certainly true for the teachers of teachers in particular.

The question then is how do we characterize the activity of teaching so as to distinguish it from all other activities? How, for instance, on entering a classroom can one tell whether the teacher is in fact teaching? What exactly has to be going on? To begin to answer the problem here we must surely distinguish two obviously different senses in which we talk about teaching. In the first sense we talk about teaching as an *enterprise* in which a person may be engaged for a long period, say all afternoon. In this sense, a teacher spends the afternoon not in shopping, sunbathing, or taking the dog for a walk, but in fact in teaching. The term teaching is here functioning at a very general level, labelling a whole enterprise which may be broken down into many much more specific activities. And if indeed we look at these more detailed elements of the enterprise, it is perfectly plain that many of them are not activities we would in a more restricted sense of the term wish to call 'teaching' at all. Opening the window to let in more air, sharpening a few pencils, preventing a squabble between two pupils, all these may be legitimate parts of the enterprise of teaching as a whole. But we do surely use the term teaching in a much more specific sense whereby we can say that these activities are not the activities of teaching. In this second sense then we can speak of specific teaching *activities* which do not include in their number the sharpening of pencils, the opening of windows, and all other such activities which might form a legitimate part of the teaching enterprise as a whole. In the rest of this paper I am not concerned with the enterprise use of the term and would add only one point about it. Clearly for an enterprise to be that of teaching at all it is necessary that it must contain certain specific teaching activities. If a teacher spent the whole afternoon opening windows, sharpening pencils, cleaning her glasses, and so on, she would do no teaching in any sense at all. It is necessary therefore to the teaching enterprise that it should include specific teaching activities, and all other specific activities are part of that enterprise only because of their relation to these.[1]

But how are specific *teaching* activities to be distinguished from all other specific activities? Why exactly is opening a window or sharpening a pencil not teaching? Manifestly teaching is no one specific activity readily identifiable in general circumstances like, say, walking or running or riding a bicycle. There are an enormous number of specific activities which may in fact be teaching. One might be describing a historical situation and this could be called teaching. One might on the other hand be saying nothing at all, but be drawing on a blackboard, or doing a chemical experiment in front of the pupils. All these would seem to be teaching activities in a specific sense, so that there is no one immediately recognizable activity which the term teaching picks out. Is there then a limited number of specific activities which constitute teaching, so that to be teaching at all one would have to be carrying out one of these? A teacher would then have to know how to question, how to prove things, how to demonstrate, etc. If this were what teaching involved, it would greatly simplify the business of teacher training and indeed it seems to me that there is a large grain of truth in this idea. Such an approach is, however, too simple-minded, if only because many, if not all, of the specific activities which occur within teaching, also occur when one is certainly not teaching. One can tell a story to a child who knows it backwards but who just simply enjoys hearing it over once more. One might demonstrate something to entertain a nightclub audience. In proving something, one may be actually discovering the proof, not teaching someone else. One may be translating something, without teaching anything to anybody. None of these activities implies that teaching is taking place at all. It therefore seems to be the case that we cannot hope to get clear what teaching is simply by producing an exhaustive list of activities of this kind.

Nevertheless, teaching is what is technically known as a polymorphous activity; it quite literally takes many different forms. Its parallels are thus activities like work and gardening, and explicit comparisons with these might help in the process of clarification. What does a person have to be doing to be working? Driving a truck, working a lathe, solving mathematical problems, drawing beer, all these activities constitute somebody's work. Indeed any activity would seem to be in principle a possible form of work. On the other hand, gardening is much more limited in what it embraces. Digging, mowing the lawn, pruning are activities of gardening, but one cannot be doing *anything* as one might in the case of work. What then about teaching? Is it in this respect more like work or like gardening? Looked at one way teaching can take so many different forms that, like work, there seems pretty well no limit to the activities it can involve. Standing on one's head could in fact be part of teaching something, so could driving, working a lathe, solving a problem. Provided one looks at the whole range of things that can be taught, it would seem that any activity might occur as a teaching activity. Which activities might be involved in any particular instance will depend on exactly *what* is being taught. Yet it might be insisted that though teaching, say, to drive, might *involve* driving, when teaching one must in fact do more than merely drive. One must, say, *demonstrate* driving. This would seem to imply that though any activity might be subsumed under the notion of teaching, for that to be the case it must be carried out in some special way. And this in turn suggests that all the legion activities that can figure in teaching, to figure in that way, must be seen as occurring within a framework of the kind of specific activities mentioned earlier, such as demonstrating, proving, telling, etc. This view is I think correct and the analogy between teaching and other polymorphous activities would seem to be most helpful at the level of, say, gardening rather than at the level of, say, work. Yet the parallel with gardening is strictly limited. Activities like pruning and mowing the lawn are necessarily forms of gardening and that concept may be exhaustively analysable in such terms. Yet it was insisted above that demonstrating and proving are not necessarily forms of teaching and it is by no means obvious that, limited though the range of activities of teaching may be, there is an exhaustive list of distinct activities into which the concept of teaching could be even partially analysed. I conclude therefore that we cannot hope to characterize specific teaching activities simply in terms of the activities of proving, demonstrating, telling, etc. Rather, teaching must be characterized some other way which will make it clear to us when these activities are indeed involved in teaching and when involved in, say, entertaining. It will perhaps also make plain why these activities are peculiarly important in teaching.

How then are we going to characterize specific teaching activities at all? I think the answer to this is that they can only be characterized in the way in which we fundamentally characterize all human activities, by looking at their point or purpose. It is by clarifying the aim, the intention of what is going on, that we can see when standing on one's head to demonstrate something, or any other activity, is in fact teaching and not, say, simply entertaining. The difference here is in the different, overriding intentions involved in each case. What a particular activity is, what a person is doing, depends crucially on how he himself sees the activity. To take a standard example, if a person is seen to place a glass of liquid to his lips and slowly drain it, what is he doing? He may be quenching his thirst, committing suicide, or engaging in a religious ritual. Which of these if any it is, depends on the point, purpose, or intention that lies behind the physical movements. Clearly the physical state of affairs can be described without knowing the person's intention. It can be seen that the glass is moved by a certain force so many inches towards his lips, and so on. But an account of what is observed does not tell us what the activity is. Perhaps in a particular context we may be able to infer very readily the most likely point of the movements and thus what activity is involved; nevertheless it is only by reference to the intention that we can describe the activity, and of course there is no guarantee that our external judgement of the intention, based upon our observation, is in fact correct.

Yet if a 'sufficient' characterization of an activity can only be given in terms of its intention and not in terms of its observable features, that is not to say that certain observable features are not necessary to many particular activities. Clearly not all observable events could be described as quenching one's thirst or celebrating Mass. Unless liquid of some sort is being consumed, a person cannot be quenching his thirst and on empirical evidence alone we can dismiss such a description of many of his activities. From observation we can rule out many possibilities of what a person is doing even if we cannot from observation say which of the remaining possibilities he is engaged in. The points here are fundamentally quite simple. First, any activity is characterized by its intention, but many intentions cannot, logically cannot, be ascribed unless certain observable conditions hold. Secondly, for a given set of observable conditions a number of quite different intentions may be ascribable. Thirdly, in so far as there are necessary observable conditions for a particular activity, they are necessary conditions for there being the intention concerned in this case. They are not conditions of a logically independent character.

What we want to know then about teaching is first, what is the intention by which its activities are picked out from all others and secondly what necessary observable features are there by which we can judge that some activities could not possibly be teaching, whereas others might well be, though we can never be certain from such external characterization alone.

A crude answer to the first of these questions is I think simple. The intention of all teaching activities is that of bringing about learning. But simple and banal though this answer might seem, it is I suggest an extremely important answer. It involves the claim that the concept of teaching is in fact totally unintelligible without a grasp of the concept of learning. It asserts that there is no such thing as teaching without the intention to bring about learning and that therefore one cannot characterize teaching independently of characterizing learning. Until therefore we know what learning is, it is impossible for us to know what teaching is. The one concept is totally dependent on the other. Because of the tightest conceptual connection then, the characterization and *raison d'être* of teaching rests on that of learning. If therefore a teacher spends the whole afternoon in activities the concern of which is not that the pupils should learn, but, say, the inflation of his own ego, then in fact he cannot have been teaching at all. In these terms it could be the case that quite a large number of professional teachers are in fact frauds most of their lives, because their intentions are never clear. Perhaps quite a lot of our work is misdirected because this necessary intention is lost in a welter of secondary intentions, by neglect, if not deliberately. Of course pupils may learn many things when a teacher is not in fact teaching. That is another matter. What would seem to be particularly important here is that in taking a job as a professional teacher one is presumably being paid to carry out this intention whatever else one is paid to do. If one is not going into the classroom to bring about learning, if that is not the intention, then one cannot, logically cannot, be teaching. That is not to say that one may not be doing many other things which are of value. There are many ways of occupying children's time, some of them profitable, but that does not make them teaching. I wish to maintain therefore that the notion of teaching is totally dependent for its characterization on the concept of learning and that this has important practical consequences for how teachers see their job and therefore for what they do in the classroom.

Before going further, two particular points need commenting on. First, there are two ways in which we talk about teaching activities in the classroom context. The most common relates to the case in which a person may teach in the fullest sense of that word and yet, in spite of the intention and the appropriateness of the activities involved, the pupils learn absolutely nothing. Here the notion of teaching is simply that of trying to get people to learn and no more. But there is another use of the word, which involves the implication that not only has there been the intention to bring about learning, but that the pupil has in fact learnt what was intended. To say that Mr. Brown taught me to ride a bicycle, usually means not merely that Mr. Brown tried to get me to learn to ride a bicycle, but that I have in fact succeeded in learning this. There is thus not only a 'task' sense to the verb to teach, where trying or intending alone is implied; there is also a 'success' or 'achievement' sense, where in addition to the intention, there is the implication that learning has in fact occurred. For the rest of this paper I shall be concerned with teaching in the 'task' sense only, and in this sense it is *not* the case that teaching necessarily implies learning. What teaching implies is merely the intention to bring about learning.[2]

Secondly, if teaching activities are intentional, what are we to say about all the learning that goes on in a classroom, or anywhere else, which is not intended by the teacher? Is there not such a thing as unintentional teaching after all? Certainly, we do sometimes talk in this way, when a particular situation has been the occasion for significant learning. What is important here is surely the recognition that no teacher intended the learning, though significant things might have been picked up in the context. It will be suggested later that it is because of certain important features in the context that make the situation similar to that in which there is the intention to bring about learning that we use the term teaching here, though in a somewhat different sense. In schools we are not primarily concerned with unintended learning. What we are concerned with is the task of bringing about learning because we believe there is much that we can do towards making learning more than a random business. Of course, taking the education of children as a whole, what they pick up in the context of our unintentional teaching may indeed be important. Still this does not alter the fact that in schools we are centrally concerned with intentional teaching and that as soon as we turn our attention to what has been unintentional teaching, we thereby necessarily change its character.

The characterization of teaching given thus far makes the concept entirely parasitic on that of learning. That being so, it would seem important in clarifying the notion further to look at what is meant by 'learning'. Even if teaching is not the label of one specific activity, is learning? The answer I think must again be clearly no. One may learn things by trial and error, by discovery or observation, by being told and by many other means. But if there are many different activities of learning, what makes them cases of learning? I suggest the answer is again found, as in the case of teaching, by looking at the intention of the activities concerned. If the intention of teaching involves a concern for learning, what in turn is the intention of learning? Fortunately the answer seems not to be another type of activity whose intention would in turn have to be clarified. The end or aim of learning is, I suggest, always some specific achievement or end state. There are many such end achievements: believing something which one did not believe before, knowing something one did not know before, being able to do something one could not do before, having a habit one had not got before, and so on. As a result of learning one may know a scientific theory, know how to ride a bicycle, know how to calculate a square root, know that Henry VIII had six wives, appreciate the symphonies of Beethoven, or keep one's engagements punctually. The achievements or end states with which learning is concerned are of enormous variety and not surprisingly therefore the activities of learning are equally varied. Learning like teaching is a polymorphous activity. If then learning is the activity of a person, say B, the intention of which is the attainment of some particular end, we can say that B necessarily learns something, say X, where X may be a belief, a skill, an attitude, or some other complex object that characterizes this end.

For the purpose of this paper there is no need to pursue the nature of learning further, though two particular points must be stressed. First, it is I think important to note that the end achievements of learning are new states of the person and that these differ radically from each other. We seem to be under a perpetual temptation to think that all learning results in knowledge. Clearly this is false. Along with this too goes the temptation to think that what we learn, X, is necessarily a truth or fact of some kind. Clearly this is also false. To thoroughly disabuse oneself of these myths is a first step towards getting rid of many common but quite fallacious ideas about the nature of learning and, as a consequence, about the nature of teaching.

Secondly, it must be noted that I have assumed learning to be an activity on the part of the learner. But just as we have a use of teaching to cover cases when there is in fact no intention to bring about learning, so we have uses of learning where the pupil does not in fact intend to achieve the appropriate end which he nevertheless attains. In this sense we can speak of non-intentional learning, where as the result of a causal process as in hypnotism, conditioning, sleep-teaching, or even the unconscious acquisition of something, the intention of the learner is not involved. It is important to recognize here that the term learning is being used for a quite different process, in this case causal and not intentional. Nothing is to be gained by trying to legislate one meaning for the term, cutting across general usage which now covers both these processes. Yet the distinction between them needs to be kept clear. Whether or not causal processes are educationally desirable is a matter with which I am not here concerned.

Putting together what has been said about learning with what was earlier said about teaching, we have the following account of teaching. A teaching activity is the activity of a person, A (the teacher), the intention of which is to bring about an activity (learning), by a person, B (the pupil), the intention of which is to achieve some end state (e.g. knowing, appreciating) whose object is X (e.g. a belief, attitude, skill). From this it follows that to understand what is involved in teaching, one must start at the other end of a logical chain of relations, with an understanding of the end achievements to which everything is being directed. From this one can proceed to understand what is involved in B's achieving such ends, in learning X, and then proceed to an understanding of what is involved in A teaching B, X. This logical dependence of teaching on learning, and learning on the nature of the achievements to which it is directed is thus once more no mere academic matter. If teachers are not clear what end achievements their teaching is concerned with, they cannot know what is involved in B's learning X. And until they know what is involved in B's learning X, they cannot know what is involved in A's teaching B, X. Any notion of learning which is not the learning of some particular X is as vague as the notion of going somewhere but nowhere in particular. Equally some particular person B is necessarily learning this X. Following the logical chain, it is therefore only in a context where both what is to be learnt and who is learning it are clear, that we can begin to be clear about teaching B, X. Just as a pupil B cannot simply learn, but must necessarily be learning X, so A cannot simply teach, he must be teaching B, and he must be teaching B, X. It is as much a logical absurdity to say 'One teaches children not subjects' as it is to say 'One teaches subjects not children'. Both of these phrases might have their slogan use, but the serious discussion of teaching ought surely to reject such slogans in the name of the simple logical truth, that one necessarily teaches somebody something. Not that of course one is necessarily teaching a 'subject' in the traditional sense, but there must always be an end achievement which somebody is learning. A great deal of discussion of modern educational methods seems in danger of going seriously astray because of a refusal to accept the full implications of this simple logically necessary truth.

I have so far argued that in its central use, teaching is the label for those activities of a person A, the intention of which is to bring about in another person, B, the intentional learning of X. In addition, there would seem to be uses of the terms when the intention on the part of A is missing, but the intentional learning on the part of B remains, and also uses when the intention on the part of A is present, but the intention on the part of B is replaced by a causal process. But even in the central case, the intention on the part of A to bring about the learning of X by B might be thought to leave the characterization of teaching activities too open. On this account, might not the strangest events count as teaching a pupil say to count, provided this was the intention of the teacher? This would indeed be the case if there were no necessary conditions which an activity must satisfy before it could possibly be described as a teaching activity. Just as not all activities could be gardening surely not all activities could be teaching? What then are the necessary features of a publicly observable kind which all teaching activities must possess? There are I suggest at least two. As it is necessarily the case that A teaches B, X, there is one necessary demand on the activities in relation to the particular X that is being taught, and there is a second necessary demand in relation to the particular person B concerned.

The first of these demands is far from easy to express. But I suggest that in so far as one is necessarily teaching X, the specific teaching activity involved must be what I will call 'indicative' of X. By this I mean that the activity must, either implicitly or explicity, express or embody the X to be learnt, so that this X is clearly indicated to the pupil as what he is to learn. In this way the teacher makes plain in his activity *what* he intends to be learnt. It is not I think at all the case that what is to be learnt must necessarily be explicitly discernible in the activity, yet it must be so available in some sense that the pupil's learning activity can be directed to this as its object. It is because activities like demonstrating, telling, and proving can provide such excellent means for indicating an X that it is intended the pupil will learn, that they play such a central part in teaching. Yet just because these activities are such effective means for expressly indicating a given X, they can be significant not only in teaching but in such other concerns as entertaining. It is only when such activities are used in a learning context, to indicate what is to be *learnt* that they can become teaching activities. The fact that specific teaching activities must indicatively express what is to be learnt also helps to make clear why at times we speak of teaching in an unintentional sense. We do this, I suggest, when certain features of a situ-

ation can be legitimately interpreted as indicatively expressing something to
be learnt, though this in fact may not be anyone's actual intention. The situation is thus interpreted as a teaching situation by the learner, when in fact,
from an intentional point of view, it is no such thing. First, then, specific teaching activities must be indicative of what is to be learnt and it is for this reason
that the opening of windows and the sharpening of pencils could never be
themselves the teaching of historical facts or of Pythagoras's Theorem.

In the second place, as a specific teaching activity is necessarily concerned with the teaching of X to a particular pupil B, it must be indicatively expressed so that it is possible for this particular pupil B to learn X. One might
teach an undergraduate class in philosophy Wittgenstein's criticism of the idea
of a private language, by reading to the students sections from the *Philosophical
Investigations.* But to carry out such an activity with a class of average six-year-
olds would, I suggest, not constitute teaching at all. Indicative though the activity might be, as the six-year-olds could understand practically nothing that
was being said, this could surely not constitute teaching *them* Wittgenstein's
views on private languages. There is a gap between the knowledge, skills, or
state of mind of the learner and what he is to learn, which it seems to me any
teaching activity must seek to bridge if it is to deserve that label. Teaching activities must therefore take place at a level where the pupil *can* take on what it
is intended he should learn. It must be possible, and this seems to me a logical
point, for learning to take place. This logical demand is for the teacher to have
psychological and other knowledge about the learner, and it clearly means that
many specific things cannot possibly be taught to a given pupil given his present state of knowledge, skill, etc. I conclude therefore that a specific teaching
activity must necessarily indicatively express the X to be learnt by B and be so
related to the present state of B that he can learn X.

It might be objected to my second necessary demand for teaching activities, that to misjudge the present state of the pupils does not disqualify a person's activities from properly being described as teaching. Surely he has taught
X whether the pupils have learnt X or not. Certainly teaching does not necessarily imply learning, but it does necessarily imply the intention of bringing
about learning by someone, and if from one's activities it is impossible for that
someone to learn what is intended, it does seem very odd to describe such activities as teaching. One reason why we are inclined to think that there could
be teaching even when the present state of the pupils is grossly misjudged, is I
think that we spend so much of our time teaching classes, not individuals, and
the condition I am insisting on seems to make almost impossible demands.
Must it not be the case that in any class with a wide ability range, what is presented is in fact inappropriate for some of the pupils? If we are to stick to the
individualistic model I have used, must we not say that in even the 'task'
sense, only some of the class have been taught X, and not others? Strictly I
think the answer to that must be yes. But perhaps it would be better simply to
recognize that we do use the word teaching both for activities aimed at group
learning as well as individual learning. In the case of a group, what a teacher

does if he is teaching them all the same X is to work with an appropriate norm for the attainments of that group. What constitutes an appropriate norm cannot I think be generally stated; nevertheless it seems to me that without working to such a norm there could be no activities that could properly be described as teaching the group. It might of course be argued, and with some justice, that properly understood, teaching a group necessarily involves attention to the individual differences of the pupils.

As a final comment on the two criteria which I have suggested are necessary to any teaching activity, it is I think instructive to note that in these terms opposing virtues and defects have tended to characterize both traditional formal teaching methods and more contemporary progressive alternatives. Traditional teaching methods have above all concerned themselves with the indicative features of these activities, often meeting the present learning state of the pupils in an over-generalized and inadequate way. In reaction, more progressive methods have tended to cater extremely well for the present learning state of individual pupils, but at the expense of the necessary indicative features that teaching activities must embody. It is not that either group of methods is of itself necessarily deficient as teaching activity, and each might well have its place according to what exactly is being taught and to whom. What is important is that we come to realize that in all teaching activities both these necessary features need the fullest responsible consideration.

In concluding this paper I would like to return to the problem of clarifying the nature of such activities as indoctrinating, conditioning, preaching, training, instructing, and so on, as the characterization of teaching that I have outlined can I think help in this process. As here considered, teaching activities form a very broad category indeed, one which is in no sense restricted to those activities we think it appropriate for schools to undertake. I have been concerned with teaching and learning in general, whatever the ends concerned, be they bad habits, perversions, concepts, facts, physical skills, etc. In so far then as indoctrination and other activities involve the intention to bring about learning of some kind, they involve teaching and in so far as they are themselves processes for bringing about learning of certain kinds they are themselves forms of teaching. From all that has been said about teaching, different categories of teaching activity can clearly be distinguished in a number of distinct ways. The object or objects to be learnt can be of one particular kind rather than another. The activity of learning may be of a specific sort, or the activity of the teacher may be restricted in some particular way. Clearly there are likely to be labels for certain types of teaching which become important for specific purposes and it is, I suggest, by looking at the particular sub-class of teaching activities involved that we are most likely to distinguish indoctrination, instruction, and so on.

Indoctrination, for example, would certainly seem to be picked out, at least in part, by the distinctive end state of mind of the learner, to which the teaching is directed. An indoctrinated person would seem to hold certain beliefs unshakeably.[3] In this case what the person is intended to learn, the X, is distinctive here, though in exactly what way it is important to note. On this criterion, it is nothing about the beliefs themselves that distinguishes indoctrination, but some higher-order beliefs about their status, or some attitude to them. But however this characterization is given, it is expressible in terms of certain distinctive objects for learning. Some have suggested that there is in fact something distinctive about the beliefs themselves in that one can only indoctrinate in matters of opinion or doctrines. Again this is to distinguish the teaching activities of indoctrination in terms of *what* is being taught. It can also be argued that indoctrination is restricted to certain learning processes, or that unintentional indoctrination is a contradiction. My point here is not to decide exactly what is meant by indoctrination or any other of these terms, but rather to indicate how a clarification of them might be helpfully approached.

What is however plain from the work that has already been done on the concept of indoctrination is that most terms in this area are likely to be in some respects unclear, being used in a number of interrelated ways. What matters then is not what any 'correct' use might be, but rather the conceptual distinctions that arise in this area. If, for instance, the notion of 'believing unshakeably' is seen as a distinctive result of some forms of teaching, and we for our purposes call these forms indoctrination, then indoctrination is being sharply distinguished from teaching leading to the holding of beliefs rationally, which many regard as a necessary part of education. Once we know the possible meanings of these very tricky terms we know our way around their relationships much better. We are clearer too about the significance of many of the things we do when engaged in teaching.

The distinctive features of such processes as conditioning and sleep-teaching would seem to be that they involve causal and not intentional learning, or if it is intentional, it is intentional in some very particular sense. Whether or not these processes ought to figure within indoctrination or education will of course depend on one's account of these latter processes. Training and instructing on the other hand would seem to be concepts connected unmistakably with intentional learning, the difference between them being determined by the particular group of end achievements with which each is concerned.

And finally, what of teaching machines: can such machines be properly said to teach? In terms of the analysis I have here given the idea that a piece of hardware can of itself teach is nonsense, for it itself can have no intentions and cannot engage in activities. But taken in the proper context I see no reason why a machine, properly programmed, should not be the instrument of a teaching activity. It is indeed the machine programmed so that it indicatively expresses what is to be learnt, in such a way that the pupil can in fact learn, because it meets his current state of mind, that must be thought of as the teaching agent. The appropriate programming of the machine is of course an essential part of the teaching activity as a whole. What the invention of books, let alone teaching machines, made possible, was a separation in time between the teacher's expression of what is to be learnt and the pupil's encounter with this. Nothing new in principle is introduced into the idea of a teaching activity. What is, however, available here to the pupil is a programme of indicatively expressive activities drawn up after expert consideration of the problems involved in pupils' learning that might be much better for the task than the live activities of the teacher available. As the teaching activities that involve the use of such machines must be completely predetermined, it is of course important that the details of the programme be constructed with the utmost care and that it be appropriate to the learning state of the pupils. It is of course only when these conditions are fulfilled that in using the machine these pupils could be said to be being taught.

Throughout this paper I have been concerned with mapping the features that distinguish teaching activities from all others. It has not been my concern to lay down the criteria for good teaching or even successful teaching. Successful teaching would seem to be simply teaching which does in fact bring about the desired learning. Good teaching, however, is much more difficult to discern. I am not even sure that successful learning is a criterion for good teaching. Certainly in a given particular case there is no contradiction in saying that a person was successfully yet badly taught. Yet in so far as this account of teaching is correct, it has at least indicated which activities we are concerned to study in a critical comparison of teaching activities. What is more it must have at least some important implications for the methods whereby such comparisons must be made. But what these are, will not be gone into here, if only because such elaboration would be rather premature when the criteria for what teaching is are not yet agreed. It is towards establishing what these criteria are that this paper has been primarily directed.

Notes

1. I am here using terminology which is in part the same as that used by B. Paul Komisar: "Teaching: Act and Enterprise," in C. J. B. Macmillan and T. W. Nelson (eds.), *Concepts of Teaching* (New York: Rand McNally, 1968). In spite of certain similarities in both terminology and approach, however, our accounts are clearly in radical disagreement over the precise relationship between teaching and learning, and the necessary characteristic of at least certain of his "teaching acts."
2. The commonplace distinction I am here making leaves unnoted a complexity which any full task/achievement analysis of teaching cannot disregard. If teaching is directed towards another activity, that of the pupil's learning, then the task and achievement uses of "teaching" need to be carefully related to possible task and achievement uses of "learning." We are inclined to assume that both uses of "teaching" are directed to the achievement use of "learning." It is, however, far from obvious that this is always the case. Just this problem arises again with activities like demonstrating and proving as Dr. Komisar shows very plainly (see note 1). I am, however, unhappy about his account of these activities, though I am far from certain that I have always understood him.
3. See J. P. White, "Indoctrination," in R. S. Peters (ed.), *The Concept of Education* (London: Routledge & Kegan Paul, 1967).

15 Education at the Crossroads*
Jacques Maritain

> The French philosopher Jacques Maritain (1882–1973) was a foremost interpreter
> of the thought of St. Thomas Aquinas, the medieval philosopher and theologian,
> whose system of thought was declared the official Catholic philosophy. In this
> essay Maritain explains the role of the teacher in the educational process, arguing
> against what he terms "old" and "progressive" education, although, in fact, his
> use of the latter term reflects ideas espoused by A. S. Neill, not John Dewey. Mari-
> tain's writings illustrate the ways in which metaphysical considerations can influ-
> ence educational thought, as, for instance, his understanding of human perfection
> as expressive of divine purpose.

THE PUPIL'S MIND AND THE ART OF THE TEACHER

In order to discuss the dynamic factors in education, we must naturally reckon
first with the Platonic conception: that all learning is in the learner, not in the
teacher. Every reader of the *Phaedo* recalls that according to Plato knowledge
preexists from the very start in human souls, which before descending into the
body have contemplated the eternal Ideas; but when these souls are bound to
a body, they are prevented from freely considering those truths of which they
already possess knowledge. The student, in this way, does not acquire knowledge from the teacher, who has no real causal influence and who is at best only
an occasional agent: the teacher only awakens the attention of the student to
those things which he already knows, so that to learn is nothing else than to remember.

There are great truths in these exaggerated views of Plato. And one cannot but wonder at the nobility and delicacy of his Socratic way of teaching
which so ennobles the one who is taught—surely—since it deals with him as
with an angel, asleep indeed, but nevertheless an angel. These educational
views have been taken up afresh by many modern educators, though from
quite different philosophical standpoints. In reality, however, things are not as
Plato saw them who, after all, when treating of education from the political
point of view in his *Laws* was to overemphasize so surprisingly the authoritative aspect of education. The teacher does possess a knowledge which the student does not have. He actually communicates knowledge to the student
whose soul has *not* previously contemplated the divine Ideas before being
united to his body; and whose intellect, before being fecundated by sense-per-
ception and sense-experience, is but a *tabula rasa*, as Aristotle put it.

Yet what is the kind of causality or dynamic action exerted by the
teacher? Teaching is an art; the teacher is an artist. Is the teacher, then, like a
sculptor, a powerful Michelangelo who belabors the marble or despotically im-

---

*From Jacques Maritain, *Education at the Crossroads*, 1943, Yale University Press, by permission of
the publisher.

poses the form he has conceived on the passive clay? Such a conception was not infrequent in the education of old. It is a coarse and disastrous conception, contrary to the nature of things. For if the one who is being taught is not an angel, neither is he inanimate clay.

It is rather with the art of medicine that the art of education must be compared. Medicine deals with a living being that possesses inner vitality and the internal principle of health. The doctor exerts real causality in healing a sick man, yes, but in a very particular manner: by imitating the ways of nature herself in her operations, and by helping nature, by providing appropriate diet and remedies that nature herself uses, according to her own dynamism, toward a biological equilibrium. In other words, medicine is *ars cooperativa naturae,* an art of ministering, an art subservient to nature. And so is education. The implications of this are far-reaching indeed.

Ready-made knowledge does not, as Plato believed, exist in human souls. But the vital and active principle of knowledge does exist in each of us. The inner seeing power of intelligence, which naturally and from the very start perceives through sense-experience the primary notions on which all knowledge depends, is thereby able to proceed from what it already knows to what it does not yet know. An example of this is a Pascal discovering without any teacher and by virtue of his own ingenuity the first thirty-two propositions of the first book of Euclid. This inner vital principle the teacher must respect above all; his art consists in imitating the ways of the intellectual nature in its own operations. Thus the teacher has to offer to the mind either examples from experience or particular statements which the pupil is able to judge by virtue of what he already knows and from which he will go on to discover broader horizons. The teacher has further to comfort the mind of the pupil by putting before his eyes the logical connections between ideas which the analytical or deductive power of the pupil's mind is perhaps not strong enough to establish by itself.

All this boils down to the fact that the mind's natural activity on the part of the learner and the intellectual guidance on the part of the teacher are both dynamic factors in education, but that the principal agent in education, the primary dynamic factor or propelling force, is the internal vital principle in the one to be educated; the educator or teacher is only the secondary—though a genuinely effective—dynamic factor and a ministerial agent.

EDUCATION BY THE ROD AND PROGRESSIVE EDUCATION

Here, we teachers and professors may sometimes find consolation for our failures—we can think of them as due to the defect of the principal agent, the inner principle within the student, and not to our own deficiencies. And such an excuse is often valid. Yet quite apart from this kind of solace to teachers, the very simple considerations which I have just laid down in paraphrasing Thomas Aquinas, are, to my mind, of great import to the philosophy of education. I think that they illuminate the whole conflict between the old form of education by the rod and progressive education, which centers upon and stresses the freedom and the inner natural vitality of the child.

Education by the rod is positively bad education. If from a love of paradox I were to say something on its behalf, I should only observe that it has been able, actually, to produce some strong personalities, because it is difficult to kill the internal principle of spontaneity in living beings, and because this principle occasionally develops more powerfully when it reacts and sometimes revolts against constraint, fear, and punishment than when everything is made easy, lenient, and psychotechnically compliant to it. Strangely enough, we may wonder whether an education which yields itself entirely to the sovereignty of the child, and which suppresses any obstacle to be overcome, does not result in making students both indifferent and too docile, too passively permeable to anything the teacher is saying. However that may be, it is still true that birch and taws are bad educational measures, and that any education which considers the teacher as the principal agent perverts the very nature of the educational task.

The actual merit of modern conceptions in education since Pestalozzi, Rousseau, and Kant, has been the rediscovery of the fundamental truth that the principal agent and dynamic factor is not the art of the teacher but the inner principle of activity, the inner dynamism of nature and of the mind. If there were time we could insist, in this connection, that the search for new methods and inspiration, as emphasized by progressive education and what is called in Europe the "active school," should be valued, developed, and expanded—on condition that progressive education gives up its out-of-date rationalistic prejudices and utopian philosophy of life and does not forget that the teacher, too, is a real cause and agent—though only coöperating with nature—a real giver whose own dynamism, moral authority, and positive guidance are indispensable. If this complementary aspect is forgotten, the finest endeavors which arise from the mere cult of the freedom of the child will be washed away in the sands.

The freedom of the child is not the spontaneity of animal nature, moving right from the start along the fixed determinate paths of instinct (at least we usually think of animal instinct in this form, which is really too simplified, for animal instinct has a first period of progressive fixation). The freedom of the child is the spontaneity of a human and rational nature, and this largely *undetermined* spontaneity has its inner principle of final determination only in reason, which is not yet developed in the child.

The plastic and suggestible freedom of the child is harmed and led astray if it is not helped and guided. An education which consisted in making the child responsible for acquiring information about that of which he does not know he is ignorant, an education which only contemplated a blossoming forth of the child's instincts, and which rendered the teacher a tractable and useless attendant, is but a bankruptcy of education and of the responsibility of adults toward the youth. The right of the child to be educated requires that the educator shall have moral authority over him, and this authority is nothing else than the duty of the adult to the freedom of the youth.

THE TRUE AND THE FALSE FREEING OF PERSONALITY

It is possible to get a more profound view of the matter if one remembers the distinction between "personality" and "individuality". . . . Here we are confronted with the crucial problem of the education of man, in the broadest sense of this word. Let me recall that the distinction of which I am speaking is a metaphysical distinction which must be carefully understood, and which considers two different aspects of a same whole, of that same human being whom ordinary language calls equally an individual and a person.

The same man in his entirety is an individual and a person: he is a person by reason of the spiritual subsistence of his soul, and he is an individual by reason of that principle of nonspecific diversity which is matter, and which makes the components of a same species different from each other. My individuality and my personality, thus defined, are two aspects of my whole substantial being, to which correspond two different poles of attraction for my inner and moral development. I may develop along the lines of personality, that is, toward the mastery and independence of my spiritual self. Or I may develop along the lines of individuality, that is, toward the letting loose of the tendencies which are present in me by virtue of matter and heredity.

Such being the case, certain educators confuse personality with individuality, and mistake the display of sheer individuality for the development of personality. Personality means interiority to oneself; this internal selfhood grows in proportion as the life of reason and freedom dominates over the life of instinct and sensual desire—which implies self-sacrifice, striving toward self-perfection and love. But individuality, in the strict Aristotelian sense in which I am using this word, individuality means the material ego, the displaying of which consists in giving a free hand to the irrational trends of this ego. Thus, while becoming the center of everything, the ego is in reality scattered among cheap desires or overwhelming passions, and finally submitted to the determinism of matter.

I have insisted that education must center on the development and liberation of the individual person. What I am criticizing is that false form of appreciation of the individual person which, while looking at individuality instead of personality, reduces the education and progress of man to the mere freeing of the material ego. Such educators mistakenly believe they are providing man with the freedom of expansion and autonomy to which personality aspires while at the same time they deny the value of all discipline and asceticism, as well as the necessity of striving toward self-perfection. As a result, instead of fulfilling himself, man disperses himself and disintegrates.

Other educators, contrariwise, misconstrue the distinction between personality and individuality as a separation. They think that we bear in ourselves two separate beings, that of the individual and that of the person. Such partisans of the rod advocate "Death to the individual! And long live the person!" Unfortunately, when you kill the individual you also kill the person. This *despotic* conception of the education and progress of man is no better than the *anarchical* one. The ideal of the despotic conception is first to take out our heart, with anesthetics if possible, and next to replace it by some perfect organ standardized according to the rules of what everyone ought to be. The first operation may perhaps succeed, the second one is more difficult. Instead of a genuine human personality, sealed with the mysterious face of its Creator, there appears a mask, that of the conventional man or that of the rubber-stamped conscience, "incorporated."

If it is true that the internal principle, that is to say, nature—and grace too, for man is not a merely natural being—is what matters most in education, it follows that the entire art consists in inspiring, schooling and pruning, teaching and enlightening, so that in the intimacy of man's activities the weight of the egoistic tendencies diminishes, and the weight of the aspirations proper to personality and its spiritual generosity increases.

It should be added that the very term "self-perfection," which I used a while ago, needs to be properly understood. Man's perfection consists of the perfection of love, and so is less the perfection of his "self" than the perfection of his love, where the very self is in some measure lost sight of. And to advance in this self-perfection is not to copy an ideal. It is to let yourself be led by Another where you did not want to go, and to let Divine Love Who calls each being by his own name mold you and make of you a person, a true original, not a copy.

16   Pedagogy of the Oppressed*

Paulo Freire

The author is a Brazilian educator, who served as Professor of the History and Philosophy of Education at the University of Recife and worked to develop methods of teaching the city's illiterates. Forced by political pressure to leave the country, he went to Chile, where he participated in the United Nations Educational, Scientific, and Cultural Organization (UNESCO) programs of adult education. His writings stress the political nature of education and the role of learning in achieving liberation.

A careful analysis of the teacher-student relationship at any level, inside or outside the school, reveals its fundamentally *narrative* character. This relation-

*From *Pedagogy of the Oppressed* by Paulo Freire. Translation Copyright © 1970 by Paulo Freire. Reprinted by permission of The Continuum Publishing Company.

ship involves a narrating Subject (the teacher) and patient, listening objects (the students). The contents, whether values or empirical dimensions of reality, tend in the process of being narrated to become lifeless and petrified. Education is suffering from narration sickness.

The teacher talks about reality as if it were motionless, static, compartmentalized, and predictable. Or else he expounds on a topic completely alien to the existential experience of the students. His task is to "fill" the students with the contents of his narration—contents which are detached from reality, disconnected from the totality that engendered them and could give them significance. Words are emptied of their concreteness and become a hollow, alienated, and alienating verbosity.

The outstanding characteristic of this narrative education, then, is the sonority of words, not their transforming power. "Four times four is sixteen; the capital of Pará is Belém." The student records, memorizes, and repeats these phrases without perceiving what four times four really means, or realizing the true significance of "capital" in the affirmation "the capital of Pará is Belém," that is, what Belém means for Pará and what Pará means for Brazil.

Narration (with the teacher as narrator) leads the students to memorize mechanically the narrated content. Worse yet, it turns them into "containers," into "receptacles" to be "filled" by the teacher. The more completely she fills the receptacles, the better a teacher she is. The more meekly the receptacles permit themselves to be filled, the better students they are.

Education thus becomes an act of depositing, in which the students are the depositories and the teacher is the depositor. Instead of communicating, the teacher issues communiqués and makes deposits which the students patiently receive, memorize, and repeat. This is the "banking" concept of education, in which the scope of action allowed to the students extends only as far as receiving, filing, and storing the deposits. They do, it is true, have the opportunity to become collectors or cataloguers of the things they store. But in the last analysis, it is the people themselves who are filed away through the lack of creativity, transformation, and knowledge in this (at best) misguided system. For apart from inquiry, apart from the praxis, individuals cannot be truly human. Knowledge emerges only through invention and re-invention, through the restless, impatient, continuing, hopeful inquiry human beings pursue in the world, with the world, and with each other.

In the banking concept of education, knowledge is a gift bestowed by those who consider themselves knowledgeable upon those whom they consider to know nothing. Projecting an absolute ignorance onto others, a characteristic of the ideology of oppression, negates education and knowledge as processes of inquiry. The teacher presents himself to his students as their necessary opposite; by considering their ignorance absolute, he justifies his own existence. The students, alienated like the slave in the Hegelian dialectic, accept their ignorance as justifying the teacher's existence—but, unlike the slave, they never discover that they educate the teacher.

The *raison d'être* of libertarian education, on the other hand, lies in its drive towards reconciliation. Education must begin with the solution of the teacher-student contradiction, by reconciling the poles of the contradiction so that both are simultaneously teachers *and* students.

This solution is not (nor can it be) found in the banking concept. On the contrary, banking education maintains and even stimulates the contradiction through the following attitudes and practices, which mirror oppressive society as a whole:

(a) the teacher teaches and the students are taught;
(b) the teacher knows everything and the students know nothing;
(c) the teacher thinks and the students are thought about;
(d) the teacher talks and the students listen—meekly;
(e) the teacher disciplines and the students are disciplined;
(f) the teacher chooses and enforces his choice, and the students comply;
(g) the teacher acts and the students have the illusion of acting through the action of the teacher;
(h) the teacher chooses the program content, and the students (who were not consulted) adapt to it;
(i) the teacher confuses the authority of knowledge with his or her own professional authority, which she and he sets in opposition to the freedom of the students;
(j) the teacher is the Subject of the learning process, while the pupils are mere objects.

It is not surprising that the banking concept of education regards men as adaptable, manageable beings. The more students work at storing the deposits entrusted to them, the less they develop the critical consciousness which would result from their intervention in the world as transformers of that world. The more completely they accept the passive role imposed on them, the more they tend simply to adapt to the world as it is and to the fragmented view of reality deposited in them.

The capability of banking education to minimize or annul the students' creative power and to stimulate their credulity serves the interests of the oppressors, who care neither to have the world revealed nor to see it transformed. The oppressors use their "humanitarianism" to preserve a profitable situation. Thus they react almost instinctively against any experiment in education which stimulates the critical faculties and is not content with a partial view of reality but always seeks out the ties which link one point to another and one problem to another.

Indeed, the interests of the oppressors lie in "changing the consciousness of the oppressed, not the situation which oppresses them";[1] for the more the oppressed can be led to adapt to that situation, the more easily they can be dominated. To achieve this end, the oppressors use the banking concept of education in conjunction with a paternalistic social action apparatus, within which the oppressed receive the euphemistic title of "welfare recipients." They are treated as individual cases, as marginal persons who deviate from the general configuration of a "good, organized, and just" society. The oppressed are regarded as the pathology of the healthy society, which must therefore adjust these "incompetent and lazy" folk to its own patterns by changing their mentality. These marginals need to be "integrated," "incorporated" into the healthy society that they have "forsaken."

The truth is, however, that the oppressed are not "marginals," are not people living "outside" society. They have always been "inside"—inside the structure which made them "beings for others." The solution is not to "integrate" them into the structure of oppression, but to transform that structure so that they can become "beings for themselves." Such transformation, of course, would undermine the oppressors' purposes; hence their utilization of the banking concept of education to avoid the threat of student *conscientização*.

The banking approach to adult education, for example, will never propose to students that they critically consider reality. It will deal instead with such vital questions as whether Roger gave green grass to the goat, and insist upon the importance of learning that, on the contrary, *Roger* gave green grass to the *rabbit*. The "humanism" of the banking approach masks the effort to turn women and men into automatons—the very negation of their ontological vocation to be more fully human.

Those who use the banking approach, knowingly or unknowingly (for there are innumerable well-intentioned bank-clerk teachers who do not realize that they are serving only to dehumanize), fail to perceive that the deposits themselves contain contradictions about reality. But, sooner or later, these contradictions may lead formerly passive students to turn against their domestication and the attempt to domesticate reality. They may discover through existential experience that their present way of life is irreconcilable with their vocation to become fully human. They may perceive through their relations with reality that reality is really a *process*, undergoing constant transformation. If men and women are searchers and their ontological vocation is humanization, sooner or later they may perceive the contradiction in which banking education seeks to maintain them, and then engage themselves in the struggle for their liberation.

But the humanist, revolutionary educator cannot wait for this possibility to materialize. From the outset, her efforts must coincide with those of the students to engage in critical thinking and the quest for mutual humanization. His efforts must be imbued with a profound trust in people and their creative power. To achieve this, they must be partners of the students in their relations with them.

The banking concept does not admit to such partnership—and necessarily so. To resolve the teacher-student contradiction, to exchange the role of depositor, prescriber, domesticator, for the role of student among students would be to undermine the power of oppression and serve the cause of liberation.

Implicit in the banking concept is the assumption of a dichotomy between human beings and the world: a person is merely *in* the world, not *with* the world or with others; the individual is spectator, not re-creator. In this view, the person is not a conscious being (*corpo consciente*); he or she is rather the possessor of *a* consciousness: an empty "mind" passively open to the reception of deposits of reality from the world outside. For example, my desk, my books, my coffee cup, all the objects before me—as bits of the world which surround me—would be "inside" me, exactly as I am inside my study right now. This view makes no distinction between being accessible to consciousness and entering consciousness. The distinction, however, is essential: the objects which surround me are simply accessible to my consciousness, not located within it. I am aware of them, but they are not inside me.

It follows logically from the banking notion of consciousness that the educator's role is to regulate the way the world "enters into" the students. The teacher's task is to organize a process which already occurs spontaneously, to "fill" the students by making deposits of information which he or she considers to constitute true knowledge.[2] And since people "receive" the world as passive entities, education should make them more passive still, and adapt them to the world. The educated individual is the adapted person, because she or he is better "fit" for the world. Translated into practice, this concept is well suited to the purposes of the oppressors, whose tranquility rests on how well people fit the world the oppressors have created, and how little they question it.

The more completely the majority adapt to the purposes which the dominant minority prescribe for them (thereby depriving them of the right to their own purposes), the more easily the minority can continue to prescribe. The theory and practice of banking education serve this end quite efficiently. Verbalistic lessons, reading requirements,[3] the methods for evaluating "knowledge," the distance between the teacher and the taught, the criteria for promotion: everything in this ready-to-wear approach serves to obviate thinking.

The bank-clerk educator does not realize that there is no true security in his hypertrophied role, that one must seek to live *with* others in solidarity. One cannot impose oneself, nor even merely co-exist with one's students. Solidarity requires true communication, and the concept by which such an educator is guided fears and proscribes communication.

Yet only through communication can human life hold meaning. The teacher's thinking is authenticated only by the authenticity of the students' thinking. The teacher cannot think for her students, nor can she impose her thought on them. Authentic thinking, thinking that is concerned about *reality*, does not take place in ivory tower isolation, but only in communication. If it is true that thought has meaning only when generated by action upon the world, the subordination of students to teachers becomes impossible.

Because banking education begins with a false understanding of men and women as objects, it cannot promote the development of what Fromm calls "biophily," but instead produces its opposite: "necrophily."

> While life is characterized by growth in a structured, functional manner, the necrophilous person loves all that does not grow, all that is mechanical. The necrophilous person is driven by the desire to transform the organic into the inorganic, to approach life mechanically, as if all living persons were things. . . . Memory, rather than experience; having, rather than being, is what counts. The necrophilous person can relate to an object—a flower or a person—only if he possesses it; hence a threat to his possession is a threat to himself; if he loses posses-

sion he loses contact with the world. . . . He loves control, and in the act of controlling he kills life.[4]

Oppression—overwhelming control—is necrophilic; it is nourished by love of death, not life. The banking concept of education, which serves the interests of oppression, is also necrophilic. Based on a mechanistic, static, naturalistic, spatialized view of consciousness, it transforms students into receiving objects. It attempts to control thinking and action, leads women and men to adjust to the world, and inhibits their creative power.

When their efforts to act responsibly are frustrated, when they find themselves unable to use their faculties, people suffer. "This suffering due to impotence is rooted in the very fact that the human equilibrium has been disturbed."[5] But the inability to act which causes people's anguish also causes them to reject their impotence, by attempting

> . . . to restore [their] capacity to act. But can [they], and how? One way is to submit to and identify with a person or group having power. By this symbolic participation in another person's life, [men have] the illusion of acting, when in reality [they] only submit to and become a part of those who act.[6]

Populist manifestations perhaps best exemplify this type of behavior by the oppressed, who, by identifying with charismatic leaders, come to feel that they themselves are active and effective. The rebellion they express as they emerge in the historical process is motivated by that desire to act effectively. The dominant elites consider the remedy to be more domination and repression, carried out in the name of freedom, order, and social peace (that is, the peace of the elites). Thus they can condemn—logically, from their point of view—"the violence of a strike by workers and [can] call upon the state in the same breath to use violence in putting down the strike."[7]

Education as the exercise of domination stimulates the credulity of students, with the ideological intent (often not perceived by educators) of indoctrinating them to adapt to the world of oppression. This accusation is not made in the naïve hope that the dominant elites will thereby simply abandon the practice. Its objective is to call the attention of true humanists to the fact that they cannot use banking educational methods in the pursuit of liberation, for they would only negate that very pursuit. Nor may a revolutionary society inherit these methods from an oppressor society. The revolutionary society which practices banking education is either misguided or mistrusting of people. In either event, it is threatened by the specter of reaction.

Unfortunately, those who espouse the cause of liberation are themselves surrounded and influenced by the climate which generates the banking concept, and often do not perceive its true significance or its dehumanizing power. Paradoxically, then, they utilize this same instrument of alienation in what they consider an effort to liberate. Indeed, some "revolutionaries" brand as "innocents," "dreamers," or even "reactionaries" those who would challenge this educational practice. But one does not liberate people by alienating them. Authentic liberation—the process of humanization—is not another deposit to be made in men. Liberation is a praxis: the action and reflection of men and women upon their world in order to transform it. Those truly committed to the cause of liberation can accept neither the mechanistic concept of consciousness as an empty vessel to be filled, nor the use of banking methods of domination (propaganda, slogans—deposits) in the name of liberation.

Those truly committed to liberation must reject the banking concept in its entirety, adopting instead a concept of women and men as conscious beings, and consciousness as consciousness intent upon the world. They must abandon the educational goal of deposit-making and replace it with the posing of the problems of human beings in their relations with the world. "Problem-posing" education, responding to the essence of consciousness—*intentionality*—rejects communiqués and embodies communication. It epitomizes the special characteristic of consciousness; being *conscious of*, not only as intent on objects but as turned in upon itself in a Jasperian "split"—consciousness as consciousness *of* consciousness.

Liberating education consists in acts of cognition, not transferrals of information. It is a learning situation in which the cognizable object (far from being the end of the cognitive act) intermediates the cognitive actors—teacher on the one hand and students on the other. Accordingly, the practice of problem-posing education entails at the outset that the teacher-student contradiction be resolved. Dialogical relations—indispensable to the capacity of cognitive actors to cooperate in perceiving the same cognizable object—are otherwise impossible.

Indeed, problem-posing education, which breaks with the vertical patterns characteristic of banking education, can fulfill its function as the practice of freedom only if it can overcome the above contradiction. Through dialogue, the teacher-of-the-students and the students-of-the-teacher cease to exist and a new term emerges: teacher-student with students-teachers. The teacher is no longer merely the-one-who-teaches, but one who is himself taught in dialogue with the students, who in turn while being taught also teach. They become jointly responsible for a process in which all grow. In this process, arguments based on "authority" are no longer valid; in order to function, authority must be *on the side of* freedom, not *against* it. Here, no one teaches another, nor is anyone self-taught. People teach each other, mediated by the world, by the cognizable objects which in banking education are "owned" by the teacher.

The banking concept (with its tendency to dichotomize everything) distinguishes two stages in the action of the educator. During the first, he cognizes a cognizable object while he prepares his lessons in his study or his laboratory; during the second, he expounds to his students about that object. The students are not called upon to know, but to memorize the contents narrated by the teacher. Nor do the students practice any act of cognition, since the object towards which that act should be directed is the property of the teacher rather than a medium evoking the critical reflection of both teacher and students. Hence in the name of the "preservation of culture and knowledge" we have a system which achieves neither true knowledge nor true culture.

The problem-posing method does not dichotomize the activity of the teacher-student: she is not "cognitive" at one point and "narrative" at another. She is always "cognitive," whether preparing a project or engaging in dialogue with the students. He does not regard cognizable objects as his private property, but as the object of reflection by himself and the students. In this way, the problem-posing educator constantly re-forms his reflections in the reflection of the students. The students—no longer docile listeners—are now critical co-investigators in dialogue with the teacher. The teacher presents the material to the students for their consideration, and re-considers her earlier considerations as the students express their own. The role of the problem-posing educator is to create, together with the students, the conditions under which knowledge at the level of the *doxa* is superseded by true knowledge, at the level of the *logos*.

Whereas banking education anesthetizes and inhibits creative power, problem-posing education involves a constant unveiling of reality. The former attempts to maintain the *submersion* of consciousness; the latter strives for the *emergence* of consciousness and *critical intervention* in reality.

Students, as they are increasingly posed with problems relating to themselves in the world and with the world, will feel increasingly challenged and obliged to respond to that challenge. Because they apprehend the challenge as interrelated to other problems within a total context, not as a theoretical question, the resulting comprehension tends to be increasingly critical and thus constantly less alienated. Their response to the challenge evokes new challenges, followed by new understandings; and gradually the students come to regard themselves as committed.

Education as the practice of freedom—as opposed to education as the practice of domination—denies that man is abstract, isolated, independent, and unattached to the world; it also denies that the world exists as a reality apart from people. Authentic reflection considers neither abstract man nor the world without people, but people in their relations with the world. In these relations consciousness and world are simultaneous: consciousness neither precedes the world nor follows it.

> La conscience et le monde sont dormés d'un même coup: extérieur par essence à la conscience, le monde est, par essence relatif à elle.[8]

In one of our culture circles in Chile, the group was discussing (based on a codification) the anthropological concept of culture. In the midst of the discussion, a peasant who by banking standards was completely ignorant said: "Now I see that without man there is no world." When the educator responded: "Let's say, for the sake of argument, that all the men on earth were to die, but that the earth itself remained, together with trees, birds, animals, rivers, seas, the stars . . . wouldn't all this be a world?" "Oh no," the peasant replied emphatically. "There would be no one to say: 'This is a world'."

The peasant wished to express the idea that there would be lacking the consciousness of the world which necessarily implies the world of consciousness. *I* cannot exist without a *non-I*. In turn, the *not-I* depends on that existence.

The world which brings consciousness into existence becomes the world *of* that consciousness. Hence, the previously cited affirmation of Sartre: *"La conscience et le monde sont dormés d'un même coup."*

As women and men, simultaneously reflecting on themselves and on the world, increase the scope of their perception, they begin to direct their observations towards previously inconspicuous phenomena:

> In perception properly so-called, as an explicit awareness [*Gewahren*], I am turned towards the object, to the paper, for instance. I apprehend it as being this here and now. The apprehension is a singling out, every object having a background in experience. Around and about the paper lie books, pencils, inkwell, and so forth, and these in a certain sense are also "perceived", perceptually there, in the "field of intuition"; but whilst I was turned towards the paper there was no turning in their direction, nor any apprehending of them, not even in a secondary sense. They appeared and yet were not singled out, were not posited on their own account. Every perception of a thing has such a zone of background intuitions or background awareness, if "intuiting" already includes the state of being turned towards, and this also is a "conscious experience", or more briefly a "consciousness of" all indeed that in point of fact lies in the co-perceived objective background.[9]

That which had existed objectively but had not been perceived in its deeper implications (if indeed it was perceived at all) begins to "stand out," assuming the character of a problem and therefore of challenge. Thus, men and women begin to single out elements from their "background awareness" and to reflect upon them. These elements are now objects of their consideration, and, as such, objects of their action and cognition.

In problem-posing education, people develop their power to perceive critically *the way they exist* in the world *with which* and *in which* they find themselves; they come to see the world not as a static reality, but as a reality in process, in transformation. Although the dialectical relations of women and men with the world exist independently of how these relations are perceived (or whether or not they are perceived at all), it is also true that the form of action they adopt is to a large extent a function of how they perceive themselves in the world. Hence, the teacher-student and the students-teachers reflect simultaneously on themselves and the world without dichotomizing this reflection from action, and thus establish an authentic form of thought and action.

Once again, the two educational concepts and practices under analysis come into conflict. Banking education (for obvious reasons) attempts, by mythicizing reality, to conceal certain facts which explain the way human beings exist in the world; problem-posing education sets itself the task of demythologizing. Banking education resists dialogue; problem-posing education regards dialogue as indispensable to the act of cognition which unveils reality. Banking education treats students as objects of assistance; problem-posing education makes them critical thinkers. Banking education inhibits creativity and domesticates (although it cannot completely destroy) the *intentionality* of consciousness by isolating consciousness from the world, thereby denying people their ontological and historical vocation of becoming more fully human. Problem-posing education bases itself on creativity and stimulates true reflection and action upon reality, thereby responding to the vocation of persons as beings who are authentic only when engaged in inquiry and creative transformation. In sum: banking theory and practice, as immobilizing and fixating forces, fail to acknowledge men and women as historical beings; problem-posing theory and practice take the people's historicity as their starting point.

Problem-posing education affirms men and women as beings in the process of *becoming*—as unfinished, uncompleted beings in and with a likewise unfinished reality. Indeed, in contrast to other animals who are unfinished, but not historical, people know themselves to be unfinished; they are aware of their incompletion. In this incompletion and this awareness lie the very roots of education as an exclusively human manifestation. The unfinished character of human beings and the transformational character of reality necessitate that education be an ongoing activity.

Education is thus constantly remade in the praxis. In order to *be*, it must *become*. Its "duration" (in the Bergsonian meaning of the word) is found in the interplay of the opposites *permanence* and *change*. The banking method emphasizes permanence and becomes reactionary; problem-posing education—which accepts neither a "well-behaved" present nor a predetermined future—roots itself in the dynamic present and becomes revolutionary.

Problem-posing education is revolutionary futurity. Hence it is prophetic (and, as such, hopeful). Hence, it corresponds to the historical nature of humankind. Hence, it affirms women and men as beings who transcend themselves, who move forward and look ahead, for whom immobility represents a fatal threat, for whom looking at the past must only be a means of understanding more clearly what and who they are so that they can more wisely build the future. Hence, it identifies with the movement which engages people as beings aware of their incompletion—an historical movement which has its point of departure, its Subjects and its objective.

The point of departure of the movement lies in the people themselves. But since people do not exist apart from the world, apart from reality, the movement must begin with the human-world relationship. Accordingly, the point of departure must always be with men and women in the "here and now," which constitutes the situation within which they are submerged, from which they emerge, and in which they intervene. Only by starting from this situation—which determines their perception of it—can they begin to move. To do this authentically they must perceive their state not as fated and unalterable, but merely as limiting—and therefore challenging.

Whereas the banking method directly or indirectly reinforces men's fatalistic perception of their situation, the problem-posing method presents this very situation to them as a problem. As the situation becomes the object of their cognition, the naïve or magical perception which produced their fatalism gives way to perception which is able to perceive itself even as it perceives reality, and can thus be critically objective about that reality.

A deepened consciousness of their situation leads people to apprehend that situation as an historical reality susceptible of transformation. Resignation gives way to the drive for transformation and inquiry, over which men feel themselves to be in control. If people, as historical beings necessarily engaged with other people in a movement of inquiry, did not control that movement, it would be (and is) a violation of their humanity. Any situation in which some individuals prevent others from engaging in the process of inquiry is one of violence. The means used are not important; to alienate human beings from their own decision-making is to change them into objects.

This movement of inquiry must be directed towards humanization—the people's historical vocation. The pursuit of full humanity, however, cannot be carried out in isolation or individualism, but only in fellowship and solidarity; therefore it cannot unfold in the antagonistic relations between oppressors and oppressed. No one can be authentically human while he prevents others from being so. Attempting *to be more* human, individualistically, leads to *having more*, egotistically, a form of dehumanization. Not that it is not fundamental *to have* in order *to be* human. Precisely because it *is* necessary, some men's *having* must not be allowed to constitute an obstacle to others' *having*, must not consolidate the power of the former to crush the latter.

Problem-posing education, as a humanist and liberating praxis, posits as fundamental that the people subjected to domination must fight for their emancipation. To that end, it enables teachers and students to become Subjects of the educational process by overcoming authoritarianism and an alienating intellectualism; it also enables people to overcome their false perception of reality. The world—no longer something to be described with deceptive words—becomes the object of that transforming action by men and women which results in their humanization.

Problem-posing education does not and cannot serve the interests of the oppressor. No oppressive order could permit the oppressed to begin to question: Why? While only a revolutionary society can carry out this education in systematic terms, the revolutionary leaders need not take full power before they can employ the method. In the revolutionary process, the leaders cannot utilize the banking method as an interim measure, justified on grounds of expediency, with the intention of *later* behaving in a genuinely revolutionary fashion. They must be revolutionary—that is to say, dialogical—from the outset.

Notes

1. Simone de Beauvoir, *La Pensée de Droite, Aujord'hui* (Paris); ST, *El Pensamiento politico de la Derecha* (Buenos Aires, 1963), p. 34.
2. This concept corresponds to what Sartre calls the "digestive" or "nutritive" concept of education, in which knowledge is "fed" by the teacher to the students to "fill them out." See Jean-Paul Sartre, "Une idée fundamentale de la phénomenologie de Husserl; L'intentionalité," *Situations* I (Paris, 1947).
3. For example, some professors specify in their reading lists that a book should be read from pages 10 to 15—and do this to "help" their students.
4. Erich Fromm, *The Heart of Man* (New York, 1966), p. 41.
5. *Ibid.*, p. 31.
6. *Ibid.*

7. Reinhold Niebuhr, *Moral Man and Immoral Society* (New York, 1960), p. 130.
8. Sartre, *op. cit.*, p. 32.
9. Edmund Husserl, *Ideas—General Introduction to Pure Phenomenology* (London, 1969), pp. 105–106.

17   Caring*
Nel Noddings

> The author is Lee L. Jacks Professor of Education at Stanford University. In this selection she considers teaching from what she has termed "the feminine view." Her aim is not to deny the important role of moral reasoning but to emphasize the equal importance of cultivating moral concern, that is, caring. She thereby seeks to develop an approach to ethics and moral education that transcends considerations of gender.

Whatever I do in life, whomever I meet, I am first and always one-caring or one cared-for. I do not "assume roles" unless I become an actor. "Mother" is not a role; "teacher" is not a role.[1] When I became a mother, I entered a very special relation—possibly the prototypical caring relation. When I became a teacher, I also entered a very special—and more specialized—caring relation. No enterprise or special function I am called upon to serve can relieve me of my responsibilities as one-caring. Indeed, if an enterprise precludes my meeting the other in a caring relation, I must refuse to participate in that enterprise. Now, of course, an enterprise by its very nature may require me to care for a problem or set of problems. If I am a bus driver, or airline pilot, or air traffic controller, or surgeon, I may properly "care" for the problems and tasks presented. My major responsibilities focus on the other as physical entity and not as whole person. Indeed, as traffic controller, I do not even meet the other whose safety I am employed to protect. In such enterprises I behave responsibly toward others through proficient practice of my craft. But, even in such enterprises, when encounter occurs, I must meet the other as one-caring. It is encounter that is reduced and not my obligation to care. Clearly, in professions where encounter is frequent and where the ethical ideal of the other is necessarily involved, I am first and foremost one-caring and, second, enactor of specialized functions. As teacher, I am, first, one-caring.

The one-caring is engrossed in the cared-for and undergoes a motivational displacement toward the projects of the cared-for. This does not, as we have seen, imply romantic love or the sort of pervasive and compulsive

*Nel Noddings, *Caring: A Feminine Approach to Ethics and Moral Education*, pages 175–182. Copyright © 1984 The Regents of the University of California. Reprinted by permission of the University of California Press.

"thinking of the other" that characterizes infatuation. It means, rather, that one-caring receives the other, for the interval of caring, completely and nonselectively. She is present to the other and places her motive power in his service. Now, of course, she does not abandon her own ethical ideal in doing this, but she starts from a position of respect or regard for the projects of the other. In the language of Martin Buber, the cared-for is encountered as "Thou," a subject, and not as "It," an object of analysis. During the encounter, which may be singular and brief or recurrent and prolonged, the cared-for "is Thou and fills the firmament."

When a teacher asks a question in class and a student responds, she receives not just the "response" but the student. What he says matters, whether it is right or wrong, and she probes gently for clarification, interpretation, contribution. She is not seeking the answer but the involvement of the cared-for. For the brief interval of dialogue that grows around the question, the cared-for indeed "fills the firmament." The student is infinitely more important than the subject matter.

The one-caring as teacher is not necessarily permissive. She does not abstain, as Neill might have, from leading the student, or persuading him, or coaxing him toward an examination of school subjects. But she recognizes that, in the long run, he will learn what he pleases. We may force him to respond in specified ways, but what he will make his own and eventually apply effectively is that which he finds significant for his own life. This recognition does not reduce either the teacher's power or her responsibility. As we saw in our earlier discussion of the cared-for, the teacher may indeed coerce the student into choosing against himself. He may be led to diminish his ethical ideal in the pursuit of achievement goals. The teacher's power is, thus, awesome. It is she who presents the "effective world" to the student.[2] In doing this, she realizes that the student, as ethical agent, will make his own selection from the presented possibilities and so, in a very important sense, she is prepared to put her motive energy in the service of his projects. She has already had a hand in selecting those projects and will continue to guide and inform them, but the objectives themselves must be embraced by the student.

Buber suggests that the role of the teacher is just this: to influence. He says:

> For if the educator of our day has to act consciously he must nevertheless do it "as though he did not." That raising of the finger, that questioning glance, are his genuine doing. Through him the selection of the effective world reaches the pupil. He fails the recipient when he presents this selection to him with a gesture of interference. It must be concentrated in him; and doing out of concentration has the appearance of rest. Interference divides the soul in his care into an obedient part and a rebellious part. But a hidden influence proceeding from his integrity has an integrating force.[3]

When, out of intrinsic interest or trust and admiration for the teacher, the student does embrace an objective, he may need help in attaining it. The teacher, as one-caring, meets the student directly but not equally. Buber says that the teacher is capable of "inclusion," and this term seems to describe accurately what the one-caring does in trying to teach the cared-for. Milton Mayeroff, for example, in his discussion of caring, emphasizes this duality in the one-caring:[4] the "feeling with" that leads the one-caring to act as though for herself, but in the projects of the other and the accompanying realization that this other is independent, a subject. In "inclusion," the teacher receives the student and becomes in effect a duality. This sounds mystical, but it is not. The teacher receives and accepts the student's feeling toward the subject matter; she looks at it and listens to it through his eyes and ears. How else can she interpret the subject matter for him? As she exercises this inclusion, she accepts *his* motives, reaches toward what *he* intends, so long as these motives and intentions do not force an abandonment of her own ethic. Inclusion as practiced by the teacher is a vital gift. As we saw earlier, the student's attempts at inclusion may result in a deterioration of the learning process.

The special gift of the teacher, then, is to receive the student, to look at the subject matter with him. Her commitment is to him, the cared-for, and he is—through that commitment—set free to pursue his legitimate projects.

Again I want to emphasize that this view is not romantic but practical. The teacher works with the student. He becomes her apprentice and gradually assumes greater responsibility in the tasks they undertake. This working together, which produces both joy in the relation and increasing competence in the cared-for, was advocated, we may recall, by Urie Bronfenbrenner in his discussion of cooperative engagement in tasks, and it was also implied by Robert White's discussion of competence as the desired end of "effectance motivation." The child wants to attain competence in his own world of experience. He needs the cooperative guidance of a fully caring adult to accomplish this. The one-caring as teacher, then, has two major tasks: to stretch the student's world by presenting an effective selection of that world with which she is in contact, and to work cooperatively with the student in his struggle toward competence in that world. But her task as one-caring has higher priority than either of these. First and foremost, she must nurture the student's ethical ideal.

The teacher bears a special responsibility for the enhancement of the ethical ideal. She is often in contact with the ideal as it is being initially constructed and, even with the adult student, she has unique power in contributing to its enhancement or destruction. In dialogue, she can underscore his subjectness—encourage him to stand personally related to what he says and does. He is not just part of the lesson, a response to be recorded as "move 15" or whatever. He is a human being responsible for his words and acts, and the one-caring as teacher meets him thus. Why he thinks what he thinks is as important as what. The domain to which he refers for justification is significant. How he relates to others as he does all this is important.

Besides engaging the student in dialogue, the teacher also provides a model. To support her students as ones-caring, she must show them herself as one-caring. Hence she is not content to enforce rules—and may even refuse occasionally to do so—but she continually refers the rules to their ground in caring. If she confronts a student who is cheating, she may begin by saying, *I know you want to do well,* or, *I know you want to help your friend.* She begins by attributing the best possible motive to him, and she then proceeds to explain—fully, with many of her own reservations expressed freely—why she cannot allow him to cheat. She does not need to resort to punishment, because the rules are not sacred to her. What matters is the student, the cared-for, and how he will approach ethical problems as a result of his relation to her. Will he refer his ethical decisions to an ethic of caring or to rules and the likelihood of apprehension and punishment? Will he ask what his act means in terms of the feelings, needs, and projects of others, or will he be content with a catalog of rules-of-the-game?

A teacher cannot "talk" this ethic. She must live it, and that implies establishing a relation with the student. Besides talking to him and showing him how one cares, she engages in cooperative practice with him. He is learning not just mathematics or social studies; he is also learning how to be one-caring. By conducting education morally, the teacher hopes to induce an enhanced moral sense in the student. This view was held, also, by John Dewey. Sidney Hook describes the relation in Dewey's thinking:

> How, then, does Dewey achieve the transition from what we have called the morality of the task to the task of morality? His answer—original for his time and still largely disregarded—is to teach *all* subjects in such a way as to bring out and make focal their social and personal aspects, stressing how human beings are affected by them, pointing up the responsibilities that flow from their inter-relatedness.[5]

Everything we do, then, as teachers, has moral overtones. Through dialogue, modeling, the provision of practice, and the attribution of best motive, the one-caring as teacher nurtures the ethical ideal. She cannot nurture the student intellectually without regard for the ethical ideal unless she is willing to risk producing a monster, and she cannot nurture the ethical ideal without considering the whole self-image of which it is a part. For how he feels about himself in general—as student, as physical being, as friend—contributes to the enhancement or diminution of the ethical ideal. What the teacher reflects to him continually is the best possible picture consonant with reality. She does not reflect fantasy nor conjure up "expectations" as strategies. She meets him as he is and finds something admirable and, as a result, he may find the strength to become even more admirable. He is confirmed.

The sort of relatedness and caring I have been discussing is often dismissed as impossible because of constraints of number, time, and purpose. Richard Hult, in his discussion of "pedagogical caring," notes that such requirements seem to require in turn close personal relationships of the I-Thou sort. He says: "While these may sometimes occur and may be desirable, most pedagogical contexts make such relationships implausible if not undesirable."[6] He concludes that caring as Mayeroff has described it, and as I have described it, "cannot be the kind of caring demanded of teachers." I insist that it is exactly the kind of caring ideally required of teachers.

I think that Hult and others who take this position misunderstand the requirement that Buber has described as an I-Thou encounter; that Marcel has described in terms of "disposability"; that Mayeroff has described as identification-with-recognition-of-independence; that I have described as engrossment and displacement of motivation. I do not need to establish a deep, lasting, time-consuming personal relationship with every student. What I must do is to be totally and nonselectively present to the student—to each student—as he addresses me. The time interval may be brief but the encounter is total.

Further, there are ways to extend contact so that deeper relationships may develop. If I know how my student typically reacts to certain topics and tasks, I am in a better position to guide him both sensitively and economically. Why can we not opt for smaller schools, for teachers and students working together for three years rather than one, for teachers teaching more than one subject? We are limited in our thinking by too great a deference to what is, and what is today is not very attractive. Our alternative is to change the structure of schools and teaching so that caring can flourish, and the hope is that by doing this we may attain both a higher level of cognitive achievement and a more caring, ethical society.

When we begin our educational planning, we may start with schools as they are, identify their primary functions, and ask how they may best be organized to serve their functions. Or we may start with our picture of caring and education and ask what sort of organization might be compatible with this picture. When James Conant made his influential recommendations concerning the organization of secondary education,[7] he began with the intellectual function of schools and, assuming a national need for high-powered curricula in mathematics and science, suggested that larger schools were required to support such programs. I have begun by identifying the maintenance and enhancement of the ethical ideal as the primary function of any educational community, and so I shall be interested first not in the establishment of programs but in the establishment and evaluation of chains and circles of caring. To establish such chains and circles, we may need to consider small schools. . . .

We should remind ourselves, before we leave this initial discussion on the one-caring as teacher, that there is another in the caring relation. The student also contributes to caring. The one form of mutality that is excluded from the teacher-student relation is an attempt at inclusion on the part of the student. A focus of student attention on the teacher's instructional strategies is fatal to the relationship—and to the student's learning. The student may, however, care for the teacher as a person. He may be fascinated by her and hold her in the highest regard. He may be willing to help her with physical tasks and, indeed, to assist her in teaching other students. Nothing in our discussion was meant to preclude the possibility of the student's caring but, within the teacher-student relation, his caring is different from that of the teacher.

The student has his greatest effect on the relationship as the one cared-for. If he perceives the teacher's caring and responds to it, he is giving the teacher what she needs most to continue to care. As the infant rewards his caring mother with smiles and wriggles, the student rewards his teacher with responsiveness: with questions, effort, comment, and cooperation. There is some initiative required of the cared-for. Just as the one-caring is free to accept or reject the internal "I must" of caring, so the cared-for is free to accept or reject the attitude of caring when he perceives it. If the cared-for perceives the attitude and denies it, then he is in an internal state of untruth.

Many of our schools are in what might be called a crisis of caring. Both students and teachers are brutally attacked verbally and physically. Clearly, the schools are not often places where caring is fulfilled, but it is not always the failure of teachers that causes the lapse in caring. Many urban teachers are suffering symptoms of battle fatigue and "burn-out." No matter what they do, it seems, their efforts are not perceived as caring. They themselves are perceived, instead, as the enemy, as natural targets for resistance.

The cared-for is essential to the relation. What the cared-for contributes to the relation is a responsiveness that completes the caring. This responsiveness need not take the form of gratitude or even of direct acknowledgment. Rather, the cared-for shows either in direct response to the one-caring or in spontaneous delight and happy growth before her eyes that the caring has been received. The caring is completed when the cared-for receives the caring. He may respond by free, vigorous, and happy immersion in his own projects (toward which the one-caring has directed her own energy also), and the one-caring, seeing this, knows that the relation has been completed in the cared-for.

We see another cogent reason for insisting on relation and caring in teaching. Where is the teacher to get the strength to go on giving except from the student? In situations where the student rarely responds, is negative, denies the effort at caring, the teacher's caring quite predictably deteriorates to "cares and burdens." She becomes the needy target of her own caring. In such cases, we should supply special support to maintain the teacher as one-caring. Communities are just barely awakened to this need. But no indirect caring can fully compensate for the natural reward of teaching. This is always found in the responsiveness of the student.

What am I recommending? That students should be more responsive to their teachers? Can we command them to respond? This approach seems wrong, although parents might reasonably talk to their children about the difficulties of teaching and ways in which students can support and encourage their teachers simply by exhibiting a spontaneous enthusiasm for their own growth. But, realistically, such a recommendation seems unlikely to be productive. What I am recommending is that schools and teaching be redesigned so that caring has a chance to be initiated in the one-caring and completed in the cared-for. Sacrifices in economies of scale and even in programs might be called for. These would be minor if we could unlock our doors and disarm our security guards. Schools as institutions cannot care directly. A school cannot be engrossed in anyone or anything. But a school can be deliberately designed to support caring and caring individuals, and this is what an ethic of caring suggests should be done.

Notes

1. For the opposite view, see Jessie Bernard, *The Future of Motherhood* (New York: Penguin Books, Inc., 1974).

2. Martin Buber discusses the teacher's "selection of the effective world" in "Education," in *Between Man and Man* (New York: Macmillan Publishing Co., Inc., 1965), pp. 83–103.

3. Ibid., p. 90.

4. Milton Mayeroff, *On Caring* (New York: Harper & Row, Publishers, 1971), pp. 3, 5, 10, and passim.

5. Sidney Hook, Preface to John Dewey, *Moral Principles in Education* (Carbondale: Southern Illinois University Press, 1975), p. xi.

6. Richard E. Hult, Jr., "On Pedagogical Caring," *Educational Theory* (1979), 239.

7. See James B. Conant, *The American High School Today* (New York: McGraw-Hill, 1959); also, *The Comprehensive High School* (New York: McGraw-Hill, 1967).

18   The Philosophy of Childhood*

Gareth B. Matthews

The author is Professor of Philosophy at the University of Massachusetts, Amherst. In this selection he challenges the idea, defended in its most influential form by the psychologist Lawrence Kohlberg, that moral development consists of attaining increasingly sophisticated concepts of morality. Matthews suggests that on occasion adults may learn from children as well as teach them.

Is it a good idea to think of moral development as concept displacement? That is, is it a good idea to conceive moral development as exchanging a less adequate concept of honesty, courage, justice, obligation, or whatever, for a better one, and then exchanging the concept for a still better one?

How would the story go? Well, consider the concept of moral obligation. One might say that a child starts out with only a very external concept of obligation. According to this "stage-one concept," an obligation is something someone *else* holds one responsible for, not a responsibility one lays on oneself. The relevant "somebody else" would be an authority figure—Mother, Father, Teacher, Priest, Police Officer. The embedded concept of being held responsible would also be external in that it would have to do with the threat of physical punishment and the promise of material reward.

Thus suppose Mother tells me not to raid the cookie jar. She goes off to the grocer's and leaves me alone in the house. I am obliged not to eat any cookies while she is away. If I am very small, perhaps my understanding of being held responsible for keeping my hands out of the cookie jar would be limited to the realization that, if I do take another cookie and Mother finds out, I will probably be spanked.

*Reprinted by permission of the publisher from *The Philosophy of Childhood* by Gareth Matthews, Cambridge, Mass.: Harvard University Press. Copyright © 1994 by the President and Fellows of Harvard College.

Getting a more advanced concept of obligation might then consist in getting a more nearly internal concept of being responsible for keeping my hand out of the cookie jar. The threat of physical punishment and the promise of material reward might come to play no essential role in my understanding of my obligation. Instead, the fear that Mother might show disappointment by the look on her face would, perhaps, be threat enough. At this point, though, my concept of obligation would still be somewhat external in that there would have to be someone outside me, some external authority figure, to hold me responsible for whatever it is I am obligated to do.

At a third stage of moral development, on this concept-displacement model, I might eventually learn to function as my own authority figure, my own "lawgiver." I could then recognize an obligation to respect the wishes of my mother, or the obligation to be brave, or to tell the truth, even when there was no likelihood that Mother or Father, Teacher or Priest, would be able to check up on me. To be sure, I might want the approval of some authority figure. I am only human. And if I lied or behaved in a cowardly fashion, I would doubtless prefer that no authority figure find out. But at the third stage I would find nothing odd or paradoxical in the suggestion that I have an obligation, say, not to read my office-mate's electronic mail, even though that responsibility has never been specifically laid on me by my parents or teachers, even my boss, and it is not backed by the promise of external reward or the threat of external punishment.

Is this a good way to think of moral development? One thing that should give us pause is the realization that, according to this model of moral development, those children who are at the first stage in the process are really only "pre-moral" beings. The reason they are only pre-moral is that their concept of obligation as the realization that they will likely be punished if they do such-and-such is not a concept of *moral* obligation at all.

To see that this is so, imagine that I live in a police state. I may agree to report to the police the daily activities of my neighbor; I may agree to do this even though I consider such reporting distasteful, perhaps even wrong. I may do it anyway out of fear that I will otherwise lose my job. In any case, I can accept the obligation the police lay on me to spy on my neighbors without my thinking of it as being a moral obligation, and without its being for me a moral obligation.

If the concept of obligation that children have includes no recognition, on any level, of the moral appropriateness of at least some of the things they feel obligated to do, then their concept of obligation is not a concept of moral obligation at all. It is just the recognition that there are some things we get punished, or rewarded, for doing.

Some people may welcome this consequence of the concept-displacement model of moral development. They will agree that young children are, in fact, only pre-moral agents. For them the concept of obligation a child has at, say, age five has to do with morality only in the very minimal sense that one needs to have this concept so as to be able to exchange it later on for a concept with real, moral content. It is thus a genuinely pre-moral concept.

I, myself, consider this consequence enough by itself to discredit the concept-displacement approach to understanding moral development. It is not that I think young children are morally better than the concept-displacement approach allows. It is rather that I think young children, even very young children, are at least genuinely moral agents. By that I do not mean just that they are capable of sometimes doing the right thing. I mean that they are capable of sometimes doing the right thing for the right reason, or, at least, for a good reason, a genuinely moral reason. They may not be able to articulate well the reasons they have for fulfilling their obligations. But they are capable of recognizing and accepting a moral obligation as a claim on them that is something different from a threat of punishment or a promise of reward.

What I have in mind is something rather ordinary, but yet also profound. One can see it, I think, in this description of and commentary on the behavior of an infant, Michael, then only fifteen months old:

> [Michael] was struggling with his friend, Paul, over a toy. Paul started to cry. Michael appeared concerned and let go of the toy so that Paul would have it, but Paul kept crying. Michael paused, then gave his teddy bear to Paul, but the crying continued. Michael paused again, then ran to the next room, returned with Paul's security blanket, and offered it to Paul, who then stopped crying.

The psychologist Martin L. Hoffman, perhaps the leading researcher on empathy in young children, comments:

> First, it does seem clear that Michael assumed that his own teddy, which often comforts him, would also comfort his friend. Second, its failure to do this served as corrective feedback, which led Michael to consider alternatives. Third, in considering the processes underlying Michael's final, successful act, three possibilities stand out: (1) he was simply imitating an effective instrumental act observed in the past; that is, he had observed Paul being comforted with the blanket. This can be tentatively ruled out, since Michael's parents could not recall his ever having such an opportunity. (2) In trying to think of what to do, he remembered seeing another child being soothed by a blanket, and this reminded him of Paul's blanket—a more complex response than might first appear, since Paul's blanket was out of Michael's perceptual field at the time. (3) Michael, as young as he was, could somehow reason by analogy that Paul would be comforted by something that he loved in the same way that Michael loved his own teddy.[1]

Hoffman adds: "I favor the last interpretation, although it does postulate a complex response for a young child."

It is worth noting that the interpretation that Hoffman says he favors does not account for Michael's behavior unless we also assume that Michael somehow thought he *ought* to comfort Paul.

However exactly one interprets this particular incident, it seems to me obvious that *some* very young children *sometimes* act in genuinely moral ways, not just in pre-moral ways. That means, they act with some kind of understanding that what they are doing is a good thing to do because, say, it will help someone out, or comfort someone, and not just that it might be a way to avoid being punished or a way to get rewarded. Since the concept-displacement approach to moral development allows children at the earliest stages only a pre-moral understanding of what they are doing, it is for that reason defective.

Let's see how this point plays itself out within the terms of the most influential contemporary theory of moral development, that of Lawrence Kohlberg. Kohlberg presents subjects with moral dilemmas and then grades their responses, in particular, the *justifications* they offer for their solutions to the dilemmas, so as to locate each subject at one of six or so stages of moral development.[2] The most famous of Kohlberg's dilemmas is this one:

> In Europe, a woman was near death from a special kind of cancer. There was one drug that the doctors thought might save her. It was a form of radium that a druggist in the same town had recently discovered. The drug was expensive to make, but the druggist was charging ten times what the drug cost him to make. He paid $400 for the radium and charged $4,000 for a small dose of the drug. The sick woman's husband, Heinz, went to everyone he knew to borrow the money, but he could only get together about $2,000, which is half what it cost. He told the druggist that his wife was dying, and asked him to sell it cheaper or let him pay later. But the druggist said, "No, I discovered the drug and I'm going to make money from it." So Heinz got desperate and considered breaking into the man's store to steal the drug for his wife.[3]

As I say, subjects are assigned by Kohlberg to a stage of moral development, not according to what they say Heinz should do (for example, steal the drug), but rather according to the *justification* they offer for whatever they say that Heinz should do. (For example, the subject might say, "He should steal the drug and give it to his wife because saving somebody's life is more important than whether you steal.")

At Stage 1 a subject will exhibit what Kohlberg calls "the punishment and obedience orientation." At Stage 2 an elementary reciprocity emerges, but it amounts only to "You scratch my back and I'll scratch yours." Stages 1 and 2 constitute what Kohlberg calls the "Preconventional Level" of moral development.

Stages 3 and 4 make up the "Conventional Level." At Stage 3 one has achieved the "good-boy-nice-girl orientation"; Stage 4 is the "law and order" orientation.

Stages 5 and 6 constitute what Kohlberg calls the "Postconventional," "Autonomous," or "Principles" level. Stage 5 is based on the idea of a social contract. And, finally, at Stage 6 "right is defined by the decision of conscience in accord with self-chosen *ethical principles* appealing to logical comprehensiveness, universality and consistency."[4]

During some thirty years of investigation, Kohlberg and his collaborators amassed a staggering amount of evidence to show that the order of this development is fixed, in that no one reaches stage $n + 1$ without first going through stage n, and there is no regression to an earlier stage.[5]

Kohlberg's scheme seems to show little interesting cultural bias. (By 'interesting cultural bias' I mean bias that cannot be eliminated by the sensitive redescription of Kohlberg's dilemmas to fit other cultures.) As one recent investigator has put the matter,

> The evidence suggests that Kohlberg's interview is reasonably culture fair when the content is creatively adapted and the subject is interviewed in his or her native language. The invariant sequence proposition was also found to be well supported, because stage skipping and stage regressions were rare and always below the level that could be attributed to measurement error.[6]

For these and other reasons, Kohlberg's theory is one of the best articulated and most thoroughly supported theories in all developmental psychology. Nevertheless, many people are profoundly dissatisfied with it. Perhaps my comments about the inadequacy of the concept-displacement approach to understanding moral development reveal an important source of that dissatisfaction.

Does Kohlberg's theory make clear why the concept of obligation a child has at Stage 1 ("punishment and obedience orientation") or Stage 2 ("you scratch my back and I'll scratch yours") is a moral concept at all, even if only a primitive moral concept? The answer is no.

A Kohlbergian might reply by pointing out that the first two stages are characterized as the "pre-moral level." The idea is, presumably, that the concepts of obligation a child has at these stages are moral only in the sense that one has to develop each of them and move on to something else in order to arrive at a genuinely moral concept. Such a reply seems unsatisfactory for two reasons. First, it is surely implausible to suppose that not a single subject at Stage 1 or 2 has any understanding at all of what real morality consists in. Second, a similar difficulty recurs anyway at Stage 3, and perhaps even at Stage 4. One who conforms to expectations simply to avoid disapproval (Stage 3) or even one who acts to maintain the "given social order for its own sake" (Stage 4)[7] has not, it seems, *or at least not for those reasons*, attained a specifically moral understanding of obligation.

It begins to look as though all stages before Stage 5, or even Stage 6, are really pre-moral stages. Since, according to Kohlberg's research, hardly anyone, perhaps no one, reaches Stage 6, and only a small minority reach even Stage 5, we are driven to the unwelcome conclusion that the vast majority of people do not have a specifically moral concept of obligation. It is not just that most people do not usually act morally; that would hardly be a surprising conclusion. What is both surprising and objectionable is the conclusion that the vast majority of people do not have any real understanding of what morality consists in.

This worry is underlined by the fact that Kohlberg himself defines morality in terms of impartiality, universalizability, reversibility and prescriptivity. If Kohlberg is right and a judgment is moral if, and only if, it exhibits those formal features, then the concepts of obligation one has at lower stages of development are not even primitive moral concepts; they are not moral concepts at all.

This worry can be made concrete by appeal to a hypothetical example. Suppose Susan, age six, is given a Kohlberg interview and is found to be at Stage 1. What this means is that Susan's ability to reason her way through a moral *dilemma* and to resolve a moral *conflict*, and especially her ability to articulate such a resolution, are very primitive. Now suppose that when cookies and orange juice are distributed to Susan's class in school, Susan herself happens to get two cookies, whereas James, through a simple oversight, gets none, and everyone else gets one. We can imagine that Susan first rejoices in her good fortune, but then, noting that James got no cookie at all, gives one of hers to him. She has done the fair thing; she has done what she ought to do, what, in those circumstances, morality requires.

Of course Susan might have given James her extra cookie out of fear that she would be reprimanded for accepting two cookies when James had none. Or she might have given him a cookie in the hope of praise from her teacher, or a favor, later on, from James. She might have had these motivations. But there is no reason to suppose she *has* to act out of fear of punishment or hope or reward. In particular, and this is the crucial point, the fact that she scores at Stage 1 in a Kohlberg interview does not mean that she *cannot* act out of a sense of fairness when she is *not* confronted with a moral dilemma, let alone confronted with the need to resolve and justify her resolution of a moral dilemma.

A Kohlbergian might reply that Susan does not really have a sense of fairness if her moral *reasoning* is at Stage 1. She may be modeling behavior that she observes in others, or conforming to pressures from adults or peers, but she is not really acting from a sense of fairness unless she can give Stage 5 or Stage 6 *reasoning* to resolve a moral dilemma.

In my view, this Kohlbergian response focuses on only one of the several dimensions of moral development and ignores all the rest. To make this point clear, let me outline an alternative conception of moral development.

Each of us can bring to mind, for each major term of moral assessment in our active vocabulary (for example, 'moral,' 'immoral,' 'fair,' 'unfair,' 'honest,' 'lying,' 'brave,' 'cowardly,' and so on) at least one paradigmatic situation to which we think the term applies. Our understanding of what these terms mean includes our ability to assimilate other cases to these paradigms.

Our first paradigm of bravery is, perhaps, succeeding in not crying in the doctor's office when we are about to be stuck with a needle. For telling a lie my paradigm may be denying, falsely, that I ate little brother's piece of candy when he was out playing. For fairness, the paradigm may be dividing the cookies evenly among the members of a school class so that each one gets the same number of cookies.

It will be objected that I am making a naive mistake here of the kind that Socrates' hapless interlocutors are always making in the early Platonic dialogues. An example of lying, even a paradigm example, is not *what lying is*. Surely, the objection continues, only someone who can define 'lying' satisfactorily really knows what lying is, and only such a person has succeeded in latching onto the immoral behavior that is properly called "lying."

My reply is twofold. First, it is an open question whether any of us can give an entirely satisfactory definition of 'lying.' (We should not be surprised that the early Platonic dialogues end in perplexity!) Yet most of us have a working grasp of what lying is. Therefore, having a working grasp of what lying is, is something other than being able to give an entirely satisfactory definition of 'lying.' In fact, it can consist in having a basic understanding of central paradigms of lying and the ability to compare other cases to these paradigms so as to determine whether they, too, should count as cases of lying.

Second, Socrates' technique in the early Platonic dialogues requires his interlocutors (and his readers!) to test out suggested definitions with their own intuitions. Thus Socrates in Book I of the *Republic* rejects Cephalus's definition of 'justice' ('telling the truth and paying your debts') by asking, rhetorically, whether one should return a weapon to its owner if, in the meantime, the owner has gone mad. As readers, we are expected to answer, "No, of course not." But on what basis can we give that answer if we have, as yet, no satisfactory definition of 'justice'? Clearly such testing of suggested definitions by counterexample is a futile exercise unless we already have a working grasp of the relevant term of moral assessment. Having such a grasp may consist simply in having a basic understanding of central paradigms and the ability to assess other cases by reference to those paradigms.

In my view moral development takes place across at least five different dimensions. First, there is the dimension of *paradigms.* A fabrication to escape punishment is a good first paradigm for lying. A misrepresentation to gain some advantage for oneself may be a second paradigm. (Lisa says she doesn't know what time it is—though she does, really—so as to be allowed to watch the rest of her TV program.) A group conspiracy to flout authority may be a third paradigm. (Albert tells the teacher he did not see who shot the spitwad even though he saw Leonard do it.)

A second dimension of moral development is relative success in offering *defining characteristics.* 'Saying something naughty the way Louis did' may be a simple, but appropriate, beginning. 'Uttering a falsehood' will be an improvement. 'Uttering a falsehood when you know better' is still better. 'Saying something you know is false to deceive someone else' is even better than that.

It is important to recognize, however, that none of these definitions is entirely satisfactory. Consider the last one ('Saying something you know is false to deceive someone else'). Suppose the teacher wants to find out who spread mustard on the washbasins in the school washroom. She already has circumstantial evidence that my school chum Ben did it. Moreover, she has good reason to think that I witnessed the awful deed. But she cannot punish Ben unless a witness comes forward. She asks me and I deny that Ben did it. The teacher may realize that I am protecting my friend. (I have often done that before.) There is no deception involved. I may even realize that the teacher realizes that I am protecting my friend. Still, when I say that I didn't see Ben spread mustard on the wash basins, I tell a lie.

So the last definition is also defective. Moreover, I do not know how to repair it. Perhaps someone can offer a definition of 'lying' that fits all our cherished intuitions and is also informative. But the important point is that no one *need* be able to do this to have a working grasp of what lying is. To begin with, one need only have a basic understanding of one central paradigm.

A third dimension of development concerns the *range of cases* that fall under each term of moral assessment and how we deal with borderline cases. Is writing a bad check, when one knows that one's balance is insufficient to cover the check, a case of lying? Can a photograph lie? Is it lying for a student who was thrown out of college to wear the college tie?

A fourth dimension of moral development concerns the *adjudication of conflicting moral claims,* or to put the matter less tendentiously, the adjudication of apparently conflicting moral claims. Sometimes telling a lie is not being naughty; sometimes it is one's duty. How can this be? Though it is *prima facie* wrong to tell a lie, other moral claims may override the demand to tell the truth. We develop morally as we get better and better at thinking our way through such conflicts, or apparent conflicts.

Fifth, there is the dimension of *moral imagination.* Michael, at fifteen months, seems to have had the imagination to understand Paul's distress and to think of getting Paul's security blanket so that Paul would be comforted. Even at that very young age, Michael was quite advanced along the dimension of moral imagination.

Of course Michael's experience of the world and his understanding of how it works will be very limited at fifteen months. A very young child will not be able to empathize with, say, a victim of racial or gender discrimination because the child's experience and understanding of society are too limited. In general, we may hope to advance along the scale of moral imagination as we grow older and our experience of life becomes broader and deeper.

Yet this need not happen. People become overwhelmed by the problems of the society around them, or increasingly preoccupied with their own personal agendas. When that happens, even a very young and inexperienced child can catch us adults up short with a direct, empathetic response to, say, a homeless person trying to keep warm in a cardboard box under a bridge. A child's naive question can awaken our sleeping imagination and sympathy, and even move us to take moral action.

On the view I advocate, then, moral development takes place across these five different dimensions. Kohlberg concentrates on only one, namely, the fourth dimension (adjudicating moral conflicts or dilemmas). But long before a child will have to deal with moral dilemmas, let alone give a justification for resolving a dilemma, the child can have a strong empathetic response to the victims of suffering, or injustice, and a working understanding of central paradigms for terms of moral assessment.

Most of us never lose the paradigms we first assimilated in childhood. The equal division of cookies remains for us a paradigm of distributive justice. As Susan grows and develops we hope she will enlarge her stock of paradigms from handing out cookies fairly to distributing work assignments fairly among workers of varied abilities, to, perhaps, refusing to change the rules in the middle of a game. And we hope Susan will grow along other dimensions of moral development as well. But the simple paradigms of distributive justice will stay with her permanently. And no contrast between the virtuosity of her later reasoning and the naiveté of her early appeal to simple paradigms can establish that those early actions were not really performed from a sense of fairness.

Parents sometimes report to me that one child in their family got recognized early on as the "justice person" in that family. Perhaps it all began with cookie distribution at age three. But it continued through middle childhood, late childhood, and adolescence. This particular child would always be the person in that family who would ask, "But is that really fair?" Mother or Father might be called on to reassess things in answer to a question like that from a child. And the "justice person" needn't be the oldest child of the family, either.

Theories of cognitive and moral development often encourage us to distance ourselves from children—both from the children around us and from our own childhood selves. Such distancing sometimes produces a new respect for children. After all, it warns us against faulting children for shortcomings that express, according to the theories, immature cognitive and moral structures that are entirely normal for children of the given age range.

Yet such distancing can also encourage condescension. If we suppose that children live in conceptual worlds that are structurally different from ours, but that will naturally evolve into ours, how can we fail to be condescending toward children as moral agents?

The condescension, though understandable, is unwarranted. One reason it is unwarranted is that . . . later structures are not entirely unquestionable accomplishments; characteristically, they are problematic in ways that philosophers never tire of exposing. Thus it is an open question whether anyone at all can provide an entirely satisfactory theory of justice or, as I remarked earlier, even an entirely satisfactory definition of 'lying.'

Another reason such condescension is unwarranted is that children, in their simple directness, often bring us adults back to basics. Any developmental theory that rules out, on purely theoretical grounds, even the possibility that we adults may occasionally have something to learn, morally, from a child is, for that reason, defective; it is also morally offensive.

Notes

1. Martin L. Hoffman, "Empathy, Role-Taking, Guilt, and Development of Altruistic Motives," in *Moral Development and Behavior,* ed. Thomas Lickona (New York: Holt, Rinehart and Winston, 1976), 129–130.
2. There are complications; Kohlberg and his associates came to speak of heteronomous and autonomous substages for each of the regular stages and also of the possibility of a "soft" Stage 7. At the same time they seemed to become less confident of Stage 6. See Lawrence Kohlberg, *Essays on Moral Development,* vol. 2: *The Psychology of Moral Development: The Nature and Validity of Moral Stages* (New York: Harper and Row, 1984), chap. 3 and appendix C.
3. Ibid., 640.

4. Lawrence Kohlberg, "From Is to Ought: How to Commit the Naturalistic Fallacy and Get Away with It in the Study of Moral Development," in *Cognitive Development and Epistemology,* ed. Theodore Mischel (New York: Academic Press, 1971), 165.
5. For a time it seemed that there was indeed regression, but refinement of the theory seems to have dealt with the problem. See Kohlberg, *Psychology of Moral Development,* 437-438.
6. J. R. Snarey, "Cross-cultural Universality of Moral Development," *Psychological Bulletin* 82 (1984), 226.
7. Kohlberg, "From Is to Ought," 164.

C

Curriculum

19   Education for Modern Man*

Sidney Hook

> Sidney Hook (1902–1989) was Professor of Philosophy at New York University
> and a prolific and trenchant contributor to the intellectual debates of his time. He
> extended and developed the philosophical views of his teacher, John Dewey.
> Whereas Dewey wrote almost exclusively about elementary and secondary edu-
> cation, Hook published extensively concerning issues in higher education. In this
> chapter he outlines and justifies the essential elements of a liberal education.

What, concretely, should the modern man know in order to live intelligently in
the world today? What should we require that he learn of subject matters and
skills in his educational career in order that he may acquire maturity in feeling,
in judgment, in action? Can we indicate the minimum indispensables of a liberal education in the modern world? This approach recognizes that no subject
per se is inherently liberal at all times and places. But it also recognizes that
within a given age in a given culture, the enlightenment and maturity, the freedom and power, which liberal education aims to impart, is more likely to be
achieved by mastery of some subject matters and skills than by others. In
short, principles must bear fruit in specific programs in specific times. In what
follows I shall speak of studies rather than of conventional courses.

   (1) The liberally educated person should be intellectually at home in the
world of physical nature. He should know something about the earth he in-
habits and its place in the solar system, about the solar system and its relation
to the cosmos. He should know something about mechanics, heat, light, electricity, and magnetism as the universal forces that condition anything he is or
may become. He should be just as intimately acquainted with the nature of
man as a biological species, his evolution, and the discoveries of experimental
genetics. He should know something about the structure of his own body and
mind, and the cycle of birth, growth, learning, and decline. To have even a
glimmer of understanding of these things, he must go beyond the level of primary description and acquire some grasp of the principles that explain what
he observes. Where an intelligent grasp of principles requires a knowledge of
mathematics, its fundamental ideas should be presented in such a way that
students carry away the sense of mathematics not only as a tool for the solution of problems but as a study of types of order, system, and language.

   Such knowledge is important to the individual *not* merely because of its
intrinsic fascination. Every subject from numismatics to Sanskrit possesses an
intrinsic interest to those who are curious about it. It is important because it
helps make everyday experience more intelligible; because it furnishes a continuous exemplification of scientific method in action; because our world is literally being remade by the consequences and applications of science; because
the fate of nations and the vocations of men depend upon the use of this

*Reprinted by permission of Ernest B. Hook.

knowledge; and because it provides the instruments to reduce our vast help-lessness and dependence in an uncertain world.

Such knowledge is no less important because it bears upon the formation of *rational belief* about the place of man in the universe. Whatever views a man professes today about God, human freedom, Cosmic Purpose, and personal survival, he cannot reasonably hold them in ignorance of the scientific account of the world and man.

These are some of the reasons why the study of the natural sciences, and the elementary mathematical notions they involve, should be *required* of every-one. Making such study required imposes a heavy obligation and a difficult task of pedagogical discovery upon those who teach it. It is commonly recog-nized that the sciences today are taught as if all students enrolled in science courses were preparing to be professional scientists. Most of them are not. Nat-urally they seek to escape a study whose wider and larger uses they do not see because many of their teachers do not see it. Here is not the place to canvass and evaluate the attempts being made to organize instruction in the sciences. The best experience seems to show that one science should not be taken as the exemplar of all, but that the basic subject matter of astronomy, physics, chem-istry, geology, in one group, and biology and psychology in another, should be covered. For when only one science is taught it tends to be treated profession-ally. Similarly, the best experience indicates that instruction should be interde-partmental—any competent teacher from one of these fields in either group should be able to teach all of them in the group, instead of having a succession of different teachers each representing his own field. This usually destroys both the continuity and the cumulative effect of the teaching as a whole.

(2) Every student should be required to become intelligently aware of how the society in which he lives functions, of the great forces molding con-temporary civilization, and of the crucial problems of our age which await de-cision. The studies most appropriate to this awareness have been convention-ally separated into history, economics, government, sociology, social psychology, and anthropology. This separation is an intellectual scandal. For it is impossible to have an adequate grasp of the problems of government with-out a knowledge of economics, and vice versa. Except for some special do-mains of professional interest, the same is true for the other subjects as well.

The place of the social studies, properly integrated around problems and issues, is fundamental in the curriculum of modern education. It is one of the dividing points between the major conflicting schools of educational thought. The question of its justification must be sharply distinguished from discussion of the relative merits of this or that mode of approach to the social studies.

The knowledge and insight that the social studies can give are necessary for every student because no matter what his specialized pursuits may later be, the extent to which he can follow them, and the "contextual" developments within these fields, depend upon the total social situation of which they are in some sense a part. An engineer today whose knowledge is restricted only to technical matters of engineering, or a physician whose competence extends only to the subject matter of traditional medical training, is ill-prepared to plan intelligently for a life-career or to understand the basic problems that face his profession. He is often unable to cope adequately with those specific problems in his own domain that involve, as so many problems of social and personal health do, economic and psychological difficulties. No matter what an individual's vocation, the conditions of his effective functioning depend upon pervasive social tendencies which set the occasions for the application of knowledge, provide the opportunities of employment, and not seldom determine even the direction of research.

More important, the whole presupposition of the theory of democracy is that the electorate will be able to make intelligent decisions on the issues before it. These issues are basically political, social, and economic. Their specific character changes from year to year. But their generic form, and the character of the basic problems, do not. Nor, most essential of all, do the proper intellectual habits of meeting them change. It is undeniably true that the world we live in is one marked by greater changes, because of the impact of technology, than ever before. This does not necessitate changing the curriculum daily to catch up with today's newspapers, nor does it justify a concentration on presumably eternal problems as if these problems had significance independent of cultural place-time. The fact that we are living in a world where the rate of cultural change is greater than at any time in the past, together with its ramifications, may itself become a central consideration for analysis.

The construction of a social studies curriculum is a task of the greatest difficulty even after the artificiality of departmental lines of division has been recognized. For the integration of the material demands a historical approach, set not by bare chronology, but by the problems themselves. It must incorporate large amounts of philosophy and the scientific disciplines of evaluating judgments of fact and value. It must abandon misconceived interpretations of the "institutional approach" which describe social practices without confronting the challenge of theories and problems. It must not shrink from considering "solutions," and at the same time must guard against indoctrination of conclusions. It must learn how to use our life in cities, factories, and fields as a kind of "laboratory," not as occasions for sight-seeing excursions of dubious educational significance.

Properly organized studies of this kind are not something which already exist. They are something to be achieved. Their content must be definite and yet not fixed in detail. They do not exclude treatment of historical background but relate it to something of momentous issue in the present. They do not exclude great books of the past and present, nor bad books, nor material not found in books.

One of the reasons for the low estate in which the social studies are held is the failure to recognize the distinction between the general pattern of inquiry, whose logic holds for all fields in which truth is sought, and the specific criteria of validity, which are appropriate to special domains. We are all familiar with the type of historian who thinks "geometrically," i.e., who believes he can reach conclusions about human beings in historical situations with almost the same degree of rigor he uses to reach conclusions about triangles and circles. The warning against taking certain standards of precision as a model for all fields is at least as old as Aristotle.

> Discussion," he says, "will be adequate if it has as much clearness as the subject-matter admits of, for precision is not to be sought for alike in all discussions . . . it is the mark of an educated man to look for precision in each class of things just so far as the nature of the subject admits; it is evidently equally foolish to accept probable reasoning from a mathematician and to demand from a rhetorician scientific proofs.[1]

Nonetheless, most discussions of the content of a liberal education which are heavily accented with a bias towards classic studies sin against this wisdom. In such accounts, mathematics and physics are justified as models of precise thought on which the social sciences are to pattern themselves. It is overlooked that the "logic" of mathematics and physics is a specific application of the general pattern of inquiry. Its precision reflects the nature of the subject matter considered. A physician, an economist, an anthropologist—even a biologist—who sought to carry into his domain the same standards would get grotesque results. *The models of correct thinking in each field must be the best illustrations of thinking in that field, not the pattern of another field.* "The type of exercise in consistent thinking" in mathematics is one thing, in the field of psychosomatic medicine it is quite another; "fidelity to empirical data" in astronomy is something else again from "fidelity to empirical data" in linguistics. This is blurred over in passages like the following from books on liberal education which, even when they give the social studies a place in the liberal arts curriculum, do so in a grudging and suspicious way:

> The social studies cannot compete with pure mathematics and the natural sciences in exhaustive analysis, rigorous inference, or verifiable interpretations. Their methods are by nature such as to forbid the substitution of these studies for the more precise and established disciplines. The latter must continue to supply a distinctive and fundamental type of exercise in consistent reasoning and fidelity to empirical data.[2]

Literally read, this may seem to provide for the independence of social studies: but it is obvious from its overtones that an invidious distinction is being drawn between the mathematical-physical sciences on the one hand, and the social sciences on the other.

(3) Everyone recognizes a distinction between knowledge and wisdom. This distinction is not clarified by making a mystery of wisdom and speaking of it as if it were begotten by divine inspiration while knowledge had a more lowly source. Wisdom is a kind of knowledge. It is knowledge of the nature, career, and consequences of *human values*. Since these cannot be separated from the human organism and the social scene, the moral ways of man cannot be understood without knowledge of the ways of things and institutions.

To study social affairs without an analysis of policies is to lose oneself in factual minutiae that lack interest and relevance. But knowledge of values is a prerequisite of the intelligent determination of policy. Philosophy, most broadly viewed, is the critical survey of existence from the standpoint of value. This points to the twofold role of philosophy in the curriculum of the college.

The world of physical nature may be studied without reference to human values. But history, art, literature, and particularly the social studies involve problems of value at every turn. A social philosophy whose implications are worked out is a series of proposals that something be *done* in the world. It includes a set of *plans* to conserve or change aspects of social life. Today the community is arrayed under different banners without a clear understanding of the basic issues involved. In the press of controversy, the ideals and values at the heart of every social philosophy are widely affirmed as articles of blind faith. They are partisan commitments justified only by the emotional security they give to believers. They spread by contagion, unchecked by critical safeguards; yet the future of civilization largely depends upon them and how they are held. It is therefore requisite that their study be made an integral part of the liberal arts curriculum. Systematic and critical instruction should be given in the great maps of life—the ways to heaven, hell, and earth—which are being unrolled in the world today.

Ideals and philosophies of life are not parts of the world of nature; but it is a pernicious illusion to imagine that they cannot be studied "scientifically." Their historical origins, their concatenation of doctrine, their controlling assumptions, their means, methods, and consequences in practice, can and should be investigated in a scientific spirit. There are certain social philosophies that would forbid such an investigation for fear of not being able to survive it; but it is one of the great merits of the democratic way of life and one of its strongest claims for acceptance that it can withstand analysis of this sort. It is incumbent upon the liberal arts college to provide for close study of the dominant social and political philosophies, ranging from one end of the color-spectrum to the other. Proper study will disclose that these philosophies cannot be narrowly considered in their own terms. They involve an examination of the great ways of life—of the great visions of philosophy which come into play whenever we try to arrange our values in a preference scale in order to choose the better between conflicting goods. Philosophy is best taught when the issues of moral choice arise naturally out of the problems of social life. The effective integration of concrete materials from history, literature, and social studies can easily be achieved within a philosophical perspective.

(4) Instruction in the natural, social, and technological forces shaping the world, and in the dominant conflicting ideals in behalf of which these forces are to be controlled, goes a long way. But not far enough. Far more important than knowledge is the method by which it is reached, and the ability to recognize when it constitutes *evidence* and when not; and more important than any particular ideal is the way in which it is held, and the capacity to evaluate it in relation to other ideals. From first to last, in season and out, our educational institutions, especially on the college level, must emphasize *methods* of analysis. They must build up in students a critical sense of evidence, relevance, and validity against which the multitudinous seas of propaganda will wash in vain. They must strengthen the powers of independent reflection, which will enable

students to confront the claims of ideals and values by their alternatives and the relative costs of achieving them.

The objections to this stress on method come from the most diverse quarters and are based on the crassest misunderstanding of the nature of methodological analysis and the reasons for making it central, not exclusive, in every educational enterprise. These objections we shall consider in a special chapter. We shall first indicate the way in which this emphasis on method is to be incorporated in the curriculum.

It is taken for granted that every subject taught will be taught in a fashion that will bring home the ways in which warranted conclusions are reached. But it is well known that the habits of correct thinking are not carried over from one field to another unless the second field is similar in nature to the first. We do not need to wait for the results of experiments on transference of training to realize that a great many able scientists who pontificate on matters outside their fields display not only ignorance but utter inability to grasp essential points at issue or to make valid elementary inferences. More and more, thinking is becoming thinking in specialized domains, largely professional, accompanied by the feeling that outside that domain it is unimportant what conclusions are reached, or by the feeling that any conclusion is as valid as any other.

Those who believe that this state of affairs can be rectified by giving a course in some special subject matter like mathematics or Latin have never confronted the challenge to provide evidence for their claim. To teach something else in order to teach *how to think* is not a short cut to logic but a circuitous way to nowhere.

There are some who deny that there is a power of general thought, that thinking is a habit that always has a specific locus in a definite field, and that there is no carry-over from one field to a widely dissimilar one. In a certain sense, this is true. But we certainly can distinguish between domains or fields of interest which are broad and those that are narrow; and between those domains in which everyone has an interest because it affects him as a human being and citizen, and those domains that are more specialized.

The field of language, of inference and argument, is a broad field but a definite one in which specific training can be given to all students. How to read intelligently, how to recognize good from bad reasoning, how to evaluate evidence, how to distinguish between a definition and a hypothesis and between a hypothesis and a resolution, can be taught in such a way as to build up permanent habits of logic in action. The result of thorough training in "semantic" analysis—using that term in its broadest sense without invidious distinctions between different schools—is an intellectual sophistication without which a man may be learned but not intelligent.

Judging by past and present curricular achievements in developing students with intellectual sophistication and maturity, our colleges must be pronounced in the main, dismal failures. The main reason for the failure is the absence of serious effort, except in a few institutions, to realize this goal. The necessity of the task is not even recognized. This failure is not only intellectually reprehensible; it is socially dangerous. For the natural susceptibility of youth to enthusiasms, its tendency to glorify action, and its limited experience make it easy recruiting material for all sorts of demagogic movements which flatter its strength and impatience. Recent history furnishes many illustrations of how, in the absence of strong critical sense, youthful strength can lead to cruelty, and youthful impatience to folly. It is true that people who are incapable of thinking cannot be taught how to think, and that the incapacity for thought is not restricted to those who learn. But the first cannot be judged without being exposed to the processes of critical instruction, and the second should be eliminated from the ranks of the teachers. There is considerable evidence to show that students who are capable of completing high school can be so taught that they are aware of *whether* they are thinking or not. There is hope that, with better pedagogic skill and inspiration, they may become capable of grasping the main thought of *what* they are reading or hearing in non-technical fields—of developing a sense of *what validly follows from what*, an accompanying sensitiveness to the dominant types of fallacies, and a habit of weighing evidence for conclusions advanced.

My own experience has led me to the conclusion that this is *not* accomplished by courses in formal logic which, when given in a rigorous and elegant way, accomplish little more than courses in pure mathematics. There is an approach to the study of logic that on an elementary level is much more successful in achieving the ends described above than the traditional course in formal logic. This plunges the student into an analysis of language material around him. By constant use of concrete illustrations drawn from all fields, but especially the fields of politics and social study, insight is developed into the logical principles of definition, the structure of analogies, dilemmas, types of fallacies and the reasons *why* they are fallacies, the criteria of good hypotheses, and related topics. Such training may legitimately be required of all students. Although philosophers are usually best able to give it, any teacher who combines logical capacity with pedagogic skill can make this study a stimulating experience.

(5) There is less controversy about the desirability of the study of composition and literature than about any other subject in the traditional or modern curriculum. It is appreciated that among the essentials of clear thought are good language habits and that, except in the higher strata of philosophic discourse, tortuous obscurities of expression are more likely to be an indication of plain confusion than of stuttering profundity. It is also widely recognized that nothing can take the place of literature in developing the imagination, and in imparting a sense of the inexhaustible richness of human personality. The questions that arise at this point are not of justification, but of method, technique, and scope of comprehensiveness.

If good language habits are to be acquired *only* in order to acquire facility in thinking, little can be said for the conventional courses in English composition. Students cannot acquire facility in clear expression in the space of a year, by developing sundry themes from varied sources, under the tutelage of instructors whose training and interest may not qualify them for sustained critical thought. Clear thinking is best controlled by those who are at home in the field in which thinking is done. If language instruction is to be motivated only by the desire to strengthen the power of organizing ideas in written discourse, it should be left to properly trained instructors in other disciplines.

But there are other justifications for teaching students English composition. The first is that there are certain rules of intelligent reading that are essential to—if they do not constitute—understanding. These rules are very elementary. By themselves they do not tell us how to understand a poem, a mathematical demonstration, a scientific text, or a religious prayer—all of which require special skills. But they make it easier for the student to uncover the nature of the "argument"—what is being said, what is being assumed, what is being presented as evidence—in any piece of prose that is not a narrative or simply informational in content. In a sense these rules are integral to the study of logic in action, but in such an introductory way that they are usually not considered part of logical study which begins its work after basic meanings have been established, or in independence of the meaning of logical symbols.

Another reason for teaching English composition independently is its uses in learning how to write. "Effective writing" is not necessarily the same thing as logical writing. The purpose for which we write determines whether our writing is effective. And there are many situations in which we write not to convince or to prove but to explain, arouse, confess, challenge, or assuage. To write *interestingly* may sometimes be just as important as to write soundly because getting a hearing and keeping attention may depend upon it. How much of the skills of writing can be taught is difficult to say. That it is worth making the effort to teach these skills is indisputable.

The place of language in the curriculum involves not merely our native language but *foreign* languages. Vocational considerations aside, should knowledge of a foreign language be required, and why?

Here again the discussion reveals great confusion. Most of the reasons advanced for making knowledge of a foreign language required are either demonstrably false or question-begging. There is a valid reason for making such study prescribed, but it is rarely stated.

It is sometimes asserted that no one can understand the structure of his own language unless he understands the structure of another. By "structure" is usually meant the grammar of the language.

> The study of Greek and Latin has a special value in increasing an American student's understanding of his own language. . . . The study of Greek and Latin provides one of the best introductions to the role of inflection in our grammatical methods and, by contrast, to an understanding of the function of other devices we now use in place of inflections.[3]

> One's own language should be known as well as possible in terms of its peculiar genius; and at least one other language—Greek is still the best one for the purpose, and indeed for any purpose [*sic!*]—should be equally known. The lines of any two languages converge in the structure of language itself.[4]

The assumption behind these passages is that mastery of the intricacies of English grammar makes for greater ability in writing, reading, and understanding modern English prose. No evidence has ever been offered for this statement and many intelligent teachers of English deny it. The best grammarians are conspicuously not the best speakers and writers of English. It is one thing to have grammar "in the bones" as a consequence of acquiring good habits of speech and writing. It is quite another to learn grammar as a means of acquiring those habits. There are better and more direct ways to that goal. But let us grant the questionable assumption. The recommendations in the quoted passages would still be a horrendous *non sequitur.* For there is every reason to believe that if the time spent on learning the grammar of foreign languages were devoted to more intensive and prolonged study of English, the result would be far greater proficiency in English than if the available time were divided between the two languages.

A second reason often advanced for making the study of foreign languages mandatory, especially Greek and Latin, is that it contributes to the enrichment of the English vocabulary of students, and gives them a sense for shades of meaning in use which is necessary for even a fair degree of mastery of our language. The following is representative of claims of this character:

> Although many of these words have now certain semantic values that were foreign to their use in their original settings, still an experience of these words in contexts of Greek and Latin provides an insight into their functioning in English *which no other experience can give.*[5]

What a breath-taking piece of dogmatism! All the evidence is begged. Once more, the obvious advantage of devoting the time spent on foreign language to additional study of English words in use is evaded. It is further assumed that Greek and Latin must be systematically studied in order to learn the historical derivation of the English words we owe these languages. Courses have been devised in which Greek and Latin words in current English use are studied without intensive study of these languages. It is still an open question whether an intensive study of the English language helps students understand the meanings of the words they encounter in the study of Greek and Latin rather than vice versa. It has often been observed that in sight reading of Greek and Latin, when students cannot consult dictionaries, those who are already most proficient in English do much better than those whose English vocabularies are limited.

The main reason why students should be requested to learn another language is that it is the most effective medium by which, when properly taught, they can acquire a sensitivity to language, to the subtle tones, undertones, and overtones of words, and to the licit ambiguities of imaginative discourse. No one who has not translated prose or poetry from one language to another can appreciate both the unique richness and the unique limitations of his own language. This is particularly true where the life of the emotions is concerned; and it is particularly important that it should be realized. For the appreciation of emotions, perhaps even their recognition in certain cases, depends upon their linguistic identification. The spectrum of human emotions is much more dense than the words by which we render them. Knowledge of different languages, and the attempts made to communicate back and forth between them in our own minds, broaden and diversify our own feelings. They multiply points of view, and liberate us from the prejudice that words—*our* words—are the natural signs of things and events. The genius of a culture is exemplified in a preeminent way in the characteristic idioms of its language. In learning another language we enable ourselves to appreciate both the cultural similarities and differences of the Western world.

So far as I know, this argument for the teaching of foreign languages was first advanced by Warner Fite.[6] But it is allied with a disparagement of "abstract thinking" on the ground that, since symbolic or conceptual thought strives to dissociate itself from the particularities of images and qualities, in the nature of the case it must falsify the fluidities of experience. This is a very serious error. Two things do not have to be identical in order to be characterized by identical relationships. And it is the relationships between things which are expressed in the symbols of abstract thinking. There is no opposition between "abstract thinking" and "concrete" or "qualitative" thinking. They involve differences in emphasis, subject matter, and interest, not different logics or formal criteria of validity.

The place of literature in the curriculum is justified by so many considerations that it is secure against all criticism. Here, too, what is at issue is not whether literature—Greek, Latin, English, European, American—should be read and studied in the schools but what should be read, when, and by what methods. These are details, important details—but outside the scope of our inquiry.

Something should be said about the unique opportunity which the teaching of literature provides, not only in giving delight by heightening perception of the formal values of literary craftsmanship, but in giving insight into people. The opposite of a liberal education, William James somewhere suggests, is a literal education. A literal education is one which equips a person to real formulas and equations, straightforward prose, doggerel verse, and advertising signs. It does not equip one to read the language of metaphor, of paradox, of indirect analogy, of serious fancy in which the emotions and passions and half-believed ideas of human beings express themselves. To read great literature is to read men—their fears and motives, their needs and hopes. Every great novelist is a *Menschenkenner* who opens the hearts of others to us and helps us to read our own hearts as well. The intelligent study of literature should never directly aim to strengthen morals and improve manners. For its natural consequences are a delicacy of perception and an emotional tact that are defeated by preaching and didactic teaching.

A liberal education will impart an awareness of the amazing and precious complexity of human relationships. Since those relationships are violated more often out of insensitiveness than out of deliberate intent, whatever increases sensitiveness of perception and understanding humanizes life. Literature in all its forms is the great humanizing medium of life. It must therefore be representative of life; not only of past life but of our own; not only of our own culture but of different cultures.

(6) An unfailing mark of philistinism in education is reference to the study of art and music as "the frills and fads" of schooling. Insofar as those who speak this way are not tone-deaf or color-blind, they are themselves prod-

ucts of a narrow education, unaware of the profound experiences which are uniquely bound up with the trained perception of color and form. There is no reason to believe that the capacity for the appreciation of art and music shows a markedly different curve of distribution from what is observable in the measurement of capacity of drawing inferences or recalling relevant information. A sufficient justification for making some study of art and music required in modern education is that it provides an unfailing source of delight in personal experience, a certain grace in living, and a variety of dimensions of meaning by which to interpret the world around us. This is a sufficient justification: there are others, quite subsidiary, related to the themes, the occasions, the history and backgrounds of the works studied. Perhaps one should add—although this expresses only a reasonable hope—that a community whose citizens have developed tastes would not tolerate the stridency, the ugliness and squalor which assault us in our factories, our cities, and our countryside.

One of the reasons why the study of art and music has not received as much attention as it should by educators, particularly on the college level, is that instruction in these subjects often suffers from two opposite defects. Sometimes courses in art and music are given as if all students enrolled in them were planning a career as practicing artists or as professional *teachers* of the arts. Sometimes they are given as hours for passive enjoyment or relaxation in which the teacher does the performing or talking and in which there is no call upon the students to make an intelligent response.

The key-stress in courses in art and music should be *discrimination* and *interpretation*, rather than appreciation and cultivation. The latter can take care of themselves, when the student has learned to discriminate and interpret intelligently.

Briefly summarized: the answer to the question *What should we teach?* is selected materials from the fields of mathematics and the natural sciences; social studies, including history; language and literature; philosophy and logic; art and music. The knowledge imparted by such study should be acquired in such a way as to strengthen the skills of reading and writing, of thinking and imaginative interpretation, of criticism and evaluation.

Notes

1. Aristotle: *Nicomachean Ethics* (tr. Ross; Oxford: Oxford University Press; 1942), 1094b, 12–14, 24–27.
2. Greene, *et al: Liberal Education Re-Examined* (New York: Harper & Brothers; 1943), pp. 56–7.
3. Ibid., p. 58.
4. Mark van Doren: *Liberal Education* (New York: Henry Holt & Company: 1943), pp. 131–2.
5. Greene, *et al: Liberal Education Re-Examined*, p. 59. My italics.
6. Warner Fite: "The Philosopher and His Words," *Philosophical Review,* Vol. 44, No. 2 (March 1935), p. 120.

20   Two Dogmas of Curriculum*
Jane Roland Martin

The author is Professor Emerita of Philosophy at the University of Massachusetts, Boston. In this article she explores the principles that should guide those entrusted with the formation of a curriculum. She emphasizes that subjects are constructed, not merely conserved, and that curricular development calls for critical examination of our intellectual beliefs, moral values, and social visions.

A cluster of second order assumptions is so deeply entrenched in our thinking about curriculum that its existence is seldom recognized and the assumptions themselves are almost never challenged. In this essay I will examine two such assumptions and will argue that they are untenable. I call the Dogma of God-Given Subjects and the Dogma of the Immutable Basics *second order* assumptions because they speak about and analyze curriculum instead of prescribing what it should be. Thus the Dogma of God-Given Subjects does not tell us what to teach or when. Rather, it tells us that the subjects of curriculum are "givens," that they are found, not made; in other words, it speaks about the nature of curriculum itself. Similarly, its special case, the Dogma of the Immutable Basics, does not tell us how the basics of education should be taught or to whom, but that they are unchanging and eternal.

The prospects of constructing an adequate theory of curriculum are dim so long as the dogmas to be discussed here remain intact, and so are the prospects for true curricular reform. Reform which goes beyond mere tinkering with existing curricula requires that proposals for new subjects be taken seriously and that the present hierarchy of subjects be challenged.[1] These dogmas of curriculum serve as barriers to such change. An adequate theory of curriculum must illuminate clearly the choices confronting those who develop curriculum. To do this it must adopt a generous conception of subjects and acknowledge the fact that our subjects are complex human constructions to which we ourselves attach value. So long as these dogmas of curriculum are allowed to go unexamined, theoretical illumination will continue to elude us.

I. THE DOGMA OF GOD-GIVEN SUBJECTS

What Things Can Be Subjects?

We tend to assume that the subjects we are accustomed to—the 3Rs, the sciences, foreign languages, the humanities, the fine arts—are the only subjects there are. In fact our subjects are not limited in number.[2] We assume they are because we wear blinders and recognize as subjects only those things which in the past have been considered suitable candidates for a general and a liberal education. There is a much greater range to choose from than we realize. Nei-

---

*From *Synthese*, vol. 51 (1982), pp. 5–20, by permission of Kluwer Academic Publishers.

ther Chairs, Hamburgers nor Humphrey Bogart has the ring of a bona fide subject to most of us. Yet if we shed our narrow frame of reference we realize not only that these can be subjects, but that they undoubtedly are—Chairs a subject in a curriculum for furniture makers, Hamburgers a subject in a curriculum for McDonald trainees, Humphrey Bogart a subject in a curriculum for film enthusiasts. Even a brief glance at the wide variety of curricula there are should convince us that anything can be a subject; that French, Mathematics and Physics can give way to Identity, Community and the Reality of Material Objects or to the Rights of Animals, Mary Queen of Scots and Dying.

Anything can be a subject because subjects are made, not found. They are not "out there" waiting for us, but are human constructions. Think for a moment about the subject Physics. From the standpoint of teaching and learning, although not perhaps from that of writing the history of science, the *science* physics is a given. The *subject* Physics is something quite different from the science physics, however. People engage in the science physics, whereas they study the subject Physics. To be sure, physicists study things, but not the identical set of things students of Physics study, for physicists study physical phenomena, while students of Physics study also the laws and theories developed by those who study physical phenomena. The subject Physics is both more and less than the science physics. It depends on the latter for its very existence: were there no science physics there would scarcely be the subject Physics. Yet if the science physics provides the *raison d'être* for the subject Physics, the latter draws its subject matter not merely from the former but from the history and philosophy of science, the sociology and the politics of science and from numerous other sources as well.

Every subject takes as its point of departure something "out there" in the world which for want of a better term I will call a *subject-entity*. The subject-entity of each of the subjects Physics, Chemistry, Biology is a science; of each of the subjects French, Spanish, Latin, a language; of the subject Driving, a practical activity and of the subject Drama, a performing art. The question "What things can be subjects?" is really a question about subject-entities; thus when I said above that anything can be a subject, what I meant was that anything can be a subject-entity. So far as I can see, there are no limits to the kind of thing that can be the subject-entity of a subject. Some things might seem too "small" to serve in that capacity, for example a Chopin Waltz or, better still, one phrase of a Chopin Waltz. However, judgments of the size of a subject-entity are really judgments of importance and these must be assessed in relation to some context of study. If the purpose is to acquaint non-musicians with Western music, it is obviously a mistake to offer as a subject of study something whose subject-entity is a single work or a part thereof, but if the purpose is, e.g., to sensitize accomplished musicians to innovations of the Romantic period, the study of a subject whose subject-entity is a Chopin Waltz or even a phrase of a waltz may not be so far-fetched.

The Dogma of God-Given Subjects addresses the question "What *can* be our subjects?" not the question "What *should* be our subjects?" To say that anything can be a subject-entity is simply to say that those in the curriculum field *can* look far and wide for the points of departure of the subjects they construct. It is not to say that everything in heaven and earth *ought* to be a subject in the curriculum. It is important to recognize, however, that there are all kinds of curricula for all kinds of purposes and that something which seems too trivial to serve as the subject-entity of a subject in relation to one educational purpose might acquire significance in relation to a different educational purpose. There is no reason whatsoever to suppose that everything which can be a subject-entity will or should become the point of departure for a subject in a curriculum. Yet the possibility remains that something which has consistently been overlooked or rejected for that role might one day serve it well.

The distinction between a subject and its subject-entity has been ignored, perhaps because a subject usually takes its name from its subject-entity. It is an important distinction to maintain, for while every subject has a subject-entity, no subject is identical with its subject-entity: on the one hand, the function of a subject is educational; on the other, a subject has not only a subject-entity belonging to it but a body of subject matter which ranges far and wide. Thus, for example, the subject matter which belongs to the subject Cooking comes from the subject-entity of Cooking, namely the practical activity of cooking, but also from a variety of other sources including the disciplines of biology, chemistry, anthropology, history, politics.

Just as the distinction between a subject and its subject-entity is overlooked, so is the distinction between both of these and subject matter. This is perhaps because curriculum theorists tend to assume that except for the so-called interdisciplinary subjects the subject matter of each subject comes from a single source. They assume too that subjects are neat, ready-made bundles of subject matter which one finds on one's doorstep. Thus they worry about content selection—which parts of the bundle should be pulled out and tied together for seniors in high school? which parts for fifth graders?—but they take the initial bundles for granted. Such complacency is not justified: the bundles of subject matter which belong to our subjects are not out there waiting to be recognized, but are themselves human creations. Think of the subject matter of that relative newcomer to curriculum, Women's Studies. It ranges over the social sciences, the natural sciences, the arts, the humanities. Yet there was no ready-made bundle of subject matter out there waiting to be found. Over time a bundle has simply been constructed.

The wisdom of my introducing Women's Studies into a discussion of subjects may be questioned, for it may be doubted that Women's Studies really is a subject. Yet what is Women's Studies if not a subject? It is taught and studied and is an integral part of many college curricula. What property does it lack? The answer most likely to be given to this question is that Women's Studies is not a field of knowledge. What is meant by this, presumably, is that the subject-entity of Women's Studies is not a field of knowledge. This is, of course, true: its subject-entity is women, not some discipline which studies women. But this fact is scarcely relevant to the claim that Women's Studies is not a subject since there are many subjects in the same boat. The subject-entity of the subject the Far East is a geographical location, the subject-entity of the subject French is a language, the subject-entity of the subject Reading is a practical activity. Subjects can take intellectual disciplines as their subject-entities, but they certainly do not have to. As I have already said, anything at all can play that role.

The classic text books on the theory of curriculum development do not recognize this fact.[3] They catalogue several different patterns of curriculum organization, one of which they call the "subject curriculum." That, of course, is the standard liberal curriculum whose subjects are History, Literature, Mathematics, Physics and the like. They fail to recognize that some of the other types of curricula they distinguish are also subject curricula, because they do not realize that what they call "broad fields"—combinations of fields of knowledge such as the natural sciences or the humanities—can themselves be the subject-entities of subjects as can "social processes" such as earning a living or making a home.[4] Although these texts do not distinguish between a subject and its subject-entity, they tacitly assume that the subject-entity of a subject must be a field of knowledge.

Women's Studies really is a subject. However, it does not follow from this fact that it *should* be a subject in a given curriculum. Subject construction no more dictates the makeup of curriculum than does epistemology.[5] The point of the present discussion is not to promote particular subjects, but to make clear the deficiencies of the received view of subjects and to urge that a generous conception of them be incorporated into curriculum theory and practice.

It will perhaps be granted that curriculum theorizing would profit from a broad conception of subjects, yet be denied that such a conception is required for true curricular reform. Members of the radical school reform movement of the late 1960s and early 1970s seemed inclined to reject subjects altogether on the grounds that subjects carry with them rigid teaching methods and institutional structures and hence were not compatible with curricular reform. Does not such reform require that subjects be abandoned rather than that our conception of them be expanded? This suspicion of subjects was based on a confusion between tradition and necessity. To be sure, subjects have in the past been taught by lecture and recitation methods and have been tied to very formal administrative arrangements, but these are not inevitable accompaniments of subjects. Mathematics and French can be taught informally at skill centers of the kind envisioned by Ivan Illich, and Physics can be taught in the laboratory or the kitchen. In sum, there is neither a short list of subjects nor a pre-established pattern of human behavior to which every subject must accommodate itself, and thus there is no reason at all to fear them. Perhaps true curricular reform can occur through the exclusion of subjects in general from the curriculum, but before they are banned it behooves reformers to search for new and better subjects and better patterns for relating them to one another.

Subject Construction

New subjects such as Women's Studies and Black Studies are not the only ones whose legitimacy has been questioned. Well-established subjects such as Social

Studies have come under attack for being conglomerations of subjects rather than subjects themselves.[6] The complaints seem to be that "real" subjects like Physics have unity and integrity whereas Social Studies does not because it is made up of history, geography and the various social sciences. Each one of these has unity, it is said, but together they do not form an integrated whole.

Interestingly enough, the criticism of traditional school subjects made by those curriculum reformers of the post-Sputnik era who developed the so-called New Curricula was of just this sort. In their eyes Physics, as taught in the schools, was nothing but a collection of unrelated topics such as heat and light, and History was nothing but a collection of unrelated facts.[7] They did not go so far as to say that these were not school subjects; they simply rejected the way in which they were conceived. Insofar as Social Studies is conceived of and taught as a collection of unrelated disciplines perhaps it deserves to be criticized. But it does not have to be conceived of in that way any more than Physics or History has to be presented as a group of discrete units.

The trouble with this complaint is that it uses a double standard. Subjects have different *versions*. It is quite unfair to compare a well-integrated version of one subject with a badly integrated version of the other and to conclude on this basis that the latter is not a subject at all. Every subject has parts. Their degree of integration depends on whether the parts are conceived of as related to one another in some sensible way or whether they are conceived of in "one thing after another" fashion. To be sure, some sets of parts may lend themselves better than others to attempts at integration. One ought not to assume, however, that because the parts of a subject *are* not well-integrated, that they *cannot* be. A Social Studies in which psychology, sociology and economics are all brought to bear on selected historical events or eras can readily be imagined as can be a Social Studies in which history, geography and the social sciences are all used to illuminate other cultures. Social Studies can have unity although there is no one right way to achieve it.

Actually there is no one right set of parts into which to divide a subject. The New Curricula rejected the topics which had long been considered the proper parts of Physics, Biology, Chemistry, Mathematics and substituted for them the methods, theories and basic concepts of the related discipline. Integration was then easy. Social Studies does not have to be divided up into history, geography, and the social sciences. Its parts could be social institutions such as family, church, government, business or it could be different kinds of cultures. There are any number of ways to divide up a subject and any number of ways to integrate the resultant parts.

Subject construction is in fact a creative activity. In choosing a subject-entity—the science physics, women, the environment—one's work has just begun. There are parts to be chosen and relationships among them to be traced. There is also the question of how the subject-entity is going to be viewed. The New Curricula for the most part took intellectual disciplines as their subject-entities.[8] What distinguished them from earlier efforts at subject construction was that they viewed the disciplines as fields of inquiry rather than as accumulations of knowledge. This was no slight change. Although the aspects under which a subject is viewed does not dictate its parts and the degree to which they are integrated, it surely influences these decisions. One who views history as a field of inquiry will normally be led to a very different version of the subject than one who views history as an account of the past.

Consider the subject English. View its subject-entity, namely English, as a language and one naturally thinks of its structure, its history, its various functions. View it instead as a means of communication and one thinks of composition and literature and speech. This is not to say that either view of English carries with it one and only one set of parts. The point is simply that some things seem to fall into place naturally in relation to one view of English, but not another. The classic texts in curriculum development give the impression that one curriculum decision leads inexorably to the next. In fact, subject construction—something they scarcely touch on—is a creative art. One decision may make certain others seem inappropriate or out of place, but they do not flow from one another in accordance with the rules of deductive logic.

Anything can serve as the subject-entity of a subject and when something does, any number of versions of the subject can be constructed. Some of those versions will have grave flaws, the lack of unity and integrity perhaps being one. But flaws are reasons for improving a particular version of a subject or for selecting a different version. They do not justify the claim that something which people are studying is not "really" a subject at all.

Subjects and Learning Activities

Additions can be made to the list of subjects, yet it would be a mistake to assume that every significant change in education brings with it new subjects. The open classrooms advocated by one wing of the radical school reform movement are a case in point.[9] They embodied a number of significant changes in educational practice, but they were not bearers of serious *curricular* reform, for the standard subjects of the elementary school curriculum were all preserved in open classrooms, albeit in disguised form.

The traditional conception of the classroom had led people to see relatively few things as educational materials: books, maps, pencils, paper, chalk, blackboards. The very different conception of the open classroom encouraged people to see as educational materials things they would previously have overlooked: costumes, wallpaper sample books, old tires, egg cartons, sand, water. It extended radically the range of things acknowledged to be useful in learning. Similarly, it extended the range of activities acknowledged to be promoters of learning. The traditional conception of the classroom limited people's sights to reading and writing and to drill, memorization and recitation. The theory and practice of the open classroom opened their eyes to painting, building robots, dramatizing stories, dancing and countless other activities which engage children's interest.

Open education did not, however, extend radically the range of things people take to be subjects. Visitors to open classrooms looked around in dismay crying "Where have all the subjects gone?" They saw children doing woodwork and messing around with water, but science, spelling and mathematics had apparently vanished. In fact they had simply donned disguises. The vast changes in learning activities and educational materials and the emphasis on informal, incidental learning served as masks for subjects which were, in the main, the subjects of the traditional classroom.

In education, as in life, appearances can be deceptive. To discover what is taking place one must look behind and beyond the overt behavior of both students and teachers for intentions which are not always obvious to the naked eye. One must also differentiate between the point of view of the student and the point of view of the teacher. Had one looked behind the surface goings on of the typical open classroom and examined the teachers' intentions, one would have found the standard school subjects. When the children in an open classroom baked cookies *they* did not take themselves to be learning to multiply fractions, nor did they take themselves to be learning to spell when they ran printing presses or gave titles to their art work. Yet from their *teacher's* standpoint baking cookies was primarily a vehicle for learning arithmetic while running a printing press was a vehicle for learning to spell.

The theory and practice of open classrooms was not concerned with significant *curricular* reform. In such classrooms informal learning—that is learning through engaging in activities one enjoys—was the rule, and the creative energy of teachers was spent devising new and better materials to use and activities to do. One great contribution of open education was its stress on the fact that from a single activity many very different things can be learned. Thus the search for activities and materials was really a search for especially fruitful ones: for activities and materials from which a wide range of results would flow. Nonetheless, the search was one-sided. Perhaps because subjects were considered to be inherently conservative, activities, not subjects, were sought. The traditional subjects were not banned from the classroom, however. Instead, they were taken as givens and the creative task was seen to be that of discovering how to teach those subjects without doing the kind of psychological and moral damage to children which traditional classrooms were thought to do.

To be sure, activities can themselves serve as subject-entities. The subjects Reading and Writing, Cooking and Sewing, Woodwork and Drama all testify to this fact. However, when students engage in activities, those activities often serve as aids to learning some other subjects and are not themselves subjects of study. Take the activity reading. It is a subject-entity of the subject Reading in grade school, but when a high school student reads a biology textbook, reading functions as a learning activity harnessed to the subject Biology, and not as a subject in its own right. So too with the activity cooking. It can be a subject, but it can also be harnessed to the subject Arithmetic or to the subject Reading or even to Biology and Chemistry in order to make learning more efficient and pleasurable.

To change curriculum radically it is not enough to introduce new ways of learning old subjects as open education did. The old subjects must be abandoned or else made to cede some of the curriculum space they now occupy to new subjects. When true curricular reform is wanted, simply extending the range of learning activities and materials, important as this may be, is not sufficient. Nor is it sufficient simply to give students the freedom to make their own curriculum, as some radical school reformers tended to assume. New subjects must be seen to be chosen and they must be created in order to be seen. Unless the eyes of students are opened to a wide range of alternative subjects, there is no reason at all to suppose that they will see, let alone choose, new ones. The grip of tradition and habit is strong. To make curriculum the province of untutored free choice—be it student, teacher or parental choice—is to minimize the likelihood of significant curricular reform.

II. THE DOGMA OF THE IMMUTABLE BASICS

What Makes Something Basic?

The 3Rs are subjects. In calling them our basics we give them a near monopoly over the curriculum of the early years, but subjects they nonetheless are. Now one of our most deeply entrenched assumptions about curriculum is that the basics are immutable givens. Thus teachers believe that theirs is not to reason why, theirs is but to teach the 3Rs or die in the attempt. However, the 3Rs are not given to us as subjects, but are made by us. We construct them as we do all subjects, and once constructed they become basics by our decision.

It will be protested that we do not choose our basics, they are given to us. To understand that the subjects we call the basics not only are human constructions, but that they serve as basics at our pleasure, it is necessary to ask what qualifies something to be one of the basics of education. What, for example, do Reading, Writing and Arithmetic have that Cooking and Driving lack? The answer to this question cannot be that Reading, Writing and Arithmetic are essential for everyone to study whereas Cooking and Driving are not, for we take the 3Rs to be essential subjects of study *just because* they are so basic.

One of the directors of the Council for Basic Education has said that the 3Rs are basic because they have "generative power."[10] A consideration of the philosophical notion of a basic action contributes to an understanding of this metaphor.[11] One opens a door by turning the knob, one pushes a stone by kicking it, one signals a right turn by moving one's arm and one nods assent by moving one's head. Compare these acts with those one just does. One turns the knob by moving one's hand, but one just does move one's hand and one just does move one's arm when one signals a right turn. Those acts which require no other act in doing them are called "basic actions" since they are the starting point, the "building blocks" out of which all other acts are formed. Indeed, they have been described as *generating* all other acts.[12]

Of course, from the standpoint of a general theory of human action, reading, writing and arithmetic are not basic at all: one does not just do them; one does them by doing a variety of other actions. Yet from the standpoint of education it makes good sense to call the 3Rs basic. The central concern of education is learning, and learning is one of those acts one does by doing other things, in particular by reading, by writing and by doing arithmetic. Just as moving one's hand is a building block or generator of the act of opening a door, so reading, writing and arithmetic are building blocks or generators of the act of learning.[13]

Learning is not the only action generated by the 3Rs, however. The 3Rs are generators of the act of living as well as learning—at least of living in modern, industrial society. Reading, writing and arithmetic enter into our work and play, our jobs and recreation. We use them in our roles of consumer and parent, citizen and neighbor. One may vote by pulling a lever and pull the lever by moving one's arm, but one chooses one's candidates by keeping informed about the issues and one does this by reading the appropriate literature. One may buy bread by taking it off the shelf and giving money to the salesperson and one may do this by moving one's arms and legs, but one decides which bread to buy and determines how much money to give by calculating costs and counting coins, both of which one does by doing arithmetic. At home one writes notes to one's children's teachers and reads school announcements, at work one writes and reads memoranda and one does calculations concerning one's income. The list of everyday activities central to living which are done by doing the 3Rs is endless.

The answer to the question "What makes the 3Rs basic?" is that we perform the acts or activities of learning and living by reading, writing and doing arithmetic. To generalize, a subject qualifies as a basic of education if its subject-entity generates those acts. Of course, for some acts of learning and living the 3Rs are all but irrelevant. Moreover, many acts which can be generated by the 3Rs can also be done without their help: one can vote without reading the relevant literature and can buy food without calculating costs. Thus we take the 3Rs to be the basics of education not because they generate all acts of learning and living, but because we believe that so many of the valued acts of learning and living must be done by doing them if those acts are to be done well.

Choosing the Basics

We take the 3Rs to be our basics because we perform many of the activities of learning and living we value by doing them. Yet the 3Rs are by no means the *only* constituents of those activities, nor are they *absolutely fundamental* constituents of them. We do not just read, although once we know how to read it may seem as if we do; rather, we perform this activity by doing a number of other things. Exactly what one does in reading is itself an interesting question. A look at the scholarly literature on the topic gives the strong impression that there are almost as many accounts of its constituents as there are experts in the field of reading.[14] There are competing theories about the constituents of writing too. Indeed, even arithmetic—whose components one might have naively assumed to be addition, subtraction, multiplication and division—is divided up in different ways by different interested parties. The precise nature of the elements of the 3Rs is not the issue, however. The point is that since the 3Rs are done by doing other things, in calling them our basics we make a practical decision. After all, we could have continued our search for the basics past the 3Rs, stopping at their components or perhaps at the components of their components—for there is no reason to suppose that the things we do in reading, writing and arithmetic are themselves unitary activities.

Assuming for the sake of argument that something *can* be absolutely un-complex, we do not make this a requirement which our educational basics must meet for the very good reason that our basics play a central role in curriculum. Were we to push our search for them too far back, we would find ourselves in the absurd position of designing educational programs around such things as eye movements or perhaps even brain waves. That we call the 3Rs *rather than their components* our basics is, then, a matter of practical decision. That we consider the 3Rs *rather than some other components* of the activities of learning and living our basics is a matter of decision too. One may learn science, history, literature and mathematics by reading, writing and doing arithmetic, but one does not learn them by the performance of these skills alone. One learns them by doing a host of things including listening and speaking, by asking questions and testing assumptions, by using one's imagination to conjecture about what might be the case and inventing ways of testing hypotheses. When one performs the activities of living by reading, writing and doing arithmetic, these skills are not exercised in isolation either, but are done in conjunction with other skills as well as with attitudes, values and numerous character traits. We could call some of these other things our basics, but we do not. Instead we single out the 3Rs for this honor.

Of course not everything which is a constituent of living and learning is a qualified candidate for the office of educational basic. Thus the 3Rs are not in competition with things which cannot be taught or learned. Some of us have blue eyes and some of us do not, but none of us has learned to have blue eyes and it is quite futile to try to teach someone to have blue eyes. In choosing our basics from among the many constituents of learning and living, we are limited to the kind of thing over which students and teachers can exercise some control. We are limited also to the kind of thing which would not develop in any case as human beings mature. Walking can no doubt be taught, but except in unusual circumstances it would be unnecessary to make it a basic of education since it is learned anyway. Finally, the 3Rs face no competition from those constituents of living and learning which lack generative power. To choose as the basics of education things such as the inside and outside edges of figure skating, or major scales on the piano, which have very specific application would be foolhardy.

In choosing basics a grasp of the larger picture is essential. If mastery of figure skating is the goal, skating on one's edges is indeed basic. If mastery of the piano is the goal, playing the major scales is certainly a strong candidate for that office. When the activities of learning and living are at stake, however, neither of these skills has sufficient generative power, whereas the 3Rs seem to fit the bill. Yet generative power is not a constant. As the world changes and we change, the activities of learning and living generated by the 3Rs can fall into disuse or disfavor, and other activities, ones not generated by the 3Rs, can come to overshadow those we once held to be especially valuable. Even if the activities the 3Rs generate remain important to us, substitute ways of doing them can become available and, if they do, the generative power of other constituents of those activities may increase, for generative power can grow as well as diminish over time.[15]

The generative power of the 3Rs is neither universal nor eternal. Given a training program in figure skating, skating on one's inside and outside edges, not the 3Rs, has wide ranging application; given a program designed to teach the 3Rs, some components of reading, writing and arithmetic, rather than the 3Rs themselves, will have great generative power. Even when one's primary concern is learning and living, the generative power of the 3Rs will not everywhere be the same. For the Ntsetlik Eskimos portrayed in the social studies curriculum, 'Man: A Course of Study,' the generative power of fishing and hunting will be far greater than that of the 3Rs.[16]

Since we choose our basics—since they are a matter of decision, not discovery—we must make quite sure that the special status we thereby confer upon them is deserved. There is no doubt about the fact that rank and privilege attach themselves to the basics of education. No one would ever call one of the basics a "frill"; no one would try to push a basic subject out of the curriculum in favor of some non-basic subject. Programs are designed around the basics; for better or worse the basics are never far from the thoughts of curriculum planners and designers.

It might seem that the decisions of what to make our basics could depend in a straightforward way on the facts of the case. Just do a survey of the activities of learning and living and see what things generate them, then select the ones with the greatest generative power. This method is not adequate however, because it begs the important question of *which* activities of learning and living people *should* perform. In this regard it is important to remember that the decision of what to make the basics of education, like every major curriculum decision, depends not simply on the way the world is but on the way we think it should be, on the kind of life we believe to be worth living, and on the kind of society we believe to be worth living in.

Notes

1. For an example of the kind of reform I have in mind see "Needed: A New Paradigm for Liberal Education," chapter 9 in Jane Roland Martin, *Changing the Educational Landscape: Philosophy, Women, and Curriculum* (New York and London: Routledge, 1994).
2. The next few paragraphs draw on Jane R. Martin, "Toward an Open Curriculum," *Futurist Working Papers: The Teacher in 1984*, New England Program for Teacher Education, 1972.
3. See, for example, Hilda Taba, *Curriculum Development* (New York: Harcourt, Brace & World, 1962); B. Othanel Smith, William O. Stanley, and J. Harlan Shores, *Fundamentals of Curriculum Development* (New York: Harcourt, Brace & World, 1957), Rev. Ed.
4. The typologies of the classic texts differ. Thus, for example, Smith, Stanley and Shores, *op. cit.*, isolate the subject, the activity and the core curriculum while Taba, *op. cit.*, isolates the subject, the activity and the social processes curriculum. Smith, Stanley and Shores call the broad fields curriculum a modified subject curriculum (pp. 255 ff.). Taba lists it separately but then refers to it as a "type of subject organization" (p. 395).
5. On the role of epistemology in relation to curricular decisions see "Needed: A New Paradigm for Liberal Education," chapter 9 in *Changing the Educational Landscape: Philosophy, Women, and Curriculum*.

6. For a more detailed discussion of this topic, see Jane R. Martin, "The Anatomy of Subjects," *Educational Theory* (Spring 1977), pp. 85–95.
7. The classic formulation of the theory behind the New Curricula is to be found in Jerome S. Bruner, *The Process of Education* (Cambridge: Harvard University Press, 1961).
8. For a discussion of the role of the disciplines in curriculum decisions see "The Disciplines and Curriculum," chapter 7 in *Changing the Educational Landscape: Philosophy, Women, and Curriculum.*
9. For an account of these classrooms see Joseph Featherstone, "The British Infant Schools" in Ronald and Beatrice Gross (eds.) *Radical School Reform* (New York: Simon & Schuster, 1969); Charles Rathbone (ed.) *Open Education* (New York: Citation Press, 1971); Ewald B. Nyquist and Gene R. Hawes (eds.) *Open Education* (New York: Bantam Books, 1972).
10. Clifton Fadiman, "The Case for Basic Education" in James D. Koerner (ed.), *The Case for Basic Education* (Boston: Little, Brown, 1959), p. 6.
11. The classic work on this topic is Arthur C. Danto, "Basic Actions," *American Philosophical Quarterly 2* (1965), pp. 141–148. For criticisms of Danto's account see Frederick Stoutland, "Basic Actions and Causality," *The Journal of Philosophy 65* (1969), pp. 467–475; Myles Brand, "Danto on Basic Actions," *Nous 2* (1968), pp. 187–190.
12. Alvin I. Goldman, *A Theory of Human Action* (Englewood Cliffs, N.J.: Prentice-Hall, 1970).
13. The analogy to the standard account of basic actions breaks down at several points: (1) the 3Rs must be learned; (2) they are themselves done by doing other actions; (3) the action generated does not necessarily have the same time boundaries as the generating action. Still, the analogy serves to illuminate the reasons for calling certain subjects rather than others the basics of education.
14. For one theory of the component skills of reading see Magdalen D. Vernon, "Varieties of Deficiency in the Reading Processes," *Harvard Educational Review 47* (1977), pp. 396–410.
15. In "Literacy and Learning," an address given to the New England Philosophy of Education Society, October, 1980, I have treated this topic in greater depth.
16. See Jerome S. Bruner, *Toward a Theory of Instruction* (Cambridge: Harvard University Press, 1966), pp. 73–101.

21 The Passions of Pluralism: Multiculturalism and the Expanding Community*

Maxine Greene

The author is Professor Emerita of Philosophy and Education and William F. Russell Professor in the Foundations of Education at Teachers College Columbia University. In this essay she seeks to convey through numerous examples the plural-

*Reprinted by permission of the author.

istic quality of American society. The challenge she poses is for a community, through expansion, to be strengthened, not fragmented.

There have always been newcomers in this country; there have always been strangers. There have always been young persons in our classrooms we did not, could not see or hear. In recent years, however, invisibility has been refused on many sides. Old silences have been shattered; long-repressed voices are making themselves heard. Yes, we are in search of what John Dewey called "the Great Community"[1]; but, at once, we are challenged as never before to confront plurality and multiplicity. Unable to deny or obscure the facts of pluralism, we are asked to choose ourselves with respect to unimaginable diversities. To speak of passions in such a context is not to refer to the strong feelings aroused by what strikes many as a confusion and a cacophony. Rather, it is to have in mind the central sphere for the operation of the passions: "the realm of face-to-face relationships."[2] It seems clear that the more continuous and authentic personal encounters can be, the less likely it will be for categorizing and distancing to take place. People are less likely to be treated instrumentally, to be made "other" by those around. I want to speak of pluralism and multiculturalism with concrete engagements in mind, actual and imagined: engagements with persons, young persons and older persons, some suffering from exclusion, some from powerlessness, some from poverty, some from ignorance, some from boredom. Also, I want to speak with imagination in mind, and metaphor, and art. Cynthia Ozick writes: "Through metaphor, the past has the capacity to imagine us, and we it. Through metaphorical concentration, doctors can imagine what it is to be their patients. Those who have no pain can imagine those who suffer. Those at the center can imagine what it is to be outside. The strong can imagine the weak. Illuminated lives can imagine the dark. Poets in their twilight can imagine the borders of stellar fire. We strangers can imagine the familiar hearts of strangers."[3]

Passions, then, engagements, and imagining: I want to find a way of speaking of community, an expanding community, taking shape when diverse people, speaking as *who* and not *what* they are, come together in speech and action, as Hannah Arendt puts it, to constitute something in common among themselves. She writes that "plurality is the condition of human action because we are all the same, that is, human, in such a way that nobody is ever the same as anyone else who ever lived, lives, or will live."[4] For her, those present on a common ground have different locations on that ground; and each one "sees or hears from a different position." An object—a classroom, a neighborhood street, a field of flowers—shows itself differently when encountered by a variety of spectators. The reality of that object (or classroom, or neighborhood, or field of flowers) arises out of the sum total of its appearances. Thinking of those spectators as participants in an ongoing dialogue, each one speaking out of a distinct perspective and yet open to those around, I find a kind of paradigm for what I have in mind. I discover another in the work of Henry Louis Gates, Jr., who writes about the fact that "the challenge facing America in the next century will be the shaping, at long last, of a truly common public culture, one responsive to the long-silenced cultures of color." (It is not long, it will be remembered, since the same Professor Gates asked in a *New York Times* article, "Whose canon is it anyway?"). More recently, he has evoked the philosopher Michael Oakeshott and his notion of a conversation with different voices. Education, Gates suggests, might be "an invitation into the art of this conversation in which we learn to recognize the voices, each conditioned by a different perception of the world." Then Gates adds: "Common sense says that you don't bracket out 90% of the world's cultural heritage if you really want to learn about the world."[5]

For many, what is common sense for Gates represents an attack on the coherence of what we think of as our heritage, our canon. The notion of different voices conditioned by different perspectives summons up the specter of relativism; and relativism, according to Clifford Geertz, is the "intellectualist Grande Peur." It makes people uneasy because it appears to subvert authority; it eats away at what is conceived as objectively real. "If thought is so much out in the world as this," Geertz asks, as the uneasy might ask, "what is to guarantee its generality, its objectivity, its efficacy, or its truth?"[6] There is irony in Geertz's voice since he knows and has said that "for our time and forward, the image of a general orientation, perspective, *Weltanschauung*, growing out of humanistic studies (or, for that matter, out of scientific ones) and shaping the direction of the culture is a chimera." He speaks of the "radical variousness of the way we think now" and suggests that the problem of integrating cultural life becomes one of "making it possible for people inhabiting different worlds to have a genuine, and reciprocal, impact upon one another."[7] This is troubling for people seeking assurances, seeking certainties. And yet they, like the rest of us, keep experiencing attacks on what is familiar, what James Clifford calls "the irruption of otherness, the unexpected. . . ."[8] It may well be that our ability to tolerate the unexpected relates to our tolerance for multiculturalism, for the very idea of expansion, and the notion of plurality.

We are well aware, for all that, that Arthur Schlesinger, Jr., among others who (like Schlesinger) must be taken seriously, sees a "disuniting of America"[9] in the making if shared commitments shatter, if we lose touch with the democratic idea. Proponents of what is called "civism"[10] are concerned that pluralism threatens the existence of a democratic *ethos* intended to transcend all differences." The *ethos* encompasses the principles of freedom, equality, and justice, as well as regard for human rights; and there is fear that the new relativism and particularism will subvert the common faith. And there are those like E. D. Hirsch, Jr., who sees the concept of "background knowledge" and the shared content it ensures undermined by "variousness" and the multicultural emphases that distract from the common. What they call "cultural literacy" is undermined as a result; and the national community itself is eroded.[11] At the extreme, of course, are those on the far right who find a conspiracy in challenges to the so-called Eurocentric canon and in what they construct as "Politically Correct," signifying a new orthodoxy built out of oversensitivity to multicultural concerns.[12] As for the religious fundamentalist right, says Robert Hughes (writing in *The New York Review*) one of the motives driving men like Jesse Helms is to establish themselves as defenders of what they define as the

"American Way" now (as Hughes puts it) "that their original crusade against the Red Menace has been rendered null and void. . . ."[13] Not only do they argue for their construct against the National Art Endowment's grants to *avant garde* artists; they attack such deviations as multiculturalism. It is important to hold this in mind as we try to work through a conception of pluralism to an affirmation of the struggle to attain the life of "free and enriching communion" John Dewey identified with democracy.

The seer of the life of communion, according to Dewey, was Walt Whitman. Whitman wrote about the many shapes arising in the country in his time, "the shapes of doors giving many exits and entrances" and "shapes of democracy . . . ever projecting other shapes." In "Song of Myself" (in total contradiction to the fundamentalist version of the "American Way") he wrote:

Through me many long dumb voices,
Voices of the interminable generations of prisoners and slaves,
Voices of the diseas'd and despairing and of thieves and dwarfs,
Voices of cycles of preparation and accretion,
And of the threads that connect the stars, and of wombs and of
the father-stuff,
And of the rights of them the others are down upon. . . .

Through me forbidden voices. . . .[14]

He was, from all appearances, the seer of a communion arising out of "many shapes," out of multiplicity. There is no suggestion of a melting pot here; nor is there a dread of plurality.

For some of us, just beginning to feel our own stories are worth telling, the reminders of the "long dumb voices," the talk of "the rights of them the others are down upon" cannot but draw attention to the absences and silences that are as much a part of our history as the articulate voices, the shimmering faces, the images of emergence and success. Bartleby, the clerk who "prefers not to" in Herman Melville's story, may suddenly become exemplary.[15] What of those who said no, who found no place, who made no mark? Do they not say something about a society that closed too many doors, that allowed people to be abandoned like "wreckage in the mid-Atlantic"? What of those like Tod Clifton in Ralph Ellison's *Invisible Man*? A former youth leader in the so-called Brotherhood, he ends up selling Sambo dolls in front of the Public Library. When the police try to dislodge him, he protests; and they kill him. The narrator, watching, wonders: "Why did he choose to plunge into nothingness, into the void of faceless faces, of soundless voices, lying outside history? . . . All things, it is said, are duly recorded—all things of importance, that is. But not quite; for actually it is only the known, the seen, the heard, and only those events that the recorder regards as important are put down. . . . But the cop would be Clifton's historian, his judge, his witness, his executioner, and I was the only brother in the watching crowd."[16] The many who ended up "lying outside history" diminished the community, left an empty space on the common ground, left undefined an aspect of reality.

It is true that we cannot know all the absent ones; but they must be present somehow in their absence. Absence, after all, suggests an emptiness, a void to be filled, a wound to be healed, a flaw to be repaired. I think of E. L. Doctorow painting a landscape of denial at the beginning of *Ragtime,* appealing to both wonder and indignation, demanding a kind of repair. He is writing about New Rochelle in 1906; but he is presenting a past that reaches into the present, into *our* present, whether or not we ride trolleys anymore.

> Teddy Roosevelt was President. The population customarily gathered in great numbers either out of doors for parades, public concerts, fish fries, political picnics, social outings, or indoors in meeting halls, vaudeville theatres, operas, ballrooms. There seemed to be no entertainment that did not involve great swarms of people. Trains and steamers and trolleys moved them from one place to another. That was the style; that was the way people lived. Women were stouter then. They visited the fleet carrying white parasols. Everyone wore white in summer. There was a lot of sexual fainting. There were no Negroes. There were no immigrants.[17]

The story has focally to do with a decent, intelligent black man named Coalhouse Walker, who is cheated, never acknowledged, never understood, scarcely *seen,* and who begins his own fated strategy of vengeance which ends when promises are broken and he is shot down in cold blood. Why is he unseen? Why were there no Negroes, no immigrants? More than likely because of the condition of the minds of those in power, those in charge. Ellison may explain it when he attributes invisibility to "a peculiar disposition of the eyes of those with whom I come in contact. A matter of the construction of their inner eyes, those eyes with which they look through their physical eyes upon reality."[18] But that disposition must itself have been partly due to the play of power in discourse as well as in social arrangements. We may wonder even now what the assimilation or initiation sought by so many educators signified when there were so many blanked out spaces—"no Negroes . . . no immigrants," oftentimes no full-grown women.

Looking back at the gaps in our own lived experiences, we might think of silences like those Tillie Olsen had in mind when she spoke of literary history "dark with silences," of the "unnatural silences" of women who worked too hard or were too embarrassed to express themselves,[19] of others who did not have the words or had not mastered the proper "ways of knowing."[20] We might ponder the plight of young island women, like Jamaica Kincaid's Lucy from Antigua, forced to be "two-faced" in a post-colonial school: "outside, I seemed one way, inside I was another; outside false, inside true."[21] For years we knew no more about people like her (who saw "sorrow and bitterness" in the face of daffodils because of the Wordsworth poem she had been forced to learn) than we did about the Barbadians Paule Marshall has described, people living their fragmented lives in Brooklyn. There was little consciousness of what Gloria Anzaldua calls *Borderlands: La Frontera* on which so many Latinos live,[22] nor of the Cuban immigrants like the musicians in *The Mambo Kings Sing Songs of Love.* Who of us truly wondered about the builders of the railroads, those Maxine Hong Kingston calls "China Men," chopping trees in the Sandal-wood and Sierra Nevada Mountains? Who of us could fill the gaps left by such a person as Ah Goong, whose "existence was outlawed by the Chinese Exclusion Acts. . . ."? His family, writes Kingston, "did not understand his accomplishments as an American ancestor, a holding, homing ancestor of this place. He'd gotten the legal or illegal papers burned in the San Francisco earthquake and fire; he appeared in America in time to be a citizen and to father citizens. He had also been seen carrying a child out of the fire, a child of his own in spite of the laws against marrying. He had built a railroad out of sweat, why not have an American child out of longing?"[23] Did we pay heed to a person like Michelle Clift, an Afro-Caribbean woman who felt that speaking in words that were not her own was a form of speechlessness? Or to a child like Pecola Breedlove in Toni Morrison's *The Bluest Eye,* the unloved black child who wanted to look like Shirley Temple so she could be included in the human reality?[24] Or to a Mary Crow Dog, who finds her own way of saying in the autobiography *Lakota Woman?* How many of us have been willing to suffer the experiences most recently rendered in Art Spiegelman's two-volume comic book called *Maus?* He tells about his father, the ill-tempered Vladek, a survivor of Auschwitz, and his resentful sharing of his holocaust memories with his son. Every character in the book is an animal: the Jews, mice; the Germans, cats; the Poles, pigs. It is a reminder, not simply of a particular culture's dissolution ("Anja's parents, the grandparents, her big sister Tosha, little Bibi, and our Richieu. . . . All what is left, it's the photos."[25]). It is a reminder of the need to recognize that everything is possible, something normal people (including school people) either do not know or do not want to know.

To open up our experience (and, yes, our curricula) to existential possibilities of multiple kinds is to extend and deepen what we think of when we speak of a community. If we break through and even disrupt a surface equilibrium and uniformity, this does not mean that particular ethnic or racial traditions ought to replace our own. Toni Morrison writes of pursuing her freedom as a writer in a "genderized, sexualized, wholly racialized world"; but this does not keep her from developing a critical project "unencumbered by dreams of subversion or rallying gestures at fortress walls."[26] In her case, the project involves exploring the ways in which what we think of as our Americanness is in many ways a response to an Africanist presence far too long denied. She is not interested in replacing one domination by another; she is interested in showing us what she sees from her own perspective—and, in showing us, enriching our understanding not only of our own culture, but of ourselves. She speaks of themes familiar to us all: "individualism, masculinity, social engagement versus historical isolation; acute and ambiguous moral problematics; the thematics of innocence coupled with an obsession with figurations of death and hell. . . ." Then she goes on to query what Americans are alienated from, innocent of, different from. "As for absolute power, over whom is this power held, from whom withheld, to whom distributed? Answers to these questions lie in the potent and ego-reinforcing presence of an Africanist population."[27] Even as Americans once defined their moral selves against the wilderness, they began to define their whiteness against what Melville called "the power of blackness"; they understood their achievement of freedom against slavery. Whether we choose to see our history that way or not, she is introducing a vision only she could create, and it offers us alternative vantage points on our world. Indeed, the tension with regard to multiculturalism may be partially due to the suspicion that we have often defined ourselves against some unknown, some darkness, some "otherness" we chose to thrust away, to master, not to understand. In this regard, Morrison says something that seems to me unanswerable: "My project is an effort to avert the critical gaze from the racial object to the racial subject; from the described and imagined to the describers and imaginers; from the serving to the served."

To take this view is not to suggest that curricula should be tailored to the measure of specific cultural groups of young people. Nor is it to suggest, as the Afrocentrists do, that emphasis should be laid on the unique experiences, culture and perspectives of Afro-Americans and their link to African roots. There is no question that what history has overlooked or distorted must be restored—whether it has to do with Afro-Americans, Hispanics, Asians, women, Jews, native Americans, Irish, or Poles; but the exclusions and the deformations have not kept artists like Morrison, Ellison, and James Baldwin from plunging into and learning from western literary works, anymore than it has prevented scholars like Gates and Cornel West and Alain Locke from working for more and richer interchanges between Afro-American and Euro-American cultures. Morrison begins her new book with a verse from Eliot and goes on to pay tribute to Homer, Dostoevsky, Faulkner, James, Flaubert, Melville, and Mary Shelley. It is difficult to forget James Baldwin reading Dostoevsky and haunting the public library, to turn attention from West's critiques of Emerson, to ignore Ellison writing about Melville and Hemingway, even as he drew attention to what he called "the Negro stereotype" that was "really an image of the irrational, unorganized forces in American life."[28] We might think of Maya Angelou as well, of her years of self-imposed silence as a child and the reading she did through those years. We might recall Alice Walker engaging with Muriel Rukeyser and Flannery O'Connor, drawing energy from them, even as she went in search of Zora Neale Hurston and Bessie Smith and Sojourner Truth, and Gwendolyn Brooks. ("I also loved Ovid and Catullus . . . the poems of e. e. cummings and William Carlos Williams."[29]) And we are aware that, as time goes on, more and more Afro-American literature (and women's literature, and Hispanic American literature) are diversifying our experience, changing our ideas of time and life and birth and relationship and memory.

My point has to do with openness and variety as well as with inclusion. It has to do with the avoidance of fixities, of stereotypes, even the stereotypes linked to multiculturalism. To view a person as in some sense "representative" of Asian culture (too frequently grouping together human beings as diverse as Japanese, Koreans, Chinese, Vietnamese) or Hispanic culture or Afro-American culture is to presume an objective reality called "culture," a homogeneous and fixed presence that *can* be adequately represented by existing subjects. (Do Amy Tan's maternal characters embody the same reality as does Maxine Hong

Kingston's "woman warrior"? Does Richard Wright's Bigger Thomas stand for the same thing as Miss Celie stands for in Alice Walker's *The Color Purple*?) Do we not *know* the person in the front row of our classroom, or the one sharing the raft, or the one drinking next to us at the bar by her/his cultural or ethnic affiliation.

Cultural background surely plays a part in shaping identity; but it does not determine identity. It may well create differences that must be honored; it may occasion styles and orientations that must be understood; it may give rise to tastes, values, even prejudices that must be taken into account. It is important to know, for example, without embarrassing or exoticizing her, why Jamaica Kincaid's Antiguan Lucy feels so alienated from a Wordsworth poem, and whether or not (and against what norms) it is necessary to argue her out of her distaste for daffodils. It is important to realize why (as in Bharaka Mukherjee's *Jasmine*) Hindus and Sikhs are so at odds with one another, even in this country, and to seek out ways in which (consulting what we believe to be the Western principle of justice) they can be persuaded to set aside hostility. Or perhaps, striving to sympathize with what they feel, we can communicate our own caring for their well-being in such a fashion as to move them provisionally to reconceive. Paulo Freire makes the point that every person ought, on some level, to cherish her/his culture; but he says it should never be absolutized. When it is absolutized, when a person is closed against the new culture surrounding her/him, "you would" (Freire says) "even find it hard to learn new things which, placed alongside your personal history, can be meaningful."[30]

There has, however, to be a feeling of ownership of one's personal history. In this culture, because of its brutal and persistent racism, it has been painfully difficult for Afro-American young people to affirm and be proud of what they choose as personal history. Poverty, hopelessness, the disruption of families and communities, the ubiquity of media images all make it difficult to place new things against a past too often made to appear a past of victimization, shadows, and shame. To make it worse, the mystifiction that proceeds on all sides gives rise to a meta-narrative of what it means to be respectable and successful in America—a meta-narrative that too often seems to doom minorities to life on the outermost borders, or, as Toni Morrison writes in *The Bluest Eye*, "outdoors" where there is no place to go. ("Outdoors," she writes, "is the end of something, an irrevocable, physical fact, defining and complementing our metaphysical condition. Being a minority in both caste and class, we moved about anyway on the hem of life, struggling to consolidate our weaknesses and hang on, or to creep singly up into the major folds of the garment."[31])

It happens that *The Bluest Eye*, because of its use of the first paragraph of the basal reader *Dick and Jane*, dramatizes (as few works do) the coercive and deforming effect of the culture's official story, the meta-narrative of secure suburban family life. As the novel plays itself out, everything that occurs is the obverse of the basal reader's story with its themes of pretty house, loving family, play, laughter, friendship, cat, and dog. The narrator of the main story, Pecola Breedlove's story, is young Claudia—also black and poor, but with a supporting family, a sister, a mother who loves her even as she complains and scolds.

A short preface, ostensibly written after Pecola's baby and her rapist father have died, after the seeds would not flower, after Pecola went mad, ends with Claudia saying: "There is really nothing more to say—except why. But since *why* is difficult to handle, one must take refuge in *how.*"[32] When very young and then a little older, Claudia tells the story; and, in the telling, orders the materials of her own life, her own helplessness, her own longings. She does that in relation to Pecola, whom she could not help, and in relation to the seeds that would not flower and those around her "on the hem of life." She weaves her narrative in such a fashion that she establishes an important connection to the past and (telling about Pecola and her family and her pain) reinterprets her own ethnicity in part through what Michael Fischer calls "the arts of memory." Whatever meaning she can draw from this feeds into an ethic that may be meaningful in the future, an ethic that takes her beyond her own guilt at watching Pecola search the garbage. "I talk about how I did *not* plant the seeds too deeply, how it was the fault of the earth, the land, of our town. I even think now that the land of the entire country was hostile to marigolds that year. . . . Certain seeds it will not nuture, certain fruit it will not bear, and when the land kills of its own volition, we acquiesce and say the victim had no right to live. We are wrong, of course, but it doesn't matter. It's too late." As Charles Taylor and Alasdair MacIntyre have written, we understand our lives in narrative form, as a quest. Taylor writes: "because we have to determine our place in relation to the good, therefore we cannot be without an orientation to it, and hence must see our life in stories."[33] Clearly, there are different stories connected by the same need to make sense, to make meaning, to find a direction.

To help the Claudias we know, the diverse students we know, articulate their stories is not only to help them pursue the meanings of their lives—to find out *how* things are happening, to keep posing questions about the why. It is to move them to learn the "new things" Freire spoke of, to reach out for the proficiencies and capacities, the craft required to be fully participant in this society, and to do so without losing the consciousness of who they are. That is not all. Stories like the one Claudia tells must break through into what we think of as our tradition or our heritage. They can; they should with what Cornel West has in mind when he speaks about the importance of acknowledging the "distinctive cultural and political practices of oppressed people" without highlighting their marginality in such a way as to further marginalize them. Not only does he call attention to the resistance of Afro-Americans and that of other long-silenced people. He writes of the need to look at Afro-Americans' multiple contributions to the culture over the generations. We might think of the music—Gospel, jazz, ragtime; we might think of the black churches; we might summon up the civil rights movement and the philosophies, the dreams that informed it; we might ponder—looking back, looking around—the images of courage, the images of survival. West goes on to say: "Black cultural practices emerge out of a reality they cannot *not* know—the ragged edges of the real, of necessity; a reality historically constructed by white supremacist practices in North America. . . . These ragged edges—of not being able to eat, not to have shelter, not to have health care—all this is infused into the strategies and styles of black cultural practices."[34] Viewed in connection with the idea of multiculturalism, this does not mean that Afro-American culture in all its variousness can be defined mainly in terms of oppression and discrimination. One of the many reasons for opening spaces in which Afro-Americans can tell their own stories is that they, far more than those from other cultures, can explain the ways in which poverty and exclusion have mediated their own sense of the past. It is true that experiences of pain and abandonment have led to a search for roots and, on occasion, for a revision of recorded history. What is crucial is the provision of opportunities for telling all the diverse stories, for interpreting membership as well as ethnicity, for making inescapable the braids of experience woven into the fabric of America's plurality.

In the presence of an increasingly potent Third World, against the sounds of increasingly eloquent post-colonial (and, now, post-totalitarian) voices, we can no longer pretend that the "ragged edges" are an exception. We can no longer talk in terms of seamless totalities under rubrics like "free world," "free market," "equality," or even "democracy." Like the "wreckage in the mid-Atlantic," like the "faceless faces," like the "unnatural silences," the lacks and deprivations have to be made aspects of our plurality as well as of our cultural identity. Publics, after all, take shape in response to unmet needs and broken promises. Human beings are prone to take action in response to the sense of injustice or to the imagination's capacity to look at things as if they could be otherwise. The democratic community, always a community in the making, depends not so much on what has been achieved and funded in the past. It is kept alive; it is energized and radiated by an awareness of future possibility. To develop a vision of such possibility, a vision of what might and ought to be, is very often to be made aware of present deficiencies and present flaws. The seeds did not flower; Pecola and her baby could not be saved. But more and more persons, paying heed, may move beyond acquiescence. They may say, as Claudia does, "We are wrong, of course . . ." but go on to overcome the "doesn't matter." At that moment, they may reach beyond themselves, choose themselves as who they are and reach out to the common to repair.

Learning to look through multiple perspectives, young people may be helped to build bridges among themselves; attending to a range of human stories, they may be provoked to heal and to transform. Of course, there will be difficulties in affirming plurality and difference and, at once, working to create community. Since the days of de Tocqueville, Americans have wondered how to deal with the conflicts between individualism and the drive to conform. They have wondered how to reconcile the impassioned voices of cultures not yet part of the whole with the requirements of conformity, how not to lose the integrity of those voices in the process, how not to allow the drive to conformity determine what happens at the end. But the community many of us hope for now is not to be identified with conformity. As in Whitman's way of saying, it is a community attentive to difference, open to the idea of plurality. Something life-affirming in diversity must be discovered and rediscovered, as what is held in common becomes always more many-faceted—open and inclusive, drawn to untapped possibility.

No one can predict precisely the common world of possibility, nor can we absolutely justify one kind of community over another. Many of us, however for all the tensions and disagreements around us, would reaffirm the value of principles like justice and equality and freedom and commitment to human rights; since, without these, we cannot even argue for the decency of welcoming. Only if more and more persons incarnate such principles, we might say, and choose to live by them and engage in dialogue in accord with them, are we likely to bring about a democratic pluralism and not fly apart in violence and disorder. Unable to provide an objective ground for such hopes and claims, all we can do is speak with others as eloquently and passionately as we can about justice and caring and love and trust. Like Richard Rorty and those he calls pragmatists, we can only articulate our desire for as much intersubjective agreement as possible, "the desire to extend the reference of 'us' as far as we can."[35] But, as we do so, we have to remain aware of the distinctive members of the plurality, appearing before one another with their own perspectives on the common, their own stories entering the culture's story, altering it as it moves through time. We want our classrooms to be just and caring, full of various conceptions of the good. We want them to be articulate, with the dialogue involving as many persons as possible, opening to one another, opening to the world. And we want them to be concerned for one another, as we learn to be concerned for them. We want them to achieve friendships among one another, as each one moves to a heightened sense of craft and wide-awakeness, to a renewed consciousness of worth and possibility.

With voices in mind and the need for visibility, I want to end with a call for human solidarity by Muriel Rukeyser, who—like many of us—wanted to "widen the lens and see/ standing over the land myths of identity, new signals, processes." And then:

> Carry abroad the urgent need, the scene,
> to photograph and to extend the voice,
> to speak this meaning.
> Voices to speak to us directly. As we move.
> As we enrich, growing in larger motion,
> this word, this power.[36]

This power, yes, the unexplored power of pluralism, and the wonder of an expanding community.

Notes

1. John Dewey, *The Public and Its Problems* (Athens, OH: The Swallow Press, 1954), 143ff.
2. Roberto Mangabeira Unger, *Passion: An Essay on Personality* (New York: Free Press, 1984), 107.

3. Cynthia Ozick, *Metaphor and Memory* (New York: Alfred A. Knopf, 1989), 283.
4. Hannah Arendt, *The Human Condition* (Chicago: The University of Chicago Press, 1958), 57.
5. Henry Louis Gates, Jr., "Goodbye, Columbus? Notes on the Culture of Criticism," *American Literary History* (Winter 1991): 712.
6. Clifford Geertz, *Local Knowledge* (New York: Basic Books, 1983), 153.
7. Geertz, *Local Knowledge*, 161.
8. James Clifford, *The Predicament of Culture* (Cambridge, MA: Harvard University Press, 1988), 13.
9. Arthur M. Schlesinger, Jr., *The Disuniting of America: Reflections on a Multicultural Society* (New York: W.W. Norton & Co., 1992).
10. Richard Pratte, *The Civic Imperative* (New York: Teachers College Press, 1988), 104–107.
11. E. D. Hirsch, Jr., *Cultural Literacy* (Boston: Houghton Mifflin Company, 1987).
12. Dinesh D'Sousa, *Illiberal Education: The Politics of Race and Sex on Campus* (New York: The Free Press, 1991), 239.
13. Robert Hughes, "Art, Morality & Mapplethorpe," *The New York Review of Books*, 23 April 1992, 21.
14. Walt Whitman, *Leaves of Grass* (New York, Aventine Press, 1931), 53.
15. Herman Melville, "Bartleby," in *Billy Budd, Sailor and Other Stories* (New York: Bantam Books, 1986).
16. Ralph Ellison, *Invisible Man* (New York: Signet Books, 1952), 379.
17. E. L. Doctorow, *Ragtime* (New York: Random House, 1975), 3–4.
18. Ellison, *Invisible Man*, p. 7.
19. Tillie Olsen, *Silences* (New York: Delacorte Press, 1978), 6.
20. Mary F. Belenky, et al., *Women's Ways of Knowing* (New York: Basic Books, 1986).
21. Jamaica Kincaid, *Lucy* (New York: Farrar, Straus, and Giroux, 1990), 18.
22. Gloria Anzaldua, *Borderlands/La Frontera; The New Mestiza* (San Francisco: Spinsters/Aunt Lute, 1987).
23. Maxine Hong Kingston, *China Men* (New York: Vintage International Books, 1989), 151.
24. Toni Morrison, *The Bluest Eye* (New York: Pocket Books, 1972).
25. Art Spiegelman, *Maus II* (New York: Pantheon Books, 1991), 115.
26. Toni Morrison, *Playing in the Dark: Whiteness and the Literary Imagination* (Cambridge, MA: Harvard University Press, 1992), 4–5.
27. Morrison, *Playing in the Dark*, p. 45.
28. Ralph Ellison, *Shadow and Act* (New York: Signet Books, 1964), 55.
29. Alice Walker, *In Search of Our Mother's Gardens* (Orlando, FL: Harcourt Brace Jovanovich, 1983), 257.
30. Paulo Freire and Donaldo Macedo, *Literacy: Reading the Word and the World* (South Hadley, MA: Bergin and Garvey, 1987), 126.
31. Morrison, *The Bluest Eye*, p. 18.
32. Morrison, *The Bluest Eye*, p. 9.
33. Charles Taylor, *Sources of the Self* (Cambridge, MA: Harvard University Press, 1989), 51.
34. Cornel West, "Black Culture and Postmodernism," in *Remaking History*, ed. Barbara Kruger and Phil Mariani (Seattle, WA: Bay Press, 1989), 93.
35. Richard Rorty, "Solidarity or Objectivity?" in *Objectivity, Relativism, and Truth* (Cambridge: Cambridge University Press, 1991), 23.
36. Muriel Rukeyser, *The Book of the Dead* (New York: Covici-Friede, 1938), 71–72.

22   Hermeneutics, General Studies, and Teaching*

Richard M. Rorty

The author, who was previously Professor of Philosophy at Princeton University, is now Kenan Professor of the Humanities at the University of Virginia. In this lecture, delivered in 1981 at George Mason University, he discusses the educational implications of the work of Hans-Georg Gadamer, a contemporary German philosopher, who has developed a theory of interpretation, according to which the meaning of a text depends in part on the historical situation of its interpreter. Rorty sees similarities between Gadamer and Dewey and defends their views against critics who, in attempting to apply these views, may undermine them.

I. HERMENEUTICS AS ANTI-PLATONISM

Any philosophy professor asked to talk about education can be expected to begin by noting that the word "education" means something like "bringing out" and then talking about Plato's Theory of Recollection. I am no exception. The idea that the student already has tacit knowledge which needs to be brought out and made explicit was basic to Plato's account of education. Something like it is still central to most explanations of why liberal education is a good thing. As Kierkegaard pointed out, the minimal form of Plato's Theory of Recollection is that we have an innate ability to recognize the truth when we hear it. On that assumption, education as training in critical thought, in the ability to reason, will be envisaged as sharpening our intellectual perceptions—clearing the line of mental sight, or shedding light on the object to make it easier for the mental eye to see, or getting the wax out of the mental ear, or something of the sort. The Platonic picture is of human beings as possessing an organ—Reason—which is naturally suited to pick out the real from the unreal, the true from the false. Education enables that organ to be efficiently used.

The reason why certain contemporary movements in philosophy, literary theory, and social theory raise problems for this traditional conception of education is that these movements take their point of departure from Nietzsche's claim that Plato was wrong. Nietzsche says, for example:

> We simply lack any organ for knowledge, for 'truth'; we 'know' (or believe or imagine) just as much as may be useful in the interests of the human herd, the species. . . . (Schlechta edition, II, 223; trans. Kaufmann)

"Hermeneutics" has become a catchword for the intellectual movements which start from this Nietzschean conviction. I shall be employing the term in this loose but useful sense. "Hermeneutics" has a primarily negative meaning: it is something which is *not* scientific inquiry, as such inquiry has been tradi-

*From *Selected Papers from the Synergos Seminars*, vol. 2, Fall 1982, George Mason University, by permission of Vernon W. Gras and the author.

tionally understood. The traditional understanding of scientific inquiry is, once again, Platonic. On this view, to inquire is to get at the reality underlying the appearance, and to do so by formulating concepts which are somehow shared with, or correspond to, that reality. The Theory of Recollection is a way of expressing Plato's conviction that there is something about the human mind which is *like* reality, that there is a natural attunement between Reason and The Nature of Things. Those who want to defend traditional conceptions of science, of literature, and of education against Nietzsche try to reconstruct something like Plato's realism—his view that there is a distinction between the right thing to say and the useful thing to say, between getting hold of reality and coping with appearances successfully.

Conversely, those who make "hermeneutics" a watchword spend a great deal of time "deconstructing the metaphysics of presence"—trying to get rid of the realism which is built into much of our language, and into practically all our cliches about the nature and method of liberal education. This realism is embodied in the notion that there is something called "The Truth" which inquiry seeks—something eternal, so that

> It gratifies my soul to know
> That though I perish,
> Truth is so.

Writers like Heidegger, Derrida and Foucault—to mention a few people often associated with the idea of hermeneutics, and equally often identified as "irrationalists"—share Nietzsche's view that this notion of "objective truth" is a survival of religious belief. Like Nietzsche, they think that truth as something which exists and endures apart from Man is an half-hearted and confused attempt to secularize and domesticate the notion of God. They see Plato as the initiator of this process of secularization, and see both Plato's conception of Reason and his realistic conception of Objective Truth, truth as correspondence to reality, as forms of what Nietzsche called "the longest lie"—the lie that there is something beyond mankind to which it is man's duty to be faithful.

I have been asked to discuss the question of how education might be conceived if one starts from Nietzschean rather than Platonic assumptions, if one sees no transcendent goal of inquiry, if one abandons the notion of "objective truth." My strategy for doing so will be to identify the hermeneutic stance with something which may seem tamer and more familiar and more manageable—namely Deweyan pragmatism. I have emphasized elsewhere, and shall be saying again here, that the stance which contemporary French and German post-Nietzschean thought adopts toward the philosophical tradition is essentially the one which the American pragmatists had already taken in the early years of this century; the difference between the two movements is a matter of tone and emphasis rather than of doctrine. In the next section of the paper, I shall try briefly to restate these similarities. In later sections, I shall touch on various controversies sparked by Deweyan notions of the nature and function of education. In particular, I shall take up the relativism of which Dewey and the pragmatists generally are often accused. I shall distinguish between vulgar relativism—the kind of jejune indifference to argument and inquiry which many critics see as the great danger in the hermeneutical stance—and pragmatism. Both Gadamer (whom I shall use as my principal example of an "hermeneutic" philosopher) and Dewey have been accused of either preaching, or at least tacitly encouraging, such vulgar relativism. I want to offer an account of the common elements in Gadamer's and Dewey's thought which enable them to defend themselves against such charges. I shall argue that what both men put in place of Reason—the Platonic organ for detecting truth—is a sense of tradition, of community, of human solidarity. The over-all argument of my paper will be that this sense is a sufficient defense against vulgar relativism. There are, to be sure, dangers in inculcating anti-Platonic views in the youth, in telling our students that there are no objective truths of the sort Plato had in mind. I shall argue, however, that these can be overcome by instilling a sense of community.

II. HERMENEUTICS AND PRAGMATISM

Perhaps the most efficient way to show the similarities between Dewey's and Gadamer's stance towards the Platonic tradition is to see both as drawing the consequences of the doctrine that, as Gadamer puts it, human experience is "essentially linguistic" (Gadamer, *Philosophical Hermeneutics*, p. 19). Gadamer explains that he made hermeneutics—the process of interpretation, of translation—his theme because "the many-layered problem of translation became for me the model for the linguisticality of all human behavior in the world." (loc. cit.) To say that our experience and our behavior is essentially "linguistic" contrasts with the view, common to Plato and Locke, that language is simply a tool, a medium, a device for expressing or communicating something non-linguistic—e.g., knowledge conceived of as unmediated relation of the mind to something non-human. To say that the hermeneutical stance is an alternative to the notion of "objective truth" is to say that true assertions are not expressive of something pre-linguistic or non-linguistic. They are not, for example, expressions of the sort of inner illumination or recognition which Plato describes in terms of the Theory of Recollection. Rather, true assertions are simply successful moves in the social practise which Wittgenstein called a "language-game." They are, in William James' phrase, "what is good in the way of belief," where belief is not construed as an inner state which assertions express, but just as a disposition to linguistic behavior—the disposition to make a certain assertion.

From the Pragmatist point of view, the only sense in which "truth is correspondence to reality" is that, within a given language, we can pair off some of our assertions with perceivable states of affairs—so that a given sentence is appropriately, and thus truly, spoken if certain sense-perceptions are had. But that sense of "correspondence to reality" is not enough to explain or justify the Platonic notion of eternal Truth, Truth with a capital "T." That notion is much more suited to truth about numbers or about values—true assertions which have nothing to do with perception or the senses, but rather, perhaps, with the sort of thing Plato had in mind when he talked about True, and hence Unchanging, Being. On the pragmatist account, as on Heidegger's, Plato has substituted Truth for God as the goal of inquiry and life. For some such tacit sub-stitution is the only way in which one can make sense of "objective truth" as something morally important or philosophically controversial. On Dewey's al-ternative account, as on Gadamer's, we need to think of the goal of inquiry and of life not as getting in touch with something which exists independently of ourselves, but as *Bildung,* self-formation, what Dewey liked simply to call "growth." In particular, we need to see education not as helping to get us in touch with something non-human called Truth or Reality, but rather in touch with our own potentialities.

I can develop this parallel further by remarking that the same two objec-tions are typically urged against the hermeneutical stance common to Heideg-ger, Gadamer and Foucault as were traditionally urged against James and Dewey. These are, first, the argument from perceptual confrontation and sec-ond, the argument from moral evil. The argument from perceptual confronta-tion says that the paradigm case of truth is the one in which our beliefs are re-futed by experience—where, for example, the negative result of a crucial experiment explodes a theoretical edifice. Hard, objective, truth is typified by the brute factuality of that disconfirming observation. According to this argu-ment, a true assertion is not one which works, one which is good to believe, but one which manifests the proper humility before such facts. Granted, this objec-tion to pragmatism says, that it is needlessly confusing to think of Truth as an entity, as something eternal, and granted that only assertions are true, never-theless we need to think of true assertions as those which get things *right.* There may be no such entity as Truth with a capital "T," but there are such entities as trees and atoms. True assertions are those that mirror such entities properly.

In reply to this argument the pragmatists said: it is quite true that our so-cial practices, our linguistic behavior, is such as to make it permissible to say certain things only when we see, or otherwise encounter, certain other things. But this does not show that truth is correspondence to reality. To show *that* we would have to find a way to say that a language *as a whole*—for example, a lan-guage which divides reality up into spatial and temporal regions bedecked with sensory qualities—corresponded to reality. It is not enough to establish the sort of correspondence which the realist has in mind to say that our lan-guage-games sometimes pair assertions with perceptual situations. We need to think that our language-games *themselves,* are, somehow, matched up with re-ality. But, James and Dewey claimed, we have no idea what that would mean, what such a match could amount to. The same point is made by Wittgenstein when he speaks of the impossibility of escaping from language, by Heidegger in his distinction between truth and correctness, and by Gadamer, once again, in his claim that all our experience is linguistic. To make sense of the notion of *languages* corresponding to reality would be to think that we could get outside of our language long enough to compare it with reality. But to say, with Gadamer, that our experience is *essentially linguistic* is just to say that that can-not be done.

The pragmatist and the hermeneuticist join, therefore, in saying that con-frontation with perception is not an illustration of the nature of truth. On their view, as on the realists', willingness to let one's theories crumble at the touch of a disconfirming experiment is a moral virtue. But this moral virtue does not give us insight into our relation to the world.

Their attitude towards their opponents' second argument—the argument from moral evil—is similar. This argument says that if truth were simply a move in a language-game then Hitler, or Stalin, or the Inner Party of *1984* could simply create their own evil game, their own evil linguistic practises, and thereby make their ghastly views true. Here Dewey and Gadamer must, I think, admit that their views offer no defense whatever against this possibility. Neither has any fulcrum outside the moral consensus embodied in our moral discourse to which they can appeal. Their only reply to this argument, therefore, is: who *has* such a fulcrum? what would such a fulcrum look like? who *can* give a "rational refutation" of Hitler or Stalin? what could such a "refutation" look like?

To say that there really are objective values out there, that there is a moral reality to be corresponded with, seems as pointless as saying that God is on our side. The two remarks are only stylistically different. Unless we have some idea how to *test* for this correspondence, or how to *test* for Divine approval, nothing has been gained by the insistence. To oppose Hitler is a moral virtue, but our certainty that we *should* oppose him is not a clue to the existence of "objective values." Thus we find Gadamer saying that "The validity of morals is based on tradition" (*Truth and Method,* p. 249), meaning, I take it, that the moral consensus built into our language is all we've got by way of back-up. To say that our experience is essentially linguistic is to say that there is no way to get behind our language to a reality against which to check it. When Dewey says that "Growth itself is the only moral end" (*Human Nature and Conduct*), I take his only answer to the question "Growth towards what?" to be "Towards realization of the potentialities which have already been sketched out in the language we are now using—towards realization of our present vaguely sensed ideals." Neither Gadamer nor Dewey thinks that one can say more than this without doing what Plato did—postulating some philosophical substitute for God and some special faculty called "Reason," which will put one in touch with this God-surrogate.

This way of dealing with the objection from moral evil lets us see that the Gadamerian claim that our experience is essentially linguistic can also be expressed as the familiar Hegelian claim that our existence is essentially *historical*—that there is no way out of our historical situation to an ahistorical view of our nature or situation or goal. Gadamer and Dewey both learned this from Hegel. Dewey can agree with Gadamer when he says:

> We may recognise that *Bildung* is an element of spirit without being tied to Hegel's philosophy of absolute spirit, just as the insight into the historicity of consciousness is not tied to his philosophy of world history. (TM, p. 15)

One way of restating the common doctrine of hermeneutics and pragmatism is to say that their emphasis upon the linguistic character of experience is an emphasis on the sheer *contingency* of the language which we use, the language in which, for example, we ask and answer such questions as "What is truth?" and "What is education?" The Platonic view is that we can *recollect* or *intuit* something which will enable us to *correct* what our language, our tradition, has told us about these matters. The Dewey-Gadamer view is that we can *invent* something which will *improve* on our tradition, on what we have been told.

When, however, one tells students that Plato was wrong, that there are no values out there to be glimpsed with the eye of the mind, that the "objectivity" of perceptual reports cannot be duplicated in the case of languages-as-wholes, they immediately reply "In that case, every view is as good as every other." For our students would still, even in this latter age, *like* to be Platonists. They have grown up on a tradition which teaches that if God, or some suitable surrogate, does not exist, then everything is permitted. The view that since God *doesn't* exist, every view is as good as every other is what I am calling "vulgar relativism." The difference between vulgar relativism and pragmatism is that pragmatism says the fact that a view is *ours*—our language's, our tradition's, *our* culture's, is an excellent *prima facie* reason for holding it. It is not, of course, a knock-down argument against competing views. But it does put the burden of proof on such views. It says that rationality consists in a decent respect for the opinions—or, in Gadamer's deliberately shocking terms, the prejudices—of mankind. With Peirce and Habermas, it sees objectivity in terms of consensus rather than correspondence.

The educational problem which the current popularity of hermeneutics raises is, on my account, the same problem which the popularity of Deweyan pragmatism and of logical positivism raised a generation ago: finding a way to guide the students between the Scylla of Platonism and the Charybdis of vulgar relativism. This comes down to the problem of getting them to realize that our having no organ for truth, no Reason in the Platonic sense, does not mean that everything must be turned over to the emotions. Or, to put it another way, it is the problem of realizing that there is a middle way between reliance on a God-surrogate and on one's individual preferences—namely, reliance on the common sense of the community to which one belongs. Dewey spent a great deal of his life urging that these simple-minded dualisms of reason-vs.-emotion, reason-vs.-prejudice, and reason-vs.-arbitrariness be set aside. In his view, they were simply remnants of the great theological and Platonic distinctions between the Eternal and the Temporal, the Real and the Apparent, Being and Becoming. Dewey, Gadamer, Heidegger and Foucault are, I think, all trying to fashion a jargon in which this sort of dualism cannot re-emerge, and thus a culture in which neither Platonism nor vulgar relativism are options. A culture, and thus an educational milieu, in which students would not feel that these were the only relevant alternatives, would be one which substituted our finite and contingent sense of human community for our trust in God. It would be one which inculcated a sense of that community as standing on its own feet, choosing its own destiny.

III. "HUMANISTIC" AND "SCIENTIFIC" EDUCATION

It would be nice if I could, in the remaining half-hour or so at my disposal, explain how such a culture could come into being—what educational apparatus could be relied upon to provide such a sense. Obviously, I am not going to do that. Instead I shall try to make some suggestions about what sort of education might at least avoid hindering the development of such a sense. My point of departure will be a *prima facie* difference between Dewey and Gadamer: the difference between Dewey's emphasis on "scientific method" and Gadamer's on "historicity." Traditionally, the inculcation of a sense of scientific procedure and an inculcation of a sense of the historicity of our existence have been seen as distinct, and often as opposed, ideals. This has given rise to debate about the relative merits of a "scientific" or a "humanistic" education. I think that the parallels which I have drawn between pragmatism and hermeneutics may help us see this opposition as factitious.

I can begin by remarking that both sorts of education began as revolts against authority. The Renaissance humanists gave us the philological and historical sense which Gadamer thinks of as basic to what he calls *wirkungs-geschichtliche Bewusstein*. Their educational schemes were designed to liberate their students, and the mind of Europe, from the Church, Aristotle, and scholasticism. When it began to be said, particularly in the nineteenth century, that the laboratory scientist, as opposed to the philological scholar, was the hero of modern culture, this was an implicit criticism of a new sort of scholasticism. For by the nineteenth century the scholar had become a new sort of priest—in some cases, as at Oxford and Cambridge, still literally a priest, but even when officially secular, nevertheless a conservative, backward-looking, figure. When Huxley challenged nineteenth-century Oxford in the name of empirical science, his intent was not too different from Erasmus' challenge to the academic institutions of his day. In both cases the cry was for a way of breaking through established notions of intellectual authority.

For my purposes, this parallel can be restated as follows: humanistic learning and laboratory science are both intellectually liberating, simply because any way to unblock the road of inquiry, to prevent thought from being imprisoned within a single vocabulary, is liberating. But neither breakout should be seen as breaking out of language or history into something different. To say that humanism in the sixteenth, and laboratory science in the nineteenth century, freed us from prejudice is perfectly true, but it did not give us something different in *kind* from prejudice. It gave us new prejudices for old, in Gadamer's harmless sense of "prejudice" in which *any* language, any framework for research or reflection, inevitably contains prejudices. On the conception common to Gadamer and Dewey and Wittgenstein, to share a language is to share a form of life—that is, a certain minimal agreement on what is reasonable to do or say under various circumstances. If one has a new language-game, a new form of life, to propose, then one will see this agreement as *mere* prejudice. All innovators see the tradition in these terms. But if we avoid Platonism, we shall not see such an opposition between superstition and prejudice on the one side, and reason and enlightenment on the other. Rather, we shall see successive stages in the attempt of the human race to solve its problems—successive attempts to create a sense of communal purpose.

From this point of view, one will see the sort of skepticism which humanistic learning made possible for Erasmus, or the sort of social hope which laboratory science suggested to Huxley, as two instances of the same phenomenon: the gradual breakup of the old sense of community, and the beginnings of a new. One will see neither as "enlightenment" but both as "progress." This will not, however, be progress towards anything like Truth in the Platonic, realist, sense. Rather, it is progress towards new possibilities for humanity—new ways in which men can think of one another and do things for one another. Similarly, one will not think of the heirs of Erasmus (e.g., Robert Hutchins) or the heirs of Huxley (e.g., Dewey) as putting forward incompatible alternatives when they emphasize the Great Books on the one hand, or hands-on experience on the other. One can see both Hutchins and Dewey as saying: a certain form of life has had undue prominence, and is in danger of closing our minds to alternatives, so let us take care that our students are educated so as to keep those alternatives in mind. Dewey was reacting to American education as it was before science and technology had become part of the educated American's image of himself and of his country's future. Hutchins was reacting, thirty years later, against the astonishingly rapid success of people like Dewey and Veblen in making the intellectuals aware of science and technology, and the naive Platonist optimism which this success inspired—the thought that all that was required was to bring the "scientific method" to bear on social and political problems.

From the pragmatist and hermeneutic point of view, both "the scientific method" and "the Great Books" are shibboleths. There is no such thing as "the scientific method" outside of a set of moral virtues—willingness to accept experimental disconfirmation, willingness to listen to alternative theories, willingness to scrap an old paradigm and begin again with a new. The conception of scientific method as putting one in touch with the Nature of Things is as much a relic of Platonism as Hutchins' neo-Thomist argument that:

> Education implies teaching. Teaching implies knowledge. Knowledge is truth. The truth is everywhere the same. Hence education should be everywhere the same. (HLA, 66)

Truth is not everywhere the same, because language is not everywhere the same and, once again, human existence is essentially linguistic and essentially historical. We do not lift ourselves out of history by doing laboratory experiments any more than by reading St. Thomas—we merely, with luck, get some new suggestions about how to solve our problems. This means that neither education in science nor education in the humanities has any special claim to centrality. All that either can do is to give the student some sense of what certain human beings at various historical periods did, in the hope of solving certain problems they had.

Thus, it doesn't make much difference whether a student's heroes are chemists or poets, or whether the discipline in which he immerses himself is philosophy or mathematics. All that matters is that the student *not* see what he's doing as less or more than what it is—participation in a community effort, learning to take a hand in what is going on, learning to speak more of the language which his time and place in history has destined him to speak. If he sees science in a Platonic way, then he may condescend to the humanities as "unscientific." If he sees the humanities in a Platonic way, then he may condescend to the sciences as "calculative," merely "empirical" and generally banausic. But if he can be got to see whatever discipline he is learning in non-Platonic terms, and can know enough about other disciplines to see workers in those in the same non-Platonic terms as he sees himself, then he may come to see *all* human disciplines as vehicles of *Bildung*, of the self-formation of the race, rather than as means for escaping the human condition by grasping eternal Truths.

Let me now return to my theme of education as aiming at a sense of human community, and of this community as foundationless, supported neither by science nor by history, but only by hope. Teaching which aims at inculcating such a sense will be Kuhnian in its approach to science and Nietzschean in its approach to history and to the humanities generally. That is, it will not describe science as approaching asymptotically to "a better representation of what nature is really like." (Kuhn, *Structures of Scientific Revolutions*, 2nd edition, p. 206). Rather, it will see successive stages in the history of the various sciences, including the present stage, as the development of what Thomas Kuhn calls "successively better instruments for discovering and solving puzzles" (loc. cit.). It will not describe the current scientific world-picture as something different in kind than Aristotle's—but rather as something of the same kind, yet *better*. It is better not because it corresponds more closely to reality, but because it enables us to do a lot of things Aristotle couldn't do. We have solved problems he could not solve, and created new problems he could not have imagined. We will see those problems not as the "real" problems, but as *our* problems. Similarly, we shall see the attempt to create "sciences of man," social sciences, not as attempts to bring Reason and Objectivity into our moral reflections, but as an attempt to solve our problems—problems which, once again, are not the "real" problems of man and society but problems about *us* and *our* society, problems whose solution or dissolution will doubtless create new and undreamt of problems for our descendants.

When we turn to history and the humanities we shall not see "monuments of unaging intellect" but a series of attempts—sometimes heroic attempts—to cope with problems which were not ours, but were similar enough to offer us useful hints. We will not get instructions about what to do, but rather models of the sort of virtue which we must exemplify. We shall not, as Hegel did, turn to History as a way of getting the Truth with a capital "T," the Truth which the Enlightenment had vainly thought to find in a knowledge of Nature. Rather we shall teach the history of philosophy, of literature, of politics, in the same way that Kuhn would have us teach the history of science. None of these will be accounts of man's encounter with Reality or with Truth, but all of them will be accounts of man's attempt to solve problems, to work out the potentialities of the languages and activities available to them. In the course of such attempts we encounter heroes who created new languages, and thus new genres, new disciplines, and new societies. These heroes of humanity are the people who dissolved the problems of their day by transcending the vocabulary in which these problems were posed. Nietzsche put this conception of what one can learn from history as follows:

> The past always speaks as an oracle: only as master builders of the future who
> know the present will you understand it. . . . You have enough to ponder and in-
> vent by pondering that future life; but do not ask history to show you the How?
> and Wherewith? . . . if you want biographies then not those with the refrain 'Mr.
> So-and-So and His Time' but rather those on whose title page should be in-
> scribed 'A fighter Against his Time.' [Schlechta edition, I, p. 251; translated by
> Peter Preuss (*On the Advantage and Disadvantage of History for Life*, Indianapolis,
> 1980, p. 38)]

From this Nietzschean angle, the difference between literature and sci-
ence fades out. The fighters against their time who are our models may include
Goethe as well as Galileo, Wordsworth as well as Darwin, Holderlin as well as
Marx and Freud.

To see the human community as engaged in problem-solving, and to see
the great figures of the past as those who solved old problems by inventing
new ones, is the Deweyan-Gadameran alternative to seeing Man as aiming at
Truth, and the great figures of the past as those who added bricks to the edifice
of knowledge. On the view I'm suggesting, the antidote to vulgar relativism is
not to reinforce a sense of factuality by explaining how laboratory experiment
can refute scientific theory. Nor is it to inculcate a sense of eternal values by
reading the Great Books. It is to give students a chance for intellectual hero-
worship by letting them see intellectual greatness as greatness at overcoming
problems. Hero-worship may seem antithetical to the sense of community, but
it is not. The sort of fighters against their time whom Nietzsche has in mind
were not solving their own individual problems, any more than they were expressing their own opinions or manifesting their own feelings. They were taking on the problems which the community around them had inherited. They
were inventing new forms of communal life by inventing new songs, new discourses, new polities. The lazy indifference which characterizes vulgar relativism is, I think, better overcome by incitement to imitate such heroic problem-solving than by assurance that there is a kind of Truth which is more than
the "mere" solution of human problems.

IV. COMMUNAL ROMANCE

In a famous essay in his *Aims of Education*, Whitehead claimed that learning
goes through three stages: Romance, Precision, and Generalization. Romance
is the stage at which the student's attention is caught—where he falls in love
with a book, or its author, or a teacher, or an activity. Precision is the stage
where he competes with fellow-lovers, fellow-students in the same discipline.
Generalization is the stage at which he is able to do something new, make a
contribution of his own, reflect and sum up what he has learned. "General
Studies" is a catchword for the sort of education which aims at Romance. The
fear that education may become merely "vocational" and no longer "liberal" is
the fear that the student will never have heroes, will never fall in love with
anything. In Platonic terms this is the fear that the student will never "use his

mind," have his higher faculties awoken, utilize the better part of his soul. In Deweyan or Gadamerean terms, however, it is the fear that he will never see himself as part of the human species, as part of the adventure of the race. The Platonist thinks that to be fully human one must learn to think abstractly, to rise above the language of the day and criticize it by appeal to something higher—Reason rather than Prejudice, Truth rather than Convention. The anti-Platonist alternative says that to be fully human one must indeed, rise above the language of the day, but that one does this by seeing it as one option among others, one set of prejudices or conventions among others. Liberality of mind and critical thought are not, on this view, matters of abstractness but of a sense of relativity, of alternative perspectives. Critical thinking is playing off alternatives against one another, rather than of playing them off against criteria of rationality, much less against eternal verities.

Given this anti-Platonic conception, and given what I was saying earlier about the difference between areas of culture being unimportant as far as hero-worship was concerned, it may seem that I ought to conclude that one should give up the notion of a "core curriculum" or of "a body of knowledge common to educated men." I want, however, to resist this conclusion. I do think that for purposes of overcoming vulgar relativism nothing will serve save hero-worship, and also that the choice of heroes is relatively indifferent. But overcoming vulgar relativism is not the only function of education. The sense of the human community which seems to me the goal of education requires that one avoid both a cold-hearted, and self-absorbed, relativism and the complacent sense that only those who have fallen in love with certain *particular* heroes are fit companions. There is a difference between the sort of love affair which is merely obsessional and the sort which frees one to love all other lovers, even those whose loves are centered on objects whose attractions one cannot understand. It is this second sort of romance which one hopes general education will produce.

The goal of general studies seems to me to make sure that no student has only *one* hero, and that there is enough overlap between the students' *sets* of heroes to permit the students to share their romantic sensibilities, to have interesting conversations with one another. The aim of such conversations is, once again, not to seek the Truth but just to bind us together. So, once again, I can put forward a kind of indifferentism and say that it does not greatly matter what the content of the conversation is. Similarly, it does not greatly matter what the core curriculum is as long as there is one—as long as each community defines itself by adopting one. It does not matter, for example, whether everybody has read a play of Shakespeare's, or can read simple Latin prose, or knows the Laws of Thermodynamics, or can handle a computer terminal. What matters is that there be *some* things they all have read and can do, some common subject of conversation. To take an example: in the 18th-century it made sense to say that nobody could call himself educated who knew no Latin. It sounds silly to say this now, for we now have a quite different set of, so to speak, sacred texts. To take another example: When C. P. Snow said that nobody could call himself educated who didn't know the Second Law of Thermodynamics what he really meant was that nobody in that predicament could talk to that segment of the community—the scientists—who seemed to him the best exemplars of moral virtue. This is a good point and a good argument for making science part of a core curriculum. But the point is not that thermodynamics is important, but that scientists are. We need to resist confusing the fact that we have trouble talking to somebody who doesn't know, or hasn't read, or can't do, this or that with the claim that somebody in that position isn't "properly educated." For the two claims only come together if we assume the Platonic notion that certain texts are windows on the Truth, or that certain activities are a necessary prelude to getting the Truth. Indeed, they would only come together if we made the further assumption that we now know which texts or activities these are.

To pick a core curriculum is, therefore, to pick a community—or, better, to decide what sort of community one would like to see come into being. When it is said that everybody in the West should learn something about non-European cultures, for example, what is being expressed is not so much the hunch that these cultures may know something that we don't as the hope that they and we may come together into a single human community. When it is said that general studies should include the history of science as well as the history of literature and religion and philosophy, what is being expressed is Snow's hope that the present gap between the "literary culture" and the "scientific culture" can be overcome. When a professor says that *everybody* should have read a certain list of books, what is usually being expressed is that professor's memory of what these books did for him when he was young and in love with books for the first time, together with his hope that his students will enjoy themselves much as he did.

In practise, the content of core curricula is whatever books the most influential members of the faculty of a given institution all happen to have liked, or all like to teach—the books which give them the greatest pleasure. This is, fortunately, the best possible way to fix a curriculum. For general education—education that is not simply learning the tricks of a trade—is basically erotic. Unless the teachers as well as the books or the laboratory apparatus are potential romantic objects, they might as well not be there. The only way in which one will get general studies teaching which does more than simple access to the library or the laboratory would have done is to have teachers whose sense of participation in the community—and thus whose sense of the point of their own lives—is somehow bound up with reading the books, or performing the activities, which they have picked for the "core." For only in that way will a sense of community and tradition be engendered in the students.

On the anti-Platonist view I have been expounding, therefore, there is nothing much to be said about general studies or the teaching of such studies save a warning against taking either as more than ways of helping the young to join the human race. What helps them to do this is—to employ a factitious antithesis—love rather than knowledge. Teaching a particular discipline (the sort of thing that goes on in the stage of Precision—when learning a non-academic trade, or when the student has chosen a major or gone on to graduate

school) is a master-apprentice relationship which may or may not have an
erotic component, but which can do without it. Teaching general studies (the
last years of high school or the first year of college—the stage of Romance)—is
erotic or nothing. Either the student is moved to think of himself as a potential
member of a community which includes both his teacher and the author of the
book being read, or nothing happens at all.

V. THE DANGERS OF HERMENEUTICS

Because there is nothing general and philosophical to be said about love, there
is nothing general and philosophical to be said about general studies. The
truth about both lies in the details. Such studies are, or should be, more like seduction than instruction. They should be an invitation to join a community, a
community of problem-solvers, united by the romantic sense that solving these
problems is the point of living. There is nothing general to be said about such
communal romances, so I shall conclude by saying some particular things
about the state of our own particular community—about American intellectuals and their relation to the various movements labeled as "hermeneutics."

   The dominant theme in intellectual circles these days is that the American Dream has been dreamt out—that the Deweyan attempt to bring "scientific method" to bear on the problems of men has failed. Marx's predictions
that the bourgeoise would simply no longer be able to keep things running are
widely felt to be coming true. This feeling has led to a suspicion that the optimistic liberalism and pluralism which have been characteristic of twentieth-
century American thought were symptoms of philosophical naivete. So now
we find American intellectuals ceasing to quote Mill and beginning to quote
Hegel, ceasing to read Freud in the light of Fromm and Erikson and beginning
to read him in the light of Marcuse or Lacan. There is an increasing turn in the
direction of contemporary French and German thought—in political theory,
historiography, and literary criticism as well as in philosophy. The generation
of academics which was in college in the '60's—the generation among whom
this turn, and the use of the word "hermeneutics" as a sort of slogan, is most
popular—is beginning to form a new intellectual community. This community
is much more sceptical about America than American thought has ever before
allowed itself to be. It tends to see our country as rich, vulgar, cruel and blind.
Unlike the Depression-induced Stalinism of the '30's, however, this new radicalism does not compare America invidiously with some other concrete alternative. But just because it lacks such an alternative, because it has nothing better to recommend, it turns towards abstractions, towards philosophy, towards
radical criticisms of the concepts in which liberal American social thought traditionally has been formulated. European writers who descend from Nietzsche
are currently being ransacked for such criticisms.

   This tendency has produced, as all such movements must, a new orthodoxy. Within this orthodoxy, it becomes impossible to deny a set of assumptions which are, so to speak, the least common denominator of Adorno, Hei-

degger, and Deleuze. This orthodoxy has now begun to spill over into undergraduate education, and in particular into the sort of interdisciplinary, non-departmental, courses which are the staple of "general education" programs. So we are beginning to meet college juniors who have already been trained to manipulate texts in the manner of Barthes, to criticize contemporary society in the manner of Freudo-Marxism, and to adopt a Nietzschean attitude towards the philosophic tradition. This tendency is illustrated by a student whom one of my colleagues told me about. The student signed up for his first philosophy course—a course in Plato—as a sophomore. He approached his instructor with some questions about how to write a term paper on Plato, explaining that thanks to his freshman literature course he had learned how to deconstruct texts, and would be glad to deconstruct Plato, but that he wasn't sure that that was wanted in a philosophy course.

The sort of pseudo-sophistication which this story illustrates is not to be deplored. Nobody gets to be intellectually sophisticated without going through a stage of pseudo-sophistication first. General education curricula will not do their job unless they do seduce students into such flights of pseudo-sophistication. But, nevertheless, there *is* a danger in all this, in the development of a new orthodoxy: perhaps Nietzsche's message will be lost, lost in the illusion that post-Nietzschean thought has now discovered the true methods, or the true principles of thought, or the true conceptual scheme which underlies all others.

What Nietzsche—and, more generally, "hermeneutics"—has to tell us is not that we need a new method, but that we should look askance at the idea of method. He and his followers should not be viewed as offering us a new set of concepts, but rather as offering a certain skepticism about all possible concepts, including the ones they themselves use. To repeat what I said at the outset, they should be seen as urging us to think of concepts as tools rather than pictures—problem-solving instruments rather than firm foundations from which to criticize those who use different concepts. To the extent that "hermeneutics" becomes the name of a movement which tells the students "These concepts are now old-fashioned; use these new ones—the recently-discovered *right* ones—instead," that movement betrays its own origins. If "hermeneutics" does become a new orthodoxy, it will eventually become as sterile as the tradition of positivistic scientism has become. Further, it may be much more dangerous than that latter tradition, because it may become just what its enemies see it as—an irrationalistic expression of resentful despair. It may culminate in a refusal to join the rest of the community in solving the problems which confront the society, a refusal produced by a preoccupation with "radicalizing" the terms in which those problems are described. If this happens, then "hermeneutics" will be the name of a cultural disaster rather than, as I have been suggesting, the name of a way to revitalize and deepen the Deweyan strain in American thought.

I shall end, therefore, by expressing the hope that as contemporary French and German thought—the sort of thought for which "hermeneutics" is often an abbreviation—becomes more and more available to our students, it will enhance their sense of communal purpose rather than diminishing it. If hermeneutics is taught as a new Truth or a new Method, then it will indeed have all the demoralizing effects which its critics fear. But if we can manage to teach it as just one more attempt to try to figure out what our problems are, an attempt no more privileged than any other, then it may contribute to the communal romance which, I have been arguing, it is the function of general education to create. It may thereby contribute to the ability of American intellectuals to see their country as still *theirs,* by letting us fall back in love with the tradition which shaped us.

23   Traditionalists and Their Challengers*

John R. Searle

> The author is Professor of Philosophy at the University of California, Berkeley. In this essay he assesses the debate between those who defend a traditional liberal arts curriculum and those who are fundamentally dissatisfied with it. His inquiry begins with controversies about multiculturalism and leads to consideration of issues in metaphysics, epistemology, ethics, and political philosophy.

There is supposed to be a major debate—or even a set of debates—going on at present concerning a crisis in the universities, specifically a crisis in the teaching of the humanities. This debate is supposed to be in large part about whether a certain traditional conception of liberal education should be replaced by something sometimes called "multiculturalism." Though the arguments are ostensibly about Western civilization itself, they are couched in a strange jargon that includes not only "multiculturalism" but also "the canon," "political correctness," "ethnicity," "affirmative action," and even more rebarbative expressions such as "hegemony," "empowerment," "poststructuralism," "deconstruction," and "patriarchalism." I find the debate at best puzzling and at worst disappointing, not to say depressing.

I believe it can be made more interesting if we approach it from a theoretical point of view. By challenging the assumptions behind the traditional conception of a liberal education, the academic left forces us to reexamine those assumptions. Even the most conservative among us will be forced to articulate them, to try to justify them, and perhaps even to alter them. Since I do not know of a neutral vocabulary, I will describe the debate as between the "defenders" and the "challengers" of the tradition. I realize that there is a great deal of variety on each side and more than one debate going on, but I am going

*Excerpted with omissions from "Is There a Crisis in American Higher Education?" *Partisan Review,* vol. LX, no. 4, 1993, by permission of the author.

to try to expose some common core assumptions of each side, assumptions seldom stated explicitly but which form the unstated premises behind the enthymemes that each side tends to use. Let us start by stating naively the traditionalists' view of higher education and, equally naively, the most obvious of the challengers' objections to it. This will, I hope, enable us to get into the deeper features of the debate.

Here is the traditionalists' view: There is a certain tradition in American higher education, especially in the teaching of the humanities. The idea behind this tradition is that there is a body of works of philosophy, literature, history, and art that goes from the Greeks right up to the present day, and though it is not a unified tradition, there are certain family resemblances among the leading works in it, and for want of a better name, we call it the Western intellectual tradition. It extends in philosophy from Socrates to Wittgenstein or, if you like, from the pre-Socratics to Quine, in literature from the Greek poets and playwrights right up to, for example, James Joyce and Ernest Hemingway. The idea is that if you are going to be an educated person in the United States, you must have some familiarity with some of the chief works in this tradition because it defines our particular culture. You do not know who you are, in a sense, unless you have some familiarity with these works, because America is a product of this tradition, and the United States Constitution in particular is a product of a certain philosophical element in this tradition, the European Enlightenment. And then, too, we think that many works in this tradition, some of those by Shakespeare and Plato for example, are really so good that they are of *universal* human interest.

So much for the naive statement of the traditionalist view. There is an objection put by the challengers, and the objection, to put it in its crudest form, is as follows: If you look closely at the reading lists of this "Great Tradition," you will discover that the books are almost all by white males from Europe and North America. There are vast areas of the earth and great civilizations whose achievements are totally unrepresented in this conception of "liberal education." Furthermore, within the population of the United States as it is presently constituted, there are lots of ethnic minorities, as well as the largest minority of all, women, whose special needs, interests, traditions, and achievements are underrepresented or in some cases not represented at all in this tradition.

What is the response of the traditionalists to this objection? At this point, the debate already begins to get murky, because it is hard to find traditionalist authors who address the objection directly, so I am going to interject myself and present what I think the traditionalists should say, given their other assumptions. The traditionalist should just accept this objection as a valid criticism and amend the "canon" accordingly. If great works by Asian authors, for example, have been excluded from the "canon" of great works of literature, then by all means let us expand the so-called canon to include them. Closer to home, if great women writers have been excluded, often because they are women, then let us expand membership in the list to include them as well. According to the traditionalist theory, one of the advantages of higher education is that it enables us to see our own civilization and mode of sensibility as one possible form of life among others. And one of the virtues of the tradition is the enormous variety within it. In fact, there never was a "canon." There was a set of constantly revised judgments about which books deserve close study, which deserve to be regarded as "classics." So, based on the traditionalists' own conception, there should be no objection to enlarging the list to include classics from sources outside the Western tradition and from neglected elements within it.

As I have presented it, the challengers are making a common sense objection, to which the traditionalists have a common sense answer. So it looks as if we have an obvious solution to an interesting problem and can all go home. What is there left to argue about? But it is at this point that the debate becomes interesting. What I have discovered in reading books and articles about this debate is that the objection to the so-called canon—that it is unrepresentative, that it is too exclusive—cannot be met by opening membership to include works by previously excluded elements of the population, since some people would accept such reform as adequate, but many will not. Why not? In order to answer that question I am going to try to state the usually unstated presuppositions made by both the traditionalists and the challengers. I realize, to repeat, that there is a great deal of variety on both sides, but I believe that each side holds certain assumptions, and it is important to try to make them explicit. In the debates one sees, the fundamental issues often are not coming out into the open, and as a result the debaters are talking past each other, seldom making contact. One side accuses the other of racism, imperialism, sexism, elitism, and of being hegemonic and patriarchal. The other side accuses the first of trying to destroy intellectual standards and of politicizing the university. So what is actually going on? What is in dispute?

I will try to state the assumptions behind the tradition as a set of propositions, confining myself to half a dozen for the sake of brevity. The first assumption is that the criteria for inclusion in the list of "the classics" is supposed to be a combination of intellectual merit and historical importance. Some authors, Shakespeare for example, are included because of the quality of their work; others, Marx for example, are included because they have been historically so influential. Some, Plato for instance, are both of high quality and historically influential.

A second assumption made by the traditionalists is that there are intersubjective standards of rationality, intelligence, truth, validity, and general intellectual merit. In our list of required readings we include Plato but not randomly selected comic strips, because we think there is an important distinction in quality between the two, and *we think we can justify the claim that there is a distinction.* The standards are not algorithmic. Making judgments of quality is not like measuring velocities, but it is not arbitrary either.

A third assumption behind the tradition is that one of the things we are trying to do is to enable our students to overcome the mediocrity, provincialism, or other limitations of whatever background from which they may have come. The idea is that your life is likely to be in large measure a product of a lot of historical accidents: the town you were born in, the community you grew up in, the sort of values you learned in high school. One of the aims of a liberal education is to liberate our students from the contingencies of their backgrounds. We invite the student into the membership of a much larger intellectual community. This third feature of the traditional educational theory, then, is what one might call an invitation to transcendence. The professor asks his or her students to read books that are designed to challenge any complacencies that the students may have brought to the university when they first arrived there.

A fourth assumption made by the traditionalists, which is related to the third, is that in the Western tradition, there is a peculiar combination of what one might call extreme universalism and extreme individualism. Again, this tends to be tacit and is seldom made explicit. The idea is that the most precious thing in the universe is the human individual, but that the human individual is precious as part of the universal human civilization. The idea is that one achieves one's maximum intellectual *individual* potential by coming to see oneself as part of a *universal* human species with a universal human culture.

A fifth feature of this tacit theory behind educational traditionalism is that a primary function of liberal education is criticism of oneself and one's community. According to this conception, the unexamined life is not worth living, and the examined life is life criticized. I do not know of any intellectual tradition that is as savagely self-critical as the Western tradition. Its hero is Socrates, and of course we all know what happened to him. "I would rather die by the present argument than live by any other," he said. This is the model we hold up to our students: the lone individual, standing out against the hypocrisy, stupidity, and dishonesty of the larger community. And that tradition goes right through to the nineteenth and twentieth centuries, through Freud, Nietzsche, Marx, and Bertrand Russell, to mention just a few. The tradition is that of the extremely critical intellectual commentator attacking the pieties and inadequacies, the inconsistencies and hypocrisies of the surrounding community.

I will mention a sixth and final feature. Objectivity and truth are possible because there is an independently existing reality to which our true utterances correspond. This view, called realism, has often been challenged by various forms of idealism and relativism within Western philosophy, but it has remained the dominant metaphysical view in our culture. Our natural science, for example, is based on it. A persistent topic of debate is: How far does it extend? Is there, for example, an independently existing set of moral values that we can discover, or are we, for example, just expressing our subjective feelings and attitudes when we make moral judgments? I am tempted to continue this list, but I hope that what I have said so far will give you a feel for the underlying assumptions of the traditionalist theory of liberal education.

I am now going to try to do the same for the challengers, but this is harder to do without distortion, simply because there is more variety among the critics of the tradition than there is in the tradition itself. Nonetheless, I am going to do my best to try to state a widely held set of core assumptions made by the challengers. Perhaps very few people, maybe no one, believes all of the assumptions I will try to make explicit, but they are those I have found commonly made in the debates. The first assumption made by the challengers is that the subgroup into which you were born—your ethnic, racial, class, and gender background—matters enormously; it is important for education. In the extreme version of this assumption, you are essentially defined by your ethnic, racial, class, and gender background. That is the most important thing in your life. The dean of an American state university told me, "The most important thing in my life is being a woman and advancing the cause of women." Any number of people think that the most important thing in their lives is their blackness or their Hispanic identity, et cetera. This is something new in American higher education. Of course, there have always been people who were defined or who preferred to be defined by their ethnic group or by other such affiliations, but it has not been part of the theory of what the university was trying to do that we should *encourage* self-definition by ethnicity, race, gender, or class. On the contrary, as I noted in my list of the traditionalist assumptions, we were trying to encourage students to rise above the accidents of such features. But to a sizable number of American academics, it has not become acceptable to think that the most important thing in one's life is precisely these features. Notice the contrast between the traditionalists and the challengers on this issue. For the traditionalists, what matters is the individual within the universal. For the challengers, the universal is an illusion, and the individual has an identity only as a member of some subgroup.

A second feature of this alternative view is the belief that, to state it crudely, all cultures are equal. Not only are they morally equal, as human beings are morally equal, but all cultures are intellectually equal as well. According to this view, the idea that we have more to learn from the representatives of one race, gender, class, or ethnic group that we do from the representatives of others is simply racism and old-fashioned imperialism. It is simply a residue of Eurocentric imperialism to suppose, as the traditionalists have been supposing, that certain works of European white males are somehow superior to the products of other cultures, classes, genders, and ethnic groups. Belief in the superiority of the Western canon is a priori objectionable because all authors are essentially representatives of their culture, and all cultures are intellectually equal.

In this alternative view, a third feature is that when it comes to selecting what you should read, representativeness is obviously crucial. In a multiculturalist educational democracy, every culture must be represented. The difficulty with the prevailing system is that most groups are underrepresented, and certain groups are not represented at all. The proposal of opening up doors just to let a few superstars in is no good, because that still leaves you, in plain and simple terms, with too many dead, white, European males. Even if you include every great woman novelist that you want to include—every Jane Austen, George Eliot, and Virginia Woolf—you are still going to have too many dead, white, European males on your list. It is part of the elitism, the hegemonism, and the patriarchalism of the existing ideology that it tries to perpetuate the same patterns of repression even while pretending to be opening up. Worse yet, the lack of diversity in the curriculum is matched by an equal lack of *diver-*

sity in the faculty. It's no use getting rid of the hegemony of *dead* white males in the curriculum if the faculty that teaches the multicultural curriculum is still mostly *living* white males. Representativeness is crucial not only in the curriculum but even more so in the composition of the faculty.

I want to pause here to contrast these three assumptions of the challengers with those of the traditionalists. The traditionalists think they are selecting both reading lists and faculty members on grounds of quality and not on grounds of representation. They think they select Plato and Shakespeare, for example, because they produced works of genius, not because they are specimens or representatives of some group. The challengers think this is self-deception at best, oppression at worst. They think that since the canon consists mostly of white European males, the authors must have been selected *because* they are white European males. And they think that because most of the professors are white males, this fact by itself is proof that there is something wrong with the composition of the faculty.

You can see the distinction between the challengers and the traditionalists if you imagine a counterfactual situation. Suppose it was discovered by an amazing piece of historical research that the works commonly attributed to Plato and Aristotle were not written by Greek males but by two Chinese women who were cast ashore on the coast of Attica when a Chinese junk shipwrecked off the Pireaus in the late fifth century B.C. What difference would this make to our assessment of the works of Plato and Aristotle? From the traditionalist point of view, none whatever. It would be just an interesting historical fact. From the challengers' point of view, I think it would make a tremendous difference. Ms. Plato and Ms. Aristotle would now acquire a new authenticity as genuine representatives of a previously underrepresented minority, and the most appropriate faculty to teach their works would then be Chinese women. Implicit in the traditionalist assumptions I stated is the view that the faculty member does not have to exemplify the texts he or she teaches. They assume that the works of Marx can be taught by someone who is not a Marxist, just as Aquinas can be taught by someone who is not a Catholic, and Plato by someone who is not a Platonist. But the challengers assume, for example, that women's studies should be taught by feminist women, Chicano studies by Chicanos committed to a certain set of values, and so on.

These three points, that you are defined by your culture, that all cultures are created equal, and that representation is the criterion for selection both of the books to be read and the faculty to teach them, are related to a fourth assumption: The primary purpose of education in the humanities is political transformation. I have read any number of authors who claim this, and I have had arguments with several people, some of them in positions of authority in universities, who tell me that the purpose of education, in the humanities at least, is political transformation. For example, another dean at a big state university, herself a former Berkeley radical, has written that her academic life is just an extension of her political activities. In its most extreme version, the claim is not just that the purpose of education in the humanities *ought* to be political, but rather that all education always has been political and always will necessarily be political, so it might as well be beneficially political. The idea that the traditionalists with their "liberal education" are somehow teaching some politically neutral philosophical tradition is entirely a self-deceptive masquerade. According to this view, it is absurd to accuse the challengers of politicizing the university; it already is politicized. Education is political down to the ground. And, so the story goes, the difference between the challengers, as against the traditional approach, is that the traditional approach tries to disguise the fact that it is essentially engaged in the political indoctrination of generations of young people so that they will continue to accept a system of hegemonic, patriarchal imperialism. The challengers, on the other hand, think of themselves as accepting the inevitably political nature of the university, and they want to use it so that they and their students can be liberated into a genuine multicultural democracy. When they say that the purpose of the university is political, this is not some new proposal that they are making. They think of themselves as just facing up to the facts as they always have been.

Once you understand that the challengers regard the university as essentially political, then several puzzling features of the present debate become less puzzling. Why has radical politics migrated into academic departments of literature? In my intellectual childhood, there were plenty of radical activists about, but they tended to operate in a public political arena, or, to the extent they tended to be in universities at all, they were usually in departments of political science, sociology, and economics. Now, as far as I can tell, the leading intellectual centers of radical political activity in the United States are departments of English, French, and comparative literature. We are, for example, in the odd situation where America's two "leading Marxists" are both professors of English. How did this come about? What would Marx think if he knew that his main impact was on literary criticism? Well, part of the reason for the migration of radical politics into literature departments is that Marxism in particular and left-wing radicalism in general have been discredited as theories of politics, society, and historical change. If ever a philosophical theory was refuted by events, it was the Marxist theory of the inevitable collapse of the capitalist economies and their revolutionary overthrow by the working class, to be followed by the rise of a classless society. Instead, it is the Marxist economies that have collapsed and the Marxist governments that have been overthrown. So, having been refuted as theories of society, these views retreated into departments of literature, where to some extent they still flourish as tools of "interpretation."

There is a more important reason, however. During the 1960s a fairly sizable number of leftist intellectuals became convinced that the best arena of social change was culture, that high culture in general and university departments of literature in particular could become important weapons in the struggle to overcome racism, imperialism, et cetera. We are now witnessing some of the consequences of this migration. As someone—I think it was Irving Howe—remarked, it is characteristic of this generation of radicals that they don't want to take over the country, they want to take over the English department. But, I would add, they think taking over the English department is the first step toward taking over the country.

So far, then, I have tried to isolate four presuppositions of the challengers: that ethnicity is important; that cultures are intellectually equal; that representativeness is crucial in the curriculum and in faculty composition; and that an important function of the humanities is political and social change. Now let me identify a fifth: There are no such things as objective standards. As one pamphlet published by the American Council of Learned Societies put it, "As the most powerful modern philosophies and theories have been demonstrating, claims of disinterest, objectivity, and universality are not to be trusted, and themselves tend to reflect local historical conditions." According to the ACLS pamphlet, such claims usually involve some power grab on the part of the person who is claiming to be objective. This presupposition, that there are no objective or intersubjective standards to which one can appeal in making judgments of quality, is a natural underpinning of the first four. The idea that there might be some objective standards of what is good and what is bad, that you might be able to show that Shakespeare is better than Mickey Mouse, for example, threatens the concept that all cultures are equal and that representativeness must be the criterion for inclusion in the curriculum. The whole idea of objectivity, truth, rationality, intelligence, as they are traditionally construed, and distinctions of intellectual quality, are all seen as part of the same system of repressive devices.

This leads to the sixth presupposition, which is the hardest of all to state, because it is an inchoate attitude rather than a precise thesis. Roughly speaking, it involves a marriage of left-wing politics with certain antirationalist strands derived from recent philosophy. The idea is that we should stop thinking there is an objective reality that exists independently of our representations of it; we should stop thinking that propositions are true when they corresponded to that reality; and we should stop thinking of language as a set of devices for conveying meanings from speakers to hearers. In short, the sixth presupposition is a rejection of realism and truth in favor of some version of relativism, the idea that all of reality is ultimately textual. This is a remarkable guise for left-wing views to take, because until recently extreme left-wing views claimed to have a scientific basis. The current challengers are suspicious of science and equally suspicious of the whole apparatus of rationality, objective truth, and metaphysical realism, which go along with the scientific attitude.

A seventh presupposition is this: Western civilization is historically oppressive. Domestically, its history is one of oppressing women, slaves, and serfs. Internationally, its history is one of colonialism and imperialism. It is no accident that the works in the Western tradition are by white males, because the tradition is dominated by a caste consisting of white males. In this tradition, white males are the group in power.

I have tried to make explicit some of the unstated assumptions of both sides, because I think that otherwise it is impossible to explain why the contestants don't seem to make any contact with each other. They seem to be talking about two different sets of issues. I believe that is because they proceed from different sets of assumptions and objectives. If I have succeeded here in articulating the two sets of assumptions, that should be enough. However, the philosopher in me insists on making a few comments about each side and stating a few assumptions of my own. I think the basic philosophical underpinnings of the challengers are weak. Let us start with the rejection of metaphysical realism. This view is derived from deconstructionist philosophers as well as from an interpretation of the works of Thomas Kuhn and Richard Rorty. The idea, roughly speaking, is that Kuhn is supposed to have shown that science does not give us an account of an independently existing reality. Rather, scientists are an irrational bunch who run from one paradigm to another, for reasons with no real connection to finding objective truths. What Kuhn did for science, Rorty supposedly also did for philosophy. Philosophers don't provide accounts that mirror how the world is, because the whole idea of language as mirroring or corresponding to reality is flawed from the beginning. Whether or not this is the correct interpretation of the works of Kuhn, Rorty, and the deconstructionists, the effect of these works has been to introduce into various humanities departments versions of relativism, anti-objectivism, and skepticism about science and the correspondence theory of truth.

Because of the limitation of space, I am going to be rather swift in my refutation of this view. The only defense that one can give of metaphysical realism is a transcendental argument in one of Kant's many senses of that term. We assume that something is the case and show how that metaphysical realism is a condition of possibility of its being the case. If both we and our adversaries share the assumption that something is the case and that which we assume presupposes realism, then the transcendental argument is a refutation of our adversaries' view. It seems to me obvious in this case that we as well as the antirealists assume we are communicating with each other in a public language. When the antirealists present us with an argument, they claim to do so in a language that is publicly intelligible. But, I wish to argue, public intelligibility presupposes the existence of a publicly accessible world. Metaphysical realism is not a thesis; rather, it is the condition of the possibility of having theses which are publicly intelligible. Whenever we use a language that purports to have public objects of reference, we commit ourselves to realism. The commitment is not a specific theory as to *how* the world is, but rather that there is a way the world is. Thus, it is self-refuting for someone to claim in a public language that metaphysical realism is false, because a public language presupposes a public world, and that presupposition is metaphysical realism.

Though I will not develop it here, it seems that a similar argument applies to objective standards of rationality. Again, to put it very crudely, one can't make sense out of presenting a thesis, or having a belief, or defending a view without presupposing certain standards of rationality. The very notions of mental and linguistic representation already contain certain logical principles built into them. For those who think that I am exaggerating the extent to which the traditional values are challenged, I suggest they read the ACLS pamphlet from which I quoted above.

Another fallacious move made by the challengers is to infer, from the fact that the university's educational efforts invariably have political consequences, that therefore the primary objective of the university and the primary criteria for assessing its success or failure should be political. The conclusion does not follow from the premise. Obviously, everything has political consequences, whether it's art, music, literature, sex, or gastronomy. For example, right now you could be campaigning for the next presidential election, and therefore this article has political consequences, because it prevents you from engaging in political activities in which you might otherwise be engaging. In this sense, *everything* is political. But from the fact that everything is political in this sense, it doesn't follow that our academic *objectives* are political, nor does it follow that the criteria for assessing our successes and failures are political. The argument, in short, does not justify the current attempts to use the classroom and the curriculum as tools of political transformation.

A further fallacy concerns the notion of empowerment. The most general form of this fallacy is the supposition that power is a property of groups rather than of individuals and organizations. A moment's reflection will reveal that this is not true. Most positions of power in the United States are occupied by middle-aged white males, but it does not follow that power accrues to middle-aged white males as a group. Most white males, middle-aged or otherwise, are as powerless as anyone else. In these discussions, there is a fallacy that goes as follows: People assume because most people in positions of power are white males that therefore most white males are in a position of power. I hope the fallacy is obvious.

Finally, in my list of criticisms of the challengers, I want to point out that we should not be embarrassed by the fact that a disproportionately large percentage of the major cultural achievements in our society have been made by white males. This is an interesting historical fact that requires analysis and explanation. But it doesn't in any way discredit the works of, for example, Descartes or Shakespeare that they happen to have been white males, any more than it discredits the work of Newton and Darwin that they were both English. Representativeness as such is not the primary aim in the study of the humanities. Rather, representativeness comes in as a desirable goal when there is a question of articulating the different varieties of human experience. And our aim in seeking works that articulate this variety is always to find works of high quality. The problem with the predominance of white males is not that there is any doubt about the quality of the work, but that we have been excessively provincial, that great works in other cultures may have been neglected, and that, even within Western civilization, there have been groups, most notably women, whose works have been discriminated against.

My criticism of the traditionalists is somewhat different from my criticism of the challengers because I do not, as a matter of fact, find much that is objectionable in the assumptions behind the traditionalist philosophy of education. The difficulty is how those assumptions are being implemented in contemporary American universities. There are many forms of decay and indeed corruption that have become entrenched in the actual practice of American universities, especially where undergraduate education is concerned. The most obvious sign of decay is that we have simply lost enthusiasm for the traditional philosophy of a liberal education. As our disciplines have become more specialized, as we have lost faith in the ideal of an integrated undergraduate education, we simply provide the student with the familiar cafeteria of courses and hope things turn out for the best. The problem with the traditionalists' ideology is not that it is false but that it has run out of gas. It is somewhat hypocritical to defend a traditional liberal education with a well-rounded reading list that goes from Plato to James Joyce, if one is unwilling actually to attempt to educate undergraduates in this tradition. I do not, frankly, think that the challengers have superior ideas. Rather, they have something which may be more important to influencing the way things are actually done. They have more energy and enthusiasm, not to say fanaticism and intolerance. In the long run, these may be more effective in changing universities than rigorous arguments can be.

24   Asia in the Core Curriculum*

Wm. Theodore de Bary

The author is John Mitchell Mason Professor of the University Emeritus, Provost Emeritus, and Special Service Professor at Columbia University. He founded the University's Oriental Studies program. In this essay he draws on his decades of experience in curricular development to explore the challenges inherent in approaching the Asian classics and striving to appreciate their vital contributions to an understanding of the human condition.

Perhaps the two most celebrated efforts to define a classic canon for modern America emerged, paradoxically, from the abandonment of a required curriculum based on the classical languages of Latin and Greek. One was the famous five-foot shelf of Harvard Classics, edited by President Eliot of Harvard, who is also responsible for introducing the elective system. In other words, Eliot put the classics on the shelf and then told undergraduates they were free to leave them there. At Columbia in the teens and twenties, John Erskine took the classics off the shelf and put them on the table for discussion in his famous Honors Course, a colloquium which became the prototype for Great Books courses of all kinds—at Chicago, St. John's, Aspen, and in the Humanities course at Columbia, required of all undergraduates from 1937 to the present.

It was as a natural extension of its earlier Honors and Humanities programs that Columbia's Asian Humanities, featuring the "Great Books of the

*Printed by permission of the author.

East," was born 40 years ago. The comparatively open and expansive view of the canon which the Asian Humanities bespoke contrasts with the educational hostilities that have broken out since. The challenge now to the so-called WASP canon, even when offered in the name of so-called "non-Western" cultures, is revealed in this negative and incoherent formulation, for "non-Western" stands for nothing in itself and is meant less to affirm these alternative traditions than to call into question the validity of any tradition at all. Indeed, it often amounts to nothing less than a radical, cultural-revolutionary challenge to any kind of canon, Eastern or Western.

In response, however, we cannot simply mount a defense of established practice, or superimpose a preconceived definition of the canon on other cultures. Rather, we must examine what other traditions have considered classic and develop criteria that may contribute to an enlarged conception of both the classics and the humanities—in short, a working, contestable canon for educational purposes.

The so-called "Western" tradition, at its inception, drew heavily on "Oriental" sources in the Near and Middle East. Much of Greek philosophy came into the hands of the medieval West through the good office of Muslim Arabs, who recognized the importance and responded to the challenge of Greek thought at a time when it had been eclipsed in Europe during the so-called Dark Ages. Long before there were any WASPs in the world, Aristotle stood as a formidable presence in the minds of the great Islamic philosophers Al Ghazali and Ibn Khaldun, as much later he would again in the eyes of modern East Asians. Plato, Aristotle, St. Augustine, Dante, Shakespeare, and Dostoevsky, when once made available to educated Japanese and Chinese, were quickly acclaimed as classic thinkers and writers of universal stature.

It is not just that "each generation chooses its own ancestors," as the saying goes, but that certain works perennially survive translation and critical scrutiny across time as well as cultures. This is what marks them as "classics"—worthy of serious consideration by each new generation—and thus deserving of attention in any structured curriculum.

In this way, the core comes to be defined through practical experience more than by an abstract definition of ideological design. A common body of required texts and source readings is used to encourage the individual's confrontation with challenging questions and ideas, as well as to facilitate discussion. Through common readings and the exchange of ideas, the core courses help students learn to think for themselves and express themselves. The curriculum promotes a shared discourse that, in an age of inescapable specialization, bridges the disciplines and sustains communication among educated persons. "Core," then, refers not just to content or canon, but to process and method.

The inclusion of Asia in the core curriculum is neither a betrayal of the West nor a capitulation to the political pressures of disaffected minorities—not anything but a natural follow-through on the original intention of a core curriculum that would be incomplete without other world traditions. What may well alarm conservatives is the more radical claim that today East and West should be treated on a par, with no privileged status reserved for traditional values or Western civilization.

I would suggest that one's own cultural tradition should have priority in undergraduate education anywhere. The globalization of culture may well produce a "global village," but there are grounds for doubt whether it will retain any real local color, distinctive culture, or sense of intimate association. Might not universities everywhere be doomed to a uniformity as anonymous, dull, and graceless as the shopping malls proliferating around the globe?

If intellectual diversity and cultural pluralism are to survive in universities, they must tend the roots of their own cultures and nurture whatever there still is of distinctive excellence in their own traditions. Which is to say, in the matter of core curricula, giving some priority to the study of those ideas, institutions or cultural traditions that make each of us—in East or West—what we are and can be at our best. No matter how well our translators do their work, studying another culture is much like learning another language. The stranger the culture, the less accessible it will be, and the greater the risks of misunderstanding and superficiality.

I question the feasibility of bringing all major traditions into a single "great books" or world civilization course. Can justice be done to the distinctive features of each tradition in a one-year survey? One can have something like "globality" in the academic equivalent of a one-year shopping mall, but nothing like the intimate personal experience of life in a village, or the sense of identification with a community for which one takes some personal responsibility.

If the choice of Asian classics is to be governed by the same selectivity as in the Western case, this selectivity has to be exercised in respect to several Asian traditions at once—indeed, all that might be included in the so-called "non-Western" world. Exercising this selectivity in the multicultural East is far more difficult than within the bounds of the more unified Western tradition. Though the "east" has something like "great books," it has nothing like the "Great Books of the East." The latter is a Western idea, both in seeing the East as one, and in imagining a common tradition shared by the people of this "East." Each of the major Asian traditions has tended to see itself as the center of the civilized world, looking inward—spiritually and culturally—toward that center rather than outward to the world or to each other. The famous "Sacred Books of the East," as published at Oxford, was a western invention. "Asia," a geographical designation, represented no common culture or moral bond among the people of that continent until, in modern times, a new unity was found in their common reaction to Western expansionism. To construct a reading list, therefore, we have to look for what each of the several Asian traditions themselves honored as essential to their own heritage.

One way of doing this is to identify the scriptures or classics already well-known within the distinct ethico-religious traditions of Islam, Hinduism, Buddhism, Confucianism, Taoism, and others. Yet one can also find recognized classics of the literary and intellectual traditions, which might or might not run parallel to the religious traditions. This method, proceeding inductively from the testimony of Asians themselves rather than deductively from some Western definition of a classic norm, produces what might seem an odd assortment of genres. Great poetry exists in each of the major traditions, though it varies considerably in form. Epics can be found in Iran and India that bear comparison to the *Odyssey, Iliad,* and *Aeneid,* but there is nothing like them in China and Japan. The reverse is true of the haiku or Noh drama—classic forms in Japan, but found nowhere else. Histories as monumental in their own way as Herodotus and Thucydides have been produced in the Islamic world by Ibn Khaldun and in China by Ssu-ma Ch'ien but by no one in traditional India or Japan.

Perhaps the greatest diversity, however, is exhibited among the religious scriptures, some of which can barely be regarded as "texts" in any ordinary sense of the term. For instance, although the Platform Sutra of the Sixth Ch'an Patriarch is presented in one sense as authoritative scripture, in another sense it points to an abjuration of all scripture.

Other problems of selection arise from the lack of geographic and cultural congruence among the four major traditions often chosen to represent the "East": the Islamic world, India, China, and Japan. The Islamic world, which covers almost half of Asia and North Africa, also includes Iran, with its own language, civilization, and religions. "Coverage" of India includes Buddhism, as well as Brahmanism and Hinduism, and in China and Japan, Buddhism as well as Confucianism and Taoism. Thus, religion cuts across cultures while it may also provide some of their underlying continuity.

If, for instance, the case for Islam and our understanding of the Koran depend heavily on how one views the distinctive claims made for it as prophecy and for Mohammed as the "seal of the prophets," the significance of that claim cannot be judged from a reading of the Koran alone, without seeing how the matter is dealt with later by Al Ghazali in relation to Greek philosophy and Sufi mysticism, or by Ibn Khaldun in relation to the patterns of human history. The contrasting claim of Hinduism that it transcends any such particular revelation and can accommodate all other religions may be difficult to evaluate except in some relation to Islam or to the Mahayana Buddhist philosophy that Sankara is variously said to have refuted and assimilated into the Vedanta. These religions or teachings may not always have acknowledged each other openly, but if we know or even suspect that there was indeed an unspoken encounter among them, some reconnaissance of the alternative positions is requisite to an understanding of any one of them.

In China, though the reception of the Confucian tradition is most directly accessible through the Analects, if one stopped there and went no further into any of the later Confucian thinkers, one would get only an archaic, fossilized view of Confucianism. In the West it would be like reading the Old Testament without the New, or the latter without St. Augustine, St. Thomas, or Dante. Yet it can equally well be argued that the encounter among the so-called "Three Teachings" in China is even more vividly brought to life in such great Chinese novels as the *Journey to the West* and the *Dream of the Red Chamber.* Thus, reading classic fiction can give access to the dialogue on China on levels not reachable through the classical and neo-classical philosophers.

The same—and more—can be said for Japanese literature as a revelation of Buddhism's encounter with the native tradition. Often that tradition is identified with Shinto, but as there were no written texts or scriptures antedating the introduction of the Chinese script, the best one can do is look to the earliest literature in Japanese—such works as the *Manyoshu*, the *Tale of Genji*, and the *Pillow Book*, to name only a few of the finest examples—if one wishes to get, in the absence of open doctrinal debate, a more intimate glimpse of what is going on in the Japanese mind and heart behind the outward show of polite professions.

Thus, unless other guests are invited, there will be no party for us to join, no way to renew the conversation with any of the great works or thinkers of the past without having others present who had engaged in the original dialogue. How long the list of participants may become is always a matter for local discretion, but in no case can just one or two works generate a real conversation. In the silence of Zen there may be such a thing as one hand clapping, but in the discourse we are entering into there is no book that speaks just to itself.

In this way, working through the natural, original associations among the recognized classics of the Asian tradition, one arrives at a provisional set of the Asian classics or Great Books of the East. Admittedly a modern creation, it is put together from material quite authentic to one or another of the Asian traditions. Yet it is an "East" that has emerged in its true reflected colors only upon being observed in a modern light.

Rabindranath Tagore, the charismatic cosmopolitan from Calcutta who thought of himself above all as a citizen of the world, was perhaps the first to appreciate this. In his new perception of the "East," brilliantly articulated in an essay on "The Eastern University," he saw the need for a curriculum in which the several Asian traditions would complement one another, highlighting each other's distinctive features in a way no solitary exposure could do.

Regrettably, the direction of modern education in Asia has taken a different turn, emphasizing technical learning and specialized training at the expense of any kind of humanistic education, Eastern or Western. In this situation, as in our own, the humanities are taught as discrete disciplines and each national tradition is a separate subject of specialization. The usual result of this process is that nothing can be seen whole and every great work is subjected to unmitigated trivialization. In most Asian universities today it is only the student majoring, say, in Sanskrit, Chinese, or Japanese studies who learns anything of the classics of his own tradition beyond the high school level, and even then it will most likely be to specialize in a single text.

In the study of other cultures or civilizations, an understanding of one's own situation and one's own past is a precondition for understanding another's. Our experience with Asian Humanities at Columbia shows how much deeper the new learning experience can be for those who have first come to an an appreciation—or even just a keen awareness—of their own tradition. The same principle applies in reverse to the Asians' understanding of the West, which may be just as advantaged or handicapped, depending on how well they have come to know their own culture. Not to come to terms with one's past is to remain hostage to it, and thus not to become fully master of oneself. In such a condition, being unable to take responsibility for one's own past, one is in a poor position to become truly responsive to others.

Such considerations are bound to enter into what I refer to as "parity of treatment." If one can appreciate what it would mean for the Great Books of the Western World to be represented only by Plato's *Republic* or the Book of Job, one can begin to appreciate why a reading of the Analects alone might not do sufficient justice to the Confucian tradition, or why the Dhammapada by itself would be inadequate to represent Buddhism.

Whatever is to be done, it seems to me, should be governed by the consideration that the reading and understanding of a text should work, as much as possible, from the inside out rather than from the outside in. This means that no reading of an Eastern text should be undertaken which is so removed from its original context as to be discussable only in direct juxtaposition to something Western. Such a reading leads almost inevitably to one-sided comparisons and does not serve genuine dialogue. Party to this new dialogue must be enough of the original discourse (i.e., writings that present alternative or contrasting views) so that the issues can be defined in their own terms and not simply in opposition to, or agreement with, the West.

The basic criterion for recognizing the Asian classics as such has been that they were first so admired in their own tradition. In quite a few cases this admiration spread to other countries, and these works came to be regarded as either scriptures or great books outside their homeland. Further, after the West made substantial contact with Asia in the 16th and 17th centuries, many of these works were translated and admired in the West as well. For at least two centuries they have been essential reading for many of the best minds in the West—philosophers, historians, poets, playwrights, and indeed major writers in almost every field of thought and scholarship. Thus, one whose education does not include a reading of the Asian classics today is a stranger not only to Asia, but to much of the best that has been thought and written in the modern West. While not perhaps to be called "Great Books of the West," many of these works and their authors have already entered the mainstream of the conversation that is going on in the West today. As that conversation is broadened to include a fairer representation of the Asian tradition, bringing out the implicit dialogue within and among them, it could indeed become a Great Conversation for all the world.